Longman business studi

Edited by D. C. Hague

Longman business studies

Edited by D. K. Hague

Management Accounting

A Conceptual Approach

Lloyd R. Amey

Professor of Accounting
McGill University

Don A. Egginton

Lecturer in Accounting
University of Bristol

Longman

LONGMAN GROUP LIMITED
London

Associated companies, branches and representatives
throughout the world

First published 1973
Third impression 1975

ISBN 0582 44021.1 (Paper)
ISBN 0582 44027.0 (Cased)
Library of Congress Catalog Card Number: 73-86099

Phototypeset by
Filmtype Services Limited, Scarborough
and printed in Great Britain by
Lowe & Brydone (Printers) Ltd, Thetford, Norfolk

Contents

Preface   1

Part 1 Entity reporting

1 The data-information transformation   6
1 The domain and nature of accounting. 2 Accounting and
information systems. 3 The theory and economics of information.
4 Measurement theory. Appendix: The value of information.
Bibliographical references. Problems.

2 The entity accounts   38
1 Fundamentals of entity accounts. 2 Uses and aims of entity
reports. 3 Double entry and the accounting identities. 4 The
principal entity reports. 5 Consolidated reports. Bibliographical
references. Problems.

3 Value and profit   75
1 The interrelationship of value and profit. 2 Value theory. 3 Value
for what? 4 Value to whom? 5 How might value be measured
for entity accounts? 6 Profit concepts. 7 Valuation and depreciation
of long lived assets. 8 Estimation in replacement cost accounting.
9 Estimation in conventional accounting. 10 General price level
changes. Appendix: 'Equivalent replacement cost' depreciation.
Bibliographical references. Problems.

4 External reports and the corporate financial image   123
1 The significance of external reports. 2 Profitability and associated
measures. 3 Financial stability. 4 Some evidence on accounting
data and ratio measures. 5 Cosmetic reporting. Bibliographical
references. Problems.

Part 2 Plans and decisions

5 Enterprise plans   140
1 Introduction and overview. 2 Definitions and classification of
economic models. 3 Production plans. 4 Investment plans.

5 Comments on long-term economic plans. 6 Accounting 'plans'.
7 A comparison of business plans as represented in economics and
accounting. 8. Program budgeting. Bibliographical references.
Problems.

6 Decision concepts   161
1 Introduction. 2 The elements of a decision. 3 Problem
identification. 4 Data specification. 5 Some comments on decision
models. Bibliographical references. Problems.

7 What to produce: product decisions   187
1 Economic theory. 2 Product mix. 3 Changes in the product line.
4 Intermediate product decisions. Bibliographical references.
Problems

8 How to produce: technique of production decisions   208
1 The nature of the problem. 2 A many-sided problem. 3 Factors
influencing choice of technique. 4 Treatment in economics.
5 Further examples of technique problems. 6 Data specification.
Bibliographical references. Problems.

9 How much to produce: price-output decisions   231
1 Market structures and pricing rules in the neoclassical theory of
the firm. 2 Conditions under which a firm may have an independent
price policy. 3 Considerations influencing choice of price policy.
4 Other behavioural assumptions. 5 Pricing in practice. 6 Costs
for pricing. 7 The role of advertising. 8 Internal sales: transfer
pricing. Appendices: (a) Multiproduct firm: general case.
(b) Joint products in variable proportions, general case.
(c) Discriminating monopoly. (d) Multiplant monopoly.
(e) Dynamic profit maximization. Bibliographical references.
Problems.

10 Price-output: some tactical aspects   270
1 'Cost–volume–profit' analysis. 2 Extensions of the break-even
approach. 3 Estimation of cost and demand behaviour.
Bibliographical references. Problems.

11 Net investment and disinvestment decisions   292
1 The nature of investment. 2 The set of problems. 3 Specifying
the data. 4. Some investment criteria. 5 Disinvestment. Appendices:
(a) Equivalence of IRR and NPV rules for independent projects in
the two-period case. (b) Non-uniqueness or non-existence of IRR:

a case where the two rules may conflict. (c) Ranking of projects with different capital outlays by their IRR. (d) Non-equivalence of max. NPV over the project set considered and max. 'profitability index' over the project set. (e) A summary of the Hirshleifer analysis, two-period case. Bibliographical references. Problems.

12 Investment under capital rationing; replacement policy; uncertainty   330
1 Capital rationing. 2 Optimal replacement policy. 3 Allowing for uncertainty in investment decision-making. Appendices: (a) Notes on the mathematics of retirement and replacement. (b) Conditional and joint probability. Bibliographical references. Problems.

Part 3 Control systems

13 Enterprise control   380
1 The enterprise control problem. 2 Background to the problem. 3 The place of control in the economics of the firm. 4 Insights from organization theory. 5 Alternative methods of control. 6 Accounting controls. Bibliographical references. Problems.

14 Cost accumulation   401
1 The elements of cost recording. 2 Process costing. 3 Job and batch costing. 4 Joint product costing. 5 Cost classifications for routine recording. 6 Proration of costs between production centres. 7 Cost absorption. 8 The data bank viewpoint. Appendix: The cost of inventory. Bibliographical references. Problems.

15 Control through standards   445
1 The rationale of standard costing. 2 Setting the standards. 3 The budgets. 4 The recording process for standard costing. 5 Direct cost variances. 6 Indirect cost variances. 7 Sales variances. 8 Reporting and evaluation. 9 Reconciliation with the planning budget. Bibliographical references. Problems.

16 Control through internal resource allocation   498
1 The significance of resource allocation. 2 Administration. 3 Marketing. 4 Research and development. 5 Capital projects. Bibliographical references. Problems.

17 Control through profitability measures   526
1 Profitability measures and responsibility. 2 Profit measures. 3 Return on investment. 4 Postscript on external reporting for segments. Bibliographical references. Problems.

18 A critique of accounting controls   551
    1 The scope of control. 2 The nature of accounting controls.
    3 The internal control process. 4 Behavioural considerations.
    5 Nonprofit controls. Bibliographical references. Problems.

Part 4 Accounting and financial management

19 Working capital management   582
    1 The working capital ambit. 2 Inventory control. 3 Trade credit.
    4 Cash and near-cash. Bibliographical references. Problems.

20 Long-term financing   610
    1 The capital structure. 2 Dividends, retentions and valuation.
    3 Debt/equity policy. 4 Cost of capital implications
    Bibliographical references. Problems.

Appendices
  A Interest   638
    Bibliographical references. Problems   648
  B Interest tables   650
  C Notes on linear programming   654
    Bibliographical references   661
Index   663

Preface

Textbooks on management accounting, usually called managerial accounting in North America, are almost as numerous as the sands of the desert. We feel under obligation, therefore, to explain why we have chosen to add to their number.

Our reasons are two-fold. First, the available books often lag as much as a generation behind advanced work in accounting and its related fields, in content and approach. We think students deserve better, and have attempted to bridge this 'generation gap' by giving a reasonably elementary account of a number of ideas from advanced work. If this aim needs any justification it is that most of our readers will be students at the threshold of their careers in a period of accelerating change. Although we claim no prescience, we have tried to provide an awareness of ideas which seem to us likely to have a significant influence in the future.

Secondly, we have sought to offer a genuine alternative to existing texts in another way, by placing much more emphasis than is customary on the conceptual aspects of our material. Many of accounting's present shortcomings, we believe, arise out of attempts to erect elaborate superstructures on what, from a logical point of view, are quicksands. Observation leads to memory leads to experience. But in the great majority of cases experience does not lead to judgment which is conscious of its reasons; it continues to be based on belief and custom, the validity of which are never tested. Furthermore, propositions and concepts from other bodies of knowledge which have applicability to accounting have not, as yet, all been identified or, if identified, sufficiently embedded in accounting thought. Before it can proceed to a higher plateau of development the take-off point of sound conceptual foundations must first be established.

Management accounting is concerned with business problems. Thinking about business problems conceptually means being able to ask the right questions. Business problems seldom have only one dimension. One class of problem, concerned with resource allocation (planning and decision), is essentially an economic problem. Another class, concerned with problems of control and evaluation of observed consequences, has behavioural, informational, control-theoretic and a number of other aspects. Both classes call for a systems approach to the business enterprise, both are likely to involve the use of quantitative techniques other than accounting, and both require data traditionally provided by the accountant. The data must, however, be properly specified, and this requires a real understanding of the essential nature of the problem.

If our philosophy is correct, it follows that the approach to business problems, if

1

it is to be at all realistic and helpful, must always straddle two or more disciplines; and the attitude which says that such-and-such a topic 'belongs' in finance, or economics, or management science can only inhibit the cross-fertilization of ideas so essential to the development of sound foundations. Professor Hague takes a similar interdisciplinary view in his companion book, *Managerial Economics*, which complements the present volume.

Whether our aims are sensible ones, and whether we have succeeded in them, is for others to judge.

The book is aimed at three classes of reader: first, those pursuing undergraduate or graduate courses in business administration (i.e. undergraduate degree or diploma courses at college level and M.B.A. courses at universities); second, undergraduate accounting specialists at universities; and third, business men, including industrial accountants, attending post-experience management courses.

After Part 1, which is intended to provide a recapitulation on global reporting, but with a management orientation and emphasis on systems and data-information aspects, the rest follows in chronological order, i.e. plans precede decisions precede controls. Users of the text may, however, wish to follow a different sequence. In particular, it is common in North America at least to offer separate one-semester courses in Accounting for Decision and Accounting for Control. We had this in mind in dividing the book into four Parts with a 'keynote' chapter leading off in each. A course in decision would include Chapters 1, 5–12 and Appendices A and C; a course in control, Chapters 1 and 13–18, while Chapters 2–4 and 19–20 have elements of each. For example, the accounts of the entity as a whole (Chapters 2–4) are a basis for decisions by external users, and serve a monitoring (i.e. control) function for management, which may lead to management decisions; the management of working capital, including inventories (Chapter 19), has both decision and control aspects; and long-term financing (Chapter 20) can be viewed either as the control of claims structure, optimally where appropriate, or as providing an important input to capital budgeting decisions (Chapters 11, 12). Several topics which we would have liked to examine at greater length – information economics is an example – had to be left for reasons of space or because a fuller treatment would have demanded more preparation on the part of the reader than we wished to assume. Most of the problems are original; a few have been borrowed, with permission. A couple of unknown authorship were inherited teaching material and the University of Bristol gave permission for the use of some problems which have appeared in degree examination papers.

Part of Chapter 1 and certain sections of Parts 2, 3 and 4 require an elementary knowledge of statistics and an understanding of the calculus. This is the only necessary prerequisite. A first course in financial accounting, while desirable, is not essential: Part 1 provides an overview for the tiro.

Where it has been necessary to assume a specific legal and institutional framework, for example in discussing external reporting, we have adopted a British context. These aspects are minimal in relation to our central purposes, however, and we have attempted to draw attention to relevant North American differences. Readers are unlikely to be harmed by the knowledge that legal and institutional frameworks are neither static nor preordained.

On terminology, we have attempted to adopt a general English-speaking usage where alternative terms exist. Thus we have used 'shares' rather than (the common North American) 'stocks' when considering equity capital, and 'inventories' rather than (the usual British) 'stocks' for goods in the firm's balance sheet, although in the inventory theory area where no possibility of confusion exists we have used 'inventory' and 'stock' interchangeably, in conformity with widespread practice.

We should like to express our gratitude to colleagues who have by their comments improved the text. All, of course, are absolved from responsibility for our personal views or for any errors which remain. Finally, our thanks go to all those who helped with the typing of the manuscript.

May 1972   Lloyd Amey
                                                            Don Egginton

Acknowledgements

We are grateful to the following for permission to reproduce Copyright material: American Accounting Association for an extract from an article by R. P. Marple in *The Accounting Review*, July 1963; American Finance Association for a Figure from 'Capital Asset Prices' by W. F. Sharpe in *Journal of Finance*, September 1964; Financial Executives Research Foundation for a Table from *Divisional Performance: Measurement and Control* by D. Solomons; Harvard Business Review for a Table from 'Misevaluation of Investment Center Performance' by John J. Mauriel and Robert N. Anthony in *Harvard Business Review*, March–April 1966; the author for the essay 'An Introduction to Replacement Theory' by M. E. Holmes; The Institute of Cost and Management Accounts and Operational Research Society Limited for a Figure from *Project Cost Control Using Networks* by C. Stafforth; North Holland Publishing Company for a figure from *Depreciation and Replacement Policy* by J. L. Meij; the author and Koninklijke Van Gorcum & Company B.V. for two figures and extracts from *The Game of Budget Control* by G. H. Hofstede.

Part 1
Entity reporting

1

The data-information transformation

In my estimation, possibly the most important variable left out of economic analysis has been information and its cost.

M. SHUBIK [34]*

1.1 The domain and nature of accounting

(a) Data and information

Accounting is a system for transmitting information about some economic activity to destinations inside and outside of the activity concerned. The accounting process may be described as one of data-information transformation. It might be useful to define a few terms at the outset. Roughly speaking, we could say that 'data' are the inputs and 'information' the outputs of the process. More precisely, *data* are recorded experiences, representations of perceived attributes of certain objects (here economic activities). Thus data already involve *measurement. Information* in the technical sense means recorded experience which is *useful* (relevant) for some *particular* purpose. This purpose is ultimately decision-making of some kind in all cases, though immediately it may be planning or control. So data collected, processed and transmitted for a particular use yield information; *knowledge* consists of data which can be put to *general* use.

In this chapter we will examine this activity of data gathering, processing and transmission from several different points of view – those of information systems, information theory, measurement theory, economics (involving decision theory) and organization theory. By bringing together conceptual ideas from each of these disciplines we hope to provide the reader with a more complete and interesting picture of the activity known as accounting.

We shall be concerned in this book almost exclusively with the transmission of information *within* the firm, to management, and beyond this with the problems involved in specifying information for a number of different purposes. As will become clear as we proceed, the perspective we adopt throughout coincides to a large extent with that of a systems analyst whose background training includes accounting, economics, quantitative methods and organization theory. Instances where these approaches (and particularly the last three) interact in business problems recur throughout the book.

(b) The scope of accounting

Anyone who attempts to define the scope of a developing discipline is either brave

* Figures in square brackets refer to Bibliographical reference.

or foolhardy. We do not intend to lay ourselves open to such a charge; the exercise in any case is inessential to our purpose in this book. A fairly standard definition of accounting will have to suffice, with the qualification that the boundary may be drawn rather wider by some. Accounting, then, involves devising and operating an information system for collecting, measuring, recording, summarizing, transmitting and interpreting the results of economic transactions, past or prospective, in resources and in claims on resources.

As applied to past transactions, the recording part, known hitherto as book-keeping but which, following developments in mechanical and particularly electronic recording, is now more often graced with the name of data processing, is usually performed by a systematic procedure called double-entry. The information produced by this procedure is periodically summarized in a set of statistical tables, the purpose of which is ostensibly to aid in evaluation and interpretation. This set of summary tables comprises a profit and loss account (or income statement), balance sheet, and sometimes a flow of funds statement. The system serves as both an external and internal information system: on the one hand management reports on its stewardship of the resources committed to the business to those who financed these resources and to other interested parties outside the business; and on the other hand management compares its own performance with what it planned.

The collection, measurement and recording of prospective transactions, by contrast, is not subject to the double-entry procedure, nor does it result in external reports. Its purpose is to generate data or information to guide planning and decision-making, i.e. it is concerned entirely with internal administration of the business. The summary statements it produces are budgeted profit and loss accounts, balance sheets and funds statements, and it is in relation to these that management judges its own performance. (In the absence of these, performance may less satisfactorily be compared with performance in earlier periods or with that of other 'similar' firms.) Besides learning whatever lessons it can from the outcomes of its past planning, the changes, trends and rates of change in the aggregates represented in these statements provide the background for future planning.

The data-information distinction is more difficult to sustain in the case of this prospective accounting. Retrospective accounting transforms data into information for the benefit of shareholders and lenders, existing and prospective, the government, trades unions, employees, customers, suppliers and the management of the business. It is true that, in the hands of some recipients (e.g. institutional investors, the government, investment analysts) this information is likely to undergo further processing, i.e. it becomes data for further calculations. Prospective accounting yields some information, in the form of budgets; but in the case of data for decision-making in many cases the accountant stops short at gathering the data. He can hardly be said to perform a data-information transformation. This is done by other specialists who develop the appropriate decision models and do the decision

7

calculations. When we are discussing this area, therefore, we will have to be a little less definite in our use of the terms data and information, and sometimes ambivalent. Later we may enter another reservation concerning these introductory remarks by questioning whether accounting data, whether retrospective, current or prospective, constitute measurements.

In this book, as the title suggests, we shall be concerned primarily with the communication of accounting data or information within the firm, i.e. to management or other specialists engaged in data processing. Questions relating to the communication of information to parties outside the firm will enter only indirectly, to the extent that they also involve management's evaluation of its own performance. Such interesting questions as whether an 'open-ended' information system can be devised which would meet the varying informational needs of different classes of external recipients will not therefore be our immediate concern. We will note only that the retrospective accounting to external recipients and to management differs in coverage and degree of aggregation, more information being available to management than is disclosed to parties outside the business. *Management accounting*, then, will be taken to comprise the gathering, processing, communication and interpretation of data within a business for the purpose of ensuring as far as possible that its expectations are realized, by seeing that decisions are consistent with the enterprise plan and with each other, that their implementation is controlled, and by management comparing its own performance with its expectations.

Our concern will be predominantly with the communication of data or information to managements of *business* enterprises – corporate enterprises in private ownership. The same ideas, with slight modification, are applicable to unincorporated businesses, non-profit organizations and public enterprises. An accounting system may be devised for any unit whose economic transactions with other organizations are of sufficient significance to make it worth while recording them. The term *entity* is used to denote the boundaries of the accounting unit. The accounting entity may be an individual, a household, a business enterprise, the government sector or the entire economy. For some purposes it is necessary or convenient to define the entity as a *legal* form of business organization (e.g. a limited company). Other purposes are best served by defining an *economic* entity, which may be broader or narrower than a single legal entity. For example, one legal entity, a holding company, may exercise control over the operations of one or more other companies. It may be more meaningful to treat the several units as one for the purpose of evaluating the efficiency with which their combined resources are utilized. On the other hand it may sometimes be desirable to subdivide a legal entity (say a divisionalized company) in order to assess the results of distinct activities conducted by it in separate and more or less autonomous divisions. The modern company is an artificial entity created by law and separate from the persons who contribute its capital. It has an indefinitely long existence of its own. Its resources (assets) are considered to be owned by the company itself, and all claims against the assets, including the claims of the owners (shareholders), are considered to be obligations of the company. Consequently all transactions with the owners are treated in exactly the same way as transactions with outside parties such as lenders.

The retrospective summary statements referred to earlier (profit and loss account, etc.) provide information on transactions between the accounting unit and other entities, i.e. they report on inter-entity but not intra-entity transactions, and reflect the point of view of the entity as distinct from that of its owners:

Accounting entity X

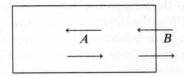

A = intra-entity transactions; B = inter-entity transactions.

Having defined the accounting entity, its retrospective summary statements (and the corresponding prospective summary statements) will report only on ΣB, although its total transactions in any period will be $\Sigma(A + B)$.*

The *accounting period* is the period of time to which the summary statements relate; interim statements may be drawn up for sub-intervals of this period. Many of the problems encountered in preparing these summary statements arise because the statements necessarily cover a year or other arbitrary period, whereas the activities of the firm (the production process) are continuous, and the whole cycle of operations is not completed within this arbitrary period. This is reflected, for instance, in the accounting treatment of inventories and the depreciation of long-lived assets. To the accountant these are two major problems, and neither would arise if it were not necessary to prepare periodic summary statements at particular dates, with the consequent need to assign ('allocate', prorate) revenue and expense between two or more accounting periods.

(c) The uses of accounting data/information

We have already commented on the management purposes which accounting data or information are required to serve. Since these will be our main focus in the remainder of the book it may not be inappropriate here to comment briefly on

---

* It will become apparent later that only type B transactions will affect the size of the aggregate profit of X over its whole life, type A transactions affecting only the time distribution of this whole-life income.

external uses. In the hands of external users accounting information serves as the basis, wholly or partly, for making decisions. Insufficient research has been conducted to enable us to state with any confidence the relative importance of the information furnished in accounting reports and other information available to external users, such as stockmarket information (e.g. the price of the shares) or a mixture of the two (e.g. price–earnings ratios, earnings or dividend yields). The existing shareholders must from time to time decide whether to leave their holdings unchanged, increase them or disinvest. A potential lender (say a bank) must decide whether or not to lend the business money, how much and for how long. Some external users (e.g. the government, in taxation and industry census returns) will require information in a prescribed form; and all public companies incorporated in the UK are required by the Companies Acts, 1948 and 1967, to prepare their published accounts in a prescribed manner which sets a minimum level of disclosure. Some users other than government, e.g. institutional investors such as insurance companies and pension funds and a bank which has granted a large overdraft, may also, by virtue of the size of their claims, be in a position to demand accounting and other information about a business additional to that provided in its published accounting statements. Increasingly, business enterprises, particularly if they are very large, must recognize their wider responsibilities to the communities in which they operate, not just to the shareholders and others who have put up the money.

Until very recently there has been no attempt on the part of the professional accountancy bodies or the government to discover what the needs of the external users of accounting information really are, what they do with it once they get it and, with these things in mind, to try to develop procedures and statements which would specify and present accounting information in these forms. The so-called 'principles' of accounting, i.e. the assumptions or conventions which underlie what is at present regarded as good accounting practice, comprise an arbitrary set of rules which have been developed pragmatically from existing accounting practice. Over much of its life the *stewardship function* has been the dominant influence on the kind of information provided in the published summary statements, i.e. it has been assumed that the accountant's main responsibility is to report the results of management's administration of the funds committed to its use by shareholders and lenders. This has had an inhibiting effect on the development of useful information, because good stewardship was interpreted as ensuring that the funds contributed by the owners were at all costs maintained intact *in money terms*, not in real terms.

Clearly the protection of invested capital must be one of the functions of accounting. But since accounting data represent something else – economic events – it is also important that accounts and the summaries prepared from them should reflect economic realities, and in particular should report in economic terms on the *efficiency* with which resources are used by a business. This latter function would call for the collection, processing and reporting of rather different kinds of information than are usually reported at present, which in turn might lead to different decisions being made by existing or prospective shareholders and lenders, possibly even by the management of the enterprise. This is something that we will be taking up in subsequent chapters.

Historically, the demand for accounting information by external users, and sometimes the form which it takes, have changed with the evolution of different forms of business organization and with changes in the degree of government regulation of industry and trade. The principle of limited liability (introduced in the UK in 1855) led directly to growth in size of business enterprises, diffusion of ownership, and later to a divorce of ownership from management. The existence of an active market in shares increased the life expectancy of companies whose shares were listed on a stock exchange: ownership claims on the corporate assets could now be transferred in circumstances in which they previously might have been permanently withdrawn, while companies for their part were enabled to finance long-term investment from funds provided, in many cases, for only a very limited period and withdrawable at will. The security of investment in business enterprises has thus undergone a mutation. Looking back to Marshall's entrepreneur [27], who borrowed capital at interest and also managed the business, it is difficult to find his counterpart in the modern company. The ordinary shareholders are sometimes said to bear the ultimate risks (and to manage, through their elected representatives, the directors), and they do. But risk is relative. As Stigler has observed [35], the ordinary shareholder in a giant company of good financial standing functions more as a lender, in terms of risk and managerial responsibilities, than a lender to, say, a mining company does.

(d) The nature of accounting data/information

Accounting data or information may be characterized in various ways, each of which may cast some light on the activity known as accounting, and help to make it a more efficient and powerful tool. Thus accounting data or information *represent* economic activities; they are a form of statistics; they may involve measurement (depending on how we define that term); and when articulated and given purpose they form an information system. It will be useful to explore these attributes.

(i) *Accounting and economics*
Business enterprises are engaged in economic activities – buying and selling goods and/or services, processing goods and financing these activities. At the level of the firm, which is one of the basic units of organization in the economy, we are con-

11

fronted with the central problem of economics, viz. that resources are scarce relative to wants, and it is necessary for someone to decide what should be produced, how, when and how much. Economists assert that the correct application of economic principles by consumers and firms will bring about optimal efficiency in the allocation and utilization of scarce resources in relation to, and in competition with, all the other wants of the community, or at least such of those wants as can be made effective with purchasing power.

It seems reasonable to suggest that accounting should assist in the achievement of this objective. It should contribute to greater efficiency in the use of scarce resources by measuring past business performance in a way which fairly truthfully and unambiguously represents economic reality, making it possible to draw the correct economic inferences from the information and learn the correct lessons of the past. Similarly prospective accounting should guide managements to make future plans and decisions which are economically sound and consistent in the light of their present knowledge, by correctly specifying the data which will in large part influence them in forming their expectations. How well conventional business accounting acquits itself in this role, and how it might be reshaped to meet this requirement which we consider to be its main function, it will be one of our main purposes to enquire.

There are parallels between accounting and economics at various levels, between business accounting and microeconomics, social accounting and macroeconomics, and international economics. For the economy as a whole there is no conflict between the two disciplines: the social accounts are prepared by economists and economic statisticians, and founded on economic principles. Elsewhere, however, conflicts arise because accounting and economics have developed independently of one another. This has led to conceptual and terminological differences which can be an obstacle to communication; for example, words such as income, capital, value and cost have different meanings in accounting than in economics.

The pictures of the firm presented in accounting and economics also differ in definition. The usual model of the firm of standard economic theory, a static model, in effect describes the firm entirely in terms of the profit and loss account (flows); the balance sheet (stocks) is missing. In other words the firm as pictured carries no inventories of goods or cash to bridge the intervals between input and output, production and sale. In dynamic theories of the firm interperiod relationships are introduced, it is true, but these feature in few standard economics textbooks. Accounting records stocks (assets and claims) as well as flows (revenues and expenses), and in comprehensiveness is a more sophisticated model than those of orthodox economics. On the score of how well it represents the economic values of the resources owned by the firm, the claims against these resources, and transactions in resources and claims, however, we shall have to conclude that the accounting model comes off very badly. Resources, except those immediately consumed, and outstanding claims upon them are not valued in any economic or even literal sense. Although it has an advantage over economic models in its comprehensiveness (it covers *all* of the activities of the firm), the accounting model forfeits this advantage by its naive treatment of economic reality.

(ii) *Accounting and statistics*

Accounting data constitute one of the richest sources of economic statistics. The effective operation of a 'mixed' economy, regulated largely by prices and profits, is dependent upon information accumulated in the accounting system and ancillary records of business enterprises. Without the various returns utilizing these data made by businesses to numerous government agencies the whole machinery of economic control of the economy as we know it would be greatly impaired, in some cases rendered impossible.

Business accounting data/information figure largely in government economic planning and in the social accounts. Since they are statistics, these data are susceptible to treatment by statistical methods. One useful application has been found in auditing; others include attempts to partition costs into fixed and variable components and to allow for uncertainty in estimates prepared for decision purposes. Statisticians would be appalled by the accountant's lack of regard for error – and any measurement, whether it involves the future or not, is subject to error. Many of the aggregates contained in accounting summary statements are estimates, yet they are given an air of precision and nothing is said about the possible error inherent in them.

Properly specified in economic terms, accounting could be a powerful tool. Some knowledge of probability theory and Statistics is also essential if the accountant is to perform his tasks sensibly. Moreover, accounting is only one among a number of quantitative methods of analysis which have application to business problems. Increasingly the management accountant needs to understand at least some of the more important of these other techniques. Without this knowledge much of his prospective accounting will fall short of producing information as defined in section 1; this task will be entrusted to those who possess these skills; and the main potentialities of the computer will remain outside his grasp.

In the remaining sections two further relationships will be examined: accounting regarded as an information system and as a measurement system. As we proceed the reader would do well to remember, however, that whatever other attributes it might be desirable for it to have, accounting data/information are proxies for economic objects and relations between economic objects; it has no *raison d'être* of its own. This is why, in presenting what we have subtitled a conceptual approach to management accounting, we have laid heaviest emphasis on economic concepts. This is not to dismiss ideas emanating from other disciplines, only to say that they are generally of secondary importance.*

* In referring to economic concepts we are of course referring to economic *reasoning*, not necessarily economic theory which, in most versions, is exclusively market-oriented, and sadly lacking in its representation of the firm's internal operations, particularly their behavioural aspects.

1.2 Accounting and information systems

(a) Systems

Accounting was earlier described as an information system. Simply defined, a 'system' is 'a set of parts coordinated to accomplish a set of goals' [8*]. Churchman elaborates:

> to make this definition more precise . . . we have to . . . spell out in detail what the whole system is, the environment in which it lives, what its objective is, and how this is supported by the activities of the parts.

He goes on to list five essential points to be kept in mind in thinking about a *particular* system:

1. The specific measures of performance of the system as a whole.
2. The environment in which the system operates, and the constraints that it · imposes.
3. The resources available for operating the system.
4. The components or subsystems of the total system and the activities they perform, their goals and measures of performance.
5. Management of the system, i.e. planning and controlling the system's performance.

Two points should be stressed about this *systems approach*. First, one of the fundamental problems is to define the 'system'. The second problem is to discover what the *real* objectives of the system (the organization and parts of the organization) are, as distinct from assumed, rationalized or stated objectives.

Very loosely, *general systems analysis*, which includes information theory and cybernetics, connotes an interdisciplinary approach to problems which is both systematic and theoretical [5]. More informatively [14†],

> it visualises an organisation in terms of a block diagram with centres connected by lines of communication. The separation of centres entails that no centre will have all the information available to the organisation . . ., and that there will be lags in transmitting information to [decision centres] . . . and in transmitting and executing instructions from executive centres . . . the problem of systems analysis [is] to deduce from the structure of information flows . . . and . . . decision rules employed . . . how the organisation will respond to changes in its environment. . . . [Its] fundamental assumption is that all decision rules can be thought of as responses to discrepancies between the actual state or performance of the organisation and some 'standard' or desired state, and are intended to reduce those discrepancies. As a corollary, [it] is concerned . . . with finding optimal information flows and decision rules.

As applied to information, this approach is personified in the systems analyst. His task is to 'identify, observe, analyse and specify the requirements for information in decision-making activities throughout the . . . organization [i.e. define the informa-

---

*p. 29.
† pp. 39–40.

tion system], to determine the sources of data, and to match information requirements with appropriate data sources . . .'. [29]. In performing this task the systems
analyst views the organization as a whole and its parts objectively, not from any
partisan functional position. His approach is interdisciplinary and conceptual:
qua organization theorist he observes how people in the organization respond to
objectives, interact with one another; *qua* information specialist he *specifies* what
information is required for various purposes, what data should be collected (compared with what *are* collected); and *qua* economist attempts to determine the best
set of information systems for the organization at any particular time. This involves
an economic assessment of alternative systems, in which the timeliness and
efficiency of the alternatives are allowed for in counting costs and benefits.

Any business organization will comprise a series of information systems (or
networks). Some will represent systems designed to provide information for major
classes of decisions. Others will be associated with plans or controls. In each case
the information system must provide for the requirements of any models involved
in the ultimate provision of information to management. A business may have
separate systems for production information, sales information, external financial
reporting, internal control accounting, and for other activities or combinations of
activities which have common or similar informational needs. Systems may also be
differentiated by the time dimension of the activity. In the limit an integrated
information system would consist of subsystems spanning all the activities of the
firm and all time frames of interest to management in planning, decision and control.

Alternative classifications of information systems might be based upon the
method of information processing (manual, mechanical, electronic) or the length
of the time-lag between data collection and the provision of information to
management, depending on the method of processing, the length of the network,
complexity of decision model, and so on. The time-lag might be considerable with
manual processing and transmission over a long network, shorter as the length of
the network is reduced (see the reference to M-form organization in Chapter 13)
and 'on-line' equipment is used, and zero with 'real time' systems.

Bound up with the development of information systems is the idea of management priorities. The intention is that the systems will provide for recurring decisions
to be routinized, by establishing standard decision rules wherever possible, thus
freeing top management to deal with planning and strategic decisions. This is what
is meant by the term *management by systems*.

As used in the technical literature, *management information system* implies two
pre-conditions: first, the information network is computer-based, and secondly
that the network is adaptive, capable of responding to change. As the name
implies, a management information system is also one which delivers final information into the hands of management. The accounting information system may or
may not be a management information system, depending upon whether it meets

the two conditions mentioned above and on whether it *alone* provides management with information for decision. Generally some other disciplines besides accounting will be involved in this process, so that the accounting information system will not constitute a management information system as strictly defined.

We have already indicated that in our view the management accountant, although concerned only with some information subsystems, needs as far as possible to adopt the broader and more conceptual approach to information of the systems analyst. As we remark in Chapter 18, existing accounting control systems clearly reflect a lack of adequate system understanding.

(b) Collection, processing and transmission

(i) *The price system as a communication system*

Consider now the information requirements of a modern firm. If it is operating in perfect markets for all of its inputs and products its main information needs are confined to future prices (inputs and outputs) and to discovering its production function (technological information). We will assume that the firm is operating (as is likely) in the region of constant average and marginal costs. The competitively determined price system signals how much to produce, buying and selling prices free of charge; this would apply also to information concerning finance. The extension to imperfect markets involves an information problem of the first magnitude. Instead of a single ruling price in any market the firm must discover its present as well as future demand function and cost function. We pass to a situation where 'the information required is a set of functional relationships which are not given by simple observation . . .' [6]. This applies to input, capital and product markets.

(ii) *Reasons for forming firms*

It is in these circumstances that there are advantages in establishing a firm, i.e. superseding the price mechanism and allocating resources over a certain set of activities independently. Market information ceases to be accurate when interdependent activities are decentralized independently of one another. There are now costs – transactions (or information) costs – in discovering relevant prices and in negotiating transactions, arising out of the double uncertainty (uncertainty about the present as well as the future) which market imperfections introduce [23], [10].*
One has only to reflect on the vast amount of information required to coordinate buyers and sellers in a single market to obtain some idea of the magnitude of the information problem which faces a large modern company. Organization of transactions within a firm can result in creation of *controlled information* (long-term contracts afford one example), which reduces uncertainty and information costs.

* Uncertainty (lack of information) is the ultimate reason for establishing a firm, whether markets are perfect or imperfect.

The price system is a means of communicating information; it is an information system which, to a greater or lesser extent depending on the market situation, influences the decisions of buyers and sellers in a particular market. When a firm supersedes the price system its internal decisions continue to depend on information – market or other information – and on the expectations which it forms. The standard version of the theory of the firm, as Cyert and March point out [12],* 'treats expectations as exogenous variables; they are given, not explained'. The firm is assumed to know its revenue function, the present state of technology (production function) and input-supply functions. The theory ignores the whole problem of data collection and processing within the firm. The new field of *information theory*, discussed in section 3, has developed in response to the vast increase in the volume of information which is needed as organizations grow in size and complexity – and the greater capacities of modern processing equipment to handle it. In order to meet decision deadlines much information must be collected, processed and transmitted to its destination rapidly. It is the task of information theory to increase the efficiency of data collection, processing and communication.

(iii) *Complete and incomplete information*
The information used by decision-makers within the firm will never be entirely accurate, never wholly complete, i.e. decision outcomes will in the strict sense be multi-valued, not unique, and in the former case information on the probability of a particular outcome will not be entirely accurate.† Thus 'the firm's efficiency in allocation decisions is not ... absolute, but rather relative ... to alternative internal and market information systems' [23].‡ Information may be deficient in various ways. There is, as just stated, uncertainty about the outcomes of future events. Secondly, the firm may not collect all the relevant data that are available or make use of the information it possesses. Third, time is of the essence: the time limit on most decisions will mean either that they must be taken on less than complete information or that the firm must pay more people to work on data collection and processing.

According to Cyert and March ([12], pp. 45, 47, 78) the typical firm does not scan all alternatives or have complete information about the alternatives selected. The set of alternatives considered, and the kind and quality of information collected, depend on features of the organizational structure and on the 'locus of search responsibility' in the firm. The information provided may also be affected by the kind of communication system the firm operates. Viewing the firm as an organizational coalition, they show that full consistency and completeness of information would in some circumstances lead to conflict situations between members of the

*p. 46.

†In the standard theory of the firm, decisions are made under conditions of complete certainty.

‡p. 419. The role of information from *outside* the firm in enterprise planning, and its monitoring for control purposes, is stressed in Chapters 5 and 13.

coalition, and should therefore not be sought. Since we may take it, then, that in all real-life situations the firm's information is less than complete, it follows that when we speak about 'optimality' we mean optimal in relation to the (imperfect) information on which the particular course of action was based. This draws attention to the fact that information has a cost. Applying economic principles, the firm should invest in information only so long as the expected value of the last increment exceeds the expected cost. This cost-benefit analysis of investment in information is the subject of *information economics*, a branch of decision theory, which we shall discuss in the next section. The marginal cost of new information is probably related in many instances to the existing stock of information in the firm's possession, being a decreasing function of the size of this stock.

(iv) *Search and collection*

Data for the firm's planning and decision-making come from a large number of sources. In addition to market data (on product demand, and on the supply of various inputs and capital) the firm may gather technological data from trade journals, while further data on all of these things may be generated within the firm (e.g. by market surveys, economic forecasts, by its purchasing, industrial relations and research and development departments). The rate of search is not likely to be constant for different parts of the business at a given time or over time. It has been suggested [12] that search for data is initiated in response to a number of factors: when existing decisions are seen to be unsatisfactory or when a problem looms up. Some firms have a hierarchy of search activities, the intensity of search varying with the circumstances, tending to be inversely related to the amount of 'organizational slack' in the firm.* The amount of data a firm needs to collect will depend, in addition, on its market structure (on whether, e.g., it is in a position of oligopolistic interdependence, an extreme case of a more general phenomenon, and must try to find out what its competitors are planning to do and how they are likely to react to its own moves), on whether its activities are simple or diverse, and whether its transactions are repetitive or varied. Firms obviously have more information about repeated than about new and different transactions, and there is some evidence to suggest that the greater the accumulation of experience of a particular type of transaction, the more the firm's expectations will be based on *past* data.†

Once collected, data must be condensed (sometimes encoded) and evaluated, and passed through the organization. The person who is the first link in the data-information chain is potentially highly important, for upon his actions depend what is collected and subsequently communicated: the wrong data, too little on some questions, too much on others. The initial screening becomes particularly important

---

* Defined as the payment to members of the ruling management coalition in excess of what is required to maintain the organization – [12] p. 36.
† Cf. the remarks on 'routinizing' of decisions in [17].

the greater the subjective element involved. On the other hand if screening rules are standardized this puts a constraint on the data entering the communication process. Clearly the task of gathering data and making a preliminary evaluation of it is a highly important one, and large businesses recognize this by having specialized functional experts to undertake it.

(v) *Communication and processing*

Like collection, data processing and communication are not costless. Someone must decide how much processing and how much communication should be undertaken. The data-information flow through the firm is illustrated in Figure 1.1: The essential elements in the system are (i) data sources, inside and outside the firm, (ii) selection of data to be communicated (involving search, collection, preliminary evaluation and condensing or encoding), (iii) transmission of data/information through the organization with or without further processing, (iv) various destinations at which the data/information is to be received, possibly after decoding. These may be inside the business (including the firm's data store) or outside. The circles interposed at various points on the network indicate 'noise' entering the system, any distortions introduced into the original data in the process; those shown are merely illustrative. The activities of storage and retrieval, while important, will not be commented on further.

The greater the amount of communication in the economy and within the firm, the easier we would expect it to be for people (consumers, firms) to form expectations and make plans and decisions, *ceteris paribus*. And we noted earlier that plans and decisions depend upon the decision-maker's information and the expectations he forms. Within the firm many plans and decisions are interdependent, and hence a mutual exchange of data/information between the activities concerned becomes essential if the activities are decentralized. The firm, after all, owes its very existence to the fact that it is cheaper to organize certain interdependent transactions internally than through the market. But while there appear to be advantages in favour of more rather than less communication we do not need to be reminded that there are obvious limits short of the point at which everyone is flooded with paper. Indeed the 'principle of exceptions' so prominent in standard costing is designed to prevent this happening. The costs, including the cost of delays, of communicating data/information through the organization must be set against the value of the decisions which result; a cost-benefit comparison of systems with varying degrees of collection, communication (consultation between decision-makers) and processing is required.*†

Before making this comparison some attempt should be made to establish the

* We take up this question in the next section.

† Failure of the organizational coalition in a particular decision area to consult other decision-makers who might have relevant data is the subject of the 'theory of teams', which is concerned with problems of imperfect communication between persons with common goals – see [25].

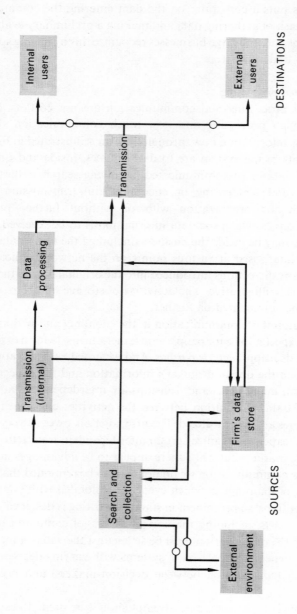

Figure 1.1 An Information System

firm's information production function, i.e. to determine the technically most efficient design characteristics (input combinations) for any given level of data/ information output. In doing this account should be taken of the fact that there are ways of transmitting data/information which are optimal in combating 'noise'. Firms which solve these problems of search and collection, communication and processing optimally will secure an informational advantage, in the same way as a firm is said to possess a production cost advantage or a marketing advantage. *In a very real sense the objective of management accounting*, as described in this book, *is to give business managements an informational advantage.*

Many firms have standard procedures to guide and regulate data/information flow. *Routing rules* specify, for any given piece of data/information, who is to send it and who receive it; these rules may or may not conform to the firm's organization chart. The length of the line will obviously affect the transmission time. The other kind of rules are *filtering rules*. Filtering refers to what we called 'noise' in Figure 1.1. At each point in the network at which data is communicated there is an opportunity to manipulate it, consciously or unconsciously, to adjust the data transmitted in accordance with the individual's personal assessment of the decision situation. There is evidence of considerable biassing of data in large firms, some of it conscious, but equal evidence of counter-biassing, i.e. recipients often do not take data/information at its face value, and correct the bias (optimistic, pessimistic) before acting upon it.*

Most standard decision models such as the standard theory of the firm – Cyert and March's behavioural theory of the firm is a notable exception – ignore information problems; i.e. the way in which data are obtained and processed through the organization, the effect of the firm's communication system on the data processed and the expectations formed, are taken as given. The substantial computation required by many decision models, and the ability of *human* decision-makers to process data, mean that in practice problems must often be considerably simplified. Biassing and time delays in communication may result. The most serious deficiencies in human decision-making, psychological research has shown,† arise in *processing* information, not in making decisions.

(vi) *Summary*
We can now attempt to sum up this discussion. Information plays a key role in planning and decision-making‡ decisions, actual or anticipated, committing resources of considerable magnitude are taken on the basis of the information

---

* [12] Chapters 4 and 5.
† [15] Part 2. Compared with the relatively simple experiments there referred to, one would wish to place much more emphasis on correct specification of the data for complex business decisions.
‡ Recent empirical studies have stressed the accumulation of information in the form of technological knowledge (rather than investment expenditure) as the main source of economic growth in mature industrial economies.

generated by the firm (meaning by this externally-generated knowledge and internally-generated information) and the expectations which result from its final evaluation. Faulty expectations may come about because too little information is collected, too little of the available information is used (insufficient communication), because they are based on irrelevant data (weaknesses in search, collection and initial screening activities) or on relevant data which has been seriously biassed in the process, or because unpredictable events supervene. The list is not intended to be exhaustive, merely indicative. Other causes will occur to the reader, such as the time limit on decisions (which restricts the information base unless data collection costs are greatly increased).

1.3 The theory and economics of information

A body of theory concerned with a number of data/information problems has grown up, mainly since World War II. The important place held by the accounting information subsystem in the firm's information system, and the crucial role of information activities in economic growth and decision-making, suggest that the accountant should try to gain whatever insights he can about information processing from this and related developments. Of the many accounts of information theory available a few are listed below,* and the reader is recommended to pursue the subject in some of these. What follows is a brief survey of some of the main ideas. Information economics is taken up in section 3(c).

(a) The 'information' concept

Information theory defines 'information' in a special way, and is concerned with providing a quantitative measure of the amount of information conveyed in a message (which may be a set of business data). Information is defined as a function of the probability that a certain 'event' will occur before a definite and reliable message saying whether or not it has occurred is received. Note that the information content of the message has to do with the *uncertainty* of the event occurring, as indicated by its *prior probability* (i.e. the probable value of the event occurring) and with the degree of surprise which the message brings. In order to measure information in this sense we need to be able to specify all possible events (outcomes) and their associated probabilities.

---

* See [37] Chapters 1 and 2; [7]; [22]; [3]; [1]. More advanced treatments will be found in [33], an important early contribution in communication theory, which is slightly narrower than information theory as here described, and in [21].

processing systems, which involve encoding of inputs and decoding of outputs.* With few exceptions at the present time, information communicated between firms must be translated by the recipient before it is of use, because firms employ different coding systems. This adds considerably to the cost of information and, of course, to the time it takes to reach its destination. The communication of information within the firm is similarly affected; the development of controlled information (see section 2(a)) works in the opposite direction. Computer systems, based upon a systems approach which sees an organization as comprising a number of sub-systems which cohere to the extent that the lines of communication between them are kept open and permit a speedy transmission of data/information, are tending to break down the conventional divisions between departments. In fact with electronic communication systems the traditional organizational subdivisions often impede the flow of information within the firm.

From such considerations it follows, first, that a supra-departmental coding system is needed in order to achieve an integrated management information system, and secondly, that standard codes need to be developed for industries, trades and commodities.† With the growing use of computers, developments can be expected in both of these directions. These new coding systems can also be expected to sweep away the traditional division between commercial and technical information, combining the two in a single record, a complete file for each commodity bought, sold or transferred by the firm. Computer-based retrieval systems for extracting information very rapidly from large-scale data banks will rank as equal in importance to the design of the information system and standardized codes.

1.4 Measurement theory

(a) Defining a 'measure'

Common usage of the term 'measure' may be stated as being the development of a method for generating a class of data/information which will be useful in a wide range of problems. In more detail, measurements seek to express qualitative differences in attributes by bringing them into a certain relationship with a set of

---

*In terms of the symbols used in the appendix, a code is determined by a given partition of X, say $X_1, X_2, \ldots, X_n$, each partition representing a different information structure. If the information sought is found on observation to belong to subset X_j, this will generate a message $y_j = \eta(x_j)$. The code is the function $\eta(x)$, determined by the state of the world, x, and the particular partitioning chosen. A code will be as many-valued as the number of subsets into which X is partitioned. As a matter of interest, it has been shown that the optimal code for any variable will in general consist of subsets of unequal size.

†In Britain the National Computing Centre has been working on development of a national commodity code – see [28]. The problem: 'How can the identifying reference number itself be made to contain the most important facets of the information about a commodity, including ... its specifications, classification, relationship to other commodities, origin, and so forth? Which are the most important facets ... ?' (p. 18).

numbers. As thus defined, measurement involves classification of the attributes, and representation. The set of numbers is not confined to a monetary scale, as in accounting; there can be non-monetary measures.

(b) Measurement theory

Measurement theory, on the other hand, an integral part of scientific method, gives a stricter definition of 'measure'. To qualify as measures the numbers must exhibit certain formal properties [39]. In particular there must be a consistent relationship between (representation of) attributes and numbers, either one-to-one or many-to-one, which ensures additivity of measures. Since accounting in general is inconsistent in its representation of economic attributes it is not a measurement system in this formal sense. More to the point, in an economic accounting, since no single concept of 'value' or 'cost' will do for all purposes, there is likewise no possibility of achieving such consistency.* The best one could hope for would be a series of different measures, each of which was universally acceptable for a particular purpose and satisfied the necessary (minimum) formal conditions. We conclude that there is no prospect of 'measurement' in accounting conforming to the requirements of measurement theory. This should not be altogether surprising in view of the fact that, unlike measurements in the natural sciences, human behaviour is involved. In other words the types of measures used in the social sciences do not possess the same mathematical properties as the types of measures used in the natural sciences, and we should be forewarned that, as a result, it may not be possible to manipulate the former in the same way as the latter. We do not find this as inhibiting as those who seek to establish uniformity throughout all sciences, however, and it should be remembered that what is said here in relation to economic measures is equally true of all social measures (i.e. it applies equally to psychology, sociology, etc.).† We suggest that the question of *representation* should be uppermost in our minds, and that whether the method of expressing (quantifying or transforming) this in numbers meets the formal requirements of a scientific measurement system is of secondary concern. While recognizing that accounting numbers are not measures in the formal sense we can, however, learn something from measurement theory.

There is no such thing as a measure of absolute accuracy; *every* measurement is subject to some error. Consequently quantitative estimates of future events, which are normally subject to a relatively high degree of error, are not on that account inadmissible as measures. Measurement theory makes a distinction between two kinds of measurement: fundamental measurement, which is based on direct

---

* Valuation involves (i) defining 'value' to a particular person for a particular purpose and (ii) finding a method of measuring (or perhaps we should say estimating) this value.

† Readers should consult [11], Chapter 15, for a statement of the minimum formal conditions for measurement; for definitions of fundamental measures and derived measures (estimates of intensive and extensive qualities, respectively), and the rarity of numerical laws in the social sciences.

observation of the attribute measured, and derived measurement, which involves a transformation of a fundamental measure. Most accounting numbers are of the second kind though, in the loose sense, both kinds will appear at some point in the process of data collection and processing. A further distinction, useful for some purposes, is based on time: measures may be retrospective, contemporary or prospective.

Fundamental measurements may be made on several different types of scale: nominal (to determine equality or inequality), ordinal (rank), interval (range), ratio (proportion) and absolute (the counting of members of a set). It is often said that this list represents a hierarchy, in ascending order, and that the nominal scale provides the least information and hence is least valuable.* One cannot make this assertion, however, without considering the other desirable criteria of a measurement system, to which we turn in a moment. To each of the fundamental measurement scales there correspond certain admissible transformations (mathematical operations) in obtaining derived measurements. Transformations which are admissible for any scale are also admissible for all 'higher' scales in the hierarchy.

(c) Desirable properties of accounting measures

Despite the fact that accounting measures do not constitute a measurement system in the strict sense, some of the desirable features which should be kept in mind in making accounting measurements are:

1. First and foremost, closeness of the representation of the economic attributes concerned, i.e. the measures should correctly record the relativities of economic values.
2. Subject to 3, accuracy.
3. Reasonable cost. As pointed out in [1], alternative measurement systems are in effect alternative information systems, which may be evaluated (as to 1 and 3) as described in section 3(c) above and in the Appendix.
4. A number of other characteristics – such as the highest measurement scale possible, objectivity, reliability, relevance, timeliness – are either subsumed in 1–3 or are of minor importance.

Some additional references are given below.†

(d) Multiple-measure reporting

As a final point we briefly examine the notion of a 'multi-dimensional accounting', mentioned in the earlier work of Ijiri and others. The suggestion is that 'instead of

*[1]. This overlaps the Report of the Committee on Foundations of Accounting Measurement [2] in the same supplement.
†[20], especially the paper by C. T. Devine; [18]; [9]. There is a useful bibliography in [39].

the reduction of all events to a single dimension with consequent loss of information'* vectors of information could be reported, including physical and other non-
monetary measures. The particular suggestion of these writers is that measurement
in terms of money only is severely constricting. It could be rejoined, of course,
that in external accounting reports at least we already have a vector of valuations in
a number of *monetary* dimensions. Our point is not directed at multi-dimensional
accounting as such but at multi-dimensional reporting to a single user. According
to research by psychologists, when people are presented with information in several
dimensions (or asked to order objects according to several dimensions) their
reaction is generally to collapse all dimensions into a single 'good *versus* bad'
dimension, with consequent loss of information. Furthermore, in general they do
not perform this dimensional compression in anything like an optimal way.†

Appendix   The value of information

The following symbols will be used:

$X = \{x\}$ The set of possible states of the firm's external environment (states of
the world)

P The probability distribution of X, assumed known (sources of
information)

a A decision in response to x

α A decision rule (function)

u Payoff (profit, or more generally utility) ‡

ω Payoff function

$H = \{\eta\}$ The set of instruments (information structures, informants) for
translating x into y, i.e. all possible ways of partitioning X

$Y = \{y\}$ The set of potential messages (channels), each y corresponding to
some subset of X (y is the value of the function η)

$U = Eu$ Expected payoff.

The processes we are visualizing (information flows, decision process, payoff) are
thus represented by the following mappings:

$$x \xrightarrow{\ \eta\ } y \xrightarrow{\ \alpha\ } a \xrightarrow{\ \omega\ } u$$

(state of	(message)	(decision)	(payoff)
the world)			
	(informant,	(decision	(payoff
	information	rule)	function)
	system)		

---

*Churchill and Stedry in [20].

†Cf. the paper by R. N. Shepard in [15].

‡This generalization to include utility relies on the von Neumann–Morgenstern axioms of consistent
behaviour under uncertainty [40].

Given these definitions the following relations hold:

$$u = \omega(x,a)$$

$$y = \eta(x)$$

$$a = \alpha(y) \quad [\alpha \text{ is the function associating message } y \text{ with decision } a]; \text{ and hence}$$

$$u = \omega(x,\alpha(y)) = \omega[x,\alpha\{\eta(x)\}]$$

$$U = U(\alpha,\eta; \omega,P), \alpha \text{ and } \eta \text{ being selected by the firm.}$$

(a) The value of exact information

Assuming the additional information to be bought is exact information on x, i.e. $\eta^*(x) = x$, the objective is to maximize U by choosing the optimal decision rule, α^*. (An optimal decision rule α^* in A maximizes U averaged over all messages y in Y.)

$$U[\alpha^*,\eta^*(x); \omega,P] = \max_\alpha U[\alpha,\eta^*(x); \omega,P] \tag{1}$$

The maximum value of U before buying further information is

$$U_0 = \max_\alpha E\omega[x,\alpha\{\eta_0(x)\}]$$

and after buying the information it is

$$U_1 = E \max_\alpha \omega[x,\alpha\{\eta^*(x)\}].$$

The value of the information is the net payoff

10
$$U_1 - U_0 = E \max_\alpha u - \max_\alpha Eu \geq 0. \tag{2}$$

$U_1 - U_0$ is called the *expected value of perfect information* (EVPI), and is equal to the *expected opportunity loss*, the expected payoff foregone by not following the decision rule α^* which would result in maximum payoff for given x.

(b) The value of inexact information

An alternative notation for $\max_\alpha U(\alpha,\eta(x); \omega,P)$ is $V(\eta; \omega,P)$. (3)

Then if η^0 is the existing information structure and η^1 some other structure (not necessarily exact information) leading to a different partition of X with greater information value, the firm should be willing to offer

$$V(\eta^1; \omega,P) - V(\eta^0; \omega,P) \geq 0$$

for the information with structure η^1.

To summarize so far, the expected value of information depends on the state of the world, x, and the functions P, ω, η and α. If the decision rule employed is an optimal one, leading to max U for given ω and P, we can express the expected value of information as a function, V, of the three functions P, η and ω. Of these, η is under the decision-maker's control; ω and P are not.

The case considered in (a) was a special case. In general the information to be acquired will not be exact. In discussing inexact information it may be useful to distinguish between lack of information about external variables and faulty information arising from the information system itself. Denoting the state of the external environment by x^e and the state of the firm's information system by x^i, the information structure is now such that

$$\eta(x^e, x^i) = y,$$

where x is now put equal to (x^e, x^i). Contrast this with the case of exact information, where $\eta^*(x) = x$, and x^i was considered constant.

Faulty information results from 'noise' and information loss in the channel. This may take many forms: actual loss of information in transmission or storage, unreliability of informants, incorrect probability assessments (p), loss due to aggregation (section 3(b)(iv)), to futurity of the states of the world, unobservability, screening, biassing, coding or scrambling ('noise'). The distortions and loss arising from the combination of these influences are summarized in the condition $\eta(x) \neq x$.

The chief differences in the analysis compared with (a) are:

1. States of the world, x, are now considered as comprising two elements, (x^e, x^i), as defined above. The variable x^i has the property that it affects the message, y, and the decision process (through the probability weights attached to different information by the decision-maker in recognition of the fact that his information system does not provide him with a true picture of the state of the world, making him, in general, more risk-averse), but it does not affect the payoff, u. It is decision-relevant but not payoff-relevant. That is:

$$\eta(x^e, x^i) = y$$

but $$\omega(x^e, x^i; a) = \bar{\omega}(x^e; a) = u.$$

It is reasonable to expect that the decision-maker will be prepared to pay more, or at least as much, for information from an informant whom he has reason to believe is highly reliable (i.e. right in a large proportion of cases) than for information having a larger probability of error – and this irrespective of how the information and the action taken upon it affect the payoff. From the earlier relations [in particular $y = \eta(x^e, x^i)$; $a = \alpha(y)$] it follows that a ranking by value of more or less reliable information will not be changed by a change in the exogenously determined payoff function, $\bar{\omega}$; $\bar{\omega}$ is independent of x^i.

2. In place of expected payoff

$$Eu = E[\omega(x,a)]$$

in (a), the function to be maximized with respect to a now becomes the *conditional* expectation

$$E[\overline{\omega}(x^e, a)|\bar{\eta}],$$

where $\bar{\eta}$ denotes the mapping of all pairs (x^e,x^i) into subsets according to the decision-maker's prior or subjective probabilities concerning the reliability of information from particular informants, as referred to above.

Bibliographical references

[1] American Accounting Association, Report of the Committee on Accounting and Information Systems, *Accounting Review Supplement*, XLVI, 1971, pp. 286–350.

[2] American Accounting Association, Report of the Committee on the Foundations of Accounting Measurement, *Accounting Review Supplement*, XLVI, 1971, pp. 1–48.

[3] Bedford, N. M. and M. Onsi, Measuring the value of information – an information theory approach, *Management Services*, Jan.-Feb. 1966, pp. 15–22; reprinted in *Accounting and its Behavioral Implications*, ed. W. J. Bruns and D. T. DeCoster, McGraw-Hill, 1969.

[4] Bierman, Bonini, Fouraker and Jaedicke, *Quantitative Analysis for Business Decisions*, Irwin, revised edn., 1965.

[5] Boulding, K.E., General systems theory: the skeleton of science, *Management Science*, II, Apr. 1956, pp. 197–208.

[6] Boulding, K. E. and W. A. Spivey, *Linear Programming and the Theory of the Firm*, Macmillan, New York, 1960.

[7] Bostwick, C. L., The use of information theory in accounting, *Management Accounting* (U.S.A.), XLIX, June 1968, pp. 11–17.

[8] Churchman, C. W., *The systems approach*, Delta Books, 1968.

[9] Churchman, C. W., *Prediction and Optimal Decision*, Prentice-Hall, 1961.

[10] Coase, R. H., The nature of the firm, *Economica*, 1937; reprinted in *Readings in Price Theory*, American Economic Association, Irwin, 1952.

[11] Cohen, M. R. and E. Nagel, *An Introduction to Logic and Scientific Method*, Routledge & Kegan Paul, 1934.

[12] Cyert, R. M. and J. G. March, *A Behavioral Theory of the Firm*, Prentice-Hall, 1963.

[13] Dorfman, R., *The Price System*, Prentice-Hall, 1964, pp. 6–7.

[14] Dorfman, R., Operations Research, in *Surveys of Economic Theory, vol. III*, American Economic Association and Royal Economic Society, Macmillan, London, 1967, pp. 29–74.

[15] Edwards, W. and A. Tversky, *Decision Making*, Penguin, 1967.

[16] Feltham, G. A., The value of information, *Accounting Review*, XLIII, Oct. 1968, pp. 684–96; reprinted in *Readings in Management Decision*, ed. L. R. Amey, Longman, 1973.

[17] Holt, Modigliani, Muth and Simon, *Planning Production, Inventories and Work Force*, Prentice-Hall, 1960.

[18] Ijiri, Y., *The Foundations of Accounting Measurement*, Prentice-Hall, 1967.

[19] Ijiri, Y., Fundamental queries in aggregation theory, *Journal of American Statistical Association*, 66, Dec. 1971, pp. 766–82.

[20] Jaedicke, Ijiri and Nielsen, eds., *Research in Accounting Measurement*, American Accounting Association, 1966.

[21] Khinchin, A. I., *Mathematical Foundations of Information Theory*, Dover Publications, 1957.

[22] Lev, B., *Accounting and Information Theory*, American Accounting Association, 1969.

[23] Malmgren, H. B., Information, expectations and the theory of the firm, *Quarterly Journal of Economics*, Aug. 1961, pp. 399–421; reprinted in *Readings in Management Decision*, ed. L. R. Amey, Longman, 1973.

[24] Marschak, J., Towards an economic theory of organisation and information, in *Decision Processes*, ed. Thrall, Coombs and Davis, Wiley, 1954, pp. 187–220.

[25] Marschak, J., Elements for a theory of teams, *Management Science*, Jan. 1955, pp. 127–37.

[26] Marschak, J., Remarks on the economics of information, in *Contributions to Scientific Research in Management*, University of California, Los Angeles, 1959, pp. 79–98.

[27] Marshall, A., *Principles of Economics*, Macmillan, London, 8th edn., 1938.

[28] National Computing Centre, *Commodity Coding*: its effect on data recording and transfer, 1968.

[29] Prince, T. R., *Information Systems for Management Planning and Control*, Irwin, revised edn., 1970.

[30] Raiffa, H., *Decision Analysis*, Addison-Wesley, 1968.

[31] Raiffa, H. and R. Schlaifer, *Applied Statistical Decision Theory*, Harvard University Press, 1961.

[32] Schlaifer, R., *Probability and Statistics for Business Decisions*, McGraw-Hill, 1959.

[33] Shannon, C. E., A mathematical theory of communication, *The Bell System Technical Journal*, XXVII, June 1948, pp. 379–423.

[34] Shubik, M., Objective functions and models of corporate optimization, *Quarterly Journal of Economics*, Aug. 1961, pp. 345–75.

[35] Stigler, G. J., *Capital and Rates of Return in Manufacturing Industries*, National Bureau of Economic Research, Princeton University Press, 1963.

[36] Stigler, G. J., The economics of information, *Journal of Political Economy*, LXIX, June 1961, pp. 213–25.

[37] Theil, H., *Economics and Information Theory*, North-Holland Publishing Co. and Rand McNally, 1967.

[38] Theil, H., On the use of information theory concepts in the analysis of financial statements, *Management Science*, 15, Series A, 1968–69, pp. 459–80.

[39] Vickrey, D., Is accounting a measurement discipline? *Accounting Review*, XLV, Oct. 1970, pp. 731–42.

[40] von Neumann, J. and O. Morgenstern, *Theory of Games and Economic Behavior*, Princeton University Press, 2nd edn., 1947.

Problems

1.1 Reflect on the quotation from Shubik at the beginning of this chapter.

1.2 'Information is a valuable resource . . . And yet . . . mostly it is ignored. . . . Some important aspects of economic organization take on a new meaning when they are considered from the viewpoint of the search for information'.

Carefully discuss this search process in relation to one of the following:
1. The identification of sellers in a market and the discovery of their prices.
2. The detection of profitable fields for investment.
3. A worker's choice of industry, location and job.

1.3 Discuss the following statements, taken from the same source, in relation to measurement in accounting:

1. '. . . the real world and the informational world interact. One is not merely a shadow of the other. . . . Of course, we should not lose the substance by grasping the shadow, but often the shadow helps us grasp the substance'.
2. 'The concept of [historical] costs . . . is the most essential element in accounting measurement . . . [it] has an advantage over other [measures in being] unique and certain'.

1.4 Enumerate ways in which a firm might bring about a reduction in uncertainty and/or information costs by generating 'controlled information'. [Reread section 2(b)(ii); see also section 1 of Chapter 18.]

1.5 How can a knowledge of statistical method help the accountant?

1.6 In the context of a very large business enterprise, the 'information explosion' is just a slogan meaning that greatly increased capability for processing and communicating data is more often than not grossly misused. Discuss this view.

1.7 Information flows in business organizations often differ from those in the official organization chart; and optimal information flows are often even farther removed from actual flows.

Assuming that this statement is correct, to what extent are accountants culpable concerning the second of these discrepancies?

1.8 'It is difficult for an organization to assemble all the information that would be recognized as relevant (if known) [to its decision-making]. In the long run [this leads to] extensive use of essentially contingent decisions. Decisions are used as devices for learning about their hidden consequences (through outcries or other quick feedback – simulation in the raw).'

Elaborate on this argument, and consider the trade-off which is involved.

2

The entity accounts

Accountancy students are normally taught to regard double entry bookkeeping as the foundation on which the rest of the structure is built. It must, however, be clear that this statistical technique can never add anything to the original data, though it may well present data in such a way that information becomes available which would not otherwise be disclosed.

RONALD S. EDWARDS (in [4])

2.1 Fundamentals of entity accounts

Entity accounts are records in which the economic transactions of an entity are classified and summarized; entity reports are summary statements of accounting information for the entity as a whole, prepared or reproduced from the accounts.

There are certain fundamentals common to all entity accounting. At first sight these fundamentals may seem self-evident, but it is important to distinguish the basic framework so that later developments can be perceived as options chosen for specific purposes. The four prerequisites to the preparation of entity accounts can be listed* as:

1. An entity.
2. Resources and transactions to be recorded.
3. Data capable of being quantified and a unit of measurement to allow data to be aggregated on a common basis.
4. A time period over which the data are to be summarized.

The components of this list are considered below.

(a) Definition of the entity

Any separable area of economic activities can be treated as an entity for accounting purposes, but the area will be chosen to serve the information requirements of those who have some effective control over the economic activities in question.

Three major classes of economic activity can be distinguished; these classes are not mutually exclusive, but can overlap in their areas of economic activities in the manner illustrated in Figure 2.1.

(i) *Legal entity*

A legal entity recognized in law as an independent 'person' with specific legal

---

* This list, and the list of entity reporting aims in section 2 are adapted from [11]. See also [6] Chapters 2–5 and [10] Chapters 2–4.

rights, in particular the rights to own property and enter legally binding contracts. A legal entity may be an individual or a body incorporated by law to represent certain interests of individuals. The latter group encompasses a variety of bodies

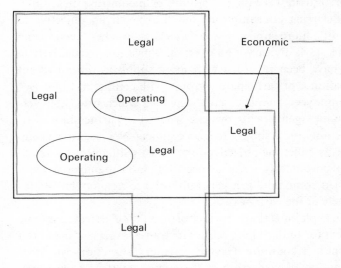

Figure 2.1 Areas of entity activities

with diverse aims; in Britain statutory corporations with powers and duties imposed by Parliament on behalf of citizens (the National Coal Board, the Post Office, etc.), bodies incorporated by Royal Charter with powers and duties imposed by the Privy Council (originating from the days of executive monarchs), trade unions registered under the Industrial Relations Act, and, most important for the purposes of this book, companies incorporated under the Companies Acts.

The Companies Acts require a company to have members, who are normally shareholders who own shares in the company and control it in law. As is well known, a company can be, and usually is, incorporated with limited liability so that legal claims against the company are confined to resources in the company's ownership and exclude members' personal resources which are not committed to the company. The entity accounts are concerned solely with transactions and resources within the ambit of the entity. A fresh contribution demanded from the members would, of course, come within the ambit of the entity.

(ii) *Economic entity*

An economic entity is an area of economic activity governed by autonomous economic objectives. On occasion this term is applied in the accounting literature to any entity which engages in economic activities; as used here the term is confined to an entity which is 'self-governing' in that its economic objectives are not subordinated to the objectives of another entity.

Classical economics divides economic entities into two classes, each with a single economic objective: individuals with an objective of maximizing their utility by consumption or by deferring consumption, and firms with an objective of maximizing profits (or a little more subtly, in neoclassical economics, maximizing the value of the firm). This stark division is an over-simplification, particularly in relation to firms, which have been regarded with more sophistication in recent economic literature as coalitions of participating groups with conflicting objectives (management, owners, employees, suppliers, etc.). Any firm which ostensibly acts as an autonomous economic agent for its owners, whether a partnership, a co-operative enterprise or a company, is subject to such conflicts. Nor are inter-group conflicts the only difficulty: conflicting objectives often exist within groups, and in the proprietorship group particularly when owners double in managerial functions; only in widely owned companies is it generally valid to assume that shareholders are interested solely in the cash nexus.

Despite its limitations in explaining the behaviour of firms, the classical economic view of the firm as an agent for undertaking economic transactions at a profit is a useful, and central, concept in accounting. The recording of transactions would be pointless without some notion of ownership of the subject matter of the transactions, and incomplete without proprietors to whom the residual effect of the transactions, profit or loss, could be assigned. Consequently entity accounts treat the entity as a vehicle for owners of some sort. The concept of the firm as an entity governed by autonomous economic objectives is important not only for entity accounts, but in the use of accounting information generally within the firm. It defines the boundaries within which the objectives of the parts can be assumed to be subordinated to the whole.

When the firm is composed of a number of subordinate sectors it is necessary to aggregate data for reporting the results of the firm as a whole. However, if the firm has only limited ownership in the subordinate sectors the rights of other owners must be recognized; thus the tinted line representing the economic entity in Figure 2.1 does not totally encompass the legal entities. The economic entity approach could be applied to an individual who controls a number of companies, but almost invariably a company which is not controlled by another company is regarded as the apex of the firm for all accounting purposes.

What constitutes effective control can be a difficult matter to determine in practice, but for a group of companies we can accept the legal definitions which impose a duty to consolidate reports for the group (to be considered in section 5); it is rare to find the aggregation of routine accounting data for a wider definition of the firm. Indeed for most internal reporting purposes the aggregation of data will be less than that required by law for external users; the problems posed by conflicting objectives in different parts of the firm are not solved by simply aggregating routinely recorded data for past transactions.

(iii) *Operating entity*

An operating entity (termed a *segment* of the firm in later chapters) is an area of economic activities for which boundaries can be defined, but within which activities are subordinated to the economic objectives of the wider entity of the firm. The requirements of the firm will determine the boundaries of the operating entity, which may be defined in relation to some subset of the wider entity's activities entrusted to agents or managers (a particular business enterprise, a division of a company), or in relation to the economic activities associated with a certain physical location (a factory, a store). Clearly an operating entity can be conterminous with a legal entity and a firm: a factory owned by an independent legal company would constitute an entity for legal, economic and operating purposes. Accounting reports for operating entities are examined in Part 3 of this book.

(b) Resources and transactions

Entity accounts are concerned with transactions involving resources, goods and services, and obligations arising from the acquisition and employment of resources. As an agent for its owners the entity is assumed to be holding and converting resources for the proprietors' benefit, and not for consumption on its own behalf.

(c) Quantification and the unit of measurement

Quantification is achieved by reference to exchange transactions with other entities, either actual or potential. Even when the accounts record intra-entity transactions which change the form of the resources commanded by the entity, the recording is based on outside exchange transactions. Timber, glue and varnish may be transformed with the aid of labour and machinery into a piece of furniture – say a desk. In one sense the new resource is already quantified, as one desk, but a variety of pieces of furniture could not be quantified on a common physical basis. The monetary unit provides the common basis of measurement for quantification, and all resources and obligations are quantified by assigning them monetary terms derived from exchange transactions.

Conventionally, only exchange transactions in which the entity actually took part are adopted as a basis for quantification; incoming resources are assigned the money prices at which they were acquired, so that they are recorded in the accounts at *historic cost*. (That describes the general rule: there are many exceptions.) Resources which change their character within the entity, like the desk, are regarded as composed of original input resources at their original prices; just which inputs

41

will be considered later. The conventional approach is not dictated by the accounting framework, but is merely one of three possible options for assigning money prices. The money prices could be determined by reference to:

1. The original past transaction which brought the resources into the entity.
2. Current transactions involving comparable resources.
3. An expected future transaction disposing of the resources.

These options are important because the money prices of resources do not remain constant over time; the selection of a particular approach will have implications for the uses made of the accounting information. Such problems of valuation will be examined in Chapter 3.

(d) The accounting period

The accounting period is a device for dividing the continuum of activities of an entity into discrete time intervals. The current time period inherits certain resources and obligations from the preceding period; in due course, when the current period has been completed, the effect of the current period's activities are apportioned between those which have *expired* (revenues and expenses) and those which bequeath resources and obligations to the next time period.

The choice of time period clearly depends on the purpose of the accounts. Traditionally the time period for full entity accounts is one year, primarily because accounts are prepared annually for external users, but also because a full year envelops seasonal fluctuations. Much shorter periods are normally adopted for internal appraisal purposes (although such accounts would not usually be in the format to be considered here), and the publication of quarterly interim reports to shareholders is now commonplace.

2.2 Uses and aims of entity reports

Entity reports may serve a variety of purposes, the most familiar being the provision of information to the external user. In the case of limited companies the external user can be literally anyone, but the major users are: existing and potential shareholders, trade unions, and employees, frequently using information filtered by financial commentators; creditors and lenders, often assisted by credit-rating agencies, and the tax authorities who uniquely require substantial adjustments to the underlying data before accepting the reports for their purposes. The reports essentially provide information to assist decision-making by the external user: to disinvest or invest in the company's shares, to press for a certain level of wages, to grant or withdraw credit, or to assess taxation at a particular level.

The legal requirements of the Companies Acts 1948 and 1967 are primarily couched in terms of the disclosure of certain items of information; they do not specify the *bases* on which the underlying accounting data are to be determined. The major guidance provided by the law is that published company accounting reports must present a 'true and fair view'; this phrase is magnificent in intention, but it provides precious little guidance on implementation. The view sought by a lender interested in assessing the safety of a short-term loan is not the same as that sought by an investor who is interested in the company's growing profitability. In effect the law delegates the implementation of the true and fair viewpoint to the directors and auditors of the company, who are in turn guided by certain conventions representing acceptable measurement practice within the accountancy profession. The law would regard an accepted convention as sufficient, although not essential, proof of truth and fairness in a company's published accounting reports. One of the difficulties of the conventions is that they encompass a wide variety of alternative treatments; auditors will usually agree to any treatment coming within the conventions, and consequently management has an area of choice in the determination of accounting data presented to the outside world.

The interest of management in entity reports generally is not clear-cut, but three major areas can be distinguished:

1. The influence, suggested above, of external reports on the decisions of external users which have implications for the firm. This aspect will be considered in Chapter 4.

2. Overall appraisal of the efficiency of the entity. This is essentially a monitoring function, in the sense that appraisal may trigger further investigation, and usually data collection, on the basis of which decisions may be made; rarely would the original entity reports be sufficient for a decision. Thus management's attitude to the entity reports will be very different from that of the external user, who must make do with the information he is given unless he has some powerful sanction to induce the production of further information (as have the tax authorities or substantial lenders). In effect the entity reports will suggest questions to management (a naive example might be 'why has profit declined?'), and may indicate partial answers ('a decline in sales'), but they rarely provide sufficient guidance for action ('can anything be done about it in the next period?').

   Nor will entity reports for management use normally be in the same form as those for external consumption; more detail, particularly on the components of profit, and comparisons with budgets would be commonplace.

3. Examination of the financing structure in relation to the resources held by the entity, with regard to financial stability and the costs of financing. Again the function of the entity reports will be primarily that of a trigger to further

investigation. Aspects of the finance function will be considered in Chapters 19 and 20.

In order to satisfy the needs of users, entity accounts should ideally conform to certain aims. Most of the problems of entity accounting arise because it is impossible to satisfy all of these aims all of the time, and the relative importance of different aims may depend upon the viewpoint of the user of the information. The major aims are considered below.

(a) Continuity

As the accounting period is merely a device for dividing up the continuum of the entity's activities into discrete intervals, the reports for a particular period should be presented in the context of the entity's continuing operations over its expected life; in other words, resources and obligations at the end of the accounting period should be determined in relation to their expected effect on the activities of future periods. Normally the life of an entity is impossible to forecast, and is potentially infinite in the case of a company; therefore life can be assumed to be indefinite unless there is evidence to the contrary. This is commonly termed the 'going concern' approach.*

(b) Objectivity

Changes affecting the entity's resources and obligations should not be recorded in the accounts until they can be recorded in objective terms. This begs the question of what is meant by objective; to avoid entering into a philosophical discussion we can accept one of the meanings given in the *Concise Oxford Dictionary* as 'exhibiting actual facts uncoloured by the exhibitor's feelings or opinions'. There is an immediate conflict with the first aim of continuity – expectations of continuance must be coloured by opinions.

(c) Consistency

Accounting procedures should be followed consistently from period to period. This aim is an attempt to provide a link between the previous two; it is perhaps the least difficult aim to achieve, but clearly its achievement does not necessarily provide either a view of the entity's continuing activities or objectivity.

(d) Stable measuring unit

Accounting reports should be based on a stable measuring unit. Money anywhere

*For example, see [7].

44

in the world patently does not provide a stable measuring unit in terms of its command over real resources (in more familiar language, its purchasing power), but the monetary unit provides the only basis for aggregating the results of diverse activities. This dilemma will be more fully examined in Chapter 3.

(e) Disclosure

Reports should disclose whatever may be necessary to avoid misleading the reader; there is an implicit assumption here of the way in which the user may employ the reports, because to avoid misleading one must know the direction in which to lead. A rider which might be added to this aim is that reports should not disclose data which are immaterial in amount, and which would merely distract the user; again some assumption of what the user would regard as material must be made.

The relative priority given to these aims might be expected to depend to a considerable extent upon the needs of the user, but the preparation of entity reports and the recording of underlying data have been overwhelmingly influenced by external reporting, where the precise use which will be made of the information is unpredictable. In this situation an 'open-ended' concept of the function of accounting information has been adopted, and objectivity has been given the highest priority. This explains the conventional emphasis on historic cost; opinions are rarely involved in the determination of the monetary amounts at which transactions with other entities were undertaken.

Conventional accounting adopts a sixth aim *in certain areas*, that of conservatism.* As used here, the term means 'cautious, purposely low', so that in situations of doubt the money amounts assigned to resources and profits err on the side of understatement. This aim, often referred to as the 'doctrine of conservatism', comes into play in the determination of the resources and obligations at the end of the accounting period. Historically the doctrine is the result of a number of influences: the belief that users are best served by cautious estimates, the desire on the part of the directors of many companies to have a buffer against the effects of bad years, and the alleged influence of inveterately pessimistic lenders as major users of accounting reports in the formative years of accounting conventions.

Inevitably the elevation of objectivity and conservatism in conventional accounting is at the expense of other aims, and particularly of disclosure. It may be objective and conservative to record a building in the accounts at its historic cost of £10 000, but not very informative if similar buildings now command a price in the region of £30 000. If the building is subsequently sold for £15 000, it may be objective to record a profit of £5 000, but not very informative of the efficiency in the use of resources in the intervening period.

Having noted the existence of the problems, we shall illustrate historic cost data

* Or, euphemistically, prudence – see [7].

in our examination of the basic accounting system; in Chapter 3 it will be seen that the recording system does *not* dictate the nature of the data to be employed.

2.3 Double entry and the accounting identities

The accounting records of an entity may take a variety of different physical forms: hand-written or machine kept files, punched cards, magnetic tapes, discs and print-outs in a computer system. The organization of recording will often involve variations in procedure between different classes of transaction, influenced by such considerations as the volume of transactions in particular classes and different peripheral requirements for the analysis of data. Few, if any, of the accounting records of a sizeable firm would nowadays be kept in the bound books of the Dickensian world, and then only at the final summary stage. Long usage has, however, made *books of account* or simply *the books* generally accepted (and conveniently brief) terms for the financial accounting records of an entity; associated terms are *book entry* for the recording of an item somewhere within the financial accounting system, and *book value* for the money amount at which an item is recorded.

Whatever the refinements of the underlying system, a complete record of the transactions of an entity can be aggregated to form a set of double entry accounts in which the effect of every transaction is represented in its dual aspect. The completion of double entry accounts, at least at the ultimate stage of the recording process, is now synonymous with accounting. Double entry is a highly efficient and adaptable technique for classifying data, but it is not indispensable; some large and successful firms used single entry methods of accounting well into the twentieth century [14].

Any transaction can be considered to involve the transfer of resources to someone or somewhere, from someone or somewhere. From the viewpoint of the entity as a whole the effect of the dual aspects of past recorded transactions can be summarized at any point of time by:

Assets: resources or rights to resources transferred into the entity which have not been extinguished by subsequent transfers in the recording process (e.g. cash, debtors, labour services, machinery);

Claims: obligations of the entity to the outside world which have not been extinguished by subsequent transfers in the recording process (e.g. loan obligations to lenders, obligations to owners).

Claims are subdivided between the claims of owners (which will be termed here the *proprietorship claim*) and the claims of non-owners, termed *liabilities*. The proprietorship claim for a company can be further subdivided between the claims of:

Preference shareholders: shareholders who have preference over equity share-holders for specified limited rights to distributions in dividends and on liquidation of the company;

Equity shareholders: *ordinary* shareholders who possess all residual ownership rights to the firm and (usually) voting rights.

Preference shareholders are more akin to long-term lenders than to owners, and henceforth will be largely ignored.

Since proprietors are treated as external to the entity, and possess residual rights against the assets, the total claims against the entity must always be equal to the total assets. This basic accounting identity can be expressed as:

$$A \equiv K$$

or
$$A \equiv S + L$$

where A is the sum of the individual assets,

K is the sum of the individual claims,

S is the proprietorship claim,

L is the sum of liabilities.

The implications of the notation are considered more fully below.

(i) $A = \sum_{j=1}^{n} a_j$, where n = number of asset accounts of the entity, and a_j = any asset account numbered 1 to n. Thus if there were 99 accounts:

$$A = \sum_{j=1}^{99} = a_1 + a_2 + \cdots + a_{99}.$$

(ii) $S = C + P$, where C = capital contributed by shareholders of a company and P = profit retained from past periods. The capital of a company must (by British law) be kept separate from the retained profits.* The capital will always include *issued capital* comprising the number of shares issued multiplied by a *nominal value* or *par value* (e.g. 100 000 shares at £1 each); it may also include an amount of *share premium* for any issues of shares made above par. For example, if 20 000 of the previously mentioned shares were issued at a price of £2 each the share premium would be £20 000.

(iii) $L = \sum_{j=1}^{n} l_j$, where l is a liability account, in the same manner as for assets.

(iv) $K = S + L = C + P + L$

and $S = A - L$

Double entry hinges on the basic accounting identity. Every transaction is repre-

---

*Retained profits can be transferred into capital by making a *bonus* (or *scrip*) issue of shares, but capital cannot be transferred into profits.

sented by two entries in the books; once on the *debit* (traditionally left) side of the 'receiving' account, which can be considered as the asset side, and once on the *credit* (traditionally right) side of the 'foregoing' account, which can be considered as the claims side.

Table 2.1 Double entry accounts

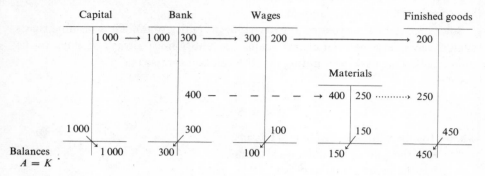

Double entry accounts are illustrated in Table 2.1; the data are complete for double entry purposes, because $A = K$, but they are incomplete for reporting purposes. Some of the resources represented by the 'asset' accounts will have yielded up their benefits; certainly wages yield benefits concurrently with, or prior to, their payment, but only part of the labour services shown above have been embodied in finished goods. Presumably the remaining wages were paid to workers who were not identifiable with the production of goods.

Normally the term 'asset' is applied only to those debit balances which represent resources which have *not* yielded up their benefits. The wider meaning being adopted here (debit balance = asset) is important conceptually, if unorthodox: debit balances are eliminated from the books when the resources they represent have expired, therefore a debit balance *should* be the same as an asset in the usual accounting sense; the fact that many expired debit balances are not eliminated concurrently with the expiry of resources, but at the end of the accounting period, is a matter of convenience in the accounting process.

The transactions of an entity take three major forms, all of which take place within the framework of the assets/claims identity. Figure 2.2 illustrates the mirror image effect on assets/claims arising from each form of transaction (although it does not illustrate all feasible transactions).

(a) Composition transactions

In the profit seeking entity the ultimate purpose of transactions can be assumed to be the achievement of reward for the proprietors, which will be reflected by a

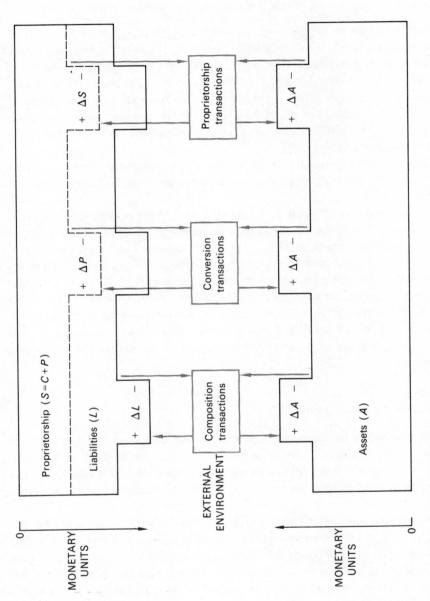

Figure 2.2 Illustration of the accounting identity $A \equiv S + L$

change in the proprietorship claim. The proximate effect of many transactions is, however, to change the composition of assets and liabilities without affecting the proprietorship claim. Transactions of this type can be divided into three categories.

1. Asset acquisitions in exchange for monetary assets, cash or bank, or in exchange for liabilities, usually trade creditors. The effect on the total assets/ claims relationship would be $\Delta A^+ = \Delta A^-$ or $\Delta A^+ = \Delta L^+$. Disposing of monetary assets and incurring liabilities cause no problems of differences between the money prices recorded in the books and the money prices at which transactions take place; the disposal of *non*-monetary assets normally gives rise to such differences (i.e. profits or losses), and is considered under conversion transactions.

2. Liability settlements, almost invariably in exchange for monetary assets ($\Delta A^- = \Delta L^-$), but occasionally by the exchange of one liability for another ($\Delta L^+ = \Delta L^-$).

3. Internal transfers of assets at unchanged money prices. These transactions represent a preliminary stage in the conversion process; in the manufacture of finished goods the incorporation of labour, materials and other resources to make up the goods will be represented by transfers from these accounts (at original money prices) to some form of goods account. ($\Delta A^- = \Delta A^+$.) In fact it will be seen later that these transfers have repercussions on the profit calculation, because they will determine the division between assets used up in the period (goods sold) and assets carried forward to succeeding periods (including finished and partly finished goods at the end of the accounting period).

(b) Conversion transactions

Conversion transactions occur when assets are sold and leave the ownership of the entity. In conventional accounting this is the usual signal (but not the only possible signal) for recognition of a change from historic cost – in exchange for the assets the entity may acquire money, a debtor for the amount, or some other class of asset.

The monetary amounts at which purchasers take assets will normally be different from (and usually more than) the amounts at which the assets are recorded in the books. The original assets have been converted into new assets of different monetary amount, and the net difference between the new and old amounts will represent a profit or loss for the proprietors.* ($\Delta A^+ = \Delta A^- \pm \Delta P$, or rarely where disposal of an asset is offset against a liability $\Delta L^- = \Delta A^- \pm \Delta P$.)

---

*At this point it can be said that a profit or loss has been *realized*, but the word is sometimes used when profit is *recognized* in the absence of a conversion transaction. See [1].

It would be impossible in reality to match the assets (resources) yielded up in each conversion transaction against the value gained by the entity in exchange. For example, when you buy a cinema ticket you buy the right to *share* in the benefits provided by the resources of the cinema on a particular evening: the building, the services of the usherettes, projectionists, cleaners, etc.; you do not purchase a particular identifiable slice of these resources. In a similar way an entity dealing in tangible goods requires a variety of back-up resources: buildings, sales staff, management, etc. Consequently the matching process for conversion transactions takes place in relation to the accounting period; all resources which have yielded up their benefits during the period are offset in aggregate against the total value gained by disposal of resources in the period. The matching concept [2] is central to profit measurement in accounting, irrespective of whether the historic cost basis or some current cost basis is adopted. Assets which have yielded up part of their benefits in the current period, say machines, are offset in part against the current profit calculation, and the unexpired portions of the assets are bequeathed to the succeeding period.

The assets which have yielded up their benefits during a period are a sub-set of the total asset balances at the end of the period (immediately before the profit calculation takes place), and are termed *expenses*; similarly the total potential increment to the proprietorship claim can be considered as a component of that claim immediately before the profit calculation, and is termed *revenue*. It is usual to refer to expense and revenue accounts as such, rather than as assets and claims, because the relevant data for items which normally expire during the period are collected in readily identifiable accounts as part of the recording process during the period (e.g. salaries, rent, sales); only items which overlap in their effect between the current and the succeeding period need to be given specific attention at the end of the period.

The effects of the conversion transactions can be summarized in terms of the notation used earlier, with a few additions.

$$A = A_1 + E$$

where A_1 is the sum of the individual asset balances which will be bequeathed to the next period and E is the sum of the expense account balances.

$$S = C + P + R$$

where R is the sum of the revenue account balances before profit is calculated. But

$$A \equiv L + S$$

$$\therefore \quad A_1 = L + C + P + (R - E)$$

$$= L + C + P \pm \Delta P$$

The entity accounts

The net effect of the conversion transaction can be seen by comparing the above equation with a hypothetical situation where those transactions had not taken place, and where it can be assumed cavalierly that no asset disposals affected the level of liabilities. Here A_0 is the sum of the individual asset balances in the absence of the conversion transactions.

$$A_0 = L + C + P$$

so that

$$A_1 - A_0 = \pm \Delta P.$$

The above equation provides the justification for illustrating conversion transactions as $\pm \Delta A = \pm \Delta P$ in Figure 2.2. The net effect of conversion transactions *alone* will usually be reflected in the change of assets available to the entity. Of course this does *not* mean that profit can be measured by the change in total assets in the accounting period; adjustments would have to be made for changes which occurred in liabilities during the period and for contributions/distributions affecting proprietors.

Liabilities were held constant above for simplicity in considering the major aspect of conversion of assets, but liabilities can give rise to conversion transactions when the amount at which they are redeemed is different from the amount at which they are recorded in the books. The most common example is the discount given by creditors for prompt payment ($\Delta L^- = \Delta A^- + \Delta P$).

(c) **Proprietorship transactions**

Proprietorship transactions can obviously take the form of either contributions to the entity or distributions from it. The powers of a company in this area are determined by law, and for distributions particularly by case law rather than the Companies Acts. Although the legal position is complex, it can be summarized broadly as follows.

1. Capital, once subscribed to the company by equity shareholders, cannot be repaid to them except by sanction of the Courts. (There can, however, be redeemable *preference* shares.)
2. Distributions must be made from profits of either current or earlier periods. In strict law it would be possible for a company to distribute a dividend from profit of the current period, even though there was an accumulated loss from earlier periods. Such a procedure would be exceedingly rare.

   Contributions and distributions are usually, although not invariably, made in cash. The effects on assets/proprietorship can be represented by:

   $$\Delta A^+ = \Delta C^+ \quad \text{and} \quad \Delta A^- = \Delta P^-, \text{ illustrated in Figure 2.2.}$$

   The first stages in the payment of a dividend are, however, a dividend declaration by the directors and approval by the shareholders; the dividend therefore appears initially in the accounts as a separate claim ($\Delta L^+ = \Delta P^-$). Occasionally a company may make a distribution to shareholders in the form of loan stock ($\Delta L^+ = \Delta P^-$), or lenders may extinguish a liability of the company in exchange for shares ($\Delta L^- = \Delta C^+$).

3. Retained profits can be capitalized (so that they are no longer available for distribution) by a bonus issue of shares to existing shareholders. This simply involves a book transfer between the two components of proprietorship claim: $\Delta C^+ = \Delta P^-$.

2.4 The principal entity reports

The principal entity reports are all concerned with the effects of the entity's activities up to the end of the accounting period, but they employ the recorded accounting data in different ways.

1. The balance sheet is a summary of the assets and claims of the entity at the *end* of the accounting period.
2. The income statements are summaries of the conversion transactions affecting the proprietorship claim *during* the period, and may be considered to include a statement of the distribution of income.
3. The funds flow statement is a summary of movements in assets and claims which took place *during* the period.

Both the income and funds flow statements are concerned with *flows* during the period.*

The first two classes of report are often called 'the final accounts'; they finalize the routine recording process at the end of the period. The Companies Acts require companies to publish a balance sheet and certain information from the income statements annually; the legal requirements and long usage have led to some degree of standardization in these reports. Funds statements have a shorter history (at least in their modern form), and are not required to be published; many companies do publish funds flow statements but forms of presentation are rather more diverse than for the final accounts.

The relationships of the double entry accounts with the balance sheet and income statements will be considered before proceeding to the presentation of the entity reports.

(a) The opening balances

The balance sheet comprises a list of the balances in the assets and claims accounts

---

*See [8] for a comparative treatment of income, funds and cash flows.

Table 2.2 Accounting data for Cog Ltd. (£000's)

ASSETS			CLAIMS	

31 December 19–0 / Balance sheet

ASSETS		CLAIMS	
‹···· 60	Freehold land	Share Capital	240 ··›
‹··· 150	Equipment	Creditors	55 ··›
‹····· 42	Materials		
‹····· 43	Bank		
295			295

Year 19–1 / Double entry accounts

Income accounts

Materials		Manufacturing		Trading		Sales revenue	
···› 42	300 ——→	300	600 ——→	600	800 ‹——	800	Δ800
Δ288	30 ··›						

Equipment						Share capital	
···› 150	15 ——→	15				‹··240	240 ‹····
	135 ··›						

Manufacturing expenses						Creditors	
Δ330	330 ——→	330	45 ··›			‹··· 95	55 ‹····
							Δ40

(Profit and Loss)

Non-manufacturing expenses				
Δ162	158 —————————→	158		
	4 ··›			

Freehold land		
···› 60	60 ··›	

Debtors		
Δ92	2 —————————→	2
	90 ··›	

Taxation ‹··18
Dividend ‹··10

Bank		
···› 43	Δ32	
	11 ··›	Retained ‹··12

31 December 19–1 / Balance sheet

60	‹······· Freehold land	Share capital	·······›	240
135	‹······· Equipment	Retained profit	·······›	12
45	‹······· Goods	Proposed dividend	·······›	10
30	‹······· Materials	Taxation	·······›	18
90	‹······· Debtors	Creditors	·······›	95
4	‹······· Prepayments			
11	‹······· Bank			
375				375

at the end of one period – and clearly the same list of balances must form the starting point for the next period.

Table 2.2 commences with a balance sheet at 31 December 19–0, representing the opening balance sheet for Cog Ltd. for the year 19–1. Cog is assumed to have commenced its activities in December 19–0, when share capital was issued. The money contributed by shareholders for 240 000 £1 shares was immediately used to acquire freehold land for a future factory and some equipment; temporary premises were rented and more equipment and materials were obtained on credit.

It will be seen from Table 2.2 that the amounts in Cog's end 19–0 balance sheet are the same as the opening balances in the double entry accounts; this carry-forward procedure is indicated by the dotted lines running from the opening balance sheet to the accounts. In fact each balance sheet item represents a *class* of asset or claim; for example, separate accounts are kept for individual creditors. The principle of the carry-forward is unaffected by the aggregation.

(b) Transactions in the period

The amounts in Table 2.2 preceded by Δ represent the *net* effect of transactions during the period which have been entered in the accounts (or in memoranda form for subsequent entry in total) as they occurred. For example, the totals for entries of transactions in the debtors account might have been derived as illustrated in Table 2.3.

Table 2.3 Double entry transactions (£000's)

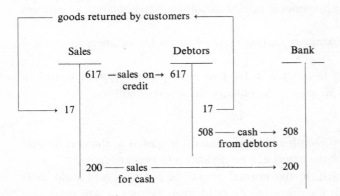

The accounts in Table 2.2 have been reduced to a minimum for illustration purposes; any number of accounts may be adopted to serve the needs of data collection.

(c) Closing the accounts

At the end of the period the unexpired balances representing assets and liabilities (non-proprietorship claims) bequeathed to the next period are carried forward in the accounts; these balances are summarized in the closing balance sheet as illustrated in Table 2.2. The remaining amounts representing unexpired conversion transactions are collected together in the income accounts; their ultimate residue constitutes profit or loss for the period, potentially an increase or decrease in the proprietorship claim.

Thus the profit calculation is inseparably linked with the determination of balance sheet values. For the present the valuation problem is deferred.

The classification of accounts in the books makes presumptions that the accounts relate to expired conversion transactions (*expense* or *revenue accounts*) or to unexpired assets or to claims. Certain accounting terminology can be most readily considered in the context of these presumptions.

(i) *Expense accounts*

Expense accounts record services, normally non-storable benefits, purchased in the period. Wages, power, rent, insurance, commission are some examples. The recording of these items takes place as they are paid for, but the receipt of the services is not necessarily concurrent with payment. Before the expenses can be transferred to the profit calculation, adjustment must be made for services not yet received (commonly a proportion of services continuing over a time interval, such as rent or insurance) and for services received but not paid for (such as wages). These adjustments are termed:

Prepayments: end-period adjustments carried forward as asset balances in expense accounts;

Accruals: end-period adjustments carried forward as claims balances in expense accounts.

A prepayment has been illustrated in the Cog example; an accrual would, of course, appear on the claims side of the balance sheet with creditors.

(ii) *Asset accounts*

These record resources representing storable benefits acquired in the current and preceding periods. Most of the assets can be divided into two groups:

Current assets: assets which, in the normal course of business, will yield their benefits within the firm's *operating cycle* (defined below) or are realizable within one year (year = usual accounting period for external reports);

Fixed assets: assets which, in the normal course of business, will yield their benefits over several years.

Current assets provide the medium through which the firm's everyday transactions occur; they are often said to *circulate*. A typical sequence might be:

cash → materials → work-in-progress → finished goods → debtors → cash

The average time period for a firm to complete the full cycle from cash to cash is termed the *operating cycle*; the length of this cycle varies with the nature of the firm's business (e.g. compare a baker and a builder).

The current asset accounts either involve exchanges with other assets or claims, or they involve use of resources which emerge eventually as expenses in the income calculation (e.g. in goods sold). When the unexpired benefits expected from an asset are less then the recorded amount at the end of the period this difference is also transferred as an expense. If the difference is considered to be objectively measurable it is treated as a reduction of the asset in the normal way; for example, the materials balance carried forward will represent the remaining physical units and the materials expensed will represent both materials used *and* any shortage. (*Separation* of the last two amounts depends on the recording of materials as they are used.) With regard to the treatment of finished goods manufactured within the firm (or work-in-progress) the balance carried forward is a matter of accounting convention, depending on which expenses are recognized as costs associated with the goods. For Cog it can be assumed that the appropriate association of costs with the manufacture of goods has been undertaken, and that a single product is manufactured of which $\frac{3}{43}$ of the units produced during the year were held at 31 December 19–1, thus:

$$\frac{3}{43} \times £645\,000 = £45\,000$$

An estimated reduction in the recorded amount of an asset is termed a *provision* and is segregated as a claims balance until its validity is known; the expense side is charged to profit calculation as before. Current assets usually subject to provisions are debtors, when a reduction is made for the amount of debtors as a whole. On past experience some proportion of debtors may be expected not to pay, or a proportion may be expected to take cash discounts on the balances they owe. Cog's reduction in debtors, if related to a general provision for doubtful debts, should have been recorded:

Debtors	Provision for doubtful debts
Balance £92 000	£2 000 ⟶ Profit calculation

Fixed assets (buildings, equipment, machinery, etc.) do not reveal their unexpired benefits in a readily identifiable form until they are sold or scrapped. The reduction in the recorded amount of a fixed asset at the end of a period, which is termed *depreciation*, is usually (but not invariably) based on the premise that the cost minus eventual scrap value of a fixed asset should be expensed equally over the periods of its expected 'useful life'. This *straight line method of depreciation* is naive but it will serve for the present. Cog's depreciation is consistent with the straight line method if the equipment's useful life is considered to be ten years, with nil scrap value. The freehold land has not been depreciated as it has an infinite expected life.

Depreciation must involve an estimated reduction in the amount of an asset, and the accumulation of depreciation is treated as a provision. On disposal of the asset, any over- or under-provision is cleared to the income account of the current period, although the adjustment strictly relates to profits calculated in earlier periods.

Another asset division is that between *tangible* assets and *intangible* assets. The former are physical assets, or financial assets involving well-defined rights against specific outsiders (such as investments or debtors). Intangible assets involve rights, sometimes ill-defined, to non-physical assets against outsiders in general (for example, trademarks, patents, research and development). Intangible assets are usually conservatively treated by swiftly 'expensing' the assets against income.

(iii) *Revenue accounts*

These record potential increments to the proprietorship claim. Most revenue, particularly sales, would be recorded during the period on the acquisition of debtors or cash. Some classes of revenue are, however, recorded during the period only when cash is received, similarly to the recording of expenses; such revenue accounts may require end-period adjustments for revenue receivable. Rent from property and investment income accruing over time are typical examples. But conventional accounting would record an end-year adjustment to revenue only when a specific legal right to the revenue exists. Thus interest accrued up to the end of the period would be considered as receivable because a legal right to sue arises, but a dividend on an equity investment which is confidently expected but not yet declared would be ignored.

(iv) *Liability accounts*

Liability accounts, which record non-proprietorship claims, are maintained at the full level of any obligation to outsiders, even though there is a strong expectation that the claim may be settled for a lesser amount. For example, cash discount for prompt payment may be expected to be taken on the creditor balances outstanding at the end of the period, but no end-period adjustment would be made in conventional accounting. Contrast the treatment of debtors; the asymmetry arises from conservatism.

(d) Presenting the balance sheet

Two simple guidelines influence the presentation of balance sheets.

1. Assets and claims are grouped. The fixed asset and current asset groups have been explained; non-conforming assets, such as investments, are given separate groups. The claims groups are: proprietorship claim; long-term liabilities, which are loans or debt not currently payable; and current liabilities, which are defined in a manner corresponding to current assets.

   In the presentation of the proprietorship claim the term *reserve* is often applied to parts of the claim other than the nominal value of share capital. Thus retained profits may be termed 'revenue reserves', share premium may be regarded as a capital (undistributable) reserve, a specific reserve may be created to 'equalize' tax charges in the accounts, etc. The claim as a whole is commonly titled *share capital and reserves* or *shareholders' equity*.

2. Assets are ranked in the order of their *liquidity* and claims are ranked in the order of their *urgency* within groups. These terms relate to the time which would elapse in the normal course of business before assets would be turned into cash and claims would be met.

In aggregation and lay-out there is substantial diversity between reports of different companies, although the Companies Acts set limits to aggregation. The balance sheet for Cog illustrated in Table 2.4 observes the major legal constraints on aggregation, such as the requirement to disclose depreciation provisions for fixed assets, but it does not demonstrate the minutiae of the disclosure requirements, which are usually met by notes. In traditional British practice claims appear on the left and assets on the right of the balance sheet, a reversal of the conventions adopted in the accounting books, but a columnar lay-out is now widely adopted in published accounts, as illustrated in Table 2.4.

(e) The income statements

Cog's income statements are presented in columnar form in Table 2.5. The presentation adopts the traditional divisions of the income statements, but the data have been severely summarized.

The make-up of expenses would normally be specified in detail for internal purposes. Published statements usually commence with profit before taxation, but in addition list certain specific data required to be disclosed by the Companies Acts, such as sales, depreciation for the year, or details of the directors remuneration. Thus the full statements are normally for internal circulation, although the figures they contain are determined by the requirements of conventional profit measurement.

Table 2.4 Cog. Ltd. – Conventional balance sheet (£000's)

Balance sheet at 31 December 19–1

	19–1		19–0	
Fixed assets				
Freehold land, at cost		60		60
Equipment, at cost	150		150	
Less accumulated depreciation	15		—	
	——	135	——	150
Current assets				
Inventories, at cost	75		42	
Debtors and prepayments	94		—	
Bank balance	11		43	
	180		85	
Less current liabilities				
Taxation	18		—	
Proposed dividend	10		—	
Creditors	95		55	
	123		55	
Net current assets		57		30
		252		240
Financed by:				
Shareholders' equity				
Issued share capital		240		240
Retained profit		12		—
		252		240

The statements divide the life cycle of conversion transactions into broad, and inevitably arbitrary, categories: the transformation of inputs into goods, in the Manufacturing account; the disposal of goods acquired or produced for resale, in the Trading account; the costs of back-up resources for the operations (administration, selling, distribution, financial expenses, etc.), in the Profit and Loss account, and finally the destination of profit (sometimes in a separately designated appropriation account).

Taxation on corporate profit is an appropriation of profit only in the strictly formal sense that it is dependent on profit being earned, although accounting profit is *not* the same as taxable profit because there are significant differences between the accounting conventions and the tax rules. More meaningfully, and very importantly from a decision viewpoint, taxation can be regarded as an expense to

Table 2.5 Cog Ltd. – Conventional income statements (£000's)

Cog Ltd.
Income statements for the year ended 31 December 19–1

Manufacturing account

Work-in-progress 1 January 19–1	—
Manufacturing costs	645
	645

Less

Work-in-progress 31 December 19–1	—
Cost of goods manufactured	645

Less

Increase in finished goods held	45
Cost of goods sold	600

Trading account

Sales	800
Cost of goods sold	600
Gross profit	200

Profit and loss account

Gross profit	200
Expenses (non-manufacturing)	160
Net profit before taxation	40
Corporation tax on taxable profit	18
Net profit after taxation	22
Proposed dividend	10
Retained profit of year	12

be incurred in obtaining a residual profit for the shareholders. For reporting after the event the distinction is trivial, and the term appropriation is commonly avoided altogether in published accounts.

(f) The funds flow statement

The funds flow statement* deals with *changes* in assets and claims, and displays the sources of funds and the uses to which they were applied during the period.

The word funds has many connotations in general usage and in accounting. Whatever the definition adopted for funds, the statement can be considered as

* For a comprehensive treatment see [3].

revealing flows in and out of 'funds'. Figure 2.3 illustrates how funds may be viewed as an asset account into which resources flow (debit to funds) from a non-funds account (credit to non-funds); thus the non-funds account constitutes the source of funds. Conversely, resources flowing out of funds will give rise to a debit entry in a non-fund account which constitutes the use of funds.

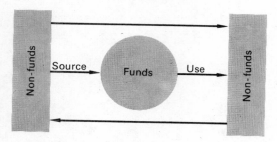

Figure 2.3 Fund flows

Transactions between *non*-funds accounts, and movements *within* funds, do not affect the level of funds and so should be excluded from any statement of the sources and uses of funds. As will be seen later, it is sometimes convenient to bend this rule a little.

The three major concepts of funds will be considered in turn.

(i) *Cash flow*

The *cash flow* concept defines funds as money, consisting of cash in hand or readily available at a bank. The flows consist simply of receipts and payments in cash, so that a funds flow statement could be prepared by listing the total entries in the cash (bank) account, with the net change in cash during the period providing the balancing item.

With some invention of figures, a cash flow statement for Cog might take the form shown in Table 2.6.

Statements similar to Table 2.6 are commonly prepared for internal use, as an outcome of the cash budgeting process. The information might well interest external users; for example, the division between cash and credit sales is not revealed in the other reports, but published funds flow statements are normally concerned with a more direct exposition of changes in the balance sheet structure. The pure cash flow concept is not employed in external reports: the concept which commonly masquerades under the name of cash flow will be considered next.

(ii) *Working capital*

The *working capital* concept of funds echoes the everyday notion of funds as 'pecuniary resources', not merely cash but resources swiftly convertible into cash.

Table 2.6 Funds flow statement (cash concept) (£000's)

Sources		
Cash sales		200
Receipts from debtors		508
		708
Decrease in cash		32
		740
Uses		
Payments to:		
Trade creditors	235	
Creditors for equipment	13	
	—	248
Manufacturing expenses		330
Non-manufacturing expenses		162
		740

Attention is concentrated on current assets which will soon be converted into cash in the ordinary course of business, and on current liabilities which will soon require settlement in cash. For the purposes of this concept net current assets (= current assets minus current liabilities) constitute funds. A current liability to pay a dividend is commonly excluded from the working capital for present purposes, and Cog's dividend will be excluded in the example which follows.

In principle the funds flow statement could be prepared by cataloguing the totals of entries between the working capital accounts and the non-funds accounts in a similar manner to the cash receipts and payments. Invariably an easier method of preparation is adopted, which commences with the changes in claims and assets between the opening and closing balance sheets. Entries between non-funds accounts during the period are then added back. This approach is illustrated for Cog in Table 2.7.

Working capital is the medium through which the transactions of the entity are normally conducted. Therefore changes in non-funds assets and claims can be considered, *prima facie*, to involve a corresponding effect on funds:

Non-funds	*Funds*
increase in asset, A^+, debit $\left.\right\}$	uses
decrease in claim, K^-, debit	
increase in claim, K^+, credit $\left.\right\}$	sources
decrease in asset, A^-, credit	

63

The columns in Table 2.7 headed *prima facie uses/sources* are based on this initial approach, from the changes between the two balance sheets displayed in Table 2.4. Cog did not buy or sell fixed assets during the year; and increase in cost between the beginning and end of the year would be a *prima facie* use of funds and a decrease would be a *prima facie* source. As the current liability for the dividend is not being considered as part of working capital it has been shown as a *prima facie* source.

Table 2.7 Non funds adjustments (£000's)

	Prima facie: uses	sources	Non-funds adjustments		Uses	Sources
	(Dr.)	(Cr.)	(Dr.)	(Cr.)	(Dr.)	(Cr.)
Depreciation		15	15			
Net current assets excluding dividend	37				37	
Proposed dividend		10	10			
Retained profit		12	12			
Retained funds from operations				37		37
	37	37	37	37	37	37

The only non-funds items which need to be added back for Cog can be obtained by examining the income statements: neither the depreciation provision nor the transfer to retained profit involved a current asset or current liability account, and the proposed dividend is being treated as a non-funds item. The elimination of these items gives *net funds from trading* – the net amount (after earmarking funds for taxation) by which funds benefited from conversion transactions during the period.

Non-funds transactions which do not involve the income accounts are rare; they have to be non-conversion transactions taking place entirely within the non-funds group of assets and claims. Typically such transactions involve the issue of shares or commitment to a long-term loan, either in exchange for non-current assets (say the acquisition of shares in another company) or by way of extinguishing retained profits/reserves to provide a 'bonus' capital issue to existing shareholders. No harm is done by failing to make this second class of adjustment if the transaction is one which would normally involve funds (i.e. any acquisition of non-current assets). Provided the nature of the transaction is specified, the user's understanding of the activities of the period may be enhanced. Certainly it would be confusing to eliminate a non-funds transaction which was associated with another involving funds: for example the issue of shares by the company in part settlement for the purchase of assets, the remainder of the purchase price being settled in cash. A simple version of such associated transactions might be presented:

Source	£
Issue of x £1 shares, in part settlement for investment in A Ltd.	x
Use	
Investment in shares of A Ltd.	$x+y$

In this example, the balance of £y would be merged with the change in working capital.

A *pro forma* statement of working capital funds flow appears in Table 2.8; relevant data for Cog have been inserted.

Table 2.8 Cog Ltd. Funds flow for 19–1, (£000's)

Operations		
Funds from operations	+	55
Corporation tax	−	18
Net funds from operations after taxation		37
Financing		
Share issue	+	
Share redemption	−	
Loan issue	+	
Loan redemption	−	
Acquisitions and disposals		
Fixed assets purchased	−	
Fixed assets sold	+	
Investments purchased	−	
Investments sold	+	
Distributions		
Dividends *paid*	−	
Working capital increase		37

The item 'net funds from operations' is commonly called 'cash flow', although it clearly does not represent cash flow in the strict sense of that term discussed earlier.* It does indicate the increase in working capital (*ex* proposed dividend) which would have occurred in the absence of the other changes specified, and it is therefore helpful to the user as an indication of the company's ability to generate a net increase in resources which would be turned rapidly into cash in the normal course of business.

(iii) *Total funds*

The *total funds* concept is the last to be considered. The essential concept is that of a

---

*To quote Mason [9] (p. 5) 'it is neither cash nor flow'. Nor is usage universally agreed: the term may refer to the calculation before taxation or after dividends – see [12] p. 35.

fund as a 'stock of something to be drawn upon'; in this sense all transactions involve funds.

This concept is capable of a number of interpretations in a funds flow statement: all entries in all accounts, net changes arising from external transactions only (which could be derived from the figures preceded by Δ in Table 2.2), or simply changes between balance sheet dates. On the widest interpretation such a statement would be excessively detailed, and on the narrowest interpretation it would cast little new light on the assets/claims structure. A judicious use of the total funds concept has, however, been seen to be helpful to the working capital treatment of funds, where consideration was given to the disclosure of certain items which were 'non-fund' from the working capital viewpoint.

2.5 Consolidated reports

Consolidated reports* present accounting information for a group of companies which together constitute a firm, an economic entity. The reports are prepared by aggregating and adjusting entity reports of the separate companies, but they represent the viewpoint of the controlling company at the apex of the group.

The company at the apex is termed the *parent* (or *holding* company) and any company which is controlled by the parent is a *subsidiary*. For the purposes of the legal requirement to prepare consolidated reports (Companies Act 1948) a company controls another if it owns more than half the latter's equity share capital, if it controls through the power of appointment of the majority of directors, or if it controls through intermediary companies.

A group rather than a single company structure may be adopted for a variety of reasons: limited liability for each company of the group compartmentalizes and limits possible losses to the resources controlled by that company, trading operations in overseas countries may be facilitated through local subsidiaries, minority shareholders in subsidiaries may be unwilling to sell their shares or their continued participation may be considered advantageous to the parent, and so on.

In principle consolidation proceeds by eliminating amounts in the separate companies' reports which arose from transactions between the companies of the group, shown as intra-group transactions in Figure 2.4. Thus the consolidated reports attempt to present statements as if the group's transactions had been recorded for a single entity. In one sense this attempt is doomed to failure: the external claims relate to each company as a separate legal entity and to that company's assets; the group as a whole does not have legal responsibility for the total claims of the group.

The basic approach to consolidation will be considered by reference to the con-

---

*[13] covers the major elements in this area.

solidation of the balance sheets of a parent company and a single subsidiary. The procedure can be considered in two stages.

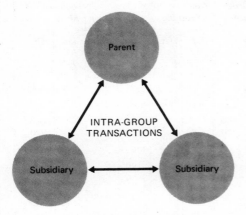

Figure 2.4 Intra-group transactions eliminated on consolidation

(a) Acquisition of control

The parent's acquisition of shares in the subsidiary will be evidenced by an asset in the parent's balance sheet; this investment in the subsidiary is effectively a proprietorship right to a slice of the net assets of the subsidiary (total assets minus liabilities) or, what comes to the same thing, a slice of the capital and reserves of the subsidiary.

For consolidation the assets and claims of the subsidiary are added to those of the parent, but the parent does not possess an investment *and* a slice of the subsidiary's net assets, nor does the parent have responsibility for its own capital/reserves *and* its own slice of the subsidiary's capital/reserves. Therefore the element of double-counting is eliminated for consolidation purposes, and any remaining balances appear in the consolidated report.

Illustrated in Table 2.9 is the procedure for consolidating the balance sheets of Multicog Ltd. and Cog Ltd.; the former company acquired 75 per cent of the share capital of Cog Ltd. for £210 000 (*ex* the proposed dividend) on 31 December 19–1.

Multicog's 75 per cent slice in the equity of Cog has been eliminated in the consolidated balance sheet; the remaining 25 per cent belongs to outside shareholders who retain a stake in the total group, and is termed a *minority interest*. When the parent has acquired the investment, as opposed to setting up the company and subscribing to shares at par (nominal value), there will normally be a difference between the acquisition cost of the shares and the book value at which this proportion of the equity is recorded in the books of the subsidiary. This difference usually emerges as an asset (excess of cost over book value, termed *goodwill*), but it may

Table 2.9 Acquisition method (£000's)

	Multicog (Parent)		Cog (Subsidiary)		Elimination		Consolidated balance sheet	
	Dr.	Cr.	Dr.	Cr.	Dr.	Cr.	Dr.	Cr.
Fixed assest	485		195				680	
Net current assets	175		57				232	
Investment in subsidiary	210					210		
Excess acquisition cost over book value					21		21	
Parent:								
Share capital		600						600
Retained profits		270						270
Subsidiary:							M/I	
Share capital				240	180			60
Retained profits				12	9			3
Minority interest in subsidiary								63
	870	870	252	252	210	210	933	933

emerge as a claim (excess of book value over cost, often termed a *capital reserve* or *undistributable reserve*). Such differences are not surprising; they emerge from valuations at different times from different viewpoints. After the acquisition their significance is purely historical.

The consolidation adjustment relates book values to the price paid by the parent for its block of shares. It is noteworthy that the minority's slice in the net assets is not similarly adjusted: if the parent's 75 per cent of the assets must be raised to £210 000 it might seem consistent to raise the minority's 25 per cent to £70 000 by the recognition of minority goodwill. The simplest explanation is the conventional one: the minority shareholders were not involved in the acquisition transaction.

The above describes the *acquisition* or *purchase* method of consolidating an investment in a subsidiary, which effectively abstracts pre-acquisition profits of the subsidiary from those of the group as a whole. Another method, termed *merger* (UK) or *pooling of interests* (USA) is of importance because it can leave pre-acquisition profits available to the group. In very general terms a major condition under which this method is 'conventionally'* appropriate, in place of the previous method, is that substantially all the 'selling' equity shareholders should have accepted compensation in the form of voting equity shares in the 'buying' company.

The merger method is demonstrated with new data in Table 2.10, where A has

---

*A convention which specifies when merger should be adopted in place of the acquisition method is not yet firmly established. Attempts of national professional bodies have encountered difficulties, particularly in the U.S.A. with a size test which would stipulate use of the acquisition method when companies are of a substantially different size and in Britain, where the merger method is not common, over legal implications of the merger method.

acquired all the share capital of B. The important difference in method is that the investment is recorded in A's books at the *nominal value* of the shares issued by A when the investment was acquired, and not at any estimate of the current value at that time. The excess of the nominal value of the shares issued by A over the nominal value of those acquired is charged against available reserves and retained profits,† but a substantial element of B's retained profits goes through into the group balance sheet. Excess nominal value in the other direction (nominal value of shares acquired in B greater than the nominal value of the shares issued by A) would be treated as undistributable reserve – effectively an increment to group capital.

Table 2.10 Merger method (£000's)

	A		B		Elimination		Consolidated balance sheet	
	Dr.	Cr.	Dr.	Cr.	Dr.	Cr.	Dr.	Cr.
Net assets	250		170				420	
Investment in B	100					100		
Share capital:								
original		200		80	80			⎫
issued in exchange for shares in B		100						⎬ 300
Retained profits		50		90	20			120
	350	350	170	170	100	100	420	420

(b) Post-acquisition transactions

In accounting periods subsequent to the acquisition of an investment in a subsidiary, the consolidation proceeds on the same basis of eliminating the double-counting arising from transactions between the group, whether the 'acquisition' or 'merger' method is adopted. The parent's slice of the *post-acquisition* profit of the subsidiary is recognized each year as a profit of the group, as illustrated for the Multicog group in Table 2.11. The elimination of a loan between the companies is also illustrated.

A troublesome area of consolidation concerns the treatment of profit on assets sold by one member of the group to another member. If the asset is resold to outsiders before the end of the accounting year there is no difficulty, because a profit can be recognized for the group as a whole in accordance with the usual accounting conventions. Nor is there any problem when the subsidiary is wholly owned; all the unrealized profit can be eliminated and the asset can be shown at cost to the original company in the balance sheet. These procedures are illustrated below:

†The excess would be set off first against 'combined other contributed capital' (effectively share premiums) under the American convention, or against any 'unrealized surplus' (from asset revaluation) under a moribund proposal of the British accountancy bodies.

		Company A		Company B		Effect on consolidated balance sheet £
		Dr.	Cr.	Dr.	Cr.	
EITHER	Cost of goods	80		100		} Profit 25
	Sale		100		105	
OR	Cost of goods	80		100		} Goods (held) 80
	Sale		100			

When the subsidiary has outside minority shareholders and the asset is still held within the group at the balance sheet date, the rights of the outside minority against the group need to be considered. From the minority viewpoint an external transaction was involved, and although consolidated accounts are prepared from the group viewpoint the separate legal rights of the minority impinge on the majority. Consequently it is widely (but not universally) accepted in conventional accounting that a consolidated report should recognize the slice of the unrealized profit which 'belongs' to the minority. There are, however, different opinions on the methods which should be adopted in calculating that slice of unrealized profit [5], and common British and American practices conflict.

It has been seen that consolidation, like most of conventional accounting, requires the adoption of conventions which are supplementary to the basic convention of historic cost.

Table 2.11 Post-acquisition consolidation (£000's)

	Multicog (Parent)		Cog (Subsidiary)		Elimination		Consolidated balance sheet	
	Dr.	Cr.	Dr.	Cr.	Dr.	Cr.	Dr.	Cr.
Fixed assets	502		218				720	
Net current assets	165		82				247	
Loan to Cog	28					28		
Investment in subsidiary	210					210		
Excess acquisition cost over book value					21		21	
Parent:								
Share capital		600						600
Retained profits		305						305
Subsidiary:							M/I	
Share capital				240	180		60	
Retained profits:								
pre-acquisition				12	9		3	
post-acquisition				20			5	15
Minority interest in subsidiary							—	68
Loan from Multicog				28	28			
	905	905	300	300	238	238	988	988

Bibliographical references

[1] American Accounting Association, The realization concept, *Accounting Review*, April 1965, pp. 312–22.
[2] American Accounting Association, The matching concept, *Accounting Review*, April 1965, pp. 368–72.
[3] Anton, H. R., *Accounting for the Flow of Funds*, Houghton Mifflin, 1962.
[4] Baxter, W. T. and S. Davidson eds., *Studies in Accounting Theory*, Sweet and Maxwell, 1962.
[5] Egginton, D. A., Unrealised profit and consolidated accounts, *Accountancy*, May 1965, pp. 410–15.
[6] Ijiri, Y., *The Foundations of Accounting Measurement*, Prentice-Hall, 1967.
[7] Institute of Chartered Accountants in England and Wales (publishers), *Disclosures of Accounting Policies*, Statement of Standard Accounting Practice No. 2, 1971.
[8] Jaedicke, R. K. and R. T. Sprouse, *Accounting Flows: Income, Funds, and Cash*, Prentice-Hall, 1965.
[9] Mason, P., *'Cash Flow' Analysis and the Funds Statement*, Accounting Research Study No. 2, American Institute of Certified Public Accountants, 1961.
[10] Mattesich, R., *Accounting and Analytical Methods*, Irwin, 1964.
[11] Moonitz, M., *The Basic Postulates of Accounting*, Accounting Research Study No. 1, American Institute of Certified Public Accountants, 1961.
[12] Parker, R. H., *Understanding Company Financial Statements*, Penguin, 1972.
[13] Stamp, E., *The Elements of Consolidation Accounting*, Sweet and Maxwell, 1965.
[14] Yamey, B. S., Accounting and the rise of capitalism, *Journal of Accounting Research*, Autumn 1964, pp. 117–36.

Problems

2.1 Name six specific accounting entities of different types.

2.2 Explain the matching concept in entity accounting.

2.3 (a) How would you determine whether a debit balance in an account represented an asset or an expense?

(b) How would you determine the amount of a provision? In what way, if any, is a provision different from a reserve?

2.4 Consider the possible needs of two major classes of users of entity reports of firms and examine the relative importance of different 'aims' of entity reports for each class of user.

2.5 Shown below are balance sheet data for Merchandise Ltd. at 31 December 19–0 and the balances appearing in the books of the company at 31 December 19–1 before the preparation of final accounts. All amounts in units of £.

	31 December 19–0 Dr.	31 December 19–0 Cr.	31 December 19–1 Dr.	31 December 19–1 Cr.
Bank	5 300		3 000	
Creditors		5 800		6 300
Debtors	8 200		9 100	
Equipment	4 400		4 900	
Long-term loans		3 400		1 600

71

	31 December 19–0		31 December 19–1	
	Dr.	Cr.	Dr.	Cr.
Accumulated provision for depreciation on equipment		1 400		1 100
Rent			1 700	
Retained profits		2 900		2 900
Share capital		8 000		8 000
Sales				45 000
Goods:				
held at 31 December 19–1	3 600		3 600	
purchased during 19–1			34 000	
Sundry expenses, including interest on loans			3 500	
Surplus on disposal of equipment				100
Wages			5 200	
	£21 500	£21 500	£65 000	£65 000

At 31 December 19–1 the following items require adjustment:

1. Rent £300 was due but unpaid.
2. A provision is to be created for doubtful debts of £150. It is expected that £50 discount (for prompt payment) will be allowed to end-year debtors.
3. Goods held at 31 December 19–1 amounted to £4 800.
4. The surplus on disposal of equipment arose when old equipment (cost £700, depreciation provided £300) was traded in for £500 against the purchase of new equipment costing £1 200. The equipment balances at 31 December 19–1 were made up:

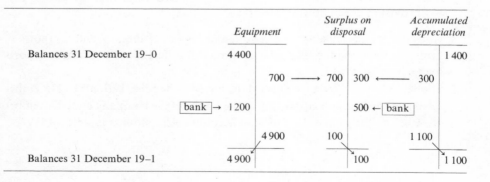

	Equipment	Surplus on disposal	Accumulated depreciation
Balances 31 December 19–0	4 400		1 400
	700 ⟶	700 300 ⟵	300
bank ⟶ 1 200		500 ⟵ bank	
	4 900	100	1 100
Balances 31 December 19–1	4 900	100	1 100

5. £400 is to be provided for depreciation of equipment during 19–1.

No dividend was proposed, and taxation can be ignored.

Prepare a balance sheet at 31 December 19–1 and income statements and a (working capital) funds flow statement for 19–1.

2.6 The balance sheets of X Ltd. and Y Ltd. at 31 December 19–0 revealed:

	X Ltd. £	Y Ltd. £
Share capital (£1 ordinary shares)	80 000	30 000
Retained profits	19 000	60 000
	99 000	90 000
Liabilities	36 000	25 000
	£135 000	£115 000
Sundry assets	£135 000	£115 000

Immediately after the determination of the above balance sheets X issued 50 000 £1 ordinary shares in exchange for the entire share capital of Y. The value of the issued shares was estimated at £110 000.

At 31 December 19–1 the balance sheet of X and Y included:

	X Ltd.	Y Ltd.
Liabilities	£48 000	£105 000
Sundry assets	£150 000	£188 000

The above liabilities and assets do not include any amounts arising from inter-company transactions, nor any amount for X's investment in Y. Neither company had any new transactions affecting share capital during 19–1.

Profits and dividends for 19–1 are shown below.

		X Ltd. £	Y Ltd. £
Retained profits at 31 December 19–0		19 000	60 000
Net profit 19–1:			
trading profit	10 000		8 000
dividend received from Y	15 000		
		25 000	
		44 000	68 000
Less dividends paid during 19–1		22 000	15 000
		£22 000	£53 000

Note that Y's dividend was proposed and paid after the acquisition of shares by X.

The entity accounts

Required:

The X group balance sheet at 31 December 19–1 on the alternative bases of:

(a) The acquisition method of consolidation.

(b) The merger method of consolidation.

Comment on your results.

3
Value and profit

3.1 The interrelationship of value and profit

This chapter will examine some of the basic conceptual problems of accounting*
which arise from the deceptively simple questions 'what is value?' and 'what is
profit?'. Value and profit are capable of a variety of interpretations;† the terms used
in economics carry substantially different implications from the same terms in the
context of conventional accounting, and worse still the meanings within each area
are far from uniform. One sample of economics textbooks produced 14 different
profit concepts and it has been estimated that the potential profit figures conforming to accounting conventions which might be produced from a single set of
accounting data exceed thirty million [8]. Fortunately some central ideas can
provide guidance in this maze of possibilities.

In broad terms the economic approach has been one of developing concepts to
explain economic activity and until relatively recently economists have not been
unduly burdened with applying their concepts, whereas the conventional accounting approach has generally been concerned with finding *ad hoc* solutions to specific
measurement problems with little regard to the validity or purpose of the overall
result. The approach we shall adopt will examine concepts before trading down to
bases which are measurable with some degree of 'objectivity'.

A useful starting point is a definition of profit, by the economist Marshall, which
is wide enough to provide a meeting point for the major concepts of profit in both
economics and accounting:

> When a man is engaged in business his profits for the year are the excess of his receipts from
> his business during the year over his outlay for the business. The difference between the value
> of his stock of plant, materials, etc., at the end and at the beginning of the year is taken as
> part of his receipts or as part of his outlay according as there has been an increase or decrease
> in value.‡

It is evident that profit is not simply the increase in cash made available from

---

* See [11] for a survey of the accounting literature relating to this area, and [18] for a comprehensive
collection of readings on income.

† They can also be expressed in different terms, such as *worth* and (*business*) *income*. In this book, with
the business context apparent, *income* is used as a neutral synonym which does not pre-empt any
particular profit concept.

‡ [15] p. 74.

business activities but includes some value (positive or negative) arising from the change in resources commanded during the period; moreover the implicit assumption that cash and value are additive begs the question of whether the value of cash can be considered constant. Thus profit and value are interrelated concepts and a consideration of value will have implications for the subsequent discussion of profit.

3.2 Value theory†

The theory of value was of major concern to classical economists. Although ideas in this area have had negligible influence on conventional accounting, they provide useful insights into the meanings which can be attached to value and indirectly into the implications of valuation for business purposes.

Throughout the economic discussions of the eighteenth and nineteenth centuries there was difficulty over the exchange value of goods (the prices at which goods are bought and sold) and their value in use (utility, in terms of the total satisfaction the possession of the goods conferred). There seemed little correlation between these two attributes, as Adam Smith observed in a famous passage:

> Nothing is more useful than water, but it will purchase scarce anything: scarce anything can be had in exchange for it. A diamond, on the contrary, has scarce any value in use, but a very great quantity of other goods may frequently be had in exchange for it.*

This seeming 'paradox of value' arose because economists at that time confused value in use (= *total* utility) with *marginal* utility. Total utility refers to the total satisfaction obtained by an individual purchaser from the total stock of a good held (or consumed) at a particular time; the concept of marginal utility refers to the satisfaction obtained by an individual purchaser from the last unit acquired. An individual purchaser would become more rapidly satiated with additional units of water than he (or she) would with additional diamonds; consequently the marginal utility of water can be considered to decline more rapidly than that of diamonds. In choosing between water and diamonds the individual will exchange so long as the increase in satisfaction from acquiring one good exceeds the sacrifice in satisfaction from foregoing the other.

But utility concerns only one side of the determination of exchange value, the demand side. In temperate climates units of water can be obtained at relatively small sacrifice (if only by collecting rain water); thus the cost of production is low and supply can be said to be plentiful. Conversely the discovery of diamonds involves considerable search effort and supply is scarce. However, the cost of

†See Bonbright [6] Chapters 1–12 for a wide ranging treatment of valuation which has much to offer accountants.
*[19], p. 25.

producing either good is unlikely to remain constant for all units; acquiring additional units per time period will require, say, storage facilities for water or considerably more search effort and mining equipment for diamonds; additional units would therefore be more costly to produce than earlier units so that *marginal cost* of production would be rising, if less rapidly for water (plentiful) than for diamonds (scarce).

It was Marshall who brought about the synthesis of utility and cost of production, showing the fundamental symmetry of the general relations of supply and demand to exchange value by way of an analogy with the blades of a pair of scissors:

> We might as reasonably dispute whether it is the upper or the under blade of a pair of scissors that cuts a piece of paper, as whether [exchange] value is governed by utility or cost of production. It is true that when one blade is held still, and the cutting is effected by moving the other, we may say with careless brevity that the cutting is done by the second.
>
> . . .
>
> . . . *as a general rule* the shorter the period we are considering, the greater must be the share of our attention which is given to the influence of demand on value; [because supply can be considered as virtually fixed in the very short period] and the longer the period, the more important will be the influence of cost of production on value [because in the long run production can be adjusted to some specific level of demand].*

In this way Marshall showed that exchange value is *jointly* governed by *marginal* utility and *marginal* cost of production.

A consumer can be said to maximize his (total) satisfaction by equalizing the marginal utility per £ spent on each and every good; in other words by equating the ratios of the marginal utilities of the goods he purchases to the ratio of their prices and to the marginal rate of substitution between them. This does not imply that utility, in the sense of satisfaction obtained, is measurable in money terms, nor is there any implication of equality of marginal utilities between different individuals.

It is only the price of the last unit exchanged by the individual which is equated at the margin but all units held can be assumed interchangeable, so that provided marginal utility declines with the acquisition of additional units the individual would have been prepared to pay rather more for earlier units rather than go without the good altogether. This difference between the exchange price of acquisitions and the notional price which individuals might have been prepared to pay is termed 'consumer surplus'.

From the above discussion it is evident that the multiplication of exchange value (current price per unit) by the number of units of a good held or acquired does *not* represent value either in the sense of total utility to the individual or in the sense of the maximum price which the individual would be prepared to pay. It *does* represent value in the limited sense of the price which could be obtained for the goods or the

*[15], pp. 348–49.

price at which the goods could be replaced *provided* such action would not affect the exchange value (e.g. cause glut or scarcity in the market) and there were no costs in undertaking transactions.

What relevance does all this have for the business firm? The firm's demand for goods is a derived demand, in the sense that the firm is concerned with purchasing goods which are sold eventually (commonly in different physical form) to consumers. The firm's proximate concern is therefore with the exchange value of its inputs in relation to the exchange value of its outputs, but any expectations of exchange values imply assumptions about the relationship of market demand for the product and its supply and about the supply/demand relationship for inputs.

The commonest (although not always stated) assumption in discussing the exchange value of a firm's assets is that the firm's own demand for inputs and its supply of output are both insignificant in relation to the total transactions of the market as a whole. Thus the firm's actions could not affect market price (which, remember, is determined at the margin), and exchange value per unit multiplied by the number of units held would provide a valid exchange value for assets held by the firm. Although this is a very convenient assumption which will be adopted for our purposes, a moment's thought will reveal that it is only a useful rule of thumb: consider what would happen to the market price of diamonds if the considerable diamond inventories of de Beers Consolidated (*the* diamond producer) were offered for sale at one time in the market. Current market price per unit provides the exchange value of assets only if asset transactions by the firm would not affect market price – a qualification which is sometimes suggested by the use of the phrase 'in the normal course of business'.

It is now appropriate to consider three major questions affecting valuation which were implicit in the above discussion: what fate is intended for the object being valued?; from whose viewpoint is value being considered?; how is value to be measured? Each question will be examined in turn.

3.3 Value for what?

If an object is not held for its own sake but for the receipts it will bring, as business assets are, the object's *eventual* fate can be assumed to be exchange for cash. When assets are held for use the benefits from the asset can be assumed to be incorporated in the firm's output – which is sold for cash. Timing is important: the firm can dispose of the asset now or at some point in a continuum of future dates; moreover the firm may face several opportunities for disposal/employment at any one time. For the present purposes it will be assumed that the firm has selected the 'best' fate for its assets.

Since assets are held for exchange (in one form or another), exchange values are patently relevant for business assets. Three possible views of exchange values* are:

Past: the price ruling in the market when the asset was acquired;

Current: the price at which the asset could be acquired or disposed of currently;

Future: the cash (net receipts) which the asset is expected to yield through employment/production and/or eventual sale.

Note that any value must relate to a specific place and time; these values will be viewed in relation to their relevance for 'here and now'.

(a) Past exchange value

The price at which an asset was acquired is, of course, historic cost. This need not necessarily coincide with the exchange value ruling in the market at acquisition – a particularly favourable or unfavourable bargain could have been made – but exchange value will be assumed here. To consider historic cost as a value of relevance to the present point of time is unduly flattering; its claim to inclusion arises from its adoption in conventional accounts. The historic cost of an asset need not approximate to any price at which this (or a similar) asset can be bought or sold currently or in the future.

(b) Current exchange values

It is now necessary to acknowledge that there are almost invariably *two* exchange values for any asset: the *entry* price at which it can be bought and the *exit* price at which it can be sold. Even in a highly competitive market there is some transaction cost of bringing buyers and sellers into contact with each other; when exchanges of a particular good are rare, or goods are not homogeneous, dealers may require very wide margins to recompense them for the time which elapses before a buyer can be matched with a seller and for the risk that the price may have to be reduced to avoid holding some goods indefinitely.

Since the objective of a firm is to sell goods for a price greater than that at which the goods were acquired, a firm will have a *normal* expectation of selling the goods in which it deals at an exit price *above* entry price. Conversely almost every firm holds some goods, usually fixed assets, for employment as agents of production in the firm rather than for sale; as the firm would not have the advantage of dealing in such goods the normal expectation would be that such goods could only be sold in their present condition at an exit price *below* the entry price. For example, a garage which currently buys a motor van for £600 (entry price) may consider the current exit price to be £800; a bookseller who buys the van for £800 (his entry price) would have considerable difficulty in selling the van brand new for anything

---

* These values can be further related to the inputs, a present partially completed form, or to the finished (output) form of an asset; see [9] Chapter 3.

approaching £800. A decision as to which exchange value is relevant to the owner of an asset clearly hinges upon expectations regarding the fate of the asset.

It may be noticed that historic cost considered earlier was in fact an entry price, corresponding to which there would have been some hypothetical exit price at the time of acquisition; such a past hypothetical price has no current significance.

In accounting, entry price is usually termed *replacement cost* and exit price (net after any costs involved in selling) is termed *net realizable value*. These terms used without qualification mean *current* exchange values; exchange values at some specified future date are termed *future* replacement cost and *future* net realizable value.

The difficult measurement problem of assigning quantities to these value concepts will be considered later.

(c) Future exchange values

A firm acquires assets with the intention of disposing of them in future time periods, either in their original form or in a transformed character through employment within the firm. The future exchange values are of fundamental importance to the firm, but in order to provide a currently meaningful value (e.g. for comparison with prices for disposing/acquiring assets currently) three major aspects must be considered in the determination of a single value based on future expectations.

(i) *Cash flows*

All the expected monetary benefits from an asset or group of assets in future time periods must be incorporated in 'value'. It would be ridiculous to consider only that the future exchange value (= future net realizable value) of the bookseller's van when he expects to dispose of it in 3 years time would be £400; possession of the van in the intervening period would allow additional revenue to be earned and would necessitate outlays on running costs, etc. These future exchange values (entry and exit prices for goods and services at the times they are expected to occur) will give rise to *cash* transactions, and are termed *cash* flows which are really exchange transactions for cash at specified future times. The bookseller's transactions (in £'s) might be:

End-year	0	1	2	3
Motor van	(800)			400
Additional sales minus (entry) price of books		1 600	1 600	1 600
Additional wages, petrol and repairs, etc.		(1 300)	(1 330)	(1 370)
Net cash flow	(£800)	£300	£270	£630

Parentheses indicate cash payments.

. Cash transactions have been assumed to take place conveniently at the end of each year, and a short *time horizon* of 3 years has been adopted. Obviously both of these assumptions are simplifications for the present purpose; in particular the bookseller may have expectations of replacing the van with another which will be used in later periods.

(ii) *Interest rate*

The cost of waiting for expected benefits must be considered. A firm would not regard £100 in one year's time as identical to £100 now, even if the future amount were entirely certain (which means that the amount and its purchasing power are beyond doubt); the difference in attitude to the same amount at two different dates arises because money now could be employed or lent to earn something in the intervening period. An interest rate provides the means for translating amounts at different times to one common point of time; the reader is referred to Appendix A for a consideration of the mechanics of such procedures.

The value which emerges from the translation of future amounts back into current terms by application of an interest rate is called *present value*. This concept will be seen to be of central importance to the consideration of value in relation to decisions by the firm.

(iii) *Uncertainty*

Asset holding, which can be interpreted as any commitment of current resources in the expectation of future benefits, involves risk and uncertainty in the sense that expectations of future exchanges of value (future cash flows) may not be achieved. Serious consideration of risk and uncertainty will be deferred until Chapter 12 but it is impossible to ignore this crucial aspect entirely at this stage.

Most expectations relate to a range of possible outcomes rather than a point estimate of a particular outcome, even though it is very common to specify expectations naively in terms of 'most likely' amounts (as in the bookseller example above). The range of possible outcomes and the level of confidence which can be attached to particular outcomes within this range can be considered as determining the 'riskiness' of expectations; the wider the range of possible outcomes and the lower the level of confidence which can be attached to particular outcomes within the range the more 'risky' is the asset concerned. As a first approximation it can be assumed that a firm will prefer to receive, say, £100 with near certainty to some 'most likely' but 'risky' expectation of the same amount; consequently some adjustment for riskiness is implicit in translating future expectations into a present value. This adjustment may take the form of scaling down future amounts or scaling up the interest rate employed in translating amounts to the present time.

Our bookseller's expected cash flows from years 1 to 3 might be discounted at an interest rate of 10 per cent per year to give a present value of £969. (Readers unfamiliar with discounting should check the derivation of this figure with the aid of Appendix A. Assume that the bookseller has already adjusted the basic data for riskiness.) Possession of the asset confers expected benefits equivalent to £969 at the present time; in this sense present value represents a very important concept of value for the firm.

From the discussion of the three major aspects which determine present value it is clearly a value 'coloured by the opinion of the exhibitor' (see section 2(b) of Chapter 2) and it is subjective. Some areas of the accounting literature use the term 'subjective value' in place of present value, which should not be interpreted as meaning that other accounting values are necessarily objective.

3.4 Value to whom?

On the question of value in relation to the firm there are two major viewpoints which might be adopted. One is that of shareholders, which is concerned with issued shares representing ownership claims against the company. The other viewpoint is that of 'the firm' as an entity, which is a quasi-managerial view concerned with resources controlled by the firm and claims against the firm.

Value concepts which might be candidates for consideration from each viewpoint are illustrated in Table 3.1. It is assumed that the shares can be readily bought or sold on a stockmarket.

Table 3.1 Major value viewpoints in relation to a firm

| | | Exchange value bases | | |
Value to whom?		Past	Current	Future
Shareholder viewpoint (shares held in company)	Entry	Historic cost to shareholder	Entry price at which shareholder can buy	
	Exit		Exit price at which shareholder can sell	Present value of future dividends and eventual disposal of shares
Firm viewpoint (net assets of company)	Entry	Historic cost to company	Replacement cost	
	Exit		Net realizable value	Present value of future cash flows

Value viewpoints have been compressed in Table 3.1. The continuum of future exchange values has again been eliminated by an assumption that the most favourable opportunities are adopted to give present value. The present values of future entry prices have been ignored; they have a tactical relevance to switching opportunities for sale and repurchase which need not detain us.

(a) Shareholder viewpoint

It might appear that a company which operates for the benefit of its shareholders should adopt a currently quoted share price (entry or exit) as the benchmark concept of value, possibly to the extent of recording the accounting value of the firm in terms of share price. Such a view is an oversimplification; certainly the multiplication of the number of issued shares by the current market price gives a value which has an attractive objectivity as a measure of value for many purposes, but it is neither the unambiguous measure of value to shareholders which it seems nor does it necessarily serve accounting and management purposes.

An individual shareholder can be assumed to have some assessment of present value of his shares based on his own expectations. The rational shareholder would sell his shares when exit price exceeds his present value and buy more shares when entry price falls below present value; since the margin between entry and exit prices of widely traded shares is normally small it would appear that current market price should approximate to the estimation of present value by all shareholders. Unfortunately complications of tax liabilities on sale of shares, investors' funds constraints and the inertia of shareholders make such a generalization suspect. Market prices are determined by dealings at the margin (by shareholders who find it worthwhile to deal) and it is observable that a substantial surplus over current exchange price is usually necessary to induce the majority of shareholders to sell their shares, e.g. in a take-over bid. Consequently share prices are only rough, although undoubtedly the most objective indicators of value to shareholders.

Most important for accounting, share prices are themselves partially determined by accounting information. The adoption of share prices for assigning value to a firm in its own accounts would be both circuitous and uninformative; data on prices of quoted shares are already easily accessible. Finally a shareholder viewpoint could not be employed where shares were unquoted.

(b) Firm viewpoint

The firm viewpoint is based on the total assets owned by the firm less the liabilities to non-owners which it must meet; these net assets represent the ownership resources which the firm controls as agent of the shareholders. The firm viewpoint can be considered (at least conceptually) as singular, in contrast to the multiplicity of views on value which might be held by shareholders.

The central concept of value from the firm viewpoint is the present value of the future cash flows arising from assets and liabilities of the firm. Future transactions between the firm and its shareholders are excluded because the firm's value belongs to shareholders *as a whole*; for example, future dividends will reduce the ownership rights of shareholders but they can be assumed to provide a corresponding increment to shareholders' personal wealth (tax makes this a cavalier assumption, but the point is that the strictly firm viewpoint does *not* enquire into individual circumstances and preferences of shareholders). If the firm's management operates solely in the interests of shareholders as a whole it will seek to maximize its subjective estimate of present value of the firm. If the expectations prove correct the benefits will eventually accrue to individual shareholders through dividends and the adjustment of market prices of shares; in other words management would not be indifferent to share price but management expectations may be several steps ahead of, or at least different from, the criteria determining current share price. In the maximizing firm any decision on the acquisition or disposal of resources implies a comparison of current exchange value with the present value of these resources to the firm, and all resources retained by the firm should have a present value greater than (or at least equal to) the exchange value currently available to the firm.

The preceding paragraph requires some qualification. Firms do not necessarily formulate their decisions explicitly in terms of present value and in any case the interdependencies of resources within the firm may often make explicit formulation exceedingly difficult; but the present value concept is not invalidated, any more than musical notation is invalidated by the fact that many people play music by ear. More important, the decisions of firms are not invariably undertaken in the interests of the owners; in some respects a concept of utility to the firm as an organization or to management as an entity may be appropriate. For example, the commissioning of works of art to decorate a company's head office may make more sense in terms of utility than in terms of present value, but it is difficult to be sure; such decisions can be, and often are, rationalized in terms of present value – say benefits from better working environment or even expected price rises for the works of art. Finally, firms may seek some 'satisfactory' performance rather than maximization; even so a satisfactory margin between present value and currently available exchange value is implied, if not the best available margin which might be obtained by an exhaustive search for opportunities.

3.5 How might value be measured for entity accounts?

The discussion of value concepts has supported present value as the fundamental concept of value to the firm. With regard to decision making the relevance of present value (explicitly or implicitly) is inescapable, but our immediate goal is value *measurement* for entity accounts. One of the major functions of these accounts is to aid in the assessment of earlier decisions, and a series of unverifiable subjective present values would be useless for this purpose. Consequently it is necessary at this stage to trade down to value concepts which are capable of measurement with some degree of objectivity.

It will be recalled that 'objective' was defined earlier as 'exhibiting actual facts uncoloured by the exhibitor's feelings or opinion'; in an accounting context a concept capable of objective measurement would be one which gave sufficient guidance to enable two or more accountants acting independently to arrive consistently at the same figures. It can be said at once that only a record of past cash transactions would ensure such objectivity in accounts, to the exclusion of information on other resources of the firm and on the profitability of those resources; the best value concept which can be hoped for is one which constrains the influence of personal opinion and yet provides information which serves the purposes of users.

With present value eliminated the candidates are historic cost and current exchange values. Determining historic cost is merely a matter of documentation and recording on acquisition; thus historic cost is undoubtedly objective. Relevance is another matter. It must be admitted that a defender of conventional accounting and historic cost would say that accounts do not purport to indicate values in any sense, but instead represent an historical record of past transactions. This view would be credible if accounts were simply chronological records of cash transactions at historic cost, but conventional entity accounts provide history without dates and yet are riddled with estimated amendments to the historical record. The conventional estimation procedures for depreciation and the rules for amending current assets to 'market value' (to be considered in section 9) lend substantial support to the view that unadorned historic cost is irrelevant to the user.

Inevitably the argument now leads to the adoption of current exchange values. These values have two important characteristics which make them useful measures:

(a) Objectivity

Exchanges taking place in a competitive market represent a consensus view of 'society' of value in money terms. Limitations of such prices determined 'at the margin' have already been examined, but the prices at which exchanges are taking place at a particular time are observable without being 'coloured by feelings or opinion'.

Even when prices cannot be observed in a competitive market, if the firm is currently exchanging assets of a particular character the price is *prima facie* the value at which it could deal with the remainder of its assets of the same class. (Only *prima facie*; recall the de Beers example in section 2.)

Considerable problems arise when neither a readily available competitive market price exists nor is the firm engaging currently in exchanges of comparable

Value and profit

assets, for example fixed assets of the firm like plant and machinery. Estimation becomes necessary, for which procedures will be examined in section 8.

(b) Value to firm

Currently available exchange values have definable relationships to present value for the firm. There are six possible permutations of the relation between present value and the current entry/exit values for a firm's assets,* ignoring the chance that one or more values might precisely coincide. These possibilities are illustrated in Figure 3.1. The exchange values available to the firm for goods in their current state may offer *exit above entry* price (say for goods which the firm itself is a dealer/processor) or an *exit below entry* price (which would be common for goods which the firm employs). For either of these alternatives present value may be above, between or below the two exchange values; the relationship should, however, determine the fate of the asset.

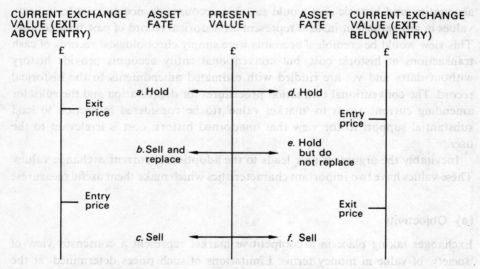

Figure 3.1 Relationships between present value and current exchange values

The firm intent on enhancing the value of its resources should hold only those assets for which expectations support a present value greater than current exit price (situations *a, d, e,* in Figure 3.1) and should sell all assets for which future expectations support a present value less than exit price (situations *b, c* and *f*). In this sense current exit price represents the *minimum* value of assets to the firm.

---

*See Solomons in [3] for a similar analysis, and also [18], pp. 17–19.

86

Entry price as an indicator of value is more complex, but potentially more fruitful. If an asset can be replaced immediately by another *identical* asset at a particular entry price it would be irrational for the firm to regard the value of the asset *by itself* as higher than current entry price. What would the firm suffer if it were suddenly deprived* of the asset? Approximately the cost of replacing the asset. Yet Figure 3.1 illustrates present values above and below entry price.

The apparent paradox can be resolved by regarding present value as being composed of two elements: the replaceable value (current entry price) of the asset and a surplus (positive or negative) which arises from the firm's expectations of using the asset *in combination with other assets of the firm.* The other assets may be physical assets or nebulous assets like the 'know-how' which will enable the firm to achieve the expected benefits. The surplus of present value for the firm as a whole over the sum of the individual values of separable assets can be termed goodwill.†

When present value of an asset is below entry price the situation is uncomfortable (see *e* in Figure 3.1). Entry price no longer represents the amount the firm would suffer if it were deprived of the (uninsured) asset – because the asset is not currently worth replacing. The problem can be evaded in one of three ways: by adopting *entry price* even though it exceeds present value; by adopting *exit price* when this is below entry price, or by adopting the *present value* below entry price. The first treats negative goodwill in a consistent manner with positive goodwill, the second adopts the minimum observable value and the third is an entirely subjective estimate which accounting measures seek to avoid.

An example may help to clarify the argument so far. Our bookseller's van, in combination with his other assets and knowledge of the trade had a present value of £969. But the bookseller would presumably not hesitate to accept say £900 for the van if he could replace immediately for £800. To the bookseller the value of the van in isolation is simply current entry price. If changes in expectations force the bookseller to adjust his present value downwards to, say, £700 (with entry/exit prices unchanged) he would continue to hold the van because it is worth more to him than the exit price of £600. But the £800 entry price becomes a value to him only in the devious sense that another identical van would cost him that much; it would not represent the loss (£700) he would suffer by being deprived of the van. The potential significance of this last qualification depends on the size of the margin between entry and exit; in general the margin will be widest for fixed assets which are specific to the firm's activities so that potential buyers are scarce and exit price is low.

Despite these difficulties exchange values offer information of current relevance to the firm's position, which is more than can be said for historic cost. Given that a

---

*The term 'deprival value' is used by Baxter [4] in the context of depreciating assets.

†This is similar to, but not the same as, goodwill recorded in conventional accounts. The latter is the difference between the price paid for a business on acquisition (≤ present value to purchasers) and the book values assigned to the net assets acquired.

choice has to be made* between exit and entry prices as value concepts for accounts, which should be chosen?

It has been seen that exit price (net realizable value) would give the minimum value of separable assets to the firm, conforming to a view of the firm in which all assets were to be realized in the short run. But continuity is a more widely appropriate assumption for firms than dissolution, and for the continuing firm exit prices would give unduly conservative fixed asset values. For example, assets specific to the firm would have to be written down immediately on acquisition, with consequences for profit measurement in current and future periods.

Entry price (replacement cost) gives an approximate measure of value to the continuing firm. It is not a perfect measure, but it is the best available.† It has prospects of being quantified with some degree of objectivity, but it would often be necessary to regard replacement cost of the particular asset under consideration as a measurement aim which is not precisely achievable. Current entry prices for identical assets (especially those which are partly used) are often not known or at least not available to the firm in a readily accessible form; consequently the application of replacement cost must involve estimation (see section 8 and Appendix to this chapter). It may be noted that most firms do have some readily available estimates of replacement cost of assets in the form of valuations for insurance purposes; disclosure of those estimates to shareholders would not be unduly burdensome.

Finally, replacement cost, like any other measure of the value of the *separable* assets of the firm, will not represent the value of the firm *as an entity*. The value of the firm as a whole can be considered to be the present value of expected future cash flows: such value depends on the complex organizational interrelationships of assets which in the last resort depend upon the abilities of management and other employees. Nor does the adoption of replacement cost give what is termed *reproduction* cost of the firm (the total cost of setting up a comparable firm *ab initio*); clearly many organizational factors like staff training and customer contacts are ignored. Of course what can be regarded as a separately indentifiable asset for accounting purposes is itself a debatable matter: any current resources committed in the expectation of future benefits are eligible, and for conceptual consistency such items as Research and Development (R & D), patents, and advertising expenditure would have to be valued at the replacement cost of the benefits still accrued. Subjective estimates would be inevitable, but arguably more informative than the present diversity of conventional accounting practice: expenditure on 'twilight' items like R & D are treated as anything from expense of a single year to assets yielding benefits over an indefinite life.

* Different accounting measures, each based on an appropriate value concept, could be calculated, so that choice would rest with the user (see e.g. [9]). Alternatively external users might be supplied with sufficient information to derive their own measures (see e.g. R. S. Edwards in [5] and also [20]).

† For broadly similar conclusions see [9], [10], and Bell in [21]; for views in support of exit prices and historic costs see [7] and Ijiri in [21] respectively.

3.6 Profit concepts

The discussion of value has narrowed the profit concepts to be considered. Profit will be examined from the viewpoint of accounting measurement in the light of the earlier conclusions on value to the firm.

A profit measure must be considered in relation to the purpose for which it is to be used. There are many possible purposes; we shall briefly consider four major candidates before turning to measurement. The list is not exhaustive; our primary concern is with the first possibility.

(a) Appraising performance

A profit measure can assist in the appraisal of the success with which a firm's operations have been conducted. If profit represents the increase in one period of the net resources owned by the firm (after adjusting for contributions from, or distributions to, shareholders) it provides a *prima facie* indicator of successful operations.

Appraisal implies some expectation of what performance should be and power to investigate and take action on inadequate performance; detailed data required for this essentially managerial function within the firm will be considered in Part 3 (Control Systems). However, the accounts of the firm as a whole can assist self-appraisal by the firm's controlling management, or appraisal by controlling shareholders. Non-controlling shareholders normally have relatively little power to appraise in the sense used here.

(b) Projecting performance

Existing and potential shareholders must usually take a relatively passive view towards profit; for the widely owned firm an investor's personal assessment can rarely be translated into action to affect profitability directly and his major sanction is to 'vote with his feet' by either buying or selling shares.

Consequently investors are primarily interested in profit as a starting point for share valuation. Certainly the most commonly used indicator in relation to share prices is the price/earnings ratio (current market price per share divided by profit after tax per share), which implies that profit earned by a company in the last accounting period has some bearing on share price. The ideal profit measure for investors might be a current period estimate of the annual increment in net resources which could be maintained in future years: many reasons, not least subjectivity, make this ideal unattainable, but it is possible that shareholders may prefer a profit measure which attempts to eliminate apparently short-run fluctuations. For present purposes however, it will be assumed that a measure of the increment in net resources, together with sufficient information on fluctuations, would serve investors equally well.

(c) Determining dividends

A company intent on using its resources to the advantage of shareholders would employ available cash to obtain a higher present value than would be available to the shareholders in general and would distribute to shareholders (either as dividends or return of capital with sanction of the Courts) cash which could not be so employed. The analysis would be vastly complicated by such considerations as taxation, the transaction costs of distribution and raising cash and the selection of the appropriate interest rate for discounting, but the principle remains that it is cash generation in relation to available opportunities which is the primary consideration: a profit measure is *not essential* for this purpose.

Profit does influence dividend payments in at least two ways. Firms commonly adopt a policy of paying some proportion of 'normal' accounting profit as dividends: the fact that such pay-out ratios differ between firms and change for a single firm over time supports a view that profit is used largely as a surrogate for the generation of available cash in the long run, although shareholder expectations affecting share price provide a further complication in dividend policy. The law requires dividends to be paid only from current or past profits: this stems from an intention that capital should be 'maintained intact' (originally for the safety of creditors), but the law allows considerable latitude to companies in their measurement of profits.

(d) As a base for taxation

From the taxation viewpoint, profit is merely an indicator of ability to pay tax. There is no reason why profit for taxation should coincide with profit measured for other purposes, and indeed there are already very considerable differences between accounting profit and taxable profit.

(e) Profit measurement

Attention can now be directed to profit as a measure of the firm's performance, which will be assumed to serve the first two purposes considered above. How is the increase in net resources to be measured? The earlier conclusions on measurement of value to the firm will apply, but there is one important qualification. Value at a single point of time involves no problems of changes in the money unit of measurement, but the increase in net resources between two points of time implies a constant 'value' of the measuring unit. The implication is unjustified if, as is often the case, the money unit is subject to changes in its purchasing power over resources *in general*. This problem of *general* changes in the measuring unit must be distinguished from changes in the *specific* money prices of resources owned by the firm: the situation is analogous to using a growing tree as a general measure for the growth in height of several different children, where the inconstant tree is simply a complication detracting from our main aim. Since specific prices change even when money 'value' is stable, our money unit will remain conveniently stable until the last section of this chapter.

The increase in present value of the firm during a period, after adjusting for ownership contributions/distributions during the period, provides a conceptual ideal for the increase in the firm's net resources. Such profit, often called *increased net worth* or *subjective profit*, could not be measured with any degree of objectivity. A corresponding measure based on the replacement cost of resources becomes appropriate for reasons previously advanced in relation to value, and subject to the same limitations.

The measurement of profit on a replacement cost basis, or indeed on any other value basis, can be approached by two alternative methods.

Net resources at one date can be deducted from net resources valued at a later date and the residue adjusted for ownership contributions/distributions to give profit or loss. This approach requires the valuation of all assets and liabilities of the firm at just two dates, the beginning and end of the accounting period. Thus a profit calculation *could* be obtained by valuing at replacement cost at the balance sheet date without considering the transactions which occurred during the year.

Alternatively activities can be recorded on the chosen valuation basis as they occur during the year, any amendments could be made to value as changes occurred during the year, and profit/loss calculated at the end of the year. This is the normal accounting approach, *although* with a different valuation basis. The final residual profit would be the same as before, but it is possible to analyse the composition of profit.

The second approach, using replacement cost, will be introduced here; the adaptation of historic cost data to estimated replacement cost at the end of the year will be examined in detail in section 8.

The data for Cog in Chapter 2 (Table 2.2) have been adapted to provide a replacement cost example in Table 3.2. Considering materials only, any items held could be updated to replacement cost by recognizing a gain or loss when price changes occur. The materials would be transferred to manufacturing at replacement cost at time of transfer and the ending inventory would appear at replacement cost – instead of the historic cost of the earlier records, shown here in square brackets.

An important point emerges. Cog has derived a benefit of £13 000 by purchasing

Table 3.2 Materials recorded at replacement cost (£000's)

Materials			Manufacturing	Profit calculation
Opening balance (assumed replacement cost 1 January)	42	[300] 311 ——	Replacement cost when used ——→	Operating gains ——→
Purchases (various dates)	288	[30] 32 ↓		
			Inventory 31 December at replacement cost	Holding gain
Holding gain	13			13 ↑
	343	343		

Italic numerals indicate changes from original data in Table 2.2.

materials some time prior to use: if the firm had operated on a hand-to-mouth basis it would have had to pay that amount more for its inputs. But most of the materials were consumed in sustaining the firm's operating activities, so that in terms of current exchange values the operating activities were some £11 000 *less* profitable than the historic cost basis would imply (finished goods inventories are being ignored). A distinction can therefore be made between:

Holding gains/losses: increase/decrease in replacement cost of assets while held during the accounting period;

Operating gains/losses: the difference between revenue and the replacement cost of resources when disposed of during the accounting period.

The sum of operating gains/losses is commonly termed *current operating profit* and the sum of all gains/losses is (rather less widely) termed *business profit.** We shall retain the gain/loss terminology, defining the sum of all gains/losses as *net gain* (or loss).

The distinction between operating and holding gains has some significance for appraisal, since that function is concerned not merely with the net result of activities but with how and why the result occurred. Holding gains/losses carry implications for buying/holding activities while operating gains/losses convey information on operating/selling activities. This division is unattainable with historic cost accounting, and so it must be noted that firms do *not* in fact distinguish gains in this manner in their entity accounts. Nevertheless an efficient management will be aware (if not precisely informed) of the major elements in each area, largely by use of detailed control information.

* These terms derive from [9].

3.7 Valuation and depreciation of long lived assets

Assets held by the firm over many years pose a major valuation problem* in accounting which requires separate attention. Even if it were decided to value such assets at the replacement cost of equivalent second-hand assets there are rarely competitive markets which will provide the necessary information (what is the replacement cost of a second-hand oil refinery?) and sometimes not even markets in similar new assets because models of a different type are currently being sold.

An everyday meaning of depreciation would be 'decline in value over time'; the conventional accountant would, of course, eschew all reference to value and define depreciation as something like 'the expenditure on an asset spread over its effective lifetime'. The latter definition does not escape value considerations but instead leads to two central aspects involving value: the estimation of the asset's life and the pattern of depreciation over that life.

(a) Asset life

There are two possible ways of interpreting the life of an asset:

Technical life: the length of time over which the asset could continue to render services to the firm;

Economic life: the length of time over which the value of the services received are expected to exceed the costs of employing the asset.

Technical life can be very long indeed if sufficient money is spent on maintaining the asset, although competition from alternative more efficient assets must eventually cause the value of services in the original use to decline; there are still stage coaches in existence with unfinished technical lives but the demand for their services as means of transport is limited.

Economic life is usually shorter than technical life for several reasons. There are costs associated with holding and using any asset: running costs, repair and maintenance costs, which tend to increase as the asset deteriorates physically with age and use, and interest foregone on the price for which the asset could be sold (although declining with age). A new asset of *identical* type may offer reductions in running/repair costs, etc., which exceed the cost of the new asset; for example, no rational person would repair a crashed car for £1 100 if a new replacement would cost £1 000. A new asset of a *different* type may become available which offers reductions in running/repair costs or increased revenue exceeding the costs involved in acquiring the new asset; this phenomenon and the possible decline in demand for the services of the existing asset are termed *obsolescence*. Without entering the complex area of putting figures on such expectations, it can be said that the complementary costs (out-of-pocket and opportunity costs) associated with holding

*For some contributions in this area see Baxter [4], Lewis and E. O. Edwards in [16], Wright in [18].

an asset will normally increase with time: when these costs exceed the value of the services from an asset in a particular time period, economic life will be ended as illustrated* in Figure 3.2. Any specification of a life over which an asset is to be depreciated implies, but may not get, some assessment along these lines; the view corresponds to that which is implicit in the original decision to purchase (which could be expressed in present value terms). Since only economic life has relevance for depreciation any further reference to life (without qualification) will mean economic life.

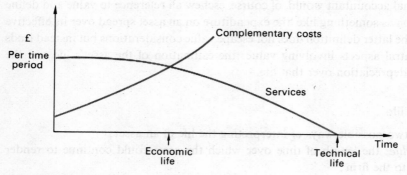

Figure 3.2 Illustration of economic and technical lives

Economic life can coincide with technical life for legal reasons, as at the end of a lease on property, and can effectively coincide when services cease through failure – but failure is usually another way of saying that repair is obviously uneconomic. Only legally determined life can be predicted with substantial confidence: all other estimates are essentially based on probabilities, with 'most likely' life implied for depreciation purposes.

(b) The depreciation pattern

The way in which an asset is depreciated over its expected economic life can be thought of as establishing a pattern, which must relate in some sense to decline in value and/or net services yielded up. Earlier arguments supported the use of replacement cost as a value concept, but how can replacement cost be approximated in the most common situation where no reliable market data are available for assets in the same partly used condition as those held by the firm? A major reason for adopting the replacement cost concept was that it represented an estimate of the amount the firm would suffer from loss of the asset. The best approach in the usual absence of market prices for fixed assets is to estimate that amount directly and to

*Adapted from Meij [16], p. 6.

use the decline in that amount over time as a measure of depreciation. We shall call this estimated amount *equivalent replacement cost*.

The analysis for economic life provides guidance here: the loss of a *separable and replaceable* asset would deprive the firm of the *asset's* unexpired residual benefits. These residual benefits can be regarded as the difference between the total periodic costs of an economically identical asset and the out-of-pocket costs of holding and using the existing asset (i.e. the residual benefits are the cost savings from not having to replace the asset). A summation of the expected residual benefits, suitably time discounted, would give the money amount for 'equivalent replacement cost' which is being sought.

An example will help to clarify the argument so far. An asset with an unnaturally convenient one period life will be taken to avoid discounting complications. Scrooge's Department Store holds the Christmas decorations and lighting which were used to decorate the store last year. These decorations will serve for the coming Christmas, after which they are expected to 'fail'; the best replacement decorations available cost £1 000 and are designed to serve one year only. Given the quantified expectations shown below, what is the equivalent replacement cost of the existing asset?

	Existing asset, £	Replacement asset, £
Services (net revenue from customers attracted)	1 400	1 700
Running costs	750	500
Outlay cost (on replacement)	—	1 000
		1 500
Gain	£650	£200

It is evident that the store would suffer a loss of £450 if deprived of the existing asset, the difference between the gain from the existing asset and that of the best available replacement. The same answer is shown below in terms of the earlier analysis of residual benefits and from an alternative viewpoint of *net cost savings*.

The reader should satisfy himself that the answer in each case would have been the £1 000 cost of the replacement asset if the economic characteristics of the existing asset had been identical with the replacement.

Depreciation in the above example would be the decline in 'equivalent replacement cost' during the past period; if the existing asset had been acquired at, say, £1 600, depreciation would have been £1 150.

For estimating purposes the apparently devious net cost savings approach is

95

In terms of residual benefits:		£
Services		1 400
Less complementary costs:		
running costs	750	
profit foregone on best replacement	200	
		950
Residual benefits		£450
In terms of net cost savings:		
Net periodic cost of replacement		
outlay/running	1 500	
Less service advantage of replacement	300	
		1 200
Less running costs		750
Net cost savings		£450

probably easiest (and certainly implicit in much of the literature and practice of replacement decisions) because the service *advantage* of a replacement can often be estimated more easily than the gross benefits from services of an asset. Gross benefits are in fact important to the replacement *decision** but not to our current concern with estimating the replacement cost of the separable asset. The appendix to this chapter illustrates an 'equivalent replacement cost' depreciation model based on the net cost savings approach.

Certain qualifications must be noted before proceeding:

1. The discussion has been dealing with estimates which are neither easy to make nor in any sense objective. It may be some small consolation that the same criticisms apply to conventional accounting depreciation; the aim has been to supply a conceptual frame of reference, not a catch-all formula.

2. The implicit assumption has been made that depreciation estimates will be re-worked in each period to take account of changes in expectations. It would be realistic to recognize that an estimation of the depreciation pattern at the beginning of the asset's life and adjustment for the grosser changes during its life is the best that can be hoped for.

3. Complementary costs of an asset can be divided between those which arise simply from owning the asset – physical decay, obsolescence, etc., termed *retainer cost* – and those costs which arise from use – running and maintenance costs, etc., termed *user* cost. Variations in use of the asset in different periods will affect expectations of remaining economic life and therefore in principle should affect the depreciation calculation. Usually accounting depreciation is related entirely to the age of the asset (which implies retainer cost), although

*See section 2 of Chapter 12.

the equally arbitrary simplification of relating depreciation entirely to use is sometimes adopted.

Even though a full-blooded incorporation of residual benefits (= net cost savings as defined here) might be too onerous for routine accounting, the approach provides guidance on the acceptability of depreciation *patterns* derived from more conventional rules of thumb. For most assets except those with lives determined by failure or by the termination of legal rights one message is clear: life ends not with a bang but with a whimper. Even technological breakthroughs which render assets obsolete commonly take years to become economically dominant. Residual benefits can usually be expected to tail off gradually* over economic life, and depreciation should reflect this. It is an exceptional asset which offers the constant residual benefits throughout life implied in much of the accounting discussion of depreciation. However, with a stable age distribution of (comparable) assets any depreciation pattern on historic cost would give an equal depreciation charge each year *if* prices also remained stable – since, say, a higher than average depreciation charge on a young asset would be balanced by a lower than average charge on a counterpart old asset.

Some conventional depreciation methods will be reviewed in relation to the expected residual benefits from an asset which would justify the particular depreciation pattern. Assume an asset which is bought currently for £250; it has an expected salvage value of £40 at the end of its life and an economic life of two years. (The last is unrealistic because the economic characteristics determining the two-year life have not been specified, but it is convenient here.) It is assumed for simplicity that residual benefits accrue at annual intervals. The appropriate interest rate is 10 per cent per year; changes in expectations and price changes are ignored.†

(i) *Constant depreciation in each year of life*
The widely used straight line depreciation method determines annual depreciation as:

$$D = \frac{C - S}{n}$$

where D = annual depreciation, C = original cost of asset, n = estimated years of asset life, S = scrap value at the end of n years.

What are the residual benefits implied by this method? Clearly in year 1 at least the £105 depreciation (see Figure 3.3a), but also 10 per cent on the £250 foregone at the beginning of the year, giving the £130 implied residual benefits shown in Figure 3.3b‡ Similarly the £145 valuation at the end of year 1 implies a residual

---

* But not necessarily at any constant rate.
† For price changes with an assumed (straight line) depreciation pattern see section 8.
‡ In Figure 3.3b and subsequent examples the implied services are shown for simplicity as constant over time; it is the *difference* between services and costs which is central to the analysis.

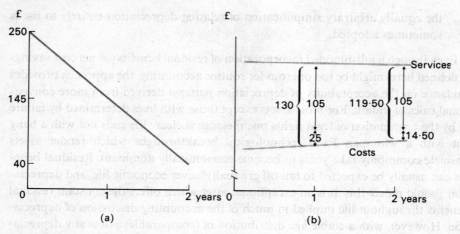

Figure 3.3 (a) Asset 'value'. (b) Implied residual benefits

benefit of £119·50 in addition to the scrap value of £40 at the end of year 2. Expected amounts of £130 at year 1 and £159·50 at year 2 discount at 10 per cent to a present value of £250 – which is not surprising in view of the way the implied residual benefits were calculated.

An asset which might be expected to produce gently diminishing residual benefits of this character would normally be long lived and free from steeply rising repair costs/maintenance/obsolescence; many buildings (*ex* land) might qualify.

(ii) *Depreciation increasing with each year of life*

The little used method known as annuity or sinking fund depreciation provides depreciation which increases with each year of the asset's life, the increase being related to some selected interest rate. The amount of depreciation in each year can be calculated from the following formula:

$$D_1 + D_1(1+i) + \cdots + D_1(1+i)^{n-1} = C - S$$

where D_1 = depreciation for year 1, $D_1(1+i)$ = depreciation for year 2, $D_1(1+i)^{n-1}$ = depreciation for year n, and i = rate of interest.

In this case depreciation, as illustrated in Figure 3.4a, can be calculated:

$$D_1 + D_1(1·10) \qquad = £250 - £40$$
$$D_1 = \frac{£210}{2·10} = £100$$
$$\text{and } D_1(1+i) \qquad = £110$$

In Figure 3.4a this approach can be compared with the effect of straight line depreciation, which is indicated by the tinted line.

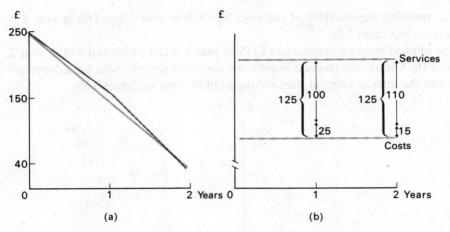

Figure 3.4 (a) Asset 'value'. (b) Implied residual benefits

What residual benefits are implied? Again these are the depreciation in year 1 (£100 this time) plus interest on the £250 foregone, giving £125; in year 2 depreciation (£110) plus interest on the £150 implied value of the asset gives £125, identical to the previous year. Thus there is an implication of *constant* residual benefits, as shown in Figure 3.4b.

An asset capable of producing constant residual benefits throughout life would not deteriorate economically until its life suddenly ended. Such an asset requires services and costs during life either to remain constant or to change in unison and requires some expected event which will terminate life. Long-lived assets with these characteristics are rare: parts of assets could qualify (for example, electrical components which fail) but they would normally be treated as repair items in formulating expectations for the total asset; one type of asset which would be appropriate is a property lease excluding responsibility for repairs.

(iii) *Depreciation decreasing with each year of life*
The reducing balance method provides depreciation which decreases with each year of the asset's life. Depreciation is calculated as a constant percentage of the asset balance for each year *after* deducting the depreciation of earlier years; thus the percentage is applied to a reducing balance in each succeeding year. The constant percentage can be derived:

$$R = 100\left(1 - \sqrt[n]{\frac{S}{C}}\right)$$

Applying the formula to our asset gives:

$$R = 100\left(1 - \sqrt[2]{\frac{40}{250}}\right) = 60 \text{ per cent}$$

Value and profit

The resulting depreciation of the asset by £150 in year 1 and £60 in year 2 is illustrated in Figure 3.5a.

The implied residual benefits are £175 in year 1 (£150+£25) and £70 in year 2 (£60+£10). Clearly the residual benefits are declining sharply, with both depreciation and the interest element diminishing as illustrated in Figure 3.5b.

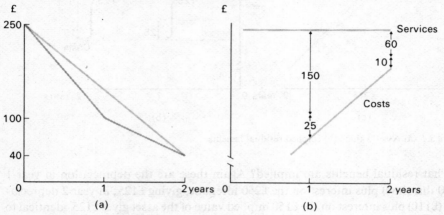

Figure 3.5 (a) Asset 'value'. (b) Implied residual benefits

The exceptionally short two year life of the asset in this example leads to an exaggerated tapering of depreciation and the implied residual benefits; in fact a percentage rate as high as 60 per cent would be rarely adopted. The method is employed fairly widely in the UK; in the USA another method, termed sum of the years' digits depreciation, produces a similar reducing depreciation effect.

Assets which might be expected to produce moderately to strongly declining residual benefits, declining more rapidly than by the rate of interest alone which is implied in the straight line method, would tend to have short to medium lives (say up to about a dozen years) and would be subject to significantly increasing physical deterioration, repairs and/or obsolescence. Many machines and vehicles owned by firms would meet these requirements. Observation of the few available competitive markets in second-hand assets (particularly commercial vehicles) reveals a decline in second-hand price with age of asset which supports this analysis of decline in 'value'; it is to be expected that second-hand prices would reflect residual benefits for firms in general.

The discussion of the three general categories of depreciation pattern is subject to qualification. An essentially static situation was assumed in which expectations were achieved and in the absence of price changes the original cost of the asset implicitly reflected current (new replacement) cost. In conventional accounting amendments may be made for changes in the expected life of an asset but price changes are ignored.

100

3.8 Estimation in replacement cost

The use of replacement cost for accounting purposes has been the subject of considerable discussion and controversy among accountants, although implementation is rare. Attention has been directed largely to measurement for published accounts, but the replacement cost concept is central to many management uses of accounting information and it is curious that an estimate of current value should be widely rejected for internal purposes in favour of an irrelevant, if 'objective', measure of past acquisition cost.

Replacement cost of goods held and frequently replenished by the firm can be ascertained from current transaction prices; one possible method of dealing with the recording aspects was indicated earlier in Table 3.2. The estimation of replacement cost for goods which the firm has manufactured or partly manufactured is more complex, but the complexity arises irrespective of the cost concept employed: the problem is to decide which inputs to attribute to particular outputs. That particular problem will be considered in Chapter 14; any procedure for attributing historic cost inputs is equally capable of being approximated to a replacement cost measure. Assets for which the firm does not have frequent dealings cause difficulties; for partly used fixed assets market information on corresponding new assets can be substituted for historic cost, and depreciation deducted appropriately.

Alternatively indices for replacement cost of *specific classes* of assets can be used as a basis for estimation, and this approach will be developed here. It need hardly be said that the resulting replacement costs are approximate, but they have the advantage of being relatively easy to obtain. For fixed assets held for long periods the divergences between historic costs and replacement costs can become so substantial that any honest attempt at updating can hardly fail to be more informative than historic costs.

As an example, an index might be prepared for changes in the purchase price of (new) heavy industrial vehicles. If the selected representatives were vehicle type A which rose in price from £5 000 to £5 500 in the period under consideration and vehicle type B which remained at £5 000, the index would be expressed as 100 at the beginning of the period and 105 end-period. The index could then be used to approximate the replacement cost of similar vehicles held by the firm.* In fact the average would usually be weighted to reflect relative purchases in the asset class.

Estimated replacement cost would be obtained as follows:

$$\frac{\text{Current index}}{\text{Index at acquisition of asset}} \times \begin{bmatrix} \text{Historic cost (less deprecia-} \\ \text{tion for depletion of asset life)} \end{bmatrix} = \begin{array}{l} \text{Estimated} \\ \text{replacement cost} \end{array}$$

---

* This approach evades the possibility that newer models may offer improved services.

Price indices for many classes of assets can be obtained from outside sources,†
alternatively indices can be prepared from the firm's own data.

The application of indices for replacement cost will be illustrated by returning
to the accounts of Cog given originally in Table 2.2. The acquisition of fixed assets
coincided (approximately) with the beginning of the year, so that beginning
replacement cost of the period coincides with historic cost. Normally many assets
would have been acquired at earlier dates; the replacement costs at the beginning
of the current year can be taken from the previous end-year replacement cost
balance sheet or can be updated from historic cost.

Assume that the index for purchase price of new equipment of the class held by
Cog was 100 at 31 December 19–0 and 93·3 at 31 December 19–1, a fall of $6\frac{2}{3}$ per
cent. The equipment's beginning replacement cost was £150 000. Depreciation can
be assumed to take place throughout the year, so it is appropriate to depreciate on
replacement cost at the average of the year (henceforth abbreviated to *average-
year*). With average-year index taken as 96·6 the average-year replacement cost
becomes £145 000 and depreciation is £14 500 (adopting the straight line depreciation and 10-year life of the original Cog data). At the end of the year, with index
93·3, the 9-year life asset has a replacement cost of £126 000. Holding loss can be
calculated in relation to the two separate half-years, or as a balancing item, as
illustrated below:

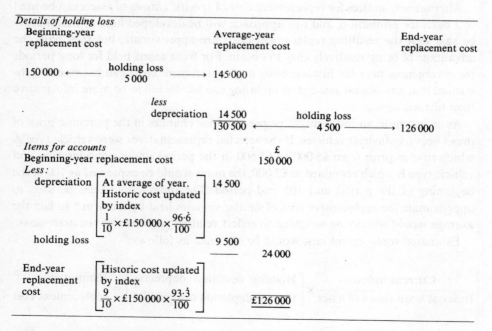

Details of holding loss

Beginning-year replacement cost		Average-year replacement cost		End-year replacement cost
150 000	← holding loss 5 000 →	145 000		
		less depreciation 14 500		
		130 500 ← holding loss 4 500 →		126 000

Items for accounts

		£
Beginning-year replacement cost		150 000
Less:		
depreciation	At average of year. Historic cost updated by index $\frac{1}{10} \times £150\,000 \times \frac{96\cdot6}{100}$	14 500
holding loss		9 500
		24 000
End-year replacement cost	Historic cost updated by index $\frac{9}{10} \times £150\,000 \times \frac{93\cdot3}{100}$	£126 000

† For example, in Britain, from The Economist Intelligence Unit.

The index for land price increased in the same period from 100 to 110. Since no depreciation is involved this gives a holding gain of £6 000 on the original £60 000.

Table 3.3 shows how these changes could be recorded in the accounting records of Cog if the original historic cost data were superseded; only items relevant to the income accounts have been shown. Note that some items in the income accounts are unaffected by the replacement cost basis; these represent the use of resources which cannot be stored (e.g. non-manufacturing expenses) or relate to items fixed in money terms* (e.g. doubtful debts).

Table 3.3 Operating and holding gains for Cog (£000's)

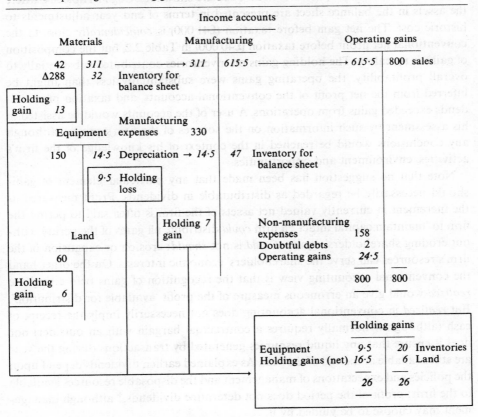

Italic numerals indicate changes from original data in Table 2.2.

The historic cost data for materials consumed, and manufactured goods sold, could have been converted to replacement cost at a weighted average of purchase prices, and production costs, for the period; the ending inventory would be cor-

---

* Borrowing at a fixed interest rate can be considered to produce holding gains/losses when changes in market interest rates occur – see [9].

respondingly converted to end-period replacement cost.* This adjustment problem has been ignored by adopting the data from Table 3.2, where it was assumed that changes in replacement cost had been recorded as they occurred during the period; a similar assumption applies to the goods manufactured by the firm.

With end-year conversion to replacement cost the adjustments can be segregated to leave the historic cost data undisturbed for the production of conventional accounts. Accounting estimates for replacement cost accounts would be *additional* to the conventional accounts. It is only in this supplementary role that replacement cost accounts have at present even the slightest prospect of widespread acceptance.†

Final accounts on a replacement cost basis are shown for Cog in Table 3.4, where the assets in the balance sheet are presented in terms of end-year adjustments to historic cost. The net gain before taxation (£41 000) is *coincidentally* close to the conventional net profit before taxation (£40 000) in Table 2.2, but the composition of gains is revealing. The holding gains on inventories contributed substantially to overall profitability, the operating gains were substantially less than might be inferred from the net profit of the conventional accounts, and taxation plus dividends exceeded gains from operations. A user of the accounts would be assisted in his assessment by such information on the sources of the firm's profits, although any conclusions would be reached in the context of his knowledge of the firm's activities, environment and opportunities.

Note that no suggestion has been made that any particular element of gains should necessarily be regarded as distributable in dividends. Profit measured as the increment in currently valued net assets of the firm is often said to permit the firm to 'maintain capital intact': a firm *could* distribute all gains of the period without eroding shareholders' equity. *Could* is not *should*; erosion or expansion of the firm's resources can serve the shareholders' economic interests. On the other hand the conventional accounting view is that the recognition of gains before they are *realized* would give an erroneous measure of the profit 'available for distribution'. But *realized* in conventional accounting does not necessarily imply the receipt of cash (although it normally requires a contractual bargain with an outsider) nor does it ensure that any liquid resources generated by transactions during the year are still available at the end of the year. As explained earlier, dividends depend upon the policies and expectations of management and the disposable resources available to the firm; profit of the period does not determine dividends,‡ although management may choose to be guided by it.

The purpose of replacement cost accounts is commonly misinterpreted with regard to depreciation. The source of the confusion is the effect of a series of price

---

* See [18], pp. 20–22 for treatments of price changes relating to inventories.

† The replacement cost accounting of the Dutch Philips Electrical Industries is the outstanding exception. See [10].

‡ Except that *absence* of current *and past* retained profit would in law require zero dividend.

Table 3.4 Cog Ltd. – final accounts in replacement cost terms

---

Balance sheet at 31 December 19–1 (£'s)

Fixed assets

Freehold land at (historic) cost	60 000	
Replacement cost adjustment	+6 000	
		66 000
Equipment at (historic) cost	150 000	
Less depreciation	15 000	
	135 000	
Replacement cost adjustment	−9 000	
		126 000

Current assets

Inventories at (historic) cost	75 000	
Replacement cost adjustment	+4 000	
	79 000	
Debtors and prepayments	94 000	
Bank balance	11 000	
	184 000	
Current liabilities	123 000	
Net current assets		61 000
		£253 000

Shareholders' equity

Issued capital		240 000
Retained gains		13 000
		£253 000

Income statement for the year ended 31 December 19–1 (£'s)

Sales		800 000
Less		
Cost of goods [from Table 3.3]	615 500	
Non-manufacturing expenses	158 000	
Doubtful debts	2 000	
		775 500
Operating gains		24 500
Holding gains/(losses):		
Freehold land	6 000	
Equipment	(9 500)	
Materials	20 000	
		16 500
Net gain before taxation		41 000
Less		
Taxation	18 000	
Proposed dividend	10 000	
		28 000
Retained gain		£13 000

Value and profit

changes over the asset's life, which will be illustrated by extending the data for Cog's equipment by a further year.

Assume that at the end of 19–2 the index for entry price of Cog's equipment (new) was 80, with base = 100 at 31 December 19–0. The calculation of depreciation and holding gains would be as follows:

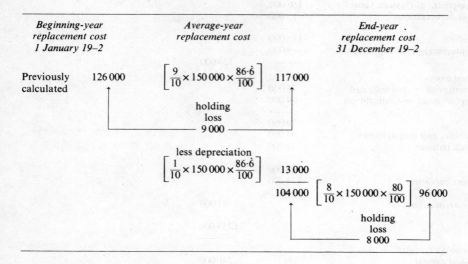

If it is desired to preserve the historic cost data the double entry records would appear as in Table 3.5.

Table 3.5 Historic cost depreciation and replacement cost adjustments (£000's)

| | Historic cost | | Replacement cost adjustment account | | | Estimated replacement cost (net amount of row). |
	Equipment	Accumulated depreciation				
19–1	150	15	Depreciation 0·5 adjustment	Holding loss	9·5	126
19–2		15	Depreciation 2 adjustment	Holding loss	17	
Balance end 19–2	150	30	2·5		26·5	96

Now consider the data from a conventional viewpoint. The deduction of the replacement cost depreciation for 19–1 and 19–2 from the replacement cost of a new asset does not produce the £96 000 estimated replacement cost for the partly used asset:

		£
Replacement cost of new asset		120 000
Less accumulated depreciation 19–1	14 500	
19–2	13 000	
		27 500
		£92 500

But such an approach would mix current values with the backward-looking conventional accounting approach. The depreciation was charged as resources were consumed, and is history by the end of 19–2; the firm has an asset for which the estimate of current value is eight-tenths of £120 000, i.e. £96 000.

Many accountants appear to regard the 'accumulation' of depreciation as some sort of piggy-bank into which money is put away to provide for the eventual replacement of an asset, and replacement cost accounts have been criticized on the grounds that they do not provide depreciation over the life of the asset to provide the unpredictable amount required for eventual replacement. There are two fundamental flaws in this eventual replacement view of depreciation:

1. Depreciation as a measure of decline in asset value during a period for profit measurement carries no implications for the past or future value: concern is with the *current period* in *current terms*. Similarly the balance sheet is concerned with the estimated separable value of an asset at a point of time and is not dependent (as in the historic cost situation) with a legacy of past adjustments.

2. Few firms can be so naive as to regard depreciation provisions in a piggy-bank manner; available funds are employed in accordance with expectations and opportunities, and the particular asset may well not be replaced at the end of its life – but if it is replaced it will hardly be from funds which have accumulated interest free from its predecessor.

Part of the misunderstanding may arise from interpreting the unfortunate term replacement cost as *future* replacement cost, instead of the generally accepted *current* entry price.

The Cog example showed a decline in replacement cost in successive years, which illustrates that the point at issue here has been the change in *specific* prices of assets and not inflation as such. In fact firms have faced *generally* rising prices for several decades, but this does not mean that all prices move in the same direction or, even less, in the same proportion; there are substantial differences in price behaviour between assets.*

* [18], p. 13, refers to a study of Australian manufacturing industries in a 4-year period of generally rising prices; in 3 years approximately one-third faced overall reductions in prices.

3.9 Estimation in conventional accounting

Conventional final accounts do not present a clear-cut historic cost record of the firm's activities and resources: they represent an amalgam of historic cost, interest free expectations and current market values. The basic conventions depend upon the class of asset, and can be *broadly* stated as:

Fixed assets: valued at historic cost less depreciation provided for the expired portion of the asset's expected life;

Current assets: valued at the 'lower of historic cost or market value'.

The treatment of current assets provides a major example of the doctrine of conservatism: market value changes are recognized only in a *downward* direction. The doctrine does not extend in this respect to fixed assets, where both upward and downward 'fluctuations' in market prices are ignored on the grounds that fixed assets are held for use, not market transaction purposes. Changes in the asset's expected life may, however, lead to the amendment of depreciation on historic cost.

The basic conventions are permissive in the sense that they offer a wide variety of acceptable treatments, but provide few criteria for selection.*

A brief review will be sufficient to make the point that conventional accounting is inherently a process of estimation. Its so-called objectivity should certainly not influence the firm intent on preparing relevant information for management purposes, even though conventions are very influential (but not binding) for external reporting.

(a) Fixed assets

The conventions permit any life and many depreciation patterns for fixed assets. The differing economic characteristics of fixed assets justify such a breadth of choice but the absence of any orthodox basis for selecting between depreciation methods is less explicable. Straight line depreciation does have a widespread acceptance which almost gives it the status of a convention, but this status is prone to erosion (e.g. in the USA for tax reasons).

The conventional treatment of fixed assets has been most frequently breached in recent years by the revaluation of property: many companies have revalued land, buildings and leases at current realizable values, often updating periodically at intervals like five years. Gains on revaluations are almost invariably treated as windfall increments to capital, leaving profit calculation on a conventional basis.

---

* Recent British 'accounting standards' are narrowing the range of conventional treatments – often by adopting current majority practice as standard practice. See [13].

(b) Current assets

The phrase 'lower of historic cost or market value' indicates the nature of the general convention on current assets, although use of the phrase is normally confined to inventories.*

In the non-inventory area the convention merely involves an adoption of estimated current value when this is below the original book value. Thus book values are reduced for debtors when bad debts are expected and for short term securities when market price is below cost.

'Lower of cost or market value' for inventories permits variations of interpretation in three areas:

1. *Lower* can entail comparison of individual items or comparison at some level of aggregation for inventory classes. The greater the number of comparisons the more likely it is that valuation will be reduced.
2. *Historic cost* is itself capable of a very many interpretations. What is the historic cost of unused goods remaining from a physically homogeneous collection of goods purchased at different prices? Historic cost of specific units or batches of goods may be identified, but more usually one of several possible simplifications is adopted, such as average cost of the period or an assumption that the goods which were bought first were sold first (first-in-first-out). For goods produced within the firm there are numerous additional possibilities arising from the allocation of inputs to the items concerned.†
3. *Market value* can refer to replacement cost or net realizable value. Conventions in this respect vary between countries; for example, British and Canadian practice favours net realizable value, American practice incorporates consideration of replacement cost.‡

These variations are not exhaustive. Certain current assets may be valued *above* cost: some mining and produce companies value inventories at net realizable value, long term contracts commonly include some portion of anticipated profit, short term securities may be recorded at realizable value, and finance companies have several acceptable options for the valuation of hire purchase contracts.

3.10 General price level changes

Until now it has been assumed that the 'value' of the money unit used for measure-

* The term 'market value' is not favoured by British professional accountants. A British 'accounting standard' [14] proposed in June 1972 would adopt the lower of cost and net realizable value of separate items or groups of similar items, with cost defined as all expenditure incurred in bringing the product to its present location and condition.
See [1] for a comparison of North American and British conventions.
† See Chapter 14.
‡ See [1].

ment remains stable, in the sense that its purchasing power over resources *in general* is constant. Rarely would such an assumption have been valid throughout the history of money, and certainly the decline in the purchasing power of the money unit (i.e. generally rising prices) has been an all too familiar experience in recent years. Thus some consideration must be given to *general price level* changes as opposed to the *specific* price changes considered so far.

The first requirement is an indicator of the general price level. Most governments publish a number of indices which have 'official' status. An index of prices paid by consumers is a widely accepted indicator for the present purpose, and CPI will henceforth refer to the official Consumer Price Index based on price changes in a selection of goods commonly purchased by a group of 'typical' consumers. If it can be assumed that firms operate for the ultimate benefit of shareholders, that shareholders are ultimately interested in personal consumption of goods and that shareholders are 'typical' consumers, then CPI offers a measure of the change in 'value' of the money unit for accounting purposes.

(a) Measurement in real terms

A change in the general price level has a similar effect to that of a change in the exchange rate between two national currencies. Assume that an individual in country R holds assets in country M. At the beginning of a period the exchange rate was $R100 = M80$ but by the end of the period M had been devalued so that $R100 = \cdot M100$. If the individual's assets valued in M rose by exactly 25 per cent (measured in M) during the period, he is no better or worse off (in R) and the rise in his assets in M can be considered as *fictional*. To the extent that his asset values in M rose by more or less than the fictional element the individual has made a *real* gain or *real* loss in terms of R. If the asset values were fixed in money terms (debtors or cash), and therefore failed to increase in M at all, the individual has made a real holding loss of 25 per cent on his assets at the beginning of the period; this can be termed a *monetary holding loss*. On the other hand, if his assets in M were negative (i.e. he borrowed in M to hold assets in R) he will have made a *monetary borrowing gain* of 25 per cent on his borrowing.

The above analysis applies to general price level changes, with CPI replacing M and money value at the end of the period ($=$ real terms at that point of time) replacing R. For the following discussion an increase in general price level will be assumed; corresponding arguments can be applied to a decrease.

Assume that the firm's accounts have already been prepared on a replacement cost basis – so that specific price changes have been recognized. The objective is to provide accounting measures in real terms by measuring consistently in end-year money 'value'. In the balance sheet at the end of the year the *net assets are already expressed in real terms* because they were valued in money at that date. Consequently the *total* shareholders' equity is already expressed in real terms (because equity = net assets). The problem therefore concerns profit measurement: to what extent was the change in the shareholders' equity fictional in that it merely compensated for the increase in the general price level, and to what extent was there a real increment?

From the balance sheet at the beginning of the year the equity measured in beginning-period money can be converted to end-period by an index adjustment, as follows:*

$$\text{Beginning-period equity (issued capital + retained gains) in beginning-period money} \times \frac{\text{End-period CPI}}{\text{Beginning-period CPI}} = \text{Beginning-period equity in end-period money}$$

The converted beginning-period equity reflects the increase in the general price level. The equity increment arising from this adjustment equals total fictional gains – therefore this increment can be deducted from money gains to give *real* gains for the period. If the user required only a global explanation of the general price level effects on equity (in addition to the detailed replacement cost accounts) these two complementary adjustments would be sufficient. Such a global adjustment is illustrated for Cog in the balance sheet of Table 3.6, where the fictional element of £20 000 has been deducted from the period's retained gains (add back dividend to obtain real gains after taxation). The replacement cost data originate from Table 3.3 and it is assumed that CPI = 120 at 1 January 19–1 and CPI = 130 at 31 December 19–1. (As 19–1 was the first year of Cog's operations there were no retained gains in equity at 1 January.)

For a detailed income statement it is necessary to adjust the component items. Considering the operating gains first, these were originally calculated at the average of the year: they are therefore measured (approximately) in average-period £'s. Note that operating gains do not include holding elements, so that no question of fictional gains on asset holding arises – *the operating gains were already expressed in real terms at average-period £'s*. However, for comparability with the balance sheet in end-period £'s the operating gains can be converted to end-period £'s by application of the index change (from assumed average-year CPI = 125 to end-year CPI = 130). This adjustment has been made to Cog's total operating gains in the income statement of Table 3.6; each individual amount in the original calculations of operating gains could be similarly converted if desired.

The holding gains were also calculated in average-year £'s, so that the original amounts can be updated to end-year £'s. But in this case there must be deducted the fictional elements which merely compensate for the rise in the general price level – on beginning assets for a full year and on asset increments from average-year to

---

* Equity contributions and distributions during the period are ignored here; they can be updated to end-period from the time at which they occurred.

Table 3.6 Cog Ltd. – final accounts in real terms

Balance sheet summary at 31 December 19–1, in end-year £'s

Net assets	[Individual items as for replacement cost]	£253 000
Shareholders' equity		
Beginning equity	$\left[\text{From beginning year £'s: £240 000} \times \dfrac{130}{120}\right]$	260 000
Less Real residual loss of year	$\left[\text{In total: £13 000} - \text{£240 000} \times \dfrac{10}{120}\right]$	7 000
		£253 000

Income statement summary for the year ended 31 December 19–1, in end-year £'s

Operating gains	$\left[\text{From average-year £'s: £24 500} \times \dfrac{130}{125}\right]$		25 480
Less Real holding losses [See calculation below]			3 760
Real net gain before taxation			21 720
Less Taxation	$\left[\text{From average-year £'s: £18 000} \times \dfrac{130}{125}\right]$	18 720	
Proposed dividend		10 000	
			28 720
Real residual loss			£7 000

Calculation of real holding losses (£'s)

	Holding gains/(losses)		Assets/(liabilities) held in year		Fictional gains (losses)	Real holding gains (losses)
	Average-year £'s	End-year £'s $[1] \times \dfrac{130}{125}$	Beginning-year assets (liabilities)	Increase (decrease) at average of year	$[3] \times \dfrac{10}{120}$ $[4] \times \dfrac{5}{125}$	
	[1]	[2]	[3]	[4]	[5]	[2]−[5]
Freehold land			60 000	. . . 5 000		
				6 000 240		
	6 000 ⟶	6 240			5 240	1 000
Equipment			150 000	12 500		
				(24 000) . . . . . . (960)		
	(9 500) ⟶	(9 880)			11 540	(21 420)
Inventories			42 000	3 500		
				37 000 . . . . . . 1 480		
	20 000 ⟶	20 800			4 980	15 820
Net monetary assets (liabilities)			(12 000)	(1 000)		
				4 000 160		
	0 ⟶	0			(840)	840
	16 500	17 160	240 000	23 000	20 920	(3 760)

end-year. The calculations are summarized in the last section of Table 3.6; the principle is shown in detail below for Cog's holding gain on land.

		£
Money holding gains converted from average-year £'s to end-year £'s	$\left[6\,000 \times \dfrac{130}{125}\right]$	6 240
Less fictional element:		
Hypothetical general price level increase on beginning-year asset value	$\left[60\,000 \times \dfrac{10}{120}\right]$ 5 000	
Hypothetical general price level increase on increment to asset value (assumed occurring average-year)	$\left[6\,000 \times \dfrac{5}{125}\right]$ 240	5 240
Real holding gain		£1 000

Assets and liabilities which are fixed in money terms deserve comment. The same calculation approach is adopted as for the other items making up net assets, but here the hypothetical nature of the general price level increase is self-evident. The general price level adjustment represents a real loss from holding monetary assets or a real gain from borrowing in a time of declining money value. Cog was a net 'borrower'* and gained £840 (end-year) by borrowing 'heavy' £'s which can be repaid with current 'light' £'s – whether the gain was in fact achieved depends on what Cog did with the funds. It should not be thought that a monetary borrowing gain necessarily shows that the firm benefited at the expense of lenders. The *costs* associated with such 'borrowing' (interest, forfeited cash discounts) are reflected in the operating gains; the compensation required by lenders cannot be assumed to be devoid of expectations of inflation, but the weight given to this element is not amenable to objective measurement.

How important is adjustment to real terms? The answer depends on the purpose for which the accounts are to be used. For appraisal of performance in a single period the accounts add little to those previously prepared in money (replacement cost) terms. The operating gains were already known in real terms at the average of the period and performance on holding activities can be assessed more meaning-fully by comparison with perceived opportunities than by adjustment for the general price level. However, adjustment is important if the accounting data are to be compared over several years; the commonly substantial cumulative effect of changes in the 'value' of the money unit make conversion to a common unit neces-sary for valid comparison. For such purposes each set of accounting data would be converted from money units at the date of the accounts into money units at a common point in time – normally the date of the last set of accounts in the series. Such a series might be considered appropriate for inclusion in external reports to shareholders, but they are not provided (in real terms as defined here).

* 'Borrowing' is used here in a wide sense of fixed money commitments. The £10 000 dividend com-mitment has been excluded on the grounds that the equity cannot make gains by borrowing from itself, and in any case the dividend is assumed to be declared end-year.

(b) Adjusted historic cost

A different view of price changes from that which has been advanced in this chapter is that accounts should be adjusted for general price level changes only, by conversion of historic costs into current money terms without any intervening adjustment for specific price changes. Thus changes in the measuring unit are recognized but changes in the items being measured are ignored until realization (subject to the usual conventional amendments). This accords with the orthodox accounting view that balance sheets and profit calculations do not involve valuation processes.*

Adjustment proceeds by amending each item in the accounts from recorded historic cost to end-period money terms:

$$\text{Historic cost} \times \frac{\text{End-period CPI}}{\text{CPI at historic cost date}} = \begin{array}{l}\text{Historic cost in end-period money}\\ \text{terms.}\end{array}$$

Transactions which occur at an approximately constant rate during the accounting period can be adjusted from average CPI of the period to end-period CPI along previous lines.

Adjusted historic cost accounts for Cog are shown in Table 3.7, where the previous assumptions for CPI have been adopted. The historic cost data derive from Cog's original accounting records in Table 2.2. The only new assumption is that inventories were acquired on average at CPI = 128.

On the adjusted historic cost basis Cog's profit for the period is £16 422 greater than the corresponding calculation in real terms. This arises largely because Cog's major assets did not increase with the general price level; Table 3.7 gives an erroneous impression that they did.

Adjusted historic cost is subject to the same basic limitation which applies to historic cost in times of a relatively stable money unit – the accounts do not reflect that particular price environment which is faced by the *firm*. A substantial danger of adjusted historic cost accounts is that they may be misinterpreted by users as reflecting current exchange values. This danger is enhanced by some of the terminology employed in (the few) published reports of such accounts – for example the use of the adjective 'real' in relation to profit calculated by this method.

Appendix: 'equivalent replacement cost' depreciation

In the absence of a competitive second-hand market it is not possible to determine depreciation of a wasting asset by the decline in replacement cost of assets in identical condition. The *'equivalent replacement cost'* (ERC) of a partially used

---

*Consequently general price level adjustments to historic cost are regarded relatively favourably by professional bodies. See [2] and [12].

Table 3.7 Cog Ltd. – final accounts in adjusted historic cost terms

Balance sheet 31 December 19–1, in end-year £'s

Fixed assets

Freehold land $\left[60\,000 \times \dfrac{130}{120}\right]$ 65 000

Equipment, less depreciation $\left[135\,000 \times \dfrac{130}{120}\right]$ 146 250

Net current assets

Inventories $\left[75\,000 \times \dfrac{130}{128}\right]$ 76 172

Less

Net monetary liabilities   8 000

Dividend (proposed end-year)   10 000

     18 000

       58 172

       £269 422

Shareholders' equity

Issued capital $\left[240\,000 \times \dfrac{130}{120}\right]$ 260 000

Retained profit [See below]   9 422

       £269 422

Income statement for year ended 31 December 19–1, in end-year £'s

Sales $\left[800\,000 \times \dfrac{130}{125}\right]$ 832 000

Costs:

Beginning inventories $\left[42\,000 \times \dfrac{130}{120}\right]$ 45 500

Purchases and manufacturing expenses $\left[618\,000^* \times \dfrac{130}{125}\right]$ 642 720

Depreciation $\left[15\,000 \times \dfrac{130}{120}\right]$ 16 250

   704 470

Less ending inventories $\left[75\,000 \times \dfrac{130}{128}\right]$ 76 172

Cost of goods   628 298

Non-manufacturing expenses, etc. $\left[160\,000 \times \dfrac{130}{125}\right]$ 166 400

     794 698

     37 302

Monetary borrowing gains   840

Adjusted accounting profit before taxation   38 142

Less

Taxation $\left[18\,000 \times \dfrac{130}{125}\right]$ 18 720

Proposed dividend   10 000

     28 720

Retained adjusted accounting profit   £9 422

---

*From Table 2.2:

                £000's

purchases of materials   Δ288

manufacturing expenses   Δ330

         618

asset can be estimated as the present value of the incremental costs the firm would incur if the remaining services of the existing asset were replaced by equivalent services of a currently available *new* asset.* Depreciation can be determined as the decline in ERC over time.

The following assumptions will be adopted:

1. The firm has a constant annual interest rate i at which all future cash flows can be discounted.
2. Cash flows occur at annual intervals.
3. The economic characteristics of the existing asset and the new asset are known with certainty, and the new asset would be adopted from among available replacement *if* the firm were replacing now.
4. The economic characteristics of *future* replacement assets will be the same as those of the (current) new asset. The effect of this assumption is to confine consideration to the current technological and cost environment in deriving the estimated current replacement cost.
5. The economic lives of the existing asset and the new asset have been estimated. (For examination of service lives see section 2 of Chapter 12.)
6. Variations in asset usage during life can be ignored, either because use is a constant in each year or because depreciation is composed entirely of retainer cost (as opposed to user cost).
7. Initially it will be assumed that the new asset has *annual* capacity and services identical with those of the existing asset (although outlay and out-of-pocket running costs may be different).

These simplifying assumptions are unrealistic, although not more so than the implied assumptions of conventional accounting depreciation.

Arising from assumption 4 the available successors to both the new asset and the existing asset at the end of their lives would be an infinite chain of replacements identical with the current new asset. The two resulting series are illustrated in Figure 3.6, where the following notation is used:

C current outlay cost of a new asset
R_t running costs (maintenance, repairs) of a new asset in year t (incurred end-year)
S_n salvage value of new asset at the end of its life of n years
P_t running cost of existing asset in year t (incurred end-year)
T_k salvage value of existing asset at the end of its *remaining* life of k years

In Figure 3.6 series A and B differ only by the life of the existing asset; ownership of that asset delays the commitment of the firm to the (hypothetical) perpetual stream of costs in series A. The value of this delay to the firm can be derived in three steps:

---

*The term 'equivalent replacement cost' has been coined for the present purposes. The valuation formula in this Appendix is developed in a different manner by Merrett and Sykes [17], pp. 466–75.

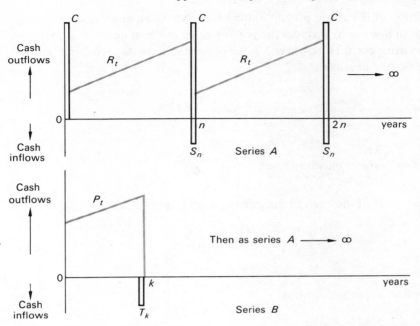

Figure 3.6 Series for new and existing asset. Series *A*, new asset and successors. Series *B*, existing asset and successors

1. The *annual* savings, constituting the avoidable costs of the new asset stream, are given by an annuity of all costs over the duration of stream *A*. In fact this annual amount can be calculated as the annuity of outlay and running costs (minus salvage) *over n years* because the pattern is repeated in perpetuity. But these savings are made only over the life of the existing asset; therefore the annuity for *k years* can be discounted to give the present value of savings arising from the ownership of the existing asset.
2. The cost of ownership of the existing asset is given by the present value of the running costs (minus salvage) during the asset's *remaining* life of *k* years.
3. The difference between the two present values is the 'equivalent replacement cost' of the existing asset.

These steps can now be expressed algebraically:

(a) Savings from owning existing asset

The present value of the outlay, running costs and salvage value of the (first) new asset at year 0 is given by:

$$C + \sum_{t=1}^{n} \frac{R_t}{(1+i)^t} - \frac{S_n}{(1+i)^n}$$

117

Multiplication of the above present value by $a_{\overline{n}|}^{-1}$ yields an annuity over n years; further multiplication by $a_{\overline{k}|}$ gives the present value of the annuity for k years, the life of the existing asset. Thus, where N is the present value of the 'avoidable' portion of the costs of the new asset:

$$N = \left(C + \sum_{t=1}^{n} \frac{R_t}{(1+i)^t} - \frac{S_n}{(1+i)^n} \right) (a_{\overline{n}|}^{-1})(a_{\overline{k}|}) \tag{1}$$

(b) Costs of owning existing asset

The present value of the costs of the existing asset is given by:

$$E = \sum_{t=1}^{k} \frac{P_t}{(1+i)^t} - \frac{T_k}{(1+i)^k} \tag{2}$$

(c) Equivalent replacement cost

The ERC at time 0 is given by $(1)-(2)$:

$$\text{ERC} = N - E$$

Depreciation would be measured as the decline in ERC from year to year; recalculation of ERC would occur each year on the basis of fresh cost data. (Negative ERC suggests that replacement should not be delayed.)

The approach requires modification when assumption 7 is inapplicable. A new asset of identical capacity may not be available, the service quality of the existing asset may decline with age (e.g. increasing wastage of inputs), or the new asset may offer improved services. Pure capacity effects could be accommodated by proportional adjustment of the new asset data. With differences in service quality the new asset offers a service advantage in each year equal to the incremental net revenue arising from the new asset. This service advantage is an opportunity cost of using the existing asset, and can be included in a redefined P_t in (2); thus ERC would represent the present value of net cost savings after incorporation of the service advantage.

Note that ERC derived by taking the differences between costs yields an approximate valuation of the *separable* asset. It does not incorporate valuation of the gross revenues from the asset; in the terminology of section 4 goodwill associated with the asset has not been recognized.

Bibliographical references

[1] Accountants' International Study Group, *Accounting and Auditing Approaches to Inventories in three Nations*, (American Institute of Certified Public Accountants; Canadian Institute of Chartered Accountants; Institutes of Chartered Accountants in England and Wales, Scotland, and Ireland, 1968).

[2] American Institute of Certified Public Accountants (publishers), Accounting Research Study No. 6, *Reporting the Financial Effects of Price-level changes*, 1963.

[3] Backer, M. ed., *Modern Accounting Theory*, Prentice-Hall, 1966.

[4] Baxter, W. T., *Depreciation*, Sweet and Maxwell, 1971.

[5] Baxter, W. T. and S. Davidson eds., *Studies in Accounting Theory*, Sweet and Maxwell, 1962.

[6] Bonbright, J. C., *The Valuation of Property*, Michie Reprint, 1965.

[7] Chambers, R. J., *Accounting, Evaluation and Economic Behaviour*, Prentice-Hall, 1966.

[8] Chambers, R. J., A matter of principle, *Accounting Review*, July 1966, pp. 443–57.

[9] Edwards, E. O. and P. W. Bell, *The Theory and Measurement of Business Income*, University of California Press, 1961.

[10] Goudeket, A., An application of replacement value theory, *Journal of Accountancy*, July 1960, pp. 37–47.

[11] Hendriksen, E. S., *Accounting Theory*, Irwin, 1970.

[12] Institute of Chartered Accountants in England and Wales (publishers), *Accounting for Stewardship in a Period of Inflation*, 1968.

[13] Institute of Chartered Accountants in England and Wales, Accounting standards – A new era, *Accountancy*, February 1971, p. 61.

[14] Institute of Chartered Accountants in England and Wales, Stocks and work-in-progress, *Accountancy*, June 1972, pp. 118–26.

[15] Marshall, A., *Principles of Economics*, 8th ed., Macmillan, London, 1938.

[16] Meij, J. L., *Depreciation and Replacement Policy*, North Holland, 1961.

[17] Merrett, A. J. and A. Sykes, *The Finance and Analysis of Capital Projects*, Longmans, 1963.

[18] Parker, R. H. and G. C. Harcourt eds., *Readings in the Concept and Measurement of Income*, Cambridge University Press, 1969.

[19] Smith, A., *The Wealth of Nations*, Vol. I, Dent, 1910.

[20] Staubus, G. J., *A Theory of Accounting to Investors*, Scholars Book, 1971.

[21] Sterling, R. R., *Asset Valuation and Income Determination*, Scholars Book, 1971.

Problems

3.1 Discuss the following statement:

'The rules by which accountants arrive at the annual income of a given enterprise are not self-consistent, and could not be derived by deduction from any major premise as to what "income" means.' [6], p. 902.

3.2 Examine the following argument, advanced by R. P. Marple (Value-itis, *Accounting Review*, July 1963):

'Value-itis is marked by a special feature – the inability to distinguish between cost prices and selling prices. The victim will argue in all seriousness that when the market price of what you buy goes up, the value of what you have increases and the value increase represents a profit which should be recognized and reported.

Proponents of this view have been known to maintain that a company earns a profit by signing a contract to pay higher wages. They argue that a wage increase, granted near the end of the year, increases the replacement cost of the inventory and that the write up of inventory should be taken as a profit. This is true, they say, because selling prices will be increased to reflect the increased costs. Somehow, those who hold this viewpoint cannot

119

see that it involves acceptance of three totally untenable assumptions:
1. That selling prices can be increased automatically whenever costs increase and in the same proportion,
2. That any price increase which is made will be made before rather than after the lower cost inventory is sold, and
3. That increased selling prices will have no effect on the volume of sales, the principal determinant of profit in this era of high fixed costs.

And, in addition ... they propose that this increased profit be "attributed" to the period of the price increase.'

3.3 '... "replacement cost" accounts ... attempt to set aside from profits sufficient funds to replace specific (usually fixed) assets ...'

Inflation and Accounts, discussion paper, Institute of Chartered Accountants in England and Wales, 1971.

Examine the suggested objective and the extent to which it could be satisfied by replacement cost accounts. Consider whether there is any other possible objective for replacement cost accounts and the extent to which it could be satisfied.

3.4 Examine this view:

'A balance sheet cannot measure the current value of a firm, either to existing owners or to potential purchasers of the whole firm, and a profit calculation cannot measure an increase in such a value, so there is really no point in preparing either of them.'

3.5 Draw a graph representing the approximate decline in market value with increasing age of a motor vehicle. Obtain your data from published advertisements or specialist price guides. Use dealers' selling price and choose a model which has been in production for several years.

Demonstrate which, if any, conventional depreciation method based on current price of a new model approximates to your observed data. (Ignore the problem of future price changes.) Provide a theoretical explanation for your observed depreciation pattern.

3.6 The balance sheet of A Ltd. at 1 January 19–1 showed:

	£		£
Share capital	8 000	Asset at cost	23 000
Retained profits	1 000	*Less* accumulated depreciation	14 000
	£9 000		£9 000

Smith and Jones have a choice of either:
1. purchasing the entire share capital of A Ltd. for £5 000,

or 2. purchasing the company's single asset for £5 000.

The asset has an expected economic life of 5 years, nil scrap value, and straight line depreciation is appropriate. Net revenue (after all costs *except* depreciation) is expected to be £1 500 per year.

Compare the expected balance sheet at 31 December 19–1 and the 19–1 profit for A Ltd. under option 1 with the balance sheet and profit for Smith and Jones in partnership under option 2. (Net revenue will be received in cash; no dividend will be paid by A Ltd. during 19–1; Smith and Jones are equal partners with no other transactions; adopt historic cost.)

Discuss the implications of the accounting treatments.

3.7 Copper Ltd. and Gold Ltd. are two independent companies. By coincidence both commenced trading on 1 January 19–1; on that day each had an issued share capital of £50 000 and borrowing of £50 000, Copper acquired for £100 000 a 10-year lease on the mineral rights of a Cornish copper mine and Gold acquired for £100 000 a 10-year lease on 'The Gold-digger', a Soho restaurant.

Purchase price for the leases included all necessary equipment in each case. Straight line depreciation can be assumed appropriate, with nil salvage values. Both leases involve negligible rental payments, which are included among expenses in the accounts below.

Conventional final accounts for both Copper and Gold for 19–1 revealed the following identical results:

Balance sheet at 31 December 19–1 (£'s)

Issued share capital		50 000
Debt		50 000
		£100 000
Fixed assets	100 000	
Less depreciation	10 000	
		90 000
Cash		10 000
		£100 000

Income statement for year ended 31 December 19–1 (£'s)

Sales		150 000
Less:		
expenses	140 000	
depreciation	10 000	
		150 000
Net profit		£0

Value and profit

All operating transactions took place at a constant rate during the year, and there were no inventories, dividends or taxation.

During 19–1 market expectations of declining copper prices led to a sharp fall in the entry price of Cornish mining rights and property development caused increases in the prices of Soho leases. Specific price indices are given below, together with general price level data.

	Specific price indices		General price index
	Cornish mining rights	Soho leases	(CPI)
1 January 19–1	100	100	144
Assumed average index during 19–1	80	120	150
31 December 19–1	60	140	156

Required:

(a) Final accounts for Copper and Gold on the following bases:

1. Replacement cost.
2. Real terms.
3. Adjusted historic cost.

(b) Comment on the implications of your results.

3.8 Gusher Ltd. purchased a drilling rig for £1 million at year 0. The rig has an expected economic life of 4 years.

Running costs in the first year were £200 000 (assume incurred end-year). Costs for running and repairs are expected to increase by £100 000 per year in each of the remaining three years of life.

The entry price of a new rig at the end of the first year is £1·1 million. Such a rig would be identical to the existing rig (when new). Neither rig will have any value at the end of its life, because costs of dismantling will precisely offset any scrap value.

Adopt an interest rate of 7 per cent per year.

Calculate (to the nearest £1 000) the 'equivalent replacement cost' of Gusher's rig at the end of the first year. What does the 4-year life imply for costs associated with the rig in the fifth year?

4

External reports and the corporate financial image

The simplest possible theory of the firm is the theory of 'homeostasis of the balance sheet', in which we suppose that there is some composition of balance sheet which the firm wishes to maintain

K. E. BOULDING. *A Conceptual Framework for Social Science*

4.1 The significance of external reports

External reports provide financial information for non-management users. Such users are described as external (to management) although they may participate to varying degrees in the activities of the firm. This chapter will consider only 'traditional' users whose reactions to financial data have major implications for the firm: investors, trade creditors and lenders.

The detailed legal and institutional requirements for external reports are outside the scope of this book. It will suffice to say that a company must publish an annual report which includes the final accounts of the period and the directors' report on activities. Thus summarized data, with little detail on such matters as individual expense categories, are made publicly available – and in the case of quoted companies the information is widely circulated. In the present context external reports are equated with the final accounts, but these do not provide the only data available to external users, nor necessarily the most important. Other published information includes brief interim reports of profit progress and dividend declarations by Stock Exchange quoted companies, and reports on contracts, plans and activities of companies and industry developments. Some users, particularly lenders, may be given access to certain internal information, but the outsider inevitably has only a small proportion of the information available to management.

(a) Management and external reports

It might seem that the content of externally published final accounts would be of only passing interest to management. Any internal reporting system worthy of the name must provide management with much more detailed and/or timely information. It has been explained that detailed entity reports, from which the external information is prepared, may well serve an appraisal function of the sort which will be considered in connection with budgets in the control area.

In fact management has a central interest in the content of external reports

123

because they may influence outsiders in relation to decisions affecting the firm. Lack of creditor/lender confidence in the firm's financial stability can have serious consequences; a fall in share price can make new capital difficult to raise or expose the firm to a takeover bid.

The measures used in the interpretation of final accounts are less than perfect, but the outsider must explore his limited information and act on it as best he can. In many cases the measures can be regarded as constraints which circumscribe the actions of the firm: management may aim for 'satisfactory' values for the measures in order to avoid trouble with external users.

(b) Some interpretation measures introduced

A wide variety of measures are used in the interpretation of accounts, of which the major indicators will be considered. For further aspects in this area the reader is referred to Bird [5] and Graham, Dodd and Cottle [11].

The indicators can be categorized as being concerned with profitability and growth, price and valuation, use of resources, and financial stability. Clearly the categories are interrelated: any user would be foolish to look at a single category in isolation from the rest.

Some of the measures which are to be examined in turn in sections 2 and 3 are shown in Table 4.1. The figures are derived from the final accounts of Cog Ltd. for 19–1 in Tables 2.4 and 2.5 of Chapter 2, *except* that it is now assumed Cog had issued share capital of £160 000 in £1 ordinary shares (previously £240 000) and long-term debt of £80 000 (previously nil), debt interest of £8 000 having been charged under non-manufacturing expenses in the original income statements.

Most measures adopted in interpretation are ratios of two figures from the final accounts. For comparison purposes a ratio eliminates the effects of scale. If both numerator and denominator are expressed in money at the same point in time the ratio also eliminates the effect of differences in monetary 'value' for comparison with the ratio of another year. Of course relatively few figures in conventional accounts are expressed in money terms at the same point in time.

The ratios may be judged by comparison with other firms in the same industry (which raises problems of comparability of both the firms and the data calculations) or by comparison with the past results of the firm for the purpose of identifying trends. Quoted companies commonly assist trend comparisons by including 10-year summaries of final accounting data in their reports. These summaries are not in real terms, so that trends in absolute amounts are likely to be upwards in periods of inflation (although a few companies do provide some trend data adjusted for *general* price level changes only) .*

---

*See section 10(b) of Chapter 3 on the dangers of such 'adjusted historic cost' accounts.

Table 4.1 Some measures used in the interpretation of external reports

Measures	Definition	Illustration (for Cog Ltd. Chapter 2) £000's unless pence stated	Measures
Profitability and growth:			
Return on capital employed	$\dfrac{\text{net profit before tax and interest}}{\text{total assets*}}$	$\dfrac{48}{375}$	12·8%
Earnings per share	$\dfrac{\text{net profit after tax}-\text{preference divds.}}{\text{number of issued ordinary shares}}$	$\dfrac{22}{160}$	13·75 pence
Price/valuation indicators:			
Price/earnings ratio	$\dfrac{\text{market price per share}}{\text{earnings per share}}$	$\dfrac{165 \text{ pence†}}{13\cdot75 \text{ pence}}$	12·0
Dividend yield	$\dfrac{\text{dividend per share}}{\text{market price per share}}$	$\dfrac{6\cdot25 \text{ pence}}{165 \text{ pence†}}$	3·8%
Dividend cover	$\dfrac{\text{earnings per share}}{\text{dividend per share}}$	$\dfrac{13\cdot75 \text{ pence}}{6\cdot25 \text{ pence}}$	2·2
Use of resources:			
Sales/inventory	$\dfrac{\text{sales}}{\text{inventory*}}$	$\dfrac{800}{75}$	10·7
Sales/total assets	$\dfrac{\text{sales}}{\text{total assets*}}$	$\dfrac{800}{375}$	2·1
Financial stability:			
Quick ratio	$\dfrac{\text{current assets}-\text{inventory}}{\text{current liabilities}}$	$\dfrac{105}{123}$	0·9
Current ratio	$\dfrac{\text{current assets}}{\text{current liabilities}}$	$\dfrac{180}{123}$	1·5
Interval measure	$\dfrac{\text{defensive assets}-\text{current liabilities}\times 365}{\text{projected expenditures}}$	$\dfrac{105-123}{745}\times 365$	−9 days
'Cash flow'	net profit after tax+depreciation	22+15	£37 000
Interest cover	$\dfrac{\text{net profit before tax}+\text{interest}}{\text{interest}}$	$\dfrac{40+8}{8}$	6·0
Debt/equity ratio	$\dfrac{\text{debt}}{\text{share capital}+\text{reserves}}$	$\dfrac{80}{160+12}$	46·5%

* Commonly calculated as average of figures in current and previous balance sheet.
† It has been assumed that Cog's ordinary shares have a current Stock Exchange price of 165 pence.

Some empirical evidence on the implications of interpretation measures, particularly ratios, will be surveyed in section 4.

4.2 Profitability and associated measures

Investors have an obvious interest in profitability, growth and associated aspects of the firm's activities. Creditors and lenders share this interest in some respects: a firm cannot be unprofitable for long and survive.

(a) Profitability and growth

(i) *Profits and sales*

The ultimate measure of profitability for shareholders is net profit after tax. This figure is commonly compared between different years, and past trends may be extrapolated for future years.

The problems of profit measurement have already been examined: clearly the limitations of accounting procedures must apply in full to the user's interpretation. The flexibility of accounting conventions is one source of difficulty, for which an example will be provided in the calculation of earnings per share.

Substantial variations in tax can occur between years (even with constant tax rates and profit), particularly because new investment provides heavy deductions for tax purposes in the year of purchase. Many companies, but not all, use tax equalization accounts to make the percentage tax charge consistent between years.

Sales may be compared on a trend basis to give an indication of growth of operations. Trends in both profits and sales may incorporate the effects of acquisitions of other companies, which increase profits and sales without necessarily benefiting existing shareholders.

A commonly used indicator of average profit margin is

$$\frac{\text{net profit before tax}}{\text{sales}}$$

The cost of goods sold is not usually available to the outsider, so that average gross profit margin

$$\frac{(\text{sales} - \text{cost of goods sold})}{\text{sales}}$$

cannot be calculated. Examination of such margins may provide the user with some clues on the nature of profit changes (sales volume versus profitability of sales).

(ii) *Return on capital employed*

Return on capital employed is defined in Table 4.1 as

$$\frac{\text{net profit before tax} + \text{interest}}{\text{total assets}}.$$

This ratio is intended to indicate the overall efficiency with which the resources of the firm have been employed in the period. The concept is often termed return on investment, particularly in connection with measuring performance for segments of the firm: in that context it will be examined in Chapter 17.

The ratio is unlikely to reflect the efficient use of resources between different periods, and almost certainly not between different companies. Historic cost

126

(ii) *Current ratio*

The firm's working capital is employed in 'circulating' short-term assets financed to some degree by current liabilities. The current ratio, calculated as (current assets)/(current liabilities), indicates the extent to which the firm provides its own working capital. In this case the mythologically safe ratio is 2. Again the differences between firms in different industries are substantial, and the ratio is used for trend and industry comparison purposes.

Both the quick ratio and the current ratio can be affected by the timing of end-year transactions. When manipulation is deliberate it is termed 'window dressing', but accidental distortions can occur.

The delay of a payment, the acceleration of a purchase or borrowing can all *add* an amount (x) to both the numerator and the denominator of the ratio. Where A is the original asset numerator (either quick or current assets) and L is the original current liabilities denominator, the addition of x to both makes the ratio $(A+x)/(L+x)$.

$$\text{If} \qquad \frac{A}{L} > 1 \quad \text{then} \quad \frac{A+x}{L+x} < \frac{A}{L}.$$

$$\text{If} \qquad \frac{A}{L} < 1 \quad \text{then} \quad \frac{A+x}{L+x} > \frac{A}{L}.$$

Thus a ratio of *less than* 1 can be improved by adding both assets and liabilities (although only towards 1, as $(A+x)/(L+x)$ approaches 1 as a limit).

Conversely the deduction of an equal amount from both assets and liabilities gives $(A-x)/(L-x)$;

$$\text{as} \qquad \frac{A}{L} \gtrless 1 \quad \text{then} \quad \frac{A-x}{L-x} \gtrless \frac{A}{L}.$$

Thus a ratio *greater than* 1 can be improved by reducing assets and liabilities equally (in theory until $L-x = 0$).

Users cross-check to some extent on the behaviour of the components of the quick and current ratios when they use the turnover ratios.

(iii) *The interval measure*

The interval measure attempts to overcome the 'manipulative' limitations of the previous two ratios. The measure was originally proposed by Sorter and Benston [20] who suggest several possible definitions. Only the 'no credit interval' will be considered here, given by

$$\frac{\text{defensive assets} - \text{current liabilities} \times 365}{\text{projected expenditures}}.$$

Defensive assets are cash, trade debtors and readily marketable securities – virtually the same as quick assets (apart from possible differences in the securities included). Projected expenditure constitutes the estimated cash outflows for the coming year. The external user would have to guess at cash expenditures on the basis of the current year's accounts: say sales – net profit – depreciation. The resulting measure estimates how many days the firm could continue operations without obtaining credit. (In Cog's case this period is negative.)

The measure is not susceptible to 'window dressing' as both assets and liabilities appear in the numerator: equal changes would cancel out. It is possible that this attribute is in fact unimportant: in a study of ratios as predictors of company failure [1] the no credit interval performed in a similar manner to the current ratio.

(b) 'Cash flow'

It was explained in Chapter 2 that the figure for short-term funds generated by operations of the firm is very commonly – and misleadingly – called 'cash flow'. This increment to working capital arising from operations of the firm is a particular period is not *cash* flow; therefore the term in its working capital sense will be shown in quotes.

'Cash flow' enables the user to compare the firm's generation of funds with anticipated commitments. One such comparison is the ratio 'cash flow'/total debt, which provides an indication of ability to service the firm's total borrowing.

An entirely different, and dubious, use of 'cash flow' in financial analysis equates the term with profit. Since the external user's 'cash flow' is net profit after tax plus depreciation the employment of the term in the profit sense ignores depreciation. An ability to generate a positive 'cash flow' will help the firm to survive (at least in the short-run) but that by itself does not indicate whether survival is benefiting shareholders; a firm can hardly be regarded as profitable in the long-run if it depletes long-term resources faster than it generates working capital.

The use of 'cash flow' in the profit sense may arise from dissatisfaction with the arbitrary nature of the accounting depreciation calculations. For examination of the use of the term in profit contexts see Paton [17] and Jaedicke, Sprouse [13].

(c) Long-term solvency

(i) *Interest cover*
Interest cover, given by (net profit before tax + interest)/interest, is an indication of the relative safety of interest payments – and of the capacity of the firm to avoid problems with its lenders. Net profit before tax is adopted in the numerator because

interest is deductible for tax purposes: thus the numerator represents total earnings potentially available to meet interest.

Usually this ratio is employed in connection with interest on long-term debt.

(ii) *Debt/equity ratio*

The debt/equity ratio shows the relative reliance on long-term debt and equity in the long-term capital of the firm's balance sheet. The debt entails a continuing legal commitment to pay interest, which pre-empts the first slice of the firm's total earnings; the consequences of non-payment would also bear heavily on the equity shareholders. Thus the debt/equity ratio indicates the risk introduced into the corporate structure by borrowing. The book values do not, of course, represent the values assigned to debt and equity (shares) in the market; in particular the equity figure is the residual of the conventional balance sheet valuations. Problems of debt and equity in the capital structure will be examined in Chapter 20.

4.4 Some evidence on accounting data and ratio measures

All accounting measurements have limitations in some degree. In view of these limitations, to what extent do accounting measures, particularly ratios, serve the purposes for which they are designed, and to what extent do managements and external users act in ways which are consistent with the implications of the measures? The present state of knowledge in this area is far from complete, but this section will consider some of the available evidence relating to these questions.

There is evidence that many ratios adjust towards the industry average in surviving firms, and that firms which fail tend to exhibit deteriorating trends in ratios for several years prior to failure. Lev [14] in a study of 900 continuing firms found a general tendency for ratios to revert to the industry mean. (The ratios examined were: return on capital employed, sales/inventory, sales/total assets, quick ratio, current ratio, equity/debt.) The nature of the adjustment process is less clear: such behaviour would be consistent with that of random variables in an uncertain economic environment, firms may deliberately adjust their operations to produce desired results (an assumption consistent with orthodox financial analysis), or in some circumstances accounting adjustments may assist in producing the desired results. Lev's evidence did suggest, however, that ratios with short-term solvency implications (quick and current ratios) were adjusted most rapidly towards the industry mean.

Regarding failure, there is evidence by Beaver [1], [2], Merwin [16] and others that company failure is markedly associated with the 'deterioration' of ratios over a number of years. This does not mean that ratios are necessarily the *best* predictors available. Beaver's second study [2] revealed that changes in market prices of

133

shares prior to the failure of firms performed slightly better as predictors than the 'best' ratios (cash flow/total debt, net profit after tax/total assets, total debt/total assets). The ratios may influence the market, but other information is obviously available.

The evidence on the implications of accounting data for investors is mixed. Little and Rayner [15] conclude from a study of share prices and profitability that 'past dividend and earnings growth . . . both appear to be of significance for the [current] valuation of shares'. (EPS was their measure of earnings growth.) This suggests that *past* accounting data influence *current* market price, but it does not mean that the measures are predictors for the future. Little and Rayner's evidence supported other work in this area which indicates an unpredictable 'random walk' of share prices (although a non-random path for dividends was apparent). In contrast, later work by Singh and Whittington [19] has suggested a positive association between past and future return on capital. Since their findings relate to return on book values, the accounting base is of some relevance. The adoption of historic cost, which does not revalue assets to reflect changes in the economic environment, means that any holding gains or losses trickle into profits over the lives of the assets. The findings by Singh and Whittington could conceivably be related to this inherent 'smoothing' phenomenon in accounting data – of which other aspects will be considered in the next subsection.

Evidence on the effect of published annual reports is also mixed. Publication has been shown by Beaver [3] to be associated with heavy trading in shares and substantial price changes, which suggests an information content for investors. On the other hand Gonedes [10] could detect no significant impact from annual reports on a model of investors' price-expectations.

4.5 Cosmetic reporting

The accounting conventions permit a substantial degree of flexibility, and management has discretion to choose between the permissible conventions for external reports. The effects of choice between the conventions become focused in the profit calculation.

Managements may have preferences for accounting treatments which 'beautify' profits. Two categories of importance can be distinguished: treatments which smooth profit (= income) and manipulative changes which improve profit.

The rationale for 'income smoothing' was originally advanced by Hepworth [12]:

 . . . owners and creditors of an enterprise will feel more confidence toward a corporate management which is able to report stable earnings than if considerable fluctuation of reported earnings exists . . . The absence of peaks and valleys in the earnings record of an enterprise may do much to maintain continuing satisfactory industrial relations.

Self-interest on the part of management is not a necessary feature of income smoothing: management may believe that short-term fluctuations in profit are misleading or irrelevant.

There are two ways in which smoothing might take place. One is by management discretion in the choice of accounting practices, mentioned above. For example, the treatment of intangibles and deferred charges (advertising, research and development) in a manner which spreads the expense over a number of periods could produce smoother profit figures than if the items were expensed immediately. The other way may be inherent in certain generally accepted accounting practices: inventory valuation which spreads current period costs into later periods, or historic cost valuation of fixed assets which spreads holding gains or losses in the manner mentioned earlier.

Copeland [7] surveyed a number of studies which sought to test the smoothing hypothesis, most of them concerned with a single discretionary smoothing variable. These studies were inconclusive. Subsequent studies by Beaver [4] and Dascher and Malcolm [9] suggested that smoothing of some sort does take place, although the sources of smoothing were not distinguishable.

The second category of accounting treatments which may affect the profit image of the firm concerns changes in accounting procedures. For example, changes in methods of valuing inventory or the treatment of depreciation or deferred charges can produce substantial profit changes. The effect of the change would be noted in the accounts, but the final profit figure incorporating the change may be regarded as the 'right' profit by users. The line between smoothing and manipulation is a thin one: the frequent use of manipulation would produce smoothing results.

Research relating to accounting changes has been undertaken by Blaine [6], Cushing [8] and White [21]. Their results are consistent in suggesting that *material* changes in accounting methods tend to have a favourable impact on profit and tend to be made in years when profit would otherwise be low.

Bibliographical references

[1] Beaver, W. H., Financial ratios as predictors of failure, *Empirical Research in Accounting: Selected Studies 1966*, supplement to *Journal of Accounting Research*, 1966, pp. 71–111.

[2] Beaver, W. H., Market prices, financial ratios, and the prediction of failure, *Journal of Accounting Research*, Autumn 1968, pp. 179–92.

[3] Beaver, W. H., The information content of annual earnings announcements, *Empirical Research in Accounting: Selected Studies 1968*, supplement to *Journal of Accounting Research*, 1968, pp. 67–92.

[4] Beaver, W. H., The time behaviour of earnings, *Empirical Research in Accounting, Selected Studies, 1970*, supplement to *Journal of Accounting Research*, 1970, pp. 62–99.

[5] Bird, P., *The Interpretation of Published Accounts*, CAS Occasional paper No. 14, HMSO, 1971.

[6] Blaine, E., Reported accounting changes and financial statement manipulation: An empirical study, *Proceedings of the Canadian Branch of American Accounting Association*, 1970, pp. 9–14.

[7] Copeland, R. M., Income smoothing, *Empirical Research in Accounting: Selected Studies, 1968*, supplement to *Journal of Accounting Research*, 1968, pp. 101–16.

[8] Cushing, B. E., An empirical study of changes in accounting policy, *Journal of Accounting Research*, Autumn 1969, pp. 196–203.

[9] Dascher, P. E. and R. E. Malcolm, A note on smoothing in the chemical industry, *Journal of Accounting Research*, Autumn 1970, pp. 253–59.

[10] Gonedes, N. J., Investor actions and accounting messages, *Accounting Review*, April 1971, pp. 320–28, and July 1971, pp. 535–51.

[11] Graham, B., D. L. Dodd and S. Cottle, *Security Analysis*, McGraw-Hill, 1962.

[12] Hepworth, S. R., Smoothing periodic income, *Accounting Review*, January 1953, pp. 32–39.

[13] Jaedicke, R. K. and R. T. Sprouse, *Accounting Flows: Income, Funds and Cash*, Prentice-Hall, 1965.

[14] Lev, B., Industry averages as targets for financial ratios, *Journal of Accounting Research*, Autumn 1969, pp. 290–99.

[15] Little, I. M. D. and A. C. Rayner, *Higgledy Piggledy Growth Again*, Blackwell, 1966.

[16] Merwin, C. L., *Financing Small Corporations in Five Manufacturing Industries, 1966–36*, National Bureau of Economic Research, 1942.

[17] Paton, W. A., The 'cash-flow' illusion, *Accounting Review*, April 1963, pp. 243–51.

[18] Schiff, M., Accounting tactics and the theory of the firm, *Journal of Accounting Research*, Spring 1966, pp. 62–67.

[19] Singh, A. and G. Whittington, *Growth, Profitability and Valuation*, Cambridge University Press, 1968.

[20] Sorter, G. H. and G. Benston, Appraising the defensive position of a firm: The interval measure, *Accounting Review*, October 1960, pp. 633–40.

[21] White, G. E., Discretionary accounting decisions and income normalization, *Journal of Accounting Research*, Autumn 1970, pp. 260–73.

Problems

4.1 Balance sheets at 31 December 19–1 are shown below for two independent companies.

	Fast Ltd. (£000's)	Slow Ltd. (£000's)
Issued share capital (£1 ordinary shares)	250	200
Retained profits	50	100
8 per cent Debentures	—	150
Bank borrowing	—	60
Creditors	300	220
	600	730
Fixed assets, less accumulated depreciation	320	200
Raw materials	—	40
Work-in-progress	—	230
Finished goods	180	70
Debtors	40	190
Bank	60	—
	600	730

The companies' profit and loss accounts for 19–1 revealed:

		(£000's)		(£000's)
Sales		3 000		750
Cost of goods sold (Fast)	2 330		—	
Materials (Slow)	—		250	
Wages and expenses	575		385	
Depreciation	30		35	
Interest	5		20	
		2 940		690
Net profit		60		60

Analyse the accounting information for Fast and Slow, using appropriate interpretation measures. (Ignore taxation.) To what extent is it valid on the information available to compare the financial performance and stability of the two companies?

(The split for inventory items and for cost of goods sold/materials/wages would not normally appear in the published accounts.)

4.2 Examine the following statements:

'The "cash flow" adopted in the interpretation of accounts is consistent with discounting future cash flows to obtain a present value: by projecting the firm's current "cash flow" into the future and discounting to a present value the investor can obtain an estimate of the value of a company.'

'Since "cash flow" equals net profit (after tax) *plus* depreciation, a firm enhances its funds position via "cash flow" if it increases its depreciation charge.'

4.3 Consider the profit measurement implications of the following quotations:

'The demise of Rolls-Royce will have but a slight effect on Lloyds and Midland, the two banks affected; both are writing off the losses over five years. [The losses refer to expected bad debts arising from the failure of Rolls-Royce.]

'... Commercial Union [insurance company] was able to charge much of the cost of hurricane Celia and another particularly expensive tornado against its extreme weather provision.'

The Economist, 27 February 1971.

4.4 'Chrysler Corp. reported a net loss of $7·6 million for 1970 ... it was the first for any year since 1959 and would have been $20 million larger if Chrysler hadn't changed the accounting method it uses to value most of its inventory.

. . .

'Chrysler said it changed to the FIFO method of evaluating inventories ... because the LIFO [last-in-first-out] method had substantially "understated" its profit during the last few years of rising costs. Under LIFO, costs are computed on the basis of the last bought inventory as it is used [balance sheet values remain at original prices until inventory level declines]. . . .

'The change . . . improved Chrysler's working capital . . . by boosting inventories, and thus current assets, by $150 million . . . over what they would have been under LIFO. As Chrysler's profit has collapsed over the last two years and its financial position tightened, auto analysts have eyed warily Chrysler's shrinking ratio of current assets to current liabilities.

'The major advantage of LIFO is that it holds down profit and thus tax liabilities. The other three major auto makers stayed on the FIFO method. . . . Chrysler now has to pay back . . . $53 million to the government over 20 years, which will boost Chrysler's tax bills by about $3 million a year.'

Wall Street Journal, 9 February 1971.

Discuss the rationale of the Chrysler decision.

4.5 In company A the stock turnover rate (cost of sales/average stock) in a certain year was 8·2 times, while in company B, a manufacturer in the same industry, it was 5·1 times. 'This means that company A was more efficient in its stock control than was company B.' Discuss.

4.6 On 1 November, 1967 Associated Electrical Industries Ltd. forecast that its profit for the year to 31 December, 1967 would amount to £10 m.

The company was taken over by General Electric Company Ltd., which later announced that A.E.I. Ltd. had incurred a loss of £4$\frac{1}{2}$ m. in 1967.

Two firms of auditors (one of which had reviewed the original forecast) issued a joint statement which included the following sentence:

'Broadly speaking, of the total shortfall of £14$\frac{1}{2}$ m. we would attribute roughly £5 m. to adverse differences which are matters substantially of fact rather than of judgment and the balance of some £9·5 m. to adjustments which remain substantially of judgment.'

Assume that the £5 m. arose from the difficulty of forecasting before the year was completed, and ignore that aspect.

Discuss the matters of accounting judgment which might have produced a difference of £9$\frac{1}{2}$ m. in the profit figures. (Do not attempt to consider the circumstances of this particular case.)

from, and unrelated to, the other activities of the firm. In fact it is not; production activity is influenced by, and in turn influences, the structure of the firm's assets and liabilities; i.e. logically production, investment and financing are all interrelated:*

> ... logical difficulties bypassed by the [partial optimization] analysis have to do mainly with the need to show a clear linkage between the production and factor employment problems on the one hand and the asset requirements and capital intensities of production processes on the other ... the amount of money capital available, and the terms on which it is available, will influence the capital intensities of the factor combinations which the capital funds are used to finance.

The linkage between production and investment is clearly expressed by Massé in the following passage:†

> Investment in equipment is a means chosen to achieve given ends, but it is by no means exclusive, since it must be combined with other factors of production ... in order to realize a desired production program. The choice of equipment should therefore be understood as forming an integral part of a broader problem: the simultaneous determination of a program for acquiring inputs X and of a program for producing products Y [where some x in X are durable inputs, i.e. the services of capital goods].

We shall continue to discuss production here, however, in the standard textbook manner.

There it is the subject of the theory of the firm, which is concerned with answering the questions 'what to produce (and for whom), how much to produce/what price to fix?' in various market structures. The further question 'how to produce' is usually assumed to have been answered already.

In perfectly competitive markets these problems, some aspects of which are examined in Chapters 7–9, are solved by the price mechanism.‡ In reality, of course, most markets are imperfectly competitive, and the effectiveness of the price mechanism is diminished by non-price competition between firms. For many products production is in anticipation of demand, not in response to it. The same kind of model can be used to deal with problems of internal resource allocation, where both purchase of commodities and sale of (intermediate) product take place within the firm.

Economics textbooks usually refer to short-run and long-run production models of the firm, the latter referring to a period where there are no constraints on the firm's use of inputs, the former to the period in which the use of some inputs is constrained. This is an arbitrary distinction, useful chiefly in explaining the cost/output relationship before and after total adaptation to the least-cost input combination. The constrained input is usually taken to be 'plant'; changes in plant

---

*[27], pp. 14 and 3.

†[19], p. 84. The need for a unified theory of production and investment is also recognized in [11], [24], [18] and [6].

‡Partially solved, to be strictly correct, since the prices in one market depend on prices in all other markets. Also the last problem (how to produce) is partly a technological problem, and only partly solved by the price mechanism.

capacity generally have the longest planning period of all inputs and this defines the 'short period' for the production model (the price-output planning horizon).

We are now ready to discuss the role of plans in production models of the firm. In terms of the classification of the previous section we will consider the following cases:

(a) Static certainty model

Plans, as defined, do not feature in this model at all, since they are not subject to replanning. All variables relate to a single time period and all outcomes are single-valued. The firm makes decisions for this single period.*

(b) Dynamic certainty model

Two types of models may be mentioned here:

(i) *Hicksian model*
The entire future of the firm is divided into discrete time periods, say N periods. Starting at time $t = 0$ the firm selects its entire best course of action up to $t = N$. The value of this best course thus depends on its actions in future periods as well as in the current period. The values assigned to the variables for the current period by the solution of this problem provide the basis for immediate decisions, those assigned to variables for the remaining $N-1$ periods constitute the future production plan. The firm replans each period. So in this model there is always a plan for $N-1$ periods, and all anticipations up to the horizon are taken into account.

(ii) *Modigliani–Cohen model*
Instead of replacing the single current set of decisions ('move') of the static model by the entire set of 'moves' up to the horizon as in the Hicksian dynamic model, the firm each period makes the best 'move' for the ensuing period. The significant difference here is that, while 'best' still means best up to the horizon, in determining the first move only those aspects of the future are taken into account which will affect the first move (these are called 'relevant anticipations' by the authors). Aspects of the future which, whatever their value, do not affect the optimum value of the first move, are irrelevant, and need not be estimated; the firm need not devote scarce resources to making irrelevant plans.† Hence 'plan' in this model has a slightly different meaning than in the Hicksian model: plans should preferably be regarded as representing the best forecast that can be made by the firm [at any

---

*Before proceeding further it is suggested that the reader should consult Chapter 6, pp. 9–11 and 25–26 on 'Planning horizon'.

†[10], p. 314.

given decision stage] about the values that certain components ['relevant anticipations'] of future moves will eventually take; this forecast is made for the purpose of deciding the *first* move, *not ... later* moves'.‡ In other words there is no comprehensive future plan; the plan at date zero comprises only those elements from periods 2 to N which will influence decisions in period 1. This latter view of business planning seems to be more in accord with reality, recognizing the cost of obtaining information about the future and that anticipations, while regarded as single-valued, may prove to be wrong.

(c) Models incorporating uncertainty

Once we regard anticipations and decision outcomes as non-unique and describable only in terms of probabilities, two further difficulties arise: how to incorporate these probabilities in the model (i.e. how the firm should evaluate outcomes which are uncertain), and what it regards as rational behaviour in the presence of uncertainty. These are questions we shall be examining in detail in Chapter 12 in relation to investment.

As far as the role of anticipations and plans is concerned, the chief difference compared with certainty models is that forecasts and estimates are now required for *all* periods (including the single period of the static model and the first period of the dynamic models). Plans relate to the same period as in the certainty case.

These ideas are summarized in the table below for a firm at the point $t = 0$:

Planning or decision model's view of time	*Period covered by:*	*State of information*	
		Certain	*Uncertain*
Static†	plans	——	——
	anticipations	——	——*
Dynamic	plans	2 to N (or elements from 2 to h)**	2 to N (or elements from 2 to h)**
	anticipations	2 to N (or elements from 2 to h)††	2 to N (or elements from 2 to h)

† In this case plans = decisions, since periods 1 to N are regarded as a single period.

* Anticipations relate to the *future* values of exogenous variables *beyond period 1*; in the static model all variables relate to the same time period, the entire future regarded as a single period. The anticipations horizon and the planning horizon need not always coincide.

** 2 to N in the Hicksian dynamics; in the Modigliani–Cohen dynamics, elements from 2 to h, where $h \ll N$ is chosen so as to make period 1 decisions optimal over the entire life of the firm.

†† In conditions of certainty, however, these single-valued anticipations involve no forecasting.

‡ Ibid., p. 317. There is a discussion of which anticipations are 'relevant' on pp. 314–7. The point is illustrated in the quadratic production smoothing model in [15].

The production models of the firm as characterized in economic theory may be thought of as comprising submodels of production (in physical units), cost, revenue and profit, together with a long-term economic plan which will be discussed in the next section.* For further discussion of the usual convention of assuming a common planning (or decision) period for all activities represented in the production model the reader is referred to [23], pp. 281–6.†

5.4 Investment plans

It is convenient to assume to begin with that long-run economic plans/decisions of the firm are confined to production, and thus almost exclusively to investment in plant (fixed assets), since this is the input usually assumed to prevent least-cost operation beyond a certain level of production in the short-run. This assumption will be relaxed later.

The theory of investment of the firm, a branch of capital theory, is concerned with the fact that the use of capital goods frequently enables the firm to adopt more efficient production processes which, however, take more time. Specifically, it is concerned with the questions of how much to invest in any given period, which projects to select within this total, when to undertake investment‡ and, indirectly, with how to finance investment. These questions are examined in Chapters 11, 12 and 20.

Investment analysis is typically confined to outlays on what the accountant calls *fixed assets*, consisting of new projects ('expansion investment') and replacement of existing assets, as represented in the term 'capital budgeting'. Other assets are not usually included in the analysis. There are practical reasons for this: fixed assets *normally* have longer economic 'lives' than assets such as inventories, and special calculations are necessary to reduce projects with different time patterns of outlays and returns to a comparable basis. Also the factor of uncertainty increases the longer the period considered. At the same time it should be realized that the division is quite arbitrary. It poses the question 'how are the returns on fixed assets and on working capital related to one another?' The firm is interested in the return earned on all of its assets, and there should be a sensible relationship between the returns on different classes of assets, after allowing for differences in the uncertainty associated with their possession. This point is taken up again in Chapter 19. For

---

*See [22], Chapter 2, for elaboration. 'Plan' is there used in the looser sense.

† See also section 2(c) of Chapter 6 below.

‡ This relates to all investment, expansion and replacement, and leads to a further question, the problem of length of service, which is discussed in Chapter 12 in relation to replacement policy. A related point, determination of the 'period of production' (i.e. the length of the investment period in capitalistic production, the total time involved in the production and use of a capital good), as a step towards measuring durable inputs, is a main topic in the theory of capital. For a discussion see [4], Chapter 13.

the present we may note that when fixed investment is undertaken, the additional working capital requirements associated with the investment should be included in the investment outlays – and any remaining working capital disinvested at the end of the asset's life should be included with the scrap value of the asset in the investment decision calculation. In projects involving heavy construction, such as steelworks, it is not uncommon for the necessary working capital investment to be as much as 60 per cent of the outlays on fixed assets.*†

The really distinguishing feature of investment decisions is that they are *intertemporal* decisions, i.e. they involve *choice* over time: outlays in earlier periods have to be set against returns spread over a number of later periods; there is a choice between returns (from production) or consumption now and returns (from investment) or consumption in the future. Production decisions involve time, but not choices over time. With that introduction we may consider investment models in terms of our earlier classification in order to see to what extent they involve planning, as defined.

(a) Static models

While investment decisions are essentially intertemporal decisions, most investment models of the firm are static models. That is, although the investment process spans more than one time period,‡ no replanning is involved, and the environmental variables for different periods are treated as constants, not parameters. Further, none of the variables contained in the model usually relates to periods outside the decision period. With two main exceptions, capital budgeting models employing, for example, the net present value or internal rate of return criterion, are static decision models.

The first exception occurs when there are resource (including budget) constraints on investment in any period. In theory though not in practice, formulation of the problem then involves dynamic elements, as will be explained in Chapters 11 and 12. Massé's linear programming model for the joint optimization of production and investment,** while recognizing the 'open-ended' nature of the investment problem – by choosing a long horizon and representing the value of all projects beyond the horizon by a lump-sum return at the horizon – nevertheless treats the problem statically.

A second exception arises as a result of the timing of investment. Although it is

---

*[17], p. 671.

† In the *production* model (i.e. after investment has taken place) interest on borrowed capital is one of the firm's costs.

‡ The term 'multiperiod' should not be used to describe this process, however; in a number of books ([13], Chapter 8 is an example) 'multiperiod' is used synonymously with 'dynamic' to convey the idea of optimization through time.

** [19], Chapter 3.

usually acknowledged only in the case of replacement, timing introduces dynamic considerations in all cases, since it involves intertemporal interdependence. In fact, just as the production of the firm is most realistically seen as a dynamic problem [20], so the investment problem is essentially dynamic in nature, though in this case the element of 'irreversibility' needs to be noted (see section 1 of Chapter 11). That is, the evironment is changing during the planning period and, as Massé asserts:*

> *Every* investment problem is 'open-ended with respect to the future' . . . [it] involves, not a single decision, but . . . an indefinite chain of decisions. . . . All previous decisions obviously affect subsequent decisions . . . the present is conditioned simultaneously by the past and the future.

Strictly, therefore, every investment problem is dynamic and sequential in nature.

(b) Dynamic models

As with other areas of economic analysis, the complexities of investment decision-making may often make it impossible to solve the entire sequential problem. A one-period dynamic treatment of the problem, as described in the Hicksian or Modigliani–Cohen production models referred to earlier, would provide a reasonable compromise.† However, even this may not be possible in practice; the computational problems are severe. Dynamic models are hard to find in the literature on investment decisions, from whatever discipline it emanates. Apart from the two situations referred to in the previous section, which contain dynamic elements but are usually not treated in a fully dynamic way as defined in section 2(b)(i), some of the very few fully dynamic treatments of investment are listed below.‡

As regards uncertainty we must distinguish more sharply between theory and practice. Many of the commonly discussed theoretical models of investment do not allow for uncertainty explicitly. That is, forecasts and estimates, while known to be uncertain, are treated in the models as though they were not. Those models that do introduce uncertainty explicitly employ a variety of different approaches. In practice, some allowance is almost always made for uncertainty, but often in a very crude manner. The main approaches to the problem of uncertainty in the context of the investment decision, both theoretical and practical, are examined in Chapter 12.

From what has been said the reader may discover for himself the role of anticipations and plans in the investment models encountered in theory and practice,

---

* [19], pp. 52 and 60. See pp. 18–20 on the general case, pp. 42, 52, 60–61 on replacement.
† See sections 5(a) and 5(b) of Chapter 6.
‡ Dynamic certainty models: [24], Chapter 11 (production-investment planning); reference [40], Chapter 9 (advertising regarded as investment); dynamic programming approaches to the replacement problem could also be cited; dynamic uncertainty models: [19], Chapter 6; [3], Chapter 7 (Arrow, Beckmann and Karlin, 'The optimal expansion of the capacity of a firm').

parallel to the classification presented earlier for production, remembering that, as here defined, anticipations and plans enter only when the model is dynamic, anticipations which involve forecasting only in conditions of uncertainty, and a planning horizon shorter than the life of the firm only in the Modigliani-Cohen dynamics.

5.5 Comments on long-term economic plans

It is now time to relax the assumption made at the beginning of the previous section, that long-run economic plans/decisions of the firm are confined to production, and thus almost exclusively to investment in plant.

It would seem reasonable to expect that, for perfectly competitive firms,* *long-term* forecasts and estimates would be confined almost entirely to investment activity, and possibly to long-term technological developments. (It should be recognized that 'long-term plans', such as those for investment the year after next, are plans in the strict sense whether or not they are incorporated in a dynamic model, since by definition they cannot be acted upon immediately, and will almost certainly be revised before they are.)

Once we move away from this unrealistic special case, however, the area of interest in the future is enlarged. Imperfectly competitive firms, and more especially monopolists and oligopolists, have reason to be concerned about the future demand for their products (the level of prices charged now may affect future sales). Such firms may accordingly form anticipations concerning their long-term sales, pricing and advertising policies. Other aspects of the future which may exercise their attention might include research and development, expenditure on human capital (training programmes and the like), the costs of entering a new industry, and future financing needs (it being assumed that capital markets are also imperfect).

As yet, none of these aspects except investment in fixed capital has received much attention in economic theory. There is, however, a growing business literature on the subject of corporate long-range planning. One of the points to emerge from this [2] is that a firm's long-term plans may include what we earlier called strategic plans (such as plans to enter a new industry or the export trade). Besides themselves being the subject of plans, strategic considerations may be reflected in the *assumptions* on which the other plans are drawn up. The problems encountered in long-term planning, particularly strategic planning, may often be relatively unstructured, and may need to be solved heuristically† or by what Ansoff [2] calls quasi-analytic methods (a compromise between rigorous mathematical methods of analysis and heuristics).

---

* Assuming *all* the conditions of perfect competition are met.
† Defined in section 6(a) of Chapter 6.

We have briefly reviewed the part played by anticipations and plans in economic models of production and investment, and in respect to proposed activities in the more distant future. The role of plans, we saw, depended on our distinction between static and dynamic models and on the possibility of revising forecasts and estimates before they were acted upon. The role of the latter, in turn, depended on the state of the firm's information, as represented explicitly in the plan. Within this framework, some of the other determinants of the firm's economic plans are:

1. *Production*: the firm's objective, possible constraints upon its achievement (cost, demand, technological and interdependency constraints), perceived alternative courses of action, the internal organization structure of the firm, managerial ability, the structure of the firm's markets,* the properties of the firm's production processes with regard to changes in scale (and to indivisibilities of inputs), input substitution (and product substitution), technological change, relative prices of inputs and products, and resources inherited from the past.

2. *Investment*: the criterion by which it is assessed, alternatives, constraints (including budget constraints), the structure of markets, availability of capital from internal sources, the price of capital goods and the relative costs of more or less capital-intensive production methods, interest rates (or more generally the opportunity cost of investing, measured at the margin), expected return, technological progress, the efficiency of existing assets (in the case of replacement), expectations with respect to the future price level, business taxation, and the time-preferences of the owners of the firm for consumption at different dates.

5.6 Accounting 'plans'

Using the word 'plan' loosely to begin with, in accounting business plans are usually thought of as being represented in budgets, which are commonly regarded as serving the dual functions of plans and controls.† Our interest accordingly centres on budgets regarded as plans. More particularly, budgetary planning consists in forming not only production, cost, revenue and profit plans, but also in:

1. disaggregating these plans by segments of the business (such as 'responsibility centres', production processes, products) and of the planning period ('control

---

*The firm is seen as an intermediary, purchasing commodities which are ultimately owned by consumers or government, and converting these into products which are ultimately bought by consumers or government [16].

†If separated, they are called forecast or planning budgets and control budgets, respectively.

periods'). The budget period is commonly one year for short-run production-related operations,* two or more years for long-term operations.
2. Planning the future structure of assets and claims.

All managements make plans, implicitly or explicitly. If these plans are made explicit and are set out systematically in quantitative terms they are called budgets. Fully developed, accounting budgets display the management's intended allocation of resources among all the perceived alternative opportunities open to the firm. The budget targets become goals for the enterprise, and subgoals for segments of the business and of the planning period.

Figure 5.1 shows some of the main components of a fully-developed system of budgets. The set of short-term budgets on the left must be internally consistent in physical and in financial terms. To the extent that they include related activities, the long-term budgets should also be financially consistent with one another (e.g. the forecast of sales revenue, capital investment and provision of the necessary money capital requirements).

Two further aspects of planning budgets are of particular interest: what the budget targets represent, and how often they are revised. On the first, the overwhelming weight of evidence seems to be that the targets are fixed conservatively and are not in the nature of optimizations of the firm's opportunity set. In fact there is some evidence that they are formed largely on the basis of extrapolations of past results or trends. For instance: †

A [budget] is a precedent. It defines the decisions of one year and thereby establishes a *prima facie* case for continuing existing decisions. Only in quite exceptional cases do firms in fact reexamine the rationale of existing functions, for example, or alter radically the expenditure for them. This tends to be particularly true of overhead functions (e.g. advertising, research and development, clerical help).

In accounting terminology, budgets are almost always of the 'currently attainable' variety rather than of the 'ideal' (or optimal) variety. The second point concerns what happens if budget forecasts, although good in the light of information available to the firm and the conditions prevailing at the time the budget was drawn up, are falsified during the budget period by the receipt of new information or a change in conditions to such an extent that they lose all meaning. The budget no longer represents the firm's plans. The firm's response will depend upon the system of budgeting in use.‡

As with economic models, we now ask the question whether the various accounting budget models which have been discussed are 'plans' in the Modigliani–Cohen

---

* Though this is not hard-and-fast: a firm producing for seasonal markets may take the season as its budget period, while in an oligopolistic firm it may cover the period during which the firm expects prices to remain fixed [12].
† [12], p. 112; the word 'budget' has been substituted for 'plan'.
‡ See Chapter 13, section 6(d).

Enterprise plans

Short-term budgets   *Long-term budgets*

In physical terms:

    production   purchases
    sales   labour
    inventories   expenses

In money terms:

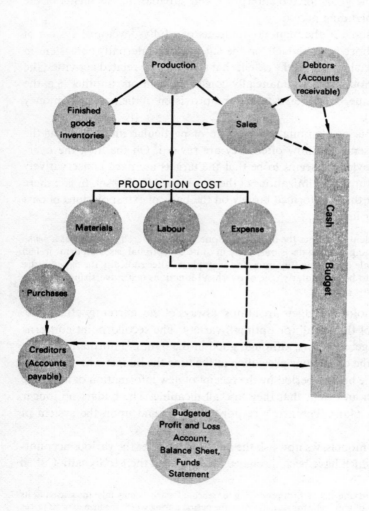

Long-term sales
    forecasts

Capital budget
    (fixed investment)

Long-term finance
    budget (capital
    requirements)

Research and
    development
    budget

etc.

Figure 5.1 A comprehensive system of budgets

sense, for there is no gainsaying that the underlying processes with which they are concerned are dynamic processes. To qualify as plans, budgets must be subject to revision (replanning), otherwise we are referring to decisions, not plans, *and* the forecasts they incorporate must be partly determined by anticipations relating to more distant periods. There is no solid evidence that we know of to show whether these conditions are met. Our feeling is that probably in most cases neither condition is met; that is, most budgets are periodic (fixed) budgets (the budget for overhead expenditure may be flexible with respect to level of output but not to time); and that dynamic considerations, in the form of the influence on the budget variables of anticipations regarding events beyond the budget period, play a very shadowy role in the formation of budgets. If we are correct, this draws attention to the need for intensive study of this aspect of business behaviour. Our interpretation of accounting budgets is that they would only be plans in the strict sense of the term if all budgets – short-term, and long-term up to some horizon date – were dynamically linked, the budgets in earlier periods were partly determined by those in later periods, and if the budgets for the shortest period (the operating budgets) were subject to more or less continuous revision.

5.7 A comparison of business plans as represented in economics and accounting

Some of the more important differences between the economic and accounting representation of business plans may now be brought together from the foregoing discussion:

1. *Role*: Plans as defined appear to play a much greater part in economics than in accounting, where it is doubtful whether they exist at all in a strict dynamic sense. In other words, most accounting models appear to be static models under certainty.* We are reminded that :†

> The static model provides an explanation of a wide range of phenomena. It is, however, quite inadequate as an explanation of anticipatory and planning activity.... In order to understand such phenomena ... dynamic models have been developed. ... In reality the current actions of ... business men are influenced by awareness that the future is uncertain and that the future is relevant.

Leaving this important difference aside, other points of departure include:

2. *Objective*: In economic models the objectives of the firm are always clearly stated; in accounting budgets they are not. Economic plans of the firm are most often optimal plans; in accounting there is no clear attempt to optimize.

3. *Type of model*: Economic models of the firm (the models of orthodox economic

---

* More precisely, uncertainty is allowed for crudely and unsystematically.
† [10], p. 310.

theory, at least) are *normative*, i.e. they show how the firm *should* act in order to achieve a particular objective (such as maximum profits). The models represent a considerable simplification of the real world. Accounting budgets, by contrast, are in effect *positive* theories of how firms *actually* plan their operations.

4. *Coverage*: Standard economic models are less comprehensive than accounting models in regard to internal variables, leaving out some important activities: there is no systematic inclusion of 'balance sheet' variables (the structure of assets and claims, and the financing of operations), even in dynamic economic models. The position is reversed in regard to external variables.

5. *Degree of disaggregation*: Economic plans are not disaggregated for segments of the business or of the planning period as accounting budgets are (except to the extent that they distinguish between the short period and the long).

6. *Data specification*: The same future events may be differently described in economic and accounting models because of different rules governing data specification. Thus 'cost' and 'capital' have different meanings in accounting than in economics. The influence of arbitrary accounting conventions and taxation regulations leads the accountant to include in *ex ante* costs some items (e.g. various 'sunk' costs) which are not economic costs and to omit some items (implicit opportunity costs) which are, while some expenditure (e.g. research and development, large-scale advertising) is treated as a cost which is really of the nature of investment. In short, accounting budgets are not in general founded on economic principles.

7. *Interdependencies*: There is a presumption that accounting budgets do not allow for intertemporal interdependencies, the dynamic interrelationships previously referred to; similarly, budgets for sections of the business (e.g. divisions or departments) rarely take into account any interdependencies between the activities concerned, but treat them as closed systems. That is, the set of budgets, while internally consistent in physical and financial terms, may often not be so in economic terms.

8. *Alternatives*: Because the firm's objective (or objectives) is usually not made explicit, it is doubtful whether all the possible alternatives are considered in drawing up the budgets.

9. *Prices*: In economic models of production, selling prices of products are usually regarded as variables; in operating budgets they are taken as given. For the imperfectly competitive firm the same applies to selling expenses (especially advertising) and product quality. Economists would be inclined to express all long-term plans in 'real' terms (i.e. allow for expected changes in the general price level); no such refinement is usually made in long-term budgets.

10. *Control*: Economic models assume that plans are always perfectly realized, i.e. that there is no communications or control problem. Accounting makes no such bold assumption.

10. *Information and computation*: Similarly, standard economic theory assumes that

no information or computation problem exists – that all data required by a particular model are already available or can be obtained at a justifiable cost, and that computation costs are not excessive. The typical accounting process is not designed to generate the data/information required by economic models, nor does it, as a matter of routine, submit itself (i.e. the data-information transformation) to cost-benefit analysis. Neither economic models nor accounting budgets consistently take account of the fact that data/information are always incomplete and inaccurate, and that this may lead to the formation of faulty expectations.

12. *Communication*: As we saw in Chapter 1, data can be biassed at the selection stage, biassed and counter-biassed at various points during its passage through the organization to management. Faulty expectations may also be formed through too little data being collected, too little of the available data being used, or through data being irrelevant as distinct from biassed (and accurate expectations at the planning stage may go awry because of unpredictable events). Neither accounting nor economics takes account of the influence of the firm's communications system on the formation of plans.

13. *Organization structure*: As we will show in Chapter 13, the form of organization structure of the firm may influence goal formation and the kind of plans that are made, as well as influencing the effectiveness of internal control devices to make performance conform to plans. This also is a missing element in both the economic and accounting representations of planning.

14. *The budgeting process*: In 2. above it was stated that business budgets are usually not optimal plans. Beyond this there is at least a possibility that the very existence of the budgeting process may constrain the firm's planning, further inhibiting efficient performance in terms of the firm's objective. The argument is best stated in its original source :*

> The budget in a modern, large-scale corporation plays two basic roles. On the one hand, it is used as a management control device to implement policies on which executives have decided and to check achievement against established criteria. On the other hand, a budget is a device to determine feasible programs. In either case, it tends to define – in advance – a set of fixed commitments and (perhaps more important) fixed expectations. Although budgets can be flexible, they cannot help but result in the specification of a framework within which the firm will operate, evaluate its success, and alter its program. . . . any budget tends to identify as given some factors that are in an absolute sense variables within the control of the organization. . . . Because of these characteristics of plans and planning, the decisions within the firm have both temporal periodicity and consistency over time that they would not necessarily have otherwise. . . . Within rather large limits, the organization substitutes the plan for the world – partly by making the world conform to the plan, partly by pretending that it does. So long as achievement levels continue to be satisfactory, budgetary decisions are exceptionally dependent on decisions 8f previous years, with shifts tending to reflect the expansionist inclinations of subunits rather than systematic reviews by top management.

*[12], pp. 110–12.

5.8 Program budgeting

At least some of the undesirable features of conventional business budgeting systems, notably points 2, 6, 7 and 8 in the previous section, are removed in the Program Planning and Budgeting System (PPBS)* approach. This approach also incorporates some desirable features, and overcomes yet other undesirable ones, which we refer to in other parts of this book, principally in Chapters 1, 6, 13 and 18. In view of this it is considered to be deserving of wider study by accountants.

PPBS evolved from traditional systems of budgeting in both the government and private sectors; new analytical tools and concepts (such as systems analysis, cost-benefit analysis, various management science techniques and computer simulation studies) were an integral part of its development. Much of the early research was undertaken in the 1950s by the RAND Corporation,† on whose urging program budgeting was introduced by the US Department of Defense in 1961. In 1965 the President ordered the implementation of PPBS throughout the US Federal Government.‡ The Canadian Federal Government followed suit in the same year.** It has since been adopted, wholly or partially, by a number of state, provincial and local authorities, universities, and some large private corporations in North America. (Though most of the applications have been in government and government agencies, the principles involved are equally applicable to private business organizations.)

Traditional systems of budgeting, whether government or private, are heavily input-oriented, with primary emphasis on detailed financial control. They are also oriented towards existing organizational units (divisions, departments, etc.). PPB, by contrast, is output- and objective-oriented,†† with main emphasis on resource allocation, based on economic analysis. It seeks to improve the quality of decision-making towards explicit objectives. It is framed in terms of programs (functional groupings of activities with a common objective), not traditional organizational subdivisions, and involves a systems approach to management (i.e. identifying, describing and analysing the total system represented by the organization and its parts, determining its real objectives, which may not be the same as its stated objectives, and appropriate measures of performance by which the total system is to be judged).

The steps necessary in developing such a system are briefly set out below:

1. What are the goals (missions) of the organization? To test whether stated goals

---

*Sometimes called Planning Programming Budgeting System. 'Program budgeting' is a well-understood short title.

† Novick, one of those involved at RAND, subsequently published [21].

‡ See [26], also [25].

** Acting on the Report of the Royal Commission on Government Organization, 1960.

†† See the reference to 'management by objective' in section 1 of Chapter 16.

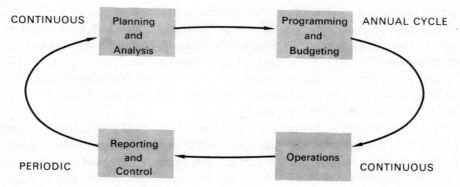

Figure 5.2 Program budgeting system

are real the management can be asked whether the system will knowingly sacrifice other goals in order to attain this set of goals.

2. Define the total system, comprising programs and activities. The system is described in terms of its goals, environment, the resources at its disposal, the goal-directed programs and activities in which it engages, and its management, which bears responsibility for the formation of goals, generation of plans and measures of performance, revision of plans, decision-making, and exercise of control over performance of the system.

3. Planning and analysis: A continuous iterative process concerned with developing and analysing alternative objective-oriented programs, each comprising a number of basic activities. Instead of thinking within the framework of the existing (pre-PPB) system, the planning of both existing and new activities here involves 'the display of alternative designs and selection of the best design in terms of the whole system objective'.* That is, planning and analysis culminates in the development of a program structure, arrived at after detailed analysis of alternatives, and firmly focused on the explicit objectives of the system. The analysis spans a rather longer planning horizon than does traditional business budgeting; i.e. it is multi-period, but not yet what we have described as dynamic, analysis. It does, however, usually make provision for examining the effects of possible changes in priority as between programs.

The analysis also includes development of appropriate measures of performance for activities, programs and the total system. The word 'appropriate' is important. For one thing the measure of performance for a subsystem, as Churchman notes,† will change if the total system changes, and therefore depends on the correct definition of the latter. For another, it means that it must be consistent with the measure of performance of the total system. Thus a measure based on a subgoal of minimiz-

* [8], p. 93.
† Ibid., p. 84.

ing costs, or more generally of carrying out each activity as efficiently as possible, may not optimize performance of the system. Contrary to popular belief, idleness in an activity *per se* does not necessarily mean inefficiency. We must think of the whole system and its objectives. To be appropriate a measure should be consistent with optimizing performance of the whole system in the pursuit of system objectives.

In many cases, one suspects, not very much systematic analysis of this kind goes into the planning process of business enterprises.

4. Programming* and budgeting: The translation of planned programs, complete with resource requirements and expected results, into detailed program budgets. The distinguishing features of PPB here are that budgets are based on programs rather than organizational subdivisions, and are much more directly tied to plans and total system objectives.

5. Reporting and control: Program budgeting requires for its implementation, in addition to systems thinking and analysis and agreement on system objectives, a considerable extension of the traditional information system, to provide information in groupings related to programs and activities for measuring progress towards system objectives, with feedbacks for control and to the planning, programming and budgeting process. Difficulty in defining system objectives, especially in non-profit enterprises (what are the real objectives of a university?), and lack of an adequate information system or the means of developing one, have probably been the two greatest obstacles towards implementing a fully functioning PPB system.

We suggest that the reader return to PPBS after reading the chapters referred to above.

* Not to be confused with computer programming or mathematical programming.

Bibliographical references

[1] Ansoff, H. I., *Corporate Strategy*, McGraw-Hill, 1965.
[2] Ansoff, H. I., A quasi-analytic method for long-range planning, in *Modern Financial Management*, ed. Carsberg and Edey, Penguin, 1969.
[3] Arrow, K. J., S. Karlin and H. Scarf, *Studies in the Mathematical Theory of Inventory and Production*, Stanford University Press, 1958.
[4] Baumol, W. J., *Economic Theory and Operations Analysis*, Prentice-Hall, 2nd edn., 1965.
[5] Buchanan, N. S., *The Economics of Corporate Enterprise*, Holt, 1940.
[6] Carlson, S., *A Study on the Pure Theory of Production*, P. S. King & Sons, London, 1939.
[7] Chandler, A. D., Jr., *Strategy and Structure*, Doubleday, Anchor Books edn., 1966.
[8] Churchman, C. W., *The Systems Approach*, Delta Books, 1968.
[9] Coase, R. H., The nature of the firm, *Economica*, November 1937.
[10] Cohen, K. J. and R. M. Cyert, *Theory of the Firm*, Prentice-Hall, 1965.
[11] Cournot, A., *Researches into the Mathematical Principles of the Theory of Wealth*, 1838, trans. by N. T. Bacon, Macmillan, New York, 1897.
[12] Cyert, R. M. and J. G. March, *A Behavioral Theory of the Firm*, Prentice-Hall, 1963.
[13] Henderson, J. M. and R. E. Quandt, *Microeconomic Theory*, McGraw-Hill, 1958.
[14] Hicks, J. R., *Value and Capital*, Oxford University Press, 2nd edn., 1946.

[15] Holt, Modigliani, Muth and Simon, *Planning Production, Inventories, and Work Force*, Prentice-Hall, 1960.

[16] Lancaster, K., *Introduction to Modern Microeconomics*, Rand McNally, 1969.

[17] Lundberg, E., The profitability of investment, *Economic Journal*, LXIX, December 1959.

[18] Lutz, F. and V., *The Theory of Investment of the Firm*, Princeton University Press, 1951.

[19] Massé, P., *Optimal Investment Decisions*, Prentice-Hall, 1962.

[20] Modigliani, F. and K. J. Cohen, The role of anticipations and plans in economic behavior and their use in economic analysis and forecasting, *Studies in Business Expectations and Planning, No. 4*, Bureau of Economic and Business Research, University of Illinois, 1961.

[21] Novick, D., ed., *Program Budgeting: Program Analysis and the Federal Budget*, Harvard University Press, 1967.

[22] Schneider, E., *Pricing and Equilibrium*, Unwin University Books, 2nd edn., 1962.

[23] Scitovsky, T., *Welfare and Competition*, Unwin University Books, 1952.

[24] Smith, V. L., *Investment and Production*, Harvard University Press, 1961.

[25] United Nations, Department of Economic and Social Affairs, *A Manual for Program and Performance Budgeting*, New York, 1965.

[26] US Congress, *The Planning Programming Budgeting System: Progress and Potentials*, Report of the subcommittee of the Joint Economic Committee on Economy in Government, US Government Printing Office, 1967.

[27] Vickers, D., *The Theory of the Firm: Production, Capital, and Finance*, McGraw-Hill, 1968; his article 'The cost of capital and the structure of the firm,' *Journal of Finance*, March 1970, pp. 35–46, covering much the same ground, is reprinted in *Readings in Management Decision*, ed. L. R. Amey, Longman 1973.

Problems

5.1 Carefully consider the implications of making a firm's planning budgets fully dynamic.

5.2 'What strikes one about the information system in most businesses is that it has evolved in response to a number of needs which generally did not include planning.' Discuss the implications of this state of affairs.

5.3 In many companies strategic planning starts with the budget. Argue the case for separating the two in time.

5.4 'A plan is a goal, schedule, theory, and precedent (as well as a prediction), . . . reducing a complex world to a somewhat simpler one.' Elaborate on each of these attributes as applied to business budgets.

5.5 What is the practical significance for optimal decision-making of the distinction between the forecasting (or anticipations) horizon and the planning horizon?

5.6 The available empirical evidence seems to suggest very strongly that corporate planning, whether it be short-run or long-range planning, commonly fails to take the environment into account adequately and explicitly (or assumes it will behave in the future as it has in the past). As an example, it is quite common to see very elaborate plans but no explicit consideration of how competitors are likely to behave.

Stated in another way:

'We expect in most firms to have contradictions between how the environment speaks to the firm and the way the firm is actually operated. If you suppress these, you will lose something of the planning process.'

Compile a list of what you consider to be some of the main exogenous variables about which firms should form anticipations in the planning process (and monitor in the control process).

5.7 Contrast business budgeting as you know it from textbooks and existing practice and the PPB (program planning and budgeting) system used by some government agencies. [As indicated in the text, students will be in a better position to answer this question after they have read up to and including Chapter 18.]

6

Decision concepts

The traditional content of such fields as accounting may [in future] apply only at lower levels of the organization. For top levels a new kind of person is needed . . . he should probably not even be called an accountant . . . he will need to know much more . . . about economics, . . . operations research, and . . . the data requirements for decision and control. [12]

6.1 Introduction

In the previous chapter we saw briefly how the future plans of a business, in the broad sense of proposed moves, are commonly expressed in a series of *ex ante* accounts and accounting statements called budgets, and that in addition to embodying management's expectations about the future and thus providing a framework within which to conduct future operations they also acted as a system of controls designed to make actual results conform to plans, as far as possible and desirable.

We consider in this chapter how plans are put into effect. Plans are activated by decisions. A *plan* is a broad statement of policy governing the future conduct of the business. Every plan implies a series of decisions to implement it. A *decision* refers to a single choice situation, a choice between future alternatives whose outcomes are uncertain. The philosophy behind this chapter, and running through Part 2, as indicated in the opening quotation, is that if the accountant is to continue to provide management with data for decision he had better know something about the logic of decision, decision concepts, and the more common types of models within which choices are posed.

The class of decisions to be discussed here will be quantitative business decisions, i.e. problems of choice which can be clearly defined, and whose elements and the relations between them are measurable. It should be recognized that not all of the decisions which are likely to have important influence on the future of the business are of this kind: whether to appoint X or Y as the senior executive, for instance, may have repercussions far transcending those of a decision to instal type I or type II equipment in the factory, and yet it is probably non-quantifiable. Quantitative business decisions nevertheless comprise a very large, important, and diverse field, as the sample presented in following chapters will show.

A common ingredient of most of these quantitative decision problems is that they rely on data relating to costs and benefits, *properly specified*, for their solution, which are expressed in terms of money. The accountant is accustomed to regard the preparation of such data for decision purposes as being his preserve. This right is not taken for granted by non-accountants, and we think rightly so. For the accountant's involvement in the process leading up to decision depends on his ability to do two things:

1. To conceptualize, i.e. to recognize the essential structure of a decision problem, and pose the right questions for its solution. Business practice and the
   accounting literature are not lacking in evidence of instances, some of which
   we will examine, in which wrong solutions have resulted from accountants
   asking the wrong questions.
2. Having done this – and only by doing this – to fit the appropriate data to the
   problem.

Business decision problems are essentially problems in applied microeconomics.
It follows that in order to fulfil the above tasks the accountant needs to have reasonable familiarity with microeconomic theory.* More important still, he needs to be
able to employ economic reasoning, the logic of business decision.

A further requirement is as much familiarity as possible with some of the more
common quantitative techniques used in business decision-making – at the least
probability theory, linear programming, and the mathematics of compound
interest and annuities, in addition to the calculus.† Many common business decisions involve the use of mathematical models for their correct formulation and
solution. Unless the accountant understands the technique in question he is unlikely to prove reliable in providing data for it, or in interpreting the solution if
called upon by management to do so. Besides acquiring some new modes of
thought and new tools, the management accountant must abandon some of his
traditional modes of thought, legacies from his role as keeper of historical records.
For example 'objectivity' is, by definition, not possible in this area, and consistency
of treatment no longer a virtue. Each decision problem calls for data which are
relevant – economically relevant – to that particular choice. It is better for decision
data to be inaccurate but relevant than accurate but irrelevant.

To remain a useful member of the team of specialists assisting management in
the decision process the management accountant must increasingly meet the
requirements stated above. To go further, and suggest that he should have primary
responsibility for making decision calculations as well as preparing data for them
would be wildly unrealistic. Decision calculations involving intricate mathematical
models belong to the specialist who is trained in the use of quantitative methods –
the operations researcher or management scientist. The task of correctly specifying
data for decision is, on its own, a large and crucial one, as will become apparent.

Although business decision-making typically involves a number of persons it
will be treated here as individual rather than group decision-making, on the grounds

---

* As presented, e.g., in [37], [11] or [18]. The last two are more mathematical than the first.

† A brief introduction to compound interest and annuities will be found in Appendix A; [25] provides
a good introduction to the calculus; probability theory is discussed in a companion volume in this
series, *Managerial Economics*, by D. C. Hague, [16], Chapter 7, or in any textbook of mathematical
statistics; a compact, but more mathematical, treatment will be found in [2], pp. 123–39; linear programming is described in many books including [16], Chapters 8–10 and [6], Chapters 5–6, and briefly
in Appendix C.

that one view ultimately prevails – whether this comes about democratically (majority rule), or is in some way imposed (dominance of the senior executive). The class of problem which plagues attempts to aggregate *individual choices* into *group choices* will thus not concern us.*

6.2 The elements of a decision

Any decision problem can be thought of as involving four parts :†

1. *an objective function*, which indicates the relative desirability of different possible outcomes,
2. a range of policy *alternatives* among which the decision-maker must choose.
3. *a model*, which specifies the empirical relations connecting the alternatives, the variables entering into the objective function, and other relevant variables, and
4. the *computational methods* by which the decision-maker chooses the values of the alternatives so as to maximize (or minimize) the value of the objective function, subject to the conditions implied by the model.

Much of the work on decision theory has been concentrated on the last point, using the term 'computation' in a very broad sense: the role of the price system as a computing device for achieving an economic optimum, for example, has long occupied the central position in economic theory. The development of an appropriate price system to govern the complex internal operations of large business enterprises, discussed in Chapter 9, is a formidable computational problem in this sense. In the more commonly understood sense of numerical solution methods, computation may also be a problem. The sheer complexity or dimensions of some decision problems is such that existing computational capabilities (computer capacity) or computational methods (numerical solution procedures) require some simplification of the problem in order to make computation possible. Our main concern here, however, is to ensure that decision data are correctly specified. The great advance in the variety and power of solution methods and in the computing machinery available is often in nothing like one-to-one correspondence with the capacity of human decision-makers to pose the right questions, and hence elicit the relevant data for formulating the problem.

The decision elements referred to above will bear some elaboration.

(a) Objective

The starting point in any decision problem is to state the firm's objective explicitly

* Readers wishing to explore this area are referred to [27], Chapter 14.
† The particular classification used here is based on [5], pp. 523–31.

and keep it clearly in mind. This will lead the decision-maker to think of all the feasible alternative ways of furthering this objective, and of any constraints on undertaking them. Firms seldom appear to pursue a single objective such as profit maximization without qualification of some kind, and may have multiple objectives. The latter case may be formulated so that the multiple goals are achieved in a certain desired order; alternatively, only the dominant goal may be represented in the objective function, the subsidiary goals being shown among the constraints.* Which method is the more appropriate can only be decided by reference to a particular case.

It is important to ensure that multiple goals are mutually consistent. As Shubik has pointed out [32], the simultaneous maximization of two or more objectives which are functionally interrelated will usually be logically inconsistent. For example, it *may* be impossible to maximize profits *and* obtain the largest share of the market. An objective of obtaining maximum output at minimum cost, on the other hand, is operationally undefined (the operational alternatives are either maximum output for a fixed outlay or minimum cost for a fixed output).

For the most part we will concentrate on a single objective, usually profit maximization in some sense (e.g. short run or long run).

Two of the main types of objective business decision-makers have been assumed to set themselves are '*optimizing*' (i.e. maximizing or minimizing, as the case may be) and '*satisficing*'. The firm of orthodox economic theory has, until comparatively recently, always been assumed to be an optimizer. Rational economic behaviour meant maximizing profits. It has been persuasively argued by H. A. Simon [33] that the 'global rationality' attributed to economic man is completely divorced from reality, and should be replaced by a principle of 'bounded rationality': instead of optimizing behaviour, rational decision-making should be defined in terms of behaviour which is compatible with the information and computational capacities actually available to the decision-makers in their particular organizational environment, and compatible also with their skills in problem formulation.† It is Simon's conviction that economic theory has almost completely ignored the human characteristics of decision-makers (individuals or groups) in organizations. The kind of rational choice to which acceptance of his principle of bounded rationality leads has been called 'satisficing', i.e. instead of maximizing, the objective becomes achievement of a 'satisfactory' level of outcome. With satisficing the objective function becomes a two-valued utility function: good enough or not good enough.

Many decision problems involve optimizing an objective function subject to one or more *constraints*. These are called problems of *constrained optimization*. The term is rather misleading, in that optimization must ultimately be constrained by

---

* See also the reference to [36] below.
† The 'information problem' is discussed by Boulding in Chapter 1 of [8].

the *domain* on which it is defined. The objective will be stated, or be capable of being stated, in the form of an objective function, say $y = f(x)$; and to describe this fully we must specify the domain X over which the function is defined. This gives the *range, Y,* of the function. In a strict sense, therefore, it is meaningless to speak of maximization or minimization without imposing some limit or limits (an upper bound in the former case, a lower bound in the latter), because strictly all optimization is constrained optimization. In common usage, however, the domain of the objective function (a set of real numbers) is rarely referred to, though the decision-maker will generally have some estimate of the order of magnitude of the relevant objective function before attempting to solve the problem,* and 'constrained optimization' means the existence of some restrictions which will not permit y to take on all possible values within the range *Y,* but confine its extreme values within upper and/or lower bounds. A firm may wish to optimize a given objective (say sales revenue) subject to both upper and lower bounds on a particular side relation (e.g. a maximum and minimum level of income). This introduces via the constraints a notion similar to that of 'satisficing'. As Baumol and Quandt have remarked [7], 'satisficing is, as it were, constrained optimization with only constraints and no optimization'.

A further interpretation has been provided by Simon in his paper 'On the concept of organizational goal' [36]. Simon here uses the term 'organizational goal' to refer to *constraints*. On this view, decisions are not directed towards achieving a single goal, but with discovering courses of action that satisfy a whole set of constraints, including certain organizational constraints. He thinks the constraints that motivate the decision-maker and guide his search for actions are sometimes more 'goal-like' than those that limit the actions he may consider, or the constraints used to test whether a potential course of action is satisfactory.

Taken together with the notion of 'satisficing', what this amounts to is that Simon sees only different sets of constraints facing the firm; and whether all of these are treated symmetrically, or some are treated asymmetrically as goals, is largely a matter of analytical convenience.

As an example of 'satisficing', in a decision problem which (assuming 'global rationality') might be formulated as a linear programming problem, instead of finding the optimal program the satisficer would be content to select a feasible program which offered a pay-off that exceeded some prescribed amount. (The minimum pay-off requirement simply means a further linear inequality must be satisfied; we are merely defining a feasible region with one additional constraint. *Any* pay-off falling within this region will do; a complete ordering of all pay-offs

---

* If the problem is one involving linear programming, a way has been devised of setting upper and lower bounds on the values of the objective function by a method of partitions applied to the constraints – see [30], pp. 352–53.

is not required.)* Another example would be the attempt to achieve a target rate of return on investment. The satisficer seeks a course of action that is 'good enough'. Like a thermostat which controls the heat produced by a furnace, subsequent decisions are governed by the idea of feedback correction (homeostasis). In this way approximate rationality is possible with a considerable simplification of the problem.

Profit maximization – and optimizing behaviour in general – is part of the tradition of normative microeconomics, which states how decisions *ought* to be taken given this objective; it has never been seriously suggested that it describes what firms actually do. Looked at from this point of view, the case for regarding economic (including business) behaviour as maximizing behaviour gains force, since it is difficult to think of any other objective which is not subsumed under a more general maximization model in which, for example, *learning* is included as one of the goals [7]. We return to the question of optimizing and the meaning of optimality in section 4(e).

(b) Criterion

For a given decision problem a criterion (or *decision rule*) is needed in order to choose the preferred alternative in terms of the firm's objective. The objective remains constant over all decisions; decision criteria will vary from one type of decision to another. The criterion translates the objective into an operational form in terms of the decision data, the costs and benefits associated with the various alternatives. For example, the firm's objective may be profit maximization; the criterion for a particular decision may be minimizing a certain class of costs, subject to any constraints on the overall problem of maximizing enterprise profits, such as the technological limitations imposed by its production function.

(c) Planning horizon

The firm has to decide over what time interval the objective is to be achieved. An objective of seeking to maximize profits year by year† is unlikely to lead to the same results as maximizing profits over periods of two or five years; one will be more nearly optimal over the firm's economic horizon. The objective and criterion are meaningless unless related to a specific planning horizon.

This raises the question of how to fix the horizon, and whether there is such a thing as an *optimal planning horizon*, which could be defined as that planning period which yields the best results in the long run (i.e. over the firm's economic horizon).

---

* [33], p. 250.
† The time unit may be months or weeks, depending on the activity which is being planned.

This second question has as yet received no definitive answer, though in practice it can be solved approximately. We discuss this in section 5(b) below. The problem is that if the horizon is too short the firm is throwing away useful information about the future; and if it is too long information relating to the more distant periods may be almost valueless because of mounting uncertainties. This might suggest that the horizon should be fixed as the foreseeable future, with the uncertainties being built into the model. The catch is that this begs the question, because the firm is continually creating new information about the future: the horizon is in part what the firm plans it to be; the meaning of the horizon cannot be defined without a plan.

There are two general approaches to planning horizons, called the fixed and shifting planning horizon methods (FPH and SPH).* These can be described with the aid of the following table:

Time	t_0	t_1	$t_2 \ldots \ldots \ldots t_{n-1}$	t_n	$t_{n+1} \ldots \ldots \ldots T$
FPH	1. $[p_1$	$p_2 \ldots \ldots \ldots \ldots \ldots p_n]$			
	2.	$[p_2'$	$p_3' \ldots \ldots \ldots p_n']$		
	3.		$[p_3'' \ldots \ldots \ldots p_n'']$		
SPH	1. $[p_1$	$p_2 \ldots \ldots \ldots \ldots \ldots p_n]$			
	2.	$[p_2'$	$p_3' \ldots \ldots \ldots p_n'$	$p_{n+1}']$	
	3.		$[p_3'' \ldots \ldots \ldots \ldots \ldots \ldots \ldots \ldots p_{n+2}'']$		

Imagine a firm at time t_0 whose economic horizon is T. Under the SPH method a constant time interval of n periods is defined as the planning horizon. Suppose the effectiveness of the activity being planned is to be measured in terms of its expected cost, based on the information (forecasts, estimates) available to the firm at this point and on what is known of the past behaviour of this cost up to t_0. The firm, we will suppose, wishes to minimize this expected cost over the horizon t_n. It draws up a plan with this purpose at t_0 and puts it into effect. At time t_1 a second plan is drawn up, based on expectations held at that time and known results up to t_1. In the light of this second plan the implementation of the first plan may be modified (i.e. p_2' may not be the same as p_2). This procedure is repeated period by period, making use of the additional information about the future which is constantly coming in.

Under the FPH method the planning horizon (t_n) remains fixed; a plan is drawn up at t_0 and there is no further planning until t_n. As in the other case the plan is based partly upon expectations and partly on what is known of past behaviour. If the latter can all be summarized in one variable, A, the plan made at t_0, $f(t)$, can be represented as:

$$f(t) = g(t_0, A)$$

*See [17], pp. 75–77.

where g is a particular function which will minimize costs over the period from t_0 to t_n, given the firm's information at t_0. The first period of this plan is implemented as before. At times t_1, t_2, ... the next stages of the plan up to t_n are determined by inserting updated information into the function g (at time t_1, the value of A up to t_1 and the value of t_1). Compared with the other method, therefore, the *particular* form of the function g is determined for all periods up to t_n at t_0, even though as the plan progresses this means ignoring more and more information which may be relevant to decisions at the first stage, whereas under the SPH-method it is possible to change this function at any stage if significant changes in the underlying relationships are detected.

(d) The alternatives

These refer to means by which the firm's objective may be accomplished. This involves perception of the possibilities: the firm must recognize that alternatives exist between which it must choose. This may involve two steps; first, what Simon* calls *perception of need*, which requires continuous collection and assessment of information of all kinds from external sources and within the firm in order to signal the need or opportunity for decision. This first step is particularly applicable to what we have called strategic planning, which would otherwise go by default or be left to intuition and judgement. The second step is the search for attractive alternatives. These often do not obligingly come to the firm; they must be sought out, particularly if they relate to a strategic problem. One characteristic of an efficient management is the extent to which it recognizes decision needs and opportunities.

Occasionally 'golden' opportunities may present themselves which require no elaborate decision calculation to justify them. At the other extreme a preliminary sifting will weed out some alternatives as being clearly infeasible. The remaining alternatives form the subject of the decision calculation. One of the alternatives may be to do nothing now in order to be in a position to undertake a more highly-valued alternative later which would use the same resources. And even refusing to choose is one kind of decision.

(e) Constraints

Restrictions on the permissible values of the independent decision variables are called constraints. These may take various forms and must be stated explicitly: resource constraints (limitations on inputs required to implement the decision alternatives); balance requirements (e.g. that the quantity sold in any period may not exceed current production plus reduction in finished goods inventory); inter-

* H. A. Simon, [34].

dependencies (discussed in section 5 below); indivisibilities or non-negativity conditions on some or all of the decision variables. If a constraint effectively limits the values that the objective function may take on it is called a *binding constraint*.

(f) A model

A decision model must be developed, explicitly or implicitly, displaying the relationships between the objective (or criterion), the alternatives and the constraints. Business decision models vary tremendously in formal complexity and in their data requirements (compare, e.g., the simple break-even model (Chapter 10) and a model for optimizing capital investment in conditions of capital rationing (Chapter 12)). A particular model may call for submodels, i.e. there may be decisions within decisions (an example would be the assessment of investment projects, some of which are mutually exclusive, when capital markets are perfect and there are no constraints on the resources, including money, needed to undertake the investment program). Models are discussed in more detail in section 5.

(g) Uncertainty

A fundamental characteristic of all decision problems is that the outcome is uncertain. Since the data are estimates of future events, it is not possible to predict decision outcomes with perfect accuracy; the outcomes are not single-valued. In a given decision model uncertainty may take various forms: it may be recognized but excluded by the assumptions of the model (e.g. an assumption that there will be no major war during the period of the decision); evaluation of the various alternatives can only be expressed as sets of estimates with probabilities attached; or there may be uncertainty about the structure of the problem (and hence about the important variables to be included). A distinction is sometimes drawn [24] between 'risk' and 'uncertainty', depending on whether the probabilities of outcomes are known (*a priori* or statistically) or not, respectively. We will, however, continue for the most part to use the two terms interchangeably.

Some of the ways in which uncertainty may be explicitly introduced in decision problems will be reviewed in Chapter 12 in the context of the capital investment decision. For the present it is important to note that the role of uncertainty in decision-making involves two distinct aspects. When the decision data have been estimated

1. There is then the uncertainty (or confidence) with which the decision-maker views these estimates (*risk estimation*).
2. There is also, however, the attitude of the decision-maker to risk-taking in general. One person will often react differently to essentially the same choice

situation at different times, or to different types of choice situation (say a purchasing decision and a marketing decision), being perhaps highly optimistic in one case and highly pessimistic in another; and different decision-makers faced with the same decision may exhibit a whole array of different attitudes to risk (*risk preference*).

As Coase has remarked [10],

> There is no decision which can be considered to maximise profits [or more generally achieve the firm's objective] independently of the business man's attitude to risk-taking.

6.3 Problem identification

Once a decision problem is seen to exist we must decide what kind of problem it is, i.e. what is its essential structure? This involves keeping the firm's objective in mind, generating all the feasible alternatives and understanding the underlying economic relationships between the decision variables. An understanding of economic principles and reasoning are all-important here; familiarity with some of the more common optimization techniques, and their assumptions, may be useful in structuring a problem. There will always be some business problems which are relatively 'unstructured', however (meaning that they do not conform to any of the classes of problems to which standard optimization techniques have been applied). The ability to return to first principles – in economics and in mathematics – is essential for the successful analytical treatment of this kind of problem.

As an illustration of incorrect problem identification, decisions involving marginal and non-marginal adjustments may be cited. Transfer prices, the accounting prices fixed for transfers of goods or services within a business, sometimes called 'sales not at arm's length', will serve as an example. If these prices are determined optimally they lead to correct output adjustments between the divisions of the firm concerned *at the margin*. It does not follow that if a division is apparently losing money at this price the firm would increase its profits by shutting down that division. Such a decision would involve a non-marginal output adjustment. In order to decide this question we would have to ask ourselves what difference it would make to costs and revenues throughout the firm if this division were to be closed down.

6.4 Data specification

(a) Whose domain?

We return to this question, referred to earlier, to make one further observation. As already stated, the task of providing data for decision is more in the nature of applied economics than accounting, and also requires some acquintance and facility with quantitative methods other than accounting. The concern which non-accountants feel as to who should be entrusted with this task is shown in the following statement by an eminent operations researcher [9]:

> Even though a [operations] researcher feels satisfied with a general form of the model of decision-making, he still has to find the data which can be used to estimate the parameters: e.g. costs and demands.... A study of data-collection problems of O.R. indicates that the split between the task of formalizing the model and collection of the data . . . is ill-conceived. It is incorrect to assume that a set of costs or profit quantities are *measures* simply because they are quantities. Measures have known formal properties which have to be tested empirically and which justify their use in models.... Thus . . . it is generally unsafe for the O.R. team to turn over to another less technically qualified team the responsibility of generating measures for models.

The point bears reiteration that it is by no means taken for granted that the part of management accounting concerned with *preparing* data for decision – and even the non-routine part of accounting for control – should be handled by accountants at all. If accountants are to continue to lay claim to this function a much more conceptual approach, as suggested by the subtitle of this volume, is imperative.

(b) Measurement problems

The question of measurement was referred to in Chapter 1. Providing data for decision is what we there called prospective accounting. Prospective accounting measures are, by their nature, unlikely to be as accurate as *ex post* (or retrospective) measures. The fact that decision data may be subject to wide margins of error is generally recognized in practice, though the allowance for uncertainty is not always made explicit, and is often crude. At the same time we should not be so blinded by the need for accounting measures to satisfy certain purely formal properties that we forget that these measures are important only to the extent that they faithfully *represent* something else, viz. economic stocks or flows. We will therefore be concerned in this book mainly with two other aspects of the data, viz. with whether a certain quantity measures what it purports to measure, and more important still, with the rules by which we should decide what should be measured.

(c) Cost concepts for decision

As stated earlier, correct specification in economic terms is of over-riding importance in preparing data for decision. The data are predominantly costs and revenues, or cash flows, though they will sometimes include physical measures as well. In this section we concentrate on cost concepts which are relevant for decision. Specification of the measures of benefits (revenues, cash flows) involves greater estimation problems than costs do, but in most business decisions it does not give rise to conceptual difficulties. The following paragraphs set out the main points to be kept in mind in ensuring that the costs of a decision are correctly specified – that all of the relevant costs are counted and those that are irrelevant to the decision are ignored. Further reading in the literature is strongly recommended in order to fix these ideas.*

(i) *Ex ante and ex post costs*

All costs of relevance in decision-making are *ex ante* costs (i.e. estimates of future costs); *ex post* costs are relevant only to the extent that they are a guide to *ex ante* costs.

(ii) *Avoidable costs*

Furthermore, we are only interested in the costs which will change as a result of adopting a particular alternative. These are the costs which could be avoided, and any revenues that would be foregone, if the particular alternative were not adopted. Any costs which will remain constant whichever alternative is adopted are irrelevant for decision-making purposes, and may be ignored. Other terms used for avoidable cost are escapable cost, additional cost, incremental cost.

If

$$q = f(x_1, x_2) \qquad \text{(production function)}$$

$$C = r_1 x_1 + r_2 x_2 + b \qquad \text{(cost equation)}$$

$$= \phi(q) + b \qquad \text{(cost function; } b = \text{fixed costs)}$$

and

$$V = \phi(q) \qquad \text{(variable cost function)}$$

the economist's *marginal cost* $\dfrac{dC}{dq} = \dfrac{dV}{dq}$ is the avoidable cost of producing one additional unit of q. *Ex ante* costs in the economic sense are always those (and only those) expenses which can be avoided.

It follows from what has been said above that avoidable costs can only be determined by reference to a particular decision; costs which are avoidable for one decision may be unavoidable for other decisions.

(iii) *Fixed costs*

Fixed costs in the economic sense are those which can not be avoided. Before dismissing them as irrelevant for decision-making purposes, however, note that there are several possible categories of fixed costs, depending on the degree of avoidability. They may be:

1. Fixed in relation to *the time period considered*: some costs are unavoidable in the short run but not in the long run: $f(t) = $ constant.

* The list would include [26], Chapter 1 on fixed costs, particularly pp. 9–15; [10]; [15] and [3].

2. Fixed in relation to *output*: some costs are unavoidable for small but not for large changes in output. More strictly, costs which are fixed in this sense must be paid regardless of how much the firm produces, or whether it produces at all. This is the usual meaning of 'fixed cost' in accounting:

$$f(q) = \text{constant}$$

$$\ldots \leq q \leq \ldots$$

3. Fixed in relation to *the time available to implement a decision* (e.g. a change in output): some costs are unavoidable if output must be stepped up sharply within a week, say, but avoidable if the same increase is to be effected in three months: $f(\tau) = $ constant.
4. Fixed in the sense of being *joint costs*: if Q_1 and Q_2 are joint products the cost of Q_1 is only avoidable by curtailing production of Q_1 and Q_2: $f(q_1, q_2) = $ constant.
5. *Fixed in a combination of the above senses*: some costs may be unavoidable in more than one of the above senses in a particular decision problem: $f(q, t, \tau) = $ constant.

The costs which may safely be ignored for decision purposes are those which will remain invariant for the whole set of alternatives considered, in each and every one of the above senses which happens to apply in the particular decision problem. In accounting, costs of a fixed *nature* (i.e. costs which are invariant with changes in output of the size encountered in normal operations), but which would vary if a certain course were adopted, are sometimes referred to as *separable fixed costs*; obviously these *are* relevant if that course is considered.* It follows that if there is no alternative use for resources they are costless for decision-making purposes (their opportunity cost is zero).

(iv) *Economic cost further considered*

We noted in (i) and (ii) that the relevant costs for decision-making are *ex ante* economic costs, and that the latter have the characteristic of *avoidability*: they are those costs which could be avoided if the action being considered were not proceeded with.

But in economics the essential nature of costs is summed up in the term *opportunity cost* (or alternative cost). The (opportunity) cost of a certain course of action is defined as the highest-valued alternative foregone – the highest value to other producers, or in certain cases to the firm itself, of the resources which would be employed by the alternative being considered. The value is measured by the net

---

*Separable fixed costs are costs which are discontinuously variable at zero output of the activity in question. They are sometimes referred to as 'start-up costs', though it should be noted that 'start-up' and 'shut-down' costs need not be equal.

receipts of the next-best alternative. We thus have two views of economic cost: first in terms of foregone opportunities (opportunity cost), and second, in terms of avoidability (avoidable cost). That the two are identical, and merely represent different ways of looking at the same thing, is a matter of definition.

The equivalence may be stated as follows (all costs *ex ante*):

economic cost $\equiv$ opportunity cost

$\equiv$ avoidable outlay costs + the implicit opportunity cost of any resources not represented by outlay costs.

Whenever they are evidenced by an exchange transaction opportunity costs are measured* by money (outlay) costs.

In approaching a decision problem we are on safer ground if we think in terms of opportunity costs, since not all of the relevant costs may be money costs; some may have to be imputed.

At the same time it is never *necessary* to impute opportunity costs in a decision problem; the correct decision can always be made by listing and comparing the avoidable costs (and revenues foregone, unless these are the same for all alternatives) for *all* the alternatives.

Which one happens to be the more operational in a particular case – avoidable costs plus imputed opportunity costs, or avoidable costs only – depends on which offers the more convenient method of calculation.

(v) *Economic cost and accounting cost*

Economic cost (opportunity cost) differs from 'cost' in the business or accounting sense, which is simply the sum which would be expended as a result of a particular course of action (i.e. *ex ante* or budgeted accounting cost). 'Cost' is thus synonymous with 'expense', and may include 'book' expenses (like depreciation) as well as expenses which give rise to a payment inside or outside the firm.

The difference between economic cost and accounting cost is represented by fixed expenses, those which cannot be avoided by not undertaking the course of action being considered (to call them fixed *costs* as we usually do is therefore really a contradiction in terms):

Accounting cost = Economic cost + fixed expenses.

We already noted that for a particular decision we could ignore any expenditure which would remain fixed in all senses relevant to that decision.

---

* Approximated – see [3].

(d) Estimation problems

All decision-making is strictly decision-making in conditions of uncertainty. The exclusion of uncertainty in the formulation of a problem is usually justified by one of two considerations: either the uncertainties surrounding the decision are thought to be small (this may be the case with many decisions of short duration), or the problem is treated as though it were deterministic as a first step, before introducing uncertainty. As already stated, the uncertainty involved in estimating the data for a particular decision is likely to be greater in the case of benefits than of costs, since fewer of the determinants of benefits are under the firm's control.

Statistics is one form of decision-making under uncertainty: on the basis of sample information alone inferences are drawn about a population. It follows that we would be foolish to disregard the considerable body of knowledge statisticians have built up for dealing with estimation problems. Detailed consideration of this subject is beyond the scope of this book, but readers are advised to consult one of the works referred to below.* The topics of particular relevance include: the distinction between point estimates and interval estimates; whether an estimate is based on sample information alone (i.e. consists entirely of forecasts) or on a combination of sample and *a priori* information; the desirable properties of point estimates (efficiency (accuracy, 'best estimate'), lack of bias, consistency, sufficiency); the maximum likelihood method (one means of choosing between estimators (sample statistics, such as mean and variance) when no single one possesses all of the above characteristics, or no estimator is dominant as regards these characteristics (the most important of these is, of course, what we have called accuracy; after that lack of bias is probably the next most desirable)); subjective (personal) probabilities (another method of choosing between estimators); confidence intervals; the application of Bayes' theorem to discriminate between estimators based on both *a priori* information (about probabilities of various outcomes) and sample information.

For present purposes two only of the terms referred to above will be defined:

1. *Accuracy*: concerns the variance of the estimator about its actual value. An estimator t_i provides a better estimate of a parameter θ than estimator t_j if

$$E[(t_i-\theta)^2] < E[(t_j-\theta)^2] \quad \text{for all values of } \theta,$$

   where E = expected value.
2. *Lack of bias*: an estimate t is an unbiased estimator of a parameter θ if $E(t) = \theta$.

---

* Any textbook on mathematical statistics, such as [20], section 3.3 and Chapter 10. The same ideas are discussed in a decision theory context in various books, e.g. [31], [14], Chapters 14–15; [23], Chapter 3.

(e) Data limitations and computation costs

As already mentioned in section 2, a possible constraint on the form which decision-making takes – even on its objectives – is imposed by cost-benefit considerations relating to the decision process itself.* As described by Baumol and Quandt [7],

> The more refined the decision-making process, the more expensive it is likely to be and therefore, especially where a decision is not of crucial importance, no more than an approximate solution may be justified. Since all real decisions are made under conditions of imperfect information, precise calculation . . . is pointless in any event.

They go on to formulate the appropriate marginal conditions for what they call an 'optimally imperfect decision', viz. one for which the marginal cost of gathering additional information or making more refined calculations equals its marginal expected gross yield.† No data collection or processing is worthwhile unless the expected benefits exceed the expected costs.

Putting this another way, a distinction can be drawn between a *maximal solution* to a problem, which is only possible if there are no data limitations and computation costs are not excessive in relation to expected benefits, and an *optimal solution*, where these conditions are not met. All attempts at maximization, Baumol and Quandt argue, strictly produce only optimal solutions in this sense, because of these limitations, and because the system to be maximized ultimately extends far beyond the particular activity and firm being considered. 'Optimizing' therefore really means maximizing in a restricted sense.‡ The notion of an optimally imperfect decision rule has some similarities to 'satisficing', referred to earlier.

6.5 Some comments on decision models

A complete classification of model types likely to be met with is unnecessary for present purposes, even if it were possible. Accounting students should, however, be aware of at least the following points.

(a) Single and sequential decisions

Some decisions are non-recurrent; an example might be fixing a price for a special government contract during a slack period. Many, however, are of a sequential nature, i.e. they comprise a series of repeated decisions, and the consequences of a decision made at one point in time become initial conditions (given data) which affect the decisions to be made at the next decision stage. A good example of a sequential decision problem is the holding of inventories: the inventory at the

---

* Refer section 3(c) of Chapter 1.
† Cf. the similar notion of 'optimally inexact information' in [28].
‡ For a striking application of these ideas, see [21], p. 59 *et seq.*

beginning of a period is in part a reflection of decisions and events occurring earlier.

In a true sequential decision problem the consequences of any decision extend to infinity. If, as often happens, the decision problem at each stage has the same form, it may be possible to solve the sequential problem analytically. If this is either not the case or computationally infeasible, a one-period problem called the proximal or proximate decision problem is substituted for the sequential one. We make the best possible decision for the first period in the light of the information we then have for all periods covered by the sequential decision (which we will for present purposes assume has a finite horizon of $t = T$ periods). Data relating to the more distant periods embodied in the objective function may be highly uncertain, but forecasting errors can be offset to some extent at subsequent decision stages.*

A one-period treatment of a sequential decision problem bears some similarities to the use of static analysis in economics to deal with problems which are dynamic in nature but incapable of being handled as such by existing tools. If the one-period proximal problem contains variables relating to later time periods, as well as relying on initial conditions resulting from earlier decisions, the analysis is dynamic (see below). Useful insights into a number of economic problems have unquestionably been gained through static analysis, but there are risks inherent in this approach.

Sequential decision problems, despite their greater complexity, have one potential advantage compared with 'one-off' problems, and that is that they usually have a greater degree of *reversibility*. If a wrong decision is made this period, due to a faulty forecast, the effect of this may be offset to some extent next period when the process is repeated using revised data. With 'one-off' decisions there will generally be less chance of doing this, and consequently the cost of wrong decisions may be relatively greater. Most business decision problems are probably sequential.

(b) Static and dynamic models †

A static model is one in which the variables are treated as being in a steady state (e.g. if the variable is rate of production, this rate is approximately constant throughout the decision period). This does not mean that they do not change at all through time, merely that the changes occur slowly enough for the system to be treated as though it were in a steady state throughout the period to which the decision relates; alternatively, the period may be made sufficiently short to exclude significant changes in most cases. If the decision period is longer or changes in the variables occur more rapidly they must be taken into account explicitly. This is done by means of a dynamic model, in which all variables are time-subscripted. In a dynamic model corresponding variables in different periods are treated as distinct variables; there may also be interperiod constraints in addition to those relating to a single

---

* See [21] for an illustration.
† Refer Chapter 5.

Decision concepts

period.* Sometimes the static/dynamic distinction is treated as synonymous with single period/multiperiod models. The single/sequential and static/dynamic distinctions are closely related: static models are concerned with a single choice among courses of action all contained within the same period; dynamic models are concerned with a sequence of choices among courses of action, where the decision in any period is influenced by variables in other periods, both earlier and later.

Dynamic models, by introducing time explicitly, raise some new problems, in particular how to ensure comparability of data for different periods, and how much of the future to include, i.e. how to fix the planning horizon. The first problem is solved by time discounting: data for all periods are reduced to present values. In short-run (production) problems it is normally unnecessary to introduce this refinement, as it would usually not affect the result significantly. In investment and other long-run problems discounting becomes essential (see Chapters 11 and 12).

The second question, how to fix the planning horizon with the object of ensuring that under constantly changing conditions and expectations plans will be optimal in the long-run, is a difficult one, which has not yet been solved. That is, the problem is to determine the planning period, n, in such a way that a sequence of n-period plans will be optimal over T periods (where $T = \infty$ or the foreseeable future).

Some brief comments can be offered, however. First, the answer will depend on whether or not decisions in different periods are interrelated.† If they are not, each period can be treated as a closed system and planning period by period will be consistent with optimizing over the long-run. Normally, of course, this is not so; decisions taken in one period are not independent of decisions taken in other periods. When such interdependencies exist plans should, in theory, cover the entire future, or as far ahead as the firm can foresee. As noted in section 3 of Chapter 5, however, not all aspects of the future are relevant to decisions to be taken in the first stage of the plan.

The second comment is that in practice the problem can be approximately answered by simulating the system under different planning horizons. Plans could be prepared in turn for n and $(n+1)$ periods, the confidence felt in forecasts and estimates suggesting the value of n. If the plan for $(n+1)$ periods shows a significant improvement, in terms of the measure of effectiveness, over the plan for n periods, the process would be continued by planning for $(n+2)$ periods, and so on, until the measure exhibits reasonable stability (i.e. approaches an equilibrium rate). The horizon determined by this trial-and-error approach should yield results which are approximately long-run optimal. This horizon will be sufficiently far ahead to make

---

* We can further clarify this by distinguishing between exogenous variables (the external environment not determined by the model) and variables controllable by the firm (endogenous, or decision, variables). The essential characteristic of dynamic systems is that the *environment* is changing over time. The controllable variables can change over time even in static systems, due to unforeseen random disturbances.

† This relationship is known as intertemporal dependence – see section 5(d) below.

the first period's decisions near optimal, and in most circumstances the planning period will be small compared with the firm's entire economic horizon (referring back to section 2(c), $n \ll T$).*

Thirdly, as noted in Chapter 5, there is no reason to suppose that the horizon will be the same for different components of the firm's plan (e.g. for production, purchasing, finance, marketing).

We have already seen in section 2(c) that there are two general approaches to planning, the fixed planning horizon method (in which the horizon is fixed but the planning period varies) and the shifting planning horizon method (in which the reverse applies).

(c) Deterministic and probabilistic models

Many processes that cause change do not necessarily result in uncertainty; an example is investment in a savings deposit. If a decision will give rise to an outcome which is single-valued (i.e. certain as a first approximation) the process is called deterministic. Alternatively, if a decision process will cause change *and* give rise to uncertainty, i.e. if it can have more than one outcome (if the model does not permit perfect predictability), the decision is probabilistic, and the process involved is called a stochastic process. It will be evident from the foregoing that most economic and business problems are of the latter kind.

(d) Interdependencies

One of the common attributes of economic and business problems is the presence of interdependencies – interactions between the primary variables in a given decision, or between different decisions (decisions made in different parts of the firm, or inside and outside the firm). There may be interdependencies between alternatives being currently considered or between present and future alternatives, and even past actions.† What makes the question of interdependencies important is that they are rife, and that they tend to be overlooked.‡

Interdependencies give rise to 'externalities' (or external effects). At the level of the individual firm this means that when they are present corrections must be made to costs and/or benefits in formulating the problem. At the level of the economy they are evidenced by discrepancies between private and social costs and/or benefits after the effects of market imperfections have been eliminated.

---

* In the case of production planning, two exceptions would be where sales have a marked rising trend from one seasonal cycle (or period) to the next, or storage costs are negligible – [29].

† See Chapters 11 and 12.

‡ The tendency when faced with large and complex decision problems is to break them up into a number of subproblems small enough to be solved. Interdependencies between the parts may, and frequently are, lost sight of in the process.

Decision concepts

The subject will not be pursued further here, as it has been treated in some detail elsewhere,* but we will have cause to mention interdependencies again in later chapters, e.g. in connection with problems of decentralization and capital investment. When strong interdependencies exist between different activities of the firm, three courses of action are open: either the appropriate corrections must be introduced into the decision problem of each activity, considered separately; or these activities must be treated as one, and jointly optimized; or they may be further decomposed, if by this means the interdependence can be eliminated.

This discussion of interdependencies brings into question the relative advantages of a piecemeal *versus* an holistic approach to the decision problems of the firm, particularly where significant linkages are suspected between its different activities. (If the interdependencies are overlooked, the combined result of partial optimizations may not be consistent with overall optimization of the firm; this is a classic problem in welfare economics.) Roughly speaking, in the 1940s 'problem reduction' was the vogue, stemming principally from developments in operations research, with occasional support from economists.† This led, and is still leading, to increasingly sophisticated models of more and more subproblems within the overall problem (enterprise optimization); that is, the overall problem was partitioned into a number of subproblems sufficiently narrow for *information* to be available to solve them,‡ and relatively easy and inexpensive to compute using one of the known optimization techniques. Throughout the years a few economists have been working, at a theoretical level, towards a more unified decision model of the firm, motivated chiefly by the need to recognize significant linkages between different parts of the firm's activity.§ There is also some evidence of growing disenchantment on the part of operations researchers, for a variety of reasons, with continued development along the 'suboptimization' road.** The extent to which it is possible to employ more general optimization models in practice will depend on whether they can be solved by existing analytical methods or whether suitable heuristic methods (discussed below) can be developed, and on whether solution of the model is computationally feasible.††

†† See [4].

† Notably C. J. Hitch [19]. According to Hitch, optimal decision-making is a planned series of sub-optimizations. The problem of enterprise optimization must be broken down, because it is too difficult (analytically or computationally) and too costly to study the overall problem. As Churchman observes in [9], p. 45, 'in this respect Hitch and Simon ("satisficing") are not too far apart, because a planned series of suboptima is one type of learning'. The term 'suboptima' is here used in the original sense employed by Hitch to mean optimization of something less than the whole system, i.e. a *partial optimization.*

‡ See Boulding, in [8].

§ A number of these more general optimization models are referred to in Vickers [38]. Vickers' own model is probably the most comprehensive (if not the most detailed) yet to appear. See also [4].

** Thus Ackoff states 'O.R. should attempt to deal with larger and larger segments of larger and larger systems so that deficiencies in procedures can be made more apparent . . .' [1], p. 31.

†† A third qualification, made in [4], is that, from an economic efficiency point of view, such an holistic approach would appear to be the opposite of what is needed in all 'second best' situations.

(e) Analytical versus heuristic solutions

Already some business problems are so complex that they cannot be solved analytically, i.e. they do not respond to any known optimization techniques. Furthermore, in some of these problems strong interdependencies are present, which might suggest a further enlargement of the problem. In such circumstances the attempt to optimize, using analytical methods, may be abandoned in favour of an heuristic solution. A few definitions may help to clarify these ideas.

The solution to a decision problem which has been formulated mathematically is called an *analytical solution* if it is computable as a closed function of the decision variables. The possibility of an analytical solution thus depends on finding an appropriate mathematical form for the problem (there is no universal optimization technique) and then on the possibility of numerical computation.

An *algorithm* is a method of generating solutions which guarantees that, if a particular problem has a solution, the method will eventually find it.

An *heuristic problem-solving method* (or simply heuristic), by contrast, is any process which *may* solve a given problem, but offers no guarantee of doing so. Heuristic methods (such as 'direct search') have the characteristics that (a) they reduce the area of search for a satisfactory solution: each trial solution is an improvement on previous ones, and there is a strategy for determining what the next trial solution will be; and (b) they are computable. In terms of the next section, heuristic methods are neither necessary nor sufficient to reach a desired objective, though they may do so pragmatically; nor do they satisfy any particular criteria of optimality [35]. At any stage of development of analytical methods and computational capacities there is the possibility of profitable trade-off between the use of analytical and heuristic methods.

Simulation has a different aim: it is an attempt to *describe* the working of a specific system. The description of the system (i.e. of the decision problem) is often so complex that it cannot be stated in the form of a mathematical model. The advent of electronic computers has made it possible to describe the operation of highly complex systems, and a computer program can be written to replicate the thought processes of the human decision-makers. The main emphasis in simulation is on the exactness with which the real system is described, in order to gain greater insights into the problem, rather than on developing a satisfactory and efficient solution to it.*

(f) Necessary and sufficient conditions

In quantitative decision problems care is needed to ensure that the result of the decision calculation satisfies the conditions for a solution, given the objective or

---

*For further discussion see [22], Chapter 14.

criterion. Readers will be familiar from the calculus with the first-order (necessary) and second-order (sufficient) conditions for the maximum or minimum value of a function.

More generally, a *sufficient* condition for the achievement of a given objective guarantees that the objective will be achieved but is not essential for its achievement; a *necessary* condition must be satisfied for the objective to be achieved but may not in itself be enough to guarantee the result; while a condition (or set of conditions) which is both *necessary and sufficient* must be satisfied and does guarantee the result. As an example, consider the inequality $x + 10 \geq 25$. For this inequality to hold it is necessary, but not sufficient, that $x \geq 0$; it is sufficient, though not necessary, for $x \geq 30$; and it is both necessary and sufficient if $x \geq 15$.

Necessary and sufficient conditions are an occasional source of confusion in dealing with business problems. Solutions sometimes stop short at necessary conditions. As we have seen, this is dangerous, and may very well lead to wrong decisions. We should try to ensure that both conditions (if they exist)* are met by our solutions, though in problems involving complicated mathematical manipulation it is not always possible to achieve this: the necessary and sufficient conditions, if they exist, are often not discoverable.

(g) Omitted variables

A decision model will usually be a simplification of the real situation. Some variables will have been omitted, because their influence is considered minor or because they are nonquantifiable, or thought to be so. The model may not explicitly include behavioural variables, such as the likely effects of the decision on the people who will be affected by it. Behaviour within the firm in such matters as the formation of goals and expectations, the influence of organizational structure, and what is to be taken as the appropriate model, becomes an important area of study in decision-making, particularly by large and complex business enterprises. The latter involve a number of decision-makers who are not usually to be identified with the owners (if they are in fact owners their shareholdings are typically small, and their goals may be rather different from those of owners who are not also employed as managers).†
In short, all optimization procedures must partly rest on certain subjective evaluations, a fact which is often obscured if these subjective elements are not explicitly represented in formal models. The distinction sometimes made between 'objective' and 'subjective' decisions is therefore a matter of degree. In view of these considerations we should be careful always to regard the quantitative solution to a decision problem as a first step, and remember to take into account all important

---

*A necessary condition for an optimum must be fulfilled at the optimum point; it may also be fulfilled elsewhere. A sufficient condition can only be satisfied at the optimum, but may not be even there.

† Readers interested in exploring this area further could begin by referring to [13], Chapters 1–6.

omitted variables of a qualitative nature, the so-called 'imponderables'. It is doubly important to do so when the margin in favour of the preferred alternative is small. We have more to say about some of the variables commonly omitted from economic analysis – corporate form and organization structure, information, financial structure, to mention a few – in other parts of the book.

These are but a few of the matters – though with the exception of uncertainty, which is to be discussed later, we hope most of the main ones – of which the management accountant should be aware in approaching business decision problems. It has not been possible within the space available to give more than a brief sketch of these points, but we hope it has been sufficient to give the reader a sense of the wider horizons of this branch of accounting, if such it is, and of the need for a logical approach based on economic principles, and often formulated mathematically. A number of the ideas are illustrated in subsequent chapters.

Bibliographical references

[1] Ackoff, R. L., ed., *Progress in Operations Research*, Vol. I, Wiley, 1966.

[2] Allen, R. G. D., *Basic Mathematics*, Macmillan, London, 1962.

[3] Amey, L. R., On opportunity costs and decision making, *Accountancy*, July 1968, pp. 442–51; reprinted in *Studies in Accountancy 1968*, Institute of Chartered Accountants in England and Wales, a revised version of which is reprinted in *Readings in Management Decision*, ed. L. R. Amey, Longman 1973.

[4] Amey, L. R., Interdependencies in capital budgeting: a survey, *Journal of Business Finance*, Autumn 1972, pp. 70–86.

[5] Arrow, K. J., Statistics and economic policy, *Econometrica*, 1957, pp. 523–31.

[6] Baumol, W. J., *Economic Theory and Operations Analysis*, Prentice-Hall, 2nd edn., 1965.

[7] Baumol, W. J. and R. E. Quandt, Rules of thumb and optimally imperfect decisions, *American Economic Review*, 1964, pp. 23–46, reprinted in *Readings in Management Decision*, ed. L. R. Amey, Longman 1973.

[8] Boulding, K. E. and W. A. Spivey, *Linear Programming and the Theory of the Firm*, Macmillan, New York, 1960.

[9] Churchman, C. W., Decision and value theory, in [1], pp. 35–64.

[10] Coase, R. H., Business organisation and the accountant, *The Accountant*, Oct. 1 to Dec. 17, 1938; reprinted in *Studies in Costing*, ed. D. Solomons, Sweet & Maxwell, 1952.

[11] Cohen, K. J. and R. M. Cyert, *Theory of the Firm*, Prentice-Hall, 1965.

[12] Cyert, R. M. and W. R. Dill, The future of business education, *Journal of Business*, July 1964, pp. 221–37.

[13] Cyert, R. M. and J. G. March, *A Behavioral Theory of the Firm*, Prentice-Hall, 1963.

[14] Dyckman, T. R., S. Smidt and A. K. McAdams, *Management Decision Making under Uncertainty*, Macmillan, New York, 1969.

[15] Gould, J. R., The economist's cost concept and business problems, in *Studies in Accounting Theory*, eds. W. T. Baxter and S. Davidson, Sweet & Maxwell, 1962, pp. 218–35.

[16] Hague, D. C., *Managerial Economics*, Longmans, 1969.

[17] Hanssmann, F., A survey of inventory theory from the operations research viewpoint, chapter 3 in [1].

[18] Henderson, J. M. and R. E. Quandt, *Microeconomic Theory*, McGraw-Hill, 1958.

[19] Hitch, C. J., Sub-optimization in operations problems, *Journal of the O.R. Society of America*, 1953, pp. 87–99.

[20] Hoel, P. G., *Introduction to Mathematical Statistics*, Wiley, 1954.

[21] Holt, C. C., F. Modigliani, J. F. Muth and H. A. Simon, *Planning Production, Inventories, and Work Force*, Prentice-Hall, 1960.

[22] Howell, J. E. and D. Teichroew, *Mathematical Analysis for Business Decisions,* Irwin, 1963.
[23] Johnston, J., *Statistical Cost Analysis,* McGraw-Hill, 1960.
[24] Knight, F. H., *Risk, Uncertainty and Profit,* Houghton Mifflin, 1921; London School of Economics Reprints of Scarce Tracts in Economics, Series No. 16, 1933; Harper Torchbooks.
[25] Lewis, J. Parry, *An Introduction to Mathematics for Students of Economics,* Macmillan, London, 1962.
[26] Lewis, W. Arthur, *Overhead Costs,* Allen & Unwin, 1949.
[27] Luce, R. D. and H. Raiffa, *Games and Decisions,* Wiley, 1967.
[28] Marschak, J., Towards an economic theory of organization and information, in *Decision Processes,* eds. Thrall, Coombs and Davis, Wiley, 1954.
[29] Modigliani, F. and F. E. Hohn, Production planning over time and the nature of the expectation and planning horizon, *Econometrica,* 1955, pp. 46–66, reprinted in *Readings in Management Decision,* ed. L. R. Amey, Longman 1973.
[30] Saaty, T. L., Approximation to the value of the objective function in linear programming by the method of partitions, *Operations Research,* 1956, pp. 352–53.
[31] Schlaifer, R., *Probability and Statistics for Business Decisions,* McGraw-Hill, 1959.
[32] Shubik, M., Objective functions and models of corporate optimization, *Quarterly Journal of Economics,* 1961, pp. 345–75.
[33] Simon, H. A., *Models of Man,* Wiley, 1957.
[34] Simon, H. A., *The New Science of Management Decision,* Harper & Row, 1960.
[35] Simon, H. A., The logic of rational decision, *The British Journal for the Philosophy of Science,* 1965, pp. 169–86.
[36] Simon, H. A., On the concept of organizational goal, *Administrative Science Quarterly,* 1964–5, pp. 1–22, reprinted in *Readings in Management Decision,* ed. L. R. Amey, Longman 1973.
[37] Stigler, G. J., *Theory of Price,* Macmillan, New York, 1952.
[38] Vickers, D., *The Theory of the Firm: Production, Capital and Finance,* McGraw-Hill, 1968.

Problems

6.1 The firm which does not pay its fixed interest charges in a slump, and lets its price fall to a level at which those interest charges are not covered, is merely recognizing the distinction between economic costs and fixed costs. Elaborate.

6.2 Discuss the problems of obtaining data for a practical application of any of the linear programming models referred to in this book. Consider also the costs of obtaining the data.

6.3 Two shares have been analysed as to immediate and long-term growth and anticipated dividend rates. The results of the analysis show:

	Share A	*Share B*
Anticipated growth in market value next year per £ invested	£0·03	£0·15
Anticipated growth in market value in next 10 years per £ invested	£2·50	£1·00
Anticipated dividend rate	2·5%	4%

What minimum investment must be made in these two shares to achieve the investment goals of (1) at least £300 appreciation in value next year, (2) at least £10 000 appreciation in value in 10 years, and (3) at least £200 yearly income? Is it possible to achieve these goals *exactly* by investing in only these two shares? Discuss.

6.4 Hogg Ltd., has multiple goals. Indicate in each of the cases below whether these are mutually consistent:

1. The goals are maximization of profits and sales revenue. The firm's revenue function is $R = 100q - 4q^2$ and its cost function $C = 50 + 20q$ (both stated in £000's).

2. The goal is to maximize sales revenue subject to a lower limit on profits of £300 000. In this case, however, in addition to production costs as represented by function C above, there are also advertising costs, represented by the function $S = 0.02R$.

3. The revenue function is as in (1); costs comprise production and selling costs, as in (2). The firm seeks to maximize profits and maintain a market share of 25 per cent (measured in terms of sales volume). Sales of the industry in the period in question are expected to be 50 units.

6.5 J. Ltd., long distance road hauliers with headquarters at A, runs a fleet of 10 trucks. Operating costs are based on the vehicle-mile (vm) as unit (cost per vm = cost/distance travelled). Charges for services are normally based on the 'commercial ton-mile' (ctm = $\frac{1}{2}$ × tons loaded at start of journey × miles travelled on return trip). Where return loads can be arranged beforehand, however, single loads are accepted on an ordinary ton-mile (tm) basis (tm = tons loaded × miles travelled).

The following is a representative operating statement for the company:

4 weeks ended . . . . .
Vehicle-miles run . . . 60 000 . . .
Commercial ton-miles carried . . . 360 000 . . .

	£	per vm (pence)
Fuel	3 000	5·00
Oil	144	0·24
Tyres	360	0·60
Drivers' wages	3 600	6·00
Licences	240	0·40
Insurance	120	0·20
Depreciation	720	1·20
Maintenance and repairs	1 896	3·16
Garage expenses	180	0·30
Administration expenses	540	0·90
Total costs	10 800	18·00
Traffic receipts	11 700	19·50
Surplus	900	1·50

	per ctm (pence)
Total costs	3·00
Traffic receipts	3·25
Surplus	0·25

During a month of normal activity when eight of its trucks are already fully booked the firm is faced with the following possibilities of employing the other two:

1. Transport 20 tons of cement from A to B (2 000 miles), requiring two trucks, at a rate of 3·6 pence per ctm. Another client in C, 250 miles beyond B on the same route, also wants 20 tons of cement picked up from A on the same date. Hearing of the enquiry from B, and that J. Ltd. is unable to accept both jobs, this client offers to pay £240 more than the price agreed upon for the haul to B. Going on to C would, however, mean missing other employment for two trucks when they return to A – namely a journey of 200 miles to D, 10 tons each truck, at 3·9 pence per tm. It is unlikely that return loads can be secured for either of the trucks from B, C or D.

2. Do a round trip with one truck, consisting of two single loads, A to E (10 tons) and E to A (8 tons), a total journey of 2 500 miles. The second truck would be left idle. Each of these jobs can be secured at a rate of 2·4 pence per tm.

3. Hire an additional truck. One similar to those in the firm's own fleet as regards capacity and cost of operation can be hired for £144 per month. It cannot be hired for any shorter period. Under this arrangement the hirer would bear the cost of fuel, oil, tyres and the driver's wages; all other costs would be borne by the owner of the vehicle.

Assuming that:

1. Depreciation is entirely a fixed cost
2. Maintenance and repair expenditure varies proportionally with mileage
3. Use of each of the firm's trucks gives rise to identical costs
4. There is no possibility of hiring more than one truck

what work should the firm take on?

6.6 'It is better to find a near-optimal solution for a real problem using a heuristic method than an optimal solution for an unreal problem.' Comment.

6.7 'Marginal cost is not the only real social cost, and indivisible cost is not necessarily fixed.' Nor is the unit of product necessarily 'the unit on which the calculation of economic cost must be based'. Comment on these three statements in relation to rail passenger transport pricing policy.

7

What to produce: product decisions

What one knows, it is sometimes useful to forget.
                        – LATIN PROVERB

7.1 Economic theory

In Chapters 6–8 and 10 we discuss, against an economic background, the main
production decisions of the firm, viz. how to produce, what to produce, how much
to produce/what price to fix. In the orthodox (marginal analysis) theory of the firm
these sets of decisions are solved simultaneously. This involves assuming that the
problem of how to produce has already been solved outside the model; technique
of production is treated as given. In practice this problem of determining the firm's
production function is often a difficult one which cannot be taken for granted but
which must be solved before what to produce and how much to produce can be
determined.

The firm will seek to produce and sell that combination of products which will
maximize its objective. For the sake of uniformity we will continue to assume this
objective to be maximum profits. As we saw in Chapter 6, this implies some time
horizon. At times it may be more profitable, over the horizon, not to produce in
order to be in a position to take on more profitable work later. Within the production decision period the two main problems facing the firm are what to produce and
whether it is getting sufficient work to cover its overhead (and total) expenses over
the period. Pursuit of this objective may mean selling some products at variable
cost in the short-run (see Chapter 10); and more generally it may pay to produce
and sell some products at a loss so long as this is more than offset by the profit
earned on other lines.

In perfectly competitive markets the question of what to produce is determined
by the price system. By means of prices – the strength of their demand at a given
price – consumers are continually indicating the usefulness to them of various
commodities (inputs, factors of production) being employed in particular uses. A
price change is the signal for a movement of resources between different uses. In the
markets for commodities the cost to firms of securing various commodities, in
particular the marginal cost, will likewise reflect consumers' judgement of the value
of their alternative uses.* An equilibrium system of prices and production emerges
after a trial-and-error process has run its course,† and the firm attains its objective

---

* This is subject to the qualification in section 3 of Chapter 5 concerning interdependent markets.
    † Advanced economics students will realize that there are still problems concerning the uniqueness of
competitive equilibrium.

by producing any given output at minimum unit cost,* 'cost' meaning opportunity cost as defined in the previous chapter. Even in perfect competition there is uncertainty concerning the future. This makes it worth while for the firm to form anticipations about some aspects of the future, e.g. via market surveys, general economic forecasting and technological research. Such surveys give the competitive firm an informational advantage in the short-run. A further consideration is that unit costs may be reduced by production smoothing, i.e. ensuring a reasonably steady rate of production. For these and other reasons (e.g. the heavy capital intensity of many productive processes, weather in the case of crops) most production is in anticipation of demand, not in response to it. It is more correct to say, therefore, that in perfect competition consumers *ultimately* decide what shall be produced.

Imperfect markets introduce several new factors, the most notable of which is that the firm now has some control over the prices it charges; it can follow an independent price policy (including policies of price stability and following a competitor's prices). In the real world most markets are imperfect and hence most prices are 'administered' prices. Marginal revenue rather than price now determines what shall be produced and, since MR < P, the imperfectly competitive firm restricts output to maximize profits. The firm's costs are similarly affected by restriction of output in commodity markets. In these circumstances several new avenues of competition are opened. Price tends to decline in importance and non-price competition to come to the fore. Whereas the perfectly competitive firm could compete only by reducing costs and gaining an informational advantage concerning its future operations,† its imperfectly competitive counterpart can also compete via selling costs (in particular advertising, which we discuss in Chapter 9), product improvement, after-sales service, and by being better informed about its *current* position than its competitors.

Other influences on what the firm produces also flow from a relaxation of the conditions of perfect competition. Products need no longer be homogeneous; the firm may differentiate its product from those of its competitors by branding, advertising and so on. The behaviour of competitors (imperfect competition), and possibly their reactions to the behaviour of the firm in question (oligopoly) must be taken into account. This includes potential competitors. What the firm produces may also be influenced by the fact that it no longer has perfect information about its *current* position (current commodity and product prices for various rates of production, prices in other markets, and information on the existing state of technology). In the widely prevailing circumstances of administered prices, product

* Except when there are increasing returns to scale which are not offset by (nontechnological) diseconomies of scale – [5], pp. 88–89.
† The latter point is subsumed in the phrase 'more efficient management'.

differentiation, and large-scale expenditures on advertising, the firm itself has a very large say in what it produces, even in the long-run.

7.2 Product mix

Most real-life firms produce more than one product in imperfectly competitive input and product markets; in the language of economic theory they are multiproduct, multifactor firms. The reasons for this are numerous, and frequently a firm will have more than one reason. Multiproduct operation may lead to a fuller and/or less fluctuating use of resources (one of the reasons why firms diversify). It may assist a firm in overcoming indivisibilities in its inputs. It may make the firm less vulnerable to adverse factors affecting its products, whether in the form of declining demand (market narrowing) or increased competition (falling market share). It may also lead to economies of scale – which may sound rather paradoxical at first. However, economies of scale apply to *all* functions within a business – to finance, marketing and management as well as to production. Higher unit production costs through increased variety may be more than offset by lower costs in these other functions. A policy of carrying a 'full line', for example, often significantly reduces marketing costs. Of course it is not even certain that production costs will rise as a result of offering greater variety, as the latter could be accompanied by increased volume and longer production runs.

(a) Marginal analysis of multiproduct firm

In deciding what to produce only the costs which could be avoided (and any revenues that would be lost) if the item is not produced are relevant. In simultaneously determining what and how much to produce this avoidable cost, measured at the margin (= marginal cost) is equated with marginal revenue. Which costs are avoidable will partly depend on the estimated 'life' of the product, which we discuss in the next section. The simultaneous determination of production rates for various products by the conventional marginal analysis is outlined in Chapter 9. The only problems that arise in this analysis are when costs and/or demands are related. Then it is no longer true, as when costs/demands are independent, that profits are maximized by equating MR and MC for each product. Marginal costs/marginal revenues must first be adjusted to take account of the interdependence.

To illustrate, suppose a firm produces two products, X_1 and X_2, whose costs and demands are both interrelated. Quantities produced are denoted by x_1 and x_2 and prices by p_1 and p_2, respectively. Total revenue is $R = p_1 x_1 + p_2 x_2$. But the marginal revenues are

$$\frac{\partial R}{\partial x_1} = p_1 + x_1 \frac{\partial p_1}{\partial x_1} + x_2 \frac{\partial p_2}{\partial x_1};$$

$$\frac{\partial R}{\partial x_2} = p_2 + x_2 \frac{\partial p_2}{\partial x_2} + x_1 \frac{\partial p_1}{\partial x_2}.$$

The first two terms on the right-hand side represent the change in R resulting from sale of an additional unit of the product concerned. The third term on the right-hand side, the cross marginal revenue, which measures the change in revenue from one product when an additional unit of the other is sold, will be positive if the products are complements and negative if they are substitutes. Similarly in the case of interrelated costs:* the cost equation is $C = c_1 x_1 + c_2 x_2 + k$, where k represents fixed costs. Marginal costs are

$$\frac{\partial C}{\partial x_1} = c_1 + x_1 \frac{\partial c_1}{\partial x_1} + x_2 \frac{\partial c_2}{\partial x_1};$$

$$\frac{\partial C}{\partial x_2} = c_2 + x_2 \frac{\partial c_2}{\partial x_2} + x_1 \frac{\partial c_1}{\partial x_2},$$

the last term on the right in each case indicating the effect of a change in the output of one product on the marginal cost of the other. This term will be positive if the products are competitive, negative if they are complementary.† It is these corrected marginal costs and revenues which must be equated in determining what and how much to produce.

In practice firms very often do not take account of these interdependencies.‡ A further problem arises as a result of the costing procedure and price-fixing rules commonly employed. If product costs include allocated overheads they will depend on the basis of allocation of *common costs* (expenses common to a number of products). Since these allocations are more or less arbitrary, if these costs are used as a *basis* for price-fixing a considerable 'blurring of the market' may result. Firms often judge the profitability of products, and whether to produce or discontinue producing them (see section 3 below), on the evidence of such irrelevant information. As a result these decisions are often reached upon arbitrary grounds within the firm, and the market may exercise little influence. An even grosser mismanagement can occur if firms *deliberately* allocate the common costs dispro-

---

*So long as the products may be produced in variable proportions.

† Cf. Stigler [9], pp. 314–20 in 1947 edn., pp. 129–32 in 1952 edn. The solution may be illustrated geometrically either by means of a three-dimensional figure (cf. Stigler, 1952) or by sets of indifference curves (constant outlay and constant revenue curves, cf. Stigler, 1947) which are horizontal sections through a three-dimensional surface.

‡ Firms tend to consider demand interdependence, if at all, only as it is evidenced *outside* the firm (i.e. the interaction between its own and rival products), or occasionally between the products of different divisions.

portionately between products, giving those which face the keenest competition a lighter share. This practice was commented on in some of the Board of Trade Working Party Reports in Britain.* As a result of either of these practices firms may continue to produce some products in which they are relatively inefficient, and instances of this are not hard to find.

Multiple products are usually distinguished from 'joint products' in the economic literature as follows:

Multiple products: If each of a number of products is manufactured from different raw materials but all products share the same plant facilities.

Joint products:† If, on the other hand, a common raw material is converted into a number of products it is not possible to associate material or even labour costs directly with particular products; the problem of relating the common material and labour costs to the different products is superimposed on the overhead cost problem. *All* costs are common; variable material and labour costs as well as variable manufacturing overheads become indirect costs in relation to the products manufactured. The multiple products are described in this case as joint products, and the common costs associated with their production are called *joint costs*.

(b) An illogical cost accounting rule

A curiously illogical rule for deciding what to produce when the availability of one input is limited appears to be widely used by cost accountants in Britain. Known as the 'limiting factor' rule, it is stated in a professional publication [4] as follows:

1. Variable costs and marginal costs are equivalent for practical purposes [para. 313].
2. For decision-making purposes, 'contribution' (= selling price minus variable cost) is the appropriate measure of profitability [para. 32].
3. If there is some obstacle in the way of achieving the maximum possible contribution (such as a scarcity of materials [para. 433] or when sales orders exceed capacity to produce [para. 52]) the final decision should be based on the course yielding the maximum contribution *per unit of the limiting factor* of output [paras. 54, 433 and App. A].

In other words in deciding whether to use certain inputs to produce $A, B, C, \ldots$ one should calculate their respective contributions per unit of the factor which limits production, i.e. the ratio

$$\left(\frac{\text{fixed overheads} + \text{net profit}}{\text{limiting factor}} \right)$$

---

* Cf., e.g., the Report of the Working Party on Hosiery.
† These are further discussed in Chapters 8 and 9.

and select the one for which this ratio is a maximum. The limiting factor may refer to any input, e.g. labour-time, machine-time, cash, or the market demand for the products.*

The trouble with these rules, as pointed out elsewhere,† is that they put the cart before the horse. More specifically, they fail to distinguish between inputs which are *available* only in limited quantities (= constraints) and that subset of these which are actually *used to the limit* in the process of maximizing contribution (= binding constraints). The 'limiting factor', in other words, cannot in general be known *a priori*, but only after optimizing, i.e. only after the production schedule which maximizes the firm's objective function (here expressed in terms of contribution) has been determined. If more than one input is in limited supply simultaneously these rules obviously cannot be applied. The important thing is what limits the value of the objective function, not what limits production. Correct solution of the problem will now be demonstrated by means of linear programming for the case where there are several constraints.

Example

Rho Ltd. produces and sells two products, X_1 and X_2, which yield unit contributions of £40 and £30, respectively. The products each pass through three manufacturing operations, which have capacity limitations of 800, 1 000 and 400 hours, respectively. Other data are as follows:

	X_1	X_2
Per unit:	*(£'s)*	
selling price	90	70
variable cost	50	40
contribution	40	30
Plant requirements (in hours) per unit of product:	*(hours)*	
Operation I	20	10
Operation II	20	20
Operation III	5	4

---

*A variation on the same theme will be found in [8], where instead of ranking the above ratio the criterion is given as equating the ratios

$$\frac{\text{contribution } j}{\text{limiting factor } j} \quad (j = 1, 2, \ldots, n)$$

for all products at the margin.

† Cf. [7] and [1].

‡ Assuming, as elsewhere in this book, that the objective function and constraints are linear functions.

If there is only one constraint the I.C.W.A. rule gives the correct solution only if this constraint is binding.

The problem is formulated algebraically and solved geometrically below:*

$$\text{maximize } z = 40x_1 + 30x_2$$

subject to:

$$(1) \quad 20x_1 + 10x_2 \leq 800$$

$$(2) \quad 20x_1 + 20x_2 \leq 1,000$$

$$(3) \quad 5x_1 + 4x_2 \leq 400$$

$$x_1, x_2 \geq 0$$

Optimal solution: produce 30 units of X_1 and 20 units of X_2 (point B in Figure 7); maximum contribution £1 800.

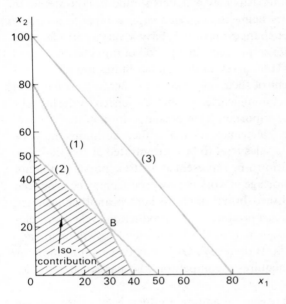

A further reason why the 'limiting factor' rule, apart from its illogicality, might yield misleading solutions occurs if indivisibilities are present, in inputs or in products. As regards inputs, a particular machine may only be available in units the smallest of which is large relative to a unit change in output. There may also be indivisibilities in input utilization as well as intake: the firm may have to work in complete shifts or complete man-hours for various contractual or practical reasons. As regards products, it may be necessary to produce an entire batch or none at all. When indivisibilities are present a different optimal production plan will in general result than when all the relevant data are continuously divisible.

*Constraint (3) is clearly redundant.

In a practical situation there may well be a number of inputs whose supply is fixed for periods of time varying from one to another.

7.3 Changes in the product line

A decision to add new products may be influenced by a great variety of factors, only some of which will be mentioned. Thus the firm may realize the advantages, in the form of lower unit marketing costs, of offering a 'full line'. Increased choice is also often considered to be a benefit to the customer, for which he is prepared to pay. The new items may be related in use to existing products. The firm's information system (market and economic surveys in this case) may uncover various reasons, e.g. changing tastes, market widening, why new products should be considered. In some industries, the fashion trades being the extreme case, competition largely takes the form of frequent product changes; products have a very short life cycle. This tends to be true for other kinds of products in a period of rapid technological advance. Thus a recent McGraw-Hill survey in the United States found that US manufacturers expected 17 per cent of their sales two years hence to come from products not yet on the market. Technological leadership, evidenced by the launching of radically new products, is an important form of competition in the 'science-based' industries (e.g. electronics, pharmaceuticals). Other additions may be related to price: for many products sales tend to be concentrated at certain 'price points' and it is important for a firm to be represented at these points if it is not already. Further reasons include shortage of work (a new product may be produced temporarily), the use of an established brand name to launch another product, production smoothing by addition of a product whose production cycle is complementary to that of existing products, increasing the firm's rate of growth or spreading risks (two of the reasons why firms diversify). Or it may come about more or less fortuitously, as when a firm acquires a competitor who has some activities outside of its main activity.*

In all cases, it would appear, the reason for adding products is either to increase (or maintain) profits or reduce risk; conversely, products are dropped when they are losing money (or earning insufficient return) or because risks are incommensurate with rewards. The *method* by which products are added (using excess capacity in one or more functions, buying new facilities, or acquiring a firm already producing the product) may have an effect on competition, and hence on the result. In terms of our classification in Chapter 5, a new product decision may be the end result of tactical planning or it may be strategic (as, for instance, when it results from diversification, or involves very large expenditure or uncertainty, e.g. the decision of an aircraft manufacturer to build an SST). This draws attention to the fact that the introduction of a new product may involve investment by the firm. If this is the

* Cf. [3], pp. 127–37.

case there is a prior decision: the investment must be justified in competition with the other investment opportunities available to the firm at the time, and at the firm's cost of capital. We examine this topic in Chapters 11 and 12.

There is a good deal of desultory discussion in the managerial economics and accounting literature on the question of when to add and discontinue products. It is worth quoting from one such source, as it illustrates the conceptual confusion. Dean [3], apparently arguing by analogy with expansion and contraction (changes in *scale* of production), seems to think that the cases of adding and dropping products are asymmetric.* As we shall demonstrate, the analogy only partly holds.

According to Dean, profitability should be the criterion, but 'profit' should be measured differently in the two cases:†

> The relevant concept is incremental profits over the probable life cycle of the candidate product. Some standard of adequate incremental return is needed for this profitability test. Ideally it should be market cost of new capital, with allowance for special risks. Sometimes the standard is average past returns, maximum alternative return, or some arbitrary profits goal. . . .
> The problem of deciding on what products to drop is the converse of the problem of adding products, except that long-run cost functions are not reversible and specialized capital [goods] is not perfectly mobile.

However, he qualifies the first part of this statement as follows:‡

> The adoption of a new product carries with it explicitly or tacitly the commitment to stay with the new venture at least until it has had a fair trial, and possibly longer. Additions to existing costs that are often unforeseen at the time of [its] introduction are likely to occur, so that the business man's rule-of-thumb of loading on the new product its full share of common overhead cost is often the most appropriate method after all.

The two cases, therefore, are asymmetric: in deciding whether to add products, overheads costs should be included, but not in deciding to discontinue products.

Dean's conclusion arises from introducing investment considerations into a production decision.§ He assumes for the most part that product additions will require capital investment (and product deletions disinvestment). This may or may not be the case; but it pinpoints the problem. The real dichotomy is not between adding and dropping, but between additions requiring and not requiring investment, and between deletions involving and not involving disinvestment. The position may be summarized as follows:

(a) Adding products

(i)

If this involves new investment, the first step is investment analysis, i.e. investment

---

*pp. 120–23 (adding), 133–37 (discontinuing).
†p. 138.
‡pp. 122–23 and p. 264.
§Cf. the second and third sentences and p. 122 in the immediately previous footnote reference.

in the new facilities must be assessed, in competition with other investment opportunities available to the firm at the time, against the firm's opportunity cost of money capital. This calculation requires estimation of the cash flows (cash costs and receipts) over the whole estimated life of the investment. If the project is justified on this criterion it is worth producing the new product; the only remaining question is 'how much?' Investment and production are distinct, though related, and the market cost of capital or alternative return on investment to which Dean refers have no place in production decisions. The production decision (how much of the new product to produce) is handled by the multiproduct analysis discussed earlier. Clearly it is desirable that the volume estimate embodied in the investment calculation should closely approximate to that obtained from the production calculation (this can be achieved by making a tentative production calculation first),* and that both should reasonably mirror reality, though this is difficult to achieve in the case of a radically new product of highly uncertain lifespan.

(ii)

If investment is not involved the usual multiproduct production analysis is all that is required, providing any interdependencies between the new and old products are taken into account. If the resources which would be used to produce the new product would otherwise be idle, their opportunity cost is zero, and the product is worth adding if it contributes any profit at all.

(iii) *Specification of costs*

Case (i): Suppose introduction of the new product requires investment expenditure of C_1 in the first year and increased cash operating expenses of $c_j \Delta q_j$ each year ($j = 1, 2, \ldots, T$), where Δq_j is the increase in output as a result of the investment and c_j is unit operating cost. The present value of this expenditure is

$$V_0 = \frac{C_1}{(1+i)} + \sum_{j=1}^{T} \frac{c_j \Delta q_j}{(1+i)^j}$$

where i is the firm's cost of capital.† There exists a value of x, the additional unit cost of production each year (here assumed constant from year to year), for which

$$x \sum_j [\Delta q_j/(1+i)^j] = V_0$$

x, the cost of expansion, approximates to the economist's long-run marginal cost.‡

* What and how much to produce are of course normally determined simultaneously; costs are meaningless except when related to rates of output, and price for the imperfectly competitive firm depends upon volume of sales – each of which calls for marginal determination in relation to the firm's other products.

† Discussed in Chapters 11–12 and particularly in Chapter 20. i is here assumed constant over time.

‡ The calculation assumes the price of the product and operating costs remain fixed over time.

Since the investment decision involves a whole-life calculation, the costs that vary include all costs relating to the investment, including some (represented by the annual equivalent of C_1) which are fixed once the decision to invest is taken. That is the investment decision, involving as it does a non-marginal adjustment, requires us to look at total conditions – total cost and total revenue for the firm as a whole are affected by the decision. The cash flows in the investment calculation will be adjusted for consequential changes in the cash flows of the firm's existing activities as a result of the investment. In the production analysis, on the other hand, we are concerned with marginal equalities and constrained production (limitations on some inputs, notably plant, in the short-run). Overhead costs which are invariant with output during this period (the capital cost component of x) are irrelevant in this analysis.

Case (ii): The production analysis for the multiproduct firm suffices, and the considerations mentioned immediately above apply.

(b) Dropping products

(i)

If this involves disinvestment total conditions apply, as in (a)(i). This is an abandonment decision. Supposing there are only two alternatives – to discontinue the product and disinvest now or at the end of the useful life of the investment. The condition for disinvesting now, here shown in terms of present values, is given by

$$C - C_N (1 + i)^{-N} - \sum_{j=1}^{N} \{(1+i)^{-j} (d_j \, \Delta q_j - f_j)\} > 0,$$

where Δq = the annual production of the product which may be dropped,

$d_j = (r_j - c_j)$ denotes per unit cash receipts less cash operating expenses in year j,

f_j = separable fixed costs as a result of dropping production of Δq_j (these are defined in Chapter 6),

C = the capital disinvested when Δq_j is dropped (scrap value of fixed assets plus working capital no longer required),

N = the remaining economic life of the investment, and

the other symbols and assumptions are the same as before.

When this calculation has been made that is the end of the matter in case (i). A numerical example of an abandonment decision is given in the questions at the end of Chapter 11.

(ii)

If no investment is involved the production analysis suffices, with slight modification, though an incremental analysis confined to the product in question will give the same result.

(iii) *Data specification*

In case (i), d_j is to be understood as including any consequential changes in receipts and expenses of other products. In case (ii) the production analysis must be modified if there are any separable fixed costs as a result of dropping the product. Denoting total profits of the firm by π, instead of the condition

$$\pi_{q(1-\Delta)} - \pi_q > 0$$

where the π's are determined by ordinary multiproduct analysis, we must now substitute

$$\pi_{q(1-\Delta)} - \pi_q > f_{\Delta q},$$

where $f_{\Delta q}$ stands for the separable fixed costs. Alternatively, and more straightforwardly, case (ii) could be decided by an incremental analysis over the estimated remaining life of the product, in terms of either present values or equivalent annuities. If the resources which would be released by dropping a product are entirely specific (i.e. have no alternative use) and, in case (i), have no resale value, the opportunity cost which can be avoided is obviously zero.

Dean is therefore right about the two decisions being asymmetric, but for the wrong reasons. And where no change in investment is involved the only difference between the two cases comes about if any fixed costs are avoidable by discontinuing production of a particular product. Apart from this, any costs which are fixed over the period of the production decision are irrelevant in all cases except the investment calculation. All costs referred to in this section are to be understood as being opportunity costs; that is, wherever use of any of the resources involved in the decisions would not result in a paid-out cost its implicit opportunity cost must be included in the calculation. On the practical side, adding products may involve difficult problems of estimation (of revenues, costs and the product's life cycle).* And as Dean observes, before dropping a product which has not become obsolete the firm may often consider ways of salvaging it, by cost reduction, price change or quality change.

The suggestion is sometimes heard† that products should be added or dropped according to whether they are earning a satisfactory *rate* of return on investment, usually calculated on the 'book' value of the assets employed. This suggestion, which implies an objective other than profit maximization would, among other things, require allocation of capital among products, a practical impossibility in most cases.

---

* In addition, failure to take account of the 'learning effect', i.e. the reduction in costs which results as experience is gained in making a new product (or performing a new process), has had unfortunate effects in some cases, e.g. government contract work by private firms, where prices were fixed on a 'cost-plus' basis. For a discussion of the application of learning theory to cost estimating see [2], pp. 342–44.
† Cf. [2], pp. 383–84.

7.4 Intermediate product decisions

By 'intermediate products' we shall mean products purchased or produced to be processed further, not for final use. Three decisions concerning intermediate goods will be examined.

(a) Sell or process further

This case concerns products at various stages of production, including the raw materials stage. The chief interest attaching to this case is (i) to show the importance of opportunity costs in all decision situations and (ii) to affirm the statement in Chapter 6 that it is never necessary to impute opportunity costs so long as all alternatives are considered and their avoidable costs compared. A simple numerical example will be sufficient to demonstrate this.

Example

Suppose a textile manufacturer makes yarn (product A) which is then woven into cloth (B), but which can also be sold without further processing. 1 000 lb of A are produced annually at a cost of £400. This can be sold to the trade for £500, or alternatively, by incurring £200 further conversion costs it can be woven into 1 000 lb of cloth (for simplicity we will assume there is no wastage), which will sell for £800. Should the firm sell or process the yarn?

In terms, first, of additional costs and receipts (ΔC and ΔR, respectively):

		Sell	Process further (£'s)	$\Delta R, \Delta C$
Receipts:	A	500	—	
	B	—	800	+300
less Costs:	A	400	400	
	B	—	200	+200
Profit		100	200	+100

(> 0, ∴ process further)

Alternatively, imputing opportunity costs:

			Process further (£'s)
Receipts:	A	—	
	B	800	
less Costs:			
yarn production cost		400	
revenue foregone by not selling A		100	
weaving production cost		200	700
Profit			100 (> 0, ∴ process further)

Whichever way the calculation is presented, further processing should not be undertaken unless it yields more than avoidable costs plus implicit opportunity costs (here the revenue foregone by not selling the intermediate product).

There are two provisos. The first is that (R_B – the full opportunity cost of producing B) > 0 is only a necessary condition for further processing *unless* the facilities used in producing B have no alternative use. If they have alternative uses (say C) the full opportunity cost involved in producing B must be redefined. The sufficient condition for processing further is the necessary condition after this cost has been adjusted [6]:

$$R_B - (\text{production cost } B + \text{opportunity cost of not selling } A$$
$$+ \text{ opportunity cost of not producing } C) > 0.$$

The second point concerns the firm's decision horizon. As stated earlier, the choice between selling or further processing may present itself at any stage of the production process, including the very beginning (raw materials). Does it follow that the firm should resell its raw materials inventory if the price of these materials has risen substantially, even though it knows they must be replaced? This draws attention to the importance of expectations and to the dangers of year-by-year optimization. Dynamic decision models allow for such considerations.

(b) Make or buy

The second case concerns the decision to make an intermediate product at present bought from outside the firm, what the economist calls 'backward integration'. It has been authoritatively claimed in the cost accounting literature [4] that when faced with this choice it will be profitable for the firm to make if the variable cost of so doing is below the outside purchase price. Some observations on this assertion are listed below:

(i)
A reduction in cost will almost always be a *necessary*, but not a sufficient, condition for making rather than buying.

1. It may not even be a necessary condition, for it is possible that making may be profitable, not because it reduces costs, but because it increases the revenue of the firm more than it increases costs. In all decision problems we need to consider how the decision will affect both revenues and costs (positive and negative cash flows) in the firm as a whole.
2. The relevant cost reductions stemming from backward integration can be divided into two categories: those relating to the price that must be paid for outside supplies, and those relating to the efficiency with which production of

existing products can be organized. In the second category come all the problems of obtaining supplies of the required kind, of adequate quality and in sufficient amount at the required times. These problems may be particularly important when the final product must conform to rigid specifications, or in rapidly growing industries where different 'stages' of the industry do not expand simultaneously; where there are close technological links between the various stages of production; where suppliers are able to exert monopolistic pressure on the firm, or where there are periodic difficulties in obtaining supplies due to severe supply or demand fluctuations.

(ii)

Even though the firm may be able to produce more cheaply than it can buy, deployment of the resources to making the component may be less profitable than some alternative way of using them. Before committing resources to making the component the firm must ensure that more profitable uses do not exist (unless the resources would otherwise remain idle, in which case they are costless). The *sufficient* condition for making is that it should increase the profits of the firm as a whole more than buying, and more than any alternative use of the resources. There may, however, be a number of other factors to take into account, some of which (e.g. uncertainty) are difficult to quantify. Some of these are discussed below. Making may or may not involve investment. If it involves investment it must be shown to be worth undertaking in competition with other available investment opportunities at the firm's cost of capital (sufficient condition). The necessary condition in this case is that either

1. the discounted cost of the investment (comprising capital outlays, variable operating expenses excluding interest and depreciation), reduced to a constant annual cost over the life of the investment (i.e. constant annual variable cost + capital cost) is less than the annual cost of buying the component,* or
2. profits of the firm increase as a result of making more than the costs enumerated in 1.†

(iii)

Evidence based on a large sample of firms who thought they could achieve decisive cost reductions by making suggests that most were deluding themselves, sometimes seriously [10].

(iv)

Care is needed to ensure that the costs of making and buying are comparable, e.g.

---

*The situation is analogous to asset replacement, discussed in Chapter 12.
† There is a tendency for firms to regard 'make or buy' decisions as a class apart from other investment decisions. Of course they are not.

refer to the same quantity and quality of output, in the same time period; that the costs of making cover all the functions which are undertaken by the supplier (such as research for product improvement), that the outside price is reliable, that the many intangible factors which may be present are accurately quantified (these tend either to be ignored or to be given undue emphasis), and that costs which will become variable as the firm expands its operations are not regarded as fixed costs.

(v)

In particular, estimates of manufacturing labour costs may prove to be seriously wrong, and need special attention. In contrast to the typical management attitude 'we can do better than they can', costs usually vary considerably between suppliers, and a firm which decides to make will seldom do better initially than the least efficient firm specializing in that particular business.

(vi)

It is frequently assumed that by freeing itself from dependence upon suppliers the firm will be assured of a reliable supply, whereas unsatisfactory performance by suppliers may reflect adverse conditions in the industries upon which they in turn depend that will affect any firm producing that product.

(vii)

Firms often disregard the costs that might arise if a decision to make has subsequently to be reversed. 'Make or buy' decisions are reversible with changing conditions, not once-for-all, and should be continuously reviewed. In other words we are really concerned with *two* decisions, not one: 'make or buy', and 'buy or make'.

(viii)

If undertaken by large firms, either of these two decisions may be self-limiting:

1. Making may lead to excess capacity and price cutting in the supplier industry; other firms may be induced to buy rather than make, possibly offsetting the effects of the initial move.
2. Buying may have the converse effect, with pressure on existing capacity of supplying firms, causing them to raise prices in the short-run.

(ix)

Making undertaken via acquisition of an existing business often tends to exaggerate the effects of a change of management.

(x)

There are strong pressures within many businesses leading them to make things they would have been better advised to buy. The greater flexibility offered by buying if demand in the firm's product markets 'turns sour' is also frequently not considered (e.g. specialist Lancashire cotton firms weathered the Great Depression better than integrated firms).

(xi)

The decision may also be influenced by the competitive position in the supplier industry: are the firm's suppliers competitive and efficient; are they so few or so large as to be able to achieve economies of scale; could the firm itself produce on a sufficient scale to achieve these economies; how would a decision to make affect the terms on which the firm could buy other things (if indeed it does) from the suppliers concerned?

These are a few of the considerations which might influence the 'make or buy' decision. They show that this decision is rather more complex than the cost accountants' rule would suggest.

(c) The role of transfer prices

The final decision concerning intermediate goods concerns fixing the prices at which they are transferred within the firm. Quite frequently these internal transactions assume considerable proportions. It is therefore highly important that they are conducted in a way which is consistent with optimizing the firm's objective. The prices which govern these internal sales, as an element in production costs, may influence how much of a particular product is produced, through their effects on the level of operation of the activities concerned, and even what is produced. We hold this topic over until Chapter 9, where it is discussed together with external pricing.

Bibliographical references

[1] Amey, L. R., Mathematical programming in accounting – a comment, *The Accountant*, June 5, 1965, pp. 765–67 and June 12, 1965, p. 813.
[2] Anthony, R. N., *Management Accounting Principles*, Irwin, 1965.
[3] Dean, J., *Managerial Economics*, Prentice-Hall, 1951.
[4] Institute of Cost and Works Accountants, *A Report on Marginal Costing*, 1961.
[5] Lancaster, K., *Introduction to Modern Microeconomics*, Rand McNally, 1969.
[6] Mathews, R. L., *Accounting for Economists*, F. W. Cheshire, Melbourne, 1962.
[7] Samuels, J. M., Mathematical programming in accounting, *The Accountant*, Feb. 27, 1965, pp. 264–68.
[8] Solomons, D., Cost accounting and the use of space and equipment, in *Studies in Costing*, ed. D. Solomons, Sweet & Maxwell, 1952, pp. 277–91.
[9] Stigler, G. J., *The Theory of Price*, Macmillan, New York, 1947, 1952.
[10] *US Senate Hearings in Economic Concentration*, part 4, 1965 (which contains expert testimony by A. R. Oxenfeldt).

Problems

7.1 Undecided Ltd. has the possibility of producing two products, *A* and *B*, which are expected to yield unit contributions of £4, and £3, respectively, according to the following technology:

$$
\begin{array}{cc}
\text{Input 1} \\
\text{,, } 2 \\
\text{,, } 3 \\
\text{Product } A \\
\text{,, } B
\end{array}
\begin{bmatrix}
3 & 2 \\
6 & 8 \\
4 & 8 \\
1 & 0 \\
0 & 1
\end{bmatrix}
$$

(the rows of the above table show the quantities of outputs and inputs, the columns relate to processes).

The company has available only 300 units of input 1, 720 units of input 2 and 640 units of input 3.

What combination of the two products will maximize the total contribution?

7.2 Zeta Ltd. has excess capacity in three plants. It is considering using this excess capacity to produce a certain product in three sizes:

	Net profit per unit
Small	£9
Medium	£10·5
Large	£12

Maximum sales are estimated at 500, 800 and 600 units per day, respectively.

The spare capacities of the plants are 500, 600 and 300 units per day, respectively, regardless of the size of product manufactured. The space for work-in-progress, however, is limited to 8 000 square feet at plant 1, 7 000 at plant 2 and 3 500 at plant 3. Required storage space per unit per day for the three sizes of products is 12, 15 and 20 square feet, respectively.

The agreement with the trade union concerned requires that the proportion of excess capacity which is used for this product should be kept the same at each plant.

Formulate the above as a linear programming problem.

7.3 Firms *A*, *B* and *C* are interdependent in the following ways:

A's costs vary with both *B*'s and *C*'s output

B's costs vary with *C*'s output

C's costs vary with *A*'s output

A's revenue varies with *C*'s output

B's revenue varies with both *A*'s and *C*'s output.

Formulate a model showing how the profits of all three firms taken together may be maximized. Also examine any device (other than joint maximization) for internalizing these externalities.

7.4 Limfac Ltd. manufactures three different types of product, X_1, X_2 and X_3. Production of each product involves three processes, A, B and C in that sequence, each requiring a different kind of labour, viz. lathe operators (process A), milling machinists (B) and assemblers (C).

Production is continuous and the set-up time required in changing over machines from one product to another is negligible. Machine capacities for process A and B are sufficient to produce any amounts of X_1, X_2 and X_3 that may be demanded: process C is entirely manual. All types of labour, however, are in limited supply.

Details of man-hours required per unit of each product, total available man-hours per week, unit selling prices (constant) and variable costs are summarized in the table below.

Labour	Product			Available man-hrs. per week
	X_1	X_2	X_3	
A	1	4	2	2 400
B	2	2	2	1 800
C	3	1	0	2 100
Per unit:				
selling price	£9·975	£15·125	£8·25	
variable cost	£7·775	£11·125	£6·25	

Wage rates are £0·5 per hour for lathe operators, £0·625 for milling machinists and £0·375 for assemblers. Fixed costs, which include depreciation on the machinery, are expected to be £1 300 for the period.

Required:

(a) Formulate the above as a linear programming problem for determining the optimal product mix. Solve, using the simplex method. Comment on your solution.

(b) Formulate (but do not solve) the dual of the above problem, and hence give a formal statement of the condition for hiring at least one additional man-hour of any class of labour which, if available, would increase the total profits of the firm.

7.5 The engineering works of Metallicus Ltd. is divided into three cost centres, X, Y and Z, in each of which the capacity available during the period of six months now about to start is 1 000 hours. The fixed and variable overheads budgeted to be incurred in each cost centre during the coming half-year are:

Cost centre	Fixed	Variable
X	£250	£0·175 an hour
Y	£300	£0·125 an hour
Z	£875	£0·150 an hour

The overhead rates chargeable to work in each cost centre are fixed accordingly.

Two orders become available. One of them is for 2 500 articles of Type *A*, at a selling price of £1 each. The other is for 2 500 articles of Type *B*, also at a selling price of £1 each. Variable materials and labour costs will amount to £850 in each case. The use which the two orders make of the capacity in the works is, however, different, being as follows:

Order A	Order B
Use of capacity in cost centre:	Use of capacity in cost centre:
X 500 hours	X 1 000 hours
Y 200 hours	Y 300 hours
Z 1 000 hours	Z 500 hours

Required:

(a) Assuming that only one or other complete order can be accepted, which would you choose? Give your reasons.

(b) Suppose that any proportion of either order or of both orders can be accepted. How would you use the available capacity during the six months so as to maximize profit?

7.6 Psi Ltd., a manufacturer, is faced with the problem of whether to take an order. Its works are running at capacity when an order is received for 2 000 units of a certain product for which it can obtain a price of £1·75 per unit. Psi could sub-contract the work at a cost of £1·275 per unit. To do the work itself would require an immediate investment of £2 500 in new machinery; its variable production costs would be £1·15 per unit.

You are given the following additional information:

1. The new machinery would have an expected life of 8 years, at the end of which time its scrap value would be zero.
2. Psi calculates depreciation by the 'straight line' method.
3. The company can earn 5 per cent on any excess cash it has available.
4. Psi has been experiencing a mild expansion: output, at present running at an annual rate of 50 000 units, has been rising on the average at a rate of

5 per cent a year, and this trend is expected to continue in the foreseeable future. The company has been investing in additional plant capacity in step with this increase in output.

5. No change is anticipated in the price of new machines, technology or the cost of money.

Ignoring tax considerations, how should Psi decide? Show your calculations. How much would its variable production costs need to change from your calculation for Psi to become indifferent as between fulfilling the order itself and subcontracting?

8

How to produce: technique of production decisions

Such labour'd nothings, in so strange a style, Amaze th' unlearn'd, and make the learned smile.

– POPE, *Essay on Criticism*

8.1 The nature of the problem

By 'technique of production' is meant the methods used in the production and sale of a given product. At any time there will be a number of different techniques of production for any given product, and technical progress adds to the number over time. The firm tries to achieve any output it produces at minimum unit cost. This involves solving a technological problem – finding the combination of inputs which will yield the maximum output per unit of the combined inputs. The best (least-cost) technique at any given time is determined by adapting these technical production coefficients to the current set of relative input prices.

The relation between the technical problem (productivity) and the economic problem (unit costs) can be clearly seen from the following diagram, due to Farrell [7];

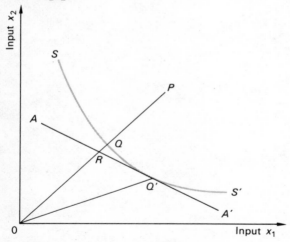

Figure 8.1 Technical and cost efficiency

Suppose a firm makes a single product with two inputs, x_1 and x_2. P represents the proportions of the two inputs per unit of output that the firm is observed to use. SS' is the isoquant (equiproduct curve) representing the various combinations of x_1 and x_2 that a technically perfectly efficient firm might use to produce this parti-

208

cular product (we assume that this information is known). The ray OP, representing the technique actually employed by firm P, cuts SS' in Q. This tells us that if the technically perfectly efficient firm Q used the same technique (input proportions) as firm P it would produce the same output with only OQ/OP as much of each input. OQ/OP measures the *technical efficiency* (or productivity) of firm P in relation to the efficient standard, represented by firm Q.

Line AA' is a price line with slope equal to the ratio of the input prices; it is tangent to SS' in Q'. Then Q' (and not R) is the optimum (least-cost) technique. We see this by noting that although Q and Q', in common with all other points on SS', represent maximum *technical* efficiency, costs at Q' are only OR/OQ of those at Q, given constant input prices. In terms of *costs*, firm P is only OR/OP as efficient as a perfectly efficient firm. Each ray from the origin represents a different technique of production. Farrell shows that the cost efficiency of firm P can be represented as the product of its productivity (OQ/OP) and what he calls its 'price efficiency' (OR/OQ), i.e. how suitably it adjusts its production methods to relative input prices. It is perhaps not necessary to add that a least-cost firm must be perfectly efficient technically, but the converse (that all technically efficient firms will be least-cost firms) is not true. Nor, of course, is it true in general that least-cost firms necessarily earn the highest profits.

We conclude this demonstration by noting that SS' is a boundary relation. Any point (such as P) above this line signifies lower productivity than any point on the line. SS' is what economists call the *production function*, or efficient production set. Operation anywhere on SS' implies that the technological part of the problem has already been solved optimally.

Thus the firm has to decide optimally upon input proportions, input quantities for its rate of output, and its rate of output. These are interdependent decisions, as as the diagram below shows, and must be solved simultaneously by a profit-maximizing firm.

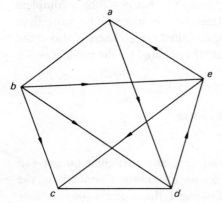

Figure 8.2 Interdependence of technique and rate of output

In the diagram a = input proportions, b = unit input prices, c = input quantities for rate of output e, d = unit costs. The directed lines mean that the symbol to which the arrow is pointing depends on the symbol (or symbols) behind the arrow(s), e.g. e depends on d, which in turn depends on a and b.

8.2 A many-sided problem

It used to be fairly common in some of the old professional costing textbooks to list the duties of the cost accountant as being (i) to check day-to-day operations of the business and pinpoint inefficiencies, (ii) to advise on the setting of product prices and (iii) to advise on questions of technique. The aspects of this last problem are extremely numerous. For example, sales seldom occur at a constant rate throughout the year. The goodwill of customers might depend significantly on the firm being able to meet incoming orders promptly. To meet fluctuations in demand a firm may either have some excess plant capacity or carry heavier stocks of finished goods, work overtime or multiple shifts, or subcontract some of its orders to cover peaks in demand. Each of these alternatives involves a cost; they may also vary in risk. If it is an optimizer, the firm will choose whichever of the alternatives is least costly, consistent with the risk it entails.

A similar sort of problem arises over the choice between flexible (i.e. multi-purpose) and specific (single-purpose) plant. A firm may often not prefer to invest in plant which produces a single product at least cost because it is too specific. That is, the firm may prefer *not* to operate at least *production* cost, but to have a plant which can be switched over to other products when the need arises – perhaps a plant to produce a complete range of a certain class of product. This does not necessarily contradict the idea that the firm seeks to operate at minimum unit cost, because there is another cost involved here which we have not yet considered, viz. the added cost of selling a limited range compared with that of selling a complete range. Lower unit production costs of the former course may well be more than offset by the greater difficulty and cost of selling a limited range. There is also in the long-run the question of greater flexibility should the demand for the single product fail.

8.3 Factors influencing choice of technique

(a) Information

The technique decided upon by a firm for producing any particular output will depend, first, on perceived alternatives, i.e. on its information concerning the technical possibilities open to it. As we saw in Chapter 1, this is one of the functions of the firm's information system. The economist's perfectly competitive firm is assumed to have perfect knowledge of its production function, and the assumption is reasonable in this case. But although the imperfectly competitive firm is not credited with possessing perfect knowledge in other respects, the assumption is usually carried over so far as its production function is concerned. In practice, by contrast, many firms undoubtedly operate well within their efficient production set. Dean gives an illustration of the difficulty of discovering the production function :*

> The lowest cost technique for a given rate of output may involve considering such alternatives as speed of machines, number of man-hours worked per day, number of days' operation per month, number of machines operated – these are only a few of the things, and they in turn might involve considering maintenance requirements, trade union rules, wage differentials as between shifts, and so on.

The gathering and sifting of technical information, and research and development activity, are aimed at keeping the firm abreast or ahead of its competitors in technology.

(b) Relative input prices

A second influence, relative input prices, has already been mentioned. This calls for more or less frequent adaptation by the firm if it wishes to remain efficient, and considerable differences exist between industries in the scope for doing this. As Dorfman notes [5],

> In oil-refining ... a given grade of gasoline can be produced from any one of a large number of combinations of crude oils. Refiners change their formulas almost weekly, as the prices of crude oils fluctuate. ... At the other extreme, many industries are 'machine-bound'; once they have built a plant they cannot change their methods of production or their raw materials without expensive alterations. Typesetting, power generation and airline operation are examples.

(c) Scale of production

The economist's long-run average cost curve (see Figure 8.5 below) purports to show the costs of producing various levels of output assuming that input prices do not change and that at each level of output the technique resulting in lowest unit cost is employed. Scale of production is one of the difficult problems confronting the business man when he is considering laying down a new plant (in capital budgeting, Chapter 11, it would be represented by a number of mutually exclusive projects of different sizes). If the firm bases its investment in new plant on an annual rate of production of, say, 500 000 tons, and demand turns out to be only 300 000, it will not be employing the best technique and will become a high-cost producer. Scale is also the basis of the distinction between short-term and long-term technique

*[4], pp. 256–57.

decisions, the former being those which do not involve investment in new plant. In the short-run the firm's choice of technique may be influenced by the limited availability of one or more inputs: least-cost technique will not be possible in the short-run if these input constraints are effective.

(d) Market structure

The market position of the firm may influence its technique of production and efficiency. A number of cases have been reported of monopolists holding up the introduction of improved processes or products, often originating in their own research departments, because they have large unrecovered investments in old processes/products, and want to 'get their money back'. Not being exposed to immediate competition they are often able to succeed in their aim, unless prevented by a government regulatory body or by the 'entry' of a large established firm from another industry.

(e) Product mix

Indirectly, technique may be influenced by product mix. Recall the earlier reference to flexible *versus* specific plant. It is perhaps cheaper, in terms of unit production cost, to specialize in the production of one kind of screw, but cheaper to produce *and sell* a range of different screws. A somewhat similar situation arises when production is constrained by the fact that certain products are manufactured jointly, can be sold only in certain fixed proportions, but need not be produced in precisely the proportions required for sale.*

(f) Management

Even supposing the optimum technique for the firm's rate of output has been implemented, and its demand forecasts have not been proved inaccurate, it remains necessary for the management to make best use of it. That is, the full fruits depend on management's ability to exploit the technique by overcoming any technical problems and ensuring that productive capacity is as fully utilized as possible (subject to the qualification in section 2). Dean wisely observes that the firm's desire to achieve the optimum technique is not, as assumed in economic theory, constant over time, but likely to vary considerably over the trade cycle and with the fortunes of the particular firm:†

> Contrary to the suppositions of economic theory, the least-cost way of making a given output is not always known, not always politic, and sometimes not even sought.

*[6], p. 154.
†[4], pp. 256–57; similar remarks will be found in [14].

The list is meant to be indicative rather than exhaustive; a number of other considerations will occur to the reader, including the influence of taxation (including inducements of various kinds ('capital allowances') made to companies to undertake particular forms of investment; indirect taxes on input use (such as a payroll tax)), interest rates (affecting the economic viability of investment), business and financial risk.

8.4 Treatment in economics

(a) Orthodox economic theory

It is necessary here to distinguish between the standard economic approach to production and that of linear programming. In the standard approach the technological possibilities open to the firm are represented in a relationship called a production function, mentioned in section 1. Outputs and inputs are measured as physical flows per unit of time. Inputs are classified as fixed or variable, depending on whether they vary with the rate of production over the production period. The production function relates outputs and *variable* inputs. Assuming a single output (q) and two variable inputs x_1 and x_2, it would be

$$q = f(x_1, x_2)$$

The function is only defined for q, x_1, $x_2 \geq 0$.

There is nothing unique about this relationship: there will generally be a number of different ways of combining x_1 and x_2 to produce q. However, as defined in economics, the production function is the *optimal* combination of inputs to produce output q. When fully specified, the coefficients of x_1 and x_2 state the amount of each of these inputs needed to produce a unit of q. That is, as mentioned earlier, the production function in standard economic theory is regarded as data of analysis, the whole problem of technique is assumed to have been solved.

The above relationships (one product, two variable inputs) may be represented in two dimensions as follows:

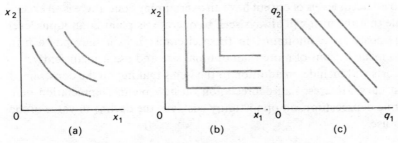

Figure 8.3 Production functions (a), (b) two inputs, (c) two products,
one product; one input

213

The inputs are represented on the two axes. The lines are isoquants which show all combinations of the inputs which yield a given output. The further the line from the origin, the greater the rate of output. In (a) the input combinations are continually variable; in (b) only one combination, indicated by the corners, is possible; it is not sensible to employ any other combination. By 'product' is normally meant any good/service which is not perfectly substitutable for any other. Substitutability is shown by the curvature of the *input* isoquants: in diagram (c), in which rates of *output* are shown on the axes and the contours represent different input rates, products q_1 and q_2 are perfect substitutes, i.e. not distinct products. 'Inputs' (formerly called factors of production) are usually defined rather loosely, e.g. 'an input is any good or service which contributes to the production of an output' [10]; or 'an input is simply anything which the firm buys for use in its production or other processes' [1] A more precise definition [18] is that inputs should be confined to 'measurable quantitative economic goods and services' explicitly included in the firm's production function. It should be noted that such things as 'organization', management and time are not regarded as inputs (time merely influences the productivity of inputs), nor is money capital, as distinct from the services of capital goods (availability of money capital is best regarded as a constraint on production, as in [22]).

Some particular kinds of production function may now be considered.

(i) Short- and long-run production functions

The production function acts as a constraint on the achievement of the firm's operating objective: the firm seeks to maximize profits subject to the technical possibilities represented in its production function. In the short-run it is prevented from adopting the least-cost technique because certain inputs ('plant') are fixed and cannot be increased. The duration of these limitations will vary with the period of the firm's commitments. The longer the period considered the more these constraints it will be able to relax.

In addition to these short-run input limitations some indivisible inputs can be employed only when output is sufficiently large. These are a principal source of economies of scale. Where indivisibilities are present, and the optimal techniques appropriate to adjacent levels of output have an overlapping zone, there is an exception to the rule that the firm will always seek to operate its plant at an input level where average costs are a minimum. In these circumstances it may pay a firm deliberately to instal a plant of more than optimal size and use it inefficiently.*

Long-run costs will include, in addition to the items making up the constrained short-run cost curve, interest and depreciation on new plant. Depreciation here means economic depreciation, an opportunity cost, viz. the decline in value of the plant through use.

*[1], pp. 264–66; [12], pp. 89–91. We will comment further on this phenomenon in subsection (vi) below.

A long-standing difference of opinion continues between economists and accountants (and other economists) as to whether the short-run average cost curve of the firm is U-shaped or L-shaped (average costs first falling, then constant; marginal cost constant over a considerable range of output). A number of empirical studies by economists, some of which are reported on by Johnston [12], have supported the latter conclusion, which is the accountant's position. As Cohen and Cyert note,* it has not always been made clear in these empirical studies over what range of output this applies. They conclude that the implication of the L-shaped short-run average cost curve has not been completely analysed. A further point is made by Hague,† that 'given the way economists define the short-run, it is inevitable that SRAC curves must rise whenever the output of the firm exceeds 'normal' capacity, since this definition precludes any increase in the size of plant'.

This is a question still awaiting resolution· As against the statistical cost function approach, which is based on regression analysis of sample observations of costs at different outputs, it should be added that the process (or activity) analysis approach to the problem has yielded results which are consistent with economic theory (i.e. confirm the U-shaped short-run average cost curve and rising marginal cost curve).‡

(ii) *Multiple products*
Generalization of the earlier single product, two inputs case to r inputs and s outputs raises no new problems. The special case of joint products will be referred to later.

(iii) *Single- and multi-period production functions*
Written in implicit form, the production function for a single period,

$$q = f(x_1, \ldots, x_n), \text{ is}$$

$$F(q_1, \ldots, q_m) = 0, \tag{1}$$

where the q's now denote inputs as well as outputs, distinguished by sign (inputs being given a negative sign). To allow for the customary time-lag between inputs and resulting outputs, and for the fact that it is generally impossible to associate a particular output with the inputs that contributed to it, the firm may plan production over a number of periods. The T-period production function corresponding to the single-period one above would be

$$F(q_{kt}) = 0, \quad k = 1, \ldots, r$$

$$t = 2, \ldots, (T+1), \tag{2}$$

---

* [3], p. 102.
† [10], p. 117.
‡ See Griffin [9]. The process analysis technique develops the production function from engineering data, then derives cost-output relationships by assuming optimizing behaviour. It was the subject of a pioneering study by Manne [16]. Nonlinearities can be overcome by using piecewise linearizations.

215

assuming a uniform lag of one year between input and sale of resulting output.*

(iv) *Technological progress*

We have seen that some of the main factors influencing the firm's costs are productivity, relative input prices and scale of operation. The relationship between the first two was shown in Figure 8.1. There the production function (*SS'*) was constructed on the assumption that available technology was fixed. Over time technological progress renders some production processes *technically* inefficient. The new process may use less of some inputs and no more, or more, of the others per unit of product, or require inputs not previously used. Technological progress is represented by a change in the production function, i.e. in the shape of the line *SS'* in Figure 8.1 (by contrast a movement along *SS'* indicates substitution among inputs due, e.g., to a change in their relative prices). It is the result of a change in the relationship between quantities of outputs and inputs not due to a change in input prices or to variations in the rate or scale of production of the firm in question. Technological progress is measured by the difference between costs in different periods after eliminating all other causes of variation.

(v) *Cost minimization*

As already stated, determination of the production function is one problem; the other consists in determining the least-cost input combination for a given set of input prices. Using the earlier example, if the production function is $q = f(x_1, x_2)$ and the cost equation $C = p_1 x_1 + p_2 x_2 + A$, where the p's are the input prices and A denotes fixed costs, the problem is to minimize C subject to q. Assuming both functions are continuously differentiable, this is done by forming the Lagrangean expression

$$L = C + \lambda[q - \bar{q}]$$
$$= p_1 x_1 + p_2 x_2 + A + \lambda[f(x_1, x_2) - \bar{q}],$$

where $\bar{q}$ is a given rate of output and λ an undetermined multiplier. The necessary conditions for a minimum are

$$\frac{\partial L}{\partial x_1} = p_1 + \lambda \frac{\partial f}{\partial x_1} = 0;$$

$$\frac{\partial L}{\partial x_2} = p_2 + \lambda \frac{\partial f}{\partial x_2} = 0;$$

---

*In (1), if there are n inputs $x_1, \ldots, x_n$ and r outputs $q_1, \ldots, q_r$ we let $q_{r+j} = -x_j, j = 1, \ldots, n$; $m = (n+r)$. See [11], p. 73. In (2), $q_{kt}, k = 1, \ldots, r; t = 2, \ldots, (T+1)$, denotes the kth output in period $(t-1)$ sold in period t; $-q_{kt}, k = (r+1), \ldots, m; t = 1, \ldots, T$, denotes the kth input purchased and used in period t. *Ibid.*, p. 241.

$$\frac{\partial L}{\partial \lambda} = f(x_1, x_2) - \bar{q} = 0,$$

from which it follows that

$$\frac{p_1}{p_2} = \frac{\partial f}{\partial x_1} \bigg/ \frac{\partial f}{\partial x_2},^*$$

i.e. a necessary condition for the least-cost technique is that the ratio of the marginal products of the inputs should equal the ratio of their prices (marginal value products in the case just footnoted); the slope of the isoquant equals the slope of the price line.

The case of *joint products*, say two products from a single input, for simplicity, in fixed and variable proportions, is illustrated in Figure 8.4. Joint products arise from the technical nature of the production process or from the nature of demand.

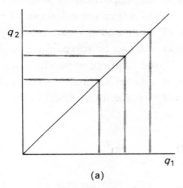
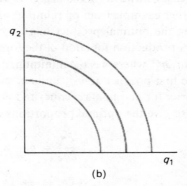

(a)   (b)

Figure 8.4 Production functions, single input, two products. (a) Fixed proportions (b) Variable proportions

When the proportions are fixed the outputs of Q_1 and Q_2 (say cups and saucers) are interdependent, and the only problem is to determine the rate of joint produc-

---

*If the firm can influence the prices it pays for inputs (i.e. is a monopsonist or oligopsonist) the left-hand side becomes

$$p_1\left(1 + \frac{1}{\varepsilon_1}\right) \bigg/ p_2\left(1 + \frac{1}{\varepsilon_2}\right),$$

where ε is the elasticity of supply of the input. In a competitive market $\varepsilon = \infty$. Elasticity in economics is a measure of the responsiveness of variables denoting effects to causal variables. For a function of one variable $y(x)$, the elasticity of y with respect to x is defined as

$$\lim_{\Delta x \to 0} \frac{\Delta y}{y} \bigg/ \frac{\Delta x}{x}$$

For a function of several variables such as $d = d(x, y, z)$, where d is quantity demanded, x the price of the product in question, y income, and z the price of a competing product, partial elasticities may be calculated with respect to each of the independent variables: in this case η_x = price elasticity, η_y = income elasticity, η_z = cross price elasticity. The symbol η is normally used for demand elasticities.

217

tion. If the proportion $q_1/q_2 = b$, a constant, a compound unit of output $(bQ_1 + Q_2)$ with a price $(bp_1 + p_2)$ may be defined and the analysis for a single output applied. If selling prices are given, this amounts to determining q', the output of the compound product, so that

$$bp_1 + p_2 = \frac{dC}{dq'},$$

where C is the cost of the compound product. If the firm can fix its prices

$$\frac{d_1(q_1)}{d_2(q_2)} = b$$

replaces $q_1/q_2 = b$ and the two conditions must be satisfied by fixing p_1 and p_2 appropriately.

In most cases, however, some degree of variability in the proportions is possible (e.g. the earlier example from oil refining), and the problem is then the usual one of determining the optimal product mix at given sets of input and product prices. Assuming a production function of the form $f(q_1, q_2, x) = 0$ can be solved for x to give $x = g(q_1, q_2)$, where x is the minimum quantity of input required to produce q_1 units of the first product and q_2 units of the second, profits (π) are maximized by equating price (or marginal revenue) and marginal cost (w is the input price) in the usual way to give the optimal proportions of q_1 and q_2:

$$\frac{\partial \pi}{\partial q_1} = p_1 - w\frac{\partial g}{\partial q_1} = 0$$

$$\frac{\partial \pi}{\partial q_2} = p_2 - w\frac{\partial g}{\partial q_2} = 0*$$

In making these calculations the relevant costs are, as usual, opportunity costs – in the first case the additional (marginal) costs as the rate of output of the joint process is increased, in the second case the additional costs of the individual process. Fixed costs, the costs that remain constant with a change in rate of output in the first case and the joint costs (the costs up to the 'split-off' point) in the second, are irrelevant to the optimizing decisions.

(vi) *Cost and demand interdependence*

It is important that cost or demand interdependencies† should be taken into account in specifying the decision data. As an illustration of cost interdependence,

---

* For imperfect competition p_i becomes $p_i + q_i\frac{\partial p_i}{\partial q_i}$.

† Cost (or technological) dependence occurs where the cost of one product depends on the quantity produced of other products, demand dependence where the quantity demanded of one product is influenced by the demand for other products.

in the variable proportions case the cost of q_1 will be represented by the function $C_1(q_1, q_2)$, and the cost of q_2 by $C_2(q_1, q_2)$. The marginal costs will then be

$$\frac{\partial}{\partial q_1} C_1(q_1, q_2) \quad \text{and} \quad \frac{\partial}{\partial q_2} C_2(q_1, q_2), \text{ respectively.}$$

(In the fixed proportions case, of course, costs are totally interdependent:

$$\text{marginal cost of } (bq_1 + q_2) = w \frac{dg}{dq'},$$

where w is the price of the input and q' is the output of the compound product.)

For a method of testing for the existence of cost interdependence between products, see Johnston [12], pp. 92–94 and 96. Johnston takes as his measure a partial correlation coefficient between the total variable costs y_j of product $j (j = 1, 2, \ldots, n)$ and an output index, I_j (Paasche type, with selling prices as weights), for the remaining $n-1$ products, with the output x_j of product j held constant. Subject to certain conditions, interdependence is established if a coefficient, $r_{yI.x}$, is positive and significant.

The kind of demand interdependence discussed above is what the economist calls cross (price) elasticity of demand, defined as

$$\frac{\Delta q_j}{\Delta p_i} \cdot \frac{p_i}{q_j},$$

where the q_j and p_i in this case all refer to a single firm. Statistical techniques have been used to estimate this relationship in a number of studies of aggregate consumption of various products in different countries, e.g. [23], [8] and [17].

(vii) *Plant indivisibilities*
In the 'long-run', when the availability of all inputs is unconstrained, the average cost curve (the envelope curve in Figure 8.5) shows the minimum cost of producing any output, given the present state of technology and input prices:

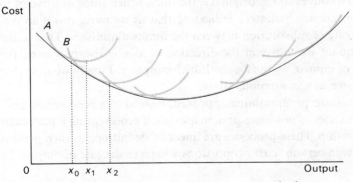

Figure 8.5 Average cost curve when all inputs are unconstrained

The firm aims to choose the plant size most appropriate to its expected rate of production. Baumol makes the interesting point* that in the short-run it will not always pay the firm to operate its plant at minimum average cost. Suppose a firm has invested in plant *A*, the first of the short-run average cost curves in the diagram, expecting its output to be in the region of Ox_1 units a year. Even when it is operated most efficiently, plant *B* can produce this output at even lower cost. Plant *A* will be confined to operating at rates of up to Ox_0 units, i.e. it will be operating well below its capacity. This emphasizes the importance of choosing the plant size which offers the greatest flexibility, and the influence of indivisibilities. Plant *B* is the most efficient in producing outputs in the range $Ox_0 - Ox_2$. A firm which has recently invested in plant *A*, if demand remains within this zone, might be unable to rectify its bad decision because of inability to raise further finance (it would also have to explain the capital loss to its shareholders).

Anticipating the next section, in terms of the linear programming approach the counterpart of the above argument is that for outputs in the intervals such as $Ox_0 - Ox_1$ along the curve in Figure 8.5 it will pay the firm to choose the larger-scale process and use it inefficiently by choice, since when operated less efficiently it is still relatively more efficient than the smaller-scale process.

(b) Linear programming

Standard economic theory was not altogether helpful because it abstracted from the technological part of the technique problem, assuming this was already optimally solved. Linear programming, in its application to problems of production, makes no such assumption. To see how it solves the problem of choosing the optimal technique we must first examine the notion of 'processes' (or 'activities') and its relation to the production function of orthodox economic theory.

In orthodox theory, as we have seen, the production function was represented by a family of isoquants on a diagram which had as its axes the variable inputs. The isoquants were drawn convex to the origin (i.e. the lines, which slope downward to the right, become progressively flatter), indicating that as we move down an isoquant the marginal rate of substitution between the inputs diminishes. That is, the lower down an isoquant we move, in the direction of *x*-intensive processes, the greater the amount of input *x* we must substitute for input *y*. Finally we note that an isoquant was drawn as a continuous curve.

Now consider the linear programming approach. Instead of a production function we will define a series of *processes* or *activities*, each representing a particular input-output relationship. These processes are linear by definition, i.e. each process involves using inputs in certain fixed proportions whatever the rate of output. To

*[1], p. 265.

increase output *all* inputs must now be increased in the same proportion, the proportion by which output is to be increased. The optimal choice of technique then becomes a question of choosing the optimal process or combination of processes.

To show how processes are represented in the LP approach we will employ a different kind of diagram which, however, bears some resemblance to that of standard theory on which the isoquants were drawn. Inputs are shown on the axes, and a process (fixed input proportions) is represented by a ray through the origin, its

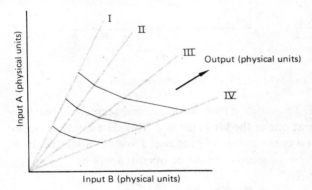

Figure 8.6 Process ray diagram for choice of technique

slope being equal to the input proportion. The line segments joining points on adjacent rays are isoquants, but here we consider only a discrete number of processes, in this case four. By drawing more rays we would approach the smooth isoquants of the standard theory of production.* The isoquants have the same meaning as before, i.e. as they move outward from the origin they indicate higher levels of output. Unlike those of the theory of production, however, these will always be parallel because of constant input proportions in processes. Each process is characterized by constant returns to scale (the processes are linear and homogeneous).† Finally it should be noted that the inputs shown on the axes are, in contrast to the earlier isoquant diagram, *fixed inputs* (or constraints). This type of diagram may be employed for any number of inputs which are available without limit but there must be not more than two fixed inputs. In the more common LP diagram of Chapter 7, it will be recalled, fixed inputs were represented by constraint lines on the diagram.

Two cases are of interest concerning technique. The first may be identified as the short-run problem, and the second as the long-run problem. They are illustrated in Figure 8.7.

In Figure 8.7(a) availability of the inputs is limited to *x* units of *B* and *y* units of *A*. *OxCy* defines the feasible region. The object is to get on the highest isoproduct curve

*Though it is an assumption of the LP model that the number of processes will always be finite.
†Constant returns to scale is shown by the fact that any ray from the origin will be divided into equal segments by successive isoquants.

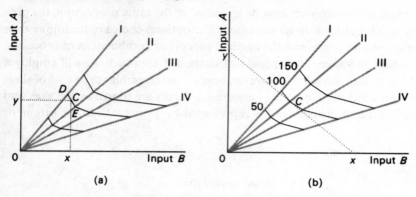

Figure 8.7 Choice of technique. (a) Two fixed factors. (b) Price-ratio constraint

and this is achieved at point *C*. The solution may occur on a line segment in between two processes (as in 8.7(a)) or at one of the kinks (as in 8.7(b)). The solution represented by point *C* means that a combination of processes I and II should be used. The levels at which each of these processes should be operated will be

$$\text{process II} \quad \frac{DC}{DE} \cdot OE$$

$$\text{process I} \quad \frac{CE}{DE} \cdot OD$$

The optimum technique is determined in this case by the relative availabilities of the fixed inputs. The example illustrates one of the basic theorems of linear programming, which states that if there are *n* fixed inputs no more than *n* processes need be used.*

Figure 8.7(b) could represent a long-run technique decision, such as which of four *types* of machines capable of performing the same task to use. This could be considered as a study undertaken prior to investment. Input *A* is investment in machines and input *B* labour-hours. As before, units of output are shown along the rays. Only one level of output need be considered, as the quantities of inputs and outputs increase proportionately along the rays. Moving from process I down to process IV means using a less expensive machine and more labour-hours.

Here process II is indicated as the best (least-cost) technique where the price line *xy* showing the relative cost of machinery and of labour per unit of time is tangent to an isoquant at *C*.† If the isoquant through *C* represents an output of 100 units a month and process II consists of employing a machine costing £50 000 and 100 hours of labour time per month, then the price line *xy* will represent the relation

---

*Cf. [1], p. 82 *et seq.*
†Cf. [5], pp. 35–37.

between the equivalent monthly cost of the machine, $50\,000\,a_{\overline{n}|}^{-1}$, where n is the expected economic life of the machine in months, and the cost of 100 man-hours of labour.

Extending the problem considered in Figure 8.7(a) to n processes and m fixed inputs, it may be expressed algebraically as follows:

$$\text{minimize} \qquad \sum_{j=1}^{n} c_j x_j$$

$$\text{subject to} \qquad \sum_{j=1}^{n} a_{ij} x_j \leq b_i, \qquad i = 1, \ldots, m$$

$$x_j \geq 0,$$

where c_j is the variable cost of operating process j at unit level, x_j is the level at which process j is operated, a_{ij} is the amount of fixed input i required per unit of output j, and b_i is the available amount of fixed input i.

As Baumol notes [1], the problem of choice of technique has the same form as the problem of what and how much to produce which we formulated in Chapter 7. There the x_j represented the quantity of product j to be produced, and the c_j denoted net revenue (price minus variable cost). In the present problem, as we have seen, x_j denotes the output of a single product produced by process j. By giving c_j the same interpretation as in Chapter 7 and introducing double subscript notation, letting x_{kj} denote the quantity of product k produced by process j, we can cover the case of multiple products and solve for optimal product mix and optimal technique simultaneously. Readers should do this as an exercise.

8.5 Further examples of technique problems

Several different types of technique problem have already been mentioned: the optimal combination of men and machines, choice between different machines, flexible *versus* specific equipment, excess plant capacity *versus* heavier inventory holdings or subcontracting, etc., and (in Chapter 7) make or buy. The problem is a recurring one with changes in the firm's production function, in the relative prices of its inputs, its scale of operation and a number of other factors. Two further examples will be given as illustrative of the many different aspects of the problem.

(a) Location of plant

The location of production is a factor which may affect the firm's costs in various ways: via transport costs, the existence of external economies at particular concentrations of production, government development grants and other inducements to locate in certain 'depressed' areas, and so on. In the early economic theory of location transport costs were given prominence, for the reason that wherever a firm locates raw materials must be brought in and products transported out. The more the firm's output grows, the greater the volume of commodities and products which must be transported. Thus the siting of operations is pulled in two directions: towards its raw materials supplies and towards its markets. Other things being equal, it was argued, a plant should be located at the point of minimum transport cost.

In practice the solution is seldom as easy as this; there are other factors to be considered, some of which were mentioned above. Moreover transport costs are more important in the case of some industries (where supplies are heavy or bulky) than in others; and in modern industry the tendency is for a declining proportion of the cost of production and sale to be represented by the cost of transporting raw materials. In particular, the cost of moving products to markets is usually not so much a function of distance as of handling charges (packing, warehousing, trans-shipment, etc.). *Speed* of delivery may also be highly important. There has been a considerable change in the character of transport facilities, with road transport becoming more important in relation to rail in the domestic distribution of many products. And in periods of full employment the single most important factor influencing choice of location of production is often the availability of the necessary kind of labour (especially since at such times the mobility of labour declines).

For a new firm about to commence operations or for an established firm which is expanding by building an additional plant, the question of location is part of the broad question of technique of production. In some heavy industries the decision on where to locate new operations (and the amount of capacity to lay down) is often a critical one. In the case of multi-national firms, decisions to establish overseas plants are subject to further influences which may be very difficult to assess. In all cases the most difficult problem is likely to be that of estimating demand areally.

Minimizing transport costs is really a subproblem within the wider problem of choice of location. It can be solved with the aid of linear programming. Suppose that production can be located at any of $i = 1, \ldots, n$ different points; these are the feasible alternatives. Annual production capacity of a plant built at location i is P_i, and the (short-run) marginal cost of production at this location is c_i.* There are $j = 1, \ldots, m$ market areas, and the estimated annual demand from market j is D_j. The number of units of product transported from plant i to market j is denoted by x_{ij}; and the cost of transporting one unit of product between these points is t_{ij}. The firm is supplied with materials from $k = 1, \ldots, p$ different locations. The number of units of materials delivered from supply k to plant i is y_{ki}, and the cost of transporting one unit between these points is s_{ki}. The number of units of materials from supply k

---

* Excluding freight charges on materials.

224

required per unit of (single homogeneous) product by plant i is a_{ki}. The programming problem is then

minimize
$$\sum_i \sum_j (c_i + t_{ij})x_{ij} + \sum_k \sum_i s_{ki} y_{ki}$$

subject to:
$$\sum_i x_{ij} \geq D_j \qquad (j = 1, \ldots, m)$$

$$\sum_j x_{ij} \leq P_i \qquad (i = 1, \ldots, n)$$

$$\sum_k y_{ki} \geq P_i \sum_k a_{ki} \quad (i = 1, \ldots, n)$$

$$x_{ij}, y_{ki} \geq 0 \qquad (\text{all } i, j, k)$$

This formulation omits inventory considerations relating to materials and products.

(b) Method of distribution

Method of distributing products is another aspect of technique. Of all sections of economic activity distribution often comes in for the most criticism, especially the distribution of consumer goods. Wastefulness and high cost of many of the methods used is in contrast to the cost reductions achieved in many branches of manufacturing, and it is a fairly widely held view that the efficiency of distribution has, at least until recently, lagged behind that of manufacturing.*

The revolution in distribution methods in the UK in the past decade or two was a belated recognition that there are economies of scale to be reaped in distribution just as in manufacturing.

Most British manufacturing firms do not sell direct to the public but rely on a chain of distributors over which they have more or less control, in most cases very little. In these circumstances the manufacturer must adapt his products and selling methods to existing distribution arrangements; it would be stupidity, for instance, to spend large sums on advertising a product of the kind usually bought in small general stores if salesmen's efforts had been concentrated on specialist shops, or to advertise nationally on a large scale if the product is sold only through non-exclusive wholesalers. Design and packaging will also depend on the method of distribution to the consumer.

In general, the extent to which a manufacturer relies on intermediaries will depend largely on whether the product reaches the final consumer mainly through a few specialist shops with fairly large turnovers or through a large number of small shops. There is some level of turnover at which supply direct to the retailer becomes

---

*In the UK it was not possible to substantiate or refute this popular view until 1950, when the first full-scale Census of Distribution was taken. (In the US they began in 1929, in Canada in 1924.)

225

economic; below this level the manufacturer will sell through wholesalers. He has to balance the advantages of being closer to the final consumer when selling to retailers or selling direct (advantages such as quicker notice of consumer reactions to product changes and price changes, which help him plan production more smoothly, with a consequent reduction in unit costs; and elimination of intermediaries' commission) against the costs of performing the intermediaries' functions (holding larger inventories, breaking bulk, supplying many small orders, and so on).

8.6 Data specification

In the course of this chapter a number of points concerning data specification in technique problems have been made. As in all economic decisions, the costs of interest to us are opportunity costs, which means that if a particular problem should involve using any resources which would not result in outlay costs being incurred, their implicit opportunity costs must be taken into account in the decision calculation. There may be substantial problems in estimating costs, and in making these estimates allowance should be made where appropriate for the 'learning effect'. In other problems estimation of demand is likely to be even more formidable. Technique is a many-sided problem. Some technique problems involve marginal adjustments and hence the calculation or comparison of marginal costs (e.g. cost minimization subject to the constraint of the production function); others involve non-marginal adjustments, and hence incremental costs (e.g. the make or buy decision in the previous chapter). The quest for optimal technique also draws attention to the importance of the firm's technical information-gathering activities. Besides being a many-faceted problem, choice of technique may also be influenced in any particular case by a large number of different factors, some of which were mentioned in section 3; the earlier examination of the make or buy decision provided further demonstration of this.

We saw that the problem has two parts, the first technological and the second economic. Subject to one qualification, standard economic theory offers a satisfactory conceptual analysis of the second part, but may not be easy to apply if the number of constraining circumstances is large or they take the form of inequality relationships. The qualification is that it assumes that (as with other decisions) once the least-cost technique has been discovered it will be put into effect without any loss of efficiency, i.e. it abstracts entirely from problems of control and the influence of organization structure. These points will be taken up later, especially in Chapters 13 and 18. Standard economic theory also completely abstracts from the first part of the technique problem. Here, as in the case of the exceptions referred to, linear programming proves invaluable. In Appendix C we make the comment that a major task in developing realistic LP models is the provision of reliable numerical values for the coefficients of the objective function and constraints. Rapid technological change makes new techniques available and speeds up the rate of obsolescence of existing techniques in the areas concerned. The management accountant should be active in examining problems of technique and keeping them constantly under review. He will be better prepared for this task in proportion to his understanding of the economic nature of the problem, and he needs to be equipped with a knowledge of linear programming.

Bibliographical references

[1] Baumol, W. J., *Economic Theory and Operations Analysis*, Prentice-Hall, 2nd edn., 1965.
[2] Boulding, K. E. and W. A. Spivey, *Linear Programming and the Theory of the Firm*, Macmillan, New York, 1960.
[3] Cohen, K. J. and R. M. Cyert, *Theory of the Firm: Resource Allocation in a Market Economy*, Prentice-Hall, 1965.
[4] Dean, J., *Managerial Economics*, Prentice-Hall, 1951.
[5] Dorfman, R., *The Price System*, Prentice-Hall, 1964.
[6] Dorfman, R., P. A. Samuelson and R. M. Solow, *Linear Programming and Economic Analysis*, McGraw-Hill, 1958.
[7] Farrell, M. J., The measurement of productive efficiency, *Journal of the Royal Statistical Society*, A, 120 (1957), pp. 253–81.
[8] Girshick, M. A. and T. Haavelmo, Statistical analysis of the demand for food, in *Studies in Econometric Methods*, eds. W. C. Hood and T. C. Koopmans, John Wiley, 1953.
[9] Griffin, J. M., The process analysis alternative to statistical cost functions: an application to petroleum refining, *American Economic Review*, March 1972, pp. 46–56.
[10] Hague, D. C., *Managerial Economics*, Longmans, 1969.
[11] Henderson, J. M. and R. E. Quandt, *Microeconomic Theory*, McGraw-Hill, 1958.
[12] Johnston, J., *Statistical Cost Analysis*, McGraw-Hill, 1960.
[13] Lancaster, K., *Introduction to Modern Microeconomics*, Rand McNally, 1969.
[14] Leibenstein, H., Allocative efficiency versus 'X-efficiency', *American Economic Review*, 56, Sept. 1966, pp. 392–415.
[15] Lesourne, J., *Economic Analysis and Industrial Management*, Prentice-Hall, 1963.
[16] Manne, A., A linear programming model of the US petroleum refining industry, *Econometrica*, Jan. 1958, pp. 67–106.
[17] Prais, S. J. and H. S. Houthakker, *The Analysis of Family Budgets*, Cambridge University Press, 1955.
[18] Samuelson, P. A., *Foundations of Economic Analysis*, Harvard University Press, 1953.
[19] Schneider, E., *Pricing and Equilibrium*, Unwin University Books, 1962 (first published 1952).
[20] Schultz, H., *The Theory and Measurement of Demand*, Chicago University Press, 1938.
[21] Stigler, G. J., *The Theory of Price*, Macmillan, New York, 1947 (revised edn., 1952).
[22] Vickers, D., *The Theory of the Firm: Production, Capital, and Finance*, McGraw-Hill, 1968.
[23] Wold, H. and L. Jureen, *Demand Analysis*, John Wiley, 1953.

Problems

8.1 Why is the presence of monopolistic competition in a firm's product markets important in considering the firm's technique of production?

8.2 Johnston ([12]) states that one of the major impressions he formed from a review of statistical cost studies was 'that the various short-run studies more often

227

than not indicate constant marginal cost and declining average cost [i.e. an L-shaped short-run average cost curve] as the pattern that best seems to describe the data that have been analysed'. Among the English studies supporting this hypothesis are P. J. D. Wiles, *Price, Cost and Output*, Basil Blackwell, 1956, and P. W. S. Andrews, *Manufacturing Business*, Macmillan, London, 1949.

Conventional economic theory, on the other hand, contends that the short-run average cost curve is typically U-shaped.

What might be some of the implications for decision-making in the firm if the L-shaped curve were conclusively shown to be the rule rather than the exception?

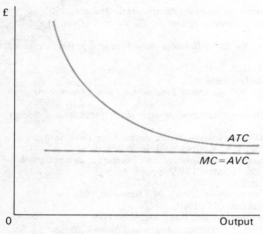

8.3 An equipment company assembles frames for four machines in three shops: (1) cutting, (2) welding, (3) painting. The pertinent data are presented in the table below:

Department	A	Type of frame B	C	D	Hours available per month
Cutting: unit time	150	80	120	120	4 500
unit cost ($)	1 000	500	850	700	
Welding: unit time	230	140	180	160	6 400
unit cost ($)	1 100	650	900	800	
Painting: unit time	50	40	40	30	1 600
unit cost ($)	450	300	350	350	
Profit contribution per unit ($)*	400	250	300	350	

* Unit sales revenue less the three variable costs above.

228

Painting can be subcontracted to an outside shop at a 20 per cent increase in cost.

Required:
(a) What should be the rate of production of each type of frame in order to maximize the monthly profit contribution if no restriction is placed on the number of each type of frame produced?
(b) How much would the monthly profit contribution be increased by a 10 per cent increase in the capacity of the welding department?
(c) What are the optimal production rates if no more than 10 frames of types C and D are to be produced? Assume the capacity of the welding department remains at 6 400 hours.

8.4 Hudson Electronics Ltd. has been contemplating using funds currently surplus to requirements to purchase 40 000 ordinary shares in Madison Valves Co. as a trade investment. Madison's £1 shares stand in the market at £1·4 each, and its last annual dividend was at the rate of 7 per cent on nominal value.

X, Hudson's purchasing officer, at this point comes forward with an alternative proposal. Through his professional contacts he has learned that a certain material of which his company uses 150 000 units per annum, maintaining an inventory of 12 500 units, is purchased in small lots by a number of other manufacturers in the area, at an average unit price of £0·60. His own company obtains it at £0·55 per unit.

If Hudson were to purchase 480 000 units of the material at a uniform rate throughout the year and keep one month's supply in stock, they could secure a price of £0·48 a unit from the supplier and meet all requirements of the area, reselling it to the other firms at £0·55 a unit.

To store the additional material X suggests recommissioning a company-owned warehouse now leased to another firm at an annual rental of £7 000. He estimates that labour costs in handling and delivering the material would rise by about £9 500 a year and that administrative expenses would be £4 500 a year higher.

His plan would, however, also entail acquiring six new delivery vans at a total cost of £30 000. These would have an estimated working life of 7 years, at the end of which their combined sale value would be £2 500. The delivery vans would be depreciated by the straight line method in the accounts.

Required:
(a) Should X's plan to effect a reduction in materials cost by acting as a distributor to other firms be adopted, or would Hudson be better advised to follow the first idea? (Ignore taxation.)
(b) On what points, if any, would you like further information?

8.5 We hear a lot about the speed of technological change in recent years. How would you measure the effects of technological change in a business enterprise over a period of time?

8.6 Argue the case for a firm being (a) a leader, (b) a follower in the matter of technological innovation in its field.

9

How much to produce: price-output decisions

People who like this sort of thing will find this the sort of thing they like.
— ABRAHAM LINCOLN

A market, as we noted in Chapter 1, is a communication system linking potential buyers and sellers of some commodity or commodities. In this chapter we shall be concerned with the pricing decisions of firms. It is as well to make clear at the outset that, except when they relate to internal sales (section 8 below), firms do not *fix* prices. Firms *announce* provisional prices. Actual prices are fixed by a consensus of buyers and sellers in the market. In economic theory markets are classified according to the number of *sellers*, whether large or small, and according to whether the product is homogeneous or differentiated. In reviewing these market structures we will assume initially a large number of buyers in each case, later examining some of the cases where this is not so.

9.1 Market structures and pricing rules in the neoclassical theory of the firm

The main categories distinguished in economics are:

1. A large number of sellers
   (a) Homogeneous product: perfect competition
   (b) Differentiated product: monopolistic competition
2. A small number of sellers
   (a) A single seller, homogeneous or differentiated product: monopoly
   (b) Few sellers, homogeneous or differentiated product: oligopoly.

Except in case 2(b), a goal of profit maximization is assumed throughout. In case 1(a) this is shown to imply a pricing rule of price = marginal cost (as in the other cases this is a tautology: given the objective, it follows automatically). No seller exerts a perceptible influence on price and must be content to accept the ruling price in the market. In case 1(b), because its product is differentiated the firm may pursue an independent price policy. It maximizes its objective by charging a price at which marginal revenue (MR, and not price) equals marginal cost (MC). In the long run the large number of competitors in both 1(a) and 1(b) will ensure that prices are competed down to a level at which only 'normal' profits are being earned. The difference between the two cases is that in 1(b) this 'long run equilibrium' position will not coincide with the most efficient scale of production (minimum average cost). This is demonstrated in Figures 9.1(a) and 9.1(b), where 'normal' profits have been included in the cost curves and p_2 is the long run equilibrium price:*

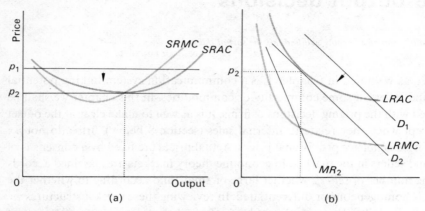

Figure 9.1 (a) Perfect competition. (b) Monopolistic competition

Pure monopoly, case 2(a), differs from case 1(b) not only in regard to the number of sellers, but also in the closeness of substitutes (the monopolist's demand curve is steeper than that of the monopolistically competitive firm). For the monopoly to be sustained there must be barriers to the 'entry' of new firms into the industry. There are two kinds of monopoly: the cartel type, where a single firm has cornered the market by gaining control of the whole supply of some necessary input or possesses exclusive legal rights in the production of some commodity (a patent)†; and a technical monopoly where, due to the nature of the productive process, economies of scale persist over such a range of output that one large firm will eventually emerge to produce the entire output. The monopolist maximizes profits at a price at which $SRMC = MR$. In the long run the corresponding condition is $LRMC = SRMC = MR$ (see [12]). Compared with the competitive firm depicted in Figure 9.1(a), output will only by chance be at the minimum AC level; and since there is no-one to compete down his profits, equilibrium price (short run and long run) will be greater than AC (rather than equal to it as long run equilibrium price p_2 was in cases 1(a) and 1(b)).

The perfectly competitive firm can determine only its output; the monopolist or monopolistically competitive firm can determine either price or output, but not both. If price is fixed too high or too low the firm or its customers build up stocks.

---

*To avoid possible confusion later when dealing with transfer prices, it should be pointed out that 'normal' profits are included in costs only for the purpose of long-run *equilibrium* analysis. In all other cases costs include only payments to the contracting factors.

† Alternatively, it may be a group of oligopolists acting in concert. In each case the firm (or group) is conscious of its downward-sloping demand curve, and exploits its position by varying its output.

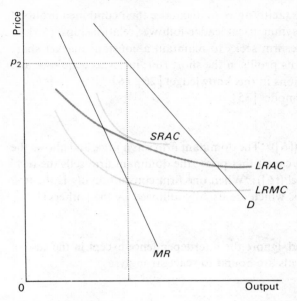

Figure 9.2 Monopoly

The remaining case, 2(b), is complicated by the fact that sellers are sufficiently few that the behaviour of one affects the behaviour of its competitors. The previous analysis is insufficient to explain the strategies which such firms may adopt concerning level of output (if the product is homogeneous), output *or* price (if the product is differentiated). A number of different theories have been offered purporting to describe the nature of the interdependence between firms and the resulting strategies. These are listed below; some of them will be referred to later in this chapter:*

(a) Models within the neoclassical framework

(i) *Conjectural variation models* (i.e. models which depend on various hypotheses concerning rivals' reactions)†

1. Cournot model‡ (rivals will not react to an output change by altering their output).
2. Edgeworth model§ (rivals will not react to a price change with a price change).

* See [26] or [18] for a fuller description.

† If there are two oligopolists whose outputs are denoted by q_1 and q_2 the conjectural variations are

$$\frac{dq_2}{dq_1} \text{ and } \frac{dq_1}{dq_2}.$$

‡ See [7].

§ See [13].

3. Collusion model (the rivals tacitly agree to maximize their combined profits).*
4. von Stackelberg model (asymmetrical leader-follower relationships) [33].
5. Market shares model (one firm seeks to maintain a constant market share regardless of the effect on its profits in the short run; its rivals acquiesce and maximize their own positions in this knowledge) [26], [6].
6. Sweezy's kinked demand model [35].

(ii) *Price leadership models*

1. The dominant firm model ([6]): 'The dominant firm sets a price and allows the minor firms to sell all they can at that price; the dominant firm sells the rest.'
2. The barometric firm model ([6]): 'When one firm conventionally is the first to announce price changes, which are usually followed by the [others].'

(iii)

The firm may, on the other hand, ignore the interdependence except in the case of major decisions to which its rivals are bound to react strongly.

(b) Other models

Fairly obviously the above list does not exhaust the possible conjectures which could be made. Some other approaches are:

1. Game theory models [20], [32]: Here instead of conjecture the firm calculates the optimal strategies of its rivals and designs its own counter-strategies accordingly.
2. Behavioural models [8], [9], [10], [5].

As a form of market organization, oligopoly is very common in advanced industrial societies. The interdependence between firms has the general characteristic of producing a strong desire to maintain the *status quo*; short run objectives are subordinated to long run considerations, an understanding (overt or tacit) is reached between firms, and certain acceptable rules of behaviour are established, among them price leadership. Price change is seldom part of the oligopolist's strategy. Instead competition takes non-price forms: promotional activities (particularly advertising) and product improvement. We will examine the question of advertising in section 7.

Throughout the foregoing it has been assumed that there is a large number of buyers on the other side of the market – perfect competition among buyers. But of course other situations are possible. In particular buyers may be very few (oligopsonists) or there may be a single buyer (monopsonist). Various permutations are

---

*See [26], [6].

possible; the single buyer – single seller situation is called bilateral monopoly.*

In the appendix to this chapter the following further cases are outlined: the multiproduct firm; joint products; price discrimination; multiplant, multimarket monopoly and dynamic profit maximization.

9.2 Conditions under which a firm may have an independent price policy

With this background we are now in a position to define the domain over which price may be treated by firms as a variable.By price policy we mean the ability of a firm to alter its prices independently at any time. A general answer to this question involves substitutability of products. In perfect competition there is perfect substitutability between the products of all firms. As soon as substitutability between the products of different firms becomes imperfect (there is a gap in the chain of substitutes) and is recognized as being imperfect by consumers, each firm may elect to charge a higher or lower price than other producers.†

But we can be more specific. The following are cases in which a firm may *not* have an independent price policy:

(i) Perfect competition: the individual firm is a 'price-taker'

(ii) Central price control by

1. The government, by fixing a single price or a maximum price (regulatory board).
2. A trade association fixing minimum prices, including the practice known as group resale price maintenance, now outlawed in Britain.

(iii) Oligopoly

1. Following the price leader, generally the firm with the largest market share. This does not mean that each firm will not follow an independent course in non-price competition. Oligopoly is not a necessary condition; this may occur in monpolistic competition, in which case the price leader need not be the dominant firm.

---

*See [17], pp. 98–101 for a discussion of the various cases, and the need to distinguish between private and industrial buyers.

† In technical language this is indicated by the numerical value of an important concept called the elasticity of substitution. Between two products x and y this is defined as

$$\sigma = \frac{\dfrac{x}{y} \cdot d\left(\dfrac{y}{x}\right)}{\dfrac{1}{r} \cdot dr} \quad (0 \leqslant \sigma \leqslant \infty),$$

where r = the marginal rate of substitution of y for $x = -\dfrac{dy}{dx} = \dfrac{\phi_x}{\phi_y}$. If the products are poor substitutes (i.e. the more curvature their indifference curves have, these being defined by an equation of the form $\phi(x, y)$ = constant), $\sigma \to 0$.

235

2. Price stability, by tacit agreement between firms, e.g. few producers of a homogeneous product (though where there is freedom to change prices, in market structures other than oligopoly, this amounts to a price policy).

(iv) Monopoly: if the monopolist determines his output and takes the price which clears this output.

(v) Finally, some firms may not have a clear-cut policy on price, tied to a certain objective or objectives, but may set prices in an *ad hoc* manner.

In most other circumstances a firm is free to follow an independent price policy, though within the area described as monopolistic competition the relative emphasis of price and non-price competition may vary considerably from one end of the spectrum (the competitive end) to the other (the monopolistic end). The same firm selling in several markets with different structures may need to adopt different pricing policies in each.

9.3 Considerations influencing choice of price policy

As we have seen, the zone of discretion within which a firm is free to vary its price at will is determined more or less closely by the structure of the product market: the pricing policy must match, or not be inconsistent with, the firm's competitive situation.* Some of the other considerations which may affect a firm's choice of price policy are as follows:†

1. To summarize the factors already mentioned: the number and size of competitors, whether the product is homogeneous or differentiated, the closeness of substitutes in the latter case, the configuration of buyers, the likelihood of potential competition (new entrants), whether the market can be split up and different prices charged in each section, the relative importance of price and non-price competition.
2. The stage of consumer acceptance of the product (compare old and new products), real and imagined differences between the product and other products and how long these can be sustained; whether the product is storable.
3. Whether the product is part of the firm's standard production or a special line (e.g. a government contract).
4. Whether there are economies of scale in its production.
5. The proportion of variable to total costs.
6. The method of distribution.

---

* Besides the number of sellers (and buyers) and the degree of substitutability of the product, market forms and hence price structure are also influenced by technological conditions, the financial structure of producers (and buyers) and by institutional limitations of the kinds mentioned above.

† See [11].

7. The state of trade (whether the industry demand for this type of product is growing, steady or declining).
8. The opportunities for competition through after-sales service, product improvement, quantity discounts, and so on.
9. The firm's overall objectives (e.g. if the objective is achieving a profit within some 'satisfactory' range this would rule out a policy of charging 'what the traffic will bear' in the short run).

Other influences may occur to the reader, or be mentioned subsequently.

9.4 Other behavioural assumptions

In section 1 and associated appendices the influence of market structure on the price-output policy of the firm was examined. Excepting the case of oligopoly, the models discussed all belonged to the neoclassical theory of the firm; that is, they employed the traditional marginal analysis, they treated the firm as usually having a single goal, viz. profit maximization, and they were highly aggregative models. By the last statement is meant that the theory treats the interests of the firm, its owners and managers as identical (sharing the common goal of profit maximization), and telescopes the whole current operations of the firm into two sets of decisions, one set concerned with inputs and one with outputs, which are taken simultaneously, not independently of each other. The theory is normative in that it states what the firm *should* do if it behaves rationally, rationality being interpreted in terms of the marginal calculus. Hicks's dynamic model of the multiproduct, multi-input firm represented the culmination of development within this framework [19].

As we have noted earlier, there has been a growing tide of dissent from this neoclassical view of the firm, in favour of theories which are more descriptive of *actual* behaviour, i.e. positive economic models of the firm. Recent developments have challenged the behavioural assumptions of the neoclassical theory, the assumption that the firm has a single objective, and that this is profit maximization; the assumption that it always acts with complete rationality in the sense described above (rather than 'satisficing', for example, or using heuristic methods or questionable rules-of-thumb); that it takes decisions on various different fronts simultaneously rather than sequentially; that these decisions comprise only those indicated here in the titles of Chapters 7–10; and that the influence on the firm's decision-making of its organization form and structure and information system may be ignored. These are just a few of the considerations which have motivated the dissenters from the neoclassical view.

It will not be possible in the space available to trace the kind of price-output decisions to which each of these developments might lead. For the most part we can only draw readers' attention to the fact that changing some or all of the behavioural assumptions of the neoclassical theory (referred to elsewhere in this book as the 'standard' or 'orthodox' theory of the firm) will in general lead to different price-output decisions being taken. Collectively, however, the new developments are too important to be ignored completely. Brief reference will therefore be made to some of them. In what follows no mention is made of another important departure from the neoclassical model, viz. the more flexible representation of the firm's production transformation process in terms of 'activities' in mathematical programming models. Nor will anything more be said, except incidentally, about the role of organization form and structure and the information system. These aspects are considered in other chapters.

(a) Maximizing models

Papandreou [28] and Williamson [36], [37], [38],* among others, have made proposals which continue to treat the firm as a maximizer, but of utility rather than profits. In [28], utility takes the form of a general utility function, usually considered to be almost impossible to discover empirically. Williamson, in several different models, suggests that management maximizes its own utility. In [36] this is represented as a function of staff, managerial emoluments and 'discretionary spending for investment', defined as the difference between 'reported profits' (actual profits less 'organizational slack' absorbed as cost) and minimum profits and taxes (minimum profits after taxes being the amount which just satisfies the other members of the organizational coalition, i.e. shareholders, suppliers and customers). This function is maximized subject to reported profits being not less than minimum profits demanded:

Maximize $$U = U(S, \pi_A - \pi_R, I_D)$$
subject to: $$\pi_R \geq \pi_0 + T$$
$$0 \leq \rho \leq 1,$$

where π_A = actual profits = revenue (R) − production cost (C)
$\qquad$ − staff expenditures (S).†

π_R = reported profits = $\rho \pi_A$

π_0 = minimum required profit

ρ = the fraction of actual profits reported

$I_D = \pi_R - (\pi_0 + T)$ and

T = taxes.‡

* See also [6].

† Williamson interprets S as including advertising expenditure.

‡ Since the first constraint has the same form as the last variable in the objective function (and assuming that second-order conditions are met), it is redundant, and the problem is a straightforward maximization problem. (The second constraint is also rendered redundant by the necessary conditions for a maximum, which require a positive proportionality between the second and third terms of U.)

It is shown that maximization implies equating MR and MC, but staff will be added beyond the point at which its marginal value product equals its MC.

Price and output are variables in the model, price being defined as a function of output level, staff and a demand-shift parameter:

$$p = P(X,S,\varepsilon).$$

The price-output decision rules under this objective, while of the same form as for a profit-maximizing objective, lead to different results because MR is an implicit function of staff emoluments (S), and the optimal values of S will generally differ in the two models.*

Baumol's firm in [2]† is a revenue maximiser subject to a minimum level of profit. The problem is to choose values of x (output) and A (advertising expenditure)‡ so as to

maximize $\qquad R = px.$

subject to $\qquad \pi \geq \pi_0$

where $\qquad \pi = (1-t)\{R-C-A\},$

$\qquad\qquad \pi_0 = $ the minimum desired level of profits,

$\qquad\qquad t = $ the tax rate,

and the other symbols are as in the previous model. This model may be solved using Lagrangean methods:

$$L = R + \lambda[(1-t)(R-C-A)-\pi_0].$$

It follows from the necessary conditions for $R_{\max}$ that

$$\frac{\partial R}{\partial x} < \frac{\partial C}{\partial x} \quad \text{and that} \quad \frac{\partial R}{\partial A} < 1.$$

The first condition means that a firm with such an objective will adopt (price)-output policies (here meaning 'produce at a level') at which its MR is less than its MC, sacrificing some profits in order to achieve its objective of maximum revenues. An increase in turnover resulting from increased advertising, unlike that following a price cut, always increases revenues. The revenue maximizer will therefore carry his advertising expenditure to the limit of the profit constraint, i.e. (using the symbols of the previous model, with meaning modified as above) until $\pi_A = \pi_0$. Here

---

* [6], p. 360: so long as staff expenditures have a positive marginal utility,

$$\frac{\partial R}{\partial S} < 1.$$

† Described also in [3], Chapter 13; [26], Chapter 18 and [6], Chapter 17.
‡ Treatment of price as given reflects oligopoly (price stability or following a price leader).

is a further example of how different enterprise goals lead to different production decisions.

Maximizing the rate of return on capital rather than absolute profits has been advanced as another possible goal [16]. The relevant portion of the argument here for present purposes is the view of the authors concerned that the firm takes an essentially long run view of things, as evidenced by the fact that it allocates overhead costs to products or processes, and is attached to the idea of a norm (standard cost).* It is shown by them that, as long as the nature of the firm's production remains relatively constant, an objective of maximizing the rate of return implies operating at estimated minimum *LRAC*, and pricing under normal circumstances according to what the traffic will bear, with appropriate long run qualifications as mentioned in a later footnote.

(b) Non-maximizing models

Other *behavioural theories* or descriptions of the firm are far more sweeping in their departures from the neoclassical theory. Some of their characteristics are as follows :

(i)
Unlike the neoclassical model they allow the firm to have multiple objectives. For example, Cohen and Cyert† allow the firm to have a small set of operational goals, all of which must be met. In the case of decisions concerning price, output and general sales strategy they suggest the set contains five goals: a production goal (made up of a production level goal and a production smoothing goal), a finished goods inventory goal, a sales goal (or a market share goal), and a profit goal.

(ii)
These goals need not be optimizing goals; usually they are satisficing goals.

(iii)
Decision rules are not tautologies as under the marginal analysis, but standard operating rules or sometimes rough rules-of-thumb.

(iv)
Problems in each of the firm's decision areas (in the traditional theory the problems of how to produce, what to produce, how much to produce/what price to set) may be solved independently of one another and sequentially, not simultaneously as in

---

* When it is short of work, the firm does not add more for overheads, but rather the reverse, and conversely if it has too much work.

† [6], p. 336.

the traditional theory, by means of standard decision rules which are loosely related to a set of non-maximizing goals. According to the traditional theory, a change in anything which affects profits (e.g. technology, relative input prices, indirect taxes, demand conditions, advertising expenditure, rivals' reactions to this) leads the firm to take a single new set of simultaneous decisions. But in real life there are literally hundreds of factors which might change, 'too many to review simultaneously, and the interactions are only approximately and vaguely known, where they are known at all' ([34], p. 1).

(v)

It is not only market considerations which influence the decisions taken by the firm;* other important determinants are:

1. The firm's organization structure.
2. The particular goals the firm sets itself, how they are determined, and how they come to be revised.
3. The firm's information system – its form, the process of search and collection, and whether information is biased or lost as it passes through the organization. Uncertainty is assumed to be the rule rather than the exception.
4. How expectations (plans and anticipations) are formed, and whether plans (budgets) constrain the firm's decisions by defining in advance fixed expectations and a fixed commitment of resources to implement them.

(vi)

The new theories are positive rather than normative: they give attention to the processes by which decisions are reached. In the eyes of their authors they supplement the traditional theory, asking 'a different set of questions', . . . 'questions not all economic, concerning the internal decision-making structure of the firm' and resource allocation within the firm, rather than questions about the way in which the price system allocates resources among markets.†

(vii)

The theories are to a large extent empirically based,‡ and are often embodied in simulation models. By this means they are able to handle the qualitative as well as the quantitative aspects of decision-making, to 'incorporate adaptive and learning behaviour and include . . . aspects of heuristic reasoning' [5] – refer (iii) above.

(viii)

They are much less aggregative than the neoclassical theory which, because of its

* Not only that, but the neoclassical theory sees no difference between selling to private consumers and to industrial consumers [34].
† [6], p. 330.
‡ They also import a number of concepts from organization theory into the theory of the firm.

market orientation, sees the firm as taking only two types of decisions – input decisions and output decisions. Computer simulation has enabled models to be developed which are highly disaggregated.

(ix)
Simulation has also enabled dynamic problems (such as the holding of inventories) to be included in operational models.

(x)
It is recognized that an internal control problem exists, i.e. that the relationship between decisions made and the final outcomes may not be one-to-one, for reasons other than external ones.

These are just some of the features of the models which depart from the traditional economic model of the firm. Interested readers will find it particularly useful to examine the three models included in [9] and [6]: a duopoly model, an oligopoly model, and a department store (also oligopoly) model. The last one (see Chapter 7 of [9]) is particularly interesting in that price and output decisions are made on the basis of different goals. Yet other models of the firm under risk and uncertainty rest on a statistical decision theory framework.*

9.5 Pricing in practice

In perfect competition, it will be remembered, the equilibrium price in any market occurs where supply equals demand; prices are fixed independently of any producer at 'what the traffic will bear'. Once any degree of monopoly is admitted this is no longer necessarily true; each firm can exploit its downward-sloping demand curve to raise price above its competitive level by restricting output. According to the neoclassical theory, profit-maximizing firms that are able to pursue an independent price policy determine price and/or output by equating MC and MR. There has been considerable dissent from this view for two principal reasons. First, information on these marginal equalities is not available to the decision-makers. Secondly, there is of course no reason why pricing should follow the marginalist rule unless the firm has only a single objective, and that is profit maximization. As we have already seen, empirical studies seem to cast doubt on this being the case.

(a) Formula pricing

When asked how they fix prices, firms commonly reply that they use some formula (a standard decision rule). Some of the more commonly mentioned of these decision rules are listed below.

*See [26], Chapter 12; [6], Chapter 15.

(i) *'Cost-plus' pricing*

According to this rule prices are entirely cost-determined; demand has no influence at all. A percentage margin, which varies from trade to trade or within a given firm from product to product, is added to costs. This margin appears to be related to risk – products which 'turn over' less quickly than others (e.g. jewellery compared with bread), and hence tie up capital for longer periods, carry a higher margin than low-risk lines – and tends to remain fixed over fairly considerable periods of time. The costs to which this percentage margin is applied vary from case to case: they may be average variable costs (in which case the margin is a gross margin), or average total costs including allocated overheads,* and in either case it may be actual or standard costs. Two other forms of 'cost-plus' pricing are described below.

(ii) *Backward 'cost-plus' pricing*

Instead of building up to a price, costs are tailored to price under this method. Reasons for following this 'price-minus' rather than a 'cost-plus' approach might be seen in the existence of 'conventional prices' (for any product at a given time sales may tend to concentrate at several 'price points' in the price range, a result probably of consumer psychology), in a policy of following the price leader or what competitors are charging, or expected to charge. The extent to which price is demand-determined under this rule varies from case to case.

(iii) *Pricing for a target rate of return on investment*

This takes a form somewhat as follows:

$$\frac{\text{Budgeted profit}}{\text{Standard cost}} = \frac{\text{Capital invested}}{\text{Standard cost at standard volume}} \times \frac{\text{Budgeted profit}}{\text{Capital invested}}$$

i.e. 'capital turnover' × target rate of return = mark-up on standard cost. For a multiproduct firm, where different products required widely different amounts of capital in their manufacture, in order to make this calculation it would be necessary to allocate capital invested by product groups. This can only be done arbitrarily, and hence unsatisfactorily. There are, of course, other questions: how invested capital is to be valued, and why, having settled for a 'satisficing' goal, it should be a rate of return rather than absolute profits. To say that commitments of resources to a firm contain pricing implications is a matter of degree: committed resources determine, at least to some extent, the type of output it can produce and (again within limits) its production costs;† they need have no further influence on price policy.

* What the Americans call 'full cost'. Outside of N. America 'full cost' means average total cost plus mark-up.

† Capital invested will vary, *inter alia*, with the scale of output and the nature of the production process (how capital-intensive it is).

(iv) *Pricing for a target market share*

As shown by Cohen and Cyert,* if there are four oligopolists, one of whom (firm 4) wishes to maintain a fixed market share regardless of the effects on its profits in the short run (the firm believes long run advantages will more than offset any short run disadvantages), then:

$$\frac{q_4}{\sum_{i=1}^{4} q_i} = k,$$

where the q's are physical quantities. This firm determines its output

$$q_4 = \frac{k \sum_{i=1}^{3} q_i}{1-k}$$

on the assumption that the other firms' outputs remain fixed. Such a policy can only succeed if firms 1–3 acquiesce in it.

(v) *The form and the substance*

It is difficult to judge, without careful empirical investigation, whether pricing decision rules such as the above are really the substance of what firms actually do, or whether they stop short at the form. In the case of the various forms of 'cost-plus', for example, these describe a ritual [31] about which there is no argument. The only argument is over whether this ritual is *all* that the firm does, or whether it adjusts the 'cost-plus' price in a way which reflects its judgement as to what the market will bear (i.e. brings the demand side, which is entirely unrepresented in the 'cost-plus' theories, into the picture), and competition (what competitors are charging or expected to charge). Empirical work† has shown that in particular firms the 'cost-plus' estimated price is only a first approximation, and is in most cases adjusted for the factors just mentioned. As already noted, the power to fix prices, in substance though often not in form, resides in the market collectively.‡ The firm announces a tentative price; this price and/or its level of output (sales) change in the light of demand conditions in the market and changes in the firm's costs.

It is suggested above that in most cases the tentative prices will already reflect the firm's estimate of what the market will bear rather than a pure 'cost-plus' calcula-

---

* [6], pp. 239–40.
† See, e.g., [14], [29], [30]. Further empirical investigations are reported in [21].
‡ [12]. At the same time it should be realized that charging what the market will bear, in its pure form, is a short run pricing policy. In the long run price policy will be determined by supply. 'What the traffic will bear' is usually qualified to allow for long run considerations such as potential new 'entrants' and customers' goodwill.

tion. This is not to say, however, that in certain cases pure 'cost-plus' might not be a sensible price policy to follow. Consider the case of a monopolist, for example. Here 'what the market will bear' depends in an indeterminate way on output: the monopolist can fix price *or* output, but not both. In order not to attract new entrants into the market, and to minimize the risk of government regulation, cost plus a reasonably low percentage margin might well be the most sensible long run pricing policy for the monopolist to follow. The same policy could be used to penetrate a new market which is considered to have large potential, and carve out a large share of the market before other producers are attracted in.

(b) A multistage approach to pricing

We have already referred to behavioural models of the firm in which price and output decisions are taken independently, and satisfy different objectives. It has been suggested by Oxenfeldt [27] that this separation of decisions should be extended to the pricing decision itself, i.e. that the pricing decision could be made in stages, to be undertaken in a certain prescribed sequence. These stages are what Oxenfeldt considers to be the major elements in the pricing decision, viz.

1. Selecting market targets – the types of customers, or sections of the market, to be served.
2. Creating a favourable brand image of the product or the firm.
3. Deciding on the marketing mix, the combination of promotional devices to be employed. At this stage the expenditure on advertising would be decided, and a role assigned to price.
4. Determining price policy, taking into account competitors' prices, whether price competition will be matched (or alternatively whether the firm should price above the market and strive for prestige), whether and how often prices should be varied (there are costs involved in changing prices as in changing output levels).
5. Deciding on a pricing strategy (policy is to meet anticipated and foreseeable situations of a recurrent type, strategy to deal with special situations, e.g. 'entry' of a large new competitor or a sharp decline in demand for the whole industry).
6. Fixing price for a specific product.

While this approach is rich in its specification of the variables involved in the pricing decision, it appears to involve a certain amount of arbitrariness and subjectivity rather reminiscent of the description of price fixing in the early writings on 'marginal costing' in the United Kingdom.*

* See [22].

(c) Pricing in special situations

Special pricing situations are numerous, and only some of these can be mentioned. The multiproduct firm must decide on the relationship between prices in its product line, how to price products which are jointly produced or jointly demanded (complementary products) or are new to its range (skim or penetration pricing).* If production is to order,† or consists of items of very high unit value (e.g. ocean-going vessels, supersonic aircraft), prices are subject to individual negotiation; especially in the former case, there may be more room for flexibility in pricing. The same is true for non-standard production. The special short run pricing problems associated with the technique known as variable costing are discussed in the next chapter. Potentially important in all cases are the related questions of the distribution channels by which manufacturers deliver their products to final consumers; this is briefly referred to in Chapter 8.

Competitive bidding for contracts is another special case. The problem here is as follows: How should a firm fix its price in tendering for a contract in competition with other firms? If it sets its bid too low it risks incurring losses if its cost estimates prove to be low; too high a price will lose the contract. A possible strategy would be for the firm in question to estimate the highest, lowest and most likely prices its competitors will bid. It may consider, for example, that the price is unlikely to exceed its last bid, or be less than its own present estimate of cost, while the 'most likely' price may be the mean of this range. Looking at the position now from the customer's point of view, the firm may consider that its bid must be at least £x lower than that of its competitors in order to entice the customer away from them. This 'price sensitivity' is the rate at which the probability of the firm winning the contract increases (decreases) if its bid is just under (over) the lowest competing bid. A correction may then be made to this price for estimated customer bias against, or in favour of, the firm if all firms tendered at this common price. Then, using a Bayesian approach (involving subjective probabilities), the expected profits at this and every other price in the range between 'high' and 'low' estimates are generated. ‡

From this series the (say) ten bids offering the greatest expected profit (the bids which most nearly approach the optimal trade-off between profit margin and probability of winning) are selected. The firm chooses one of these prices, trying to increase its probability of winning without sacrificing too much profit. Obviously, this is no more than an outline of the method.§ Other factors which might be taken into account include how important it is to the firm to obtain the particular contract

---

* The *information* costs may be very high during the trial-and-error period which is necessary to discover the best price to fix for a new product – see [23].

† 'Discontinuous producers' sometimes fix (or estimate) their prices on an *ex post* full cost basis.

‡ Expected profit = probability of winning at each firm's bid/competitor's bid price pair, as calculated from the sensitivity and bias estimates, multiplied by the probability that a competitor will make this bid, multiplied by the firm's profit margin at this bid price.

§ The method described was developed by RCA and is described in detail in [25].

(in view of the current state of its order book); whether costs have been correctly specified (e.g. there may be opportunity costs, in the form of earnings foregone by not being in a position to take later work, to be imputed against the contract); possible interactions between 'sensitivity' and 'bias', and how the subjective probabilities are formed.

Government defence contract pricing raises special problems. These contracts often cover research and development work as well as production. Because of the very specialized nature of the work a competitive situation may not exist; in the United Kingdom, for example, only something like 5 per cent of Ministry of Aviation contracts are placed by competitive tendering. Prices must then be negotiated on some formula basis, known as 'prices to be agreed' contracts. Two principal methods have been used. Under the first, known as the fixed price contract, the price is agreed on the basis of cost estimates made before or during production. Price may here be cost plus a percentage profit or plus a fixed profit; alternatively, the parties may agree on the profit that will be paid if actual cost equals some agreed target cost figure, and on the basis of sharing differences between the two. A further alternative is some combination of 'cost-plus' and the fixed price or target cost method. Under the second method prices are agreed on the basis of actual costs after production is completed. (A further possibility is single tendering.)

In 1968, following two official investigations into suspected cases of over-charging on aviation contracts (by Ferranti and Bristol Siddeley Engines*), the British Government reached agreement with industry on new arrangements for placing and pricing non-competitive Government contracts. These provided for higher rates of return under a revised profit formula (equal on average to the overall return earned by British industry in 1960–66;† a higher rate is provided for 'risk' work); the contractual right of the Government to equality of information (to prevent the contractor from withholding vital information affecting price); post-costing of individual contracts (to price follow-on orders, not to renegotiate agreed prices); periodic revision of the profit formula; and the setting up of an impartial review board to which both parties could refer contracts where earned profits were too high or too low.

In both of the cases which were the subject of official inquiries the main cause of the excessive profits was found to have been a considerable over-estimating of direct labour-hours or cost. In the Ferranti case, where these estimates were often double what they should have been, a marked 'learning effect' had not been foreseen;‡ this error was amplified over five times by charging overheads on the basis of direct labour cost. In the Bristol Siddeley case there was also evidence of bad

---

*See [15] and [1], respectively, for accounts of these inquiries.

†A figure which, interestingly, was slightly lower than the rate assumed by the Government for the purpose of setting the financial targets for the nationalized industries in their 1961–67 White Papers.

*This problem arises, of course, whenever a new type of product is manufactured.

over-estimation of labour-time, to which (as with Ferranti) the withholding of information by the contractor and lack of coordination between Ministry director-ates contributed. Ferranti also contained a lesson for accountants concerning the size of the unit costed and the traceability of costs. It turned out in this case that almost half the expenses which were treated as overheads were in fact direct costs traceable to the Guided Weapons Division. They were treated as overheads because no-one had bothered to define the unit being costed (at the time, virtually all the work of this division was on the Government contracts concerned).

9.6 Costs for pricing

About all that can be said which is true of all the cases that have been referred to is that, as for all decision-making, the costs which are used as a basis for setting prices should be opportunity costs: the maximum amounts the resources concerned (including management time) could earn in other uses is the cost to the firm using them.

Beyond that statement it is impossible to generalize because of the great variety of theories and practices which have been mentioned. The exact specification of costs will depend, for one thing, on the objective (or objectives) towards which pricing is directed; it need not be marginal cost, for instance, unless the objective happens to be profit maximization or an objective which is equivalent so far as the price-output decision is concerned (e.g. the Williamson model examined earlier). And where marginal cost (= variable cost) is appropriate, whether this is short run or long run MC will depend on the firm's price policy (whether it is a short- or long-run maximizer) or whether the production in question calls for an increase in scale (i.e. new investment).

On a minor point, throughout much of the discussion of actual business practice – the 'cost-plus' literature is a notable example – the costs which the business man says he uses (as a basis) for setting prices are average direct costs. This reinforces the writers' view that the variability of costs with output is often not analysed very carefully in practice, if at all. Much more attention seems to be given to the trace-ability of costs to particular activities or products. The direct/indirect and variable/fixed distinctions are, of course, based on quite different attributes; direct costs and variable costs (which are the ones we should really be concerned with here)* are not necessarily the same or even approximately the same.

The chief omission in the foregoing, however, has been to confine discussion to production costs. There has been no mention of distribution and selling costs. The

---

*In decisions where a change in output is not involved we fall back on the more general category, avoidable costs.

relevant cost is the opportunity cost, measured at the margin, of producing, distributing and selling the product. This cost, measured precisely, cannot be generated by any formula, or predetermined; it will depend on the circumstances prevailing at the time the decision is taken.* At the same time it has been recognized that there is a cost involved in changing prices; if the changes are very frequent this may include loss of customers or of customers' goodwill.

We turn now to the matter of selling costs, and in particular advertising.†

9.7 The role of advertising

We must now recognize explicitly that, in highly industrialized societies, in which many industries are oligopolistic or near-oligopolistic, non-price competition assumes tremendous importance. Among the various forms of non-price competition are various promotional expenditures (selling costs), product improvement, after-sales service, and so on. Advertising is often the largest item in selling costs. Ignoring the other items, we may say as an approximation that in monopolistically competitive industry the firm seeks to influence the demand for its products by both price and advertising (even the monopolist may advertise to launch a new product or enter a new market). In oligopoly, however, and in certain other situations where price is not a competitive device and it is believed that advertising can influence demand, 'advertising comes fully into its own' . . . 'a life-and-death matter'.‡ High start-up costs in the form of heavy advertising expenditure may here discourage new entrants as effectively as heavy plant costs in a non-oligopolistic industry.

(a) The nature of advertising

Advertising is an 'innovation' in the sense in which the economist Schumpeter used that word: a firm innovates when it no longer takes its cost or demand curves as given, but directs its activity towards shifting these curves, and so *itself* changes the conditions under which profit maximization (or more generally its objective) is achieved. That is, 'innovation' takes the form of either (i) manipulating demand, by advertising or other means, or of (ii) changing the production function, which reflects the technological possibilities open to the firm at a given time. Normally the discussion is confined to the cost side when innovation is referred to.

Since the influence of the firm on the prices of inputs and products is already

---

* See also [4].
  † Distribution costs will not be referred to further. Their importance, however, should not be overlooked: in the US, for example, they represent 9 per cent of GNP and are still rising.
  ‡ [3], p. 328.

taken account of in the cost and demand curves, innovation on the demand side *implies a change in the type of product.* A firm may find it profitable to change the type of commodity it produces (i) if its views about consumers' tastes change, or (ii) if it thinks it can bring about a change in consumers' tastes by its own action. Advertising, then, can be viewed as a change or modification in the type of product sold; this will in all likelihood bring about a change in the firm's production function at the same time. That is, consumers' preferences for a product may be influenced by changing the product either physically or psychologically. A successfully advertised product can be made to *seem* just as different from an unadvertised one as a completely different physical product.

Together with other forms of selling cost, advertising seeks to shift the demand curve of the firm to the right, with or without a change in its price-elasticity, i.e. to push the demand curve out *at all prices*, and/or to make it more inelastic, thus giving the firm more flexibility in its pricing, subject to the qualifications mentioned earlier. (A price change, it should be noted, is *not* an alternative device: price influences the amount bought with a *given* demand curve; a price change is represented by a movement along the curve, not a shift or a tilt in the curve.)* Most successful advertising is on a national scale and is accompanied by branding of the product.

We may distinguish between (i) informational and persuasive advertising (the former merely informing the public of the existence of the product and stating its price; most advertising is persuasive to some extent); and between (ii) autonomous and defensive (competitive) advertising (much advertising is competitive: one firm advertises because its competitors do so). This is not the place to enter into a long discussion on the ethics of advertising or its social effects. Given existing arrangements in so-called developed societies, we need only note that it is a very powerful, widely used, and costly device, accounting in the US, for instance, for more than 3 per cent of GNP. Our concern here is with how a particular firm's advertising budget should be determined, and with some of the practical problems that may be encountered.

As with pricing, this will depend on the firm's market structure and on its objectives. The discussion will be confined to the former (two cases: monopolistic competition and oligopoly) under a single objective, profit maximization. The analysis, if carried out in terms of geometry, requires either three dimensions (price, advertising expenditure, revenues/costs) to allow for the interdependence between advertising and price, or the use of indifference curves.† It will be more convenient, however, to formulate the problem algebraically, using a static model.‡

* What are some possible alternatives which *would* have the same effec.
† For an illustration of the latter, see [42], Chapter 14.
‡ The model described below is that of Dorfman and Steiner [39], ignoring the details concerned with optimal quality.

(b) A static model

(i) *Monopolistic competition or monopoly*

Assume, then, that the firm can determine both the price it charges and its expenditure on advertising, and that these are the only variables affecting the demand for its product (incomes, tastes, and so on are constant), i.e.

$$q = f(p,s) \tag{1}$$

where q is the quantity demanded per unit of time, p is price and s is the advertising budget. The problem is to determine the optimal price-advertising-quantity combination.

As a first step, assume q is fixed, and determine the optimal (p,s) combination for selling this predetermined output.* (By this device production costs can be left out of the first part of the analysis. q will later be allowed to vary and find its optimal level.) If the price and advertising expenditure are both varied by a small amount, dp and ds respectively, the resulting change in q, assuming the function f to be continuous and differentiable, will be the total differential of equation (1):

$$dq = \frac{\partial f}{\partial p} dp + \frac{\partial f}{\partial s} ds.$$

But in order for q to remain constant, as assumed, dp and ds must have equal and opposite effects on q, so that $dq = 0$. Equating the RHS to zero, therefore, we have

$$dp = -\frac{\partial f/\partial s}{\partial f/\partial p} ds \qquad \left(\frac{\partial f}{\partial p} \neq 0, \text{ by assumption}\right) \tag{2}$$

What has happened is that revenue has changed by $q\, dp$ and advertising by ds, leaving q and total *production* costs unchanged. The net effect on profits is therefore

$$q\, dp - ds = -\left\{ q\frac{\partial f/\partial s}{\partial f/\partial p} + 1 \right\} ds \tag{3}$$

Two cases may now be considered: where the expenditure on advertising from which the variation was measured was positive, and where it was zero. These initial expenditures are denoted by s_0. By general reasoning, it can be shown that (i) a positive level of advertising cannot be optimal unless the quantity in parentheses in (3) is zero, and (ii) if there was no advertising previously, profits could not be maximized if the quantity in parentheses were negative. Thus the following necessary condition for profit maximization at any, and therefore all, levels of output is derived:

$$q\frac{\partial f/\partial s}{\partial f/\partial p} + 1 \begin{cases} = 0 \text{ if } s_0 > 0 \\ \geq 0 \text{ if } s_0 = 0 \end{cases} \tag{4}$$

* Sales and output are here regarded as synonymous, i.e. all output is sold immediately; there is no making for stock.

251

Denoting the price elasticity of demand, $-\dfrac{p}{q}\dfrac{\partial f}{\partial p}$, by η and the marginal value product of advertising (analogous to marginal revenue product in the case of price),* $p\dfrac{\partial f}{\partial s}$, by μ, substituting in (4) and simplifying, we have:

$$\mu = \eta \quad \text{if} \quad s_0 > 0$$
$$\mu \leq \eta \quad \text{if} \quad s_0 = 0 \tag{5}$$

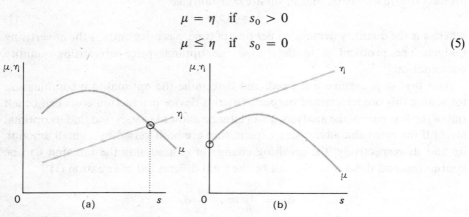

Figure 9.3 (a) $s_0 > 0$. (b) $s_0 = 0$

In words, this method consists essentially in equating MR and the sum of marginal production and selling costs. The analysis shows that the necessary condition for profit maximization can be expressed in terms of (i) the marginal value product of advertising (μ) and the price elasticity of demand (η), the particular form of the condition depending on whether the existing level of advertising expenditure (s_0) is positive or zero. (Students should prove for themselves that $\mu > \eta$ is a necessary condition for advertising to pay at all.) To each level of advertising expenditure there corresponds a certain price which will maximize profits, taking that advertising expenditure as given. This is the optimal price, p^*. μ^* is the marginal value product of advertising and η^* the price elasticity of demand corresponding to this optimal price.

Several comments can be made as a result of this analysis: (i) in perfect competition $\eta = \infty$ and μ is always less than η; consequently there will be no advertising; (ii) the greater the degree of product differentiation the lower the price elasticity η for a given brand, and the higher the optimal expenditure on advertising; (iii) uncertainty on the part of consumers reduces the effectiveness of changes in price differentials between brands, but at the same time increases the marginal effectiveness of advertising, encouraging heavy advertising effort.

In the first stage of the analysis output (q) was assumed to be constant. It is

*The rate of increase of revenue as advertising expenditure is increased, price being held constant. This is indicated by the height on the graphs in Figure 9.3 of the μ curve, the shape of which implies diminishing returns to advertising.

argued, in the second step, that if a firm's position can be improved without changing its sales volume, then *a fortiori* it can be improved if this possibility is open to it. In other words the result obtained above has full generality. We then have three variables, MR, production and selling costs, and output, which must be solved for simultaneously to determine the firm's optimum.

(ii) *Price fixed*

We turn now to the special case where price is a constant, not a variable in the optimisation as in (i). That is, $q = f(s)$. This is particularly likely to be the case in oligopolistic firms – and this is the market situation in which most advertising occurs. With price given, the necessary condition for profit maximization is that level of sales and advertising expenditure at which the expenditure on advertising required to increase sales volume by one unit $(\partial s/\partial q)$ just equals the difference between price (fixed) and marginal production cost, MC, on this marginal unit, i.e.

$$p - MC = \frac{\partial s}{\partial q}.$$

Remembering that the marginal value product of advertising is $\mu = p\frac{\partial q}{\partial s}$, this condition can be written

$$p - MC = \frac{p}{\mu}$$

i.e.
$$MC = p\left(1 - \frac{1}{\mu}\right).$$

As Dorfman and Steiner point out, the RHS has the same form as the well-known expression* for marginal revenue in terms of price and price-elasticity of demand, the difference being that here we have μ instead of η.

Solving this equation for μ shows that advertising expenditure is optimized when the marginal value product of advertising equals the reciprocal of the mark-up (i.e. $p/(p - MC)$) on the marginal unit sold. If rivals are not taken into account, it follows that the greater the mark-up in relation to price, the lower the marginal value product of advertising, and the greater advertising expenditure will be.

If the reason why price is treated as fixed is an oligopolistic market situation, a crucial element in the above analysis will be the accuracy with which rivals' reactions are estimated and allowed for in specifying the function $q = f(s)$.

(c) Advertising viewed dynamically

The above analysis provides the necessary conditions for profit maximization when

$$*MR = p\left(1 - \frac{1}{\eta}\right).$$

the only variables affecting demand are price and advertising expenditure, or the latter alone. The analysis left out one very important aspect of advertising, namely that its effects are usually distributed over a period of time;* advertising throughout this period may affect current and future sales. Advertising was also regarded as a current operating expense, which certainly accords with business practice in most cases.

A more realistic approach would be to regard advertising – large-scale advertising outlays – as being in the nature of investment rather than a current expense, yielding up its benefits over a number of periods just as durable equipment does. This would call for use of a dynamic model, as defined in Chapters 5 and 6. The introduction of time into the analysis would suggest that we should include, in addition to price and advertising, other variables such as incomes, population and the prices of substitute and complementary products. Allowance should also be made for the effects of advertising causing a change in the shape, as well as a shift, in the firm's demand curve, and for the effects of the expenditure diminishing over time.

Such an approach has been followed by Nerlove and Arrow [40]. They represent the effects on demand of current and past advertising outlays as an asset, goodwill, which depreciates in a manner similar to capital goods (in their model a constant percentage rate of depreciation is assumed). The corresponding expression for quantity demanded is now

$$q(t) = f[p(t), A(t), z(t)],$$

where t denotes time, A goodwill and z the variables not under the firm's control (incomes, population, etc.). The firm attempts to maximize the present value of revenues net of production and advertising costs by adopting appropriate price and advertising policies over time, i.e. the problem is to determine the optimal time paths of price and advertising outlays. This analysis will not be outlined further; the results are a dynamic generalization of those of Dorfman and Steiner.†

There is an interesting tailpiece to the Nerlove–Arrow paper, viz. that under plausible assumptions,‡§ the necessary conditions for maximizing the present value of future net revenues lead to a decision rule which is similar to a rule-of-

---

*A fact established empirically by Palda [41].

† The condition corresponding to equations (4) and (5) in section 7(b)(i) above, in words, is 'that at the optimal price (price = marginal production costs) the marginal revenue from increased goodwill net of the marginal costs of producing the increased output should be equal to the marginal opportunity cost of investment in goodwill' – [40], p. 134n.

‡ The assumptions are that (i) total production costs are linear (i.e. marginal production cost is constant) and (ii) demand is linear in logarithms (i.e. q changes at a constant proportional rate (which may be zero) with changes in p, A or z : $f(p, A, z)$ has the form $kp^{-\eta}A^{\beta}z^{\zeta}$, where η, β and ζ are the elasticities of p, A and z and k is a parameter defining the units of z.

§ As one of our students remarked, 'While the authors regard the common business rule-of-thumb as supporting their analysis, particularly the special case, curiously they do not argue that, with equal coincidence, their model might have identified a widespread malpractice among firms.'

thumb widely used in practice, and which hitherto seemed completely illogical, that advertising outlays should bear a constant ratio to sales revenue.

(d) Measurement problems

The foregoing analyses gloss over some formidable measurement problems in assessing the effectiveness of advertising (the benefits compared with the cost). This may very well explain why so many firms resort to rules-of-thumb in determining their advertising budgets. As Dean says,* 'the economist's assumption that the entrepreneur knows the least-cost combination of production factors is rarely correct for marketing activities . . .'. The benefits are usually even more difficult to measure. Some of the main difficulties are listed below.

1. The effect of advertising on sales is very difficult to measure because there are so many interdependencies between the demand determinants: quantity demanded depends partly on price, quality, design and packaging, consumers' incomes and tastes, the prices of substitutes and complementary products, and there are interactions between these.
2. Advertising typically has cumulative effects: an immediate (impact) effect and delayed effects. Consequently sales this period are likely to depend in part on past advertising. The time-lag between impact and delayed effects is extremely difficult to measure.
3. For the oligopolist the effectiveness of advertising will, in addition, depend on rivals' past and present advertising and on their reactions to the firm's advertising effort. They may react by reducing price, improving product quality, offering better service (repairs, credit, etc.). Retaliation is in general much more difficult against non-price competition than against price-cutting, which helps to explain why the former is so prevalent. Effectiveness will depend on how much of the advertising expenditure is purely defensive.
4. It will also depend on the quality of the advertising, its degree of persuasiveness, which often cannot be measured at all closely in terms of money, and on the type of advertising (how much will be national and how much point-of-sale, and how will the total budget be allocated as between different media?).
5. Advertising effectiveness depends also on the kind of product (e.g. whether it is a consumer good or a producer good), on whether the product is an old or new one, and if the former, on the point it has reached in its acceptance cycle.†
6. The state of the market is also relevant – whether sales of the *type* of product in question are increasing or relatively steady (there are very few recorded

* [11], p. 134.
† Also of relevance to the foregoing analysis is the fact that the price elasticity of demand for most products increases with time.

instances of advertising reversing a declining demand, though there are some). Analogous to the income and substitution effects of a price change we can distinguish two possible effects of advertising: an income (or market widening) effect and a substitution (or market sharing) effect. If the demand for the class of product in question is increasing (as, e.g., in the early stages of a product's life), advertising may expand the total market, with the result that increased sales by any single firm are not at the expense of its competitors. If demand is fairly stable, on the other hand, advertising will have a substitution effect, if it has any effect at all, i.e. it will result in a revision of market shares.

7. Effectiveness measured as the money difference between costs and benefits will depend on the rate of taxation on business profits.

9.8 Internal sales: transfer pricing

Sections 1–6 have been concerned with the prices charged by firms in outside markets. We now distinguish between such external sales and the allocation of resources to the firm, on the one hand, and internal sales and the utilization of resources within the firm on the other. Transfers of goods or services between parts of a firm, or what are sometimes called 'sales not at arm's length', may assume considerable proportions: a figure of 20–25 per cent of total sales to all sources is not uncommon in large integrated companies.

The reason why it is important to inquire how the prices governing these internal movements of resources are fixed is that these prices will affect the level of operation of the activities concerned, the performance measure by which they are judged, and the profitability of the firm as a whole. In practice a number of different methods are used for fixing transfer prices; they include pricing at cost (direct cost, direct cost plus some portion of overheads, cost plus some prescribed rate of return, standard cost), at rates negotiated by the managers of the activities concerned, or market price if there happens to be an active outside market for the item transferred. (In yet other cases allocations are determined in aggregate by budgeting, as discussed in Chapter 17.) These methods are arbitrary and will not, in general, correspond to the optimal transfer price, which should measure the *opportunity cost* of the item concerned *to the firm as a whole, measured at the margin*. Only such a price will ensure that the transferred good or service is used at the optimum level relative to all alternative uses, and relative to all constraints on enterprise optimization.

The neoclassical theory of the firm, as Coase has pointed out [45], makes the implicit assumption that all internal allocations of resources are made under perfectly competitive conditions. This ignores a number of external (market) and internal (organizational) factors, and would not in general be an optimal rule.

Behavioural theories of the firm, which assume objectives other than profit maximization or indeed maximization of any quantity, while believing that price-guided allocations as referred to above are likely to be useful approximations, are sceptical as to whether 'all of the major relevant factors in allocation decisions . . . can [be identified] *a priori*'.* In their positive theory of the firm, in which the organization is viewed as a coalition of participants among whom conflict is only partially resolved, the concept of an 'efficiency price' (the opportunity cost transfer price referred to above) has limited usefulness. In this view transfer payment rules are arbitrary within fairly wide limits, and are the result of a long-run bargaining process rather than the solution to a properly specified economic pricing problem. The same factors that produce organizational slack with respect to the external environment, they consider, will produce slack with respect to transfer payments (e.g. activities which have negotiated favourable transfer payments will be less concerned with negotiating revised rules than will activities that have been less successful).†

Just as in the choice between economic socialism and free enterprise organization for management of national economies, there is a choice between centralization and decentralization of decision-making within the firm. Under the latter system, authority and responsibility in some matters is delegated by the central management to sub-units of the business, including divisions. In a national economy resource allocations are guided by the price system under the free enterprise system, and by a system of accounting prices under economic socialism (e.g. the USSR). The transfer price problem, at least under the assumptions of the neoclassical theory, is a problem in the adaptation of price mechanisms to the internal environment of the firm. Contrary, however, to the neoclassical assumptions that the firm is under wholly centralized direction, in practice some degree of decentralization is widespread, suggesting that managements believe this is a more efficient form of organization.‡ It represents an attempt to halt the decline in efficiency which usually results as the volume of transactions organized internally increases.

Whether such prices are determined locally (i.e. by the activities concerned) as market prices are in a free enterprise system, or globally (by central management for all activities) as they are under socialism, will depend on the degree of decentralization which is desired and possible. The latter will depend, *ceteris paribus*, on the market structure for the good transferred and whether there is interdependence between the activities, that is, whether some of the relevant decision variables may not be completely controllable by the activity concerned, but depend on actions by

* [9], p. 271.
† [9], p. 276.
‡ An organization may be said to be optimally decentralized when the net effect of all individual actions will be more favourable to the firm than the actions of any other array of decision centres – [50].

other activities.* (The attempt to operate an artificial pricing system is, of course, only worth making if the estimated benefits through greater efficiency exceed the costs involved: costs of coordination, computation and data transmission. The cost of any necessary incentives, and of operating the reward-penalty system, to make the internal pricing system effective, should also be included.)†

Since one of the authors has dealt with the topic at some length elsewhere‡ it is not proposed to duplicate the analysis here. Readers are referred to this source; they may also wish to consult Hirshleifer ([47], [48]) for a marginal analysis of the problem, and [44] and [51] for more detailed mathematical programming formulations. A survey of the methods actually used by firms (American) will be found in [49] and [51].

Some of the main results for the case where there are no interdependencies between the activities concerned are set out in Table 9.1, where:

p^* = optimal transfer price

p = price in intermediate market

P = price in final product market

mc_s, mr_s = marginal cost/revenue of selling activity

mc_b, mr_b = marginal cost/revenue of buying activity

nmr = net marginal revenue = $mr_b - mc_b$

MR = the (horizontal) sum of mr_s and nmr.

In the first two cases we see that the transfer price should equal the marginal cost of the selling activity, and in the second case, in addition, equal the price in the intermediate market. In the third case the transfer price should always be less than the market price in the intermediate market.

In the first case neither activity can fix its (common) output level independently of the other; both problems must be solved simultaneously. This can usually only be done iteratively, either by an exchange of information between the activities (administratively or via a mathematical programming formulation which is solved on the computer), or the same must be done by central management, resulting in a retreat from decentralization. In the third case the firm is in a position like a discriminating monopolist (see the appendix to this chapter), and the same analysis is used. The problem here can be solved in a way which is consistent with decentralization by an exchange of information – as in the first case either administratively or by mathematical programming.

---

* See section 4(a)(vi) of Chapter 8.

† Once again our attention is drawn to the role of the reward–penalty system in inducing behaviour which is consistent with enterprise objectives.

‡ Amey [43], Chapter VII and Appendix V.

Table 9.1 Optimal transfer price rules

		Final product market	
		perfectly competitive	imperfectly competitive
Intermediate product market	Nonexistent (or where, for other reasons, a joint level of intermediate and final output is necessary)	$p^* = mc_s$ Overall solution for firm: $mc_s + mc_b = P$	$mc_s + mc_b = mr_b$
	Perfectly competitive	$p^* = mc_s = p$ $mc_b = P - p$	$mc_b = mr_b - p$
	Imperfectly competitive	(perfectly and imperfectly competitive) $p^* = mc_s$ Firm: $mc_s = MR$, i.e. $mc_s + mc_b = mr_s + mr_b$ *Supplier activity:* *Purchasing activity:* p^* given by output at $p^* = nmr$ gives output which $mc_s = MR;$ of final product; $p^* = mr_s$ gives external this is equivalent to sales; balance trans- setting ferred internally $mc_s + mc_b = mr_b$	

Once the assumption that there are no interdependencies is relaxed the problem must be formulated in mathematical programming terms (see [43], appendix).

It should be noted that the analysis to which we have been referring provides solutions only in terms of the determination of *marginal* rates of output of the activities concerned. For non-marginal changes in output, including changes in the *scale* of the activities (expansion of capacity or the closing down of an activity), the optimal transfer prices are not relevant. For we are then dealing with a non-marginal decision, as discussed in Chapter 6, and would have to look at the change in total revenues and costs for the firm as a whole if we expanded/contracted/closed down the activity. Some examples of abandonment decisions (closing down of an activity) are given at the end of Chapter 11.

In closing it is useful to compare the method of pricing internal transfers discussed above with transfers at standard cost, a system which is believed to be used by many British and American companies. This is left as a question for the reader to consider, in problem 9.1.

As well as being decision rules, transfer prices serve as controls on the efficiency of intrafirm activities involving resource allocations. The reader is referred to Chapters 17 and 18 on the control aspects of transfer prices. In section 5 of Chapter 18 we offer some observations on the practicality of operating an economic transfer price system in a large business enterprise.

Appendices

(a) Multiproduct firm: general case [*][†]

The chief difference here compared with the single-product case is that in any period the firm cannot increase its output of one product without decreasing its output of the remaining products.

The production function, in implicit form, is

$$Q = f(q_1, \ldots, q_m; x_1, \ldots, x_n) = 0$$

where the q's are outputs and the x's inputs, both in physical units per unit of time. The constraint imposed by the production function can be written

$$f(q_1, \ldots, q_m) = g(x_1, \ldots, x_n).$$

If the firm's revenue function is $R = R(q_1, \ldots, q_m)$ and its cost function is $C = C(x_1, \ldots, x_n)$, this expression including variable costs only, the problem is to maximize

$$\pi = R_i - C_j, \quad i = 1, \ldots, m$$

$$j = 1, \ldots, n$$

subject to
$$f(q_i) - g(x_j) = 0.$$

Forming the Lagrangean expression

$$L = R_i - C_j - \lambda [f(q_i) - g(x_j)],$$

the necessary conditions for a maximum are given by:

$$\frac{\partial L}{\partial q_i} = r_i - \lambda [f'(g_i)] = 0;$$

$$\frac{\partial L}{\partial x_j} = -w_j + \lambda [g'(x_j)] = 0,$$

$$\frac{\partial L}{\partial \lambda} = -[f(q_i) - g(x_j)] = 0$$

where r_i is the marginal revenue from product i, w_j is the marginal factor cost of input j, $\lambda [f'(q_i)]$ is the marginal cost of any one product i and $\lambda [g'(x_j)]$ the marginal value product of any one input j.

From this it follows that

$$\frac{\partial f / \partial q_1}{r_1} = \frac{\partial f / \partial q_2}{r_2} = \ldots = \frac{\partial g / \partial x_1}{w_1} = \frac{\partial g / \partial x_2}{w_2} = \ldots = \frac{1}{\lambda}.$$

[*] Perfect or monopolistic competition.
[†] For further details and a description of the sufficient conditions, see [26], pp. 123–28.

(b) Joint products in variable proportions, general case

This can be seen by extension of the analysis in section 4(a)(v) of Chapter 8.

(c) Discriminating monopoly

One form of monopoly – price discrimination – is of particular interest. If the market can be split up into separate markets with different elasticities of demand it will pay the monopolist to charge different prices in these markets (higher prices in the market with the more inelastic demand), provided that it is not possible for customers to switch between markets (buying in the cheaper and selling in the dearer), and that the costs to the firm of keeping the markets separate is small relative to the differences in demand elasticities. In these circumstances profits will be maximized by the condition

$$MR_1 = MR_2 = \ldots = MC.$$

This is illustrated in Figure 9.4, where the curve MR is the horizontal sum of the separate curves MR_1 and MR_2:

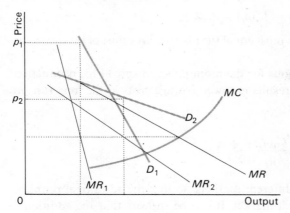

Figure 9.4 Discriminating monopoly

Price discrimination may take various forms: (i) it may be direct, as when different consumers are charged different prices for the same product; or (ii) indirect, when a given product is sold at the same price to all consumers, but different products contribute disproportionately to the firm's overhead costs; or (iii) different quantities may be offered at different prices (the discrimination being between increments of sales rather than between buyers, as with electricity tariffs); (iv) the discrimination may also be in respect of time or place as well as persons. The discriminating monopoly analysis has a number of applications in other fields. Two examples are internal transfer pricing where both intermediate and final product markets are imperfectly competitive (section 8 of this chapter) and joint production in variable proportions (section 4(a)(v) of Chapter 8).

(d) Multiplant monopoly

Suppose a monopoly operates two plants, whose outputs are q_r and q_s, respectively. Profit is denoted by π, and the other symbols are as in Chapter 7. Assume initially that all output is sold in a single market. Then the problem is how much to produce in each plant.

$$\pi = R(q_r+q_s) - C_r(q_r) - C_s(q_s).$$

Using primes to denote derivatives,

$$\frac{\partial \pi}{\partial q_r} = R'(q_r+q_s) - C'_r(q_r) = 0$$

$$\frac{\partial \pi}{\partial q_s} = R'(q_r+q_s) - C'_s(q_s) = 0$$

i.e.
$$R'(q_r+q_s) = C'_r(q_r) = C'_s(q_s);$$

i.e. the marginal cost of each plant must equal the marginal revenue of the output as a whole.*

It will in general be advantageous for the monopolist to spread his production over more than one plant if this results in lower average costs in the long run; in particular if:†

$$\sum_{j=1}^{n} \left(\frac{C_j(q_j)}{q_j} \cdot \frac{q}{\Sigma q_j} \right) < \frac{C(q)}{q}$$

Now suppose there are three different markets, so that the additional problem arises of how much to sell in each market. It can be shown‡ that the additional condition is that marginal revenue should be equal in all markets, and equated to ΣMC. The analysis can be extended to a monopolist with $j = 1, \ldots, n$ plants and $i = 1, \ldots, m$ markets.

(e) Dynamic profit maximization

The static analysis of the previous models is a special case of a dynamic system in

---

* Second-order conditions require that the MC in each plant must be increasing more rapidly than the MR of output as a whole.

† [6], p. 196.

‡ By combining with the discriminating monopoly analysis (in which the MR's were added horizontally) a curve for ΣMC obtained by adding the MC's of each plant horizontally.

which tastes, technique and resources remain constant through time. In static conditions firms, acting on past experience, are likely to assume these conditions will continue into the future. It is not therefore necessary for them to form expectations, because expectations (e.g. expected price) and outcomes (actual price) are always the same.

Once this assumption is dropped and the firm is considered dynamically, the problem is to find that production plan which will maximize the present value of the stream of profits over the period of the plan. That is, we wish to determine the series of output rates which will maximize the present value of the firm, given initial resources and subject to the constraint of the firm's production function.

If V = the present value of the plan, which we will assume extends over T periods,

q_{rt} = output of product r in period t (if $q_{rt} > 0$), or the input of r in period t (if $q_{rt} < 0$),

$\beta_t = (1 + i_t)^{-1}$ is the discount rate in period t, assumed constant in all periods,

p_{rt} = the expected price of r in period t,

then with perfect competition in product, input and capital markets (all p's and β's given), the problem is of the general form:

$$\text{maximize } V = \sum_{r=1}^{n} \sum_{t=1}^{T} (\beta_t^t p_{rt} q_{rt})$$

subject to $f(q_{11}, \ldots, q_{rt}, \ldots, q_{nT}) = 0$.

Forming the Lagrangean expression

$$L = \sum_{r=1}^{n} \sum_{t=1}^{T} (\beta_t^t p_{rt} q_{rt}) - \lambda f(q_{11}, \ldots, q_{rt}, \ldots, q_{nT}) = 0,$$

the conditions for a maximum are:

$$\frac{\partial L}{\partial q_{rt}} = p_{rt} \beta_t^t - \lambda \frac{\partial f}{\partial q_{rt}} = 0$$

$$\frac{\partial L}{\partial \lambda} = -f(q_{11}, \ldots, q_{rt}, \ldots, q_{nT}) = 0,$$

and the appropriate second-order conditions. It is also necessary that

$$\frac{-\partial q_{rt}}{\partial q_{\rho\tau}} = \frac{\partial f}{\partial q_{\rho\tau}} \bigg/ \frac{\partial f}{\partial q_{rt}} = \frac{p_{\rho\tau} \beta_\tau^\tau}{p_{rt} \beta_t^t},$$

where $t, \tau = 1, \ldots, T; r, \rho = 1, \ldots, m$ denote outputs and $r, \rho = (m+1), \ldots, n$ denote

263

inputs; and it is assumed that all inputs are used and outputs sold in the period in which they were purchased/produced.

If product and input markets are imperfectly competitive, p_{rt} must be replaced by $\dfrac{\partial R}{\partial q_{rt}}$ (marginal revenue if $q_{rt} > 0$, marginal revenue product if $q_{rt} < 0$), R being the revenue function.

As noted in Chapter 5, there are differences of opinion over the period of the plan. In Hicks [19], $t = \infty$, in Modigliani and Cohen [24] it covers varying periods beyond the first, depending on what aspects of the future ('relevant anticipations') need to be taken into account in order to make optimal decisions in the first period.

Bibliographical references

Price-output decisions

[1] Amey, L. R., The Bristol Siddeley Affair, *Journal of Business Finance*, Spring 1969, pp. 53–54.

[2] Baumol, W. J., *Business Behavior, Value and Growth*, Macmillan, New York, 1959.

[3] Baumol, W. J., *Economic Theory and Operations Analysis*, Prentice-Hall, 2nd edn., 1965.

[4] Baxter, W. T. and A. R. Oxenfeldt, Approaches to pricing: economist *vs.* accountant, *Business Horizons*, 1961, pp. 77–90; reprinted in *Modern Financial Management*, eds. B. V. Carsberg and H. C. Edey, Penguin, 1969.

[5] Clarkson, G. P. E. and H. A. Simon, Simulation of individual and group behavior, *American Economic Review*, 1960, pp. 920–32.

[6] Cohen, K. J. and R. M. Cyert, *Theory of the Firm*, Prentice-Hall, 1965.

[7] Cournot, A., *Researches into the Mathematical Principles of the Theory of Wealth*, trans. N. T. Bacon, Macmillan, New York, 1897.

[8] Cyert, R. M., E. A. Feigenbaum and J. G. March, Models in a behavioral theory of the firm, *Behavioral Science*, 1959, pp. 81–95.

[9] Cyert, R. M. and J. G. March, *A Behavioral Theory of the Firm*, Prentice-Hall, 1963.

[10] Cyert, R. M. and J. G. March, Organizational factors in the theory of oligopoly, *Quarterly Journal of Economics*, 1956, pp. 44–46.

[11] Dean, J., *Managerial Economics*, Prentice-Hall, 1951.

[12] Dorfman, R., *The Price System*, Prentice-Hall, 1964.

[13] Edgeworth, F. Y., *Mathematical Psychics*, London School Reprints of Scarce Works, No. 10, 1881; reprinted 1932.

[14] Edwards, R. S., The pricing of manufactured products, *Economica*, August, 1952.

[15] Flower, J. F., The case of the profitable bloodhound, *Journal of Accounting Research*, Spring 1966, pp. 16–36.

[16] Gabor, A. and I. F. Pearce, A new approach to the theory of the firm, *Oxford Economic Papers*, 1952.

[17] Hague, D. C., *Managerial Economics*, Longmans, 1969.

[18] Henderson, J. M. and R. E. Quandt, *Microeconomic Theory, A Mathematical Approach*, McGraw-Hill, 1958.

[19] Hicks, J. R., *Value and Capital*, Oxford University Press, 2nd edn., 1946.

[20] Hurwicz, L., The theory of economic behavior, *American Economic Review*, 1945, pp. 909–25; reprinted in *Readings in Price Theory*, American Economic Association, 1953.

[21] Lanzillotti, R. F., Pricing objectives in large companies, *American Economic Review*, 1958, pp. 921–40.

[22] Lawrence, F. C. and E. N. Humphreys, *Marginal Costing*, Macdonald & Evans, 1947.

[23] Malmgren, H. B., Information, expectations and the theory of the firm, *Quarterly Journal of Economics*, 1961, pp. 399–421; reprinted in *Readings in Management Decision*, ed. L. R. Amey, Longman 1973.

[24] Modigliani, F. and K. J. Cohen, The role of anticipations and plans in economic behavior and their use in economic analysis and forecasting, in *Studies in Business Expectations and Planning No. 4*, Bureau of Economic and Business Research, University of Illinois, 1961.

[25] Montgomery, D. B. and G. L. Urban, *Management Science in Marketing*, Prentice-Hall, 1969.

[26] Naylor, T. H. and J. M. Vernon, *Microeconomics and Decision Models of the Firm*, Harper, Brace & World, 1969.

[27] Oxenfeldt, A. R., Multistage approach to pricing, *Harvard Business Review*, July-August 1960, pp. 125–33.

[28] Papandreou, A. G., Some basic problems in the theory of the firm, in *A Survey of Contemporary Economics*, ed. B. F. Haley, Irwin, 1952.

[29] Pearce, I. F., A study in price policy, *Economica*, 1956, pp. 114–127, reprinted in Carsberg and Edey, *ibid.*

[30] Pearce, I. F. and L. R. Amey, Price policy with a branded product, *Review of Economic Studies*, 1957, pp. 49–60.

[31] Robinson, E. A. G., The pricing of manufactured products, *Economic Journal*, 1950.

[32] Shubik, M., *Strategy and Market Structure*, Wiley, 1959.

[33] Stackelberg, H. von, *The Theory of the Market Economy*, A. T. Peacock trans., Oxford University Press, 1952.

[34] Steuer, M. D. and A. P. Budd, Price and output decisions of firms – A critique of E. S. Mills' theory, *Manchester School*, March 1968, pp. 1–25.

[35] Sweezy, P. M., Demand under conditions of oligopoly, *Journal of Political Economy*, 1939, pp. 568–573; reprinted in *Readings in Price Theory*, American Economic Association, 1953.

[36] Williamson, O. E., Managerial discretion and business behavior, *American Economic Review*, December 1963, pp. 1032–1057.

[37] Williamson, O. E., *The Economics of Discretionary Behavior:* Managerial Objectives in a Theory of the Firm, Prentice-Hall, 1964.

[38] Williamson, O. E., A model of rational managerial behavior, in [9].

Advertising

[3] Baumol, W. J., *ibid.*

[9] Cyert, R. M. and J. G. March, *ibid.*

[11] Dean, J., *ibid.*

[39] Dorfman, R. and P. O. Steiner, Optimal advertising and optimal quality, *American Economic Review*, 1954, pp. 826–36.

[40] Nerlove, M. and K. J. Arrow, Optimal advertising policy under dynamic conditions, *Economica*, 1962, pp. 129–42.

[41] Palda, K. S., The measurement of cumulative advertising effects, *Journal of Business*, April 1965; and a book bearing the same title, Prentice-Hall, 1964.

[42] Stigler, G. J., *The Theory of Price*, Macmillan, New York, 1946 edn.

Transfer pricing

[9] Cyert, R. M. and J. G. March, *ibid.*

[43] Amey, L. R., *The Efficiency of Business Enterprises*, Allen and Unwin, 1969.

[44] Arrow, K. J., Optimization, decentralization, and internal pricing in business firms, in *Contributions to Scientific Research in Management*, Western Data Processing Center, University of California, Los Angeles, January 1959, pp. 9–17.

[45] Coase, R. H., The nature of the firm, *Economica*, 1937, pp. 368–405; reprinted in *Readings in Price Theory*, Allen and Unwin, 1953.

[46] Gordon M. J., The use of administered price systems to control large organizations, in *Management Controls*, eds. Bonini, Jaedicke and Wagner, McGraw-Hill, 1964.

[47] Hirshleifer, J., On the economics of transfer pricing, *Journal of Business*, 1956, pp. 172–84; reprinted in *Modern Financial Management*, eds. Carsberg and Edey, *ibid.*

[48] Hirshleifer, J., Economics of the divisionalized firm, *Journal of Business*, 1957, pp. 96–108.
[49] National Association of Accountants, Accounting for intra-company transfers, *Research Series No. 30*, June 1, 1956.
[50] Shubik, M., Incentives, decentralized control, the assignment of joint costs and internal pricing, *Management Science*, 1962, pp. 325–43; a slightly modified version appears in *Management Controls*, ed. Bonini *et al.*, *ibid*.
[51] Whinston, A., Price guides in decentralized organizations, in *New Perspectives in Organization Research*, eds. W. W. Cooper, H. J. Leavitt and M. W. Shelly II, Wiley, 1964.

Problems

9.1 Evaluate the relative merits of (i) accounting prices fixed according to economic principles and (ii) pricing at standard cost as means of securing an optimal allocation of productive resources within a business.

9.2 'The computer offers a kind of break-through in managerial technology, the possibility of setting up a sensitive nervous system in the rather unwieldly bodies of the larger corporations, and hence of attaining the speed of response, adaptability and economy which we should like.'

What, in your opinion, is likely to be the effect of this development on the question of centralization *vs.* decentralization of decision and control?

9.3 A certain multi-product paper board mill produces board varying in thickness between 0·01 and 0·05 in. The running speed of mill machinery is unaffected by the thickness of board being produced. The company lumps together all costs, direct (excluding materials) and indirect, for each machine. A record is kept of the tonnage throughput for each machine, and costs are allocated to the various products manufactured by means of a machine-ton rate. Prices are then fixed on a 'cost-plus' basis, as an approximation.

What are the possible implications of this pricing policy?

9.4 In the course of an interview a business man says 'We have come to the conclusion that we would not sell any more if we reduced prices, even by as much as 50 per cent. I don't know why it is. We have tried countless times, sometimes under a different brand name.' Later in the same interview the business man added, in reply to the hypothetical question as to what he would do in the event of a marked reduction in cost confined to his firm, that he would rather take only the normal profit margin on costs and sell a lot.

Comment on these statements. Do they suggest to you possible areas for further investigation?

9.5 So what are some of the possible alternatives which would have the same effect as advertising, i.e. shift the demand curve (see footnote in section 7(a))?

9.6 Given the following information, formulate a linear production scheduling model. [The problem is to determine the production schedule which satisfies the production constraints, meets the demand requirements and minimizes the sum of production and storage costs]:

1. A single homogeneous product.
2. An n-period shifting planning horizon.
3. A fixed work force.
4. No production time-lag: any units sold in period j must have been produced in period j or earlier.
5. Opening inventories zero.
6. x_{ij} denotes the number of units produced on regular time in period i for sale in period j and y_{ij} the number of units produced on overtime in period i for sale in period j.
7. M_i denotes the number of units which can be produced in period i on regular time and N_i the number of units which can be produced in period i on overtime (N_i does not include M_i).
8. c_i is the constant unit production cost in period i on regular time and d_i the constant unit cost in period i on overtime.
9. h_i denotes storage cost per unit of product for period i, here assumed constant in all periods. No storage charges are incurred in the period in which the sale takes place.
10. r_j is the number of units demanded in period j.

9.7 In addition to the production decisions mentioned in section 1 of Chapter 7 there is often the problem of production smoothing (or scheduling), referred to in the previous problem. That is, if future sales do not occur at a steady rate, how (assuming the firm's objective is profit maximization) will it optimally absorb these fluctuations?

One of the models proposed for dealing with this problem is that of Holt *et al.*, referred to as the HMMS model (see reference [21] of Chapter 6). In this model sales in each future period up to the (shifting) planning horizon are assumed to be known with certainty (i.e. both sales volume and price). The work force is variable, and if an item ordered by a customer cannot be supplied from stock it is always possible to backorder it (i.e. place an order with the factory and let the customer wait). The model for determining production rate, work force and finished goods inventory level each period in respect of all products taken together is a dynamic model extending over T periods.

The problem takes the form of minimizing the sum of the relevant costs, which are represented by a quadratic cost function:

$$\text{minimize} \quad E(k_T) = k_T = \sum_{t=1}^{T} k_t,$$

where
$$\sum k_t = [k_1 W_t + k_{13} \quad \text{(regular payroll costs, including idle time cost)}$$

267

$$+ k_2(W_t - W_{t-1} - k_{11})^2 \quad \text{(hiring and layoff costs)}$$

$$+ k_3(P_t - k_4 W_t)^2 + k_5 P_t - k_6 W_t + k_{12} P_t W_t$$

$$\text{(overtime costs)}$$

$$+ k_7(I_t - k_8 - k_9 S_t)^2] \quad \text{(inventory and backorder costs)}$$

subject to $\qquad I_{t-1} + P_t - S_t = I_t \quad (t = 1, \ldots, T)$

where P denotes production rate, W the number of workers employed, I inventory less back-orders, S sales, and the k's are parametric constants. There are three decision variables, W, P and I, of which two (W and P or W and I) are independent (P is related to I through the constraint equation). Past values of the decision variables (W_{t-1}, I_{t-1}) are of course known.

Taking partial derivatives and setting them equal to zero yields two linear decision rules of the form:

$$P_1 = \sum_{t=1}^{T} a_t S_t + c W_0 + (b - d I_0)$$

$$W_1 = \sum_{t=1}^{T} \alpha_t S_t + \gamma W_0 + (\beta - \delta I_0)$$

where the coefficients (a, b, . . .; α, β, . . .) depend only on the coefficients (k's) of the cost function.

Given this description of the model, answer the following questions:

1. The model allows for sales fluctuations to be absorbed in three different ways, or some combination of three ways: (a) maintain constant P, adjust by hiring or laying off workers; (b) maintain constant W, adjust P by working overtime or undertime; (c) maintain constant P and W and allow inventories and order backlogs (I) to fluctuate. Looking at the cost function to be minimized, have all the relevant costs *of these alternatives* been included?

2. Are there *other* alternative ways of meeting sales fluctuations not considered by the model?

3. Indicate three feedbacks incorporated in the two decision rules.

4. Supposing you wanted to make the model more realistic, and made future orders (S) a variable, so that the decision problem became a profit maximization rather than a cost minimization problem. If the methods of responding to sales fluctuations remained as originally stated (i.e. the three ways mentioned in 1), would the model as stated in the question still correctly specify the relevant costs? If not explain why not.

5. As an exercise, reformulate the cost minimization model in the question as a production smoothing model for *individual* products (assume there are n products, $i = 1, 2, \ldots, n$).

9.8 '. . . the setting of, and attempt to follow, specific target returns on investment are manifest at two separate levels of operations: short-run pricing [i.e. target rate of return pricing] and investment decisions. The investment decision presupposes a price (and usually a market share) assumption which, in turn, determines short-run price decisions thereafter. Thus investment decisions in effect are themselves a form of pricing decision, and over time become an inherent part of price policy.'

What do you make of this argument?

9.9 Most advertising occurs in conditions of oligopoly. Indicate how an oligopolist whose objective is profit maximization should fix his advertising budget (1) on the assumption that his rivals do not react to changes in his level of advertising expenditure and (2) on the assumption that they do. Contrast these decision rules with that which would be used by a monopolistically competitive firm whose objective is to maximize sales revenue subject to a profit constraint.

9.10 A farmer can operate three processes at any levels, subject to the technology described below, viz.:

Process	I	Raise pigs
,,	II	Grow wheat
,,	III	Produce pigs and wheat as joint products

The technology is as follows:

Commodity (input +, output −)	*Unit*	*Process* *I*	*II*	*III*
Labour	man-months	50	25	75
Land	acres	5	50	60
Wheat	100 tons	$\frac{1}{2}$	−1	−1
Pigs	100 head	−1	0	$-\frac{1}{2}$

(*Note*: column 1 indicates that in pig production a unit output (100 head) requires 50 tons of wheat, 5 acres of land and 50 man-months of labour.) The availability of labour and land is limited to $31\frac{1}{4}$ man-months and 75 acres. Each of the commodities can be bought or sold at constant market prices, pigs at £20 per head, wheat at £20 per ton.

At what level should each process be operated in order to maximize profits on the assumption that there are constant returns in each process?

10

Price-output: some tactical aspects

How to live well on nothing a year.
       W. M. THACKERAY

Chapter 9 examined the major elements of price-output decisions. This chapter has a narrower focus. Attention will be directed to certain tactical aspects, including a consideration of the 'break-even' model and related approaches to price-output decisions, and a cursory examination of the problems of estimating short-run cost and demand behaviour. Concern will be with the short-run, with production subject to constraints in the current period. There will be one digression on long-run problems in section 2 to mention suggestions which have been made for the use of the break-even technique in investment decisions.

10.1 'Cost–volume–profit' analysis

Price-output decisions encompass examination of price and cost of output (volume) in relation to the profit outcome. Consequently such examination is commonly termed *cost–volume–profit analysis* in the accounting literature.

Two cost concepts are central to analysis in this area:

Variable costs: Costs which vary with the level of activity in a period.

Fixed costs: Costs which do not vary with the level of activity in a period, over a
    particular range of activity.

For the present purposes the term 'activity' refers to volume of output. Differences between the volume of goods produced and the volume of goods sold in a period obviously emerge as inventory changes. It will be assumed that output = sales, although some reference will be made to the limitations of ignoring inventory changes.

In the short run the potential limit of the range of output is capacity in the sense of the productive capability of fixed assets, but other constraints (e.g. scarce labour) may be binding at a lower level. Investment in capacity must involve long-run considerations beyond the current period. The lower end of the output range assumes something more than zero output: at that point questions of costs avoidable during a shut-down and of disinvestment would again change the nature of the problem. For graphical and calculation purposes it is usually convenient to assume that fixed costs of production go right back to zero output.

A clear example of a variable cost would be the cost of material input and of a fixed cost the rent of a factory: it will be seen that the determination of variable and fixed costs is not always so straightforward.

If the firm is committed to production in the short run *and* there are no alternative uses of capacity, any increment to sales revenue which exceeds the variable cost of producing the increment will increase profit or decrease loss of the firm: if there are competing opportunities they must, of course, be compared.

Discussion in the following sections will assume that identical units of output are sold at identical prices, but there are many circumstances in which a firm may adopt discriminatory pricing.* With different prices for different customers† or markets the firm can exploit the nature of the demand function for each market segment; a prerequisite is that the segments are in some way insulated from each other. Two examples which can be considered as forms of differential pricing are the granting of discounts for large orders and the practice of selling in different tariff-protected international markets at prices which do not yield a constant net revenue per unit (selling price minus tariff). Products which are virtually identical for production purposes may be different for market purposes: some manufacturers sell identical consumer products at different prices via different outlets or brand labels. Whenever a product or service is specific to an individual customer, that customer effectively constitutes a separate market segment. Thus discriminatory pricing can provide a firm with flexibility: in the short-run (given no better opportunities) it will be profitable for the firm to sell at any price above the relevant variable cost in the 'marginal' market.

(a) The simple break-even model

The basic assumptions of the break-even model are that variable cost and selling price are both constant per unit of output (= sales), and that fixed costs are constant irrespective of output in the period. Thus total costs and total revenue are linear functions of output. In its simplest form the model relates to a single product; the multiproduct case is examined later.

The graph employing these assumptions for total costs and total revenue is termed a *break-even graph* (or chart), as illustrated in Figure 10.1. The corresponding assumptions for unit costs and revenues are shown in Figure 10.2.

The intersection of total costs and total revenue indicates the *break-even point* of output: output beyond this point yields a profit (sales revenue – fixed costs – variable costs) and output below this level produces a loss. Profit or loss is measured in both cases by the vertical distance between the lines for total revenue and total costs.

In algebraic terms profit or loss will be given by:

$$\pi = Pq - (F + Vq) \tag{1}$$

* See also Chapter 9.
† In the United States the Robinson Patman Act prohibits discriminatory prices which are not based on cost differences.

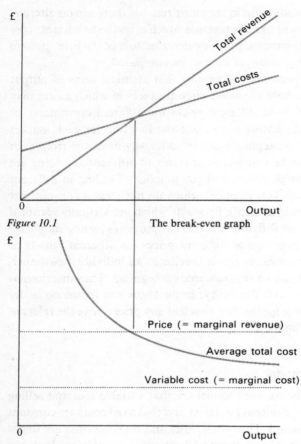

Figure 10.1   The break-even graph

Figure 10.2   Unit costs and revenues

where π is profit or loss, q is the number of units produced *and* sold in the current period, P is the selling price per unit, F is fixed cost and V is variable cost per unit. (P, F and V are constants in the period.)

The break-even point, at which profit is zero, must occur when total revenue equals total costs, thus:

$$Pq = F + Vq \qquad (2)$$

(1) can be alternatively expressed as:

$$\pi = q(P - V) - F \qquad (3)$$

The difference between selling price per unit and variable cost per unit, $P - V$, is termed *variable profit per unit*; total revenue minus total variable costs, $q(P - V)$, is *variable profit*.

The assumption that each unit makes an equal contribution towards fixed costs/ profit is central to the break-even model. A corresponding assumption of linear contribution to profit is made in linear programming, but with this important difference: the constant returns relate to processes* and not to the production of the product as a whole.

(b) Comparison with the economic model

The major assumptions of the break-even model are stated below.

1. Productive efficiency and capacity are given for the period.
2. Output = sales.
3. Selling prices and costs are known. (Alternatively the effects of price changes can be examined by assuming that the units which can be sold at a particular price and the associated costs of those units are known.)
4. Either output relates to a single product or in the multiproduct situation a constant mix of products is assumed at all levels of output. (It will be seen later that the effects of different product compositions can be examined by a series of graphs.)
5. Total costs and total revenue are linear functions of output.

Traditional economic theory shares the first two assumptions. It assumes that demand and cost functions are known and that product mix for the multiproduct case will be optimally determined in relation to those functions. Finally total costs are assumed to be curvilinear, with total revenue linear under perfect competition and curvilinear in imperfect markets. Thus the intersection of rising marginal cost and constant or declining marginal revenue determines optimal output, as discussed in Chapter 9.

The break-even model will be compared with the economic model under the imperfect market assumption of declining marginal revenue, where differences between the models are greatest. Figure 10.3 shows economic assumptions for total costs and total revenue; the corresponding unit costs and revenues are shown in Figure 10.4. These graphs are comparable with Figures 10.1 and 10.2.

Figure 10.3 shows *two* break-even points, where total costs cut total revenue from above and below; similarly for *average* total cost and *average* revenue in Figure 10.4. But the break-even points are irrelevant here, because the graphs indicate the optimal output. Maximum profit is obtained when the excess of total revenue over total costs is at its greatest in Figure 10.3: at the same output the marginal revenue curve cuts the marginal cost curve from above in Figure 10.4.

The important differences between the two models depend on two things: the

---

*See section 4(b) of Chapter 8 and Appendix C.

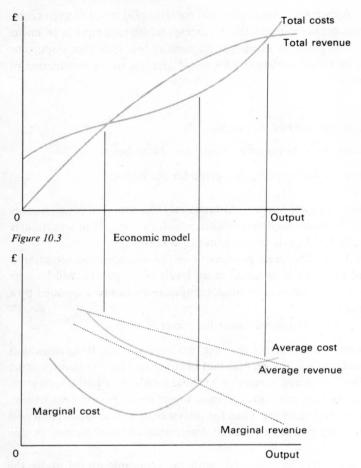

Figure 10.3 Economic model

Figure 10.4 Unit costs and revenues

validity of the assumptions about the behaviour of costs and revenues, and the purposes for which the models are used.

The shape of the short-run average cost curve of the firm has been the subject of controversy, considered earlier in section 4(a)(i) of Chapter 8. Whatever the shape of typical average cost curves, a firm must investigate cost behaviour for its individual operations (processes). The effects of increasing production beyond a certain point may be relatively simple to estimate for some costs (e.g. overtime premiums for labour hours); firms must and do consider such implications. For example, inventory may be built up in anticipation of high cost/demand periods.

The shape of the total revenue function depends upon the nature of the market. The break-even assumption may not be too unrealistic for firms which are price-takers, either in a market which approaches perfect competition or in a market which follows the price leadership of a major firm. The price-making firm must take into consideration the likely demand function, in a manner analogous to that implied in the economic model; but the firm's approach is inevitably iterative, because at best it will have only fragmentary indications of the demand function in an imperfect market. Where advertising is important it would seem to strengthen the assumptions of the economic model: the advertising firm may well have to spend increasing increments on advertising in order to sell additional units at a given price. This suggests increasing marginal cost, or alternatively decreasing marginal revenue if costs are defined as *production* costs and revenue is expressed net of advertising.

The most common adjustment of the break-even model towards the assumptions of the economic model involves the incorporation of certain increases in fixed costs as step costs. The expansion of output beyond a certain point may require 'lumpy' increments to costs (e.g. hiring another supervisor); such a step cost treatment is illustrated in Figure 10.5. Investment outlays are *not* admissible for such treatment; they bring future benefits which must be analysed outside the current period.

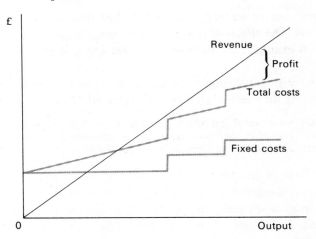

Figure 10.5 Break-even graph with step costs

Perhaps the major difference between the two models relates to their purposes. The neoclassical economic model provides a summary *explanation* of profit maximizing behaviour: it is not a technique for supplying management with the 'right' answer, but it does provide a useful conceptual framework for understanding the considerations which affect profit maximization. The break-even model is an exceedingly simple technique for approaching certain decisions or for summarizing decisions which have been taken; it must be judged on how well it serves in those roles.

275

(c) Some uses of break-even analysis

The break-even graph derives its name from the importance attached to the break-even point by early users of the graph. Certainly the break-even point is of some interest: if volume cannot be maintained above the break-even point in the current period a temporary or permanent shut-down must be considered. Operations above break-even are of more usual interest to the firm.

The break-even point has certain risk implications. A break-even point at the upper end of the output range indicates that profit is vulnerable to demand fluctuations because fixed cost is a major component of total costs; the hypothetical all-variable cost firm could always avoid a loss. Interpretation must depend on the firm's expectations of probable demand, as will be seen in the next sub-section.

Break-even analysis has a major use as a form of sensitivity analysis: calculation of the effects of changes in the assumed selling price, costs or output will indicate how 'sensitive' profit is to these changes. For example the impact of an increase in variable cost per unit, ΔV, can be swiftly estimated from:

$$\pi = Pq - F - q(V + \Delta V).$$

The new break-even point can be similarly calculated. The results may, of course, be put into graph form. The effects of changes in product mix can also be examined in this manner – an example will be provided when the multiproduct case is considered.

Such analysis is associated with satisficing behaviour in firms: if the initially indicated profit is not satisfactory the effects of changes are examined. For example:

> Several of the companies interviewed stated that they prepare cost-volume-profit analyses from preliminary budget figures and, when the profit structure thus indicated is not satisfactory to management, changes are made where possible before the budget is approved.*

Assumptions similar to those of the break-even model are very commonly employed for control purposes. Budgets are prepared on assumptions about the behaviour of variable and fixed costs, and those budgets provide the basis for appraising the costs incurred. These uses will be explored further in the control area, particularly in Chapter 15.

A problem concerning inventory must be mentioned. If the firm uses variable cost assumptions for decisions or control, but includes some element of fixed cost in the valuation of inventory, inventory changes can make the profit outcome different from that projected even though sales, selling price, fixed cost and variable cost per unit are all as anticipated – because output $\neq$ sales. This is particularly important in internal control uses, where the control period will be short (say one month) and an inventory change can be relatively large in relation to the profit of the period. The potential impact of such inventory changes on profit are examined

*[14], p. 42.

276

in the appendix to Chapter 14. A solution, which is not universally accepted as legitimate,* is to value inventory at variable cost – at least for internal purposes. In this way fixed costs are not transferred between periods via the inventory valuation.

(d) The profit–volume graph

The profit–volume graph shows the effect of output on profit/loss in a similar manner to the break-even graph, but profit and loss are graphed instead of costs and revenues. Profit and loss related to output are determined by the equation previously given:

$$\pi = q(P - V) - F$$

Such a graph is illustrated in Figure 10.6. Note that the profit line is determined by variable profit, $q(P - V)$, because F is constant.

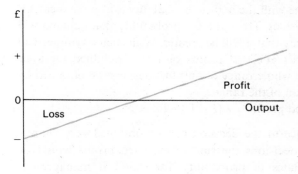

Figure 10.6 Profit–volume graph

The effects of different assumptions about costs, revenues and output can be explored through the profit–volume approach in the same way as for break-even.

The purpose of a separate approach is to concentrate attention on the profit outcome. Management may wish to examine the vulnerability of profit to different output (= sales) results, in which case the graph is being used as a basis for risk analysis. The graph may be used by management in the light of subjective expectations about risk, or these subjective expectations could be explicitly formulated as a probability distribution.† Such a distribution need not necessarily take any particular shape, but a conveniently continuous symmetrical distribution (specifically a 'normal' distribution) lends itself most easily to statistical manipulation. Such a distribution has been superimposed over the profit–volume graph in Figure 10.7.

* e.g. see [15].
† See Chapter 12 for a discussion of risk, uncertainty and probability.

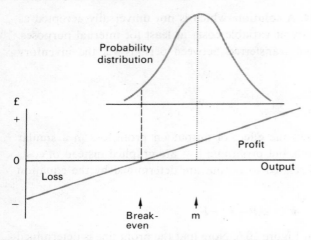

Figure 10.7 Profit–volume graph with probability distribution

It can be seen that the outcome with the highest probability is also the mean (*m*) of the probable range of output/sales. There is a 0·5 probability that demand will be less than *m* and a 0·5 probability that it will be greater. With such a symmetrical curve the *expected profit* (the net effect of profits or losses weighted for their associated probabilities over the whole range of output/sales) can be obtained by calculating the profit for the mean of the range:

$$\text{Expected profit} = m(P-V)-F.$$

Thus one estimate of relevance to the decision can be obtained very simply. (Over a large number of such decisions the sum of expected profits would be achieved, *if* management estimates of probability are valid.) If management attaches more importance to a potential loss than to an equally probable profit it will be necessary to consider separately the probable loss area, as indicated by the area under the probability curve to the left of the break-even point. The derivation of expected loss and other measures in this context are examined by Bierman [2] (Chapter 2) and by Jaedicke and Robichek [8].

(e) The multiproduct case

The commonplace situation of several products sharing the same production facilities has so far been largely avoided. Here the traditional break-even approach is entirely inadequate.

The term multiproduct firm will be used for simplicity, although it is remotely feasible that a multiproduct firm might have independent single processes for each of a number of independent products.

For the determination of break-even sales it is necessary to express disparate units of output in money terms. Translation into money terms for the single product will be considered first.

The break-even point in units, from (2), is

$$q = \frac{F}{P-V}$$

To convert the units into money terms multiply both sides by the selling price, P:

$$Pq = P\frac{F}{P-V}$$

The formula is usually expressed by taking P (on RHS) into the denominator, thus:

$$\text{Break-even sales revenue \\ (for single product)} = \frac{F}{(P-V)/P}$$

The expression $(P-V)/P$ is termed the *variable profit ratio* or contribution ratio: it is a measure of the profitability of the product in terms of the variable profit percentage yielded by sales. This ratio is unlikely to be uniform for all products, and it must therefore be expressed for multiproduct break-even as an overall profit ratio, weighted for each product. Where $n =$ number of different products (and $j = 1, \ldots, n$) the overall variable profit ratio is given by:

$$\frac{\sum_{j=1}^{n} [q_j(P_j - V_j)]}{\sum_{j=1}^{n} P_j q_j}$$

Thus for the multiproduct firm:

$$\text{Break-even sales revenue} = \frac{\text{Fixed costs}}{\text{Overall variable profit ratio}}$$

$$= \frac{F}{\sum_{j=1}^{n} [q_j(P_j - V_j)] \Big/ \sum_{j=1}^{n} P_j q_j}$$

Profit is given by:

$$\pi = \text{Total variable profit} - \text{Fixed costs} = \sum_{j=1}^{n} [q_j(P_j - V_j)] - F.$$

The calculation of break-even sales for the multiproduct case is illustrated for two products in Table 10.1. The data are based on the linear programming example for Rho Ltd. in Chapter 7, *except* that fixed costs of £800 are now assumed and it is

279

assumed that the firm is using profit–volume analysis to approach a solution to its production decisions, i.e. the optimal solution is not already known by the firm. Rho makes a preliminary assumption of 10 units of X_1 and 40 units of X_2, perhaps based on the sales of the preceding period: at this output sales revenue is £3 700 and profit £800.

Table 10.1 The multiproduct case

	Product X_1	Product X_2
Per unit:		
selling price (P)	£90	£70
variable cost (V)	50	40
variable profit margin (P−V)	£40	£30
Product variable profit ratios	= 44·4 %	= 42·9 %
Preliminary sales assumption	10 units	40 units
Total variable profit (10 × £40)+(40 × £30)	£1 600	
Total sales revenue (10 × £90)+(40 × £70)	£3 700	
Fixed costs	£800	
Overall variable profit ratio:		
$\dfrac{\text{variable profit}}{\text{sales revenue}}$	$\dfrac{£1\ 600}{£3\ 700} = 43\cdot2\%$	
Break-even sales revenue:		
$\dfrac{\text{fixed costs}}{\text{overall variable profit ratio}}$	$\dfrac{£800}{0\cdot432} = £1\ 850$	
Profit for £3 700 sales revenue:		
variable profit−fixed costs	£1 600−£800 = £800	

The next step would be to examine the effects of changes in the product mix. The model indicates that profit would be increased by a switch to the product(s) with relatively high variable profit ratio(s), in this example product X_1. The sale of only the product with the highest variable profit ratio may not be a serious proposition: usually less dramatic adjustments in product mix are considered. Figure 10.8 illustrates the profit graphs for the preliminary assumption and for the two extreme assumptions of 100 per cent of product X_1 and 100 per cent of product X_2, all on the originally assumed revenue of £3 700. In the Rho example the variable profit ratios of the two products are very close, and the (net) profit for £3 700 sales of X_1 would be about £845 (£3 700 × 0·444 − £800) and for £3 700 sales of X_2 about £785 (£3 700 × 0·429 − £800).

There are two fundamental weaknesses in the results from the profit–volume graph for Rho, both stemming from the fact that constraints are not explicitly considered. The first is that although the indicated 'best' profit of £845 is better than the preliminary profit of £800, the required production of X_1 would exceed the constraints on Rho's output (see section 2 of Chapter 7):

$$\frac{\text{Revenue}}{\text{Selling price}} = \frac{£3\ 700}{£90} = 41\tfrac{1}{9}\ \text{units} > \text{maximum output 40 units}\ X_1$$

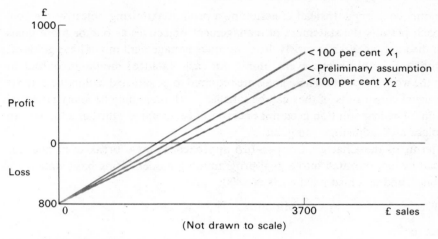

Figure 10.8 Profit–volume graphs for Rho

The second weakness is that £845 profit would fall short of the optimal solution, which will not be discovered by assuming sales of £3 700. In section 2 of Chapter 7 the optimum was 30 units of X_1, 20 units of X_2 which would give revenue £4 100 and (net) profit £1 000.

Thus the model does not provide an adequate framework for the utilization of resources in the multiproduct situation. Constraints must be considered outside the analysis, a complex undertaking for a large number of products. The multiproduct case can be analysed much more efficiently with linear programming, which if desired can be used equally well for sensitivity analyses employing a variety of assumed data.

10.2 Extensions of the break-even approach

Two techniques which have links with break-even analysis will be considered briefly.

(a) Goal programming

It has been suggested, originally by Jaedicke [7], that the technique of linear programming can be looked upon as an extension of break-even analysis. However, it has been seen that linear programming, unlike break-even, incorporates consideration of the constraints. In its basic form linear programming is an optimizing technique, whereas break-even is associated with satisficing.

Charnes, Cooper and Ijiri [3] applied goal programming, a variation of the linear programming technique, to the class of problem with which break-even analysis is

281

commonly concerned. Instead of assuming a profit maximizing objective the goal approach permits the statement of management objectives as one or more goals which the analysis seeks to satisfy. For example, management might have goals of: £x profit (or simply break-even); minimum cash balance; minimum output to retain the work-force, etc. These goals are required to be satisfied within the context of the usual constraints; if they can be satisfied at all there may be many potential solutions. The first solution need not necessarily be accepted – further analysis can take place after adjustment to goals.

In terms of the Charnes–Cooper–Ijiri approach a single break-even goal for Rho can be incorporated into a goal programming model. Using basic data from Chapter 7, and assumed fixed costs of £800:

$$\text{Minimize} \quad y_4^- + y_4^+.$$

Subject to:

(1) $\quad 20x_1 + 10x_2 + y_1 \qquad\qquad\qquad = \quad 800$

(2) $\quad 20x_1 + 20x_2 \quad + y_2 \qquad\qquad = 1\,000$

(3) $\quad\ \ 5x_1 + 4x_2 \qquad\quad + y_3 \qquad\quad = \quad 400$

(4) $\quad 40x_1 + 30x_2 \qquad\qquad + y_4^- - y_4^+ = \quad 800$

$$x_1, x_2, y_1, y_2, y_3, y_4^-, y_4^+ \geqslant 0$$

Equation (4) represents the break-even goal: variable profit = fixed costs. 'Slack' variables y_1, y_2, y_3, have been introduced to convert the previous constraint inequalities to equalities; these non-negative variables take up any 'slack' when a constraint is not binding. The terms y_4^-, y_4^+ appear in the objective function, indicating that a solution is sought in which these two terms are as near zero as possible; if they are both zero the break-even goal will be achieved precisely in the solution. A solution which under-achieved (here a variable profit < £800) would be indicated by $y_4^- > 0$, which is necessary to satisfy equation (4); conversely a solution which over-achieved would give $-y_4^+ < 0$.*

The feasible region for the satisfaction of Rho's break-even goal could be given for Rho in Figure 7.1 by introducing a 'break-even line'. Its extremities would be:

$$x_1, \frac{£800}{40} = 20; \quad x_2, \frac{£800}{£30} = 26\cdot6.$$

This line would bound the new feasible region from below. A break-even goal

---

*The objective function, $y_4^- + y_4^+$, therefore represents the sum of the absolute deviations from the goal, here zero profit. Underachievement of this goal ($40x_1 + 30x_2 < 800$) results in $y_4^+ = 0, y_4^- > 0$, overachievement ($40x_1 + 30x_2 > 800$) in $y_4^- = 0, -y_4^+ < 0$, and exact achievement in $y_4^+ = y_4^- = 0$. The distinguishing feature of goal programming is that at least one of the constraints is incorporated in the objective function. See Simon (ch 6 [36]), referred to in section 2(a) of Chapter 6.

would be satisfied (i.e. either precisely achieved or overachieved) by *any* point in this region.

The break-even goal is not, of course, essential to goal programming. A profit goal is more usually and usefully employed, and multiple goals can be incorporated. The technique can be used in a satisficing decision context and in exploring for control purposes the implications of goals for different segments of the firm.* The term 'goal programming' was first applied to the programming formulation of the problem of coming as close as possible to a set of simultaneously unattainable goals. This is done by ordering the goals in terms of preferences from an overall operations point of view, and weighting under- and over-achievement of each goal.

(b) A digression: the break-even model and long-run decisions

Suggestions have been made by Manes [11] and Moore [13] for the use of break-even graphs in investment decision making. The focus is entirely different from that discussed so far: in the short run relevant costs are those which must be incurred in order to produce during the period; for investment decisions† the expected future net cash flows must exceed the investment outlay and associated costs of providing capital. The break-even graph is no more than a graph: any assumptions can be imported provided they are relevant to the purpose in hand.

Costs, made up of investment outlay and all future cashflows expected to be incurred in using the asset for production, can be discounted to present values for the range of potential annual output. Similarly the estimated revenue cash flows can be discounted to present values over the range of potential output. The results can be graphed as shown in Figure 10.9. The vertical distance between the present values of cash inflows and outflows for a particular output level measures positive net present value about the break-even point, and negative net present value below it.

The purpose is one of sensitivity analysis: the effect on net present value of different annual outputs can be seen from the graph. Alternative cash flows for different cost and revenue assumptions can be tested, along the lines previously discussed. Both Moore and Manes also test alternative discounting rates which imply an internal rate of return decision criterion,** but this is not fundamental to the use of the graph.

The method provides a simple means of introducing some consideration of risk into an investment decision: there are more sophisticated methods available.‡ The graph does imply that output in the first year will determine output in subsequent

---

* See [5], Chapters 1–4 and [12], Chapters 4–5.

† Investment decisions will be examined in Chapters 11 and 12. For the mechanics of discounting see Appendix A.

** To be considered in Chapter 11.

‡ To be considered in Chapter 12.

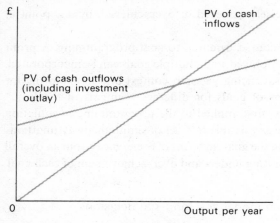

Figure 10.9 Net present value break-even graph

years, because for each specific output constant annual cash flows are discounted for the asset's expected life.

10.3 Estimation of cost and demand behaviour

In this section we are again concerned with the short-run.

(a) Cost behaviour

Methods of estimating cost behaviour in relation to output (or other activities of the firm) can be divided into three major categories:

1. The classification of data in the accounting records on the basis of the assumed nature of particular costs, e.g. rent as fixed and material costs as variable. Many costs give difficulty in classification (e.g. maintenance); such hybrids are termed semi-variable costs, and a guesstimate of the fixed and variable elements is adopted.
2. Investigation to determine the cost of undertaking a specific operation; e.g. how long it takes to paint a widget. Such investigations involve industrial engineering or work studies; they commonly carry implications of what costs 'should' be.
3. Investigation of past cost data, with varying degrees of statistical sophistication.

These methods are not mutually exclusive: they may provide valuable bases for cross-checking the validity of data. The results indicate the patterns of cost behaviour, but of course for decision (and control) purposes assumptions about

284

future changes must be incorporated. In multiproduct operations it is usual to relate certain cost elements (overheads) to an input activity such as machine hours worked as a surrogate for output; this effectively aggregates diverse products on a common basis.

The use of the first two categories will be developed in Chapters 14 and 15. Some methods in the third category will be considered here.

It is necessary to ensure that data are relevant to the activity being examined. Relevance is not so simple as it may sound: accounting data may include many arbitrary elements which are not related to the activity, or may exclude elements which are related; adjustments may have to be made for the purposes of an investigation. Time period is also important: a period of more than a few weeks is liable to yield data influenced by a variety of factors (e.g. input price changes) unrelated to activity levels.

The two simplest methods of examining past cost behaviour are the 'high-low' approach and visual graph fitting to a scatter diagram of observed costs. The former means drawing a straight line between the highest and lowest observed points, and the latter means drawing the curve or line which looks the best fit. Cost equations can then be calculated from the resulting graphs. A scatter diagram is in any case a useful preliminary to more elaborate examination.

Another approach is linear regression analysis, using the method of least squares. By this method a 'line of best fit' for the data can be obtained, *provided* an assumption of linearity is in fact valid, and cost behaviour can be assumed to take the form:

$$C_t = a + bq + \varepsilon$$

where C_t = total cost at time t, a = fixed component of cost, b = variable component of cost, q = measure of activity (here output) and ε = an independent random variable which explains observed variations from the total cost line.

The cost function $C = a + bq$ provides the 'best estimate' of cost behaviour with output. It can be obtained by substituting observed data in the following two equations:

$$\sum_{j=1}^{n} C_j = na + b \sum_{j=1}^{n} q_j \tag{1}$$

$$\sum_{j=1}^{n} C_j q_j = a \sum_{j=1}^{n} q_j + b \sum_{j=1}^{n} q_j^2 \tag{2}$$

where n = number of observed values, $j = 1, 2, \ldots, n$.

The insertion of observed data for q and Cq permits the simultaneous solution of the two equations. An example of such calculation for a small number of observations is provided in Table 10.2.

Table 10.2 Least squares method for linear costs

Time	Activity volume (output units) q	Total costs (£) C	Cq	q^2
	Observed data 000's omitted			
1	13	36	468	169
2	11	34·5	379·5	121
3	10	34·5	345	100
4	12	36	432	144
5	14	37·5	525	196
6	16	42	672	256
7	17	43·5	739·5	289
8	18	48	864	324
9	14	42	588	196
10	12	39	468	144
	137	393·0	5 481·0	1 939

$$\Sigma C = na + b\Sigma q$$
$$393 = 10a + 137b \qquad (1)$$
$$\Sigma Cq = a\Sigma q + b\Sigma q^2$$
$$5\,481 = 137a + 1\,939b \qquad (2)$$

Substituting $a = 39\cdot3 - b(13\cdot7)$ in (2) and solving gives:

$$a \simeq £17\,700 \text{ (fixed element)}$$
$$b \simeq £1\cdot576 \text{ per unit (variable element)}$$

The results from Table 10.2 can be expressed in the accounting terms previously adopted: total costs $= F + Vq = £17\,700 + £1\cdot576q$. The data could be graphed in the usual manner.

Three problems of this approach must be mentioned. Linearity is assumed; the assumption will depend on the validity of a rough visual check using a scatter diagram. There may be few observations available outside a narrow range of output; extrapolation beyond that range is obviously dangerous. There may be a tendency for costs to be 'sticky' in falling with output (e.g. it may be difficult to lay off workers), but this effect is submerged in the calculation of the cost line.

The least squares method can be used to fit curvilinear relationships. For these and other aspects of the method the reader is advised to consult a statistical textbook* or Lyle [10] who examines applications specifically in the cost area.

The use of simple regression analysis for investigating cost behaviour implies that only changes in the level of activity 'cause' changes in costs, apart from purely random variations. In fact other variables, such as seasonal factors, may affect costs. Multiple regression analysis can be used to determine the effects of several

*e.g. [4].

independent variables. Benston [1] and Lyle [10] examine the uses and problems of this technique in estimating cost relationships.*

(b) Demand behaviour

It has been mentioned that firms in imperfect markets usually have only fragmentary evidence about the nature of the demand function. Price changes are rarely as frequent as the costs/output changes which provide data for cost behaviour, but any price change which does occur provides the firm with two points (new and old price) for estimating demand behaviour over that price range. Since a short period is involved in which extraneous factors can be assumed constant the firm learns something about price-demand behaviour. It may also learn something about the behaviour of competitors, but that is intrinsic to the price change from the firm's viewpoint. Extrapolation beyond the observed range must obviously be treated with caution, but possible actions may be suggested: only an actual price change can test their validity.

Certain factors may discourage frequent short-run price changes, quite apart from the 'price-taking' stance of some firms. Full exploitation of current price opportunities may provide smaller gains than the (discounted) expected future losses through diverting customers to substitutes or encouraging the advent of new competitors. Price changes can also be administratively costly in advertising, informing sales outlets, etc.

The investigation of price–demand relationships for a sufficient number of observed price changes to permit a thorough estimation of the demand function involves long-run analysis. In the long-run both price and income of consumers are interrelated in their effects on demand, and are not easily disentangled. For such analysis the reader is referred to Wold and Jureen [17].

For forecasting volume of demand, at least in the short-run, the interrelationships are less serious provided the recent past structure can be assumed to persist. Forecasting methods may take the form of establishing a trend line for sales in past periods by a method such as least squares,† and the line may be extrapolated to provide a forecast.

A widely used method is the moving average updated for each new period, given by:

$$m_{t=n} = \frac{1}{n}\left(\sum_{t=1}^{n} d_t\right)$$

where $m_{t=n}$ = the moving average for the latest period, n = number of time periods

*See also [9].
† See [4].

for which the moving average is calculated, and d_t = observed demand in time t.

In its simplest form the moving average can be extrapolated by eye to give an estimate of current (or future) period demand. The forecasting characteristics can be improved by weighting the demand data in favour of more recent periods, by the inclusion of a trend variable for the periodic rate of change of demand, and by the inclusion of a further variable when there is evidence that the trend itself is changing.* The method also provides the basis for the analysis of seasonal variations: patterns established from past years can be superimposed on the moving average.

Bibliographical references

[1] Benston, G. J., Multiple regression analysis of cost behavior, *Accounting Review*, October 1966, pp. 657–72; reprinted in Solomons [16].
[2] Bierman, H., *Topics in Cost Accounting and Decisions*, McGraw-Hill, 1963.
[3] Charnes, A., W. W. Cooper and Y. Ijiri, Break-even budgeting and programming to goals, *Journal of Accounting Research*, Spring 1963, pp. 16–43.
[4] Chou, Y., *Statistical Analysis with Business and Economic Applications*, Holt, Rinehart and Winston, 1969.
[5] Ijiri, Y., *Management Goals and Accounting for Control*, Prentice-Hall, 1965.
[6] Imperial Chemical Industries (publishers), *Short-term Forecasting*, I.C.I. Monograph No. 2, 1964.
[7] Jaedicke, R. K., Improving B-E analysis by linear programming technique, *N.A.A. Bulletin*, March 1961, pp. 5–12.
[8] Jaedicke, R. K. and A. A. Robichek, Cost–volume–profit analysis under conditions of uncertainty. *Accounting Review*, October 1964, pp. 262–74; reprinted in Solomons [16].
[9] Johnston, J., *Statistical Cost Analysis*, McGraw-Hill, 1960.
[10] Lyle, P., *Regression Analysis of Production Costs and Factory Operations*, 3rd edn., Oliver and Boyd, 1956.
[11] Manes, R., A new dimension to break-even analysis, *Journal of Accounting Research*, Spring 1966, pp. 87–100; reprinted in Solomons [16].
[12] Mao, J. C. T., *Quantitative Analysis for Financial Decisions*, Macmillan, New York, 1969.
[13] Moore, C. L., The concept of the P/V graph applied to capital investment planning, *Accounting Review*, October 1962, pp. 721–29.
[14] National Association of Accountants (publishers). *The Analysis of Cost–Volume–Profit Relationships*, Research Report 16–17–18, 1949–50.
[15] Patrick, A. W., Some observations on the break-even chart, *Accounting Review*, October 1958, pp. 573–80.
[16] Solomons, D., *Studies in Cost Analysis*, Sweet and Maxwell, 1968.
[17] Wold, H. and L. Jureen, *Demand Analysis*, Wiley, 1953.

Problems

10.1 'Break-even analysis merely tells you that the more you sell the more profit you make.' Do you agree? Discuss the uses and limitations of the break-even (or cost–volume–profit) approach.

*See [6] for use in short-run forecasting.

10.2 Solo Ltd. manufactures a single product. Estimated data for the coming month are:

Capacity	1 000 units

Fixed costs

1–750 units	£2 100
751–850 units	£2 400
851–1 000 units	£2 800

Variable costs

1–900 units	£6 per unit
901–1 000 units	£7 per unit for the incremental 100 units

Solo could sell 900 units (or less) at £10 each; sales of more than 900 units would require that the price be reduced to £9·50 for all units sold.

Required:
(a) A graph of the data, and calculations showing the output (= sales) which would give the maximum profit. Suggest causes for the cost changes at different levels of output.
(b) Solo has an opportunity to make its variable costs £6·20 per unit over the whole range 1–1 000 units. Comment.

10.3 Trio manufactures three products, *A*, *B* and *C*. Data for last month were:

Fixed costs £25 000			
	A	*B*	*C*
Variable costs per unit	£7	£11	£18
Selling price per unit	£10	£20	£30
Sales: units	5 000	1 000	1 000
£	£50 000	£20 000	£30 000

Calculate the variable profit ratio for each product and the overall variable profit ratio for the given product mix. What were break-even £ sales?

From the available data draw a profit–volume graph for the given sales mix, and show the effect of a change to a £ sales mix of 40:40:20 for *A*:*B*:*C*. What information would you require in order to make a decision regarding the mix for the coming period?

10.4 'At present we incur fixed costs of £1 500 per month and variable costs of £3 per unit, getting a selling price of £7 per unit. The new equipment will cost us an additional £1 000 per month, but it will save about £1·50 per unit in labour costs. In a reasonably good month that will increase our profit by £200.'

Show how the £200 was calculated. What happens in a 'bad' month?

10.5 Liquids Ltd. has a plant which is engaged solely in the manufacture of HT, a cleaning fluid. HT is sold to industrial users at £3 per gallon, through agents who receive 15 per cent commission.

The HT plant has for some time produced and sold 21 000 gallons per month, which is 70 per cent of capacity. The plant's accounts show that costs per month are currently:

	Total costs £	Average costs per gallon £
Materials	13 650	0·65
Wages	16 800	0·80
Depreciation	5 250	0·25
Rent	6 300	0·30
Sundry plant expenses	6 720	0·32
Delivery costs	1 470	0·07
Sales commissions	9 450	0·45
	£59 640	£2·84

A chain store company offers to buy 7 000 gallons of HT next month at £2 per gallon; further orders are likely. The cleaning fluid would be retailed in small quantities under a different brand name at more than £3 per gallon, so that existing sales to industrial users would be unaffected.

The additional sales would not incur sales commission or delivery costs (the chain store company would collect). Sundry plant expenses (all out-of-pocket costs) would increase by £1 000. Wages are linearly variable with output to 25 000 gallons; beyond that level wage costs will be £1·10 per gallon.

The plant manager considers it would be foolish to incur the additional costs in order to sell at significantly below the usual price. Give your assessment on the basis of the available information, adding any qualifications you consider appropriate.

10.6 A factory produces a variety of frozen fruit and vegetables. There are three production lines (for preparing and quick-freezing) and a cold store. During the high season all three lines are run on 24-hour basis with the aid of temporary labour; at this time many inputs are quick-frozen in bulk for storage in an ungraded or partially processed state. For the remainder of the year an 8-hour shift usually operates two lines, processing fresh or stored inputs.

Examine the problems of estimating cost behaviour with output.

10.7 The following data for total costs of production in an engineering workshop have been observed over the past 10 weeks:

Week	Quantity (units)	Costs £
1	8 500	16 000
2	10 500	18 000
3	11 500	19 500
4	11 000	19 000
5	10 000	18 000
6	9 000	17 000
7	7 500	15 200
8	8 500	16 800
9	6 000	15 000
10	9 500	17 500

(No imputed costs of shared facilities are involved.)

Plot a scatter diagram, compute a linear cost function by the least squares method, and comment on your results.

Planned production next week is 12 000 units; what estimate can you offer for total costs?

291

11

Net investment and disinvestment decisions

Forsan et haec olim meminisse juvabit. (Perhaps even these things it will some day give pleasure to recall).

VIRGIL, *Aeneid*

In the last four chapters we have discussed some of the main classes of decisions which arise in the course of the current operations of a business, i.e. production operations. We now leave production and turn in this and the following chapter to investment. For the time being we will treat these two areas of decision as distinct. Later we will question whether we are justified in doing so.

Though capital investment decisions are among the most important in their impact on the firm, their treatment in management accounting texts is highly superficial and conceptually inadequate. Furthermore, the bulk of the attention tends to be given to the question of investment criteria, which as we will show is only one of the questions involved.* In what follows we will attempt to lay a more adequate foundation, without which this subject cannot be sensibly discussed.

11.1 The nature of investment

All economic activity is ultimately directed to satisfying wants, i.e. to consumption. Economists had long realized that it was possible to increase the efficiency of production by adopting round-about methods. That is, by postponing some consumption and investing in capital goods (machines and so on) a greater satisfaction of wants was made possible in the long run for a given outlay on resources as a result of the use of the more round-about (capital-intensive) methods. But the greatest contribution to the theory of capital at the micro level (i.e. the theory of investment of the firm) was made by the economist Irving Fisher over 40 years ago [9]. Fisher showed that capital investment decision-making required, essentially, a balancing of consumption alternatives over time. The upshot of his analysis is that in the *general* case we cannot consider investment on its own; we must consider consumption and investment alternatives together. 'Investment' to Fisher meant not only expenditure in acquiring new capital goods but also financial investment (the purchase or sale of securities); consumption may be transferred through time equally by borrowing and lending as by investment in a machine or

---

*There is some argument as to whether capital budgeting lies in the field of accounting or of finance. Our position on this and other such issues is clearly stated in the preface.

292

sale of a machine before its economic life is terminated.* 'Consumption,' as used by Fisher, needs a little clarification. It means the income received in future periods as a result of the investment, the income *available* for consumption. In the case of a business this is the amounts withdrawn in different periods by the owners (the dividends received by the ordinary shareholders in the case of a company). In their hands it may or may not be immediately consumed. As we proceed it will be well to remember that, in general, investment cannot be considered independently of the time-preferences of the owners for income. We will see that in one special case this advice can be ignored and left to take care of itself, but this does not disprove the rule, which will be a central strand in our subsequent discussion.

There are certain other characteristics of investment activity which we should note. Investment decisions are an example of what we have previously referred to as '*long-run*' *decisions*. We define the 'short-run' as that period of time during which the firm is constrained from using the optimal combination of inputs, that combination which would yield minimum unit costs. The long-run is the period of time necessary for the firm to be able to adapt completely to its optimal technique of production. The length of this period will depend on a number of factors to do with the nature and magnitude of the changes to which it is adapting. In the long-run all of the firm's inputs may be varied. When the quantities of all inputs change *simultaneously in the same proportion* economists say there is a change in the *scale* of production. In the short-run, by contrast, the quantities of only some of the inputs (the variable inputs) can be changed, i.e. it is possible to change input proportions, within limits, but not the scale of operations. Not only may the quantities of all inputs be changed in the long-run, but it becomes possible to make substitutions between current inputs and capital inputs. At the same time it should be recognized that not all investment involves a change in scale. A useful distinction may also be drawn between net investment (expansionary investment) and replacement investment. Net investment involves a change in productive capacity; replacement investment may or may not, depending on whether assets are replaced by assets of the same capacity.

Another characteristic of investment which has already been alluded to in referring to Fisher but which needs elaboration is that while, like production, investment is a process involving time, it is unlike production in involving *choice* over time [14]. (Production choices are regarded as timeless.) It is an intertemporal decision. Production is pictured as resource allocation within a single time period, investment as resource allocation over a number of time periods. The introduction of time requires the recognition of uncertainty.† Hirshleifer [12] has provided a useful exposition which links the key concepts of timeless resource allocation (price theory) to their counterparts in the theory of allocation over time

---

* Borrowing is a device for substituting present for future income, lending for doing the reverse.
† Fisher's model did not allow for uncertainty.

(capital theory, specifically the theory of investment of the firm). The brief summary below may help the reader to see the parallels between ideas discussed in Chapters 7–10 and those to be examined in this and the succeeding chapter.

	Price theory	*Theory of investment of the firm*
Concerned with:	'timeless' resource allocation	resource allocation over time
Objects of choice	current consumption alternatives	dated consumption claims
Opportunity set (the range of combinations of objects of choice attainable) depends on:		
(a) Endowment	commodities (inherited inputs)	time-distributed commodities
(b) Exchange opportunities	market transactions in commodities	market transactions in financial claims (exchanges of funds of different dates by borrowing and lending)
(c) Production opportunities	production opportunity set (the opportunities for transforming commodities into other commodities of enhanced value, i.e. into current consumption alternatives)	productive investment transformation function or investment opportunity set (the opportunities for transforming current consumption claims into future consumption claims)
Method of ordering alternative combinations of desired objects	preference function ———————	time-preference function
Exchange ratio	price	interest rate (i.e. the price ratio between current and future consumption claims)
State of the world	certain (as an approximation)	uncertain
Behaviour rule (neoclassical)	maximization of profit (or utility)	maximization of present value of the firm (or of utility of dated consumption claims)
Criterion for the allocation decision (first behaviour rule above only)	$MR = MC$	discounted value of consumption stream minus discounted value of endowment stream > 0

The disinvestment decision, though it may be completed in a single period, nevertheless involves choice over time in the same way as the investment decision does.

This brings us to a further characteristic of investment, viz. *irreversibility*. Investment, it is argued, represents a 'sunk' cost, i.e. a fixed cost which is irrecoverably committed. Once investment has taken place the cost is irretrievable, irreversible, unless the asset is sold. We are concerned here, however, with a related point, viz. the extent to which the physical amounts of capital inputs to production can be varied over time. Before they are installed, capital inputs* (such as the services of machines) are, subject to indivisibilities, freely variable. After it has been installed the amount of a capital input can be varied in the short-run by using the asset more or less intensively† (the stock of the input is fixed, but not the flow of its services). In the long-run‡ it can be varied as follows:

Upward (to meet a permanent increase in demand)	*Downward* (to meet a permanent decrease in demand)
1. If it is divisible, by adding more units of it immediately, without waiting for existing units to wear out.	1. Disinvestment
2. If it is indivisible, by replacement (i.e. wait until it wears out and replace with a unit of larger capacity)	2. Replacement with a unit of smaller capacity when the existing asset falls due for replacement
3. If 'scale obsolescence'§ occurs, replacement with a larger unit can be made before existing units wear out or become obsolete as a result of technological improvements.	3. Abandonment

Our purpose in mentioning this last characteristic was to show that, when replacement is possible (i.e. if the asset is not indestructible) or there is investment in multiple units of the asset, the effects of 'irreversibility' of investment expenditure on production may not be as complete in the long-run as often claimed. According to Smith [23], it is an observed fact that firms often operate multiple units of capital inputs in parallel, even when production is subject to increasing returns to scale. This policy could be regarded as a rational response to fluctua-

---

* Inputs which yield up their services over a number of time periods, compared with current inputs which are entirely consumed within one period.

† If it is not completely specific it may be possible to transfer it to another use without great loss.

‡ The length of this period will depend on the durability of the asset or on 'scale obsolescence'.

§ The term used by Smith [23] to describe obsolescence due entirely to changes in demand rather than technological improvements in the performance of the capital good.

tions in demand, another method of adapting to changing conditions given the fact that investment expenditure otherwise represents an irreversible cost. As a result of these two factors, Smith believes capital inputs can be made more or less continuously variable in an upward direction in the long-run, i.e. that irreversibility of under-investment can ultimately be completely offset. At the same time he believes long-run variations in capital inputs are likely to be asymmetrical: while they may approach continuous variability when expanded, contraction is likely to occur in discrete steps (i.e. because of the prevalence of multiple units working in parallel, declining demand is likely to lead to the shutting down of individual units).

One final point needs to be made before leaving this section. In the above we have talked about production ('timeless' resource allocation) and investment (allocation over time) as two quite separate things. While it will be beyond the scope of this book to develop the idea, in fact they are not. In terms of Chapter 8, the firm's production function may be thought of as a 'stock-flow' function which includes stocks of capital goods as well as flows of current inputs like labour and materials. Determination of the optimal investment program depends on prior or simultaneous determination of the optimal production program, because the amount and kind of investment undertaken influences production costs. Investment decisions are not really separable from the problem of optimal technique, any more than they are in general separable from consumption decisions.* In fact the interdependence goes further than that, as we shall see in the next section when we discuss the coverage of 'investment'.

11.2 The set of problems

Investment decision-making comprises a set of problems. These are listed below.

(a) How much to invest in any given period

In part this will depend on perceived opportunities for investment.

(b) Constraints

Whether the amount of investment which may be undertaken in any period is constrained. Constraints on investment may take the following forms:

(i) *Externally-imposed constraints*
 1. Quantitative limits on borrowing.
 2. Beyond a certain point a sharply rising marginal cost of borrowing.

*This point is brought out in [23], [18] and [25], among others.

3. Nonavailability of factors other than money required to implement the investment program.

(ii) *Internally-imposed constraints*

Limitation of internal funds for investment in any period to a fixed amount or imposition of an arbitrary 'cut-off' rate of return.

Cases (i)1. and (i)2. are often referred to as external capital rationing, case (ii) as internal capital rationing.

(c) Which projects to select

This involves the use of some criterion (decision rule). Some of the possibilities will be discussed in section 4. The criterion will depend on the firm's overall objective (behaviour rule) if this is a maximizing objective as in neoclassical theory; as we saw in Chapter 9 in discussing behavioural theories of the firm, however, where the firm has multiple objectives generally of a 'satisficing' nature and different kinds of decisions are taken independently of one another, standard operating rules may be used which are only loosely related to the goals of the firm.

The criterion is used to make accept/reject decisions in respect of physically independent projects, and to rank dependent projects. As will be shown later, it is necessary to rank all 'projects' in conditions of capital market imperfection and capital rationing. Dependent projects are defined by two conditions: *either* the returns from the projects are non-additive, *or* investment decisions cannot be optimized by looking at the set of projects coming forward in any particular period alone. Some of the main kinds of dependence are described below.*

(i) *Physical dependence*

This arises where the feasibility and profitability of accepting any set of projects affects the feasibility and profitability of accepting any different set. It is the result of technological (cost) dependence and/or demand dependence† between the expected operating cash flows of the projects in question if they were all implemented. The literature generally discusses only the two limiting cases, although there may be various degrees of dependence short of these limits. They are:

1. Mutually exclusive or competitive projects, where acceptance of one reduces the feasibility and profitability of undertaking the others in the set to zero. One project handicaps another. An example might be building a new plant of annual capacity 50 000 tons or 100 000 tons.
2. Contingent or complementary projects, where acceptance of one or more

---

*For a fuller discussion see [2].
† Refer section 4(a)(iv) of Chapter 8.

projects is only feasible and profitable if one or more prerequisite projects are first undertaken. One project supports another. An example would be building an industrial complex in an underdeveloped country which would require prior investment in power utilities.

(ii) *Dynamic dependence*

A special case of (i)1. but with separate features concerns the *timing of investment*. Here we have a case of mutually exclusive alternatives which are out of phase. An example of this is afforded by assets which have finite lives: should we buy the asset now, or in n years' time ($n = 1, 2, \ldots$)? As in (i)1., returns from the projects are non-additive. The projects must first be ranked according to some criterion of their economic value. Only the highest-valued alternative is included in the set of independent projects under consideration. It will pay to postpone a project, *cet. par.*, as long as the reduction in the capital outlays exceeds the loss of net returns from postponement, after making allowance for time. The case is further discussed below.

(iii) *Serial dependence*

In a general sense *all* investments are interdependent, in that assets earn in combination: the marginal contribution of a single asset derives from the aggregate contribution of the particular combination of assets of which it forms a part. The return from a project undertaken now will be influenced by the other assets with which it cooperates throughout its economic life, whether pre-existing, acquired at the same time, or yet to be acquired.

Dynamic dependence, as evidenced in the timing of investment, requires only that we ensure *comparability* between alternatives (variants of the same decision) which are separated in time. There is no interaction between earlier and later decisions. To bring about comparability between out of phase alternatives we adopt some device such as continuing each cash flow stream to infinity, or a terminal value convention.

Optimal replacement policy, as we shall see in Chapter 12, involves both dynamic and serial dependence: in addition to deciding when to replace (involving dynamic dependence) there is the prior question of whether or not to replace. The answer to this question, as we shall see, depends partly on the immediate past decision and on a chain of future decisions. That is, there are *interactions* between the decisions in the sequence. As Massé has put it:*

Not only does the replacement of machine N by machine $N+1$ depend on the time when machine N replaced machine $N-1$; it also depends on the time when machine $N+2$ will replace machine $N+1$.

*[18], p. 60.

This is because the optimal length of service of the asset (the existing asset, its replacement, and so on indefinitely, a recurring relation) becomes a variable in the decision.

These interactions, as already stated, are a quite general phenomenon applying to all investment. In analysis, however, it is usual to assume that their effects are negligible, and hence to ignore them, except in the case of optimal replacement and when investment is undertaken in conditions of capital market imperfection.* This latter case is examined later in the chapter. To sum up, thinking of the general case, serial dependence exists in all circumstances, dynamic dependence only when questions of timing of investment are involved.

(iv)

In categories (i) and (ii) above only those interdependencies were included which could be causally explained (e.g. projects were mutually exclusive, or differed in timing). Other interdependencies may occur between projects in these categories: one example would be *statistical dependence*, which might occur as a result of uncertainty.†

(v)

The other kinds of dependence have to do with interactions, not between individual projects or even sets of projects, but between investment decisions and other classes of decisions taken by the firm.

1. One of these has already been referred to in section 1, viz. the interdependence between *investment and production*,‡ i.e. between short-run and long-run decisions.
2. It has been argued by Vickers [25] that this should be extended to *production, investment and financing*.
3. It was stated earlier that *investment and consumption* must be considered together. The special case referred to in section 1 where consumption (in the form of the time-preferences of the owners of the business for income in different periods) can be omitted from the analysis is the case where capital markets are perfect. Here the firm's investment policy and the shareholders' time-preferences for income are separable. With *imperfect capital markets* the firm's productive investment and opportunities for the owners to attain a more desired time-distribution of income by themselves engaging in financial investment (borrowing or lending) become interrelated. The owners' time-

---

* The interactions may be ignored if capital markets are perfect, as has been shown by Hirshleifer [11], p. 227 and [12], p. 203.
† Two events A and B defined on a common sample space are statistically dependent if

$$P(A, B) \neq P(A) . P(B).$$

‡ We add a rider to this in section 4(d) below.

preferences must be taken into account by the firm in determining its optimal productive investment. Point (e) in the appendix to this chapter describes the relevant analysis. The statement above also applies to situations involving capital rationing. A constraint on resources other than money required to implement the investment program has a similar effect to a funds limitation.

(d) What precisely does 'investment' include?

In economics, as we have seen, investment refers to resource allocation through time. This is reflected in expenditure on durable capital goods such as machines and also on items like inventories. 'Capital budgeting,' with which we shall be concerned in this and the following chapter, is restricted in two ways, first to *business* investment, and secondly to investment by firms in what the accountant calls *fixed assets*. Investment in working capital is not included unless it is associated with the acquisition or sale of fixed assets. We discuss the question of working capital in Chapter 19. Clearly there should be some sensible relation between the investment in fixed and current assets, after allowing for differences in risk. As was stated in Chapter 8, investment in inventories of product and investment in excess plant present a choice of technique. They are substitutes, albeit imperfect substitutes, alternative ways of smoothing the impact on production of fluctuations in demand. If we were approaching the problem dynamically, and order rate fluctuations were frequent and large, we should therefore build into the cost function, in addition to the normal components of production cost, the costs of alternative ways of smoothing the impact or demand fluctuations of different size and duration.*

'Cost-benefit analysis' is the name applied to the assessment of the desirability of projects in which the indirect effects on third parties outside the decision-making unit are taken into account. That is it involves, in addition to the principles to be discussed in connection with capital budgeting, various other considerations drawn from welfare economics or public finance, political and social as well as economic considerations, and takes a wider view of the decision. It is sometimes thought of as being concerned with public sector investment. The 'project', however, may refer to any resource allocation decision (e.g. a proposed change in prices by a public enterprise or a change in government regulations affecting firms or private consumers).

(e) Uncertainty

Since the investment decision is extended in time it becomes essential to allow in some way for mounting uncertainties as the period increases. Various approaches to this problem will be examined in Chapter 12.

*For further details see [13].

300

(f) Planning horizon

As with current operations, so with investment will the solution of the problem depend on the length of the planning period. The presence of uncertainty encourages short horizons. The longer the horizon the greater will be the possibilities of substitution between current and capital inputs. Just as with the optimization of production, what constitutes optimal investment in any period will be a function of the planning period adopted. As noted in Chapter 5, most investment models are static models, and the discussion of this and the following chapter will be confined to this case.

11.3 Specifying the data

One cannot say which data are relevant without knowing the particular circumstances in which investment is undertaken; there is no single best method of economically evaluating business investment. Below we have shown separately data which are required in all circumstances and data applying only to particular situations:

Relevant in all cases. Estimates of:
1. The capital outlays (the price of the capital asset to be purchased or the cost of constructing it).
2. The economic life of the asset to be acquired (technological change leads to a discrepancy between economic life and physical life; as already seen, changes in demand may have the same effect).
3. The additional cash operating receipts and payments to which the investment will give rise.
4. The discount rate to be used.
5. The uncertainties attaching to the above estimates (and to those appearing below).

Relevant in particular cases. Estimates of:
6. (Imperfect capital markets) The future net operating receipts from employment of the *existing* assets.
7. (Imperfect capital markets) The time-preferences of the owners of the business.
8. Any other interdependencies which may be involved.
9. (Replacement) The variable operating costs of the asset at present in service.

(a) Why *cash* flows?

The first question that arises in the reader's mind, after reading points 1., 3., 6. and 9., is likely to be 'why is the investment calculation formulated in terms of cash flows

301

rather than profit (revenue and expense) flows?' The answer is that in any decision problem we are concerned with the whole life of the decision. We only need to measure profit when we are concerned with incomplete periods – periods shorter than a single decision, the full production cycle or the life of the business. Secondly, the difference between profit flows and cash flows, in the context of the investment decision, is represented by two items: depreciation and interest. Interest is allowed for in the calculation, via discounting; depreciation is not, and should not be. The reason is that the capital outlay is already represented as a negative receipt (cash outflow), and to include depreciation would therefore involve double-counting.* The only role of depreciation in the capital investment decision is in determining the tax payments on the net operating cash flows from the project.

(b) What should they include?

The cash flows should include, first, all outlays on acquiring the assets. 'Assets' should here be understood to mean the fixed assets and the associated working capital necessary to implement the project. Lundberg [16] has instanced a case where an investment to increase the capacity of an iron and steel works by 50 per cent implied increasing working capital by an amount equal to 60 per cent of the outlays on plant.† Correspondingly, the cash flows should allow for disinvestment at the end of the project: the resale or scrap value of the durable assets and any working capital which is released should be included as cash inflows. The cash flows should, furthermore, include any consequential effects of the investment on cash flows in other parts of the business; these are costs/benefits of the decision in question. In private business investment decisions the cash flows will be calculated after tax.‡ Consistency demands that the discount rate or rate of return used as a standard of comparison in deciding whether projects should be accepted or rejected should likewise be on an after-tax basis.

As in all other decision problems, the costs included in the investment decision calculation are opportunity costs, not accounting costs, and the cash inflows the benefits which would be lost if the decision were not taken.

(c) Why discount?

Any serious attempt to evaluate investment opportunities involves discounting (or compounding) of the cash flows. It is important to understand why this is done.

---

*Contrast the reason given by Bierman and Smidt [7], 1st, 2nd and 3rd edns.

† More generally, the lives of many newly-formed small businesses have ended prematurely due to a serious under-estimation of working capital needs.

‡ If we were considering investment from a social point of view (e.g. investment by public enterprises whose actions are governed partly by welfare considerations) we should use before-tax cash flows, on the grounds that tax payments represent for the most part transfer payments from one group to another within the community; they are not in general closely correlated with the costs to the community of the activity in question.

It is done because, providing the rate of interest is not zero, money has a net productivity over time; a given sum of money in 10 years' time and now do not have the same value. That is, we discount for the time productivity of money; we are not discounting for risk or uncertainty.*

11.4 Some investment criteria

(a) Crude methods

We mention, only to dismiss, various crude methods which do not allow for the time distribution of cash flows. The reason for so doing was given above.

(b) Payback period

This is a 'break-even' concept applied to investment. Writing x_t for the net cash flow in period t, payback period may be defined as the smallest value of d for which

$$\sum_{t=0}^{\tau} x_t \geq 0 \quad \text{for every } d \leq \tau \leq h,$$

where h is the decision horizon. That is, payback is the time from which the aggregate net cash flows become positive. The criterion accepts a project whose payback period is less than some predetermined time, and within this constraint selects those projects with the shortest payback periods. It will be seen, first, that this rule takes no account of the time distribution of the cash flows, and secondly that it ignores all cash flows after the 'break-even' date is reached. Since it ignores some of the data it cannot be classed as a method of economic evaluation at all. However it is widely used in practice (and enjoys official recognition in the Soviet Union). That it does so is some indication of the importance the business man attaches to uncertainty.

(c) Methods involving discounting

(i) *Internal rate of return (IRR)*

This is what Keynes called the 'marginal efficiency of capital'. Its validity was the subject of a famous debate between Boulding and Samuelson in about 1936.†
More recently the IRR rule has been espoused in certain professional and even academic accounting journals, sometimes under the guise of '*the* discounted cash flow (DCF) method'. Most of its advocates are less than fully aware of its real limitations.‡ There are indications also that its use might be widespread.

---

*This point is further discussed in Chapter 12.
† See [22].
‡ Which are not the fact that the IRR may be non-unique or not exist. Attempts to overcome these difficulties by 'normalizing' the IRR, as in [8] for example, are therefore interesting but have little utility.

Net investment and disinvestment decisions

The IRR is that number, ρ, that satisfies the equation

$$\sum_{t=0}^{h} x_t(1+\rho)^{-t} = 0,$$

providing a solution exists in the range $\rho > -1$ and is unique. That is, it is the discount rate which equates the aggregate net cash flows of the project to zero. (It can be shown that this is the rate of return on the unrecovered portion of the capital outlay, assuming that the net proceeds of the project are reinvested at the IRR.)*

The decision rule here is: (1) accept independent projects if $\rho > i$, where i is what we shall call the cost of capital, to be defined shortly; (2) ρ should be sufficiently $> i$ in each case to allow for uncertainty. It will be noted that the cost of capital is here used as the standard against which ρ is compared. This implies that i is constant from period to period ($i_1 = i_2 = \ldots = i_r = i$), or that, if it is not, the project's cash flows can be adjusted for comparison with the constant-equivalent rate.

(ii) *Net present value (NPV)*
Denoting the NPV of a project (discounted net cash flows from operations less discounted capital outlays) by V_0, and writing β_t for $(1+i)^{-t}$,

$$V_0 = \sum_{t=0}^{h} \beta_t x_t.$$

In the general case, where the discount rate is expected to vary from period to period,†

$$V_0 = \sum_{t=0}^{h} \left[x_t \prod_{T=1}^{t} (\beta_T) \right], \quad \text{where} \quad \beta_T = (1+i_r)^{-1}.$$

The decision rule for independent projects is: (i) accept a project if $V_0 > 0$ (this does not apply to dependent projects); (2) the set of projects selected should maximize V_0; (3) V_0 should be sufficiently greater than zero to allow for uncertainty.

There are several variants of this method, among them the net terminal value (NTV) criterion, which merely substitutes compounding for discounting:‡

$$V_h = \sum_{t=0}^{h} \beta_{t-h} x_t$$

(iii) *Comparison of IRR and NPV criteria*
Some comments on these two decision rules are set out below. Where the comment requires substantiation (usually mathematical), the reader is referred to the appendix to this chapter or to the appropriate source.

1. The IRR and NPV rules have different implicit reinvestment assumptions:

---

*See [6] and point (c) in the appendix to this chapter.
† $\prod$ is the multiplication notation corresponding to Σ for summation.
‡ One possible exception to the NPV and NTV criteria being equivalent is cited by Porterfield [20], pp. 38–41.

the former implicitly assumes that the net proceeds of a project are reinvested * at the IRR, ρ, the latter that they are reinvested at the cost of capital rate, i. Both of these assumptions are arbitrary. The latter one leads to incorrect results less often than the former, however.

2. The two rules are only equivalent for accept/reject decisions in the case of two-period projects (i.e. outlays in one period, entire proceeds in the following period): see points (a) and (b) in the appendix.

3. The IRR rule may lead to problems of non-uniqueness (multiple solutions) or no real solutions where projects are not of the point input–continuous output type. For projects of this kind the IRR and NPV rules may give conflicting advice. The NPV solution is the correct one – providing capital markets are perfect. See point (b) in appendix.

4. The IRR rule is unreliable as a ranking device for projects (including two-period ones) which have different outlays – see appendix, point (c). The IRR rule may be unreliable for ranking even when outlays are equal, depending on the time patterns of cash flows. *Any ratio method* is unreliable for ranking purposes. Further, if mutually exclusive projects have different lives, ratio methods must be modified so that all other alternatives are compared with the longest-lived. The NPV rule correctly ranks projects with unequal outlays or lives provided capital markets are perfect (in the former case the rule becomes: choose the alternative with the highest NPV; accept this alternative if its NPV is positive). The NPV method is unsatisfactory for dealing with cases involving physical or dynamic dependence if capital markets are imperfect.

5. The IRR rule as usually stated cannot without modification deal with the case where the cost of capital, i, is variable over time, since the rule calls for comparison of ρ with a unique rate i.

6. The IRR *rule* does not generalize to projects beyond $t = 2$. The n-period *equivalent* of the rule requires the IRR to be redefined as a series of one-period rates. Then in the general case where $\rho_1 \neq \rho_2 \neq \ldots \neq \rho$ and $i_1 \neq i_2 \neq \ldots \neq i$, the rule is:

> for periods r ($r = 1, 2, \ldots, n$) when $x_r < 0$ (i.e. for periods in which the net cash flow is negative, when the firm can be considered as being a lender to the project), $\rho_r > i_r$; and for periods r when $x_r > 0$ (the firm is a borrower from the project), $\rho_r < i_r$.

These redefined *single-period* IRRs do in fact feature in the solution of the investment decision problem in conditions of capital market imperfection and capital rationing.†

*The reinvestment rate for period s is based on the capital outstanding in period $(s-1)$, not on the initial outlay.

† As shown by Fisher [9], Hirshleifer [11] and others.

7. Net present value, V_0, is sometimes expressed in ratio form and called by such names as 'excess present value index' (EPVI) or 'profitability index'.* Two variants of the measure have been suggested from time to time. If for simplicity we write v for the present value of net cash inflows from the project and c for the present value of capital outlays, one version is $(v-c)/c$, the other v/c. An *independent* project is then accepted, subject to risk, if

$$\left(\frac{v-c}{c}\right) > 0 \quad \text{or} \quad \frac{v}{c} > 1,$$

providing capital markets are perfect and there is no capital rationing. In these circumstances the two variants of the 'profitability index' and the NPV rule are equivalent for individual projects. Like IRR, the 'profitability index' is unreliable for ranking projects which are physically or dynamically interdependent.

A word of warning is here in order. It will be recalled from subsection (c)(ii) that the NPV rule, in the circumstances in which it applies (in particular, perfect capital markets, which implies no rationing), comprises a condition on individual projects (accept independent projects whose NPV > 0) *and* a condition on the project set (the set selected should maximize NPV). In the circumstances stated these two conditions are mutually consistent. Certain other criteria have been proposed by economists which correspond to the second (aggregate) condition as applied to the two versions of the 'profitability index', i.e. maximize the 'profitability index' over the project set. Point (d) in the appendix shows that these aggregate versions are *not* equivalent to the NPV rule.

8. When capital markets are imperfect or capital rationing is present the IRR rule as usually understood (viz. as referring to a single whole-life rate) cannot be applied. The NPV rule, while continuing to indicate correct solutions for independent projects, becomes in general non-operational, as will shortly be explained (it can be used only on a limited class of projects and under certain conditions).

9. Both rules, even if they could be applied, offer only partial solutions once we drop the assumption of perfect capital markets. In optimizing investment decisions the owners' time-preferences must then be taken into account explicitly; we can no longer use 'utility-free' rules.†

(d) The meaning of the discount rate

When capital markets are perfect the rate i which was used as the standard of

* See [26].
† Section (e) of the appendix should be read at this point.

comparison under the IRR rule and as the discount rate under the NPV rule is the *cost of capital*. More generally, the cost of capital is the opportunity cost of investing in the firm, which is the cost of postponing receipts of money, measured at the margin of investment.*

Whereas production is the transformation $M_1 \rightarrow C \rightarrow M_2$, in the expectation that M_2 will be greater than M_1, M denoting money and C commodities, productive investment is the transformation $M_1 \rightarrow C_1 \rightarrow C_2 \rightarrow M_2$, i.e. a switching from money into commodities (C_1) which are used to produce other commodities (C_2), with the further feature that the last stage of this transformation, $C_2 \rightarrow M_2$, typically occupies considerably more time than does $C \rightarrow M_2$ in the first transformation.

How we *describe* this opportunity cost depends on our viewpoint, in particular whether it is that of the firm or its owners.

To the management, the opportunity cost of postponing receipts by investment depends on the alternatives to investment in the firm and on how such investment would be financed if undertaken. Taking three 'pure' financing alternatives:

1. If the investment is to be internally financed, the alternative is lending outside the firm, and the opportunity cost is given by the lending rate.
2. If it is to be externally financed and there is no capital rationing, the alternative is not borrowing, and its cost is the interest or dividend payment which would be avoided.
3. If the investment is to be externally financed subject to limits on borrowing, the alternative is the highest-yielding project squeezed out by the borrowing constraint, and its cost is the marginal rate of return on this project.

The opportunity cost of investing to the firm will be one of the above, or some combination of them, depending on how investment is financed. From the point of view of the firm further investment is only justified if it will increase discounted future earnings. As stated earlier, it is assumed in most treatments of capital budgeting that the proceeds of investment are all distributed to the owners, after paying the cost of borrowing.

From the owners' point of view, the opportunity cost of postponing receipts of money (or of trading current income available for consumption or financial investment for the prospect of a larger future income) is not measured by the same cold economic calculus as in the case of the firm, but rather by their individual personal preferences for income in different periods, which may be influenced by purely subjective factors. That is to say, of two possible investments by the firm they may prefer the one with the lower NPV (always provided this is positive) if it happens to conform more to their preferred time-pattern of income. To the owners,

*See [4], p. 426 and [5], p. 322 for statements of this view.

then, the opportunity cost is measured by their marginal rate of substitution between current and future income.

These two viewpoints are reconciled when the firm determines the level of investment which will maximize the owners' collective utility (or time-preferences for income). The margin of investment is found by equating the marginal rate of return from productive investment in the firm with the owners' marginal time-rate of substitution. When capital markets are perfect, maximizing the owners' utility and maximizing the present value of net cash flows from productive investment are consistent; the margin found by equating the productive rate of return and the market rate of interest will then be consistent with the owners reaching their preferred time-preference positions. If capital markets are not perfect the statement in the next to last sentence is still true, but in this case it may involve two steps. If borrowing or lending by the owners in any period will enable them to achieve a more desired time-preference position, the firm's investment margin is first obtained by equating the productive rate of return with the borrowing or lending rate. The overall optimum is then found by equating the borrowing or lending rate with the owners' time-rate of substitution. Which of these three rates should be equated with the productive rate of return in any period, and hence the opportunity cost discount rate for any period, is no longer ascertainable in advance, but must be determined by the analysis.

This interpretation of 'cost of capital' as the opportunity cost discount rate to be used in capital budgeting is not universally accepted. As Baumol and Quandt note, 'the cost of capital is an ill-defined concept which has been the subject of a great deal of controversy in the literature'. Readers are forewarned of the ambiguity attaching to this term. In the finance literature 'cost of capital' is frequently used to mean the rate at which the market capitalizes the expected income from *existing* assets of a company in a given risk class.* In this literature the firm's objective is usually assumed to be maximization of the *stockmarket* value of the firm, which for the all equity firm is given by the number of issued ordinary shares multiplied by the current market price per share.† In share valuation models future dividends (rarely earnings) are discounted at the rate of return required by shareholders, the market capitalization rate, as evidenced by the current yield of the shares and its expected

---

* Financial, not business, risk. 'Cost of capital' on this view is not, therefore, to be confused with the risk-adjusted discount rate discussed in section 2 of Chapter 12, where 'risk' means 'business risk' (or the uncertainty surrounding decision outcomes). Financial risk (leverage) is discussed again in Chapter 20.

† As applied to the total ordinary shares, this value is notional, since it is composed of the market price of shares traded at the margin. Continuing shareholders presumably may value their shares more highly than the market; large blocs of shares may command a different price; the value of the total equity to a controlling shareholder could differ from the sum of the market values of minority interests. Thus stock-market value of the firm involves a fallacy of composition, which is inherent in a summation of separate asset values (see Chapter 3).

rate of growth. In the Gordon–Shapiro model, for example, discussed more fully in Chapter 20:

$$r = \frac{D_0}{P_0} + g,$$

where r = the cost of equity capital, the rate at which future dividends are being discounted,

D_0 = the current dividend rate,

P_0 = the current market price of the shares, and

g = the expected annual rate of growth in dividends ($r > g$).

The confusion is compounded when this rate (r) is carried over and used in new investment decision calculations, either alone or as part of a weighted average 'cost of capital' if investment is to be financed from a variety of different sources.* The same dual usage is evident in the writings of Modigliani and Miller [19]. According to this second view the rate of return required by the owners from the firm's existing investment is also appropriate in evaluating new investment, and the criterion for undertaking new investment should be maximization of market value.

Two points may be made about this. First, as Hirshleifer has shown,† whenever capital markets are imperfect the correct formulation of the investment decision problem does require consideration of the future returns from the existing assets as well as those of the project set, but with an important difference: they are considered together. That is, the problem involves comparing all possible combinations of cash flow streams from the existing assets and the projects under consideration, because it can no longer be assumed that maximization of the present value of the project set alone, and of the firm's existing wealth as augmented by this increment, will be equivalent. The owners' subjective time-preferences intervene. The finance view, by contrast, extrapolates a rate of return based on past investment to new investment by the firm.

Secondly, the assumed objectives of the firm in the two cases (maximization of market value and of discounted earnings) are equivalent only in the absence of uncertainty.

We conclude that to define 'cost of capital' in the finance sense in capital budgeting is to misunderstand the nature of the investment decision. It should be reserved for the purpose for which it was originally intended, viz. analysis of the *stockmarket* valuation and financing policy of the firm. To avoid confusion the capital budgeting discount rate could be called the cost of investment.

(e) The limitations of utility-free rules

It follows from what was said about the nature of investment in section 1 – that it

---

* E.g. see [7], 2nd. edn., pp. 152–58.
† In the two references given in section 2(c)(v) above.

essentially involves balancing consumption alternatives over time – that investment cannot be considered independently of the time-preferences of the owners for income. The section 4.3 discussion, by contrast, has for the most part abstracted from the owners' point of view and considered investment solely from the firm's point of view. This omission must now be rectified. Two situations may be distinguished. When capital markets are perfect and there is no rationing Fisher's 'separation theorem' holds, permitting a complete separation of the firm's investment, financing and dividend policies from the owners' consumption policies. This is so because if the firm's investment policy does not enable the owners to reach their individual time-preference optima in any period, the remedy can be assumed to lie in their own hands. That is, shareholders can adjust their current incomes by borrowing or lending, switching their holdings to other securities, or the firm might bring about the same result by changes in its dividend policy. We can therefore ignore the shareholders' position and employ utility-free rules such as NPV.

Once capital market imperfections or capital rationing appear the utility-free rules no longer apply. We have then to decompose projects into sequences of two-period projects which equate their present value to zero. If borrowing and lending rates are nonconstant over time the solution (the optimal set of discount rates and the optimal amount of investment to be undertaken in any period) involves equating at the margin the owners' time-preference rate each period and either the borrowing rate, the lending rate or the one-period IRR.* This depends on the form of the time-preference function and on whether borrowing, lending or neither is needed to reach the time-preference optimum in each period. The optimal set of discount rates needed to formulate the objective function becomes known only after optimizing, and is therefore of no use in determining the optimum position. The problem is formally indeterminate. Further understanding may be gained from Hirshleifer's geometrical analysis of the two-period case, a brief summary of which appears as point (e) in the appendix.

(f) Multi-period investments† in conditions of capital market imperfection

A good deal has already been indicated as to the nature of the investment decision problem with imperfect capital markets. For this Hirshleifer's article [11] is absolutely essential reading.‡ The capital rationing case is held over until the next chapter. What is presented below is intended only as a guide to the formulation of the problem, bringing together the various strands mentioned earlier.

---

* It should be understood that, although we are talking about one-period IRRs, the criterion is still maximizing NPV.
† Projects extending over more than two periods.
‡ The argument is reviewed at some length in [2], including various programming models.

(i) *Conditions*
1. The projects under consideration, which may include physically or dynamically dependent projects, may be of any length (n may be > 2 in $(x_0, x_1, \ldots, x_n)$).
2. Denoting borrowing and lending rates by appropriate subscripts, $i_B \neq i_L$ in any period.

(ii) *Requirements to be met in formulating the problem*
1. Conditions 1. and 2. above together require that each n-period project be decomposed into all possible sequences of two-period projects which make its present value zero.* (The solution involves arranging these assumed projects for each pair of successive periods to form a contour in n-dimensional space. The series of such contours yields an investment opportunity surface, whose tangency with the highest possible time-preference surface gives the solution. Where financial as well as productive investment opportunities are included the opportunity surface is enlarged to the n-dimensional envelope. Capital rationing has the effect of truncating the opportunity surface (or envelope in the case of increasing marginal borrowing rates). Projects can no longer be considered independently, and the relevant discount rates for different periods become interrelated, making a mathematical programming formulation almost essential.)
2. Capital market imperfections mean that
   (a) Separate rates must be introduced for borrowing and lending each period.
   (b) The future earnings of the existing assets must be included in the objective function.
   (c) The problem becomes at least partially indeterminate if an objective criterion (such as NPV) is used.
       (i) If the borrowing and lending rates for each period to the horizon can be estimated in advance and, while variable over time, are not variable with the amount borrowed/lent, the NPV criterion alone can be used for a limited class of projects. With constant marginal borrowing and lending rates over the relevant ranges of borrowing/lending, the situation may be regarded as equivalent to one of perfect capital markets with fixed per unit transactions costs.† Extending the concept of 'dominance' suggested by Pye [21], Hirshleifer‡ then calculates the present value of each representation of a project, as described in subsection (ii) 1. above, at each point $t = 0, 1, 2, \ldots, n$. Project A is dominant over projects $B, C, \ldots$ if

$$V_t^A \geq V_t^B \geq \ldots \text{ for all } t,$$

* [3]. This article generalizes the Hirshleifer two-period analysis.
† [12], p. 196.
‡ *Ibid.*, p. 203–4.

with the equality holding for at least one t. In calculating these present values cash flows before t are compounded at the lending rate and those after t discounted at the borrowing rate. Some projects, however, will be neither accepted nor rejected by this procedure. For these the NPV criterion must be abandoned and a model incorporating utility adopted.

(ii) If marginal borrowing and lending rates are non-constant there is no way of avoiding a utility formulation. The problem then involves specifying the appropriate group utility function. As Weingartner has pointed out [27], this requires the firm to assign a utility index to each period's withdrawals before dividend possibilities in that period are known. Though in principle determinate this model, which would require substitution of a subjective utility function for NPV in the objective function, seems non-operational because there is no obvious way of determining the appropriate utility function. We examine this question further in Chapter 12.

11.5 Disinvestment

Before closing this chapter a further comment will be juxtaposed concerning disinvestment. Some aspects of the disinvestment decision were discussed in section 1 ; the reader will also recall the discussion in section 3(b) of Chapter 7 in connection with dropping a product. Excluding non-replacement, which is referred to in the following chapter, disinvestment raises few problems of its own and avoids the main theoretical problems which beset the investment decision (e.g. disinvestment may involve dynamic dependence but not serial dependence). Other similarities and dissimilarities will occur to the reader. Some numerical problems involving disinvestment will be found in the exercises at the end of this chapter.

Viewing the matter from the point of view of *production* (i.e. after net investment or disinvestment has occurred), in the short-run the marginal cost of contraction (i.e. the MC of current inputs) is likely to be greater than the MC of expansion, due to 'stickiness' in labour costs as output is reduced. However, the short-run MC's of expansion and contraction are substantially reversible.

In the long-run there is no reason why the costs of expansion and contraction should be equal. The analysis is complicated by indivisibilities in the capital inputs and by the possibility of different responses to changes in demand of different magnitude. Abstracting from difficulties due to indivisibilities, the position may be described as follows [23] :

If MC_1 = marginal cost with existing plant,

MC_2 = marginal cost with a new plant operated in parallel with the existing unit,

MR = marginal revenue before the increase in demand,

MR' = marginal revenue after an increase in demand,

MR'' = marginal revenue after a decrease in demand,

$SRMC$ = short-run MC,

$LRMC$ = long-run MC.

(a) Expansion (from initial position where MR = LRMC₁ = SRMC₁)

1. Small increases in output will be met by working existing plant more intensively in the short-run. This will be continued to the point where $SRMC_1 = MR'$, at which point $SRMC_1 > LRMC_1$.
2. At this point it becomes feasible to meet further increases in output by building another plant and operating the two units in parallel. The condition for installing the second unit is $SRMC_1 = SRMC_2 = LRMC_2 = MR'$. (The two units should be operated so as to equate the MC's of the current inputs of the existing plant ($SRMC_1$) and the MC of current and capital inputs (including depreciation and interest charges) of the new plant ($LRMC_2$).)
3. If output rises sufficiently, it may pay to close down the existing plant ('scale obsolescence') and invest in a new plant of larger capacity; this becomes feasible when $SRMC_1 > LRMC_2$.

(b) Contraction (initial position MR = SRMC = LRMC)

1. Output will be decreased in the short-run until $SRMC = MR'' < LRMC$.
2. This will also be the optimal adjustment in the long-run unless it pays to retire the existing plant and substitute a smaller one. The latter becomes feasible when $LRMC_2 < SRMC_1$, as before, except that now $LRMC_2 = MR''$.

Appendices

(a) Equivalence of IRR and NPV rules for independent projects in the two-period case

The project is (x_0, x_1),

$$(x_0 < 0, x_1 > 0).$$

The IRR is the rate, ρ, which satisfies the equation

$$x_0 + x_1/(1+\rho) = 0$$

Net investment and disinvestment decisions

The NPV is

$$V_0 = x_0 + x_1/(1+i)$$

If $\rho > i$,

$$x_1/(1+i) > x_1/(1+\rho)$$

and

$$V_0 > \{x_0 + x_1/(1+\rho) = 0\}.$$

Therefore

$$V_0 \begin{cases} > 0 & \text{if} \quad \rho > i \\ < 0 & \text{if} \quad \rho < i \\ = 0 & \text{if} \quad \rho = i \end{cases}$$

(b) Non-uniqueness or non-existence of IRR: a case where the two rules may conflict

(i)

If the project is of the following form (here denoting cash outflows by a minus sign):

$$-x_0, x_1, -x_2, x_3, - \ldots, x_n$$

the IRR is found from the equation

$$-x_0 + \frac{x_1}{(1+\rho)} - \frac{x_2}{(1+\rho)^2} + \frac{x_3}{(1+\rho)^3} - \cdots + \frac{x_n}{(1+\rho)^n} = 0.$$

If $a = 1/1 + \rho$), Descartes' rule of signs tells us that a polynomial of degree n such as the above has at most as many positive roots of a (i.e. as many roots in the range $\rho > -1$) as there are sign changes in the sequence of terms in x.

There are three possibilities: the project may have (1) a unique yield, (2) multiple yields, (3) no real yield.

(ii)

Consider the project $(-x_0, x_1, -x_2, x_3)$ under each of the rules. Suppose the IRR equation has been solved uniquely and that $\rho > i$.

It then follows, assuming i to be constant from period to period, that

$$\frac{x_1}{(1+i)} + \frac{x_3}{(1+i)^3} > \frac{x_1}{(1+\rho)} + \frac{x_3}{(1+\rho)^3}$$

and

$$\frac{x_2}{(1+i)^2} < \frac{x_2}{(1+\rho)^2}.$$

In other words

$$V_0 = -x_0 + \frac{x_1}{(1+i)} + \frac{x_3}{(1+i)^3} - \frac{x_2}{(1+i)^2} \qquad (1)$$

$$0 = -x_0 + \frac{x_1}{(1+\rho)} + \frac{x_3}{(1+\rho)^3} - \frac{x_2}{(1+\rho)^2}. \qquad (2)$$

To determine whether $V_0 > 0$ we need to know the value of each of the terms on the RHS of (1). It is possible that $\rho > i$ (by IRR rule) but $V_0 \leq 0$ (by NPV rule); and similarly in the cases where $\rho < i$ or $\rho = i$.

(c) Ranking of projects with different capital outlays by their IRR

Consider first two two-period projects, A and B, their IRR's being given by the equations

$$a_0 + a_1/(1+\rho_A) = 0$$

$$b_0 + b_1/(1+\rho_B) = 0,$$

where $a_0 \neq b_0$ and $-1 \leq \rho_A, \rho_B \leq \infty$.

ρ_A is the rate of return on a_0; ρ_B the rate of return on b_0. Fairly obviously these rates are not comparable, since they are related to different bases. (Suppose, e.g., that $\rho_A = 0\cdot20$, $\rho_B = 0\cdot50$, $a_0 = £1\text{m.}$, $b_0 = £1\ 000$.) The measure cannot be divorced from the size of the investment base.

In the general case where projects extend over more than two periods the IRR, as already stated, is the rate of return on the capital outstanding. Moreover, as we explain later, the IRR needs to be redefined as a series of single-period rates of return. (The IRR rule is the special case where $\rho_1 = \rho_2 = \ldots = \rho_r = \rho$.) However, the point can be made more clearly by abstracting from this further complication for the moment. The equation for determining the (whole-life) IRR of an n-period project is

$$x_0 + \frac{x_1}{(1+\rho)} + \frac{x_2}{(1+\rho)^2} + \ldots + \frac{x_n}{(1+\rho)^n} = 0.$$

The unrecovered outlays are shown in the appended table,* assuming $x_0 < 0$ and all other x's > 0:

Period (t)	Capital outstanding in the project (U_t)
0	$-x_0$
1	$-x_0(1+\rho)-x_1$
2	$[-x_0(1+\rho)-x_1](1+\rho)-x_2$
	$= -x_0(1+\rho)^2 - x_1(1+\rho) - x_2$
n	$-x_0(1+\rho)^n - x_1(1+\rho)^{n-1} - \ldots - x_{n-1}(1+\rho) - x_n$

That is, the capital outstanding at any time $t = r$ is $U_r = U_{r-1}(1+\rho)-x_r$, $r = 1, 2, \ldots, n$.

*From [6]. The IRR is the rate which reduces the unrecovered outlay, U_r, to zero at the end of the project's life.

Consequently the n-period counterpart of the statement for the two-period case (subject to the further complication from which we are still abstracting) is that the IRR rule is unreliable as a ranking device for comparing projects A and B which have different capital outlays because comparison of ρ_A and ρ_B implies that they are both based upon approximately the same unrecovered balance.

Now consider two two-period mutually exclusive projects, A and B, with equal outlays:

$$A: \quad (-1,1,4) \qquad\qquad B: \quad (-1,2,2)$$

It will be found that $\rho_A = 1\cdot562$ and $\rho_B = 1\cdot732$. On this basis we should therefore adopt B, providing $\rho_B > i$. Suppose $i = 0\cdot5$. Then $V_0^A = 1\cdot444$ and $V_0^B = 1\cdot222$, indicating that A should be selected. This is the 'cross-over case' (Figure 11.1):

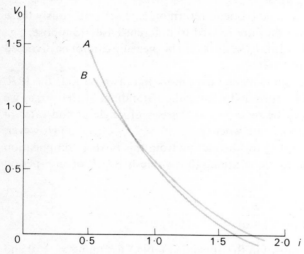

Figure 11.1

The source of the difficulty may be discovered by looking at the unrecovered outlays on the projects:

Period (r)	A		B	
	1	2	1	2
U_{r-1}	1	1·562	1	0·732
x_r	1	4	2	2
ρU_{r-1}	1·562	2·438	1·732	1·268
U_r	1·562	0	0·732	0

The unrecovered outlay at the end of period 1 is 1·562 for A and 0·732 for B. Hence

316

ρ_A and ρ_B are calculated on different bases in period 2, and are therefore not comparable.

(d) Non-equivalence of (1) max(NPV) over the project set considered and (2) max ('Profitability Index' over the project set)

Let $f(x) = \sum\limits_{t=1}^{T} x_t$ = net cash inflows from a project,

x_0 = capital outlay (assumed instantaneous for convenient partitioning of the cash flows, without loss of generality),

i = the market rate of interest,

ρ' = marginal IRR,

ρ = average IRR,

Projects range over periods $t = 1, 2, \ldots, T$; there are $j = 1, 2, \ldots, n$ projects in the set considered. It is assumed that all projects are independent, and that investment takes place in conditions of perfect capital markets (which implies no capital rationing).

	A: Single project	*B: Project set**
1. NPV rule	$f(x)e^{-it} - x_0 > 0$	max. $\Sigma [f(x)e^{-it} - x_0]$
2. IRR rule	$-x_0 + f(x)e^{-\rho t} = 0,$ $\rho > i$	
3. Profitability Index, 1st version	$\dfrac{f(x)e^{-it}}{x_0} > 1$	max. $\Sigma \left[\dfrac{f(x)e^{-it}}{x_0}\right]$
4. Profitability Index, 2nd	$\dfrac{f(x)e^{-it} - x_0}{x_0} > 0$	max. $\Sigma \left[\dfrac{f(x)e^{-it} - x_0}{x_0}\right]$
5. Max. (average IRR)		max. $\Sigma \left[\dfrac{f(x)e^{-\rho t} - x_0}{x_0}\right]$

The aggregate conditions for each of these five rules are set out below.

(i) Condition for 1B:

$$\frac{dV_0}{dx} = f'(x_j)e^{-it} - 1 = 0, \quad j = 1, \ldots, n \qquad (1.1)$$

whence
$$i = \frac{1}{t}\ln f'(x_j) \qquad (1.2)$$

(ii) Condition for 2B:

The equation for the IRR in 2 is

$$f(x)e^{-\rho t} = x_0$$

*Criterion 1B is associated with the economists Irving Fisher, Hicks, Samuelson, Massé and others, 2B with R. G. D. Allen, 5B with Böhm-Bawerk, Wicksell, F. H. Knight, Boulding, Hayek and Gabor-Pearce.

Differentiating with respect to ρ,

$$f'(x_j)e^{-\rho't} = 1.$$

Solving for ρ' gives

$$\rho' = \frac{1}{t} \ln f'(x_j). \tag{2.1}$$

But we have from (1.2) that

$$i = \frac{1}{t} \ln f'(x_j)$$

i.e. the condition for 2B is

$$\rho' = i \tag{2.2}$$

(iii) Condition for 3B:

$$f(x_j)e^{-it} - x_0[f'(x_j)e^{-it}] = 0;$$

i.e.
$$\frac{f(x_j)}{x_0} = f'(x_j); \tag{3.1}$$

i.e. when $\rho = \rho'$, which is when $\rho = \rho_{max}$. $\tag{3.2}$
(iv) Condition for 4B:

$$\frac{x_0 f'(x_j)e^{-it} - f(x_j)e^{-it}}{x_0^2} = 0;$$

i.e.
$$f'(x_j) = \frac{f(x_j)}{x_0}, \tag{4.1}$$

which is the same as the condition for 3, viz. that $\rho = \rho' = \rho_{max}$. $\tag{4.2}$
(v) From (2.1) we have that

$$\rho = \frac{1}{t} \ln\left[\frac{f(x_j)}{x_0}\right]$$

ρ is a maximum when $\quad \dfrac{d\rho}{dx} = 0 = \dfrac{1}{t}\left[\dfrac{f'(x_j)}{f(x_j)} - \dfrac{1}{x_0}\right]$ $\tag{5.1}$

i.e. when $\quad f'(x_j) = \dfrac{f(x_j)}{x_0}, \quad$ or when $\quad \rho' = \rho.$ $\tag{5.2}$

This is the condition for 5B.

It will be seen that 1B and 2B are equivalent in the conditions stated, as are 3B, 4B and 5B. The latter, however, are not equivalent to the former. In particular, from

(1.1) and (3.1) or (4.1) it will be seen that the aggregate forms of the 'profitability index' would only be equivalent to NPV_{max} if

$$\frac{f(x_j)e^{-it}}{x_0} = 1, \quad j = 1, 2, \ldots, n.$$

Criterion 2 tells us, however, that the LHS must be greater than one for all j.

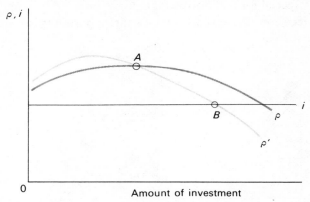

Figure 11.2

Figure 11.2 illustrates the five rules. Point A: ρ_{max} and aggregate forms of the 'profitability index' (rules 3, 4, 5). Point B: IRR and NPV rules (two-period case). (All projects assumed independent.)

Finally, it can easily be shown that, in the conditions assumed (viz. that the firm has unrestricted access to the capital market at the rate i), condition 1B is also the condition for maximizing the present value of the firm. Accordingly there is no need to include the returns from the existing assets with those of the project set in these conditions. If W_0 is the present value of the existing assets and W_1 the value of the firm after adoption of the current project set,

$$W_1 = W_0 + f(x_j)e^{-it} - x_0.$$

Treating W_0 as a constant,

$$\frac{dW_1}{dx} = f'(x_j)e^{-it} - 1 = 0, \quad \text{as before.}$$

(e) A summary of the Hirshleifer analysis, two-period case

Hirshleifer, in the references given, has extended Fisher's investment analysis to the case of imperfect capital markets. Projects are still considered deterministically, i.e. all cash flows are assumed to be known with certainty. The two-period case enables some of the essential features of the problem to be illustrated geometrically.

319

Net investment and disinvestment decisions

Besides the one mentioned in the text, Fisher's other contribution was to distinguish between productive investment and financial investment. Each is a means of transferring funds (income, consumption claims) through time. The analysis, in common with that found in most of the capital budgeting literature, assumes that the proceeds of productive investment, after meeting any costs of borrowing, are paid over in full to the owners of the firm, the ordinary shareholders (preference shares may be regarded as a special form of borrowing).

Figures 11.3(a), (b) and (c) show the owners' investment opportunity set in different situations.

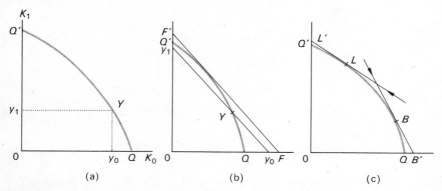

Figure 11.3

In diagram (a) the curve QQ' shows the investment opportunities open to the firm. It is a boundary relation: all points nearer the origin represent projects which are less desirable than some point on the curve in respect of income in *both* periods. The projects comprising the set shown along QQ', here all assumed to be independent (dependent projects lead to an irregular curve) are ranked in descending order of their 'productive rate of return', beginning from Q.* The marginal productive rate of return, given by the slope of QQ' at any point, equals the marginal IRR in the two-period case, but not otherwise. In other words the shape of the curve QQ' as drawn (concave to the origin) indicates diminishing returns to investment. This need not always be the case: investment in underdeveloped countries affords an example.

Y represents the firm's initial position at the beginning of period 0, its endowment or wealth. This is shown as the combination of income y_0 in period 0 and y_1 in period 1. (It is possible for Y to lie in the second and fourth, as well as the first, quadrant.)

---

*While it will be convenient to assume that a point like Q is the starting point, as noted in [24], p. 206, the 'starting point may . . . be a point on either axis (initial income falling all in period 0 or all in period 1), or . . . a point in the positive quadrant (initial income falling partly in [each period, or] It may even lie in the second or fourth quadrants, [involving] negative income either in period 0 or in period 1).' Hirshleifer is here not distinguishing between investment by firms and by individuals.

320

If the firm is free to engage only in productive investment it can use its endowment in production to yield income OQ in period 0, or it can transform it by productive investment into income OQ' in period 1. The line FF' in diagram (b) represents financial investment undertaken in a perfect capital market (a single 'price line' for borrowing and lending, showing the terms on which the market is willing to exchange units of K_0 for units of K_1 and vice versa). A slope of -1 would indicate a zero rate of interest between the periods. If confined to financial investment the firm can (by borrowing) convert its endowment Y into income y_0 available for current consumption, or (by lending) into y_1 for consumption in period 1. Putting productive and financial investment opportunities together gives the opportunity set OFF' in diagram (b).

Diagram (c) shows the same situation when capital markets are imperfect.* The lending line (arrow points upward) and the borrowing line (arrow points downward) no longer coincide; the borrowing line is steeper than the lending line ($i_B > i_L$). Straight lines indicate that the marginal borrowing and lending rates are constant. There are three possibilities in this case, depending on the slopes of the curves: productive investment by the firm will be carried to the point of tangency of QQ' with a lending line (in which case the opportunity set is $OQLL'$), with a borrowing line ($OB'BQ'$), or somewhere between the two (OQQ').

The final element is a function showing the terms on which the owners are willing to make exchanges between K_0 and K_1. Just as the financial investment relationships were represented by a family of lines parallel to LL' and BB' at different income levels, so the shareholders' time-preference or utility-indifference function is represented by a series of curves for different income positions. The relationships are set out below, where the symbol r stands for the productive rate of return:

	Equation	*Slope*
Productive investment opportunity curve	$-K_0 + \dfrac{K_1}{1+r} = 0$	$-(1+r)$
Borrowing curves	$-K_0 + \dfrac{K_1}{1+i_B} = c$, a parameter	$-(1+i_B)$
Lending curves	$-K_0 + \dfrac{K_1}{1+i_L} = d$, a parameter	$-(1+i_L)$
Owners' time-preference curves	$U(K_0, K_1) = e$, a parameter	$\left.\dfrac{\mathrm{d}K_1}{\mathrm{d}K_0}\right|_U$

*Anticipating Chapter 20, if capital markets are imperfect and incomplete (see [12], p. 244 for a definition of an incomplete market), it is possible for the firm to have an optimal capital structure. That is, a certain ratio of debt to equity capital will simultaneously maximize the value of the firm to its present owners and minimize the firm's average cost of capital in the 'finance' sense. This, in turn, makes it possible to visualize an optimal dividend policy. There are implications here for the financing of investment by the firm – and for the financing of dividend payments. If the firm's capital structure is optimal before investment is undertaken, for example, financing entirely by borrowing will be nonoptimal.

Net investment and disinvestment decisions

Which of the three possibilities mentioned will be involved in the solution depends on the slopes of the above curves. The objective of the owners is to get onto as high a U curve as possible. This requires us to separate the actions which can be taken by the owners from the action taken by the firm. The firm carries productive investment to the point of tangency of QQ' with a borrowing line, a lending line or a U curve. That is, the condition for determining productive investment by the firm will be one of the following:

$$-(1+r) = -(1+i_B) \quad \text{(tangency with borrowing line)}$$

$$-(1+r) = -(1+i_L) \quad \text{(tangency with lending line)}$$

$$-(1+r) = \left.\frac{dK_1}{dK_0}\right|_U \quad \text{(direct tangency with } U \text{ curve)}$$

If the tangency is of either of the first two kinds, it represents only the first stage towards attainment of the owners' optimum position. For in those cases it will be possible for the owners to get onto a higher U curve by engaging in financial investment (borrowing or lending). In Figure 11.4, movements along the borrowing or lending lines represent private financial transactions by the owners, aimed at achieving their preferred pattern of income, here shown by the point R.

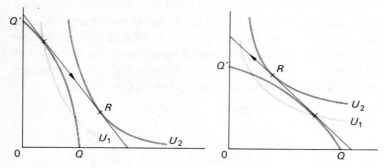

Figure 11.4

The analysis shows how a solution might be reached if the owners' time-preferences are considered, as they should be when capital markets are imperfect. The difficulty is in determining the collective time-preference function, U. The NPV criterion would be capable of providing only a partial solution in these conditions; but, as we have seen, with such a criterion the problem is indeterminate.

Bibliographical references

[1] Amey, L. R., On opportunity costs and decision-making, *Accountancy*, July 1968; reprinted in *Studies in Accountancy, 1968*, Institute of Chartered Accountants in England and Wales; reprinted in *Readings in Management Decision*, ed. L. R. Amey, Longman, 1973.

[2] Amey, L. R., Interdependencies in capital budgeting: A survey, *Journal of Business Finance*, Autumn 1972.

[3] Bailey, M. J., Formal criteria for investment decisions, *Journal of Political Economy*, October 1969, pp. 476–88.

[4] Baumol, W. J., *Economic Theory and Operations Analysis*, Prentice-Hall, 2nd edn., 1965.

[5] Baumol, W. J. and R. E. Quandt, Investment and discount rates under capital rationing: A programming approach, *Economic Journal*, June 1965, pp. 317–29.

[6] Bernhard, R. H., Discount methods for expenditure evaluation: A clarification of their assumptions, *Journal of Industrial Engineering*, Jan.-Feb. 1962, pp. 19–27.

[7] Bierman, H. and S. Smidt, *The Capital Budgeting Decision*, Macmillan, New York, 1960, 1966 and 1971.

[8] Duguid, A. M. and J. G. Laski, The financial attractiveness of a project: A method of assessing it, *Operational Research Quarterly*, vol. 15, no. 4, pp. 317–28.

[9] Fisher, I., *The Theory of Interest*, Macmillan, New York, 1930.

[10] Gordon, M. J. and E. Shapiro, Capital equipment analysis: The required rate of profit, *Management Science*, October 1956, pp. 104–6; reprinted in [24].

[11] Hirshleifer, J., On the theory of optimal investment decision, *Journal of Political Economy*, 1958, pp. 329–52; reprinted in [24] and in *Modern Financial Management*, eds. B. V. Carsberg and H. C. Edey, Penguin, 1969.

[12] Hirshleifer, J., *Investment, Interest, and Capital*, Prentice-Hall, 1970.

[13] Holt, C. C. *et al.*, *Planning Production, Inventories, and Work Force*, Prentice-Hall, 1960.

[14] Lancaster, K., *Introduction to Modern Microeconomics*, Rand McNally, 1969.

[15] Lesourne, J., *Economic Analysis and Industrial Management*, Prentice-Hall, 1963.

[16] Lundberg, E., The profitability of investment, *Economic Journal*, Dec. 1959.

[17] Lutz, F. and V., *The Theory of Investment of the Firm*, Princeton University Press, 1951.

[18] Massé, P., *Optimal Investment Decisions*, Prentice-Hall, 1962.

[19] Modigliani, F. and M. H. Miller, The cost of capital, corporation finance and the theory of investment, *American Economic Review*, June 1958; reprinted in [24].

[20] Porterfield, J. T. S., *Investment Decisions and Capital Costs*, Prentice-Hall, 1965.

[21] Pye, G., Present values for imperfect capital markets, *Journal of Business*, January 1966, pp. 45–51.

[22] Samuelson, P. A., Some aspects of the pure theory of capital, *Quarterly Journal of Economics*, 1936–37, pp. 469–96.

[23] Smith, V. L., *Investment and Production*, Harvard University Press, 1961.

[24] Solomon, E., ed., *The Management of Corporate Capital*, Free Press, 1959.

[25] Vickers, D., *The Theory of the Firm: Production, Capital and Finance*, McGraw-Hill, 1968.

[26] Weingartner, H. M., The excess present value index, *Journal of Accounting Research*, Autumn 1963, pp. 213–24.

[27] Weingartner, H. M., Criteria for programming investment project selection, *Journal of Industrial Economics*, Nov. 1966, pp. 65–76.

Problems

11.1 Explain precisely the role of depreciation in investment appraisal calculations.

11.2 Suggest at least one investment criterion for comparing projects with different capital outlays and different terminal dates.

11.3 Should allowance be made in investment decision calculations for forecast changes in the *general* price level? Give your reasons.

11.4 A company uses a pump to remove surplus water at the end of a manufacturing process. The demand for the manufactured product and (except as mentioned below) the technology and costs of the manufacturing process are expected to remain unchanged in the future.

323

The present pump cost £7 000 six years ago. It has a remaining technical life of four years (with uniform efficiency), a nil scrap value, and running costs of £1 000 per year.

A superior pump is now available which costs £7 000. It has a technical (and uniformly efficient) life of ten years, a negligible scrap value throughout its life and running costs of £700 per year.

A major reconstruction of the company's factory is planned to take place in two years' time. At that time a pump could be dispensed with entirely by constructing a drainage system at a cost of £20 000. Instantaneous construction and cash outlay in two years' time can be assumed. The drainage system would last indefinitely if regularly maintained at a cost of £100 per year.

The company's cost of capital is 7 per cent per annum.

The company's capital project analyst submits the following report:

	£
Drainage outlay (P.V. of £20 000, approx.)	17 500
New pump outlay	7 000
Excess capital outlay of drainage	£10 500
Cost of capital at 7 per cent on £10 500	735
Annual savings of drainage	600
Annual cost advantage of new pump over drainage	£135
Annual cost advantage of new over old pump	£300

Immediate purchase of new pump recommended.

Required:
Your analysis of the problem. Confine consideration to the above data, and ignore taxation.

11.5 A small engineering works has already decided to implement two investment projects, *A* and *B*. The only question at issue is timing. Each project involves a capital outlay of £40 000 irrespective of when it is undertaken. The company has £40 000 available for investment in year 0 and another £40 000 in year 5. Each project takes one year to construct. The proceeds of the earlier investment are not available for reinvestment in year 5. The alternatives are evaluated below:

Project	NPV at 5 per cent if construction started in:	
	year 0 (£000's)	year 5 (£000's)
A	164	157
B	98	87

The company reasons that the more profitable project (*A*) should be undertaken in year 0 and the less profitable one in year 5.

(1) Do you agree with this conclusion?

(2) Provide a linear programming formulation of the problem.

11.6 A Middle East government is considering plans for the building of a multipurpose dam of a certain size at a cost of £100m., the purposes to be served by the project being power generation, irrigation and flood control, etc. The value of the total benefits is set at £110m., of which £70m. is expected to result from irrigation and £40m. from power.

It has also been estimated that the cost of the additional capacity and features included for power generation would be £30m., and the costs due solely to irrigation (consisting again of added capacity and facilities) also £30m. If either of these functions were dropped from the plan £30m. would in each case be taken off the cost of the project. The remaining £40m. is regarded as a joint or common cost, treating these two terms as synonymous. All costs and benefits above are expressed in terms of present values.

From the various parties interested in the project the following conflicting advice has been received as to how the total construction costs should be divided between the three functions for the purpose of the investment decision:

  I. Each function should bear its total cost, i.e. the added cost of including each separable function plus a 'fair share' (interpreted as equal shares) of joint costs.

 II. Separable, as well as joint, costs should be allocated among functions ('the project that looks good should support the project that looks bad').

III. There should be no allocation of costs between the joint purposes.

     The results are shown below:

Allocation of Construction Costs, £m.

Method	Power	Irrigation	All other purposes	Total
I	50	50	0	100
II	35	65	0	100
	(25, 10)	(35, 30)		
III		?		100

The figures in parentheses are the separable and joint costs, respectively.

Discuss these recommendations, including the assumptions which you consider might underlie I and II. What general principles, if any, can you suggest for the guidance of any government contemplating investment in such a multipurpose utility?

11.7 Gamma Ltd. produces three different products in three workshops:

Current Annual Budget

Workshop	A	B	C
Sales: in units	4 000	10 000	5 000
in value (dollars)	60 000	30 000	50 000
Costs: Direct materials	10 000	5 000	10 000
Direct labour	8 000	5 000	16 000
Variable factory overhead	6 000	3 000	12 000
Fixed factory overhead	10 000	5 000	10 000
Administration and distribution overheads	10 000	7 000	18 000
Total departmental costs	$44 000	$25 000	$66 000
Departmental profit (or loss)	$16 000	$5 000	($16 000)

As a consultant not previously acquainted with the firm you have elicited the following additional information as a result of preliminary enquiries:

1. All three workshops are budgeted for, and working at, an output which represents practicable full capacity, but the firm believes that the sales volume for product C is only being maintained in the face of a slowly contracting market because of the firm's policy of pricing the product 50 cents per unit cheaper than does the principal competitor, Firm X, which produces only the one product.

2. Workshop C could be converted to produce more of products A or B, as suggested by the Works Director, but this would require an additional capital investment that the Board feels unwilling to make in the near future, especially in view of rather pessimistic forecasts as to the growth rate of the market for products A and B.

3. Sixty per cent of each fixed factory overhead allocation is traceable to costs arising inside the respective workshops.

4. Depreciation charges included in the traceable factory overheads of the three workshops are as follows:

   A $3 000; B $1 200; C $3 000. All other depreciation totals $5 800. Workshop depreciation charges consist of machinery (80 per cent), and buildings (20 per cent)

5. Administrative and Distribution Overhead allocations are considered to consist of 25 per cent variable costs.

6. Departmental profit or loss is shown before tax, which may be assumed to be at an effective rate of 50 per cent after allowing for time-lag in payment. Assume that annual investment allowances for tax purposes are equal to the recorded straight-line depreciation charges.

7. Permanent closure of workshop *C*, as recommended by two directors, would result in estimated annual savings in addition to traceable workshop *C* costs, as follows: fixed factory overheads, $2 000; fixed administrative and distribution overheads $6 000.

8. Workshop *C* is so located as to make it impracticable to sell the building even if the workshop is closed down permanently. It could, however, be leased at $200 per month as a warehouse, with the lessee paying all maintenance, rates, etc., once the workshop machinery had been removed and sold at a net salvage value of $5 000 (net book value is presently $12 000).

9. Net working capital presently required for financing production in workshop *C* is estimated to be $3 000. If workshop *C* were closed, it is proposed to use all released capital to reduce the existing large bank overdraft (6 per cent interest).

Required:

(a) Select the information that you consider to be relevant in support of your conclusions as to the wisdom or otherwise of permanently closing workshop *C*.

(b) Are there any other alternatives that you would wish to consider, and is there any additional information that you would like to have before making final recommendations to the firm?

11.8 The Yellow Press Ltd. are printers in London. The works consist of a composing room, where the type is set up, a machine room, containing the presses, and a process engraving department in which blocks are made for diagrams and illustrations. Some of these blocks are supplied to other printers, and some are made for use by the firm itself. The whole output of this department is valued at trade selling prices, and on this basis the department has made an annual loss for many years, as is shown in the accompanying Departmental Profit and Loss Account.

Hitherto this loss has been accepted, as the department has made some contribution to overheads each year: but now the possibility of closing the department and buying all blocks from outside specialists is being reconsidered, as the space it occupies would be suitable for an extension to the composing room, now regarded as urgent. If this is not done, then a separate temporary extension to the composing room will have to be built, pending the removal of the whole works to new premises at some future date.

327

If the engraving department were closed, it is considered that not all the expenses apportioned to it would be eliminated. The company's electricity bill might be cut by £20 p.a., general overheads would fall by £100 p.a., and interest on capital invested in plant and equipment would be saved. These assets, while serviceable, are obsolescent and would only fetch £2 500 if sold now. In seven years' time, when they will cease to be serviceable, their scrap value will be about £500.

If the department is not shut down, and a composing room extension has to be built, a suitable structure to last 15 years would cost £5 000. Such a structure would involve extra property expenses of £90 p.a.

Should the engraving department be closed? Give a reasoned statement and figures in support of your answer. Assume the cost of capital is 7 per cent.

Process Engraving Department (Trading and Profit and Loss Account for the year ending December 31)

	£	£
Sales		10 000
Less Materials	1 850	
Departmental wages and national insurance	6 160	
		8 010
		1 990
Less		
Spoilage	130	
Depreciation	460	
Repairs to plant	180	
Gas	50	
*Electricity	120	
*Property expenses	160	
		1 100
Gross Profit for the year		890
Less		
*General overheads (including interest on buildings)	1 700	
*Rent charge for premises owned by the company	200	
*Interest on capital at 7 per cent on plant – book value £3 700	259	
		2 159
Net loss for the year		£1 269

*Apportionments of works and company expenses.

11.9 Patience Inc. is contemplating building a new factory. This would require an immediate investment outlay of £100 000 and would take one year to construct. Work can begin on the construction any year from 1975 onwards. The investment will begin yielding net operating receipts the year following completion of construction, at the rate of £1 000 a year for the first 20 years, and thereafter at the rate of £10 000 a year forever. The firm's investment criterion is to maximize net present value. If the cost of capital, i, is expected to be 0·05 throughout, when should the firm invest?

12
Investment under capital rationing; replacement policy; uncertainty

12.1 Capital rationing

(a) The source of rationing

In the previous chapter we discussed the case where investment is undertaken in conditions of capital market imperfection. 'Capital rationing' refers to the case where the amount of investment a firm may undertake in any period is effectively limited by a shortage of funds. As we noted earlier, shortages of other resources required to carry out the investment program would have the same effect; these might be of a particular type of labour or of management time. Rationing may come about in two ways. First, it may be market-determined, an extreme form of market imperfection. Here the firm's investment is restricted either by an absolute limit on the amount of funds it may borrow, or by the fact that additional funds may only be obtained at an increasing marginal cost which eventually becomes prohibitive. Corresponding to these involuntary funds constraints there may be voluntary constraints, imposed by the firm itself, again taking the form either of an absolute limit or some arbitrarily determined 'cut-off' rate of return. For example, the management may decide that investment in a particular year is to be restricted to the amount which can be financed from internal sources, or it may announce a cut-off rate of x per cent. In practice the latter is arrived at, and applied, in a number of different ways. Investment is restricted in the sense that these constraints prevent the acceptance of some projects which it would otherwise be desirable to undertake. We have already noted that when the source of rationing is exogenous it is some-times referred to as 'external capital rationing', and when endogenously determined as 'internal capital rationing'.

There is disagreement in the literature concerning the rationale of *quantitative* limits on funds for investment. The two opposing views have been characterized as the 'hard' and 'soft' views of rationing due to a quantitative constraint.* The 'hard' view is that the capital market may impose an absolute limit on the money capital a firm can borrow for investment at any price, because the firm is considered to be a

*See [3].

bad risk or because it is unknown.* The 'soft' view is that rationing in the form of a quantitative limit can only be rationalized as an internal administrative device, and then only over short periods.† The argument varies slightly according to whether the constraint takes the form of an upper limit on borrowing or a fixed funds quota, but is essentially that (1) such a quantitative limit cannot be market determined (the firm can borrow any amount of funds it wants, at a price) and (2) it would never be imposed by a firm (or individual investor) following a maximizing rule.

Hirshleifer (*ibid.*) illustrates the upper limit on borrowing case as follows. Suppose a firm's board of directors imposes an upper limit of zero on borrowing for investment in a given period, i.e. the firm's opportunity set is $OQLL'$ in Figure 12.1. The point Y represents this internally-imposed budget limitation (or endowment). The optimal *attainable* solution will involve either a tangency with LL' or a direct tangency in the range QL, depending on the shape of the U curves. These possibilities are shown in Figure 12.1 by the points L^* and M^*, respectively.

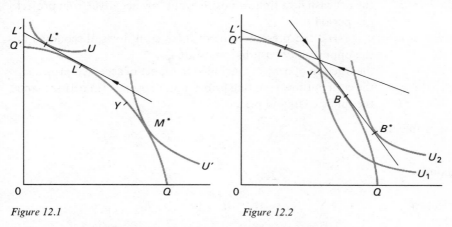

Figure 12.1   *Figure 12.2*

If the attainable solution lies in the interval QL, and $i_B > i_L$:

1. If the slope of QL is everywhere less than that of the borrowing line the only possibility is a direct tangency. If such a tangency exists in this interval the optimal attainable solution will also be the optimal solution.
2. If parts of QL are steeper than the borrowing line there is a tangency with a borrowing line (point B in Figure 12.2). In this case if the optimal attainable solution happens to be (a direct tangency) in the interval QB it will be inferior to the 'borrowing' solution, both from the firm's and the owners' point of view.

The argument about an *internally-imposed* limit on borrowing leading to non-optimal investment is, subject to the exception mentioned in 1., incontravertible.

---

*This is the view of [2], and is also subscribed to by the authors.
†[4], pp. 205–10, [8], Chapter 9, and [9].

What is less obvious is Hirshleifer's assumption that, because the management decides not to resort to borrowing, for reasons of ignorance or the risk of losing control of the firm, the shareholders are likewise precluded from borrowing.

(b) Indeterminacy with a utility-free criterion

Under conditions of capital market imperfection or capital rationing the investment decision problem becomes essentially indeterminate when an objective criterion such as NPV is used.* This is because the optimal investment program and the optimal discount rates become interdependent. The opportunity cost discount rates are required in order to formulate the objective function, but cannot be determined until the problem has been solved. The interdependence is illustrated below by means of the simplest linear programming investment decision model:†

Denote by: a_{jt} the net cash flow (inflow positive, outflow negative) from project j in period t,

$c_j = a_{jt}(1+i)^{-t}$ the present value of these cash flows, discounted at the opportunity cost discount rate i,

x_j the fraction of project j included in the set of accepted projects,‡

b_{jt} the cash outflow resulting from a unit of project j in period t, and

M_t the funds ceiling in period t.

Primal problem:

Maximize
$$\sum_{j=1}^{n} c_j x_j$$

subject to
$$\sum_j b_{jt} x_j \leq M_t \quad (t = 0, 1, \ldots, h)$$

$$0 \leq x_j \leq 1$$

Dual problem:

Minimize
$$\sum_{t=1}^{h} \rho_t M_t + \sum_j \mu_j$$

subject to
$$\sum_t \rho_t b_{jt} + \mu_j \geq c_j \quad (j = 1, \ldots, n)$$

---

*Except, as already noted, where marginal borrowing and lending rates in any period are constant, when it is possible to reach decisions on a limited class of the projects.

†Which assumes, illogically, a single rate i, the same for borrowing and lending and constant over time.

‡Fractions of projects could be eliminated from the solution by inserting a further constraint requiring all x_j to be integer.

The dual variables ρ_t are associated with the budget constraints M_t; they show the amount by which the primal objective function (the present value of the accepted set of projects) would be increased by easing the budget constraint by £1. If ρ_t^* denotes the values of these dual variables in the optimal solution, the opportunity cost discount rate $(1+i)^{-1}$ used in the primal objective function for period t is related to these values as follows:

$$(1+i) = \rho_t^* - 1/\rho_t^*$$

Consequently the primal objective function cannot be formulated until the dual problem has been solved:

$$\sum_j c_j x_j \quad \text{must be calculated as} \quad \sum_{j=1}^{n} \sum_{t=1}^{h} \left(a_{jt} \frac{\rho_t^*}{\rho_0^*} \right) x_j;$$

and if the dual problem is treated as the primal problem, it cannot be formulated until the primal problem is solved. The problem as stated is indeterminate because it is internally inconsistent: given the fact that capital is rationed, in every period in which the budget constraint is binding the opportunity cost discount rate is independent of market interest rates and can only be determined by the analysis. Continued use of the symbol *i*, previously used to denote a market rate of interest, is thus rather misleading here.

(c) Partial methods of breaking the indeterminacy

If we accept Fisher's view of investment as being directed towards balancing consumption over time, it follows that a 'utility-free' solution to the capital investment problem is not possible with imperfect capital markets or capital rationing. The problem can only be solved optimally by explicitly introducing subjective elements – the owners' time-preferences – into the analysis. To this extent, therefore, the procedures to be described in this section are really a contradiction in terms: they offer only what Hirshleifer would describe as 'partial solutions'.*

Leaving owners' time-preferences aside, however, what can be done to resolve the formal indeterminacy which was displayed in section 1(b)? One proposal would be to treat the discount rate as the variable it is, by formulating the problem as a nonlinear programming problem. As Baumol states:†

*A more sophisticated utility-free model involving capital rationing will be found in [8], Chapter 9. Readers should note that in this model the borrowing and lending is undertaken by the *firm*, not by the shareholders as in the Hirshleifer analysis (e.g. p. 141: 'We then wish to maximise the net value of assets, financial and physical, as of the horizon, where the former are expressed in terms of funds available for 'lending' at that time . . .').

†[1], p. 450n. Thus stated, the problem remains formally indeterminate, of course.

The discount rate depends upon the optimality calculation and vice versa. In principle, the solution of the problem requires a nonlinear programming analysis in which the dual prices are the marginal yields of money in the various periods, and hence the appropriate discount rates. In this problem the discounted present values ... themselves are functions of the dual prices, and hence are variable.

Two other attempts to solve the problem continue to employ a linear programming formulation. Using a simple model as in section 1(b), Lusztig and Schwab [7] preassign an initial value to the discount rate,* which they suggest might be the firm's average cost of capital on existing assets. This enables them to write down the objective function. They suggest an iterative procedure for systematic adjustment of the discount rate until it coincides with the optimum opportunity cost discount rate, and their chief concern is with the impact of these adjustments to the discount rate on the optimality of the solution. In general, the discount rate generated by this parametric variation procedure depends on the initial value chosen, and does not provide a unique optimum. By modifying the problem and stating it correctly in economic terms,† Whitmore and Amey have shown‡ that an optimum is obtained in at most one iteration, and that in general there is an infinite number of sets of opportunity cost discount rates which will yield an optimal solution in the rationing case, depending on the set initially chosen.

(d) Models employing a subjective criterion

Hirshleifer's discussion of capital rationing is confined to quantitative limitations on funds available for investment, the case we have been discussing. In his analysis, rationing by price (i.e. by a rising marginal borrowing rate) is recognized only as it relates to borrowing by the *owners* in order to reach their preferred time distribution of income, not to borrowing by the firm.

The Fisher view of investment in the quantitative limits case has, however, been formulated by Baumol and Quandt (*ibid.*) in a way which, in principle, yields true opportunity cost discount rates. This is achieved by abandoning the NPV criterion employed in the models discussed in section 1(c) and substituting a subjective criterion:

Maximize $$\sum_t U_t W_t$$

subject to $$-\sum_j a_{jt} x_j + W_t \leq M_t \quad (t = 0, 1, \ldots, h)$$

$$W_t, x_j \geq 0.$$

* I.e. they assume that the discount rate is constant from period to period.
† The earnings of existing assets are included, as this case requires; also the 'discount rate' in [7] becomes a vector of one-period rates.
‡ [11]. See also [10] for an attempt to incorporate the owners' time-preferences, which are subject to uncertainty on the part of management.

334

Here W_t represents withdrawals by the owners for consumption (dividends in the case of a company) in period t; U_t the marginal utility of these withdrawals in period t, assumed constant;* $-\sum_j a_{jt}$ is the cash outflow resulting from project j in period t as before; M_t is the borrowing limit in period t, and x_j is the number of units of project j adopted.†

The corresponding dual problem is:

Minimize

$$\sum_t \rho_t M_t$$

subject to

$$-\sum_t a_{jt}\rho_t \geq 0 \quad (j = 1, \ldots, n)$$

$$\rho_t \geq U_t.$$

The opportunity cost discount rates are then given by the ratios ρ_t^*/ρ_{t-1}^* in the optimal solution, where ρ has the same meaning as in the model of section 1(b).

By the duality theorems of linear programming, if

$$W_t > 0 \text{ in the optimal solution, } U_t = \rho_t$$

and if

$$W_t = 0 \text{ ,, ,, ,, ,, } U_t < \rho_t.$$

From this it follows that the value of withdrawals by the owners is maximized if, in any period t, the following condition is met:

$$U_t/U_{t-1} \leq \rho_t^*/\rho_{t-1}^*,$$

i.e. that the rate at which the owners discount period t funds to equivalence with period $(t-1)$ funds, their rate of substitution between income in the two periods, does not exceed the opportunity cost discount rate, the rate of exchange permitted at the margin by investment in the firm.

The reader may find it easier to follow the reasoning behind this by referring to a 'Hirshleifer' two-period diagram showing a direct tangency solution, as for example in the lower part of Figure 12.1. (Consider the relation between the slopes of the Q and U' curves before the point M^* is reached, at M^*, and after M^*.)

It may also help to consider the four possible cases, depending on whether or not there are withdrawals in each of the periods:

Withdrawals	Relation holding in optimal solution
(1) $W_{t-1} > 0, W_t > 0$	$U_t/U_{t-1} = \rho_t^*/\rho_{t-1}^*$
(2) $W_{t-1} > 0, W_t = 0$	$U_t/U_{t-1} < \rho_t^*/\rho_{t-1}^*$
(3) $W_{t-1} = 0, W_t > 0$	$U_t/U_{t-1} > \rho_t^*/\rho_{t-1}^*$
(4) $W_{t-1} = 0, W_t = 0$	undefined

* I.e., utility is assumed to be linear in money: if a shareholder's money income is doubled, his utility will also be doubled.

† Adoption of multiples of the same project can be prevented by inserting a further constraint, $x_j \leqslant 1, j = 1, \ldots, n.$

In case (2) all available funds in period t are used for investment; there are no withdrawals. Case (1) represents the limiting case, in that investment will be carried to the point where the relationship in the second column is satisfied as an equality. When this point is reached the owners' position can no longer be improved by further investment in the firm, and so funds are withdrawn. In case (3) this position is reached at the end of period $(t-1)$. In period t no investment opportunities offering higher rates of return than the rate required by the owners for postponing consumption for one period exist, and therefore all available funds are siphoned off in withdrawals. Case (4) can fall in any of the other three categories. Until we have further information – on the numerical values of U and ρ^* in each of the periods – it is undefined.

This reformulation of the rationing problem breaks the indeterminacy described in section 1(b). However it runs into two substantial practical difficulties. The first is that there is no obvious way of determining the group utility function

$$U = f(x_1, \ldots, x_n).$$

The second, pointed out by Weingartner [9], is that it requires the firm to assign, on behalf of shareholders, a utility to each period's withdrawals before dividend possibilities in that period are known. Weingartner's own response (*ibid.*), which took the form of determining productive and financial investment by the firm within a model which had as its objective function the maximization of the growth of dividends, is only rescued from indeterminacy by the introduction of an arbitrary discount rate, assumed constant over time, which is not varied parametrically as discussed in the previous section.

(e) Solution by enlarging the problem

A more promising line of approach sets investment decisions within a complete financial model of the firm, usually having as its objective the maximization of the present value of the firm, measured in terms of the value of its ordinary shares. This approach recognizes some of the weaknesses in the preceding analysis: that dividends are paid out of the firm's total cash flows, not out of the proceeds of new investment alone; that, in view of the practical difficulties in the way of determining shareholders' time-preferences, dividend policy has a rather tenuous place in the previous analysis, whereas in circumstances of market imperfection and rationing an optimal dividend policy from the firm's point of view may be defined and cannot really be divorced from the investment decision, and that the discount rates must be internally determined.

This kind of approach, which would make investment decision-making consistent with the firm's overall financial objective and clearly distinguish between the firm and its owners, has been pursued by Carleton [3].* Investment, dividend and financing decisions by the firm are jointly optimized in a two-stage model. At the first stage, by imposing certain constraints† on an aggregate corporate financial model (with objective function the maximization of the present value of the ordinary shares, defined in terms of future dividends discounted at an objectively determinable rate of return, k, required by the market), an aggregate solution is obtained for the dividend, investment and financing policies of the firm. This aggregate model yields an 'optimal' set of one-period interest rates, which we will denote by d_t^*.

Exogenously-determined capital rationing is considered arbitrary by Carleton in his model; rationing may take the form only of an administrative device used by central management.

At the second stage the interest rates so determined are used in a project selection model bearing formal similarities to the Baumol and Quandt model examined earlier, but in which

M_t becomes the capital budget for period t as determined by the aggregate model,

$U_t = (1 + d_t^*)^{-t}$,

d_t^* = the incremental rate of return on total investment in period t from the optimal solution of the aggregate problem, now used to discount project cash flows, and

W_t = funds released by the projects undertaken for further investment in the firm or withdrawal by the owners.

Subject to these redefinitions, the conditions at the optimum correspond to those for the Baumol and Quandt model.

In principle the two-stage approach has a number of desirable features. Recalling the list of requirements to be met by an investment decision model in conditions of market imperfection and rationing in Chapter 11, besides making a clear separation between the firm and its owners it represents explicitly the earnings of the existing assets and the firm's dividend policy. However, though it cannot be pursued here, this approach is also open to criticism at several points, and the 'capital rationing problem' cannot yet be said to have been solved in a fully satisfactory way.

12.2 Optimal replacement policy

Destructible assets are taken out of service, with or without replacement, for a

---

* See also [6] and [5].

† The principal one of which involves the average rate of return on total investment in each period (existing assets plus new investment opportunities considered), though the description of the model is imprecise.

number of reasons. They may fail while they are in service, deteriorate due to wear and tear (a function of their age and rate of utilization), or they may have become obsolete. Obsolescence in the normal sense is a result of technical progress: new machines are developed which are more efficient than existing ones, and this causes the economic life of equipment in service to diverge from its physical life. In the previous chapter we noted another kind of obsolescence, 'scale obsolescence', due to a marked permanent increase in demand for the product manufactured. In a period of fairly rapid technical progress such as has recently been experienced in many fields of industrial activity obsolescence often becomes the principal factor determining when equipment is retired or replaced.

By optimal (or economic) replacement policy we shall mean a systematic policy related to the objective of the enterprise, which we will take to be the maximization of discounted profits. The task, then, is to develop criteria which will be consistent with this objective in a number of different situations. In a static world in which there is no technical progress the determination of such an optimal policy is a relatively simple matter requiring merely a little arithmetic. Once obsolescence is introduced, replacement becomes a complex multi-period problem. It should be noted that the object of discussion will not be the retirement or replacement of capital goods such as machines, but of the service potential or productive capacity of capital goods.

Moreover we will not be concerned with spectacular cases of technical progress, the sort of progress that invention of the wheel meant for the transport industry. In such cases the relative advantage afforded by replacement is so great that immediate replacement is a foregone conclusion. Rather we will be concerned with the much more common case where technical progress (and hence obsolescence) is a gradual process.

In the cases that follow we shall for convenience of formulation use continuous rather than discrete discounting. Readers who are not familiar with this should consult the note in Appendix A at this point.*

(a) Retirement

Consider first the case of retirement of an asset without replacement. Suppose a firm has a single asset which is not going to be replaced, e.g. because the firm is going out of business. The asset may not be worth retaining to the end of its physical life for a number of reasons: it may have been superseded by an asset whose operating costs are lower; it may be requiring increasing maintenance and repairs; or the quality of the work it performs may be declining. For any or all of these reasons the

---

*There is a considerable literature on optimal replacement policy. Readers are referred to the following principal sources for further information: [14], Chapter 2; [17], [16], Chapter 5; [18], [19] on replacement of deteriorating assets; [12] and [13] on the replacement of assets that fail. This section follows closely the analysis presented in the first three.

difference between the benefits and costs of holding and using it may fall to zero before the end of its physical life. Our problem is when to take it out of service, or in other words to determine the optimum length of service, which we will denote by N.

Suppose the asset has just been acquired at a cost of W. Its earnings, in the form of sales revenue less user cost* throughout the period from acquisition to retirement are represented by $Q(t)\mathrm{d}t$, where $Q(t) = R(t) - C(t)$, this function representing its earning rate over a very small interval of its life, t to $(t + \mathrm{d}t)$. The symbol t represents time *measured in terms of asset age*. $S(T)$ denotes the value of the asset at the time it is retired (salvage or resale value). Then the discounted earnings of the asset from acquisition to retirement, $B(T)$, writing δ for the continuous rate of interest, assumed constant over the period, is

$$B(T) = \int_0^T Q(t)\mathrm{e}^{-\delta t}\,\mathrm{d}t + S(T)\mathrm{e}^{-\delta T} - W \tag{1.1}$$

Maximizing $B(T)$ with respect to T, we have

$$\frac{\mathrm{d}B}{\mathrm{d}T} = \mathrm{e}^{-\delta T}[Q(T) - \delta S(T) + S'(T)] = 0 \tag{1.2}$$

and $\qquad \dfrac{\mathrm{d}^2 B}{\mathrm{d}T^2} < 0,$

where the prime denotes the derivative; or

$$R(T) = C(T) + \delta S(T) - S'(T). \tag{1.3}$$

In words, the optimum length of service, T, of the single asset is such that at the retirement date the expected earnings from its continued use, $R(T)$, equal the cost of operating it for another year, $[C(T)]$, plus the loss in salvage value as a result of retiring it at the end of $(T + 1)$ rather than T years $[S'(T) < 0]$, plus the interest on the proceeds of sale in year T. This condition is shown in Figure 12.3, where T_0 represents the retirement date and N the end of the physical life of the asset. If the salvage value approaches zero, the condition reduces to $R(\dot T) = C(T)$.

Retirement of course involves a change in capacity. Note that the original cost of the asset has no effect upon the decision. It should also be understood that the interest rate used in the discounting throughout this section is the continuous equivalent of the opportunity cost discount rate referred to in preceding sections, determined according to the circumstances there discussed. It should be recognized that in order to simplify the exposition we are making the strong (and unrealistic) assumption that the interest rate remains constant throughout the period of analysis.

---

* By the convenient term 'user cost' we shall mean the variable costs associated with the asset, viz. the costs of running and maintaining it in reasonable working order; it does *not* include interest and depreciation.

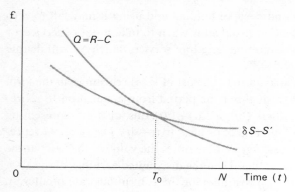

Figure 12.3

(b) Replacement of deteriorating assets

We now go on to the case where an asset is retired and replaced. This may or may not involve an increase in capacity, as we shall see. In practice there are a number of situations falling between this case and the last. 'Replacement and repair,' as Smith points out,* 'are simply two alternative ways of maintaining the "productive presence" of capital goods.' It is very difficult to draw the line between major repairs and renewals (i.e. partial replacement). In addition to maintenance expenditures many assets are kept in service beyond their original physical life by partial replacements. This introduces an additional variable into the problem, viz. the length of service of the partial replacement, as well as the retirement period for the existing asset.†

In the case outlined in section 2(a) (pure retirement) the firm's planning horizon was assumed to be conterminous with a single retirement/replacement period. As soon as we relax this assumption we have to allow for serial dependence. That is, the optimal length of service of the existing asset cannot be determined independently of the optimal life of each of a series of replacements:‡

> the economic life of the present equipment cannot be determined independently of the operating performance and economic life . . . of the equipment that will replace it. If the firm's planning horizon extends beyond the life of a single replacement, then [the economic life of the existing equipment] cannot be evaluated independently of the economic life of each [replacement] in the *chain* of future replacements . . . for as far into the future as the horizon extends.

An optimal replacement policy is then a policy that maximizes the discounted

*[17], p. 75.
†See [14] for elaboration.
‡[16], p. 136.

earnings or minimizes the discounted costs, as the case may be,* of an infinite chain of replacements of the asset in question.†

Formally, the problem involves solving a system of simultaneous equations extending to infinity. Fairly obviously some kind of convention is needed to bring this problem of a recurrent system stretching to infinity within computational bounds. The convention we shall use here as a convenient way of displaying the nature of the problem is that of the *infinitely constant chain,* i.e. we will assume that each successive replacement is identical to its predecessor. Later we will consider the limitations of this procedure and discuss another convention used by Terborgh.

The 'replacement decision', like the investment decision, consists of a set of decisions:

1. Whether or not to replace, in the course of which the optimal life of the replacement must be determined.
2. When to replace, which involves determining the economic life of the asset already in service.
3. Choosing from among all the replacement possibilities with optimal lives that one which maximizes discounted earnings (NPV) or minimizes discounted costs, as the case may be.
4. A problem arises over the case of 'replacement' which involves some element of expansion. Taking a purist view, replacement as such (i.e. pure replacement) is not an investment problem but a production problem: as Smith has pointed out, the choice is between replacement and repair (including partial renewal) of a given productive capacity. On this argument, only the incremental part of replacement involving expansion should be considered as an investment decision. If the decision is to replace immediately, and there are capital market imperfections or rationing present, whether the expansion of capacity should be authorized (and therefore whether the asset should be replaced) can only be determined after scanning the whole set of independent projects under consideration, over which NPV is to be maximized.‡ At the same time it must be remembered that replacement competes with net investment for available funds. Since in the situation just referred to all projects become interrelated, it is difficult to agree with Smith that a sharp dichotomy can be made between pure replacement and replacement involving expansion. Because of the interdependencies even pure replacement needs to be included in the investment decision.

Furthermore, we shall consider two separate cases, which explains the ambivalence over criteria in 3.: replacement involving some element of expansion, and

* The distinction is explained below.
† This was first shown by Preinreich in 1940, see [15].
‡ See [17], p. 73.

341

pure replacement which does not involve any change in capacity. The objective of maximizing discounted earnings applies to the former, and minimizing discounted costs to the latter.

(i) *Replacement involving expansion*
In practice like is seldom replaced with like; the 'replacement' often has greater capacity than the asset in service, though as Smith has pointed out, on a literal reading replacement should not affect the output dimension.

Compared with pure retirement, we now have to consider an infinite chain of replacements. We will assume that this chain is constant, in the sense that assets are identically replaced (each replacement renders the same service though not necessarily the same return). It follows that the replacement interval, L, will be constant. It will also be assumed that replacement costs and trade-in values are constant, even allowing for the moment that technical progress* as well as deterioration is occurring.

If the 'replacement' involves some expansion we must take earnings into account as well as costs. We will assume that the objective is to maximize the discounted net earnings of the entire chain. Using the same symbols as before, but with W and S now standing for cost of replacement and trade-in value, respectively, the discounted earnings of one replacement cycle will be

$$B(L) = \int_0^L Q(t)e^{-\delta t}\,dt + S(L)e^{-\delta L} - W;\tag{2.1}$$

and since under the constant infinite chain assumption each replacement cycle is identical, the total discounted earnings of the chain starting from any retirement-replacement point $T_1, T_2, \ldots$ will be a constant sum, which we will denote by B. That is,

$$B = B(L) + e^{-\delta L}B\tag{2.2}$$

$$= \frac{1}{1-e^{-\delta L}}\left[\int_0^L Q(t)e^{-\delta t}\,dt + S(L)e^{-\delta L} - W\right]\tag{2.3}$$

The optimal period of replacement, L, is then given by:

$$\frac{dB}{dL} = Q(L) - \delta S(L) + S'(L) - \delta B = 0.\tag{2.4}$$

---

*This will be qualified shortly when we examine the constant chain assumption.

Assuming the trade-in value approaches zero,

$$\delta B = Q(L) \tag{2.5}$$

or

$$Q(L) = \frac{\displaystyle\int_0^L Q(t)e^{-\delta t}\,dt - W}{\displaystyle\int_0^L e^{-\delta t}\,dt} \tag{2.6}$$

The meaning of the last two equations is as follows. Equation (2.5) says that the optimal length of service of replacements will be such that at the end of this period (L years) the interest on the total discounted value of the entire replacement chain will equal the present contribution (sales revenue less variable costs) of the asset in service. Equation (2.6) says that the present contribution of the existing asset will then equal the weighted average discounted profits* earned by this asset over the optimal replacement period, using the discounting factors as weights.

Reverting to the assumption of a constant chain, when technical progress is present it is not true to say that $L_1 = L_2 = \ldots = L$; i.e. replacement policy will strictly not be periodic. (The constant chain assumption implies that technical progress has reached its limit.) In other words, replacement does not regenerate the system if the cost structure of the replacement is not the same as that of the asset it replaces. However, the assumption of equally-spaced replacements is likely to be approximately true if the rate of technical progress is gradual and not too great, and the discount rate is high (the latter will have a strong damping effect on assets of medium or long lives). The convention will yield less accurate results if technical progress proceeds in bursts and is at a high rate, and if the discount rate is low.†

The *time to replace* is determined by a slight modification of the section 2(a) analysis. With retirement-replacement we assume that the infinite chain of replacements starts at time T when the old asset is retired. Expression (1.1) then becomes

$$B(T) = \int_0^T Q(t)e^{-\delta t}\,dt + e^{-\delta T}[S(T) + B] - W \tag{2.7}$$

and corresponding to (1.2) we have

$$\frac{dB}{dT} = Q(T) - \delta[S(T) + B] + S'(T) = 0 \tag{2.8}$$

Figure 12.4 compares this situation with that shown in Figure 12.3 for pure retirement:

---

* Net operating revenues less cost of the asset.
† See [16], p. 141.

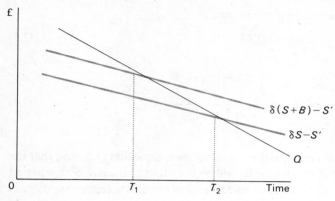

Figure 12.4

It will be understood that if the existing asset has been in service for some time, the usual situation, T is not likely to be equal to L, the constant replacement interval. Introducing the components of $Q(T)$, we have

$$R(T) = C(T) + \delta[S(T) + B] - S'(T); \qquad (2.9)$$

i.e. the date for retirement-replacement is when the revenue from operating the existing asset equals the sum of *four* cost elements. Three of these have already been referred to in the pure retirement case, viz. the decline in trade-in value if the asset is operated for a further year $[S'(T)]$, the cost of operation of the asset $[C(T)]$, and a year's interest on the trade-in value which would be foregone by retiring the asset a year later $[\delta S(T)]$.

The new element is δB, and it is important to understand how this arises. If the retirement-replacement date were postponed from T to $(T+1)$ this would affect the entire chain of future replacements. Each replacement would then benefit by a year's technical progress, reflected in improved performance and lower operating costs. The interest on the discounted value of this series of cost reductions for the entire chain represents a benefit from postponing replacement, or a cost if it is not postponed. We therefore add to the three earlier elements the opportunity cost of replacing at times T_0, T_1, . . . rather than T_{0+1}, T_{1+1}, . . ., and so on indefinitely.

In practical terms the meaning of the last paragraph is that a firm would test at the end of each year to see whether it should replace at that point. If immediate replacement is not indicated it would repeat the process in a year's time. The implication is that a necessary condition for replacement at times T_0, T_1, . . . to be optimal is that it is not less advantageous, in terms of discounted profits or costs, than replacement at times T_{0+1}, T_{1+1}, . . . The optimality of this 'next-year test' is dependent upon our (rather unrealistic) assumption of constant replacement costs, W. If the time structure of W is nonconstant, one-year testing may not prove to be optimal; it may, in fact, indicate earlier replacement than is optimal.

344

(ii) *Pure replacement*

If 'replacement' is literal, i.e. maintaining a given service potential, the problem can be formulated as one of minimizing a discounted cost stream. In the absence of technical progress the cost of replacements, salvage value and user cost will exhibit a constant pattern over the horizon. Preinreich [15] showed that in these circumstances, with an infinite horizon, the optimal policy will be periodic, i.e. the optimal economic life of each replacement will be the same $(L_1 = L_2 = \cdots = L)$. This period is determined by choosing from among all the possibilities (replace every year, two years, ...) that one for which discounted costs (user cost plus replacement cost) are a minimum.

Introducing technical progress has the effect discussed above. Under the constant chain assumption the analysis is the same as before, except that we can now omit $R(t)$ and minimize the sum of discounted costs, denoted by $E(t)$, where

$$E(t) = \Sigma\{R(t) - Q(t)\}.$$

The reader will see the formal resemblance as we proceed.

We begin with the expression corresponding to (2.2):

$$E = E(L) + e^{-\delta L}E \tag{2.10}$$

where E is the total discounted cost of the chain starting from any replacement date, i.e.

$$E = \frac{1}{1 - e^{-\delta L}}\left[\int_0^L C(t)e^{-\delta t}\,dt - S(L)e^{-\delta L} + W\right] \tag{2.11}$$

$$\frac{dE}{dL} = C(L) + \delta S(L) - S'(L) - \delta E = 0.$$

If we assume as before that $S \to 0$, the condition corresponding to (2.5) is:

$$\delta E = C(L) \tag{2.12}$$

or

$$C(L) = \frac{\displaystyle\int_0^L C(t)e^{-\delta t}\,dt + W}{\displaystyle\int_0^L e^{-\delta t}\,dt} \tag{2.13*}$$

To determine the time to retire-replace when the replacement chain starts at T we have, corresponding to $Q(T) = \delta B$ in (2.8):

$$\delta E = C(T), \tag{2.14}$$

---

*In more sophisticated models (e.g. [17]), $C(L)$ might more realistically be written $C(u,kL,t)$, where u is the rate of utilization of the asset, kL is time measured in terms of the number of replacements in a continuous chain ($k = 0, 1, \ldots$), and t is the age of the asset. This introduces obsolescence into the analysis explicitly *via* the term kL.

while a similar substitution of $C(T)$ for $C(L)$ in (2.13) gives the necessary condition for determining replacement time as being when the variable costs of the existing asset reach the average discounted variable operating plus replacement costs of the chain of replacements.

One point to be noted from this analysis is that the total variable operating costs of the existing asset and its potential replacement are not relevant, only the difference. The operating cost disadvantage of the asset already in service (called its 'inferiority gradient') is illustrated in Figure 12.5:

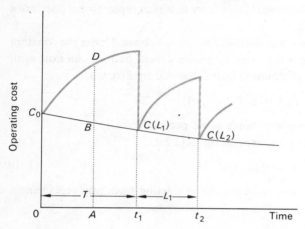

Figure 12.5

The saw-toothed curve describes the cost function $C(t)$, beginning from the acquisition of the existing asset (initial operating cost, C_0). The dashed line $C_0 C(L_1) \ldots$ shows the decreasing cost of the best available asset over time under the influence of technical progress. The distance AB represents the variable operating cost that would have been incurred if the best available asset had been used. This cost is determined by the rate of technical progress, and is independent of the replacement policy followed. BD represents the additional cost incurred because the asset in service is less efficient than the best new model available. This is the 'inferiority gradient' of the asset in use. The discounted value of the BD's over the entire chain will depend on the particular replacement policy adopted.

Hence if the objective is to minimize the total discounted cost of the chain, of which $C(t)$ is one element, since AB is independent of the policy adopted so will the discounted value of the sum of the AB's over the chain. Assuming the trade-in value is zero, this is equivalent to minimizing the discounted sum of the BD's ('inferiority gradients') and W's (replacement costs).

Readers are cautioned to remember the various simplifying assumptions that have been introduced in the above analysis, viz. the *constant* chain assumption and all that it entails (in particular that technical progress results in a slow, steady improvement in the operating characteristics of assets, not in sudden, major improvements), the assumption of a constant interest rate, and the implicit assumption that the entire future is known with certainty.

(iii) *An approximative decision rule*

Despite its simplifying assumptions and conventions, the preceding analysis is complicated, and would be difficult to apply. Terborgh, by making certain further assumptions, developed an approximative decision rule which has the advantage of simplicity.* Given these further assumptions, it has been shown by Massé and others to be essentially equivalent to the discounting analysis presented above if the operating cost function is linear and trade-in value is constant.

Terborgh's principal assumptions are that operating costs, $C(t)$, increase linearly with age of the machine,† replacement cost is constant, salvage value is zero, and that technical progress does not alter the shape of the operating cost function, only causes it to move downward over time at a constant average rate. Since technical progress is, by its very nature, very difficult to predict, little advantage is to be gained in estimating more than a simple average reduction in operating costs. Terborgh also ignores discounting.‡

If the average annual rate of obsolescence just referred to is denoted by a parameter α, measured in terms of the annual fall in acquisition cost of the asset ($\{C(L_1) - C(L_2)\}/L_1$, etc., in Figure 12.5), and the annual deterioration rate, measured by the increase in operating cost with age of the asset, is denoted by the parameter β, Terborgh's formula, which is stated in terms of costs as in our pure replacement case, is:

$$\bar{C}(L) = C_0 + \left(\frac{\alpha + \beta}{2}\right)L + \frac{W}{L} + iW, \tag{2.15}$$

where i is the annual interest rate corresponding to the continuous rate δ, i.e. iW is one year's *simple* interest§ on the cost of the asset. Instead of $C(t)e^{-\delta t}$ we are now

---

* For discussion of its limitations, see [14], pp. 72–74 and [16], pp. 142–52.

† Using Smith's more precise function $C(u,kL,t)$ referred to earlier, operating costs are assumed to be linear in kL and t, and the degree of utilization, u, is assumed constant over the life of the asset. Terborgh found this assumption to be a good approximation to the behaviour, as a function of age, of repair costs – one element in variable operating costs. Some critics of Terborgh's linearity assumption maintain that the rate of increase of operating costs is likely to decline after the 'breaking in' period, and that as a result the Terborgh formula will often recommend premature replacement. A counter-argument would be that as the cost estimates refer to machines yet to be produced (W is the constant replacement cost, assumed to be independent of the age of the traded-in asset), it is doubtful whether a great improvement in accuracy would be yielded by more sophisticated predictions – see [13].

‡ Referring back to beginning of section 2(b), an indefinitely constant chain is replaced in Terborgh's analysis by the assumption that all replacements have a constant 'adverse minimum'. (This is a less restrictive assumption, since it allows explicitly for technical progress.) The 'adverse minimum' is the sum of annual replacement cost and total operating cost inferiority ('inferiority gradient'), averaged over one replacement cycle, when an optimal replacement policy is followed.

§ See Appendix A for the relation between simple and compound interest.

in effect writing $C_0 - \alpha T + \beta t$ and working in *average costs* [$\overline{C}(L)$ is the *annual* cost averaged over one replacement cycle], where T as before is the time when the existing asset is retired.

$$\left(\frac{\alpha + \beta}{2}\right) L$$

is the average annual cost of obsolescence and deterioration over the optimal replacement period, L years,* and W/L the average annual cost of replacement. $(\alpha + \beta)$ is what Terborgh called the 'inferiority gradient' (*BD* in Figure 12.5). This reaches a maximum of $(\alpha + \beta)L$ immediately before the asset is replaced and then instantaneously drops to zero: .

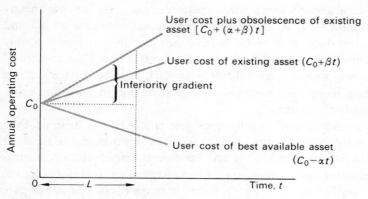

Figure 12.6

Minimizing $C(L)$ with respect to L in (2.15) leads to Terborgh's square root decision rule:

$$\frac{dC(L)}{dL} = 0 = \frac{\alpha + \beta}{2} - \frac{W}{L^2};$$

$$L^* = \sqrt{\left(\frac{2W}{\alpha + \beta}\right)}.$$

(c) Replacement of assets that fail

Space does not permit a satisfactory treatment of this case to be given. An excellent review will, however, be found in Holmes [13].† Instead of taking the form of an increase in costs of upkeep (operating, maintenance and repair costs) compared with new equipment, as in the case discussed in section 2(b), deterioration here

---

* As Smith has pointed out [16, p. 151], the dimensions of α and β are rates of change of rates of change, i.e. deceleration and acceleration, respectively.

† See also B. V. Dean [12]; Baumol [1], 2nd edn., pp. 472–74 and [20], pp. 340–46.

manifests itself as an increasing probability of failure with cumulative usage or age. Whereas the section 2(b) case usually applies to large items of capital goods, this case is more characteristic of small machines and equipment. The reader should note the distinction between the two cases, and that the methods of analysis used to deal with assets subject to deterioration will generally not be very satisfactory for dealing with assets subject to failure, and vice versa.

A brief classification of the problems that arise with replacement of items that fail is appended.

(i)

'Fail' may mean complete failure, in which case the first decision is whether or not to replace (this is characteristic of items of short life expectancy such as light bulbs); or it may be possible to repair the item, in which case the first decision to be taken is whether to repair or replace.

(ii)

In the latter case an optimal preventive maintenance schedule can be drawn up, indicating the optimal amount and frequency of repairs to each item, determined so as to minimize the expected cost of maintaining the item in operation.

(iii)

Where failure is complete the questions that arise are:

1. Should items be replaced as they fail, either as a deliberate strategy or on an unplanned basis? Or
2. Should replacement be made prior to failure, i.e. is it profitable to trade-off some remaining useful life in order to avoid the interruptions to the flow of production which failure replacement would bring? (the items can be replaced when the machine or factory is idle).* This strategy would involve replacing any item that has 'survived' for L periods.
3. A further question is whether to replace items (prior to failure) individually or in groups. Under the latter strategy all items would be simultaneously replaced at regular intervals $L, 2L, \ldots$, irrespective of their age. The justification for this kind of policy is that individual replacement may be inappropriate where a number of items of the same kind have to be kept and where there are significant interdependencies between items. The latter may take two forms [13]:

   (a) Economic interdependencies arising, for example, as a result of economies of mass replacement (if production must be shut down to replace a single item the cost of replacing other items at the same time will be less), or

---

*Failure may also diminish the efficiency of other equipment and make replacement more difficult.

349

because the act of replacement involves the use of special facilities (e.g. replacing street lights).

(b) Statistical interdependence, e.g. the failure of one item may increase the probability of failure of another item.

For this policy to be worthwhile the cost of replacing all items together must be less than the cost of replacing them all individually on failure. That is, there must be a profitable trade-off between, on the one hand, the costs avoided by group replacing before failure occurs (lost production time, costs resulting directly from failure, higher set-up costs in replacing) and higher operating costs on the other (because a smaller proportion of the item's life will be utilized, on the average, under a group policy). In addition to deciding whether or not to group replace, the other question is what is the optimal group replacement interval?*

12.3 Allowing for uncertainty in investment decision-making

(a) Introduction

Thus far we have proceeded by implicitly assuming that all the data needed to formulate the investment decision problem, and hence the decision outcomes, were known with certainty. This was a necessary expository device in order to shear away all detail other than that which was essential to convey the basic structure of the problem. We must now make good this important omission. While uncertainty will be discussed here in the context of investment decisions, the same techniques are for the most part applicable to other types of decisions. Readers should note well that uncertainty is an important dimension of all business decisions, and make the extension of the type of analysis that follows to the various decision areas discussed earlier in the book.

The reason for making investment decisions the vehicle for this discussion is that they are long-run decisions, and the influence of uncertainty usually increases the longer the decision horizon. In contrast to the fairly sophisticated techniques for dealing with uncertainty discussed in the later parts of this section, it should be said at the outset that in practice the existence of uncertainty is more likely to make the firm do two things: seek ways of avoiding uncertainty (e.g. by substituting short-run feedback data for expectational data to trigger action, and by using standardized decision rules);† and secondly, shorten the horizon over which it

---

*There are three basic types of failure: initial failures, due to defects in the quality or design of the item; wear-out failures; and random failures, due to chance. Often the initial failure rate is higher than the wear-out failure rate, making it necessary to adopt separate group replacement policies for these classes (periods).

† [23], pp. 98 and 102.

plans and thus minimize the need for predicting uncertain future events.* Though uncertainty is a fact of life in business, the firm need not be powerless in the face of it; there are ways of reducing uncertainty. One is to seek more information about the future by such activities as general economic forecasting, market research, and research and development. The firm can also allow for uncertainty by building flexibility into its production arrangements, diversifying its production, and spreading its sales over different markets and sales areas. Other devices are insurance and 'hedging'.

In Chapter 6 we drew a distinction between risk and uncertainty, which rested on whether the probabilities of decision outcomes were known or not, respectively. This distinction is followed, although not universally, in the literature of various disciplines on decision-making under risk or uncertainty. That is, if we can attach a number between 0 and 1, objectively or subjectively, to the probability of the outcome we are strictly talking about decision-making under risk, and if we cannot do so we are discussing decision-making under uncertainty. This section ought therefore more properly to be headed 'allowing for risk'. The reason we have persisted in using the term 'uncertainty' is that 'risk' has a number of different connotations, and we shall by avoiding it make clear that we are not here concerned with 'financial risk' but with the likelihood of estimated decision outcomes proving to be correct.

It is convenient at this stage to dispose of a point which will enter the discussion later. What was referred to as risk above, viz. the numerical probability which can be attached to a future event, is sometimes called first-order risk, represented by a simple probability. Second- and higher-order risks are also possible, functions of two or more probability distributions. Later we will have occasion to introduce two second-order risks, represented by joint and conditional probabilities.†

In Chapter 6 we also drew a distinction between *risk estimation* and *risk preference*. The latter, it will be remembered, is concerned with the decision-maker's attitude towards risk. Decision-makers may react to risk in various ways: some are risk-averse, some are risk seekers, and some risk ignorers, and they may change from one category to another according to the type of decision being taken and even for the same type of decision over time. Our approach to uncertainty should incorporate both risk estimation and risk preference. In what follows we distinguish between methods which do and do not allow for the latter. It is generally assumed that there are more risk-averters than risk-seekers, and a number of techniques for dealing with uncertainty are founded on the assumption that the decision-maker is risk-averse.

---

* [22], p. 312.
† These terms are explained in point (b) of the appendix to this chapter for those readers who may not be familiar with them.

(b) Deterministic methods not incorporating risk preference

(i) *Naïve or crude methods*

We may begin by briefly referring to various crude methods of dealing with uncertainty. The payback period method, which we saw involved the application of 'break-even' analysis to investment without time-discounting, is widely used by the business man as a preliminary screening device, if not as the primary method of project evaluation, and can be rationalized as a very crude way of limiting uncertainty by a risk-averter. This kind of approach may be moved back to the estimating stage, where it would take the form of lowering expected cash inflows, raising expected cash outflows, shortening the expected life of the project, or some combination of these. Some firms merely add x per cent to the cash outflows for 'contingencies'.

Another method is to use a risk-adjusted discount rate, i.e. to discount simultaneously for time and risk. Using the NPV criterion for illustration, in the formula

$$V_0 = \sum_t \beta_t x_t$$

given in Chapter 11, this would mean putting

$$\beta_t = \frac{1}{(1+i+j)^t},$$

where i is the opportunity cost discount rate and j a risk premium, i.e. i is a 'risk-free' rate. If risk is allowed for in the discount rate in this way we are assuming that it increases at a constant rate as a function of time. That is, uncertainty is being compounded in the later years of the project's life. Now it is quite likely that uncertainty will increase the longer the project extends, but it is by no means certain that it will increase exponentially, as assumed by this method. Depending on the circumstances, serious errors may result from the use of a risk-adjusted discount rate. The discount rate should not be asked to do double duty in this way.

(ii) *Sensitivity analysis on a deterministic model*

Alternatively, we could solve investment decision problems without incorporating uncertainty in the decision data, and then see how sensitive the solution was to changes in the values of one or more of the variables. That is, we could regard the variables (and constants) in the decision model as parameters. When this sensitivity testing is applied to a mathematical programming model it is known as parametric programming. In terms of our discussion in Chapter 6, the method involved is not an algorithm in that it does not provide a unique answer. What it does is to show the implications of changing the values of various parameters of the problem, by noting their effect on the objective function. In this way it can be seen how critical the values of certain parameters are, and the range of validity of the optimal solution obtained by disregarding uncertainty. Parametric programming can be carried out on the objective function itself (the undiscounted cash flows and the discount rate) or on the constraints (RHS or LHS); or a new variable or constant may be introduced into the problem. Parameters can be varied one at a time or a vector at a time. That is, taking a linear programming model for purposes of illustration, given the numerical information contained in the final simplex iteration, various post-optimality questions can be answered by formulating a series of related problems, without solving the revised model from scratch in each case. The solution of this set of problems provides a mapping of the behaviour of the optimal solution as certain parameters are varied through a range of values. Standard packages are available on many computer systems which include an extensive set of post-optimality procedures.

In conditions of uncertainty, the optimal solution to an LP investment decision model is seldom very meaningful by itself. The various probability judgements embedded in the model's assumptions and numerical coefficients are subject to error. Sensitivity analysis is useful in establishing the range of validity of the computed optimal solution. As Weingartner has argued :*

> It is by no means obvious that the use of sensitivity analysis and generalised parametric methods (which permit use of nonlinear functions and also apply to modifications of interior coefficients) is more limited than the assumption of known probability distributions.

Its limitations are that it does not allow for risk preference explicitly, and does not yield 'precise conclusions about the possible effects of combinations of errors in the estimates, even though this is the typical situation of concern'.†

(c) Stochastic methods not incorporating risk preference

The remaining methods to be discussed will involve probability analysis. The probabilities may be of two kinds. Objective probabilities are based on past data, which are regarded as a sample from an underlying process. Essentially, probability is based on relative frequency of occurrence of the event over a large number of trials in this classical view, and no meaning attaches to the probability of a single, non-repeated event. This concept of probability is accordingly not very useful when we are considering business decisions, many of which are unique. A more recent view of probability, however, claims that it is possible to assign probabilities to single events. The probabilities assigned are *subjective or personal probabilities*.‡ The decision-maker can be asked to quantify his feelings about the possible outcomes of

---

* [8], pp. 160.
† [27]. A more advanced treatment will be found in [28].
‡ See [35].

a decision on a scale from 0 to 1, by assigning numbers to the most optimistic, most pessimistic, and most likely outcomes, or by estimating the whole probability distribution of outcomes. If he should have difficulty in doing so, he can be confronted with a choice between a bet on the actual decision and a bet on a hypothetical event with known probabilities. After choosing between them, the probabilities attached to the hypothetical event are changed each time until the individual becomes indifferent as between the two gambles. By repeating this process the whole probability distribution of outcomes of the actual decision may be generated.

(i) *Certainty equivalents*

This approach bears some similarity to the risk-adjusted discount rate method, except that the adjustment is made to the numerator rather than to the denominator. Corresponding to the NPV formula given in Chapter 11,

$$\text{Net present certainty-equivalent value} = \sum_{t=0}^{h} \beta_t(\alpha_t x_t), \quad 0 \le \alpha_t \le 1,$$

where
$$\beta_t = (1+i)^{-t}$$

$$i = \text{the 'riskless' rate of interest, and}$$

$$\alpha_t = \frac{\text{certain cash flow}}{\text{uncertain cash flow}}.$$

α_t varies inversely with the uncertainty felt by the decision-maker. He would be indifferent as between a certain cash flow of $\Sigma\alpha_t x_t$ and the uncertain cash flow from the project, Σx_t. For example, if a certain project offers to yield a net cash flow of £1m. with probability 0·6 and £1·5m. with probability 0·4, and the firm would be willing to trade the project for a certain cash flow of £1·1m., $\alpha = 0·91\dot{6}$.

This method is slightly superior conceptually to the risk-adjusted discount rate method, in that it allows risk to vary from period to period. There are, however, problems of implementation. In practice α_t would probably have to be determined from the capital market, by observing how the market discounts the expected returns of companies whose activities are subject to a similar degree of business risk to the project concerned.*

Whichever way the reduction to certainty equivalents is done, there is a considerable information problem, and like the risk-adjusted discount rate method, this approach suffers from not considering explicitly the whole range of possible outcomes.

(ii) *Expected monetary value (EMV)*

Certainty equivalents and EMV are very similar in that both reduce the whole

---

* Expected returns would have to be determined from historical data.

probability distribution of outcomes to a single statistic; the difference lies only in how this is done. EMV is the mean of the distribution of monetary values of outcomes weighted by their probabilities, i.e. the weighted average return. It therefore assumes that it is possible to determine these probabilities, e.g. subjectively. This measure is open to two possible criticisms. First, while EMV is a valid measure in the great majority of cases – the decision-maker in general tends to prefer that outcome with the highest EMV – there are some important situations (e.g. gambling and insurance) which it does not explain. Secondly, the telescoping of the whole distribution of possible outcomes into a single statistic implies that the other characteristics of the distribution will not influence the decision-maker, and this is by no means always true (some of the later methods to be discussed make use of the second moment of the probability distribution, the variance (or standard deviation), to represent risk, but it may be that higher moments of the distribution, used in measuring skewness and kurtosis (peaked-ness), are also needed in order to describe it satisfactorily). We elaborate on this point in section d. Briefly, the first criticism is that EMV, like certainty equivalents, makes the strong assumption that the decision-maker is 'risk-neutral', i.e. his utility function is linear in money. Schlaifer* explains the point this way:

> Business men tend to treat acts which must have one or the other of just two possible consequences as being 'really worth' their EMV as long as the worst of the two consequences is not too bad and the best of the consequences is not too good. This immediately suggests that a business man [faced with] a great number of possible consequences can decide whether or not he should use EMV as the basis of his evaluation by looking only at the best and the worst of the consequences and asking himself whether he would act in accordance with EMV if these were the *only* possible consequences. More specifically, . . . EMV [is a valid criterion] if the [decision-maker] would use it as his criterion in choosing between (1) an act which is certain to result in receipt or payment of a definite amount of cash and (2) an act which will result in either the *best* or the *worst* of all possible consequences of the real decision problem.

Example

In the following example the firm's criterion is taken to be maximization of expected NPV, which we will denote by $E(V_0)$. Suppose a firm is considering investing in plant to produce a new product which, once produced, may be marketed nationally or regionally. The example is concerned with the probabilities of outcomes if one of these alternative marketing schemes is followed, and with how this will affect the $E(V_0)$ of the project. We assume that the probability distribution of all possible outcomes may be approximated by considering a small number of alternatives. The subjective probabilities assigned to these are as follows:

* [36], pp. 28–29.

National demand	Regional demand	(Joint) probability
large (N)	large (R)	0·5 [P(N, R)]
small (n)	large	0·2 [P(n, R)]
small	small (r)	0·3 [P(n, r)]
		1·0

The possibilities open to the firm are:

  (i) to launch the product on the national market at the outset, or

  (ii) to enter the regional market in the first instance, and extend to the national market if regional success is apparent.

The NPV's of all alternatives have been calculated and are shown in Figure 12.7:

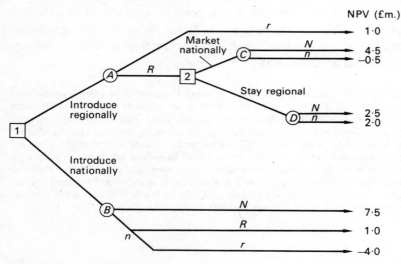

Figure 12.7

The above diagram is known as a *tree diagram or decision tree.* A tree diagram is a connected graph with no closed loops. The graph below (Figure 12.8) is *not* a tree

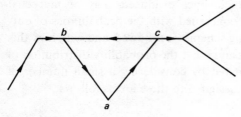

Figure 12.8

356

diagram, because it contains a closed loop *bacb*. Decision trees show the various paths the decision-maker may take, and are a handy way of representing a decision problem, especially if the number of alternatives is large and some are inter-dependent. The squares on the diagram indicate points at which a decision must be made by the firm; circles represent chance events, in this case decisions made by the market.

Take the top fork, leading to *A*. At *A* the firm has experience of the regional market only; it knows nothing about the national market. The probability of a large regional demand alone, when nothing is known about national demand, is (from the last column of the table)

$$P(N,R) + P(n,R) = 0.5 + 0.2 = 0.7.$$

So the probability of a small regional demand, when nothing is known about national demand, is $1 - 0.7 = 0.3$.

Now move to square 2. Here the firm must decide, having entered the regional market, whether to stay regional or extend to the national market. If it decides to try the national market (point *C*) the probability of a large national demand, given that there is a large regional demand, is the *conditional* probability $P(N|R)$ – see the appendix to this chapter. In this case entering the regional and the national markets are independent events, and so

$$P(N|R) = \frac{P(N,R)}{P(N)} = \frac{0.5}{0.7} = 0.71$$

It follows that the probability of a small national demand, given a large regional demand, is $1 - P(N|R)$, or 0.29 (alternatively, it is $P(n,R)$ from line 2 of the table, divided by $P(R) = 0.2/0.7$).

Taking the other fork at square 2 and moving to *D*, the probability of a large national demand subsequently developing is exactly the same situation as shown in the top branch from *C*, i.e. the probability is $0.5/0.7$, or 0.71. (Point *D* should be visualized as being reached later than point *C*.) Similarly the probability of a small national demand, given a large regional demand, is again 0.29.

Looking at the bottom fork from square 1, at *B* the firm is in the reverse situation to that at point *A*: it is entering the national market, but has no information about the regional market. (Reverting to the table of joint probabilities, it will be noted that $P(N,r)$ is not shown: the full possibilities are (N,R), (n,R), (N,r) and (n,r). Since the sum of the joint probabilities must be 1, we deduce that $P(N,r) = 0$. If the national market is entered and is large, the regional market cannot be small. This explains why there are only three branches from *B*. At the same time the size of the regional market is *not* conditional upon the size of the national market; the two are discovered simultaneously. In the bottom fork of the diagram we will therefore be

357

concerned with the joint probabilities of independent events.* These are given in the table.)

$$P(R,N) = 0.5$$

$$P(R,n) = 0.2$$

$$P(r,n) = 0.3.$$

In the tree diagram another column may now be inserted at the right showing the probabilities associated with each of the NPV's. The results so far are shown in Figure 12.9.

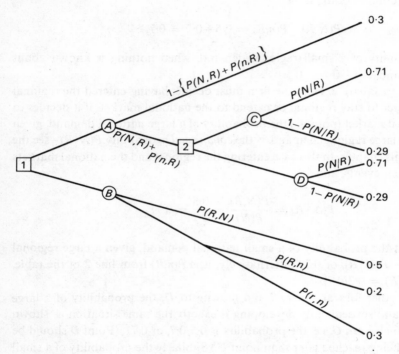

Figure 12.9

We can now calculate $E(V_0)$. Looking at the top fork (A) first, and considering the outcomes after decision 2:

	$E(V_0)$, £m.
(i) Market nationally	
$(0.71 \times 4.5) + (0.29 \times -0.5)$	3.050

---

* Readers may verify that the events are independent by showing that $P(R|N) = P(R) = 0.7$. In the course of doing so $P(N)$ will be found to be 0.71.

(ii) Stay regional

$$(0.71 \times 2.5) + (0.29 \times 2.0) \qquad\qquad 2.355$$

Therefore since $E(V_0)$ is the firm's criterion it should go to C from 2. At point 1 we have:

(iii) Introduce regionally (fork A)

$$(0.3 \times 1.0) + (0.7 \times 3.05) \qquad\qquad 2.435$$

(assuming the optimal decision is taken later, at C, as shown above)

(iv) Introduce nationally (fork B)

$$(0.5 \times 7.5) + (0.2 \times 1.0) + (0.3 \times -4.0) \qquad\qquad 2.750$$

We therefore conclude that the product should be introduced nationally from the beginning. Note that, after calculating $E(V_0)$ for each of the paths, we worked from right to left across the diagram in order to select the path with the highest expected value.

(iii) *Probability distribution of NPV*

In the normal calculation of NPV the cash flows, x_t, are represented by a single estimate which usually corresponds approximately to the mean or the mode of the whole distribution of cash flows in period t. What we have been regarding as constants are actually random variables. It follows that V_0 must also be a random variable. By the Central Limit Theorem the distribution of x_t's may not be nearly normal and yet the distribution of Σx_t will be approximately normal if the number of projects over which x_t is summed is large (say greater than 50). If this is the case the distribution of V_0 will be approximately normal. If we were able to estimate one further statistic of the distribution in addition to its mean, viz. its standard deviation, we would to all intents and purposes have generated the entire distribution. We would then have:

$$\mu_{V_0} = \sum_{t=0}^{h} [\mu_t \beta_t] \qquad \text{and}$$

$$\sigma_{V_0}^2 = \sum_{t=0}^{h} [\sigma_t^2 \beta_{2t}]$$

where μ and σ^2 denote expected value and variance, respectively, and $\beta_t = (1+i)^{-t}$ as in the previous chapter.

These expressions assume that the x_t's for different periods are independent. If they are completely interdependent, due for example to some circumstance causing the cash flows in each period to vary from their expected value in precisely the same way,*

$$\sigma_{V_0} = \sum_t (\sigma_t \beta_t).$$

Hillier formulates the case where the net cash flow of a project in any period can be split into an independent flow and a flow which is perfectly correlated over some or all periods. Suppose the life of the project is h periods as before, the independent stream is y_t, and that another stream, $z_t^{(k)}$ is perfectly correlated in periods $k = 1$, $\ldots, j, j \le h$. Hillier gives as a possible example investments in facilities to produce a new product, where the cash flows associated with production costs and investment outlays (y_t) are completely independent over time, and those associated with marketing the product, z_t, representing sales revenue less selling costs, are perfectly correlated in j of the periods. In practice, of course, something between the two extremes of complete independence and no independence would be likely. But for the case described the expected value and variance of the distribution are:

$$\mu_{V_0} = \sum_{t=0}^{h} (\mu_t \beta_t) = \sum_t \beta_t \left[E(y_t) + \sum_{k=1}^{j} E(z_t^{(k)}) \right]$$

$$\sigma_{V_0}^2 = \sum_t \left[\mathrm{var}\,(y_t)\beta_{2t} \right] + \sum_k \left[\sum_t (\beta_t \sqrt{\mathrm{var}\,z_t^{(k)}})^2 \right]$$

For a given value of σ_t, σ_{V_0} will be smallest when the cash flows are completely independent over time and largest when they are perfectly correlated. The analysis in section 3(d)(ii) (portfolio theory) introduces another kind of interdependence, between the expected values of different projects. For two projects A and B this is measured by the covariance of returns, σ_{AB}.

This method provides more information for evaluating risk and considering trade-offs between risk and the expected value of returns. It can be applied to criteria other than NPV. As remarked earlier, it assumes that risk can be identified with variance of expected return. In the possible trade-off between risk and expected

---

*On all of this see Hillier [27]. If $z = x + y$ is a normally distributed random variable, then in general

$$\sigma_z^2 = \sigma_x^2 + 2\rho_{xy}\sigma_x\sigma_y + \sigma_y^2,$$

where ρ is the coefficient of correlation. If $\rho_{xy} = 0$ (the first case above, where the project cash flows were independent over time)

$$\sigma_z^2 = \sigma_x^2 + \sigma_y^2 \quad \text{and} \quad \sigma_z = \sqrt{(\sigma_x^2 + \sigma_y^2)}.$$

If $\rho_{xy} = +1$ (corresponding to the second case, where there was a perfect direct correlation between cash flows over time),

$$\sigma_z^2 = \sigma_x^2 + 2\sigma_x\sigma_y + \sigma_y^2 = (\sigma_x + \sigma_y)^2$$

and

$$\sigma_z = \sigma_x + \sigma_y.$$

The above results may be extended to the case where $z = x_1 + x_2 + \ldots + x_n$. If readers should require further information they should consult [29] or a similar work.

return we see one method of allowing for risk preference. Presumably this would reflect the risk attitudes of *management*, shareholders being left to make their own adjustments through the market by rearranging their holdings.

(iv) *Stochastic and chance-constrained programming*

When the net cash flows for each project in each period are treated as random variables, the LP formulation of the problem corresponding to that described in the previous section is known as stochastic linear programming (see Appendix C). One particular type of stochastic linear programming is known as chance-constrained programming. This method of dealing with uncertainty is applicable when it is desirable, but not essential, that the constraints should hold. No method is yet available for solving the general chance-constrained LP problem. In the special case formulated below a solution is possible by assuming (1) all the a_{ij} are constants, (2) some or all of the c_j and b_i are random variables, (3) b_i has a known multivariate normal distribution, and (4) c_j is statistically independent of b_i.

The problem involves maximizing EMV subject to probabilistic constraints on maximum loss. Taking the general LP problem:

Maximize (1) $$z = \sum_{j=1}^{n} c_j x_j$$

subject to (2) $$\sum_{j=1}^{n} a_{ij} x_j \leq b_i, \quad i = 1, \ldots, s,$$

(2) would be replaced in chance-constrained programming by a constraint of the form:

(2′) $$P\left\{ \sum_{j=1}^{n} a_{ij} x_j \leq b_i \right\} \geq \alpha_i$$

where P denotes probability, $0 < \alpha_i < 1$, and c_j, a_{ij} and b_i are random variables. If any of the c_j are random variables z becomes a random variable. Since the maximization of a random variable is meaningless, z must be replaced by some deterministic function. The constraints must also be reinterpreted if any of the a_{ij} or b_i are random variables.

It is shown by Hillier and Lieberman [29] that the problem can be reduced to deterministic terms as follows:

Maximize $$E(z) = \sum_{j=1}^{n} E(c_j) x_j$$

subject to $$\sum_{j} a_{ij} x_j \leq E(b_i) + K_{\alpha_i} \sigma_{b_i}$$

$$x_j \geq 0,$$

361

where E denotes expected value and σ standard deviation. The relationship between the symbols constituting the RHS of the constraint should be evident from Figure 12.10, where the probability density function of b_i is exhibited :*

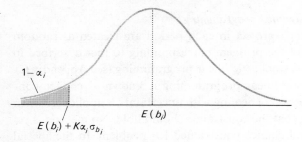

Figure 12.10

Two applications of this technique to capital budgeting under uncertainty will be found in [34] and [21]. The limitation of the chance-constrained programming approach is that, at the present time, a solution is obtainable only in special cases such as the one defined by the assumptions above. There are also some limitations inherent in this technique, a discussion of which however is beyond the scope of this book.

(v) *Simulation*

This method, which can be employed with any of the standard criteria, consists first of examining all the variables which influence the decision outcome and attaching subjective probabilities to them. (A method commonly employed in practice confines these to pessimistic, optimistic and most likely estimates of each of these factors.)† Alternatively, the simulation could start with the cash flows rather than with the factors which influence them. The next stage is to select a certain value of one of the variables from the distribution and, using chance devices such as the Monte Carlo technique, combine it with certain values of all the other variables, similarly chosen at random. By numerous repetitions of this procedure, recording the number of times outcomes of a given value occur, a frequency distribution of outcomes is generated which can be tabulated in the form of a probability distribution. The same procedure can, if desired, be followed for a number of different criteria.

Providing the subjective probabilities can be obtained, this is probably the most promising method of investigating the effects of uncertainty discussed so far. Hertz, in a simulation study [26], concludes that most business men will choose,

---

* [29], pp. 536–42. Stochastic linear programming is discussed on pp. 531–36.
† One of the standard distribution functions, e.g. a beta distribution, can then be fitted to these probability estimates. See [29], pp. 228–30 for a method of converting these estimates into estimates of expected value and variance.

not the alternative with the highest expected value, but the one which combines the lowest risk of total loss with at least as high a chance of substantial gain:

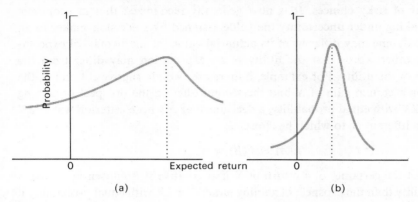

Figure 12.11

Because most business decision-makers are, he believes, risk-averters, they will pass over the alternative offering the highest expected return unless it also offers a smaller probability of losses; they would usually prefer the alternative shown in Figure 12.11(b) to that in Figure 12.11(a). Thus Hertz introduces a new factor into the analysis, albeit implicitly, viz. risk preference. As Hertz and others have stated, risk preference may be the single most important factor influencing the final decision. In the final section we discuss possible ways of incorporating risk preference into the analysis explicitly.

(d) Methods incorporating risk preference

It is well known that individuals differ in their attitudes towards risk-bearing. The same individual may also vary from one type of decision to another, and in relation to the same type of decision at different points in time (i.e. the same person, when confronted with an otherwise identical decision situation at different times, may choose quite differently). It becomes especially important to incorporate these risk attitudes into the analysis in the case of investment decisions, which often involve relatively large sums of money and have strategic effects on the whole business over an extended period.

Two principal methods have been developed for taking account of risk preferences: utility theory, and risk-return indifference curves. These will now be discussed.

(i) *Utility analysis of risk*

The idea of introducing a subjective concept, utility, into problems of choice under

363

uncertainty goes back to Daniel Bernoulli, an eighteenth century mathematician, who proposed the maximization of expected utility as the criterion to be followed in problems of risky choices. It is now generally recognized that in economic decision-making under uncertainty the value assigned by a decision-maker to an uncertain outcome may differ from its actuarial value (or mathematical expectation), or in other words that the utility of an expectation may differ from the expectation of the utility. For example, if there are two alternatives, A and B, the first offering a certain gain of X and the second offering the prospect of gaining either 0 or $2X$ with equal probability, a decision-maker whose criterion was EMV would be indifferent as to which he chose, since

$$E(A) = E(B) = X.$$

But in fact the certainty of a return of X if alternative A is chosen may have a different utility than the prospect of gaining either 0 or $2X$ with equal probability if alternative B is chosen, i.e. although $E(A) = E(B)$, it is not necessarily true that $U\{E(A)\} = U\{E(B)\}$, writing U for utility value. And in general

$$U\{E(\alpha)\} \neq E\{U(\alpha)\}.$$

Usually, though not always, an uncertain income will be valued at less than its expected value. Nor will a decision-maker necessarily be indifferent between two projects with the same EMV and the same dispersion of expected return. In practice the decision-maker may remain indifferent if the investments A and B are both small (i.e. fall within the 'normal' range of gains and losses, or the 'normal' risk pattern for the firm concerned). In this case maximization of EMV and of expected utility are likely to lead to the same decision.* If they are not small, he is likely to be influenced by his risk preferences.

An explanation for the statement above that the utility of an expectation may differ from expected utility is to assume that utility is a function of both expected monetary value and the variance of the distribution of monetary returns:

$$U = f(E,V).$$

As we shall see in section 3(d)(ii) below, the indifference curve approach is based upon such a utility function (i.e. a function of the first and second moments of the distribution of monetary returns), and assumes in particular that

$$\frac{\partial f}{\partial E} > 0 \quad \text{and} \quad \frac{\partial f}{\partial V} < 0,$$

i.e. that returns are desirable, and uncertainty (represented by the variance of returns) is undesirable.

---

*Suggestions have been made by Luce and Raiffa [30] and Schlaifer [36] as to how this 'normal' range might be determined.

The idea behind the first approach is that risk preferences* can be represented explicitly in the investment decision by means of a utility function, utility being measured in units (called 'utiles') on an arbitrary scale.† The modern version of utility which results in this cardinal measure is due to von Neumann and Morgenstern (1944) and is a complete reinterpretation of the meaning of 'utility'. The suggestion is that the decision-maker's utility function may be generated by asking him to choose between a certain sum of money and a gamble. The probabilities attached to the gamble are then changed until he becomes indifferent. In Figure 12.12 utility functions are plotted for a decision-maker who is risk-averse (a), risk-neutral (b) and risk-seeking (c):

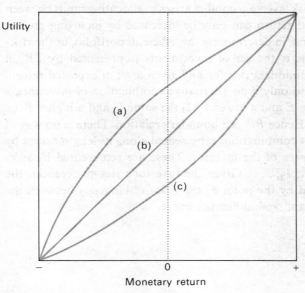

Figure 12.12

If the utility function can be thus generated, the expected utility of projects is obtained by multiplying utility value by probability of occurrence. The firm would then choose that set of projects which maximizes expected utility.

Despite the theoretical appeal of this method, there are substantial problems to be overcome before it can be put to practical use. These concern such things as whose utility should be represented, management's or shareholders', whether it is possible to specify a *group* utility function, and whether the utility of an actual productive investment project can in fact be measured by the utility of a hypothetical gamble, i.e. whether utility curves like those shown above represent the decision-maker's true risk preferences.

* Of management?
† It is not an absolute measure, but consists in putting numbers to rankings.

(ii) *Risk-return indifference curves and portfolio selection theory*

The economists Edgeworth (1881) and Pareto (1906) were the pioneers of the representation of utility by means of indifference curves (i.e. curves of constant utility). In this analysis risk preferences are reflected in the trade-offs a decision-maker would be willing to make between various levels of risk and return. This approach has been followed and developed in portfolio selection theory.* Only a very brief account of this can be given here.

As originally presented, this theory was designed to show how private investors could choose an 'efficient' portfolio of securities. Assuming that risk may be measured by the variance (or standard deviation) of expected monetary return and that investors are in general risk-averse, a conflict arises in allocating funds between investments because expected return can only be increased by incurring greater risk. The solution consists, first, in determining the 'efficient' portfolio, or the risk-return possibility curve. This is the set of investments (represented by BB' in Figure 12.13 below) which minimizes risk for any given level of expected return. The portfolio is efficient if and only if no alternative combination of investments exists with either (1) the same E and a lower V, (2) the same V and a higher E, or (3) a higher E and a lower V. Hence BB' is a boundary relation. There is no way of choosing between the efficient combinations represented along its length except by introducing the risk-preferences of the investor. These are represented by risk-return indifference curves (I_1, I_2, . . .). Given the investor's risk-preferences, the optimal trade-off is indicated by the point F, the point of tangency between the risk-return possibility curve and an indifference curve.

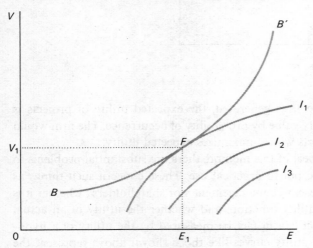

Figure 12.13

* See [32], [31], [37], [38]. Descriptions of this technique may also be found in most texts on finance.

In mathematical form the problem is as follows: If there are n securities with expected returns, variances and covariances μ_i, σ_i and σ_{ij} respectively, $(i = 1, \ldots, n; j = 1, \ldots, n)$, the proportion of total funds available for investment allocated to

security i is x_i $\quad \left(x_i \geq 0, \quad \sum_{i=1}^{n} x_i = 1 \right)$, then

total expected returns, $\qquad E = \sum_i \mu_i x_i$

and total variance (risk), $\qquad V = \sum_i \sum_j x_i x_j \sigma_{ij}$

$$= \sum_i \sum_j x_i x_j \rho_{ij} \sigma_i \sigma_j,$$

where ρ_{ij} is the coefficient of correlation between the expected returns of securities i and j. The μ_i and σ_{ij} are to be estimated by a combination of practical judgement and statistical analysis of past data. The level of risk attached to the portfolio depends on the value of ρ_{ij}; the lower its value over all i and j (i.e. the greater the degree of negative correlation) the lower the total risk of the portfolio, measured in terms of variance. Under the assumption of risk aversion this usually leads the investor to diversify his holdings: instead of choosing the single security with the highest expected return his portfolio will reflect his risk preferences. That is, given risk-aversion the problem typically takes the form:*

Minimize V

subject to $\qquad \sum_i \mu_i x_i = 1$

$$x_i \geq 0.$$

This is a quadratic programming problem. Algorithms are available for solving this problem. Alternatively, if i is small Lagrangean methods may be used.†

Leaving aside the estimation problems in obtaining μ_i and σ_{ij}, our chief interest lies in whether, as frequently suggested,‡ this analysis can be applied to productive investment undertaken by a firm. One difference between the two cases is that productive investment projects are not highly divisible as financial securities are. The time horizons are also of a different order in the typical case, as are the transactions costs.§ There is also the question of whether the firm should take account of risk preferences by diversifying its investments or whether shareholders should be

---

*For a fuller account see [33].

†Form the Lagrangean expression $L = V + \lambda_1(\Sigma x_i \mu_i - E) + \lambda_2(\Sigma x_i - 1)$; differentiate it partially with respect to x_i, giving $(n+2)$ equations in $(n+2)$ unknowns. These may then be solved by inserting the desired value of E.

‡E.g. [39].

§ I.e. we are suggesting that the markets in capital goods are in general more imperfect than the market in securities.

left to do so by diversifying their security holdings. For the typical firm, following the portfolio selection path may very well run counter to its established goals. We have also noted, in relation to some of the earlier methods, that moments of the probability distribution of returns other than the mean and variance may influence behaviour, and that objectives of maximizing expected value and maximizing utility may not lead to very different results except in the case of investments which are either very large or very risky by the firm's own standards.

There we must leave this brief survey of alternative approaches to uncertainty in investment decision-making. There is a number of unresolved issues in this area. Having examined an array of more or less complicated methods of dealing with the problem, and questioned the possibility of making some of them operational, we suggest that the reader return again to our opening remarks in section 3(a). As Cohen and Cyert remark:*

> Empirical evidence suggests that a firm will not make an important decision under conditions of complete uncertainty [defined by them as a situation in which the decision-maker cannot formulate a meaningful subjective probability distribution of possible outcomes], but rather that it will attempt through search activity to obtain greater knowledge or that it will redefine its decision problem so that uncertainty is no longer critical.

Appendix

(a) Notes on the mathematics of retirement and replacement

The derivation of (1.2) may be explained as follows:

$$B(T) = \int_0^T Q(t)e^{-\delta t}\,dt + S(T)e^{-\delta T} - W$$

If an expression on the RHS is a continuous function, the derivative of the integral of the function is the function itself. Q is a continuous function with fixed lower limit of integration of zero and variable upper limit T. Since $Q(0) = 0$, differentiation of this integral is carried out by substituting the value of the upper limit in the integrand. That is,

$$\frac{d}{dT}\left\{\int_0^T Q(t)\,dt\right\} = Q(T).$$

The function S cannot be integrated since only one value, $S(T)$, is of interest. It is differentiated in the usual way.

$$\frac{dB}{dT} = 0 = Q(T)e^{-\delta T} + e^{-\delta T}S'(T) - \delta e^{-\delta T}S(T)$$

$$= e^{-\delta T}[Q(T) + S'(T) - \delta S(T)].$$

*[22], p. 323.

368

Equation (2.4) is obtained as follows:

$$B(L) = \int_0^L Q(t)e^{-\delta t}\,dt + S(L)e^{-\delta L} - W$$

(one replacement cycle)

$$B = B(L) + e^{-\delta L}B$$

$$= \frac{1}{1 - e^{-\delta L}} \cdot B(L)$$

(infinite chain of replacements)

Then

$$\frac{dB}{dL} = (1 - e^{-\delta L})^{-1} \cdot B'(L) + B(L) \cdot \frac{d}{dL}(1 - e^{-\delta L})^{-1}$$

The derivative of $B(L)$ was explained in the previous note. The derivative of $(1 - e^{-\delta L})$ involves using the function of a function rule, i.e.

$$\frac{dy}{dL} = \frac{dy}{dz} \cdot \frac{dz}{dL}.$$

Let $z = (1 - e^{-\delta L})$.

Then

$$y = \frac{1}{z} = z^{-1}$$

$$\frac{dy}{dL} = -\frac{1}{z^2}[0 - (-\delta e^{-\delta L})]$$

$$= \frac{-\delta e^{-\delta L}}{(1 - e^{-\delta L})^2}$$

We then have

$$\frac{dB}{dL} = (1 - e^{-\delta L})^{-1}[e^{-\delta L}\{Q(L) + S'(L) - \delta S(L)\}] - \delta e^{-\delta L}(1 - e^{-\delta L})^2 B(L) = 0.$$

Simplifying,

$$[Q(L) + S'(L) - \delta S(L)] = \frac{\delta B(L)}{1 - e^{-\delta L}} = \delta B.$$

Noting that $(1 - e^{-\delta L})$ is $\delta \int_0^L e^{-\delta t}\,dt$, and making use of (2.3), if $S \to 0$ this last result may be expressed as in (2.6).

Similar reasoning applies in the pure replacement case in (2.12) and (2.13).

369

(b) Conditional and Joint Probability

Given two future events, A and B, with probabilities

$$0 \leq P(A) \leq 1; \quad 0 \leq P(B) \leq 1,$$

where $P(A)$ stands for the probability of A occurring.

(i) *Conditional probability*
The conditional probability of A occurring, if B has already occurred (or is certain to occur) is written $P(A|B)$ and is defined as

$$P(A|B) = \frac{P(B|A)P(A)}{P(B)}, \quad P(B) \neq 0,$$

where $P(B|A)$ means 'the probability of B, given the probability of A'. By transposition it may be seen that, if the order of the events is reversed,

$$P(B|A) = \frac{P(A|B)P(B)}{P(A)}, \quad P(A) \neq 0.$$

(ii) *Joint probability*
The probability of both A and B occurring is written $P(A,B)$ and is defined as the probability of B multiplied by the conditional probability of A given the probability of B:

$$P(A,B) = P(B)P(A|B) = P(A)P(B|A), \quad P(A),P(B) \neq 0.$$

If $P(A|B) = P(A)$, so that the conditional probability of A given B is independent of B, and $P(A)P(B) > 0$, the events are said to be independent, and the expressions immediately above reduce to:

$$P(A,B) = P(A)P(B).$$

It is important to remember the formulae for the joint probability of both non-independent and independent events.

These results are summarized below.

	Independent events	*Non-independent events*
Joint probability $P(A, B)$	$P(A)P(B)$	$P(B)P(A\mid B) = P(A)P(B\mid A)$
Conditional probability $P(A\mid B)$	$\dfrac{P(A,\,B)}{P(B)}$	$\dfrac{P(B\mid A)P(A)}{P(B)}$

Bibliographical references

Capital rationing

[1] Baumol, W. J., *Economic Theory and Operations Analysis,* Prentice-Hall, 1965.
[2] Baumol, W. J. and R. E. Quandt, Investment and discount rates under capital rationing: A programming approach, *Economic Journal,* June 1965, pp. 317–29.
[3] Carleton, W. T., Linear programming and capital budgeting models: A new interpretation, *Journal of Finance,* Dec. 1969, pp. 825–33.
[4] Hirshleifer, J., *Investment, Interest, and Capital,* Prentice-Hall, 1970.
[5] Lerner, E. M. and W. T. Carleton, *A Theory of Financial Analysis,* Harcourt, Brace and World, 1966.
[6] Lintner, J., The cost of capital and optimal financing of corporate growth, *Journal of Finance,* May 1963, pp. 292–310.
[7] Lusztig, P. and B. Schwab, A note on the application of linear programming to capital budgeting, *Journal of Financial and Quantitative Analysis,* Dec. 1968, pp. 427–31.
[8] Weingartner, H. M., *Mathematical Programming and the Analysis of Capital Budgeting Problems,* Prentice-Hall, 1963.
[9] Weingartner, H. M., Criteria for programming investment project selection, *Journal of Industrial Economics,* Nov. 1966, pp. 65–76; reprinted in the Markham Publishing Co. edn. of [8], 1967.
[10] Whitmore, G. A., 'Remote clients' and uncertain preferences in financial decision-making (submitted paper).
[11] Whitmore, G. A. and L. R. Amey, Capital budgeting under rationing: Comments on the Lusztig and Schwab procedure, *Journal of Financial and Quantitative Analysis,* January 1973

Optimal replacement policy

[12] Dean, B. V., Replacement theory, in *Progress in Operations Research, Vol. I,* ed. R. L. Ackoff, Wiley, 1961.
[13] Holmes, M. E., An introduction to replacement theory; in *Readings in Management Decision,* ed. L. R. Amey, Longman, 1973.
[14] Massé, P., *Optimal Investment Decisions,* Prentice-Hall, 1962.
[15] Preinreich, G. A. D., The economic life of industrial equipment, *Econometrica,* January 1940, pp. 12–44.
[16] Smith, V. L., *Investment and Production,* Harvard University Press, 1961.
[17] Smith, V. L., The theory of investment and production, *Quarterly Journal of Economics,* 1959, pp. 61–87.
[18] Terborgh, G., *Dynamic Equipment Policy,* McGraw-Hill, 1949.
[19] Terborgh, G., *Business Investment Policy,* Machinery & Allied Products Institute, Washington, 1958.
[20] Wagner, H. M., *Principles of Operations Research,* Prentice-Hall, 1969.

Risk and uncertainty

[8] Weingartner, H. M., *ibid.*
[21] Byrne, R., A. Charnes, W. W. Cooper and K. Kortanek, A chance-constrained approach to capital budgeting with portfolio type payback and liquidity constraints and horizon posture controls, *Journal of Financial and Quantitative Analysis,* vol. 2, pp. 339–64.
[22] Cohen, K. J. and R. M. Cyert, *Theory of the Firm,* Prentice-Hall, 1965.
[23] Cyert, R. M. and J. G. March, *A Behavioral Theory of the Firm,* Prentice-Hall, 1963.
[24] Edwards, W. and A. Tversky, eds., *Decision making,* Penguin, 1967.
[25] Grayson, C. J., The use of statistical techniques in capital budgeting, chapter 5 in *Financial Research and Management Decisions,* ed. A. A. Robichek, Wiley, 1967.

[26] Hertz, D. B., Risk analysis in capital investment, *Harvard Business Review*, Jan.-Feb. 1964, pp. 95–106; reprinted in *Contemporary Issues in Cost Accounting*, eds. H. R. Anton and P. A. Firmin, Houghton Mifflin, 1966, and in *The Theory of Business Finance*, eds. S. H. Archer and C. A. D'Ambrosio, Macmillan, New York, 1967.

[27] Hillier, F. S., The derivation of probabilistic information for the evaluation of risky investments, *Management Science*, April 1963, pp. 443–57; reprinted in *Foundations for Financial Management*, ed. J. Van Horne, Irwin, 1966, and in Archer and D'Ambrosio, *ibid*.

[28] Hillier, F. S., *The Evaluation of Risky Interrelated Investments*, North-Holland, 1969.

[29] Hillier, F. A. and G. Lieberman, *An Introduction to Operations Research*, Holden-Day, 1967.

[30] Luce, R. D. and H. Raiffa, *Games and Decisions*, Wiley, 1967.

[31] Markowitz, H. M., Portfolio selection, *Journal of Finance*, March 1952, pp. 77–91; reprinted in Archer and D'Ambrosio, *ibid*.

[32] Markowitz, H. M., *Portfolio Selection, Efficient Diversification of Investments*, Wiley, 1959.

[33] Martin, A. D., Mathematical programming of portfolio selection, *Management Science*, 1954, pp. 152–66.

[34] Näslund, B., A model of capital budgeting under risk, *Journal of Business*, April 1966, pp. 257–71.

[35] Savage, L. J., *The Foundations of Statistics*, Wiley, 1954.

[36] Schlaifer, R., *Probability and Statistics for Business Decisions*, McGraw-Hill, 1959.

[37] Sharpe, W. F., A simplified model for portfolio analysis, *Management Science*, January 1963, pp. 277–93.

[38] Sharpe, W. F., Capital asset prices: A theory of market equilibrium under conditions of risk, *Journal of Finance*, September 1964, pp. 425–42; reprinted in Archer and D'Ambrosio, *ibid*.

[39] Van Horne, J. C., Capital-budgeting decisions involving combinations of risky investments, *Management Science*, October 1966, pp. 84–92.

Problems

12.1 Two of the leading writers on capital budgeting, J. Hirshleifer and H. M. Weingartner, believe that quantitative limits on a firm's ability to borrow in order to finance investment are not likely to be imposed by the capital market, and will only be imposed by management:

1. on investment centres within the firm as a convenient administrative device, or
2. out of ignorance.

Design your own enquiry to test the validity of these arguments; if possible carry out the test by undertaking field studies in actual firms; and finally list, and if possible obtain, any information you would need from other sources, or from the records of the firm, in order to corroborate or refute the findings of your initial (questionnaire) enquiry.

12.2 Delta Ltd. operates two laundries. The firm is small, both in absolute size (turnover, assets, income) and in terms of market share. Production processes are heavily capitalized, and in its capital investment the firm has for some years ₊followed a policy of demanding of all new projects a rate of return at least as high as that earned by the business as a whole in the previous year. This return is calculated from the accounts, and is after depreciation, but before tax.

Discuss this policy and explore its implications.

12.3 Epicure Ltd. is considering a project for the manufacture of plastic frying pans.

Data for the project appear below:

(i) Two alternative sizes of manufacturing plant are contemplated:

Plant *A* would require an outlay (year 0) of £60 000

Plant *B* would require an outlay (year 0) of £110 000

Either plant would have an economic life of 10 years, at the end of which plastic frying pans can be assumed to be obsolete, i.e. no question of replacement arises. Neither plant will have any realizable value.

(ii) It is estimated that there is a 0·3 probability that demand for the product will be low, producing a constant annual net cash flow for either plant of £10 000 per year (commencing year 1). There is a 0·7 probability that demand will be high, producing constant net cash flows of £30 000 per year for plant *B* (but the net cash flows of *A* will be limited by capacity to £10 000). These figures are subject to the qualifications in (iv) 2. and 3. below.

(iii) If demand is low, Epicure Ltd. is certain that competitors will not enter the market for plastic frying pans.

(iv) If demand is high:

1. It is estimated that the chances of competititors entering the market at year 1 will differ according to Epicure's *initial* choice of plant size;

    If Epicure chose *A* at year 0, probability of competition 0·4, probability of no competition 0·6.

    If Epicure chose *B* at year 0, probability of competition 0·2, probability of no competition 0·8.

2. Epicure Ltd. could double capacity of plant *A* at year 1 for a further outlay of £60 000. Capacity of the enlarged plant (*AA*) would then be sufficient to provide a total net cash flow of £30 000 per year for the remaining 9 years. The decision on increased capacity will be made with knowledge of market demand (high or low), but the decision will have to be made before competitors' reactions are known – delayed expansion would not capture the larger market.

3. If competitors enter the market, it is estimated that from year 2 onwards the net cash flows of *A* would be reduced by £2 000 per year, and those of *AA* or *B* by £15 000 per year.

The above cash flow data can be summarized as follows (C = competition, NC = no competition).

Epicure Ltd. considers that the appropriate riskless rate of interest for the next 10 years is 6 per cent. It can be assumed that the company has no capital rationing problem.

Plant	Years: 0	1	2–10
A		Low 10 000	Low 10 000
		High 10 000	High NC ⌠10 000
			C ⌡ 8 000
	(60 000)		
AA		Low 10 000	Low 10 000
		High 10 000	High NC ⌠30 000
			C ⌡15 000
	(60 000)	(60 000)	
B		Low 10 000	Low 10 000
		High 30 000	High NC ⌠30 000
			C ⌡15 000
	(110 000)		

Required:

(a) A decision tree showing relevant net present values (at year 0) for the options open to the firm.

(b) Comments. If you would prefer any further information about Epicure before reaching a decision, discuss how that information might affect the outcome.

(c) Discuss (but do not attempt to calculate) the application of a risk-adjusted discount rate to this project.

12.4 Discuss the following proposition:

A constant discount rate applied to cash flows expected in different future time periods implies constant risk.

12.5 Comment on the following argument:

'One of the oldest and most widely used methods for explicitly recognizing uncertainty in [the investment decision] is the payback calculation. . . . payback has been subjected to relentless war from the [discounting school], and yet many business men continue to use it. Why? One obvious answer is that payback is simple and quick. . . . an equally significant reason is that . . . business men view with some suspicion (quite correctly) the effectiveness or accuracy of using the discount rate to adjust for the effects of *risk* on the investment decision:

1. They still know that the 'most likely' estimates on which both the payback and discounted rates of return computations are based are just 'ball park' estimates.
2. They see that an overall firm-wide discount rate may have little relevance to the risk of a particular investment under consideration.
3. They have an intuitive uneasiness over having the time-preference concept of discounting extended to include risk preferences also.

Thus, until they can be assured that the discounting-for-risk technique is superior and safe to rely on, . . . many decision makers will continue to give payback a prominent role in their decision processes.'

12.6 Karriers Corporation operates a fleet of heavy haulage vehicles. At the end of 197x it is considering the following replacement alternatives:

	Capital outlay, £	Remaining life, years	Expected annual net cash flows, £
Trucks at present in service: (five units)		3	3 000
Alternative 1:			
Group-replace all five units at the end of their working lives	25 000	6	5 000
Alternative 2:			
Replace two units immediately	8 000 ⎫		1 800
Replace two units in one year's time	8 500 ⎬	6	1 900
Replace one unit in two year's time	4 500 ⎭		1 000

Assuming that these are the only feasible alternatives, that the Corporation's cost of capital (on an after-tax basis) is 5 per cent, and that scrap values are negligible in all cases, which replacement policy should the firm adopt?

12.7 In appraising investment opportunities, explain the complications which result if a project's net cash flows in different periods are correlated. Give some examples of components of project cash flows which you would expect to be (1) highly independent, (2) highly correlated over time.

12.8 It is sometimes argued against a policy of diversification that such firms should 'keep all their eggs in one basket' and leave it to their shareholders to diversify their holdings if they so desire. What are your views on this argument?

12.9 (a) Skyscrapers Ltd. owns some cranes which are used in construction work. All cranes are of identical age and operating characteristics. They were bought two years ago for £10 000 each; their current saleable value is £5 000 each.

A crane of new design is available at £11 000. It does precisely the same work as an old crane, but its superior safety characteristics will reduce the maintenance necessary under safety regulations.

Operating costs and saleable values for old and new cranes are shown below (estimated where relevant):

	Old crane		New crane	
	Realizable value £	Operating cost £	Realizable value £	Operating cost £
Year −2	*10 000			
−1	7 000			
0	5 000		*11 000	
1	3 500	4 300 rising by £500 p.a.	8 000	3 000 rising by £400 p.a.
2	2 500		5 500	
3	1 500		4 000	
4	500		3 000	
5	0		2 000	
6			1 000	
7			500	
8			0	

*Initial outlay.

375

In addition to the operating costs above, it is estimated that the 'obsolescence cost' of the cranes will increase by about £100 per annum. (Implicitly, developments in the crane industry are expected to produce, on average, a superior model each year which will have lower costs/higher returns of £100 per annum compared with the preceding year's model. Thus a newer model purchased at the *end* of year 1 can be assumed to have an outlay cost equivalent to £11 000 and initial operating costs in year 2 equivalent to £2 900.)

The market in cranes is imperfect; the realizable values shown above represent trade-in prices. Skyscrapers Ltd. could buy second-hand cranes (of the old type) but purchase price would be some 30 per cent above the quoted realizable value for the relevant age.

Additional assumptions:

1. Taxation and investment grants can be ignored.
2. Skyscrapers Ltd. is expected to use the cranes to derive benefits in excess of cost in all relevant years.

     (In part (b) below, where a crane *might* be idle for part of the year, assume for simplicity that benefits from use for the remainder of the year would nevertheless cover all costs for a full year.)
3. Cost of capital is constant at 10 per cent in all periods.
4. All cash flows occur at end of year.

(b) There are variations in the number of cranes which Skyscrapers Ltd. requires over the year. These requirements, which can be assumed to apply for all relevant future years affected by the current decision, are:

Quarter 1	5
2	8
3	10
4	7

In the above, 5 represents 100 per cent feasible usage of five cranes throughout January to March, etc.

It can be assumed that the operating costs given earlier comprise wages, fuel, removal expenses, etc., of £3 000 per annum for both old and new cranes; thus that sum represents the user costs which would be avoided, *pro rata*, for any period in which the cranes were not used. The incremental operating costs represent maintenance, safety checks, etc., and cranes must be maintained even in a period of idleness in order to preserve the effectiveness for use in later periods.

At present Skyscrapers Ltd. has five (old) cranes and intends to follow its usual practice of hiring the remaining requirements in the coming year. The hire company will charge £9 000 per year for the use of a new crane (*pro rata* for shorter periods), and will be responsible for *all* operating costs under this arrangement.

Additional assumptions:

1. Any hire charges are paid at the *end* of the year in which a crane is hired.
2. The hire company will adjust its charges in future years in line with the assumptions of technological advance made earlier.

Required:

(a) Calculations (in discrete terms) which will assist Skyscrapers Ltd. in choosing between the retention of old cranes and replacement with new cranes.
(b) Calculations and recommendations on the 'mix' of old/new/hired cranes which Skyscrapers Ltd. should adopt for the coming year.
(c) Comments.

Table for 10 per cent

n	v^n	$a_{\overline{n}\rceil}^{-1}$
1	0·909	1·100
2	0·826	0·576
3	0·751	0·402
4	0·683	0·315
5	0·621	0·264
6	0·564	0·230
7	0·513	0·205
8	0·467	0·187
9	0·424	0·174
10	0·386	0·163

Part 3
Control systems

13

Enterprise control

A beggarly account of empty boxes.
  − ROMEO AND JULIET

13.1 The enterprise control problem

The *firm* in economics describes any business organization, whatever its legal form, that *controls* certain productive activities, where 'production' is as defined in section 3 of Chapter 5. The question with which we shall be concerned in this chapter is 'who or what controls the firm?'. In order to answer this question we shall have to cast our nets much wider than is customary in accounting treatments of the problem, as we have already done in relation to planning and decision. As in those cases, a deeper understanding of this set of problems will be gained by introducing inputs from economics and organization theory. The behavioural aspects of control will be deferred, in the main, until Chapter 18.

The reason why it is necessary to enlarge the problem is that the firm is subject, in greater or lesser degree, to both external controls and internal controls. Discussion of the former, which are never mentioned in accounting treatments, is essential for two reasons: first, that (especially in conjunction with the organization theory inputs) they throw considerable light on the nature of the control problem, and secondly, that there are important interactions between external and internal controls.* The whole spectrum of controls operating on the firm needs to be considered.

(a) The meaning of 'control'

The particular meaning we attach to 'control' depends upon the stance we take − whether the problem of control of the firm is looked at from the social point of view or from the point of view of its owners or management and, in the case of management, on the opportunity set in relation to which control is exercised and the organization structure within which management functions. Quite generally, however, we shall mean by 'control' the *control of efficiency*, i.e. efficient use of resources by the firm in both production and investment. In the broadest (social) sense this is identified with perfectly competitive markets and, for the firm, a profit-

---

*The ideas expressed in this section are drawn from several important works, most of which are written from an organizational theory of the firm or behavioural theory of the firm standpoint: [13], [11], [30], [19], [26], [27] and [21], which readers are strongly urged to consult.

maximizing objective and least-cost performance. From the point of view of the individual firm control means observation of results to see whether plans are being carried out. More especially, it implies corrective action as a result of this evaluation, or possibly replanning.

13.2 Background to the problem

Recognition of the control problem dates back to the passing of the Limited Liability Act in 1855. The corporate form led inevitably to a growth in the size of business enterprises. Corporate firms came to dominate most industries, and a few very large firms ultimately to assume economic importance quite out of proportion to their number. This change in the structure of the population of business enterprises led in turn to loss of control over the resource allocation process in two distinct ways. First, it upset market relationships. With diminished competition in product and capital markets there emerged discretionary opportunities for the corporate enterprise, particularly the large one, to exploit in a way which suited its self-interests. These did not necessarily or even probably coincide with the social view of efficiency; and it should be remembered that the volume of such imperfectly competitive resource allocations was assuming larger and larger proportions.

Concurrently, the new form of enterprise structure led to the divorce of ownership and control. A new managerial class emerged to administer the new corporate firms, and their objectives were not necessarily those of the owners.* Considerable power thus came to be concentrated in the hands of corporate managements as a result of both market and institutional forces. The dimensions of the problem it will be seen, vary directly with the degree of market imperfection and with firm size.

13.3 The place of control in the economics of the firm

To see the role played by control in the economics of the firm we focus on two points: the standard theory of the firm, and the arguments adduced by economists in an attempt to explain why growth of the firm should reach a definite limit.

---

*This second development is commented on in [7] and [9]. Note, however, the later remarks of Baumol [5]: 'In practice . . . managements will naturally identify to a different degree with different stockholder groups and separation of ownership from management, instead of amounting to a sharp cleavage, takes the form of a gradual shading-off in the degree of coincidence between managerial and stockholder objectives . . . instead of treating stockholders and managements as two well-defined polar groups each of which is completely homogeneous in its objectives.' We elaborate on this point in section 4 below.

(a) Theories of the firm

To say that the theory of the firm completely ignores the control problem, as is sometimes done is, of course, overstating the case. The influence of external market control is recognized explicitly, in the form of models of the firm for a series of different market structures (perfect competition, imperfect competition, monopoly, oligopoly, monopsony, oligopsony). In fact the whole thrust of the theory of the firm is market-oriented: it pictures the firm as looking outward towards its input and product markets. A similar orientation is apparent in the theory of investment of the firm.

This by no means includes all of the external controls operating on the firm, however, as we shall see later. In the case of internal controls the omission is complete: the theory assumes that the firm knows its production function (operates on the boundary of its production opportunity set) and optimally adjusts this set of technological possibilities to relative market prices. That is, least-cost operation is assumed; all plans and consequential decisions are perfectly executed. Similarly, the implementation of investment decisions raises no control problem. The presence of uncertainty, which increases with market imperfection and (normally) as the planning/decision horizon lengthens, may falsify the firm's expectations; but it is never acknowledged that the latter may also be falsified as a result of internal controls being less than fully effective. Dynamic deterministic versions of the model offer slightly greater control over uncertainty, by allowing the firm partially to offset the effects of earlier forecasting errors at subsequent decision stages, but still abstract from the problem of internal control.

(b) Limits to growth of the firm

In fact, the only place at which there has been explicit recognition that an *internal* control problem exists has been in the controversy over whether, and what, forces ultimately halt the growth of the firm. Perhaps the earliest pronouncement on this issue was that of Marshall, in his famous 'trees of the forest' analogy.* Marshall argued that the growth of the firm could not continue indefinitely because the abilities and energy of the entrepreneur (or his heirs) were likely to decay after a time. This 'decay of entrepreneurial faculties' was postulated as a kind of sociological law. The argument, of course, has lost much of its force as a result of institutional changes, although Marshall considered it applied in principle to the joint stock company as to other forms of business unit. With the divorce of ownership from management the supply of able and energetic managers, although not inexhaustible, has not proved to be a limit to growth in the way Marshall predicted.

To state the matter more generally, economists became concerned about the 'costs of growth' of the firm, i.e. with the costs to a firm of increasing its output of

*[20], pp. 286, 315–16 and 457.

a single product. They looked to various factors to explain why growth of a firm should ultimately reach a definite limit. Without some limit the theory of the firm would become indeterminate. Some of the things they have considered* have been the limitations of *management*, leading to increased costs of production in the long run; the *size of the market* (causing decreasing marginal revenue from sales) and *uncertainty* about the future (leading to both decreasing revenue and increasing costs, because of the necessity of making allowance for risk). Economists have suggested that there must be some limit to growth of the firm's output, caused either by the marginal cost of producing a product rising after a certain point as additional quantities of it are produced, or partly as well by falling marginal revenue as additional quantities have to be put on the market.

A common argument was that the cost of management, in particular the cost of coordinating all the activities of the business as it grew larger and larger, tended to increase more than proportionately with scale. And it was often argued that this increase in the cost of management *alone* was sufficient to set an upper limit to the size of the firm. As more and more operatives are put under each foreman, more and more foremen under each departmental manager, and so on up through the organization (i.e. as the span of control lengthens) the task of coordination becomes *progressively* more difficult; it will be done less efficiently, or if equally efficiently at increasingly greater cost because of the need for more elaborate systems of control.

In order to establish that 'management' is a factor limiting growth of the firm it is necessary to treat 'management' as a fixed input to the production process,† the source of this fixity usually having been identified with respect to the nature of the managerial task of coordination. While asserting that this identification has never been conclusively demonstrated, Mrs. Penrose [21]‡ continues to argue that this view is still correct – i.e. that 'management' constitutes *a* limit to firm size – providing one looks to the *dynamic* rather than static aspects of coordination. That is, there is no loss of control due to this cause when the firm is in a steady state, but there is when it is expanding. Expansion requires skilful planning and coordination; these are functions of management experience, and top management experience is an input in very inelastic supply.

Subsequently, proposals for the *overall* control of corporate power (i.e. limiting of the zone of management discretion), as chronicled in [30], have led in diverse directions. Competition in the capital market would act as a partial substitute for weak competition in the product market; or the public regulation of monopoly and restrictive trade practices, mandatorily fuller disclosure in external accounting reports, and so on would fill the breach. Taken together, such measures as these

---

*These are well summarized in [21].
† Cf. [10], [21], [16], [23], [24] and [8] for the main strands in the controversy.
‡ And [16].

might be expected to exert some impact on the problem, but they hardly answer it completely.

Williamson, in a recent work,* takes a different view which involves two of the limiting factors considered earlier, uncertainty as well as 'management'. In his view the control problem still exists in static conditions, though in a different way from that previously supposed, and is in no way dependent only on growth. Briefly, static conditions are only static in the sense of a stochastic equilibrium, and 'stochastic changes require adaptation whatever the size of firm'. Whereas in a deterministic equilibrium 'the data are unchanging, in [stochastic equilibrium] the firm is required to adapt to circumstances which are predictable in the sense that although they occur with stochastic regularity, precise advance knowledge of them is unavailable'. Throughout all sorts of

> disturbing influences of a transitory nature . . . the management of the firm is required to adapt to new circumstances: request the relevant data, process the information supplied, and provide the appropriate instructions. Coordination in these circumstances is thus essential. If, simultaneously, a general expansion of operations accompanies these quasi-static adjustments, additional direction would be required. But in no sense is growth a necessary condition for the coordinating function to exist.

As to why increases in scale should eventually come up against a limit, Williamson believes there are two reasons. First, as the firm expands it is exposed to a wider range of disturbances from environmental and experiential factors, and this increases the task of inter-functional coordination at the top until it eventually becomes insupportable. Secondly, loss of control is also experienced as a result of cumulative error in 'the information transfer and operationalizing† processes'. Two methods of offsetting these limitational forces are open to the firm, each of course involving a cost: delegation of responsibility and 'decoupling', i.e. reduction in internal information transmission needs. These factors will be explained further in the next section, where innovation in form of organization structure will also be seen to contain the problem temporarily for large firms for which the internal structure in question is appropriate. Ultimately, however, expansion will exhaust the capacity to provide the necessary control at the top, and together with the build-up of 'noise' in the communication system will lead to a control loss which is limiting, whatever form of organization structure is employed.

The task of coordination has been described in an earlier quotation. The following description of the two-way information flow vividly portrays the communication problem:

---

* [30], pp. 24–25.
† 'Operationalizing' is defined as the transmission of instructions down the line across hierarchical levels in such a way as to ensure that the recipient's range of choice is consistent with enterprise objectives.

[Regarding the upward flow] Raw data are sampled, screened, condensed, compiled, coded, expressed in statistical form, spun into generalizations and crystallized into recommendations* [and as regards the downward flow] General instructions are issued at the top which are consistent with a wide range of eventual behavior, not all of which outcomes have the same utility value.†

Amid these managerial diseconomies of scale a possible counter-tendency of especial interest to us here has been noted by at least two writers [21], [30]. According to Mrs. Penrose, techniques for decentralizing administrative organization have been developed to a fairly high degree, and operating control of these decentralized areas of responsibility within the firm is now effected to a considerable extent through *accounting devices* which are highly centralized. The task of top management is not to keep track of everything but to intervene in a relatively few crucial areas, i.e. management by the 'principle of exception', as exemplified in the techniques of standard costing and budgetary control, to be examined in later chapters.

Though it will be remembered that Mrs. Penrose believes that the dynamic aspect of lack of effective coordination ultimately limits the size of the firm, the gist of her argument would seem to be that, short of this limit, accounting devices of the kind mentioned tend to give management a technical advantage. The techniques of predetermining balance sheet, income statement, costs and revenues, feeding information on the latter down to all levels within the firm comparing performance with plan, rewarding/penalizing over-fulfilment and under-fulfilment, financially or otherwise, is a means of treating each 'responsibility centre' as though it were a separate entrepreneur or quasi-entrepreneur, i.e. almost a separate business. The underlying philosophy is that by this means cost- and profit-consciousness can be inculcated right down to the shop floor. Taking this a step further, what may very well happen over time is that by means of such centrally operated control devices firms may succeed in pushing out the optimum size of production or in holding it steady in the face of general increases in costs, i.e. in moving the bottom of the U-shaped long-run average cost curve to the right. If so, these accounting devices would represent a potential managerial economy of scale. This argument, it should be noted, is premised on accounting controls being capable in practice of doing what is here attributed to them in theory, and of all instructions being appropriately 'operationalized'. We shall have more to say on this in Chapter 18; for the present we reserve judgment.

The other argument does not concern accounting control systems specifically, but rather data processing within the firm. Williamson speculates that, although most of the economies of scale resulting from specialization and indivisibilies are ordinarily exhausted at a relatively modest firm size, according to Bain [4], 'the economies that result from a large data processing capability may well extend

---

*J. Gardiner, quoted in [15], p. 114.
†[15], p. 129 and [30].

considerably beyond this size'; and 'since for a given level of control loss, increases in information processing capability permit the span of control to be expanded, the association of an increasing span of control and large firm size may be due in part to this information processing – firm size relation' [30].

13.4 Insights from organization theory

The contributions of organization theory and behavioural science* in the past two decades to development of more realistic theories of business behaviour, taken together, have been very impressive. It should come as no surprise, therefore, that each of these developments should have been influential in the writing of this book, which attempts to present the student of management accounting with a (highly condensed) summary of reasonably current 'frontiers of knowledge' research in a number of areas bearing on this subject. As stated earlier, behavioural aspects of business, and particularly of accounting controls, will be referred to in Chapter 18. In this section a necessarily brief statement of some of the main strands in recent organization-theoretic approaches to the problem of enterprise control is presented.

An early participant in this discussion, N. S. Ross, *op. cit.*, thought that the whole economic approach to the question of limits to firm size missed the mark, and argued that by decentralizing and adopting appropriate control devices the firm could offset the costs of growth over the whole range of possible expansion.† The recent work by Williamson [30] analyses the problem in terms of different forms of organization structure, the possibility, open to most firms probably, of changing from one form of structure to another, and the effects of this on control. His line of argument, though its conclusion is in conflict with behavioural theorists who have argued against profit maximization as the over-riding objective of the firm,‡ nevertheless stands up well against an extensive review of the literature on the subject, has intuitive appeal, and is not inconsistent with such empirical facts as are known at present. It is convenient, therefore, to follow Williamson's terminology in this review of developments.

Of critical importance to an understanding of the enterprise control problem, Williamson believes, is the need to distinguish between external and internal controls. The external control class may be further subdivided into 'will-ful' and 'system' categories, described more fully in the next section. The first of these, with certain exceptions (represented by, e.g., big lenders and institutional investors), has limited access to control information. The second refers to the exercise by the firm§

* Representing, respectively, a macro and micro view of human behaviour in organizations.
† Recall also the observations of Mrs. Penrose [21].
‡ Such as [13].
§ Williamson's focus is deliberately on the large and very large firm.

of functions taken over from the product and capital markets. In the disposition of the discretionary opportunities* opened up to management as a result of internalizing market functions and of growth in size, significant differences appear, according to the form of internal organization employed. Indeed organization form is the new variable introduced into the analysis by Williamson.

Two forms are singled out for special study: the centralized unitary form of organization (U-form) and the multidivision form (M-form). Organization form influences goal formation and the effectiveness of internal control devices. Expansion of a U-form organization takes the form of amplification. Simon's concept of 'bounded rationality'† explains why this will lead to the introduction of additional hierarchical levels of management, with a consequent increase in information transmission across these levels. 'Simple control loss' varies directly with the volume of information transferred; 'compound control loss' involves, in addition, communication bias. 'Decoupling' (shortening the transmission network) provides only temporary relief from this problem. Cumulative control losses of these types eventually limit growth of the firm when they are no longer declining in relation to market transactions costs, of which they are the internal equivalent. Expansion of the U-form organization meets the capacity problem at top management level by adding the heads of functional divisions (i.e. operational executives) to the management team. Direction of the enterprise (the strategic decision-making process) becomes the joint responsibility of the managers (the entrepreneurs of Chapter 5) who have been used to taking an overall view and those (the managers of Chapter 5) who have taken a partisan view. Members of the latter group are likely to continue using opportunities for discretion to advance their own individual and functional interests, subject to certain constraints (the degree of imperfection of product and capital markets – competition in the latter being only a partial substitute for lack of competition in the former). As a result, the goals of the enterprise and of the augmented top management group may now diverge, the new members of the group may pursue subgoals (e.g. have an interest in introducing organizational slack). Further loss of control may occur through communication biassing.

The M-form organization, which evolved in the US in the 1920s as an adaptive response to the inherent weaknesses of the U-form organization, has as its distinguishing feature the recognition of quasi-autonomous 'natural decision units'.‡

*On managerial discretion see Williamson [31] and his paper in [13], Chapter 9. A summary of Williamson's model appears in Cohen and Cyert, *ibid.,* pp. 354–63.

†H. A. Simon, [26]. Bounded rationality also implies a certain attitude towards response to environmental disturbances: instead of adapting to every change, the organization employs response thresholds. Response to disturbances below the threshold is routinized, above it takes the form of step function adaptations of the firm [2].

‡The M-form organization does not include holding companies; while quasi-autonomous operating divisions are found in both forms, the distinguishing feature is a sharp separation of policy-making and day-to-day administration: 'the multidivisional structure [has] a general office whose executives . . . concentrate on entrepreneurial activities and . . . autonomous, fairly self-contained operating divisions whose managers . . . handle operational ones'. [11], p. 369.

Multidivisionalization is substituted in the expansion strategy for functional amplification. On the available evidence, significant advantages appear to have stemmed from this organizational innovation: control loss is minimized through a strong concentration of staff advisory and auditing (performance checks) functions centrally; the number of hierarchical levels, information flow and the size of the internal communication network are all reduced, and the 'psychological commitment' of the strategic decision-makers is more closely identified with the pursuit of enterprise goals. Moreover, a strong interaction is likely to develop, Williamson believes, between this form of internal organization and competition in the capital market: since it considers competing uses of capital by the divisions, the resulting allocation can be 'plausibly . . . represented as being made according to a profit maximization criterion' [30], thus more nearly performing the functions of a competitive capital market. The threat of takeovers by other M-form organizations (of which the 'conglomerate' is a special case) also acts to eradicate inefficient resource use. In sum, compared with other forms the M-form organization is likely to lead to increased competition (internalized) and efficiency in production and investment, but may be less progressive than *smaller* U-form firms in technical innovation, because of its different attitude towards risk (being more risk-averse).

If we accept the essence of the foregoing analysis, its main message for the management accountant would seem to be that business behaviour is a joint function of market organization and firm organizational structure.* Control systems will be more effective if they incorporate both sets of variables, and the interdependencies between them. In practical terms, this would imply a control system *considerably richer in the coverage and monitoring of exogenous variables*, and embodying *double-feedback* [3], [6]. The latter amounts in effect to formalizing the criteria and procedures for revision of budgets and standards and joining this to the conventional single-loop accounting control system.† One loop monitors performance and responds to *small* changes ('variances') in the variables by direct action at the operating level, without changing existing performance standards; the other acts on *large* changes at top management level by developing and implementing revised performance standards, a step-function response. This is just another way of saying that 'variances' between observed results and internal standards may reflect not only deficiencies in control but also failure of the environment to conform to management's expectations. The former should lead to corrective action, the latter to adaptation and possibly replanning [25]. According to Ashby [3], double feedback is a necessary condition to ensure that a system elicits fully adaptive behaviour. Apart from the formal difference referred to in its responses

---

* On the latter see also [12].

† Traditional accounting control systems are here characterized as single-loop systems not because the second loop does not exist at all, but because in terms of coverage of variables and frequency of monitoring this is the best first approximation.

to changes in kind, the other lesson from this, affirmed by other sources,* is that the boundaries of the control system must be extended to include all relevant external variables; the total system to be controlled must be correctly defined. Further, 'relevance' must here be interpreted in a way not customary in accounting, as meaning not only those elements of the environment which are subject to some degree of control by the firm, *but also elements normally regarded by the firm as non-controllable, because of the interaction between these and internal organizational factors.*

13.5 Alternative methods of control

Due to the general inability of outside forces collectively to control the behaviour of large complex enterprises *in the interests of efficiency*, the need increases to develop systems which tend to be self-regulating with respect to this objective. Subject to certain minor qualifications, Williamson considers the M-form enterprise comes closest to meeting this test at present.

The foregoing discussion leads to a rather different conception of control than that held by most accountants. Table 13.1 is an attempt to present a reasonably comprehensive picture of the spectrum of quantitative business controls of which existing forms of accounting control form a subset.† Assembly of this set has benefited considerably from Williamson's study [30] at certain obvious points, as well as incorporating our own classification of existing accounting controls, elaborated in Chapters 15–17.

Some of the items in this list are self-explanatory and will not be commented on. Thus categories (3) to (8) under 2(ii)(e) describe the usual accounting controls. Among the external controls, product (and factor) markets often exercise little control over the large enterprise and the capital market is only indirectly effective, since such firms seldom need to go to the market for funds.‡ 'Will-ful external control agents' describes any group outside of the firm which tries to enforce its expectations; it would include shareholders, creditors, the public at large, and various government regulatory agencies. By 'system' controls is meant the resource allocation functions of the product and capital markets which are internalized by the firm.§ Together with organization form, this bypassing of the market is a main source of managerial discretion. The 'other' category would include some of the things mentioned earlier such as fuller accounting disclosure.

Internal controls may be exercised in relation to external or internal criteria.

* E.g. [22].
† It needs to be remembered that there are qualitative as well as quantitative controls, an important example of the former being senior staff appointments. Maintaining a proper balance between the two is a central and constant problem of management – cf. [14].
‡ The indirect sanctions are described in [5].
§ They are regarded as external controls because market functions are only partially supplanted.

Table 13.1 Methods of control

1. *External controls*
    (i) Market control
       (a) Product market
       (b) Capital market
    (ii) Will-ful external control agents
    (iii) 'System' controls
    (iv) Other

2. *Internal controls*
    (i) By reference to external criteria
    (a) Response to interfirm cost, profit, rate of return, market share, etc., comparisons, preferably classified by firm size and type of organization structure
    (b) Anticipatory response to forecasts of general or local economic conditions
    (ii) By reference to internal criteria
    (a) Planning
    (b) Scheduling, supervision
    (c) Incentives (reward system)
    (d) Auditing (anticipatory and contemporaneous performance checks)
    (e) Response to *ex post.* feedback comparisons
       (1) automatic
       (2) statistical
       (3) technical standards
       (4) performance standards
       (5) via resource allocations
       (6) profitability measures
       (7) investment centre measures
       (8) aggregate (enterprise) comparisons
    (f) Response to intertemporal comparisons
    (g) Manipulation
    (h) Organizational innovation (step-function response)

Interfirm comparisons of various kinds are one example of the first sort. These are often not particularly helpful;* before making them an attempt should be made to ensure comparability as to firm size and organization form, at least. Management may also respond in an anticipatory way (or conceivably contemporaneously) to external conditions.

Planning is included as a method of control because a plan implies some sort of control to enforce it, and the plan becomes an integral part of this control. Scheduling and supervision are concerned with smoothing the flow of production, preventing bottlenecks and unnecessary idle time. The reward structure of the firm, encompassing methods of wage payment including 'payment by results', promotion and training policies, is an essential part of any control system. All controls must be less than fully effective if the reward structure is not geared to induce the desired performance, and completely useless if the two are mutually inconsistent. Performance checks by management ('auditing') need not be confined to the one-off, *ex post* kind exemplified in accounting controls. They may be contemporaneous or occur at the planning stage. Furthermore, as pointed out in [30], benefits in control

---

*Cf. [1], Chapter V.

may accrue from *repeated ex post* checks in response to *persistent* adverse 'variances'. The penultimate category refers to the feedback of deliberately distorted performance figures in an attempt to bring about closer conformance to plans.* The final item has been explained in the previous section.

13.6 Accounting controls

Not all controls are quantitative controls, and not all quantitative controls are accounting controls, although the latter, when coupled with planning, are the most important subset if they are effective and operate to increase efficiency. In this concluding section some observations will be offered on this subset as an introduction to the next five chapters.

(a) The dimensions of control

In the previous section we spoke of control as having an external as well as an internal dimension. In what follows, while keeping in mind the social viewpoint (control of the enterprise in the interests of economic efficiency) and the functional relationship between internal control and organizational structure, the focus will be on internal controls of the conventional type, i.e. related to internal standards. The former topics indicate some deficiencies in present systems (others will be mentioned in Chapter 18) and some directions for accounting research. Thus delimited, the dimensions of control comprise control over current operations (including control over physical as well as financial measures), control of finances, control over asset and claims structure and rate of growth of the firm.

(b) The accounting control continuum

Control measures consist of a variety of devices designed to bring about conformance with planned objectives. They operate subject to a multitude of constraints which should have been taken into account at the planning stage: resource availabilities, human abilities, existing technology, and environmental factors – the firm's competitors, government economic policies, legal and institutional requirements, and so on. Within the thus constrained opportunity set different activities will vary in their amenability to control, and some constraints will be more restrictive (shrink the opportunity set more) than others.

The major control devices used within the firm constitute a continuum, ranging from close to loose control, depending on the amenability to control of the activi-

*This is referred to again in Chapter 18.

ties in question. In Table 13.2, items (1) to (7) of the feedback controls listed in Table 13.1 are arrayed in descending order of degree of control:

Table 13.2 The feedback control continuum

---

(1) Automatic
    mechanical (e.g. a steam valve)
    biological (e.g. bees providing pollination for fruit trees)
    human (e.g. rules like 'when inventory falls to n units, reorder')
(2) Statistical (e.g. quality control)
(3) Technical standards (e.g. n lbs. of metal per widget)
(4) Performance standards (e.g. 5 widgets per direct labour-hour)
(5) Via resource allocation (spending allowances)
    (e.g. research and development, advertising expenditure; this form of
    control implies some subjective evaluation)
(6) Profitability measures (e.g. departmental contribution)
(7) Investment centre measures (e.g. divisional rate of return on investment)

The continuum relates not only to the degree of control which can be exercised, but also inevitably to the degree of responsibility delegated. The more difficult it is to provide detailed rules covering every eventuality, the more it becomes necessary to avoid detailed interference in areas where top management can neither legislate in advance nor get sufficiently rapid feedback to exercise centralized control.

The point at which a particular activity falls in the continuum is not determined for all time. Three major influences which may lead to changes in placement are:

1. Particularly technological, but sometimes organizational, changes designed to bring more activities towards the closely controlled end of the spectrum. Much of the thrust of technological innovation is designed to do precisely that (e.g. the development of machines to replace manual work, automation, O.R. techniques such as inventory control).

2. Changes in the firm's environment may force the firm to take a different stance on control areas, e.g. legislative action might require greater concern for technical standards, a competitor's action might lead to a change of emphasis from cost control to profitability control.

3. Changes within the firm, sometimes following indirectly upon environmental changes, may lead to a restructuring of controls. This is particularly evident with the growth in size and complexity of firms as we have seen, often producing a movement towards decentralization and divisionalization of operational functions with a simultaneous centralization of strategic decision-making [11], [30].

As a very broad generalization it might be said that as firms succeed in moving more activities and problems towards the 'tightly controlled' end of the spectrum there is a tendency for new 'loosely controllable' activities to appear at the other end, such things as multinational activities, diversification, and more complex technologies which are only partially understood by top management.

There is a brief reference to statistical control in Chapter 15 and to automatic control (viz. inventory control) in Chapter 19. The *control of time* (critical path analysis), often of vital importance in such activities as research and development, one of the elements in the 'control via resource allocation' group, and the joint control of time and cost (PERT/cost technique),* are discussed in Chapter 16.

(c) The main control techniques

The two principal accounting control techniques are known as budgetary control and standard costing. Each involves determining internal standards of performance and feeding back to those concerned comparisons of their actual results with these predetermined targets or norms. Control takes the form of *response* to these feedback comparisons. Deviations from target performance are called 'variances'.† Management acts on the principle of exceptions, i.e. only 'variances' of more than $\pm £x$, or more than $\pm x\%$, of the target figure are reported to top management, to be investigated and explained.

Historically, the first description of standard costing appeared in the USA in 1908, a little after the 'scientific management' movement (F. W. Taylor, Gantt, etc.), but was really part of the same development. Budgetary control, derived from governmental budgeting, had earlier beginnings. In the early stages the two techniques developed separately. Standard costing was applied in the factory, to production costs; budgetary control was applied to the financial aspect of the business. Later it was realized they were both applications of the same principle and were complementary to each other, part of a complete system of accounting control. The precise relationship between budgeted performance and standard performance, as represented in standard costs, depends on two things: first, on whether there are separate planning and control budgets, and secondly on whether or not target performance is defined identically in the budgets and standards (e.g. 'ideal' performance or 'currently attainable' performance in both cases). The budgets normally incorporate the standards. If the two do not coincide, the difference is reconciled by including the expected 'variance' between budgets and standards (called 'budget variance') in the budgets. The other difference between the two techniques relates to coverage. The budgets relate to the whole business (all activities, whether represented by cost, revenue, profit or investment centres);‡ standard costing *may* only relate to cost centre activities, and sometimes only to

---

* These techniques are described more fully in numerous texts and articles, e.g. [18], [29].

† Not to be confused with 'variance' in statistics; accounting 'variances' correspond to 'deviation' in statistics.

‡ These terms will be defined shortly.

manufacturing cost centres as in its early days, though it should be noted that the name is rather misleading, and that the technique can be and is applied to revenue, as well as cost, centres.

Apart from providing a means of financially controlling all activities within the business, it is claimed for budgetary control that it makes management think about the future – the alternative courses of action open to it, the constraints under which it is likely to operate – and to write down its thoughts in a systematic way. Everyone within the organization then knows, within limits, what is expected of them. The budgets thus represent an integrated plan of business operations, and a means of controlling these operations to ensure that, as far as possible and desirable, they conform with the plan. As stated earlier, the idea is to treat each cost, revenue, profit or investment centre as though it were a separate quasi-entrepreneur, *but in a way which is consistent with achievement of the firm's objective.* This means that in fixing the targets for individual activities allowance should be made for the fact that they are frequently not closed systems, but have interdependencies with other activities. In other words the system should encourage goal congruence: people at all levels of the organization should be made to realize that what appears to be best for their particular section is not necessarily best for the organization as a whole. The firm's reward structure has an important part to play in bringing this about. In Chapter 18 we will examine how well this aim is realized.

Control is not the only reason why many firms keep standard costs as well as a record of actual (*ex post*) costs, though it is the principal one. Standard costs, as we have seen, may be useful in the construction of budgets. Beyond this, attachment to the idea of a norm is often evident in actual business behaviour. In relation to costs the business man's norm reflects the ideal conditions under which he would wish to produce, rather akin to the economist's long-run minimum average cost. Some firms consider this norm (standard cost) provides a convenient basis for valuing inventories. And in the presence of uncertainties standard rather than actual costs are sometimes used as a basis for deciding what (provisional) prices to set and what to produce.

(d) The control process

The essentially single feedback control process employed in these techniques involves delineating the system to be controlled, partitioning it into 'responsibility centres', fixing performance standards for each of these, feeding back comparisons of actual and budgeted/standard performance, investigating the exceptions (variances of more than $\pm$...), and either taking direct corrective action on the variables concerned at the operating level or step-function action at top management level (including possibly revision of the performance standards).

We have already had occasion to comment on the boundaries of control, and will have more to say about this in Chapter 18. In budgetary control and standard costing as normally practised the boundary of control is coextensive with the boundaries of the firm. The organization is partitioned into responsibility centres, each of which is responsible for performing some activity as efficiently as possible. One of the problems in installing the control system is to fix the boundaries of these responsibility centres in the correct manner, the significance of which is explained in subsequent chapters. The responsibility centres comprise cost (or expense) centres, revenue centres, profit centres and investment centres, according to which of these is the measure of performance of the centre in question (i.e. whether the centre is *responsible* only for incurring costs, or for earning revenue, or both, or for the use of capital in addition to these, the latter usually being confined to the operating divisions of the multidivisional firm referred to earlier). Managers of profit and/or investment centres will usually have subsidiary cost and revenue centres reporting to them. In all cases accounting reports for control purposes need to be consistent with assigned responsibility at each level. The effectiveness of control depends not only on correctly designing the system and partitioning it into control areas (responsibility centres) but also on a correct interpretation of 'controllability'. In the feedback comparisons a centre should not be held responsible (asked to account) for something over which it has no control. Responsibility is sometimes a matter of degree; and in accounting controllability is usually interpreted as meaning that the centre in question has significant, though not necessarily complete, influence over the amount of the item concerned. Central to the two control techniques being discussed, therefore, is the distinction between *controllable and noncontrollable* items (costs, revenues, etc.). Noncontrollable items, by definition, are unaffected (or more precisely not significantly affected) by any possible action taken within that centre, though they may be included in the feedback reporting for information. *Controllability, therefore, only has meaning when related to a particular responsibility centre.*

Virtually all business organizations (except one-man businesses and small partnerships) are hierarchical in form. As Simon has pointed out [28], this is characteristic of all complex systems, almost universal. Each level of the pyramid controls the activities of its immediately lower level, and at the apex of the pyramid the ordinary shareholders in theory control the entire activities of the company through the board of directors, though it is significant that in practice shareholders' control of the boards of public companies is passive in most circumstances,* and effective control resides with management. Accounting reports communicate information about the activities controlled at each level of the pyramid. It follows from this pyramidal control structure that every activity is controllable by someone, i.e. at some level in the organization: in the limit an item can be controlled by

* I.e., the ordinary shareholders become 'will-ful control agents' only in exceptional circumstances.

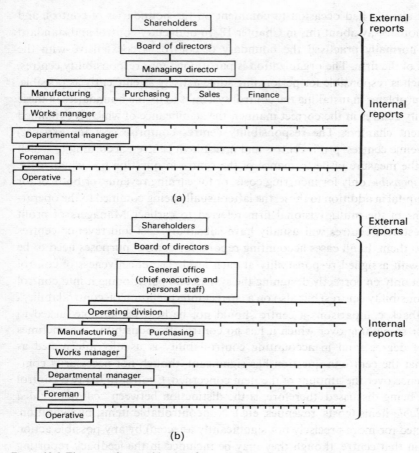

Figure 13.1 The control pyramid (a) U-form organization, (b) M-form organization

eliminating the activity which gave rise to it. At the topmost level all items are controllable.* The term 'controllable', then, refers strictly to a *particular* responsibility centre.

The other point arising from this has to do with the speed of control. Clearly if an item moves out of control in a way that is inconsistent with the firm's objective, the sooner it is brought back within the control limits the better. In accounting four periods are relevant to this discussion:

1. *The accounting period*, the period for which external reports are drawn up (typically one year).

* In the staff areas (fourth hierarchical level) the box marked 'Finance' can be thought of as embracing the accounting, finance and systems functions. Increasingly, however, the last two are being treated as separate functions in large companies.

2. *The budget period*, which usually coincides with the accounting period, though in some systems the budget estimates are reviewed at shorter intervals (e.g. quarterly, monthly), and possibly revised. More specifically, it is usual to prepare short-term (or operating) budgets, for which the period is typically one year, and which relate to production, financing and investment activity during this period, and long-term budgets, embodying the plans relating to these same activities for the more distant future.

3. *The costing period*, which is usually much shorter than the accounting and budget periods (e.g. monthly, even weekly), and

4. *The control period*, a variable period, defined as the shortest time in which intervention by management is feasible, i.e. the shortest period in which the effects of corrective action can be observed. The periodicity of control will vary as between and even within responsibility centres, depending on the time taken to adapt and the urgency of doing so (e.g. where the quality of the product is specified subject to minute tolerances, control must be almost continuous).

In other words, control reports must be timely to be useful, but timeliness is relative. As a very crude generalization, most accounting reports for a particular period would tend to be 'stale', and quite likely misleading as guides to action, after halfway through the next period (accounting, costing or control period, as the case may be).

Accounting information is, as a broad rule, increasingly condensed the higher one proceeds up the pyramid. At the base of the pyramid departmental managers and foremen need detailed information on the activity for which they are responsible. At the other end, the board of directors may require only highly condensed summaries for individual works or even divisions. Effective control carries the right of access to detailed information, but over-detailed control reports are likely to be neither fully read nor fully understood.

Attention needs to be drawn to the distinction between the costing period and control period. The costing period is the reporting period to top management, and is constant for all responsibility centres which are the subject of internal reports. The control period is the period of reporting to the person in charge of the responsibility centre concerned, and is variable as stated. The length of the control period, as a result of the factors mentioned in 4., usually varies at different levels of the pyramid. In general the lower levels require very rapid and relatively simple feedback of information for effective control of operations, while the higher one goes the longer the period of interest becomes. Top management is not interested in the minutiae of day-to-day operations (or should not be!), or with random short-term disturbances.

The precise meaning of control depends, of course, upon the nature of the norms (budget targets, standards) which are set, a question which is examined later. If, as a result of large disturbances experienced by the firm, bad estimating, or additional information coming into its possession, norms lose all meaning and no longer measure the performance it is sought to achieve, they may be changed during the budget period. Three systems are in use in this respect:

1. *Periodic budgeting*, in which the norms are never altered during the budget period.
2. *The interim revision system of budgeting*, in which systematic interim revisions are made during the budget period if the planning data change substantially ('systematic' means that the revisions include all consequential as well as direct changes).
3. *Continuous* (rolling, progressive) *budgeting*, a moving budget, in which budgets are revised every quarter, say, by adding one quarter and dropping one quarter – the same principle as is employed in a shifting planning horizon.*

Similar remarks concerning revision apply to standards as to budgets.†

(e) Plans and controls

In the previous section we alluded to the fact that it is not possible to say what control means, except in a superficial way, until we know what the planning data represent. The former question cannot be pursued until the latter one has been examined, in Chapter 15. Arising out of this there is another question, viz. whether budgets do double duty in practice, serving both as plans and as controls, and whether they should be expected to do so. That is, budgets may simultaneously serve as control devices and determine feasible programs, in each case defining 'in advance a set of fixed [resource allocations] and . . . fixed expectations'.‡

(f) Behavioural implications

We shall also need to consider the impact of budgets and standards on the people involved in the activities controlled who, unlike the other resource inputs, are not will-less; the relationship between their personal goals and those of the organization, and what motivates them in the direction of goal congruence. These matters are discussed in Chapter 18.

---

* See Chapter 6.
† See also the remarks on flexible budgets in Chapter 15.
‡ [13], pp. 110–11.

Bibliographical references

[1] Amey, L. R., *The Efficiency of Business Enterprises*, Allen and Unwin, 1969.
[2] Ashby, W. R., *An Introduction to Cybernetics*, John Wiley, 1956.
[3] Ashby, W. R., *Design for a Brain*, John Wiley, 2nd edn., 1960.
[4] Bain, J. S., *Industrial Organization*, John Wiley, 1959.
[5] Baumol, W. J., *The Stock Market and Economic Efficiency*, Fordham University Press, 1965.
[6] Beer, S., *Decision and Control*, John Wiley, 1966.
[7] Berle, A. A. and G. C. Means, *The Modern Corporation and Private Property*, Macmillan, New York, 1932.
[8] Boulding, K. E., The economics of knowledge and the knowledge of economics, *American Economic Review*, 58, May 1968, pp. 1–13.
[9] Burnham, J. H., *The Managerial Revolution*, Putnam, 1942.
[10] Chamberlin, E. H., Proportionality, divisibility and economies of scale, *Quarterly Journal of Economics*, 62, February 1948, pp. 229–262.
[11] Chandler, A. D., Jr., *Strategy and Structure*, Doubleday, Anchor Books edn., 1966.
[12] Churchman, C. W., *Prediction and Optimal Decision*, Prentice-Hall, 1961.
[13] Cyert, R. M. and J. G. March, *A Behavioral Theory of the Firm*, Prentice-Hall, 1963.
[14] Drucker, P. F., Controls, control and management, in *Management Controls: New directions in Basic Research*, eds. C. P. Bonini, R. K. Jaedicke and H. M. Wagner, McGraw-Hill, 1964.
[15] Emery, J. C., *Organizational Planning and Control Systems: Theory and Technology*, Macmillan, New York, 1969.
[16] Kaldor, N., The equilibrium of the firm, *Economic Journal*, 44, March 1934, pp. 70–71.
[17] Leibenstein, H., Allocative efficiency *versus* 'X-efficiency', *American Economic Review*, 56, Sept. 1966, pp. 392–415.
[18] Lockyer, K. G., *An Introduction to Critical Path Analysis*, Pitman, 2nd edn., 1967.
[19] March, J. G. and H. A. Simon, *Organizations*, John Wiley, 1958.
[20] Marshall, A., *Principles of Economics*, Macmillan, London, 8th edn., 1938.
[21] Penrose, E. T., *The Theory of the Growth of the Firm*, Basil Blackwell, 1959.
[22] Roberts, E. B., Industrial dynamics and the design of management control systems, in *Management Controls*, ed. Bonini *et al.* (see [14]).
[23] Robinson, E. A. G., The problem of management and the size of firms, *Economic Journal*, 44, June 1932, pp. 240–54.
[24] Ross, N. S., Management and the size of the firm, *Review of Economic Studies*, 19, 1952–53, pp. 148–54.
[25] Shillinglaw, G., Divisional performance review: An extension of budgetary control, in *Management Controls*, ed. Bonini *et al.* (see [14]).
[26] Simon, H. A., *Models of Man*, John Wiley, 1957.
[27] Simon, H. A., On the concept of organizational goal, *Administrative Science Quarterly*, 9, June 1964, pp. 1–22, reprinted in *Readings in Management Decision*, ed. L. R. Amey, Longman, 1973.
[28] Simon, H. A., *The Shape of Automation for Men and Management*, Harper and Row, 1965.
[29] US Department of Defence and NASA, *Guide to PERT/Cost systems design*, US Government Printing Office, June 1962.
[30] Williamson, O. E., *Corporate Control and Business Behavior*, Prentice-Hall, 1970.
[31] Williamson, O. E., *The Economics of Discretionary Behavior: Managerial Objectives in a Theory of the Firm*, Markham Publishing Co., 1967.

Problems

13.1 Farmer Giles is a wheat grower. 'The price of my product is determined in the market,' he says; 'therefore there is no need for me to calculate my costs.' What would be your reply?

13.2 How does management accounting differ from financial accounting?

13.3 'All controllable costs are direct costs, but not all direct costs are controllable.' Discuss.

13.4 'Accounting control systems should encourage goal congruence.' Explain this statement. Do the systems operated by actual firms usually succeed in meeting this condition? If not, what needs to be done to ensure that they do?

13.5 Individual budgets should be mutually consistent technically, physically, financially, dynamically and economically. Explain.

13.6 Control is a matter of degree. It is also a function of speed of response. What does this suggest to you concerning the 'variances' that the accountant normally labels 'noncontrollable' because they originate outside the firm?

13.7 '[In economic theory] the firm was constructed much in the fashion of the atom in classical physics. No effort was made to pierce the interior; that is, the atom itself was not regarded as a subject of study.' Accounting took a diametrically different view. Discuss the implications of these statements.

13.8 'In the field of organization, the knowledge on which what we call responsible control depends is not knowledge of situations and problems and of means for effecting changes, but is knowledge of other men's knowledge of these things ... so fundamental is it for understanding the control of organized activity, that the problem of judging men's powers of judgement overshadows the problem of judging the facts of the situation to be dealt with. And if this is true of knowledge it is manifestly true of uncertainty.' – F. H. Knight.

Do you agree with this assertion that qualitative controls are more important to the top management of a firm than quantitative controls?

13.9 Carefully examine the influence of organizational structure on the problem of corporate control.

14

Cost accumulation

. . . if cost accounting sets out, determined to discover what the cost of everything is and convinced in advance that there is one figure which can be found . . . which will furnish exactly the information which is desired for every possible purpose, it will necessarily fail, because there is no such figure.

J. MAURICE CLARK [3]

14.1 The elements of cost recording

The routine recording of accounting data provides the raw material from which accounting information is developed. For information to be available for summarization and presentation to management, data must first be recorded and accumulated in an accessible manner.

The bulk of accounting data concerning activities of the firm relates to costs, and so the activity of providing accounting data on the internal operations of the firm is termed *cost accounting* or *costing*. Only in recent years has cost accounting blossomed into management accounting; the latter title has come to mean much more than cost recording, but concern with costs still remains central to internal accounting functions.

Although our consideration of cost accumulation leads to later chapters concerned with accounting for control purposes, the routine recording of costs does in fact assist in all three major accounting areas of providing data for decisions, control and external reporting. Recorded past costs can provide a *starting point* for making cost estimates for decision making. Control can be served by the provision of a readily available record of costs as work proceeds, although the use of such data for control purposes implies some assessment of what costs ought to be. Finally the accumulation of costs permits the matching of costs against related revenues in the profit calculation for external reporting.

The diverse uses of routinely recorded cost data give rise to a fundamental danger: information prepared for one purpose can be grossly misleading in another context. The danger can be avoided by regarding the routinely recorded costs as providing a data bank from which relevant selections must be made to suit the needs of the user. This data bank viewpoint will be referred to again later; initially the mechanics of recording will be examined.

Routine cost recording is built on two basic techniques. The resulting system can be exceedingly complex, but the foundations are simple: they are double entry accounts and the 'spreading' of costs to accounts by means of some averaging calculation.

Cost accumulation

(a) Double entry for cost recording

The double entry accounting system can be elaborated to any desired extent by inserting accounts into which costs are recorded, subdivided, and summarized before eventual transfer to the profit calculation. Elaboration is usually achieved by splitting off the cost accounts from the financial accounts while concurrently maintaining a 'control account' in the financial ledger to summarize what is going on in the costing system. The detailed costing for segments of the firm can thus be conducted in subsidiary accounts.

For example, the data for Cog Ltd. in the financial accounts originally shown in Table 2.2 could be elaborated in the following manner for cost purposes:

Table 14.1 Cost recording

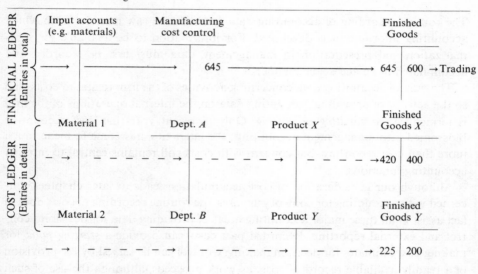

Thus the cost recording system is subsidiary to the financial accounting system in a technical double entry sense. Unfortunately the seductive symmetry of double entry can lead to the cost system being subordinated in a conceptual sense also, because financial accounting conventions for external reporting require certain information from the costing system – particularly total product cost per unit for stock valuation purposes. Some accountants use the external reporting conventions as an excuse for rigidity in their management accounting information, but in fact financial accounting requirements need never prevent management information requirements from being equally well served. Double entry is a very flexible technique and a multiplicity of data can be collected and summarized within the cost system in different ways; the use of computers is eliminating the only valid argument which ever existed against multiple summarization, that of expense. Even so, the accountant must never forget that double entry is merely a technique;

402

if the technique gets in the way of serving management information needs it is always possible to record memorandum data entirely outside the double entry system and a great deal of management information gets produced in that manner.

(b) Averaging in cost accumulation

Much of the routine collection of cost data depends on an averaging process of some sort. In the most simple situation physical units of production constitute the denominator in the averaging process: more elaborate strategems will be considered involving such terms as 'proration', 'absorption' and 'activity index'. The major danger of averaging is that the result may be interpreted as *the* cost of something: there is nothing intrinsically wrong with averaging costs, provided the calculation is suited to its purposes and elaborate jargon does not mislead the user (or the preparer) into believing that something more elaborate is afoot.

Before the cost accountant can employ his basic recording techniques he must have answers to some interrelated questions which are crucial to the information which will emerge from the recording process. The questions are posed here to provide an overview which will be illustrated in Figure 14.1: later sections of this chapter will consider more fully how the questions may be answered.

(i) *Cost centres*

What accounts should be set up for the accumulation of costs?

An account will be set up for each *cost centre*; a cost centre is the basic unit for cost accumulation and it simply represents any segment of the firm for which costs are to be routinely recorded. A cost centre can be a job (building a bridge), a product category (Mark II refrigerators), a machine (No. 2 lathe), a process (paint spraying), a department producing goods (the cake department) or a department producing services (the accounting department).

It will be useful to have some general terms to describe cost centres which are operating segments of the firm (e.g. the paint spray shop or the accounting department) as opposed to cost centres which represent products (e.g. Mark II refrigerators). These terms are

Production centre: a segment of the firm in which production is undertaken and for which costs are routinely recorded;
Service centre: a segment of the firm which provides services to other segments of the firm and for which costs are routinely recorded.

A major reason for distinguishing in costing between production and service centres is that physical production (whether of final or intermediate output) is usually easier to quantify than the provision of services: for the present we shall concentrate on the former.

Cost accumulation

The choice of cost centres will be determined partly by technology and partly by judgment. The nature of the cost centre (what the segment does and what it is called) will depend upon the technology of the firm; the number of cost centres (the degree of segmentation for recording) will be the result of judgment on the information and organization needs of the firm, balanced against the expense of providing detailed data. Sections 2, 3 and 4 consider some basic types of cost centre.

(ii) Cost classification

The problem of cost classification can be expressed as: 'how should costs be split into categories for the routine recording of costs?'

The answer depends on the nature of the information sought from the recording process. Most cost classifications used in accounting are simple dichotomies distinguishing between costs which have some characteristics of particular interest to the user or the preparer of the information, and costs which do not have that characteristic: not all cost dichotomies are adaptable to routine recording however. The most widely adopted classification for routine cost accumulation is the division between *direct* and *indirect* costs; this distinguishes between direct costs which are traced directly to a production centre *or* to units of output, and those indirect costs which are not so traced. (Note that this cost dichotomy, as defined here, concerns the manner of data preparation and not the behaviour of costs.) The direct (traced) costs are those uniquely identified with the activities of the account to which they are charged – say the cost of clay and the wages paid to the potter in the manufacture of pottery. The indirect costs are those incurred for the common benefit of several activities (say the rent paid for a multiproduct factory); consequently they are often termed *common costs* or *overhead costs*. Such costs may be averaged over the activities which are considered to benefit from the expenditure.

The use of the term direct cost for *either* costs traced directly to production centre *or* for costs traced to a specific product is a source of confusion in cost terminology. In order to avoid ambiguity the following definitions will be adopted:

Traced segment cost: costs traced to a segment of business operations (e.g. to a production centre);

Direct product cost: costs traced to a specific product or units of output.

An example of a traced segment cost is the salary of a supervisor who works in a production centre. The cost of raw materials used in one of the products of the centre would be a direct product cost.

(iii) Proration of costs between production centres

If overhead costs incurred for the common benefit of production centres are to be assigned to those centres by some averaging process, what denominators are to be used in averaging?

404

Any firm with two or more production centres will almost inevitably incur some costs for the common benefit of those centres. How such costs may be assigned to the centres and whether any meaning can be attached to the resulting calculation will be considered more fully in section 6; for the present an example of the mechanics of calculation will be sufficient.

Rent paid for a factory occupied by several production centres might be divided between the centres in proportion to the square feet of floor-space occupied by each centre. The rationale behind this assignment is a desire to charge each centre for its use of the firm's resources. But note that cubic capacity (i.e. cubic feet occupied) might appear a more rational basis if storage were important to the centres. What if one centre occupies an old and badly designed part of the building – should it be charged less? It will be evident that selection of any such assignment basis involves arbitrary choice. Assignment procedures of this kind will be defined as:

Proration: the assignment of indirect costs between cost centres.*

The term *allocation* is commonly used to describe such assignment, but it is also used to describe the tracing of segment costs *or* the assignment to cost centres or products of any costs which are not direct product costs (i.e. both proration and the tracing of segment costs). Allocation is used in this book only in the last and widest sense; allocated costs are therefore all costs assigned to a cost centre or product which are not direct product costs.

(iv) *Absorption of costs over units of output*

Most firms calculate a cost per unit of output which includes both direct product costs and elements of overhead costs. This is the total product cost referred to earlier, which is often termed simply *product cost*. Such a figure is very widely used for inventory valuation purposes in external reporting, which provides a major reason for its calculation; even for external reporting purposes its validity is questionable.

The reasoning behind the approach is that each unit of output benefits from both direct and indirect cost expenditures, and costs should therefore be *absorbed* over output proportionately to use of resources. Thus the term:

Absorption costing: the assignment to goods or services produced of all costs relating in any way to the production or acquisition of those goods or services.

Absorption is another method of averaging costs, similar to proration, but this time costs are assigned *pro rata* to units of output instead of to production centres. Two questions arise on the employment of the method (its validity is examined later).

*The term is also applied to the assignment of costs over units of output. Proration tends to be an American usage (e.g. see [11]); the corresponding common British term is apportionment (e.g. see [9]). The former has been adopted here as indicating the *pro rata* nature of the calculation.

Cost accumulation

(v) *Which costs are considered eligible for averaging?*
The definition of absorption costing indicates that any expenditures which can be considered to be for the benefit of production are eligible for absorption. Thus in broad terms the lines are drawn:

Eligible
- Manufacturing costs
  - Direct costs — e.g. direct labour, material
  - Indirect manufacturing costs — e.g. rent, depreciation
- General and administration expenditure — e.g. company management salaries, personnel training, accounting costs

Ineligible
- Financial expenses — e.g. interest on debt
- Selling expenses — e.g. salesmen's commission, advertising

The division between 'eligible' and 'ineligible' costs above is determined by financial accounting conventions. The eligible items represent the maximum costs which are conventionally acceptable for inclusion in cost of inventories for external reporting purposes; the minimum conventionally acceptable costs for external reporting are the direct costs.* In fact the overwhelming majority of companies average indirect manufacturing costs over output for the valuation of inventories; the absorption of administrative costs is not common and at the other extreme the use of only direct cost for inventory valuation is extremely rare.† Consequently manufacturing costs constitute the costs generally adopted for calculating product cost, and the resulting cost per unit of output is often called *manufacturing cost* or *factory cost*. The inventory aspects of cost determination are considered in the appendix to this chapter.

The external reporting conventions need not influence the calculation of costs for control or decision purposes, but the fact that external reporting requirements lead to the calculation of a readily available figure, coupled with the entrenched mystique that product cost somehow represents *the* cost of producing a unit of output means that conventionally determined product cost is frequently used in control situations (see Chapter 15) and in decision situations (see Chapter 9).

(vi) *How is averaging conducted?*
A production centre which produces *homogeneous* units of output poses few

---

* This refers to permissibility under British conventions (see [6]), but the direct cost minimum is in the process of being made unconventional – see [7]. North American conventions do not favour direct cost, even when that term is used in the different sense of a variable cost. See [4] for a discussion from the external reporting viewpoint.
† See [2] and [8].

calculation difficulties: the total costs which have been assigned to that centre can be averaged over the physical output of the centre. Thus a production centre producing a single type of chair might have total assigned costs of £10 000 and output of 2 000 chairs* in an accounting period: the average cost per chair (product cost) is clearly £10 000/2 000 = £5.

For production centres which produce *heterogeneous* units of output it is necessary to find some common denominator if costs are to be averaged over different types of product. If a production centre with total assigned costs of £30 800 had produced 2 000 chairs and 2 000 desks an average product cost of £7·70 per unit would ignore the fact that one product might require greater resource inputs than the other. A different approach than averaging total costs over total units is needed, and will be demonstrated in Table 14.2.

The approach for *direct* product costs in the heterogeneous output situation is quite simple: direct product costs can be traced to their respective product accounts.

The *indirect* product costs (consisting of both traced segment costs identified with the production centre and costs prorated to the production centre) can only be assigned to the products in proportion to some common measure of the volume of operations devoted to each product. An output measure is not usually available: clearly it is because one desk is not equivalent to one chair for cost purposes that a cost assignment problem existed at all in the previous example. In the absence of a common output measure an *input* measure is used instead. A popular device is the use of *direct labour hours* (DLH) as a measure of volume: this implies that if workers directly involved in the production process spend one hour in producing a chair and three hours in producing a desk, the second product consumed three times as much overhead resources (rent, depreciation, etc.) as the first. In this manner, if the total direct labour hours of the furniture production centre were 8 000 the cost of the centre might be divided as shown in Table 14.2.

Thus the basis for measuring the volume of operations in routine cost recording may be either a measure of output (e.g. the number of units produced in a homogeneous output situation) or a measure of input (e.g. the hours of labour spent on production in the heterogeneous output situation). A general term encompassing both types of measure is:

Activity index†: a measure of volume of operations.

This completes the overview of the elements of cost recording to which the reader has been subjected: later sections of this chapter will expand on the concepts which

---

* Partly finished items can be accommodated in one of two ways. The specific direct costs of a partly finished batch may be routinely recorded – and indirect costs can be assigned proportionately. Alternatively an estimate can be made, based on physical inspection, of the proportion of expected inputs which have been incurred so far – e.g. a chair might be treated as half finished for the averaging of labour and indirect costs.

† Alternative terms are *activity factor* and *index of volume*.

Table 14.2 Indirect costs assigned to products

Furniture production department costs, £		Chairs, £	Desks, £
Direct costs:			
chairs	7 000	7 000	
desks	11 800		11 800
Indirect costs	12 000	3 000	9 000
Calculation:			

$$\left[\dfrac{£12\,000}{8\,000} = \dfrac{£1\cdot50}{\text{per DLH}}\right] \qquad \left[\begin{array}{c} 2\,000 \text{ units at} \\ 1 \text{ hour} = 2\,000 \\ \text{DLH} \\ 2\,000 \times £1\cdot50 = £3\,000 \end{array}\right] \qquad \left[\begin{array}{c} 2\,000 \text{ units at} \\ 3 \text{ hours} = 6\,000 \\ \text{DLH} \\ 2\,000 \times £1\cdot50 = £9\,000 \end{array}\right]$$

	£30 800	£10 000	£20 800
Product cost per unit		$\dfrac{£10\,000}{2\,000} = £5\cdot00$	$\dfrac{£20\,800}{2\,000} = £10\cdot40$

have been introduced. The overview is summarized in Figure 14.1 which illustrates the essential components of a conventional cost recording system.

14.2 Process costing

Process costing is the name given to the recording of costs for production centres which have homogeneous output. As the name implies, costs are recorded for a particular process – but that is the same as recording product cost information, because the costs of process and product coincide in the homogeneous output situation.

Process costing is particularly appropriate to the mass production of standardized products, where production facilities turn out the same product day after day: chemical processing, some food manufacturing, and iron and steel manufacturing are examples of industries where the technique is applicable. Note that products do not have to be identical in all *physical* characteristics in order to be eligible for process costing: the criterion is homogeneity of *cost* characteristics. Vanilla ice cream is not the same as strawberry ice cream, but the lack of operating cost differences in their production would permit an ice cream manufacturer to treat them as homogeneous for product costing. Often slight differences in cost characteristics of different products are ignored and products are treated as homogeneous in order to simplify the cost recording system: implicitly someone within the firm has decided that the benefits from more elaborate information are worth less than the cost of providing it.

Many processes within industrial firms are not independent, but form part of a series of interconnected processes which lead to the production of final output.

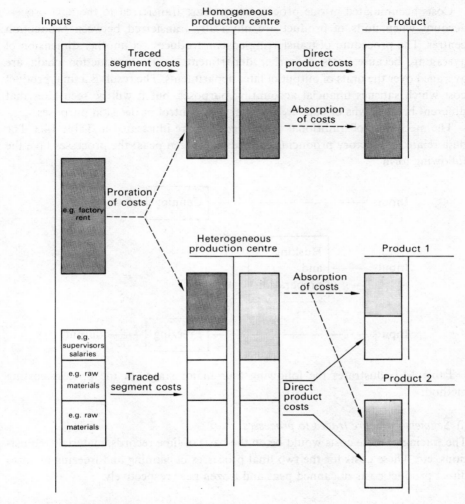

Figure 14.1 Conventional cost recording system

Process costing is commonly applied to the intermediate processes whose products are transferred largely or even entirely to other processes within the firm. For example, a simplified series of processes for the production of cotton cloth would be:

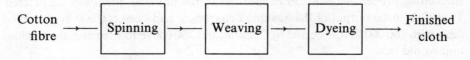

409

Cost accumulation

Costs accumulated in one process account are transferred to the next process account when units of product are physically transferred between production centres. The procedure of transferring costs introduces yet another dimension of averaging, because costs of earlier departments in the production chain are averaged over the units of output of later departments. The result is a final product cost which satisfies financial accounting purposes, but it will be seen later that different breakdowns of data are necessary for control or decision purposes.

The mechanics of traditional process costing are illustrated in Table 14.3. The data relate to a factory producing canned and frozen peas: the processes take the following form:

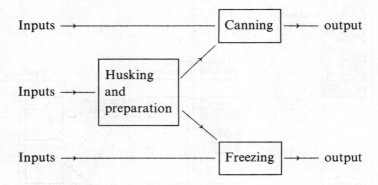

Table 14.3 illustrates the following four major stages in the process costing method.

(i) *Segment costs are traced to processes*

The tracing of these costs would be on the basis of time records, materials requisitions, etc. These costs for the two final processes of canning and freezing are also direct product costs of canned peas and frozen peas respectively.

(ii) *Overhead costs are prorated*

The overhead costs here might include such items as factory rent, staff wages (e.g. factory manager) and service centre costs (e.g. maintenance and timekeeping). For a fuller description of proration see section 6.

(iii) *Costs are transferred between processes*

Costs of completed production are transferred from the husking department to the succeeding process accounts in proportion to the physical quantities transferred. Thus if the total output of the husking department had been 600 000 lb of husked peas, with 400 000 lb transferred to Canning and 200 000 lb to Freezing, the calculation would be:

410

Table 14.3 Double entry for process costing

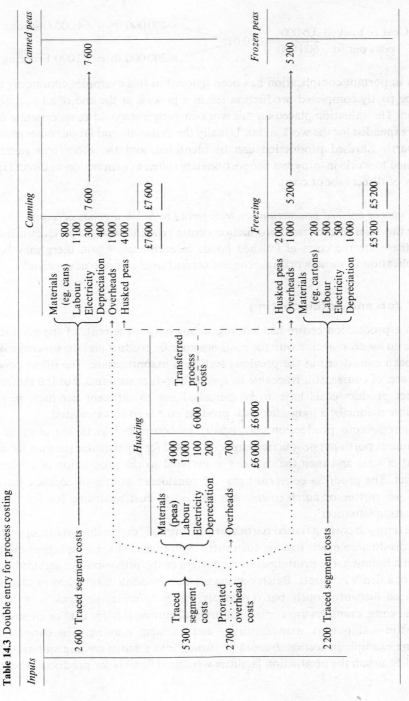

$$\text{Cost of husked} \atop \text{peas per lb} \quad \frac{£6\,000}{600\,000} = £0{\cdot}01 \begin{cases} \times\,400\,000\ \text{lb} = £4\,000\ \text{Canning} \\ \times\,200\,000\ \text{lb} = £2\,000\ \text{Freezing} \end{cases}$$

An important complication has been ignored in this example: commonly there will be partly completed production left in a process at the end of an accounting period. The valuation placed on this work-in-progress would be an estimate of the costs expended for the work so far. Usually the materials and labour costs incurred for partly finished production can be identified, and the other cost items are assigned to work-in-progress proportionately (often in proportion to direct labour hours or direct labour cost).

(iv) *Costs of finished production are transferred to finished goods accounts*
Since the costs of each final production centre relate to a single product it is clear that these are the costs of finished goods in each case. Again there may be the complication of some work-in-progress carried over into the next period.

14.3 Job and batch costing

When a production centre has heterogeneous output the costs of the production centre no longer coincide with the costs of a specific product and the process costing approach considered in the previous section is inappropriate. The direct product costs are, of course, still traceable to specific product accounts, but the remaining indirect product costs have to be parcelled out to different products in some plausible manner if a figure for total product cost is to be calculated.

Heterogeneous production can usually be considered as taking place in discontinuous portions: production capacity is used for a particular product for some period of time and then the capacity is diverted to the production of a different product. The products concerned may be considered as jobs or batches, thus the terms *job costing* or *batch costing* are applied to cost recording for the discrete production situation.

The term job costing is used particularly in 'one-off' or 'custom-made' operations when production meets specific customer requirements: for example the construction of a building, the printing of some posters or the provision of a service like the audit of a firm's accounts. Batch costing is an appropriate term when products are produced discontinuously but repeatedly, either to replenish stock or to satisfy orders: some examples are component manufacturing (say for cars or electronics), glassware and pottery manufacturing and garment making. The canning and freezing example in section 2 could be turned into a batch costing situation if (as would be usual) the production facilities were used flexibly for products other than peas.

The approach to double entry recording for job costing and batch costing can be illustrated by a single example. The chairs/desks data from section 1 could be recorded as batches of chairs and desks were completed, along the lines illustrated in Table 14.4; sources of the £12 000 indirect costs have been arbitrarily assumed for the present purpose.

Table 14.4 Double entry for batch costing

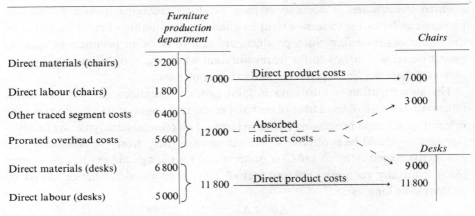

	Furniture production department			Chairs
Direct materials (chairs)	5 200 ⎫	7 000	Direct product costs →	7 000
Direct labour (chairs)	1 800 ⎭			3 000
Other traced segment costs	6 400 ⎫	12 000	Absorbed indirect costs	
Prorated overhead costs	5 600 ⎭			*Desks*
Direct materials (desks)	6 800 ⎫	11 800	Direct product costs →	9 000
Direct labour (desks)	5 000 ⎭			11 800

The stages in the job/batch costing approach are similar to those in the process costing situation, but one additional stage is added: the indirect costs of the production centre are 'absorbed' over the products emerging from the centre on the basis of an activity index. It will be recalled that direct labour hours were used as an activity index in the furniture department case.

14.4 Joint product costing

The previous section stated that heterogeneous production can usually be considered as taking place in a discontinuous manner, with operating capacity being diverted to one product after another. Joint products provide the exception: these are two or more products which are produced concurrently as the result of the technology of a production process.

Commonly joint products are produced together because the production process is essentially the separation of natural raw materials into component elements: for example, the conversion of milk into cream and skim milk, carcases into meat and hides, mineral ore into, say, zinc and copper, coal into gas and coke. Sometimes joint products are produced together as a result of the technology adopted in a particular production process, as with electricity and water for irrigation from a hydroelectric dam or electricity and heated water from a nuclear power plant. The essential characteristic of all the preceding examples is that neither product of each pair could be produced independently of the other once the technological set-up had been decided. The fact that some joint product (say zinc or gas or electricity) *could* be produced independently by another method is irrelevant to the costing of the existing production centre (although obviously such an alternative is relevant in assessing opportunities).

Often the *relative proportions* of joint products emerging from a production process can be varied to some extent by changing the quality of input materials or the extent of processing. Such products are said to be 'joint products in variable proportions', in contrast to the (rare) situation where the proportions are immutable and there are 'joint products in fixed proportions'.

The accumulation of cost data in joint product situations can provide useful information for analysis of overall cost and revenue changes arising from variations in input quality and processing effort. In terms of incremental analysis, any production change would be profitable where the revenue (ΔR_x) from the enhanced joint product(s) exceed(s) the cost (ΔC) of undertaking the change *and* any loss in revenue (ΔR_y) from any reduced joint product(s). Thus a production change would be profitable as long as:

$$\Delta R_x - \Delta R_y > \Delta C.$$

Data which may be of assistance in such an evaluation can be obtained from routinely recorded cost information by examining past cost and output changes. Unfortunately conventional joint product costing has the much more ambitious aim of providing *the* cost per unit of each joint product for financial reporting purposes, because financial accounting requires a cost figure for finished goods held at the end of the accounting period. Therefore joint product costing is concerned with finding the separate costs of products which cannot be produced separately: it is hardly surprising that the resulting figures are at best arbitrary and at worst misleading. The three most commonly adopted methods for calculating joint product costs will be considered in turn.

(a) Costs assigned proportionately to some physical characteristic

The physical characteristics chosen are commonly weight or volume, although even pseudo-scientific bases like the atomic weight of the joint products have been used.

For a creamery which separated 10 000 gallons of milk into 1 000 gallons of cream and 9 000 gallons of skim milk a simplified division of costs in proportion to the volume of the joint product would look like Table 14.5.

It might seem that skim milk caused a loss of £540, which points to the ludicrous

Table 14.5 Joint product costing – physical characteristics

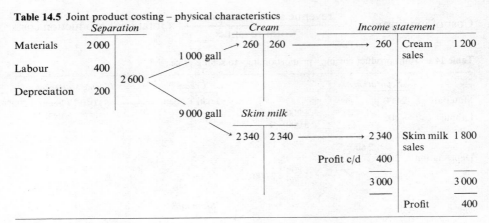

	Separation		*Cream*			*Income statement*	
Materials	2 000		→ 260	260 ⟶	→ 260	Cream sales	1 200
		1 000 gall					
Labour	400	2 600					
Depreciation	200						
		9 000 gall	*Skim milk*				
			→ 2 340	2 340 ⟶	→ 2 340	Skim milk sales	1 800
				Profit c/d	400		
					3 000		3 000
						Profit	400

conclusion that the creamery should cease producing skim milk but should continue to produce cream. Nobody would reach such a conclusion in this simple case but more complex situations involving interconnected production departments and/or inventories can lead to more serious misunderstandings.

There was no inventory in the above example: consider what would have been the income of the creamery if half the cream had been refrigerated and carried forward for sale in the next period. The income statement would look like this:

Sales		£2 400
Production costs	2 600	
Less inventory at end	130	
Cost of goods sold		2 470
Loss for period		£70

This income statement gives an unduly dismal picture of the creamery operations if the cream is saleable at current prices without depressing next period's activities. With this approach to joint product costing inventory level fluctuations can play havoc with calculations of operating profit.

(b) Costs assigned proportionately to selling price

Costs may be assigned in proportion to actual revenues obtained during a period, although rather more commonly assignment is made proportional to 'normal' selling prices which are reviewed periodically.

Using the creamery example again, the joint product 'costs' could be calculated:

$$\text{Cost of joint product} = \frac{\text{revenue from joint product}}{\text{total revenue}} \times \text{total joint production costs}$$

Table 14.6 Joint product costing – proportionately to selling price

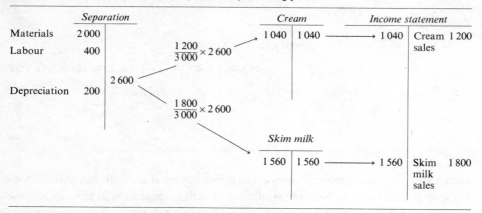

The result is that both products show profits (£160 and £240), which strangely represent identical profit percentages of $13\frac{1}{3}$ per cent on sales. Or is it so strange, when the calculation has been set up to charge costs proportionately to sales revenue?

As a method of arriving at a conventionally acceptable figure for external reporting and profit measurement this approach does have the advantage of producing a stock valuation which is related to market values. On this basis a global income statement for the joint products as a whole will be more related to economic reality than if 'cost' of stocks were determined on the physical basis previously considered. Assuming, as before, that half the cream were carried forward as refrigerated stock, the creamery's income statement would become:

Sales		£2 400
Production costs	2 600	
Less inventory at end	520	
Cost of goods sold		2 080
Profit of period		£320

For management information within the firm, however, the division of joint product costs cannot give meaningful data on the relative profitability of joint products because joint products have no relative profitability: either they are profitable together or they are not profitable at all.

(c) Major product and by-products

One product is designated as the major product to which all costs are assigned. Other products are termed 'by-products' and the full saleable value of the by-products is deducted from the costs of the major product: thus the cost of producing the by-products is always considered to be equal to the revenue received from them. More than one product may be designated as major, but that would merely require an additional division of costs between the major joint products on the lines of either method (a) or method (b) above.

Usually the by-products are chosen because they contribute relatively small amounts to total revenues of the joint products. What is small is a matter of judgment, but a rational approach would be to designate as by-products only those products which would have no effect on the level of joint production even if their selling prices fell to zero.* Clearly a product is peripheral to production activity if it will be produced at the same level irrespective of the revenue which can be obtained from it. Examples of such by-products would be scrap metal and filings in an engineering works, or straw from grain production.

In the creamery example it is unreasonable to regard cream (the smaller revenue earner) as a by-product under any usual meaning of the term, but it will be useful to remain with the creamery to illustrate the treatment of the same data by different methods. The mechanics of the cost calculation are shown in Table 14.7.

Table 14.7 Joint product costing – major product and by-product

	Separation of skim milk		By-product (cream)		Income statement	
Materials	2 000					
	1 200	By-product 'cost' → 1 200	Cream 1 200 sales			
Labour	400					
Depreciation	200					
	1 400	Major product 'cost' → 1 400			Sales	1 800
				Profit c/d	400	
				1 800		1 800
					Profit	400

The resulting cost figure of £1 400 for skim milk has no more meaning than any of the previous cost figures: production was not undertaken merely to produce skim milk and the cost figure is influenced as much by the current price of cream as by the operations of the separating department. With a more realistic by-product earning

*See [12].

417

a very small part of the revenue these objections would become less important: the by-product approach is justifiable when the by-product is so insignificant as to be irrelevant to consideration of the major product.

The examples of recording joint product costs have not explicitly shown costs identifiable specifically with one product, such as packing, further processing, etc. Such costs are not, of course, joint costs but direct costs of the particular joint product. Assignment to product accounts would occur in the usual way, and would not involve the problems discussed above.

14.5 Cost classifications for routine recording

So far consideration has been confined to the traditional direct/indirect cost classification of routine recording. The problems which arise from this classification can be seen by examining a widely accepted definition:

> Direct costs are those costs obviously traceable to a unit of output or a segment of business operations [1].

Indirect costs are those which are not direct.

Three major difficulties arise from this classification.

1. Costs which are 'obviously traceable' are not necessarily traced. The glue used in manufacturing batches of tables could be measured for each batch (or even each table) and its cost traced for each unit of output, but the expense of recording on such a detailed scale would certainly outweigh the benefits of the information obtained. Therefore such inconvenient items are treated as *indirect* costs and are not traced.

   The term traceable was avoided in section 1 by using direct costs to mean those which were treated as such by the firm. This meaning (direct = traced) is adopted throughout this book, and is commonly adopted in the literature.

2. For the production centre which has homogeneous output the costs traced to that segment of the business are the direct costs of the units of output produced. There is no such complete identity between heterogeneous output and the traced segment costs of the heterogeneous production centre, as was seen in section 3. This, of course, is a central problem of traditional cost recording, for which absorption costing is the usual answer.

3. 'Costs obviously traceable to a unit of output' can have an altogether different meaning from those suggested for direct cost so far: such costs could be those which were incurred *because* that unit of output was produced. In this sense it is similar to the economist's marginal cost (see section 4 of Chapter 6); it is not quite the same however, because routine cost recording at its most sophisticated cannot calculate the additional cost incurred for each unit but

418

only an estimate of *average* additional costs per unit. The accountant's version of this last concept was defined as *variable* cost in Chapter 10, and that term will be retained.

The variable/fixed cost classification is a major alternative to the traditional direct/indirect split, and a much more attractive classification for providing management information. The crucial difference is that the variable/fixed dichotomy relates to the behaviour of costs under certain assumptions, whereas direct/indirect relates to the behaviour of accountants in choosing which costs to 'trace'. Some of the short-run decision uses of variable/fixed cost data were examined in Chapter 10; it is also important to have some estimate of variable cost for control purposes, as will become apparent later.

Like any two-way division of costs, the variable/fixed split involves some arbitrariness in recording. It will be recalled that the division can only be applied with any meaning over some given range of output, which in the routine recording situation is some 'normal' range of output: in the final analysis all categories of cost would be susceptible to change if the implied output range were big enough.

It was seen in Chapter 10 that the costs which do not fit easily into either fixed or variable compartments are of two kinds:

Semi-variable costs: those cost items which are partially fixed and partially variable;

Step costs: those costs which change in a stepwise function with output.

Semi-variable costs can be divided into their variable and fixed components: this division can take place as part of the routine recording function or it may be done outside the records in a purely memorandum manner at the end of an accounting period. For example, payment for electricity used may entail a fixed charge on a time basis plus some charge proportionate to the electricity used. In this case it would be relatively easy to make a division on a routine recording basis (i.e. fixed electricity charge and variable electricity charge) because the amounts are invoiced by some outside supplier.

Much more difficult are items like maintenance and depreciation, for which the division between variable and fixed costs is not evidenced by any invoice. Some minimum fixed maintenance is normally necessary to keep even unused machines in working order, and additional variable maintenance is required as use increases. Depreciation is similarly eligible for division between retainer cost and a user cost variable with output (see section 7 of Chapter 3). For routine recording purposes, however, the division is not commonly made: maintenance is usually regarded as entirely fixed and depreciation almost invariably so.

In the opposite direction the cost of labour employed directly in production often entails an element of fixed cost, where there is some guaranteed wage irrespective of output levels and/or redundancy is an impractical means of adjusting to output fluctuations. Nevertheless direct labour usually gets treated as a variable cost.

Step costs are forced into the nearest applicable category. They are treated as fixed costs when the output distance between cost changes is relatively large (e.g. management salaries for a department, which might change with the addition of an assistant manager on a substantial change in output) and as variable costs when the distance between cost changes is relatively small (e.g. basic wages paid to direct labour, which might change with the addition of new men as output increased). For control purposes it is possible to incorporate expected changes in stepwise cost functions explicitly in the control system, so that the classification of costs at the recording stage assumes less importance.

The third major cost classification which can be used in routine cost recording is the controllable/noncontrollable cost dichotomy:

Controllable costs: costs for which a specific manager is held responsible;
Non-controllable costs: costs for which a specific manager is not held responsible.

This categorization indicates to a manager and his superiors those costs which are assumed to be capable of being affected by operations in a particular segment of the business: those which are not capable of being affected are not of concern at that level of responsibility. Note that non-controllable does not mean uncontrollable:* all costs in a firm are someone's responsibility, and the higher up the hierarchy a manager goes the more categories of costs he is responsible for, because he has responsibility for the costs of segments which report to him.

At the lower levels of the hierarchy controllable costs largely coincide with variable costs, because decisions on appropriate fixed costs are made higher up the tree. Controllability recording at the lower levels can therefore be provided substantially by variable cost data: at higher levels data can be either compartmentalized in the accounts on a routine basis or can be summarized periodically on a memorandum basis.

The three cost dichotomies of direct/indirect, variable/fixed and controllable/non-controllable are the major classifications of interest in routine cost recording. They are *not* mutually exclusive: each serves a different purpose, and data can be organized to serve all three classifications, as will be demonstrated in section 8 and Chapter 15.

14.6 Proration of costs between production centres

Prorated costs can potentially include all indirect costs incurred by a firm. As was explained in section 1, product cost *for the financial accounts* rarely includes

*Although the term uncontrollable is in fact widely used – see [9].

elements of administration cost and never includes such items as selling expenses, but some firms go to great lengths to assign all costs in some way to production centres for internal management purposes. Firms which go to such extremes do, of course, exclude non-eligible items from product cost for external reporting purposes: whether the original effort of proration was worth the effort is another matter.

Three major methods of proration can be distinguished, according to whether the assignment of costs is based on facilities provided, actual usage of facilities, or some activity index to represent estimated usage. Not all methods are appropriate to all cost items, but some examples are shown in Table 14.8.

Table 14.8 Three major methods of proration of costs to production centres

Nature of indirect cost	Indirect cost prorated to production centres in proportion to		
	Actual usage	Activity index for estimated usage	Facilities provided
Factory facilities:			
Rent	←——— Square feet or cubic feet occupied ———→		
Electricity	*	Machine hours of operation	—
Service departments:			
Personnel	Hours spent on personnel of production centre	Labour turnover	No. of employees
Maintenance	Hours of maintenance	Machine hours of operation	No. of machines
Canteen	Meals served to personnel of production centre	Direct labour hours worked	No. of employees
Selling expenses, administration expenses	—	Total sales	—

* If electricity from an external supplier were charged to production centres at actual *metered* cost, this would be a traced segment cost, *not* a proration.

Costs are often passed through summarizing accounts before proration: for example it is obviously informative to segregate the costs of a service department so that costs of providing that service can be reviewed by management. When proration does take place it is commonly based not upon the actual past costs of the accounting period but upon the expected level of costs in that period. The arguments for using expected costs are twofold:

Cost accumulation

1. Speed of preparation of data for internal purposes: the presentation of routine (e.g. monthly) management reports on production centres does not have to await detailed calculations on indirect costs.
2. The control function of information is strengthened because both production and service centres are made aware of cost guidelines which they must observe. This view leads to wider questions of controllability, of which more anon.

Table 14.9. illustrates proration of expected costs for a simple service department, a canteen. Costs were assigned to production centres on the basis:

$$\frac{\text{Expected net canteen costs per period}}{\text{Expected employees of production centres in period}} = \frac{£500}{250} = £2 \text{ per employee}$$

Proration compared with actual figures might turn out as shown in Table 14.9.

The extent to which proration is undertaken at all depends on how many views are accepted from the following justifications for proration, which are given in what we consider to be descending order of validity.

Table 14.9 Proration of service department costs

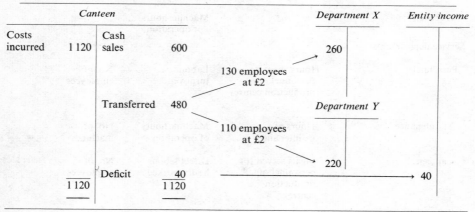

(a) Cost variability with output

Some variable costs may not merit tracing as direct costs (e.g. glue, power) but an estimate of usage based on known characteristics of the production centre may provide a useful estimate of variable cost. Thus in the electricity example (Table 14.8) the proration of electricity cost on the basis of machine hours worked provides such an estimate of variable cost, if the firm's machines consume similar amounts of electricity.

This view, confined as it is to *variable costs*, is not controversial.

(b) Controllability of facility usage

This view is that a manager of a production centre will be motivated to control the consumption of resources if his centre is charged for those resources.

There is considerable validity in this point, but it is subject to qualification. Costs must be assigned on the basis of either estimated usage or preferably actual usage: proration on the basis of facilities provided could lead to prodigal use of those common facilities. The basis for assigning costs must ensure that the manager is not encouraged to adopt goals which conflict with those of the firm, not an easy requirement; for example the charging of maintenance on an hourly basis might induce some managers to skimp on maintenance, to the long-run detriment of the firm.

A pre-set charging rate would, of course, be necessary if managers were to be influenced in their use of common resources; such a rate would be a *transfer price*, on which there is some discussion in Chapters 9 and 17.

(c) Managerial awareness of costs

The argument for assigning as many costs as possible is often justified on the grounds that managers should be made aware of the impact of the firm's overhead costs, which must be covered by their operating activities. Such assignment may produce an exceedingly crude opportunity cost estimate for higher management: if one department cannot meet 'its share' of costs, resources might be diverted to another department, but proration of all costs is neither an efficient method of approaching the problem nor of relevance to operating department managers.

If the cost is not variable with output and the manager has no control over facility usage there should not be any proration for departmental control purposes. Consider a manager whose department is charged with general administration costs at the rate of 10 per cent on sales; he would be rational (from a departmental viewpoint) to refuse an order offering a 10 per cent profit margin, even though there were no other orders available and the firm's general administration costs would be unaffected by the order. The decision would be against the firm's interests; in this situation the manager could not do harm in the absence of prorated administration costs.

(d) Accuracy in product costing

It was seen earlier that proration is a step in the calculation of product cost.

Some firms and accountants justify very complex proration methods on the grounds that they give 'more accurate' product costs. When the costs being pro-rated are either fixed or joint costs such accuracy is spurious, and the calculations involve merely arbitrary averaging over units of output. Some information implications of averaging, of which proration would be the first step, are examined in section 7.

If arbitrary averaging is to be undertaken in order to satisfy external reporting conventions there is a strong case for making the averaging as simple and cheap as possible.

14.7 Cost absorption

Absorption costing involves the averaging of costs over *units* of output whether the costs are fixed or variable. The result is a product cost which is an average of costs at a particular level of output: the cost figure gives no indication of the short-run cost of producing additional units.

It is possible to segregate fixed from variable cost elements in routine recording and calculate averages only for variable elements: such an approach, termed *variable costing,** was implicit in the consideration of short-run price-output in Chapter 10. In fact variable costing is widely used for internal management purposes, but rarely for product valuation in external reporting. The profit measurement implications of the two alternative methods are considered in the appendix to this chapter.

It will be recalled that absorption involves the assignment of indirect costs (mainly fixed) on the basis of some form of activity index. The activity index is intended to provide a measuring rod against which the proportion of common resources of a production centre devoted to different products may be determined. The major candidates for selection as an activity index will be considered briefly.

(i) *Physical output*
As we have seen, this index can be used only when a production centre produces homogeneous output.

(ii) *Direct labour hours*
This commonly used index was demonstrated in section 1. The rationale for its use is that the more labour hours which are devoted to a product the greater the common resources of the production centre (supervision, space, etc.) which are likely to be taken up by that product.

One reason for its popularity is that labour hour records (time sheets, job cards) are commonly already kept for departmental control of labour activity.

---

*Often called 'marginal costing' by British accountants and 'direct costing' by North American accountants.

(iii) *Machine hours*

The machine hour basis is widely used for absorbing costs over products, the rationale being that machines are significant resources in most production centres. A product's demands on other resources of a production centre (supervision, space, etc.) are also likely to be related to machine hours spent in production.

(iv) *Direct costs*

Possible direct cost indicators for absorption are:

1. Direct labour cost.
2. Direct material cost.
3. Prime cost (= direct labour + direct materials).

The money amount spent on any of the above direct costs would be only a very crude indicator of the product's demand on a production centre's resources. The use of such indices are not, however, uncommon; they do have the advantage of simplicity, because direct cost information is available in the most rudimentary recording system.

Whatever the activity index chosen, indirect costs are usually assigned to products at some predetermined rate on the basis of the *expected* level of costs and activity. Such a predetermined rate is termed an *absorption rate*, an *overhead burden rate* or simply a *burden rate*. Simplicity of product cost calculation and speed of data presentation are major reasons for using a predetermined rate rather than actual past costs. The basis of the calculation corresponds to that already described for prorating costs to departments in section 6. The burden rate applied to production of a department might be determined:

$$\frac{\text{Expected indirect costs of department}}{\text{Expected machine hours of work by department}} = \frac{£9\,000}{3\,000}$$

$$= £3 \text{ per machine hour}$$

In the calculation of a burden rate different interpretations of *expected* level of activity can be adopted. It could be (and usually is) the normal volume of activity in the sense of the average expected level over several time periods, it could be the expected volume in the specific time period, or it could be potential volume at full capacity. Some control implications will be considered in Chapter 15; from the cost accumulation viewpoint any burden rate based on expectations is liable to produce a difference between the total money amount absorbed over the products and the actual expenditure on indirect costs. For internal management purposes the difference can be simply transferred to the period's income statement as over or underabsorbed costs; for external purposes some adjustment of product cost for inventory valuation is appropriate when the difference is material.

Cost accumulation

So far attention has been concentrated on overhead burden rates for production centres, where an activity index is selected in each case according to the 'appropriateness' of the index to that centre. It is possible however to calculate one burden rate for the whole factory: this basis is termed a *factory-wide burden rate* as opposed to the *departmental burden rate* considered previously.

It is often claimed that departmental burden rates give 'more accurate' product cost figures than factory-wide burden rates. Certainly the departmental calculations are more detailed, but they are not necessarily any more useful to management. In the short run management is concerned with making optimal use of certain limited resources of the firm: burden rates purport to measure the cost of using those limited resources but are incapable of either indicating the relative scarcity of the resources within the firm or assisting in the determination of the optimal allocation of resources between products. In the terminology of Chapter 7 management is concerned with maximizing the value of an objective function subject to constraints, but burden rates are expressed as if they were unconstrained variable costs. From this viewpoint therefore a factory-wide burden rate is as good (or as bad) as any other.

The long-run position is a little different. It can be argued that a departmental burden rate of say £2 per machine hour based on existing cost levels gives a very rough indication of the average cost of the department's facilities if the department were given time to adjust capacity. Product costs derived by using burden rates may perform a useful function as 'trigger mechanisms' to signal the desirability of investigating the long-run future of products which are apparently out of line in terms of profitability. Unfortunately such signals should not be necessary; long-run re-assessment of all products should take place on a regular basis, and any investigation should not, of course, use burden rate information but should employ the criteria developed in Part 2 of this book.

The irrelevance of burden rates to short-run utilization of capacity can be illustrated by using data from the Rho example in section 2 of Chapter 7, where a linear programming solution indicated optimal production of 30 units of X_1 and 20 units of X_2.

Example

Assume that Rho's two products passed through three operations which were treated as separate production centres. The first operation was machining (with capacity measured in machine hours); the other two operations were predominantly manual (capacity measured in direct labour hours).

The original Rho example did not provide (or require) indirect cost data. Indirect costs adopted for the present purpose are assumed fixed (so that the original variable costs in section 2 of Chapter 7 remain valid), but it should be noted that indirect costs commonly include variable elements.

Expected indirect costs (assumed fixed) (1)		Expected total activity (2)	Overhead burden rates $\dfrac{(1)}{(2)}$
Department 1	£800	800 machine hours	£1 per machine hour
2	£500	1 000 direct labour hours	£0·50 per direct labour hour
3	£300	400 direct labour hours	£0·75 per direct labour hour
Factory	£1 600	2 000 direct labour hours	£0·80 per direct labour hour

The constraints given in section 2 of Chapter 7 have been adopted as the total expected activity for each index. If by coincidence the optimal activity for each department were adopted initially, there would be only a small change affecting department 3 (to 230 hours) – but the analysis of the relative profitability of products X_1 and X_2 would be unaffected.

For completion of the factory-wide index the direct labour hours in department 1 have been assumed to be 600 hours (e.g. three men to each group of four machines).

Costs and profit margins per unit could be calculated in three different ways, illustrated in Table 14.10.

None of the three calculations gives any indication of the mix of resources which should be devoted to each product, although section 2 of Chapter 7 showed that variable cost/contribution can provide an initial step towards solution.

The departmental burden rate approach is alone in indicating that product X_2 is more attractive than product X_1; a naive user of product cost information might be excused for believing that Rho should therefore concentrate its efforts on producing X_2. In fact it has been seen that Rho's optimal* course is to produce 30 units of X_1 and 20 units of X_2: so much for the accuracy of departmental burden rates. The sad conclusion is that if burden rates consisting of *fixed* costs are to be calculated at all, they may as well be factory-wide – they will then at least have simplicity to commend them.

14.8 The data bank viewpoint

The view has already been expressed that raw accounting data should, as far as possible, be recorded in ways which permit later selection and summarization for a variety of purposes. Clearly cost *recording* must be influenced by the known requirements of the routine *reporting* system, but all reports do not serve identical objec-

* With the assumed fixed costs of £1 600 optimal output would yield £200 profit.

Cost accumulation

Table 14.10 Three views of costs and profit margins

Per unit	X_1, £			X_2, £	
Selling price	90				70
Variable cost	50				40
Contribution	£40				£30
Selling price	90				70
Product cost with *departmental burden rate*:					
variable cost	50				40
fixed cost 1. $20 \times £1$	20		$10 \times £1$	10	
2. $20 \times £0.50$	10		$20 \times £0.50$	10	
3. $5 \times £0.75$	3.75		$4 \times £0.75$	3	
		83.75			63
Profit		£6.25			£7
Selling price	90				70
Product cost with *factory-wide burden rate*					
variable cost	50				40
fixed cost 1. 15*			7.5*		
2. 20			20		
3. 5			4		
$40 \times £0.80$	32		$31.5 \times £0.80$	25.20	
		82			65.20
Profit		£8			£4.80

* Assumed direct labour hours for department 1.

tives: the conflicting requirements of internal and external reporting provide a familiar example. Even after routine reporting requirements have been satisfied there is the likelihood that accounting data will be used for non-routine purposes, for example as starting points for the projection of costs of alternative policies. Thus the routinely recorded accounting data can be regarded as providing a data bank upon which demands may be made for a variety of uses; the essential proviso is that care must be exercised to ensure the relevance of the data to a particular use.

For the purposes of routine reporting it is possible to accommodate within the double entry recording system the direct/indirect, variable/fixed and controllable/non-controllable cost classifications. Information on these bases can be effectively provided by re-summarization of data from the recording system to be considered in Chapter 15.

Other major aspects of routine classification of data concern the purposes for which the expenditure was incurred (e.g. advertising by products and by areas), organizational responsibility (e.g. personnel hiring costs incurred on behalf of particular departments) and the nature of expense (e.g. travelling costs – and time – by road, air, etc.). With electronic data processing a variety of classifications, and subsequent re-summarization, can be cheaply accommodated; in addition cost data can be used in conjunction with information outside the conventional ambit of financial records to provide a continuing information system monitoring the activities of the firm.*

Classification of accounting data is often achieved by the use of a *code of accounts*.† A numerical code can be assigned to attributes of an accounting item – for example, in a three-figure code the range 000–100 might be reserved for direct costs of different types (material A 057, material B 058, etc.). The addition of further digits, or the use of an alpha-numeric code, permits further sub-division by attributes (e.g. responsibility for expenditure). The human element imposes a limit on the complexity of codes when source documents, such as invoices, have to be coded manually before data can be processed.

The *non-routine* uses of cost data are plainly difficult to accommodate in any routine way by such means as cost classifications: the needs of one-off investigations are rarely predictable. It is at least possible to minimize obstacles to such uses by avoiding the compression or averaging of data at a too early stage in the recording process. For example, the costs associated with specific batches of production passing through a cost centre might be needed for an investigation on cost variability; such an investigation would be impossible if data had been merged and recorded on some periodic basis instead of the batch basis needed. If the data sought in an investigation are not available in the accounting 'books' they may often be found in original source documents (job cost cards, invoices, etc.); it is not the accountant's task to record data for all eventualities, but it is his function to ensure that data are held in some accessible form for the likely needs within a firm.

Appendix: the cost of inventory

(a) Nature of the problem

Inventories comprise goods which are held by the firm pending consumption or sale: raw materials, work-in-progress and finished goods purchased or manufactured by the firm. The values attached to these items in accounts are of considerable importance. Beginning inventories effectively diminish profit of the period and ending inventories effectively increase it; assessment of performance for a segment

---

*See [10] for a straightforward treatment of a computer based information system using common data files.

†See [13].

of the firm or for the firm as a whole may therefore be affected by the inventory valuation basis employed.

The central point at issue concerns the implementation of the matching concept, which requires costs of resources to be matched (or charged) to those periods in which the resources are consumed. Two major areas of difficulty arise, where alternative assumptions about cost may be employed:

1. Cost flow assumptions – how should the flow of costs be matched with the flow of goods?
2. Cost identification assumptions – which costs are to be identified with the production of goods?

There is a third problem area concerning inventory valuation which deserves mention: the application of the financial accounting convention that inventory should be 'valued' at the lower of cost or market value. It will be recalled from Chapter 3 that net realizable value and replacement cost were candidates for the market value benchmark.

This appendix examines the first two problems mentioned above. When the 'lower of cost or market value' convention operates it has the effect of reducing ending inventory (and therefore profit of the current period) by any excess of cost over market value. Subject to this qualification the remaining discussion can be confined to the determination of cost.

(b) Cost flow assumptions

The problem of associating cost flow with goods flow arises because prices of acquiring or manufacturing goods do not remain constant. When disposals take place it is necessary to associate goods with some specific acquisition cost.

The major possible approaches will be considered in turn. Each approach is applicable to any form of inventory, but for brevity discussion will be confined to purchased materials. Table 14.11 shows the alternative double-entry records for the acquisition and disposal (issue to manufacturing departments) for one type of material.

(i) *Average cost – weighted average of the period*
Disposals during the period and inventory at the end of the period are recorded at the average cost of acquisitions (including beginning inventory) over the period. Clearly this must involve waiting until the end of the period before calculating the average cost and recording money amounts for disposals. This implies the existence of a perpetual inventory system for the recording of physical quantities during the period.

This approach has the advantage of simplicity in calculation.

430

Table 14.11

Inventory accounts for alternative cost assumptions

Date	Current acquisition cost	Physical units — Acquisitions	Physical units — Disposals or issues	Average cost – weighted average	Average cost – moving average	FIFO	LIFO	Standard cost (i) At standard cost £2·10	Replacement cost, using revaluation account (i) At historic cost (FIFO)
January	£2·04	100		£204	£204	£204	£204	£210	£204
February	2·12	100	100	212 / 216	212 / 208	212 / 204	212	210 / 210	212 / 204
March	2·20	100		232	232	232	232	210	232
April	2·32		50	108	110	106	212 / 116	105	106
May	2·30		150						
		300	150	£648 / £324	£648 / £318	£648 / £310	£648 / £328	£630 / £315	£648 / £310
Ending inventory		150		£324	£330	£338	£320	£315	£338

Date	Standard cost (ii) Variance account		Replacement cost (ii) Revaluation account	
January	2		8	
February		6	16	16*
March	22		12	
April				4 / 9*
May				
Variance, revaluation balances	£24	£6	£36	£29
	£18		£7	

* Updating of disposals.

431

Cost accumulation

(ii) Average cost – moving average

Each disposal during the period is recorded at the average cost of the units held immediately prior to disposal. It can be seen from Table 14.11 that the moving average approach (compared with weighted average) gives disposals which are influenced by costs early in the period and ending inventory which is more heavily influenced by acquisition costs later in the period. The difference between the two average methods depends on the frequency of transactions during the period; the weighted average approach is itself a long-run moving average, because a fresh calculation of the average is made each period.

(iii) Standard cost

Acquisitions and disposals are recorded at some *standard* cost, which for the present discussion can be taken to be the average expected cost forecast at the beginning of the period. Differences between acquisition cost and the standard cost are transferred to a *variance* account, so that the inventory account is relieved of the troublesome cost changes (see Table 14.11). Wider implications of standard costs will be considered in the next chapter.

Standard costs may be subject to amendment, either during an accounting period or (more commonly) at the beginning of a new accounting period. In such cases inventory at the date of change would be updated to the new standard; subsequent acquisitions/disposals and therefore ending inventory would appear at the new standard cost.

(iv) First-in-first-out: FIFO

Disposals during the period are recorded at the cost of the earliest acquired items in inventory at that time. The ending inventory therefore appears at the acquisition cost of the latest items acquired. (In Table 14.11 ending inventory is calculated: $(50 \times £2 \cdot 12) + (100 \times £2 \cdot 32)$.)

The major argument advanced in support of this approach is that the disposal of physical goods will normally proceed in a FIFO manner, particularly when the goods are liable to deterioration.

(v) Last-in-first-out: LIFO

Disposals during the period are recorded at the acquisition cost of the *latest* acquired units in inventory at that time. Inventory is therefore made up of 'layers' of items which are considered to have escaped disposal so far, with the latest layers protecting the earlier layers from disposal. Only if inventory falls to zero will the disposal of the earliest layer be considered to have occurred.

Thus in Table 14.11 ending inventory is composed of two layers, the first acquired in January $(100 \times £2 \cdot 04)$ and the second acquired in April $(50 \times £2 \cdot 32)$.

The flow of physical goods has been used to justify LIFO from an historic cost

432

viewpoint: when materials are literally stockpiled (e.g. mineral ore) the disposals will be made from the top layers of the pile. However, the major justification advanced for LIFO rejects the relevance of historic cost: LIFO charges disposals during the period at *roughly* replacement cost. Thus the profit calculation would more closely reflect current prices than with any of the approaches considered so far. This updating of the profit calculation is at the expense of an outdated valuation of ending inventory: the costs of the earlier layers can be very ancient indeed for a firm which has been operating for many years.

(vi) *Replacement cost*

A replacement cost approach to inventory would enter disposals at current cost. Appropriate updating of the inventory to replacement cost would be necessary, either directly to the inventory account or by means of a revaluation account as illustrated in Table 14.11.

This approach is rare; it was seen in Chapter 3 that replacement cost is not a conventionally favoured accounting basis.

(c) Review of cost flow assumptions

The implications of the alternative cost flow assumptions centre around the significance of current cost information for management decisions and profit measurement. If the view is accepted that accounting information is most useful when it reflects the current cost environment, the arguments about the physical flow of goods become irrelevantly tortuous. An appropriate approach would reflect replacement cost in both disposals and inventory, subject to the qualification that the benefits of continuous updating depend on the dimensions (i.e. the 'materiality') of the current cost changes.

Although this view has some acceptance in relation to the internal accounting information of firms it is certainly not widely accepted for external reporting. The historic cost approaches of FIFO and average cost are the most widely adopted approaches in external reporting; for internal purposes these approaches would figure prominently, together with standard cost. The adoption of LIFO is strongly correlated with its eligibility for tax purposes: the approach is both rare in external reports and inadmissible for tax purposes in Britain and Canada; it is both commonly adopted and admissible for tax purposes in the United States.*

*The most frequent approaches in the published accounts of 600 major American companies in 1968 (from [2]) were:

FIFO	255
Average cost	196
LIFO	168
Standard cost	27
Replacement/current cost	13

Cost accumulation

The standard cost approach can permit the firm to obtain a substantial element of current cost information internally while satisfying the generally accepted accounting conventions externally. Standard costs for internal purposes can reflect the expected replacement cost of the period, or the system can be made sensitive to replacement cost fluctuations during the period by appropriate use of variance accounts (see Chapter 15). Standard cost data can be amended to the weighted average cost approach on the following lines:

	£
Standard cost of acquisitions and beginning inventory	630
Add net variance of period	18
Historic cost of aquisitions and beginning inventory	648

Disposals at weighted average cost:

$$\text{Historic cost of acquisitions and beginning inventory} \times \frac{\text{Disposals at standard cost}}{\text{Standard cost of acquisitions and beginning inventory}} = £648 \times \frac{£315}{£630} = £324$$

Ending inventory at weighted average cost:

$$\text{Historic cost of acquisitions and beginning inventory} \times \frac{\text{Ending inventory at standard cost}}{\text{Standard cost of acquisitions and beginning inventory}} = £648 \times \frac{£315}{£630} = £324$$

All the above figures are taken from the standard cost section of the data in Table 14.11.

It should be noted that although the principal cost flow assumptions have been examined, the variations on implementation of these assumptions have by no means been exhausted. A variety of approximations are employed by firms, usually with the objective of reducing calculations and recording during the accounting period.

(d) Cost identification assumptions

Goods which are purchased by the firm have an unambiguous initial acquisition cost; the accounting difficulties arise with subsequent price changes. For goods which are manufactured by the firm there is an additional, and entirely different, dimension of the cost problem: which costs incurred by the firm are to be identified with the goods produced?

The two major methods of identifying production costs with goods produced are variable costing and absorption costing, considered in Chapter 14. The former method identifies only variable costs with products, treating fixed costs as period costs to be charged to the current period; the latter absorbs substantial elements of fixed costs over goods produced. The general effect of these two alternatives on inventory and profit can be most readily seen by examining a simple model of the profit calculation of a firm. (For a similar model with rather different interpretation see [5].)

Model of profit calculation under variable and absorption costing

The objective is to isolate the effects of the two costing methods, therefore all prices will be held constant. Non-manufacturing costs will be ignored. The firm (or production centre) manufactures a single product. All costs are either fixed or vary linearly with output. For simplicity in discussion it will be assumed that profits are being made in all situations; the analysis could be applied to loss situations with suitable amendments.

Parameters, assumed constant from period to period:

F fixed costs of production
V variable costs per unit of production
P selling price per unit of output
N 'normal' production: number of units normally expected to be produced in a period (used as denominator in the calculation of fixed cost burden rate for standard cost)

Variables:

s units sold in current period
m_0 units manufactured in preceding period
m_1 units manufactured in current period
z_0 units in ending inventory of preceding period (= beginning inventory current period)
z_1 units in ending inventory of current period
a fixed cost element in average unit cost of beginning inventory (in weighted average cost approach)
π profit of current period

(i) *Variable costing*
Profit is, of course, the revenue of the period less cost of goods sold. With beginning and ending inventory at variable cost the profit of the period is given by:

$$\pi = sP - [F + m_1 V + z_0 V - z_1 V]$$

But $\qquad m_1 + z_0 - z_1 = s$

435

Cost accumulation

Therefore
$$\pi = sP - (F + sV).$$

Thus profit is determined by sales quantity, because all other values on the right hand side are constants. The inventory quantities have no influence because they are valued at the (constant) variable cost of production: the method of identifying costs with inventory is consistent with the model's assumptions about cost behaviour.

(ii) *Absorption costing*

With absorption costing the inventory quantities do have an influence on profit, because the identification of costs with inventory is not consistent with (the model's) cost behaviour. Elements of fixed costs are transferred between accounting periods as though fixed costs were in some way dependent on production quantities, whereas the total fixed costs incurred in each period are independent of production.

Cost flow assumptions must now be reintroduced, because these assumptions determine which particular elements of fixed costs get identified with inventory. Different flow assumptions applied with absorption costing will give different profit results even though prices of purchased resources (F and V) and selling prices (P) all remain constant.

Absorption costing under three major cost flow assumptions will be considered in turn: standard cost, FIFO, and weighted average cost. (The order adopted in section (b) above has been reversed to permit the simpler effects of absorption costing to be considered first.)

1. *Standard cost* The use of standard cost implies the adoption of a 'normal' (or standard) output as denominator in the calculation of the fixed cost burden rate.

The burden rate is F/N, where N is 'normal' output, and profit of the period is given by:

$$\pi = sP - \left[F + m_1 V + z_0\left(\frac{F}{N} + V\right) - z_1\left(\frac{F}{N} + V\right) \right]$$

But
$$m_1 + z_0 - z_1 = s$$

Therefore
$$\pi = sP - (F + sV) + (z_1 - z_0)\frac{F}{N}.$$

The difference between the above profit measure and that obtained with variable costing is represented by the expression:

$$(z_1 - z_0)\frac{F}{N}.$$

Thus a portion of the profit is determined by inventory quantities. *For any given sales and beginning inventory* the profit could be increased by producing additional

436

units for ending inventory. This effect may be significant in the evaluation of profit performance, particularly for segments of the firm: it will rarely be to the long-run advantage of the firm for managers to have a built-in incentive to increase their inventory holdings. Only if demand in the future (say next period) is expected to exceed capacity, or if increased prices are expected to outweigh inventory carrying costs, will it be advantageous to the firm to encourage inventory growth.

In the standard cost situation any excess of ending inventory quantity over the quantity of beginning inventory augments profits; this is the only absorption costing situation in which such a simple relationship exists.

2. *FIFO* In this case the absorption of fixed costs on the basis of the period's actual production will be illustrated under the FIFO assumption. The absorption rate is given by F/m_0 for the preceding period and by F/m_1 for the current period. Profit is:

$$\pi = sP - \left[F + m_1 V + z_0\left(\frac{F}{m_0} + V\right) - z_1\left(\frac{F}{m_1} + V\right) \right]$$

But $\qquad m_1 + z_0 - z_1 = s$

Therefore $\qquad \pi = sP - (F + sV) - z_0\frac{F}{m_0} + z_1\frac{F}{m_1}.$

The difference from the profit under variable costing is therefore:

$$z_1\frac{F}{m_1} - z_0\frac{F}{m_0}.$$

Again it can be seen that profit is partially dependent on inventory levels, and for given sales* and beginning inventory the profit could be increased by producing additional units for the ending inventory. (With each increment to z_1 and m_1 a greater proportion of F is borne by the next accounting period.) The evaluation implications discussed under standard cost are still applicable.

Unlike the standard cost situation, a simple excess of ending inventory over beginning inventory does not necessarily augment profit.

* It has been assumed that sales exceed beginning inventory. As Ijiri, Jaedicke and Livingstone [5] point out, the profit calculation would be substantially different if $s \leqslant z_0$. In terms of our model there will be a residual quantity $z_0 - s$ of 'beginning cost' goods in the ending inventory. Thus

$$\pi = sP - \left[F + m_1 V + z_0\left(\frac{F}{m_0} + V\right) - (z_0 - s)\left(\frac{F}{m_0} + V\right) - m_1\left(\frac{F}{m_1} + V\right) \right].$$

Substituting for $m_1 + z_0 - (z_0 - s) - m_1 = s$

$$\pi = sP - (F + sV) - z_0\frac{F}{m_0} + (z_0 - s)\frac{F}{m_0} + m_1\frac{F}{m_1}$$

$$\pi = sP - (F + sV) - \frac{sF}{m_0} + F.$$

The result indicates that profit is *not* dependent in any way on the quantity of ending inventory. Clearly in this case the generalizations on evaluation of profit do not apply.

3. *Weighted average cost of the period* Both beginning and ending inventory valuations depend to some extent on an element (a) which is the fixed cost element in the average unit cost of the beginning inventory. That element is itself partially dependent on the average unit cost of the beginning inventory in the *preceding* period, and so on. The element a is therefore the outcome of a history of average cost calculations since the commencement of production.

Profit in the weighted average cost case is given by:

$$\pi = sP - \left[F + m_1 V + z_0(a+V) - z_1\left(\frac{z_0 a + F}{z_1 + s} + V\right)\right].$$

But $\qquad m_1 + z_0 - z_1 = s$

Therefore $\qquad \pi = sP - (F + sV) - z_0 a + \frac{z_1(z_0 a)}{z_1 + s} + \frac{z_1 F}{z_1 + s}.$

Which reduces to

$$\pi = sP - (F + sV) + \frac{z_1 F - z_0 as}{z_1 + s}.$$

The difference from the profit under variable costing is therefore:

$$\frac{z_1 F - z_0 as}{z_1 + s}.$$

The inventory relationship with profit is more complex than with the previous two approaches. However it is still true that given (non-zero) sales and beginning inventory the profit could be augmented by the production of additional units for the ending inventory.

(e) Review of cost identification assumptions

Only three cost flow approaches have been considered under absorption costing, but other cost flow assumptions would have the broadly similar implication that the quantity of ending inventory may affect profit. Note, however, that replacement cost is a concept which is not easily reconcilable with absorption costing: if it is valid to assume that units can be produced at something like variable cost it would seem that replacement cost must be the same as variable cost.

If the model used above is a valid representation of cost behaviour in manufacturing firms, the implication is clear that cost absorption can produce distortion of profits via inventory valuations in ways which may not be immediately evident to the user of the accounting information. The absence of such distortions in the variable costing approach provides a substantial argument for its adoption, at least for evaluation within the firm.

438

Of course the model is over-simple and many qualifications can be made about its assumptions. The major qualifications are that the linear assumptions of variable cost and the fixedness of fixed costs over all ranges of output are unrealistic, and even if they were realistic the cost recording system would rarely be sufficiently precise to disentangle them entirely. The fact remains that variable costing assumes far more plausible relationships than absorption costing, which treats *all* manufacturing costs as though they were variable with output.

Bibliographical references

[1] American Accounting Association, Report of the committee on cost concepts and standards, *Accounting Review*, April 1952, pp. 174–88.
[2] American Institute of Certified Public Accountants (publishers), *Accounting Trends and Techniques* (published annually).
[3] Clark, J. M., *Studies in the Economics of Overhead Costs*, Chicago University Press, 1923.
[4] Horngren, C. T. and G. H. Sorter, 'Direct' costing for external reporting, *Accounting Review*, January 1961, pp. 84–93.
[5] Ijiri, Y., Jaedicke, R. K. and J. L. Livingstone, The effect of inventory costing methods on full and direct costing, *Journal of Accounting Research*, Spring 1965, pp. 63–74.
[6] Institute of Chartered Accountants in England and Wales, (publishers), *Treatment of Stock-in-trade and Work-in-progress in financial accounts*, Recommendation on Accounting Principles N22, 1960.
[7] Institute of Chartered Accountants in England and Wales, (publishers), Stocks and Work-in-progress, *Accountancy*, June 1972, pp. 118–26.
[8] Institute of Chartered Accountants in England and Wales, (publishers), *Survey of Published Accounts* (published annually).
[9] Institute of Cost and Works Accountants (publishers), *Terminology of Cost Accountancy*, 1966.
[10] International Business Machines Corporation (publishers), *The Production Information and Control System*, 1968.
[11] Kohler, E. L., *Dictionary for Accountants*, Prentice-Hall, 1967.
[12] Manes, R. P. and V. L. Smith, Economic joint cost and accounting practice, *Accounting Review*, January 1965, pp. 31–35.
[13] Risk, J. M. S., *The Classification and Coding of Accounts*, Occasional Paper No. 2, Institute of Cost and Works Accountants, 1956.

Problems

14.1 'Consider the cost of manufacturing a pair of shoes. The rent of the factory in which the shoes are made and the depreciation of the machinery used in their manufacture are costs of producing the shoes, just as much as the costs of labour and materials. Equally, if the firm borrows in order to buy a factory, the interest on that borrowing is as much a cost of manufacture as if the firm were paying rent. Before the firm can make a profit *all* these costs must be covered: to ignore any of them in calculating the cost of producing a pair of shoes would be misleading.'

Examine the validity and implications of this argument.

14.2 While explaining his company's cost control policy the accountant of Spread Ltd. made the following remark:

'We make sure that all costs incurred by the firm end up somewhere in the accounts of the production departments. That way the departmental managers know that they, like the firm, must meet all these costs before showing a profit. If we left out any of the common costs the departmental managers would be living in a fool's paradise; they could all be making profits while the firm was making a loss.'

Give your views on Spread's policy.

14.3 Discuss the costing (and pricing) policy implied by this bill for repairs to a car:

	£
New starter motor	10·00
Labour 1 hour at £2·00	2·00
	£12·00

14.4 A firm produces three joint products, *A*, *B* and *C*. Each product is subjected (independently) to further processing before sale.

In determining costs for inventory in external reports and for calculation of product profit in internal reports the firm adopts the 'relative market value' method: joint costs are divided between products in proportion to sales revenue after the deduction of separable processing costs.

The firm's plant is usually operated at full capacity, and a summary of a typical internal accounting report (which allocates joint costs of £150 000) is shown below.

Product	Production = sales (1) Tons	Sales revenue (2) £	Separable processing costs (3) £	Net revenue before joint costs (4) = (2) − (3) £	Allocation of joint costs (5) £000's		Profit (4) − (5) £
A	1 200	125 000	31 000	94 000	$\frac{94}{210} \times 150 = 67\,143$		26 857
B	1 000	65 000	27 000	38 000	$\frac{38}{210} \times 150 = 27\,143$		10 857
C	500	110 000	32 000	78 000	$\frac{78}{210} \times 150 = 55\,714$		22 286
		£300 000	£90 000	£210 000		£150 000	£60 000

The firm is considering whether to sell the products in their raw state instead of processing after the 'split-off' from joint production. Processing could be dropped for any product(s) *independently*; the separable processing costs given above can be taken as the avoidable costs of processing for each product, and all the above data would be applicable for the foreseeable future. Normal production of *A*, *B* and *C* in their raw state can be sold for £75 000, £45 000 and £80 000 respectively. The firm's accountant calculates that profit for *A* using the relative market value method for calculating costs would be £18 750, i.e.

$$\left(£75\,000 - \frac{£75\,000}{£200\,000} \times £150\,000 \right).$$

Required:
(a) Complete the accountant's profit calculations under the relative market value method.
(b) Advise the firm, on the basis of the available data.

14.5 A breakfast cereals manufacturer has a department for packaging design. Change of packaging is an important marketing device for many of the firm's products; a single product may also, at any one time, have special packs for different markets.

The actual packaging for all products takes place in a single, highly mechanized, packaging department.

Examine the problem of accumulating cost data for the packaging of products.

14.6 The Vacuum department commenced production in January. Data for operations in January and February are shown below.

	January	February
Fixed costs of production, £	4 000	4 000
Variable costs per unit of production, £	3	3
Selling price per unit, £	10	10
'Normal' production (units)	1 000	1 000
Units sold	900	800
Units manufactured	1 000	800

Required:
(a) Calculate profit for February if inventory is valued at:

  (1) Variable cost.
  (2) Standard cost.
  (3) Cost using the FIFO assumption.
  (4) Cost using the weighted average of the period.

(b) Repeat the above calculations, but this time assume that production in February was 900 units, other data remaining unchanged.

(c) Comment.

441

Cost accumulation

14.7 Records Ltd. produces records which are sold at a uniform trade price of £1 each. The company made a loss in its first year, and its revenue statement is shown below:

Year 19–1

		£000's
Sales (1 m. records)		1 000
Manufacturing costs:		
Variable costs	250	
Fixed overheads	500	
Factory production cost		
(1 m. records)		750
Gross profit		250
Distribution	100	
Advertising and administration	200	
		300
Net loss		50

At the beginning of 19–2 a new managing director was appointed. His contract provided that his sole remuneration would be 25 per cent of any net profit made by the company (before charging the remuneration).

In 19–2 the company produced 2 m. records, the limit of its productive capacity. 1 m. records were sold. Selling price, fixed overheads, distribution, advertising and administration expenses were all the same as in 19–1, and variable costs remained constant at £0·25 per unit.

Records Ltd. valued inventory at full factory cost of production, using the FIFO method. Note that the company avoids ephemeral material (concentrating on e.g. language records) so that all records in inventory at the end of 19–2 have a realizable value of £1 each – eventually. The managing director resigned early in 19–3.

Required:
(a) Revenue statement for the year 19–2.
(b) Consider the implications of the statement you have prepared.
(c) Would your opinion be affected if you knew that production in 19–2 had been determined in the light of a forecast demand of 3 m. records for 19–3, which subsequently proved correct (other data remaining unchanged)?
(d) What are the implications for inventory valuation conventions?

14.8 Duplicity Ltd. recently rented a factory. The factory is divided into two departments, producing alpha and beta.

The company's accountant prepared the following accounts for the first month of operation:

	Alpha Department			*Beta Department*	
	Units	£	Units		£
Materials		5 500			20 000
Labour		4 500			7 000
Departmental expenses (including depreciation of departmental machines)		4 000			2 500
		14 000			29 500
Factory overheads:					
Rent		2 000			1 000
Depreciation of jointly used machinery		3 000			1 500
Total factory cost	10 000	19 000	50 000		32 000
(*Less*) inventories of finished goods	(2 500)	(4 750)	(10 000)		(6 400)
Cost of goods sold		14 250			25 600
Administration expenses		3 000			1 500
Net profit (loss)		(2 250)			2 900
Sales	7 500	£15 000	40 000		£30 000

Rent and administration expenses have been allocated on the basis of floorspace occupied, and the depreciation of jointly used machinery on the basis of hours of use.

The manager of the Alpha department (a friend of the accountant) saw a draft copy of the above accounts. Horrified at the implications of the large loss for his department, the manager argued that the allocation was wrong on the following grounds:

1. Cubic capacity should be the determining factor in allocating rent, because storage is important to both departments (cubic capacity occupied is in the ratio Alpha 1: Beta 2).
2. The Alpha department is relatively highly mechanized, and works a two shift system compared with Beta's one shift. Most of Alpha's use of the joint machinery takes place during the shift when Beta is not working, and Alpha should be charged less for the off-peak usage.
3. Administration expenses are not related to floorspace.

443

The accountant decided to allocate the factory overheads and administration expenses in proportion to the sales value of each department's output: he found support for this approach in a textbook statement that the method 'is considered to yield the fairest results, bearing in mind the fact that the great majority of overhead expenses are fixed charges'.

When accounts on the new basis were circulated, the manager of the Beta department complained:

1. His department was in the oldest and least accessible part of the factory, which involved his department in increased costs.
2. The product beta has a relatively high labour content, and it would be foolhardy to pay higher labour rates for a second shift to utilize the simple machines in the Beta department. If there were a second shift, it would be impossible to satisfy the requirements of both departments for use of the jointly used machinery.
3. Administration expenses are not related to the money value of turnover.

Required:
(a) Accounts for both departments, prepared on the basis of allocating the disputed items by sales value.
(b) Discuss the allocation problem.
Given the available information, how would you present the accounts?

15

Control through standards

Standard costing is the victim of its own pretensions.
D. SOLOMONS, 'The analysis of standard cost variances' [15]

15.1 The rationale of standard costing

The central notion of standard costing is very simple: predetermined measures are used as benchmarks against which outcomes are compared. A preliminary definition of a standard might be the commonplace one: 'a thing serving as basis of comparison'. However there is a widespread presumption that the standard represents what 'should be', i.e. a standard of efficiency.

In its accounting use a standard is often formulated as a *rate*, which may be defined as the numerical proportion which should prevail between two sets of things. The firm has three 'sets of things' available on which to base standard rates; money, physical inputs and physical outputs, resulting in three ways in which standard rates may be expressed.

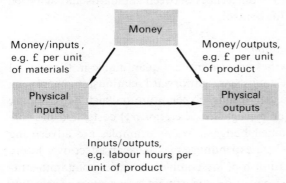

Figure 15.1 Expression of standard rates

The expression of standard rates is illustrated in Figure 15.1. Note that the term 'physical' in relation to inputs and outputs can include all forms of services, and that the inputs and outputs of any segment of the firm may come from or go to other segments.

It was explained in Chapter 13 that standard costing implies the use of budgetary control. Standard rates provide the basis on which volume assumptions can be translated into global amounts for budgets: thus a budgeted production of 100 units might be multiplied by a standard rate of £5 per unit to provide an item of

£500 in the budget. The term standard may be used to refer to the rate (£5 per unit) or to any amount against which performance is judged (e.g. for an achieved output of 80 units the standard (cost) would be £400).

Budgetary control does, however, have a wider compass than standard costing. All activities of a firm are susceptible to the *financial* control of budgets (i.e. what is spent), but the methods of control of *performance* (i.e. what is achieved) are divided into two separate categories:

(i) *Control through standards*
Applies where results of activities are routinely quantifiable in the control period, and it is possible to establish straightforward relationships for what inputs 'should be' for particular results. Such activities are commonly termed *operations* and the corresponding budgets are *operating budgets*. Manufacturing costs (labour, materials, manufacturing overhead) are controllable in this manner, but *some* other activities can be included. For example, both administration and selling include *some* activities where standard relationships between inputs and level of activity can be established (e.g. invoicing, payroll, distribution costs, sales commission). Work standards for indirect workers (e.g. clerical, maintenance) are not usually translated into standard costs for routine accounting recording; it will therefore be convenient to defer consideration until Chapter 16.

In the operations area *variances**—differences between standards and achieved results—provide a major vehicle for control.

(ii) *Control through resource allocation*
Is necessary when results of activities are *not* entirely quantifiable in the control period and/or it is not possible to establish straightforward relationships expressing what inputs 'should' be for particular results. Expenditure on such activities are commonly termed *programmed* (or *managed* or *discretionary*) costs, and the corresponding budgets are programmed budgets. Major examples are advertising and research and development, where expenditure may have an effect over future time periods and input/result relationships are complex. A variety of administration costs fall into this category (e.g. personnel department, preparation of accounting reports).

Resources are allocated through programmed budgets and any expenditure variances are routinely reported *but the variances indicate under- or over-use of allocations and not how well allocations are being used.†* It will be seen in Chapter 16 that control of effectiveness is exercised in different ways.

---

*Accounting variances for control purposes were introduced earlier in section 6 of Chapter 13. In subsequent discussion of control variances the accounting (as opposed to statistical) meaning of variances will be apparent, and the quotation marks adopted in section 6 of Chapter 13 will be omitted.

†See [6] on the distinctive natures of operating and programmed budgets.

Returning to control through standards, the reasons which are commonly advanced for the widespread use of this technique* can be summarized (uncritically at this point) under headings which represent the four stages by which control proceeds:

1. Setting up standards and co-ordinating the budget involves detailed examination and justification of activities, demands forward thinking, provides an opportunity to interrelate requirements of different activities within the firm, and provides a channel for communication of aims and ideas within the firm.
2. Implementation of the budget is aided because the standard assists in defining for the individual within the firm what his responsibilities are. At the operational level the individual or supervisor can be provided with rapid feedback when deviations from standard occur, so that swift corrective action is possible.
3. Measurement is assisted because many accounting calculations (cost transfers between segments of the firm, assignment of money amounts to inventory and work-in-progress) can proceed at uniform standard cost, with the complications of cost variations syphoned conveniently into variance accounts.
4. Evaluation of performance, particularly by middle management, is simplified: a great deal of 'noise' (irrelevant data) can be cut from reports. Variance reporting permits management by exception, the directing of attention to elements which are considered to require investigation.

It must not be thought that the above claims are entirely satisfied, or that control through standards is without significant difficulties. The problems will emerge in due course.

15.2 Setting the standards

If standards are not to be merely an average of past results their adoption entails systematic investigation of operations. Analysis, experiment and training are fundamental prerequisites to establishing standards: these were basic tenets of standard setting from the early days of the scientific management movement. The following passage by F. W. Taylor† illustrates the approach in a simple setting:

> By ... having all the conditions accompanying the work carefully observed for several weeks by men who were used to experimenting, it was found that a first-class man would do his biggest day's work with a shovel load of about 21 pounds.
> At the works of the Bethlehem Steel Company ... it became necessary to provide some

---

*A 1958 survey indicated that standards for controlling costs were used in 66 per cent of leading North American manufacturing companies [16]. A smaller sample in Britain in 1959 revealed a proportion of 40 per cent (from 30 companies) [14].

† [17], pp. 65–68.

8 to 10 different kinds of shovels, etc., each one appropriate to handling a given type of material.

With data of this sort before him . . . it is evident that the man who is directing shovelers can first teach them the exact methods which should be employed . . . and can then assign them daily tasks which are so just that the workman can each day be sure of earning the large bonus which is paid whenever he successfully performs this task.

Taylor's 'science of shoveling' provides an illustration of what is now called ergonomics or human factors engineering. Many firms have separate departments, with titles such as work study, organization and method or industrial engineering, with functions relating in some way to this area. This would not usually be considered as part of the accounting function, although accountants may find themselves involved in some firms.

For operating budgets it is often assumed that scientific investigation has established the optimum working method for the given state of technology and standards have been established in that context, *therefore* standards are a measure of optimal efficiency, representing the single best way. This implies a precision which is rarely justified. Most standards can be considered to contain technical and performance elements, the former relating to the technical requirements of the activity and the latter relating to human performance (alone or in combination with machines). To take a very simple example, it can be said that the packaging of n cartons of goods *should* require n cartons (a technical standard) but a performance element must be introduced because wastage can occur through human *and/or* machine error. The greater the importance of the performance element the more subjective the standard becomes. There is always a danger of analysis of operating activities developing into a battle of wits between observers and observed :* a rigid adherence to the 'single best way' view is likely to enhance this danger.

Alternatively standards can be regarded as goals or objectives to be aimed for, the view which will be developed here. This terminology is commonly adopted† but its implications are rarely followed through: in particular a goal is not a forecast and a goal implies a range of acceptable performance. In examining the mechanics of standard costing it will be convenient to adhere to the basic orthodox approach so that this structure is undertood before amendments are considered – to a limited extent in section 9 and more generally in Chapter 18.

The goal viewpoint begs the controversial question of how demanding should be the goals. The conventional view can be summarized as 'realistically attainable but not too loose'. There is a growing body of evidence that a tight standard can increase motivation and performance *provided* the standard is accepted as a valid goal by the budgetee; beyond that point further tightness is likely to be counter-productive.‡

*For an example, see [18], pp. 14–19.

†See [16], Chapter 4, for references by firms to objectives and 'selling the budget' to operating personnel.

‡[10], Chapter 8 provides an examination of this area.

The old proverb puts it more simply: a horse can be led to water but cannot be forced to drink.

In recent years the authoritarian approach of early standards has to some extent declined and attention has been turned to enhancing the effect of monetary incentives* to participation in goal setting, to encouragement of a sense of job achievement and to productivity sharing.† Some monetary reward schemes (often termed 'payment by results') have the advantage of enabling the employee to set his own goals within certain limits. One variant which manages to combine monetary goals with some degree of stability at the operative level is measured day-work: the operative contracts to perform at some *average* level (e.g. at intervals of 80, 90, 100, 110 per cent of standard) and movement to new goals is encouraged. However, standard setting does assume that people act as *individuals* to goals: there is substantial evidence that *group* loyalties, particularly among operatives, are major obstacles to the acceptance of goals.‡

In most firms participative developments have tended to be concerned with lower and middle levels of management rather than with operatives: moreover what a firm may call participation can be a device for obtaining the formal acquiescence of subordinates to imposed standards.§

The relationships in goal setting between participation, external reference points (e.g. work study or inter-plant comparisons) and intervention of superiors is demonstrated in the models of Hofstede in Figure 15.2. Hofstede's evidence** emphasizes that any single approach is less effective than a mixture: the most effective balance will depend largely on the budgetee's attitudes (e.g. authoritarian or libertarian) and on his perception of the impact his efforts can have on results.

Finally it must be emphasized that neither control nor standards are static. Striving for improvement is implicit in the goal viewpoint. The expectation that performance should improve over time can be justified in terms of a learning process: many activities can be performed more effectively as they become more familiar. The budgetee may not see it this way, for example:

> They make a budget and then constantly increase it. There's too much of that constant ¦ raising and raising that thing. Pretty soon the boys catch on and figure out it's the same old stuff. So they don't respond.††

The complaint is partially directed at the arbitrary way in which achieved goals are liable to be reset. One device for taking the heat out of goal revision is the establishment *and* communication of an explicit *learning curve*.

Learning curves originated in the aircraft industry, where studies of the pro-

---

* Not always successfully: see [18].
† [18], Chapter 14.
‡ See [2], [10], [18].
§ [2], p. 28.
** [10], Chapter 9.
†† [2], p. 12.

Control through standards

A. The Traditional View of the Effect of Participation in Standard-Setting

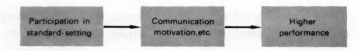

B. Improved Model of the Effect of Participation in Standard-Setting

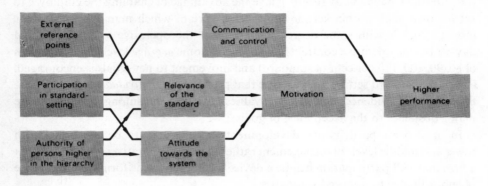

Figure 15.2 Two models for the relationship between participation in standard-setting and performmance. (Source: Hofstede [10], p. 178. Reproduced with permission.)

duction of many different types of aircraft revealed a consistent relationship between direct labour and the quantity of the production run:

> ... the fourth plane required only 80% as much direct labour as the second; the eighth plane, only 80% as much as the fourth; the one hundredth, only 80% as much as the fiftieth, and so on. Thus, the rate of learning to assemble aircraft was concluded to be 80% between doubled quantities.*

Studies in a variety of other activities have indicated similar consistent relationships; as might be expected, benefits of learning are greater in 'performance' situations (i.e. man-paced operations). There is evidence to suggest that the learning phenomenon persists in even apparently routine tasks over a long period of years.† The use of goals based on a learning curve approach would be consistent with the idea of performance goals which do not represent the 'single best way' or merely seek to make people 'work harder' but which seek to stimulate the development of better ways of doing things. Some firms do adopt an explicit learning curve viewpoint in developing performance goals.‡

---

*[9], p. 125.

† In a man-paced operation involving assembly of candy boxes . . . the learning curve was found to have persisted for the preceding 16 years during which 16 m. boxes were assembled by one person [9].

‡ See [10], p. 25.

15.3 The budgets

Budgets are usually assumed to have a planning role concerned with the co-ordination of activities and the availability and allocation of resources, i.e. they imply expectations. Standards have a control role concerned with performance measurement, based on goals. It may help to think of standards as being generally based on rates: if these rates are used to translate volume assumptions into global amounts the result can be called, for want of a better term, a *control budget*. The result is likely to be inadequate for planning: consider for example what might happen if a firm plans its cash needs on the assumption that all goals will be met in full – and those goals are tight. It would seem useful to distinguish the separate function of a *planning budget*.

The two functions can be accommodated in a variety of ways without necessarily adopting two formally distinct budgets. Usually however, the two aspects are not distinguished, probably more as a matter of principle* than through omission. Keeping 'two sets of books' carries an implication that one must be phony, a term which has been used with reference to the use of split planning and control budgets.†

For the present we shall keep one set of books by adhering to the orthodox development of the budgets, although considering the details of only control aspects. In section 9 methods of incorporating separate planning elements will be considered.

Budget development within the firm can best be considered as an iterative process. Initial proposals are most commonly developed by line managers for separate segments of the firm, with the assistance or guidance of people in staff functions: alternatively the roles may be reversed, with staff initiating [16]. The proposals would incorporate standards in the context of volume guidelines for the period. Proposals would then be reviewed by/with the next level of management and amendments may result. When budget proposals (suitably amalgamated at each level) have passed through all management levels they are incorporated into the agreed budget.

The design and content of budgets will depend on the requirements of the firm, but five major categories can be distinguished:

1. *Sales budgets.*
2. *Operating budgets* for operating segments of the firm which may be production or service centres. The operating segment to which a particular budget relates is termed a *budget centre*: responsibility for global performance in that segment will rest with one individual. The segment is likely to be divided into

---

* [10], p. 166, refers to a general resistance to the distinction.
† Becker and Green, 'Budgeting and Employee Behaviour', reprinted in [4] and [15].

451

many *cost centres* which are units of activity at the lowest level of supervision.
3. *Programmed budgets*, for programmed activities.
4. *Resource budgets*, projecting the acquisition and allocation of resources. Major examples would be the purchasing budget, cash budget and capital budget (for fixed assets).
5. *Summary budgets*, which would usually be prepared in the form of a profit and loss account and balance sheet along external reporting lines.

The operating budgets incorporate standards. Usually the sales budget is based on expectations of sales. The last three budgets are concerned with planning functions (it will be recalled that programmed budgets *authorize* expenditure and do not express goals); therefore expectations would seem appropriate. *All five* budgets are usually made to interrelate: in effect budgets 4. and 5. are based largely on data developed in the first three budgets (e.g. purchasing budget would be determined by standard quantities for operations $\pm$ projected changes in inventory).

The data originally used for Furniture production in Table 14.2 will be developed to provide an illustration of simple budgets. The original data should now be regarded *not* as actual results but as a summary of the manufacturing cost elements of Furniture's budget.

It will be helpful to elevate Furniture to the position of Furniture Ltd., a division (and subsidiary) of Conglomerate Ltd.: thus Furniture is a conveniently self-contained unit for which data can be summarized, but it is also accountable to higher management. Furniture has one factory, within which there are two production centres: Preparation and Finishing.

The budget period for Furniture will be taken as three months and the control reports on variances will be calculated for the same period. In reality firms tend to have longer budget periods (e.g. 6 months or one year) but reports would be made at much shorter intervals (e.g. weekly or monthly).

The three basic budgets for operating activities, programmed activities and sales are shown in Table 15.1a: these will be sufficient for the present purposes. Note that the standard product costs calculations in Table 15.1b summarize standards for the operating activities: traditional standard costing procedures place most emphasis on the standard manufacturing cost including absorbed overheads, but the variable costs have been shown here as alternatives (with later uses).

15.4 The recording process for standard costing

Accounting records for standard costs follow familiar double entry principles: the major differences between systems can be examined in relation to the *stage* in recording at which the direct cost variances are separated.

Actual direct cost expenditure can differ from standard for two basic reasons:

Table 15.1a *Furniture's budgets*

SALES BUDGET

	Budgeted sales quantity, units	Standard price per unit, £	Budget totals, £	
Chairs	1 900	8	15 200	
Desks	2 000	15	30 000	
				£45 200

OPERATING BUDGETS

	Standard input per unit of production	× volume (units)	= Budget quantity	Standard price of input			

Preparation department

Direct materials:							
wood–for chairs	2 ft^3	2 000	4 000				
–for desks	4 ft^3	2 000	8 000				
			12 000	×	£0·85	= 10 200	
covering–for chairs	2 ft^2	2 000	4 000	×	£0·45	= 1 800	
							12 000
Direct labour:							
for chairs	$\frac{2}{5}$ hr	2 000	800				
for desks	2 hr	2 000	4 000				
			4 800	×	£0·75	=	3 600

Finishing department

Direct labour:							
for chairs	$\frac{3}{5}$ hr	2 000	1 200				
for desks	1 hr	2 000	2 000				
			3 200	×	£1·00	=	3 200

Manufacturing overheads

Variable overheads			8 000 direct labour hours	×	£0·20 variable overhead rate	= 1 600	
Fixed overheads						10 400	
							12 000

Variable non-manufacturing overheads

Delivery expense:						
for chairs	1 900	×	£0·14	=	266	
for desks	2 000	×	£0·20	=	400	
	budgeted sales, units		standard delivery cost			666
Selling commission	2 per cent of sales (£45 200)					904

PROGRAMMED BUDGETS

Administration	3 600
Selling	3 400
	39 370

Less budgeted increase in finished goods inventory (at variable manufacturing cost: 100 chairs at £3·70)

	370
Budgeted cost of goods sold	£39 000

BUDGETED NET PROFIT

	£6 200

Table 15.1b Calculation of standard product costs and variable costs

	Standard price of input £	CHAIRS			DESKS		
		Standard input per unit of product	Standard product cost £	Standard variable cost £	Standard input per unit of product	Standard product cost £	Standard variable cost £
Direct materials:							
Wood	0·85	2	1·70	1·70	4	3·40	3·40
Covering	0·45	2	0·90	0·90	–	—	—
Direct labour:							
Preparation	0·75	$\frac{2}{5}$	0·30	0·30	2	1·50	1·50
Finishing	1·00	$\frac{3}{5}$	0·60	0·60	1	1·00	1·00
Manufacturing overheads							
Variable 1 600 0·20		1	—	0·20	3	—	0·60
Fixed 10 400							
Total £12 000							
÷ 8 000 = 1·50		1	1·50	—	3	4·50	—
Standard product cost			£5·00			£10·40	
Variable cost of manufacture			£3·70			£6·50	
Distribution (variable)			0·14			0·20	
Sales commissions			0·16			0·30	
Variable cost of sales			£4·00			£7·00	

either the *price* of the input differed from standard or the *quantity* used was different from standard. Each element must be syphoned off as a separate variance; the only question is when?

Whatever the recording system, in the *order* of separation price variance is always isolated first. An important motive is simplification of the records: once price variances have been isolated all subsequent recording can take place at conveniently constant prices. Thus embarrassing problems like FIFO are avoided: all inventory items held by the firm, whether purchased or manufactured or work-in-progress, are held at standard prices. It will be seen in the next section that this decision on the order of isolation affects the money values assigned to variances.

(a) 'Continuous' monitoring of direct cost variances

'Continuous' monitoring is shown as system 1 in Figure 15.3. At stage I price variances can be separated: by comparing invoiced and standard prices for purchased goods and by comparing actual and standard pay for time worked by direct labour.

At stage II quantity variances can be isolated as resources are consumed by the production departments. For materials this can be effected by issuing only standard quantities for specific jobs (e.g. evidenced by a white docket). The issue would provide the basis for charging production at standard cost. Additional issues for a job (e.g. red docket) would be charged to a materials quantity variance account, and any returns to store would be credited to the department's materials quantity variance. In this way there would be immediate feedback to operatives and supervisors on the progress of material usage; the approach is obviously not applicable to all situations. Analysis of work time sheets can provide frequent (e.g. daily) monitoring of direct labour costs, so that production is charged with standard cost.

Overheads, which are substantially period costs, are generally analysed at stage III, after production for the costing period (e.g. month) is completed.

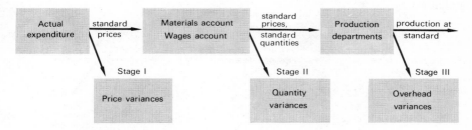

Figure 15.3 System 1 recording procedures

(b) 'Continuous' monitoring of price variances, with periodic quantity variances

In system 2 illustrated in Figure 15.4 the price variances are isolated as before, but quantity variances are calculated at the end of the costing period from the analysis of production inputs and outputs. Data collection at the operational level is simplified, but the feedback is slower; this is an acceptable trade-off for many firms.

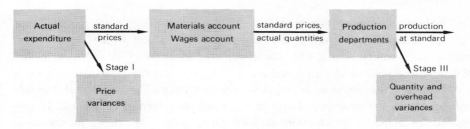

Figure 15.4 System 2 recording procedures

455

(c) Periodic calculation of variances

System 3 in Figure 15.5 separates all variances at stage III, from data on actual production costs. In fact the standards need not be recorded at all: the analysis can be conducted on a memo basis. Such analysis outside the routine recording system would be *most unusual* for direct costs, but is commonly used for other variances such as sales.

The analysis of variances after all activities of the period have been completed provides a useful vehicle for understanding the interrelationships of variances. This *ex post* approach is commonly adopted in explaining variances, and it will be used in subsequent sections. However it should be borne in mind that this is merely an *expository device*; the analysis of Furniture's variances for three months can do nothing for the operations of that period. A standard costing system must provide frequent and timely information if it is to be worth the elaborate effort of its installation.

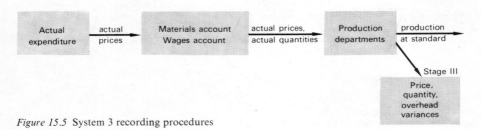

Figure 15.5 System 3 recording procedures

15.5 Direct cost variances

Direct cost variances are derived from the analysis of direct material and direct labour costs. Initially it will be assumed that these costs are linearly variable with output: overtime premiums and idle time will later provide examples of non-linearity.

(a) Direct labour

(i) *The basic price/quantity variances*
For any given achieved output the total direct labour cost which 'should' have been incurred can be obtained by multiplying standard cost by the output achieved. Note that the volume of output achieved, *not* the originally budgeted volume, is used because costs are being assumed to vary with output. Thus the total standard cost for the direct labour in Furniture's Preparation department could be calculated for achieved production of 2 400 chairs and 1 750 desks as shown in Table 15.2.

Table 15.2 Preparation department direct labour

	Standard input per unit of production	Actual × volume, units	Total = standard hours	Standard price of input (hourly pay-rate)	Total standard costs £
	Standard costs for actual volume of output:				
Chairs	$\frac{2}{5}$ hr	2 400	960		
Desks	2 hr	1 750	3 500		
			4 460	× £0·75	= 3 345
Actual costs:					
Total actual hours			4 700	× £0·80	= 3 760
Total variance			240 hr		£415

The standard data were derived from Table 15.1, but of course actual results (volume of production, hours and pay rates) are different.

Actual costs were greater than the calculated standards by £415: this is the total *unfavourable* direct cost variance. This total variance can be split to yield further information: it was composed of an increase in the average rate of pay and excess hours over standard. The pay-rate (price) element may not be the responsibility of the departmental supervisor, but the time (quantity) element certainly is.

A split of the total variance is illustrated in Figure 15.6. As a price element the *pay-rate variance* is isolated first: it can be viewed as the (average) increase in pay-rate multiplied by the actual hours (£0·05 × 4 700). The residual variance, representing labour efficiency in the use of time, is made up of the incremental hours at the standard pay-rate (240 × £0·75). This variance is often termed efficiency variance, but the term *quantity variance* will be adopted to avoid confusion with the efficiency variance commonly used for overheads.

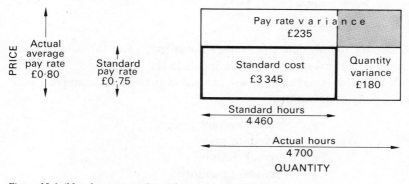

Figure 15.6 (Not drawn to scale). Direct labour variances

Note the way in which the pay-rate variance includes the incremental pay on the incremental hours (£0·05 × 240 hours = £12), indicated by the shaded area in Figure 15.6. This segment of cost was caused by the pay-rate difference *in combination with* the difference in hours: it is impossible to assign it logically to either price or quantity causes. The dilemma is solved by the arbitrary rule considered earlier: isolate price variance first. The effect of the arbitrary rule becomes serious if actual prices differ significantly from standard, in which case the quantity variance element assumes a dimension unrelated to the economic price environment.

This type of difficulty exists throughout variance analysis: when variances are isolated the order of isolation determines which variances get the 'increment × increment' segments.* Thus it is as well to remember in interpreting variances that they all have some fuzziness at the corners.

The variances can be analysed more easily by a calculation sequence which will have general application. This sequence follows the accounting procedures (e.g. system 1 of section 4). Commencing with actual costs *the analysis works progressively towards standard cost* – a simple process with the single intermediate reference point of this example.

		£	£
$p_a q_a$	Actual direct labour cost	3 760	
	PAY-RATE VARIANCE		235 *U*
$p\ q_a$	*Standard actual pay-rate* × *hours* (£0·75) (4 700)	3 525	
	QUANTITY VARIANCE		180 *U*
$p\ q$	*Standard standard pay-rate* × *hours* (0·75) (4 460)	3 345	
	Total direct labour variance		£415 *U*

It is not necessary to calculate the average actual pay-rate: the actual direct labour cost represents the total recorded payments in the accounts.

The symbols in the left-hand column will be used in subsequent examples; they can be given the general definitions:

p_a actual average price
p standard price
q_a actual quantity
q standard quantity

* See [1].

458

The signs of the variances can be designated as:

Unfavourable   Favourable
U OR F
$-$ $+$
Debit   Credit

The sign for each variance is determined in the sequence of separation: since all items $(p_a q_a, p q_a, p q)$ are costs, any *excess* of an item over its more standardized successor in the sequence must also be a cost, U. Similarly if the earlier, more 'actualized' item is *less* than its more standardized successor the difference must be a benefit, F.

(ii) *Subdivision of the basic variances*

The subsidiary variances are intended to identify component causes of the basic variances; which elements are worthwhile isolating will depend on the nature of the firm's operations, and the following examination is not exhaustive.*

1. *Labour mix variance* The first component to be considered involves a situation in which a department employs workers in more than one pay grade. If the mixture of grades actually assigned to the department is different from that assumed in setting standards, the effect on pay can be isolated. The result is called a labour mix variance, not controllable by a supervisor to whom grades are assigned by higher management.

The calculation will be illustrated this time by reference to the Finishing department. The total budgeted hours (3 200) have been divided into 800 unskilled and 2 400 skilled hours in Table 15.3. In that table the symbol Q has been introduced to represent the *budgeted quantity of inputs for each category* (here hours for each grade of labour).

The expression $Q/\Sigma Q$ defines the standard proportion of labour for each category assumed in the budget: in effect it represents the *standard mix* of labour. Therefore $\Sigma(pQ)/\Sigma Q$ is the average standard pay-rate:† the resulting figure of £1 per hour reconciles with the original total budget in Table 15.1.

*See, e.g. [8].

†The notation should strictly be defined more elaborately as

$$\sum_{j=1}^{n} \frac{(p_j^s \cdot Q_j)}{\Sigma Q_j},$$

and the standard price for the actual quantity (to be considered shortly) would become

$$\sum_{j=1}^{n} (p_j^s \cdot q_j^a)$$

where: subscript j represents individual categories (pay grades in this case), n is the number of categories and superscripts s and a represent standard and actual respectively (for p and q). The notation has been simplified, without loss of accuracy for the present purposes, so that the sequence of variance calculation can be recognized more readily.

Table 15.3 Finishing department direct labour

Budget calculation of average standard pay rate:

	Budget input, hours Q	Standard pay-rate p	Budget cost pQ
Semi-skilled	800	£0·85	680
Skilled	2 400	£1·05	2 520
	3 200 ←Average £1→£3 200		
	ΣQ	$\dfrac{\Sigma(pQ)}{\Sigma Q}$	$\Sigma(pQ)$

Standard costs for actual volume of output:

	Standard input per unit of production	× Actual volume	= Total standard hours q	Standard price of input (average hourly pay-rate) p	Total standard costs, £ pq
Chairs	$\frac{3}{5}$ hr	2 400	1 440		
Desks	1 hr	1 750	1 750		
			3 190	× £1·00	= 3 190

Actual costs:

	Actual hours q_a	Total actual costs, £ $p_a q_a$
Semi-skilled	600	
Skilled	2 500	
	3 100	3 450
Total variance	90 hr F	£260 U

The next stage of Table 15.3 calculates the total standard cost for Finishing labour along the lines already discussed for Preparation. Finally the actual results show a different labour mix from the standard assumption; the actual mix is relatively more skilled.

We now have the information to calculate the variance caused by the changed mix. This variance is the difference between total standard pay for the actual mix and standard pay for the standard (budgeted) mix, as shown below:

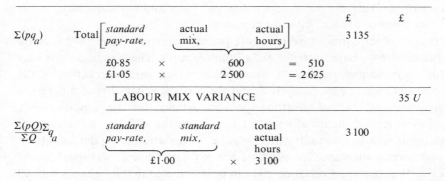

					£	£
$\Sigma(pq_a)$	Total [standard pay-rate,	actual mix,	actual hours]		3 135	
	£0·85	×	600	= 510		
	£1·05	×	2 500	= 2 625		
	LABOUR MIX VARIANCE					35 *U*
$\dfrac{\Sigma(pQ)}{\Sigma Q}\Sigma q_a$	standard pay-rate,	standard mix,	total actual hours		3 100	
	£1·00		× 3 100			

Using data from Table 15.3 the new variance can be inserted into an updated version of the original format used for the basic variances: the expression $\Sigma(pQ)/\Sigma Q$ appears in its logical place in the sequence of changing elements, as illustrated below. It would be possible to split all the variances into separate variances for each category of labour (given a split of actual pay) by dropping the first summation sign (Σ) in each expression. This approach will be illustrated later in a different mix situation.

					£	£
$\Sigma(p_a q_a)$	Total actual labour cost				3 450	
	PAY-RATE VARIANCE					315 *U*
$\Sigma(pq_a)$	Total [standard pay-rate,	actual mix,	actual hours]		3 135	
	MIX VARIANCE					35 *U*
$\dfrac{\Sigma(pQ)}{\Sigma Q}\Sigma q_a$	[standard pay-rate,	standard mix]	total actual hours		3 100	
	QUANTITY VARIANCE					90 *F*
$\Sigma(pq)$	Total [standard pay-rate,	standard mix,	standard hours]		3 190	
	Total direct labour variance					£260 *U*

2. *Overtime and idle time* Other variances can be broken out of the basic pay-rate (price) and quantity variances whenever a cause is considered worthy of separate control attention. The principle to be followed is that any amount separated

from the pay-rate variance will reflect *actual* pay-rates and any element from the quantity variance will reflect *standard* pay-rates.

An example of the former type (pay-rate/price) is overtime, where workers are paid a premium over basic rates for extra hours of work. The standard costs may allow for some normal element of overtime, in which case segregation of the variance would require payroll analysis and the periodic separation of differences between actual and normal overtime (perhaps detailed for the jobs involved). Clearly if there is no standard allowance for overtime the variance will include *all* overtime premiums. In situations where wage rates are stable during the period and there is no normal allowance for overtime, the pay-rate variance will itself constitute the overtime premium variance, and can be interpreted in this light. As with all variances the major points at issue which will determine the calculations are information costs versus information benefits. The basic rates of pay are not controllable at the lowest management levels, but overtime commonly will be.

An idle time variance can be calculated in situations where work comes to a halt for some reason, but payment does not. This implies a *fixed* element in direct labour costs (e.g. the workers are paid some guaranteed wage). Some allowance for an element of lost time is, of course, implicit in standard setting: separation of a variance is undertaken only when idle time is associated with some clearly identifiable cause like the interruption of the flow of inputs or breakdown of machinery. The separation of causes would be important in order to indicate areas for remedial action. The calculation of the variance would be based on labour time records, with lost hours priced at the standard rate.

Returning to Furniture's Finishing department, further analysis of the pay-rate variance (£315 *U*) might reveal that the skilled workers were paid overtime premiums of £300 (say 100 hours at £0·30) and the residual amount of £15 arose from a slight change in the basic pay-rates. Similar investigation of the time records might reveal idle time (caused by lack of materials from the Preparation department) amounting to 30 hours, which at the average standard pay-rate of £1 would produce an unfavourable variance of £30. Thus after adjustment the amended quantity variance would become £120 favourable: the efficiency of labour during working time was higher than was originally indicated.

The division of the variance for Finishing can be summarized as follows:

	£		£
Pay-rate variance	315 *U*	Amended pay-rate variance	15 *U*
		Overtime premium variance	300 *U*
Mix-variance	35 *U*		35 *U*
Quantity variance	90 *F*	Idle time variance	30 *U*
		Amended quantity variance	120 *F*
Total variance	£260 *U*		£260 *U*

The existence of both idle time and overtime premiums in the same period may seem inconsistent, and would certainly be worthy of attention. In fact idle time can be a contributory cause of overtime if it is necessary to complete work to a deadline. This provides a small example of the way in which the ultimate causes of variances may be interrelated.

(b) Direct materials

(i) *The basic price/quantity variances*
The analysis of the basic direct material variances proceeds on similar lines to the analysis of direct labour. There is the complication that materials are held in inventory, but as all price variances are separated first* the existence of inventory purchased at some non-standard price has no effect on the analysis of the *use* of materials.

The variances will be illustrated by data for Furniture's purchase and use of wood, given in Table 15.4.

Table 15.4 Direct materials – wood

Standard costs for actual volume of output:

	Standard input per unit × of production	Actual volume	Total = standard quantity	Standard price of input	Total standard costs, £
Chairs	2 ft³	2 400	4 800		
Desks	4 ft³	1 750	7 000		
			11 800	× £0·85	= 10 030

Materials used at standard price:

			Total actual quantity		
			11 500	× £0·85	= 9 775
Quantity variance			300 ft³		£255

Materials purchased at actual price:

			Total actual quantity		
			12 500	× £0·90	= £11 250

*Following the rule stated in section 4 and subsequently examined in connection with the pay-rate variance. The usual recording procedures (systems 1 and 2) ensure that all inventories are recorded at standard cost.

Control through standards

The analysis of the variances is illustrated in Figure 15.7. It will be seen that the price variance reflects all purchases during the period; any change in inventory (increase in this case) is accommodated by recording at standard price. With regard to the use of materials, it will be seen that actual use was less than standard, so that a favourable quantity variance is produced.

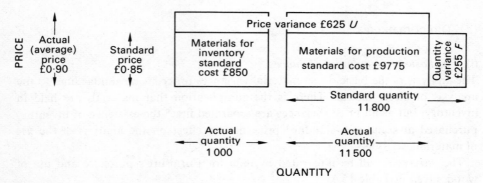

Figure 15.7 (Not drawn to scale.) Materials variances – wood

Sequential analysis of price/quantity variances can proceed in the usual way. This is shown below: variances for the covering material have been included. The

				Wood	*Covering*	*Totals*
				£	£	£
	Actual cost of purchased materials			11 250	2 050	
	+ Decrease ⎱ in inventory at					
	− (Increase) ⎰ standard price			(850)	150	
$p_a q_a$	Adjusted cost			10 400	2 200	
	PRICE VARIANCES			625 *U*	60 *F*	565 *U*
$p q_a$	*Standard*	×	actual	9 775	2 260	
	price		materials			
			used			
	QUANTITY VARIANCES			255 *F*	100 *U*	155 *F*
pq	*Standard*	×	*standard*	10 030	2 160	
	price		*materials*			
	Total direct material variances			£370 *U*	£40 *U*	410 *U*

quantity variances would be controllable by the Preparation department. Price variances (primarily arising from changes in the external environment) reflect inaccurate expectations, and may be used in the assessment of the success of buying policy (e.g. would holding costs on earlier lower cost purchases have been less than the price variance?). However, care must be exercised in interpreting the price variance because the wisdom of buying policy cannot be assessed in a single short period (e.g. an unfavourable price variance in this period may prove advantageous if further substantial price rises occur).

(ii) *Sub-division of the basic variances*
The basic variances for direct materials can be broken into subsidiary variances on the same principles as those examined for direct labour.

1. *Material mix variance* Materials can be used as substitutes for one another in the manufacture of products (e.g. a plastic component for a metal component) without changing the required characteristics of the end product. Similarly different combinations of grades of materials can be used to produce a particular end product (or set of end products, possibly in changed proportions). Chemical processes provide good examples of situations where 'richer' or 'poorer' mix of inputs can affect output volume.

Linear programming can be used as an approach for selecting optimal mix and such a mix (or an approximation to it) could be adopted as the original standard mix. Unfortunately the optimal mix does not remain constant over time: prices, demand, availability of inputs change. The standard costing approach isolates the effect of changes from the original standard mix; thus it indicates the direction of changes and permits a preliminary assessment of 'better or worse' but it does not purport to indicate whether the results were optimal in the conditions prevailing.

The Furniture example will not be further extended for material mix variances. Instead a chemical process will be considered, in which inputs and outputs are measured in common units but a loss in volume occurs through processing (e.g. through evaporation). The relevant data for budgeted inputs/outputs and actual inputs/outputs are provided in Table 15.5. Note that the standards assume each gallon of output requires 1·1 gallon of inputs. The problem has been simplified by assuming that no inventories are held.

Using the data from Table 15.5 the variances can be analysed in the usual sequence, on page 467. The price variances raise no difficulties: they reveal a favourable variance for X (£132 F) and an unfavourable variance for Y (£198 U). On price grounds there would be a case for tilting the mix emphasis towards X, and it will be seen from the mix variances that such a change has occurred (but remember that availability of inputs can also influence mix).

The mix variances are calculated on the same principle as the labour mix for Furniture's Finishing department, but on this occasion input categories are con-

Table 15.5 Input/output of 'material' for a chemical process

Budget calculation of inputs:

	Standard inputs (per gallon of output) $\times$	Budget output $=$	Budget inputs (gallons) Q	Standard price of inputs p	Budget cost, £ pQ
Grade X	0·6 ⎫	1 000	600	£3·30	1 980
Grade Y	0·5 ⎬		500	£4·40	2 200
	1·1 gallon		1 100 ⟵ Average £3·80 ⟶		£4 180
			ΣQ	$\dfrac{\Sigma(pQ)}{\Sigma Q}$	$\Sigma(pQ)$

Standard costs for actual volume of output:

	Standard inputs (per gallon of output) $\times$	Actual volume output $=$	Standard inputs (gallons) q	Standard prices p	Standard costs, £ pq
Grade X	0·6 ⎫	880	528	£3·30	1 742
Grade Y	0·5 ⎬		440	£4·40	1 936
			968		£3 678

Actual costs:

		Actual inputs (gallons) q_a	Actual prices p_a	Actual costs, £ $p_a q_a$
Grade X		660	£3·10	2 046
Grade Y		330	£5·00	1 650
		990		£3 696

sidered individually. The *total* actual inputs (990 gallons) are adjusted to standard mix and standard price assumptions by the expression $(pQ/\Sigma Q)\Sigma q_a$. Since $Q/\Sigma Q$ reflects the standard mix ratio for each category of input it would not matter whether the figures for budget quantities (600/1 100 and 500/1 100) or the standard mix ratios themselves (0·6/1·1 and 0·5/1·1) were adopted in the calculations.

The quantity or yield variance represents the over- or under-usage in terms of standard mix; it is a useless piece of information in relation to *individual* categories because individual variations have been taken into the mix variances. The total quantity (or yield) variance is a little more meaningful: it represents the total actual *physical* inputs compared with *physical* usage projected in setting standards, both valued at average standard price (i.e. $[990 - 968] \times £3·80 \simeq £84$).

466

		X	Y	Total
		£	£	£
$p_a q_a$	Actual input costs	2 046	1 650	3 696
		132 F	198 U	66 U
	PRICE VARIANCES			
pq_a	*Standard price, actual mix, actual inputs*	(£3·30 × 660) 2 178	(£4·40 × 330) 1 452	3 630
		396 U	528 F	132 F
	MIX VARIANCES			
$p\dfrac{Q}{\Sigma Q}\,\Sigma q_a$	*Standard price, standard mix, actual inputs*	$\dfrac{(£3\cdot30 \times 600 \times 990)}{1\,100}$ 1 782	$\dfrac{(£4\cdot40 \times 500 \times 990)}{1\,100}$ 1 980	3 762
		40 U	44 U	84 U
	QUANTITY (YIELD) VARIANCES			
pq	*Standard price, standard mix, standard inputs*	(£3·30 × 528) 1 742	(£4·40 × 440) 1 936	3 678
	Total material variance			£18 U

467

Variances in mix situations must be treated with caution for control purposes; three types of situation can be distinguished:

(a) Quantity variance only, with zero or negligible price variances. The quantity variance represents controllable usage at the shopfloor (i.e. lowest supervisory) level, because the standard mix, if optimal at standard prices, is applicable as a definition of the inputs which 'should' be used.

(b) Quantity and mix variances, with zero or negligible price variances. The mix and quantity variances are *jointly* controllable at the operational level at which mix decisions are taken. It is no longer possible to say categorically that the quantity variance is controllable at shop-floor level – the changed mix may cause different output ratios and therefore standard mix no longer defines what inputs 'should' be.

(c) Quantity, mix and price variances. If, as it is to be hoped, mix decisions are taken in the light of the changed price environment, the *three* variances become jointly controllable at the operational level at which mix decisions are taken. In this situation it is only possible to make some preliminary assessment of whether the variances moved in the right direction (e.g. in the chemical process they had: X became relatively cheaper and more used). When significant price changes throw the standard assumptions into the melting pot in this way, it is important to revise standards (both price and mix).

2. *Scrap and spoilage variances* It is often possible and informative to identify specific forms of material wastage by variances. A routine for measurement is essential, therefore the variance will be discussed in the context of the recording system.

When material has to be cut or machined the offcuts or shavings (e.g. metal) can be physically measured and transferred at standard price to a scrap variance account. If material standards include some provision for a 'normal' level of scrap it is necessary to adjust the scrap variance for this normal level, so that the residual variance represents abnormal scrap. The mechanics of the recording procedure are illustrated in Figure 15.8. In effect the department is credited twice for the normal scrap, once when the output is transferred out of the department at standard cost (which includes the normal scrap allowance in the standard cost calculation) and again when actual scrap is charged to the variance account. Therefore a debit for normal scrap on the actual output balances the department's accounts, and the corresponding credit to scrap variance produces a net figure representing abnormal scrap on that account.

When scrap has a saleable value an appropriate credit to the variance account (debit sale of scrap) can be made.

Spoilage is similar to scrap but refers to the wastage of partly finished products

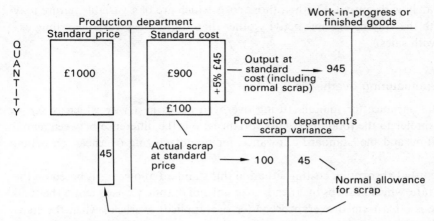

Figure 15.8 Scrap variance

and/or the cost of reworking damaged or faulty products. Thus labour inputs as well as materials are involved. A recording system for spoilage can be developed on the same principles as for scrap.*

Both scrap and spoilage are broken out of the quantity variances (the labour element of spoilage from the labour quantity variance). Whether it is worthwhile isolating these variances depends on their importance to the production problems of the firm; their controllability rests at the production level, but the assignment of causes may be informative.

In the sequential analysis of variances the scrap and/or material spoilage variances would occupy positions comparable with that of idle time for direct labour. If the approach had been applied to Furniture's materials (wood only) a breakdown might look like the following:

	£		£
Price variance	625 *U*		625 *U*
		Scrap	280 *F*
Quantity variance	255 *F*	Material spoilage	20 *U*
		Amended quantity	15 *U*

15.6 Indirect cost variances

The procedures for the separation of overhead cost variances are different from those for direct cost variances in two important respects. Substantial elements of fixed costs are involved, so that expenditure cannot be expected to vary pro-

---

*For further consideration of this area see [8].

portionately with output. Further, those costs which are of a variable nature may vary with the volume of some activity other than output (e.g. variable selling expenses with sales).

(a) Manufacturing overheads

The total variance for manufacturing overhead arises in a way which is *superficially* similar to the total direct cost variances: it is the difference between actual expenditure and the 'standard allowance' for manufacturing overhead on actual output.

In the usual absorption costing situation this standard allowance is based on the burden rate, which absorbs overheads over units of output. Consequently the total variance is often termed overabsorbed (or overapplied) overhead when the standard allowance exceeds actual expenditure, and underabsorbed (or underapplied) overhead when the standard allowance is less than actual expenditure.

But the burden rate does not provide a basis for estimating what overhead expenditure should have been (unless output is coincidentally equal to the output assumed in calculating the burden rate). Some adjustment must be made for the fixed and variable elements of overhead costs. Such adjustment is termed *'flexible budgeting'*, which merely means that fixed costs are treated as fixed costs and variable costs are treated as variable costs. However, for flexible budgeting purposes variable overhead costs need not be treated as varying linearly with output; different cost elements can be treated as varying with inputs (e.g. lighting) as step costs (e.g. indirect labour), as semi-variable – partially fixed and partially variable (e.g. maintenance) and as conventionally variable with output (e.g. indirect materials). For present purposes the simple linear assumption will be employed. Whatever the assumptions of the flexible budget it provides a third reference point which can be used to split the total variance two ways.

(i) *Two-way overhead analysis*
The three reference points will be demonstrated for Furniture on the basis of data from Table 15.6, which summarizes previous information (except actual expenditure).

1. *Actual expenditure* on manufacturing overhead is £12 140. Responsibility for control of overheads rests with the factory manager of Furniture, so there has been no allocation between departments.

2. *Absorbed overhead, or standard allowance*, of £11 475 is derived by multiplying the burden rate of £1·50 by the earned output of 7 650 direct labour hours. This is the stage at which the activity index (direct labour hours = DLH) comes into use: the *earned output* means the diverse units of physical output (chairs and desks) translated into the common activity index by application of the standard rate of

470

Table 15.6 Manufacturing overhead summary

Activity index data – direct labour hours:	Budgeted output (DLH) [= normal output in this case]	Earned output (DLH) [Achieved output at standard DLH]	Actual DLH
Preparation	4 800	4 460	4 700
Finishing	3 200	3 190	3 100
	8 000	7 650	7 800

Overhead rates per DLH:

Fixed overhead rate $\quad \dfrac{£10\,400}{8\,000} = £1{\cdot}30$

Variable overhead rate $\quad \dfrac{£1\,600}{8\,000} = 0{\cdot}20$

Burden rate $\qquad\qquad\qquad £1{\cdot}50$

Absorbed manufacturing overheads 7 650 DLH × £1·50	£11 475
Actual manufacturing overhead expenditure	£12 140
Total manufacturing overhead variance (underabsorbed)	£665

physical output to activity (1 chair: 1 DLH, 1 desk: 3 DLH). The same figure of 7 650 DLH was, in its component elements, used to indicate what total labour hours 'should' have been, but as earned output it measures the *physical output achieved*.

3. *Flexible budget allowance* of £11 930 represents the 'best estimate' of what costs should have been. It is obtained as follows:

	£
Fixed overheads (as original budget)	10 400
Variable overheads:	
Earned Variable	
output × overhead rate	
7 650 £0·20	1 530
Flexible budget for earned output	£11 930

The interrelationships and implications of the three reference points can be seen in the graph of Figure 15.9. The two lines on the graph represent the burden rate for absorption purposes (which goes through the origin, suggesting invalidly a directly proportional relationship between total overheads and output) and the flexible budget (which would meet the £ axis at fixed costs of £10 400). Against the

471

earned output of 7 650 DLH have been plotted the three reference points considered above.

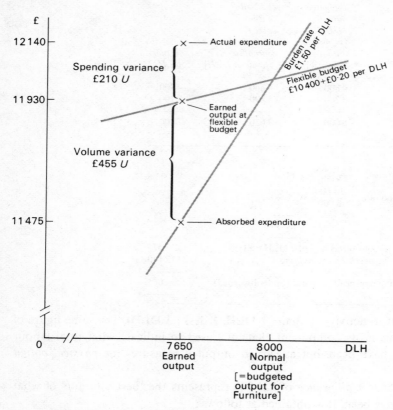

Figure 15.9 Manufacturing overheads

The difference between actual expenditure (£12 140) and the flexible budget's best estimate of what costs should be (£11 930) is termed the *spending* (or *budget* or *expenditure*) *variance*. This constitutes under- or overspending on overheads: it would usually be regarded as controllable (certainly at the factory level with which we are concerned, and commonly at departmental level), but it should be noted that it is closely comparable with the *total* variance for direct costs in that it contains both price and quantity elements. Thus Furniture's unfavourable variance of £210 could have arisen from price differences (e.g. salary changes, prices of spare parts, etc.) or from quantity differences (e.g. additional staff, power usage, etc.). In fact the total spending variance alone is not particularly informative, and a comparison of detailed actual components of expenditure against budget components (suitably adjusted for fixed/variable assumptions) would normally be undertaken as a routine part of control procedures. Thus indications would be provided of items suitable for investigation.

The difference between the flexible budget for earned output (£11 930) and absorbed overheads (£11 475) is termed the *volume variance*. This variance can be viewed in another way as:

$$(\text{Earned output} - \text{normal output}) \times \text{fixed overhead rate}$$

$$350 \text{ DLH} \qquad \times \qquad £1{\cdot}30 = £455$$

Thus the volume variance represents under/over absorption of *fixed* overheads: it can be seen from the graph that as earned output approaches normal output the variance approaches zero. There could, of course, have been a positive variance on the upper side of the crossover point.

The analysis of the spending and volume variance could be shown in the usual format (except that the *p*, *q* formulations are no longer relevant):

	£	£
Actual expenditure	12 140	
SPENDING VARIANCE		210 *U*
Earned output at flexible budget	11 930	
VOLUME VARIANCE		455 *U*
Earned output at burden rate	11 475	
Total manufacturing overhead variance		£665 *U*

There are two views of the meaning of the volume variance. The first is that it is a measure of the cost (or benefit for favourable variance) of output different from the normal level. If output had been higher the fixed costs would have been absorbed over a larger number of units.

The second view, to which we subscribe, is that the main function of the variance is to make the books balance to accommodate the use of absorption costing in the accounts. It is important to take this book-keeping element out of the total variance in order to isolate the more interesting spending variance.

Two computational reasons for this view are that the burden rate calculation can be arbitrary in two dimensions, in its numerator and in its denominator:

1. When fixed costs are arbitrarily prorated to segments of a firm the figure for overheads must, at best, be treated with scepticism. (Furniture's figures were not subject to this stricture, they applied to the whole operating entity.)

2. The choice of output on which to calculate the burden rate is arbitrary. (Furniture's budgeted output was conveniently equal to normal output: commonly they would be different and a budgeted over- or underabsorption of fixed cost would appear in the original budget.) The idea of normal output is question begging – does it mean past average or expected average? 80 per cent of capacity is a common rule of thumb, but fully practicable capacity is another acceptable alternative. Since the choice of normal output will determine the burden rate, the money magnitude of any volume variance will depend on that choice.

The volume variance is more likely to confuse than assist operating supervisors, who already know their goals in terms of output per DLH. From the viewpoint of overall assessment of capacity utilization (e.g. by the factory manager and/or his supervisors) the important consideration is not the loss or gain of overhead absorption, but the loss or gain of profit margins on output. However, a gain in output is no use if it cannot be sold. For *controlling the current situation* three major aspects must be interrelated; manufacturing capacity, margins and demand (both current *and* expected): this task is not aided by the volume variance. For *assessment of responsibility after the event* a case can be made for valuing the difference between budgeted and actual output at the variable profit (contribution) per unit [3], [11], to which should be added the proviso that excess output would merit a cost penalty (e.g. holding charge) when budgeted output was restricted through lack of demand.

(ii) *Three-way and four-way overhead analysis*

The analysis of overheads can be extended by adding *actual inputs* to the activity index axis. Furniture's actual hours of direct labour (summarized in Table 15.6) totalled 7 800 hours. This provides two new reference points potentially available for variance calculations: actual hours at flexible budget (£11 960) and actual hours at burden rate (£11 700), as shown in Figure 15.10.

Five reference points permit a four-way analysis of overheads. It is possible to combine the elements in different ways to produce three-way variances and two-way variances (potentially 4+6 different ways*); it is also possible to add to the reference points to permit further combinations! Many such combinations for overhead variance analysis have been proposed† and even used. For the most part these combinations rely on the fixed overhead element of the burden rate, so that earlier criticisms would apply. Thus we can reject the new reference point which involves the burden rate in Figure 15.10 and consider only the new flexible budget point in combination with the three original points.

---

* Actual expenditure must always be one of the reference points. From the remaining four points the choice of three points can be made in four different ways ($_4C_3 = 4$) and the choice of two points can be made in six different ways ($_4C_2 = 6$). Several of these ten possibilities are implausible.

† See [1], p. 350 for six examples.

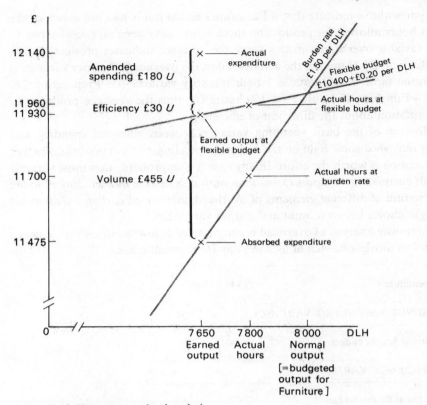

Figure 15.10 Three-way overhead analysis

The flexible budget for *actual* hours can be regarded as the best estimate of what overhead costs 'should' be in circumstances where variable overheads are strongly influenced by hours worked, i.e. variability with *input* in contrast to the earlier assumption of variability with *output*. For example, variable overhead consisting mainly of lighting and heating might behave in this manner. The new flexible budget point (£11 960) when compared with actual expenditure (£12 140) produces an *amended spending variance* (£180 *U*) as shown in Figure 15.10. The adjective amended has been used to distinguish the new variance; in fact the terms spending/budget/expenditure are commonly used irrespective of the calculation method.

An *efficiency variance* is derived from the difference between the two flexible budget points (£11 960 and £11 930). Alternatively the efficiency variance can be viewed as:

[Earned hours – actual hours] × Variable overhead rate = Efficiency variance

$$(7\,650 - 7\,800) \times £0.20 = £30\ U$$

475

The figures above indicate that if Furniture's actual hours had not exceeded the standard hours allowed for production there would have been no excess expenditure on variable overheads: in this sense the variance indicates production efficiency. But with DLH used as the activity index, the overhead efficiency variance is based on the same hourly data as labour quantity variance (i.e. Preparation 240 hours U + Finishing 90 hours F = 150 hours U); thus the variance produces no new information about the direction of efficiency.

The division of the basic spending variance between amended spending and efficiency may shed some light on the causes of spending, but it is doubtful whether the information is worth the effort. In any case it is improbable that most variable overheads correlate with inputs rather than output: a flexible budget tailored to the variable nature of different elements of overhead, mentioned earlier, would avoid the straight choice between input and output variability.

The three-way analysis of overhead is summarized below; as usual the sequence of separation moves one step at a time away from actual costs.

	£	£
Actual expenditure	12 140	
AMENDED SPENDING VARIANCE		180 *U*
Actual hours at flexible budget	11 960	
EFFICIENCY VARIANCE		30 *U*
Earned output at flexible budget	11 930	
VOLUME VARIANCE		455 *U*
Earned output at burden rate	11 475	
Total manufacturing overhead variance		£665 *U*

(b) Non-manufacturing overheads

Non-manufacturing overheads preponderantly involve programmed budgets and control through resource allocation. From the recording/reporting viewpoint in a standard costing system the programmed budgets are treated as predominantly fixed costs, but if there are costs which vary with operating activity (e.g. invoicing, payroll preparation in administration costs) an adjustment is needed on flexible budget lines. Such adjustment can be made within the recording system or on a memo basis showing detailed explanation of variances. Differences between actual expenditure and the appropriately adjusted budget are reported as spending budget variances.

The administration budget of Furniture was assumed not to contain any variable elements. Comparison with actual expenditure might produce a variance:

Actual administration expenditure	£3 480
Budgeted administration expenditure	3 600
Administration (spending) variance	120 *F*

These figures summarize detailed cost items which would appear in an administration expenditure report.

Some non-manufacturing overheads may be treated as containing a performance element. For example, this might apply to Furniture, if the company undertook its own delivery. The original variable standards (£0·14 per chair and £0·20 per desk) could represent the goals for delivery costs. However, if they are to be anything more than a very rough guideline the standards would need to be specified more clearly in a manner relevant to the operating problems (e.g. a fixed cost element plus a variable allowance for delivery distance times product sales volume); after this an understanding of price and quantity elements of variance would require separate detailed examination of expenditure. It will be assumed that Furniture's products are distributed by external carrier: any distribution cost variances will therefore lose their internal control significance.

Furniture's sales commissions have a simple expenditure forecasting role, because they are uniformly 2 per cent of sales value. Differential commissions may be used to encourage emphasis on certain (implicitly more profitable) lines: in such cases it would be informative to analyse the effect of commission changes on sales volumes; such an analysis would take place outside the standard costing system.

15.7 Sales variances

Sales variances can be used to analyse results in the sales area on broadly similar lines to those for manufacturing costs – only broadly similar, because the interpretation of variances is complicated by interrelationships between selling prices, quantities sold, product quality and marketing expenditure. Consideration of marketing expenditure will be postponed until the next chapter.

There is another important departure from the previous approach to variances. In the sales situation we are interested not only in the sales amounts, but ultimately in their profitability. Profitability analysis will be conducted here in terms of variable profit margin per unit (selling price – variable costs); similar analysis can be conducted in terms of standard profit (selling price – standard product cost).

For the remainder of this chapter the term *margin* will refer to variable profit per unit.

477

Control through standards

(a) The basic price and volume variances

Price and volume variances for sales (and margins) are isolated on the same principles as those for direct costs, subject to the qualifications that with revenues all excesses of actual over standard in the sequence of analysis represent favourable variances (i.e. opposite sign from cost variances), and volume variance means actual minus budgeted volume at standard (price or margin).

Table 15.7 Sales and margin data

Budgeted sales and margins:

	Budget sales (units)						
		Sales			*Margins*		
		Standard price	Budget revenue £		Standard margin	Budget variable profit, £	Margin per cent of sales
	Q	p	pQ		m	mQ	
		£	£		£	£	
Chairs	1 900	8·00	15 200		4·00	7 600	50
Desks	2 000	15·00	30 000		8·00	16 000	53·3
			£45 200			£23 600	52·21

Standard prices and margins for actual sales:

	Actual sales (units)					
		Sales			*Margins*	
		Standard price	Standard revenue		Standard margin	Standard variable profit
	q_a	p	pq_a		m	mq_a
		£	£		£	£
Chairs	2 300	8·00	18 400		4·00	9 200
Desks	1 700	15·00	25 500		8·00	13 600
			£43 900			£22 800

Actual prices and amended margins for actual sales:

	Actual sales (units)	Actual prices	Actual revenue		Amended margin	Actual variable profit
	q_a	p_a	$p_a q_a$		m_a	$m_a q_a$
		£	£		£	£
Chairs	2 300	8·50	19 550		4·50	10 350
Desks	1 700	15·00	25 500		8·00	13 600
			£45 050			£23 950

478

For Furniture sales and margin data are summarized in Table 15.7. The total variance of £150 U for sales can be divided between price and quantity elements in the usual manner:

Sales variances

		Chairs £		Desks £		Total £	
$p_a q_a$	Actual sales	19 550		25 500		45 050	
	PRICE VARIANCE		1 150 F		0		1 150 F
pq_a	Standard actual price × sales quantities	18 400		25 500		43 900	
	VOLUME VARIANCE		3 200 F	4 500 U			1 300 U
pQ	Standard budget price × sales quantity	15 200		30 000		45 200	
Total sales variance							£150 U

Margins can be analysed in the same way. The symbol m will be adopted to represent the standard margin. As standard *cost* variances are analysed in connection with production, it is convenient to ignore *cost* variations in analysing sales margins. Therefore the 'actual margin' reflects only selling price variations from standards, and can be defined as:

$$m_a = \text{(Actual selling price} - \text{standard variable cost of sales)}$$

This procedure could be misleading if standard costs (implying goals) are significantly different from actual costs. The use of expected margins and costs would be an improvement.

The price and quantity variances for the margins on sales are isolated on page 480: note that the price variance is the same as that produced for sales, due to the definition of actual margin.

These variances provide some preliminary indications of the price/demand relationships for the firm's products. It can be seen that a price increase *and* greater sales were achieved for chairs, whereas the desk situation looks sickly.

(b) Market variances

One approach to more informative variances involves the division of the volume variance into two elements indicating the effect on volume of *total market* demand

		Chairs £		Desks £		Total £	
$m_a q_a$	Actual margins	10 350		13 600		23 950	
	PRICE VARIANCE		1 150 *F*	0			1 150 *F*
mq_a	Standard actual margin × sales quantities	9 200		13 600		22 800	
	VOLUME VARIANCE		1 600 *F*		2 400 *U*		800 *U*
mQ	Standard budget margin × sales quantities	7 600		16 000		23 600	
	Total margin variance						£350 *F*

and the effect of the firm's relative position in the market (*market share*). Estimates on total market sales (in either unit or money terms) can be derived from a variety of sources: trade associations, market research, government publications. There are often problems in satisfactorily defining the market (in Furniture's case is it in the market for furniture, in separate markets for chairs and desks, in the market for office chairs or for office chairs in a particular geographical area?). An inadequate definition may have to be accepted in order to fit available data.

Given suitable data for Furniture, the original volume variance can be split between market volume effect and market share effect. Assume that Furniture's achieved share of its chair market (either in terms of actual units sold or actual sales value) was 9 per cent compared with 10 per cent adopted in setting standards. One-tenth of the budgeted sales were lost by this failure to maintain Furniture's share of its chair market: the market share variance was therefore

$$\tfrac{1}{10} \times £7\,600 = £760.$$

This method can be employed in the usual sequence of variances by inserting a new reference point for the updated budget figure:

$$mQ \times \frac{\text{actual share}}{\text{standard share}}.$$

The division of the basic volume variance is illustrated on page 481.

The reference point $mQ\left[\dfrac{\text{actual}}{\text{standard}}\right]$ for desks was calculated for 8 per cent actual share and 10 per cent budgeted share (£16 000 × $\tfrac{8}{10}$ = £12 800). The market volume variance means that the total market was $34\tfrac{1}{2}$ per cent above the original budget assumption for chairs, but only $6\tfrac{1}{4}$ per cent above the budget assumption for desks

Margins – market variances

		Chairs £	Desks £	Total £
mq_a	Standard margin × actual sales quantities	9 200	13 600	22 800
	MARKET VOLUME VARIANCE	2 360 F	800 F	3 160 F
$mQ \times \dfrac{\text{Actual share}}{\text{Standard share}}$	Standard margin × budget sales quantities × $\dfrac{\text{actual share}}{\text{standard share}}$	6 840	12 800	19 640
	MARKET SHARE VARIANCE	760 U	3 200 U	3 960 U
mQ	Standard margin × budget sales quantities	7 600	16 000	23 600
	Total volume variance			£800 U

$$\left(\frac{£2\,360}{£6\,840} = 34\cdot5 \text{ per cent,} \quad \frac{£800}{£12\,800} = 6\cdot25 \text{ per cent}\right).$$

The market *share* variance would be considered as controllable by the sales department, while the market *volume* variance is essentially a forecasting error.

This approach to market variances is illustrated for chairs in Figure 15.11. Note that the market *share* variance is measured in relation to the original budget assumption, and not in relation to the actual potential market. This approach can be defended on two grounds. The sales performance is being assessed in relation to the original aims given to the sales department (there would seem to have been a case for revising those aims during the period). In the reverse situation in which market volume is *below* budgeted expectations, the sales department no longer gets a 'free ride' on the corner element: it becomes relatively more important to maintain market share (which is likely to coincide with the firm's objectives).

The market variances shed some light on the sales achievement. In a market for chairs which was substantially stronger than budgeted the firm adopted higher prices at the expense of some reduction in market share. Since the price variance (£1 150 *F*) exceeded the market share variance (£760 *U*) the tactics were on balance successful *if* longer term implications are ignored and *if* Furniture had been operating close to capacity. The sales performance on desks was weak: market share was sharply lower despite adherence to standard prices in a total market which was larger than assumed in the budget. Clearly a case for investigation.

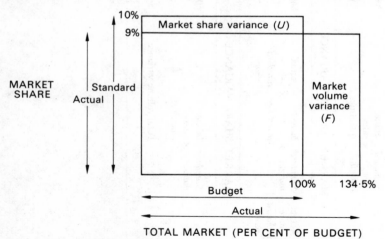

Figure 15.11 Market variances – chairs

(c) Mix variances

The previous approach attempted to assign differences in the product composition of sales to market causes for each product. Another approach examines the effect on margin of actual product composition, compared with the average margin assumed in the budget: this is the mix variance approach.

The first step splits the basic volume variance by calculating a reference point for what the contribution margin would have been if the *average margin on total sales* in the budget had been achieved, i.e. if the profitability mix assumed in the budget had been maintained. Using the data from Table 15.7 this reference point can be calculated:

$$\begin{array}{cc} Average\ margin & Total \\ on\ total & actual \\ budgeted\ sales & sales \end{array}$$

$$52 \cdot 212\% \times £43\,900 = £22\,921$$

In terms of the earlier notation this can be expressed as:

$$\frac{\Sigma(mQ)}{\Sigma(pQ)} \times \Sigma(pq_a)$$

Any difference in the profitability mix of the actual individual sales at standard margins ($\Sigma(mq_a) = £22\,800$ from Table 15.7) will constitute a mix variance. The division of the basic volume variance is shown below:

					£	£
$\Sigma(mq_a)$	Total $\begin{bmatrix} Standard \\ margin \end{bmatrix}$	, actual mix,	, actual volume $]$		22 800	
	MIX VARIANCE					121 *U*
$\dfrac{\Sigma(mQ)}{\Sigma(pQ)}\Sigma(pq_a)$	Standard margin	, standard mix	, total actual volume		22 921	
	AMENDED VOLUME VARIANCE					679 *U*
ΣmQ	Total $\begin{bmatrix} Standard \\ margin \end{bmatrix}$	, standard mix	, budgeted volume $]$		23 600	
	Margin volume variance					£800 *U*

The mix variance differs in one important respect from those calculated for labour and materials: sales quantities at standard prices are being used as an index of volume, instead of physical units alone (i.e. not $\dfrac{(mQ)}{\Sigma Q}\Sigma q_a$, as might be suggested by earlier formulations). We have seen on earlier occasions that heterogeneous products (here chairs and desks) cannot be aggregated without the aid of some

483

common index, and since the point at issue involves sales values they provide the obvious measure. (In fact ignoring relative values leads to trouble in *any* mix situation, as was seen in detail in connection with material mix.) Physical units are sometimes used in sales variance analysis;* the fact that Furniture sold *more units* than budgeted while achieving *lower sales value* indicates the irrelevance of that approach.

The total *mix* variance can be split between products by isolating the effects of variances from the average budgeted percentage margin on sales.† First it is necessary to separate the *sales* mix variances, by standardizing the sales volume of each product to the budgeted mix, i.e. what would sales of each product have been if total sales had followed the budgeted mix? This new reference point for sales is merely an individualized version of the previous mix reference point (i.e. Σ is dropped from the numerator and p substituted for m), thus:

Sales mix

				Chairs £	Desks £
pq_a	*Standard price* ,	*actual mix* ,	*actual volume*	18 400	25 500
	SALES MIX VARIANCE			3 637 F	3 637 U
$\dfrac{pQ}{\Sigma(pQ)}\Sigma(pq_a)$	*Standard price* ,	*standard mix* ,	*total actual volume*	14 763	29 137

The calculation of the new reference point uses data from Table 15.7

$$\left(\frac{£15\,200}{£45\,200} \times £43\,900 = £14\,763, \text{ etc.}\right)$$

Not surprisingly the variances sum to zero, because

$$\Sigma\left[\frac{pQ}{\Sigma(pQ)}\Sigma(pq_a)\right] = \Sigma pq_a,$$

the preceding reference point.

These sales mix variances can now be used to explain, in terms of the individual products, the margin mix of £121 U obtained earlier. The variations of percentage margins from the average (budgeted) percentage margin can be applied to the sales variances for each product, as shown below.

*See [5] and [12].
†This approach is based on Chumachenko's article [5].

	Standard margin on product %	Average budgeted margin %	Variation of standard margin %	Sales × mix variances £	Margin = mix variances
Chairs	50	52·21	−2·21	3 637 *F*	80 *U*
Desks	53·33	52·21	+1·12	3 637 *U*	41 *U*

Both mix variances are unfavourable because there was an *increase* in the sales of the *less* profitable line and a *decrease* in the sales of the *more* profitable line. Such variances can serve as warnings of changes in the profitability mix of sales and could trigger a review of pricing/selling policy. No action would seem to be indicated in the Furniture case, because the standard margins were very close and actual margins are now almost identical (chairs selling at £8·50 give a percentage margin of about 53 per cent). The variances must be treated with caution if actual prices have moved out of line with standards.

(d) Market with mix variances

After the isolation of the mix variances the amended volume variance can be split to reflect market volume and market share effects. The procedures and implications are different from those considered earlier; variations between individual products have now been incorporated into the mix variances. Therefore it is the undifferentiated market for the products which is under consideration: this approach would be appropriate in the common situation where total market information is not identifiable with product lines. It would also be relevant for the control of different sales areas, where emphasis is on total performance in the sales area rather than on individual product considerations.

The amended volume variance is split by updating the budgeted contribution as before, but this time the updating relates the firm's share of the *total* market to the *total* budgeted contribution. Furniture's share of the total market was 8·39 per cent compared with a standard share of 10 per cent.*

---

*These are consistent with the previous figures. Standard market share was 10 per cent for both products, and therefore 10 per cent overall.

Total market (projected at standard prices):

Chairs	£15 200 × 134·5%	204 444
Desks	£30 000 × 106·25%	318 750
		£523 194

Actual total sales at standard £43 900 = 8·39% of market.

Thus

$$\Sigma(mQ) \times \left[\frac{\text{actual share}}{\text{standard share}} \right]$$

gives

$$\pounds 23\,600 \times \frac{8{\cdot}39}{10} = \pounds 19\,800.$$

The resulting variances are shown below. (Derivation of the first reference point was considered at the beginning of the discussion on mix variances, section 7(c).)

				£	£
$\dfrac{\Sigma(mQ)}{\Sigma(pQ)}\,\Sigma pq_a$	*Standard margin* ,	*standard mix* ,	*total actual volume*	22 921	
MARKET VOLUME VARIANCE					3 121 *F*
$\Sigma(mQ).\left[\begin{array}{c}\text{actual}\\ \text{share}\\ \hline \text{standard}\\ \text{share}\end{array}\right]$ Total	$\left[\begin{array}{l}\text{\textit{Standard}} ,\\ \text{\textit{margin}}\end{array}\right.$	*standard mix* ,	$\left.\begin{array}{l}\text{\textit{budgeted}}\\ \text{\textit{volume}}\end{array}\right]$	$\left[\begin{array}{c}\text{actual}\\ \text{share}\\ \hline \text{standard}\\ \text{share}\end{array}\right]$	19 800
MARKET SHARE VARIANCE					3 800 *U*
$\Sigma(mQ)$ Total	$\left[\begin{array}{l}\text{\textit{Standard}} ,\\ \text{\textit{margin}}\end{array}\right.$	*standard mix* ,	$\left.\begin{array}{l}\text{\textit{budgeted}}\\ \text{\textit{volume}}\end{array}\right]$	23 600	
Amended volume variance					£679 *U*

The market variances are similar to those obtained from the totals for individual products. The differences arise partly because the present variances have excluded the mix elements, and partly through rounding. The broad implications of the variances are therefore unchanged, although it is no longer possible to draw conclusions about specific products.

The margin variance components which have been calculated in this section are summarized below.

	Chairs, £	Desks, £	Total, £
Price	1 150 *F*	0	1 150 *F*
Market volume	2 360 *F*	800 *F*	3 160 *F*
Market share	760 *U*	3 200 *U*	3 960 *U*
			£350 *F*
Price	1 150 *F*	0	1 150 *F*
Mix	80 *U*	41 *U*	121 *U*
Market volume			3 121 *F*
Market share			3 800 *U*
			£350 *F*

15.8 Reporting and evaluation

Variances provide feedback on the activities of the firm, on which corrective action may be based. The direct cost variances, because by definition they are readily identifiable with output, can be reported rapidly for lower level management reaction. Indirect cost and sales would tend to be analysed and controllable over longer time spans.

Departmental managers would be provided with variance information on the activities of their own departments, along lines already discussed. This variance information would also be made available to their immediate superiors (e.g. factory manager of Furniture) and then summarized for control purposes at that level – and so on.

A summary control report for Furniture's activities is presented in Table 15.8;

Table 15.8 Summary control report
Furniture profit and loss

	Budget £	Variances	
		£ Unfavourable	£ Favourable
Sales	45 200		
Variable costs	21 600		
Variable profit	23 600		
Fixed costs	17 400		
BUDGETED NET PROFIT	6 200		
SALES VARIANCES:			
Price			1 150
Market volume			3 160
Market share		(3 960)	
DIRECT COST VARIANCES:			
Labour Pay		(550)	
Mix		(35)	
Quantity		(90)	
Materials Price		(565)	
Quantity			155
MANUFACTURING OVERHEADS			
Spending		(210)	
NON-MANUFACTURING OVERHEADS			
Delivery expenses		(40)	
Selling commissions		(23)	
Administration			120
Selling			50
TOTAL VARIANCES	(838)	(5 473)	4 635
ACTUAL NET PROFIT	£5 362		

this assumes the use of variable manufacturing cost for inventory valuation, at least for internal reporting.* Total fixed costs have been deducted in the calculation of overhead, and there is no inventory carry forward of those fixed costs. A reconciliation of this 'internal reporting' profit with an external reporting profit based on full cost inventory will be given in Table 15.9. Reconciliation with planning reports and the balance sheet will be considered in section 9.

Having prepared the information it is necessary to add some further comments on its use.

(a) What is an exception?

If management is to be able to concentrate on exceptional items it must have some criterion for determining an exception. All non-zero variances can hardly be regarded as exceptional, so some concept of materiality must be adopted.

One view would be to regard the standard as a mean about which random fluctuations will occur. By setting control limits about the mean, and investigating only those variances outside the control limits it is possible to eliminate the majority (e.g. 95 per cent) of the random fluctuations while maintaining a high probability that non-random changes (i.e. changes in operating structure) will be caught. This type of approach is illustrated in Figure 15.12.

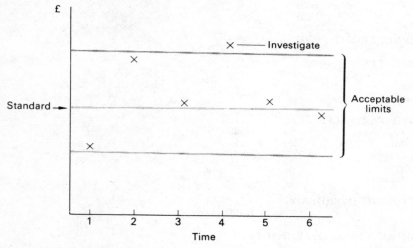

Figure 15.12 Control limits for standards

*It may be noted that the variance for selling commissions appears in Table 15.8 as £23 *U*. In this presentation the variance is 2 per cent of [actual sales (£45 050) – actual sales at standard price (£43 900)]. A favourable £26 element, 2 per cent, of [actual sales at standard price (£43 900) – budgeted sales (£45 200)], has been incorporated into the margins in the sales market variances, because those margins have been calculated using variable costs of *sales*, including commission, not on variable costs of production. Delivery expenses have been treated in a similar manner.

The approach is similar to that used by many firms for statistical sampling for quality control of output, but the formal expression of control limits is rare in standard costing.* The idea of standards as what 'should' be leaves no scope for the notion of random variations. The orthodox view of standards might be summarized as 'all variances are unacceptable, but some are more unacceptable than others'. There is, however, some tendency to adopt an asymmetrical approach, giving unfavourable variances much more attention than favourable ones of similar amount.†

Some informal view of acceptable limits must exist in the minds of managers in selecting which variances in subordinates' reports require detailed investigation, but intervention may often appear arbitrary from the subordinates' viewpoint. It has been argued, with some empirical support, that managers perform best when their responsibilities are clearly defined, and that capriciousness in investigating variances could be avoided by adopting specific control limits (e.g. $\pm x$ per cent of standard) for acceptable performance [10]. Such limits would have to be related to the operational problems for each standard (i.e. not a uniform limit on all standards).

(b) Learning or blame-laying?

The manner in which variances are regarded within the firm will influence the effectiveness of controls through standards. If standards represent anything more than average performance it is to be expected that adverse variances will commonly occur. Upper management relish in apportioning blame is liable to produce a reaction at operating level which will divert energies into ensuring that the standards are not set so tightly in future and/or into passing the blame to other departments.

Upper management has the difficult task of generating a positive attitude to variances, concerned not with who was at fault, but with learning how it will be possible to do better next time. Such an attitude has been likened to game playing [10], with the environment (not the fellow players) as opponents.

(c) Updating standards and budgets

When budgets are set six or twelve months in advance it is inevitable that many of the assumptions are outdated by the end of the budget period. This is particularly true of externally influenced elements, such as prices, sales and production volumes. The problem is substantially reduced by a rolling budget (e.g. updated monthly–

---

*See [7] and [13] for models applicable to variance investigation.

†See for example [16], pp. 245–53, for survey questions to companies regarding 'corrective action on *unfavourable* variances from standards or budgets'. (Italics added.)

although many of the recording simplifications of standards are lost) – but what is to be done with the static budget?

From the control viewpoint the only criterion for updating is the effect of the change on control. Would recognition of the changes in the standards and/or budgets influence actions at the operating level? In a sense *any* change should affect the firm's actions at the margin, but only if the change is significant in terms of goals (e.g. would bring standards or budgets close to the control limits discussed earlier), is the updating essential for control purposes.

Updating is commonly achieved by the use of *revision variances*. The original standard is maintained, but differences between the outdated standard and the hypothetical new standard are isolated into a revision variance account. This approach can be effective if managerial attention is concentrated on the new net variance and not on the original outdated standard.

15.9 Reconciliation with the planning budget

Planning is not a concern of this chapter, but this is an appropriate stage at which to illustrate the reconciliation of control and planning budgets. It has been explained that there are potential conflicts between control and planning data; these conflicts can be resolved in several different ways.

1. Dispense with goals and adopt a budget which represents average expected performance – for both planning and control.*
2. Adopt goals and use the same information for planning purposes. If the goals are on the tight side the firm can find itself in difficulties (e.g. short of cash).
3. Adopt goals and use the same information for planning purposes *but* introduce slack into the resource budgets (e.g. budget for a cash balance much higher than the financially safe minimum). This approach is not unusual, but rarely made explicit.
4. Specify the point at which the control budget does not represent a plan, and introduce budgeted variances. *With* the budgeted variances the budget represents the planning budget; *without* the variances it is the control budget. This is a long established approach.
5. Develop separate control and planning budgets, with budgeted variances to explain the differences between the two. This has virtually the same effect as the previous method.

It will be assumed that a separate planning budget was developed for Furniture. The control budget, the planning budget, and reconciliation by budgeted variances are shown in the first three columns of Table 15.9. The actual results and the con-

*This approach was reported by all but one of the companies in the Perrin survey [14].

Table 15.9 Reconciliation of control and planning budgets – Furniture

	Control budget £	Budgeted variances £ (Unfavourable) Favourable	Planning budget £	Planning variances £ (Unfavourable) Favourable	Actual £
Sales	45 200	(600)	44 600	450	45 050
Direct materials	12 000	(250)	12 250	(350)	12 600
Direct labour:					
Preparation	3 600	(100)	3 700	(60)	3 760
Finishing	3 200	(90)	3 290	(160)	3 450
Manufacturing overheads	12 000	(50)	12 050	(90)	12 140
Delivery	666	—	666	(36)	702
Sales commission	904	12	892	(9)	901
Administration	3 600	—	3 600	120	3 480
Selling	3 400	—	3 400	50	3 350
	39 370	(478)	39 848	(535)	40 383
Less increase in finished goods inventory (at variable manufacturing cost)	370	—	370	325	695
Cost of goods sold	39 000	(478)	39 478	(210)	39 688
NET PROFIT (internal reporting)	6 200	(1 078)	5 122	240	5 362
Adjustment for fixed overhead burden rate on inventory	130	—	130	195	325
NET PROFIT (external reporting)	6 330	(1 078)	5 252	435	5 687
Estimated taxation			2 100	(175)	2 275
NET PROFIT AFTER TAX			£3 152	£260	£3 412

sequent planning variances are shown in the last two columns of that table. In fact only the last three columns have any relevance for planning, and interest centres on the planning variances. These have a review function: they may provide clues on the shortcomings of this period's planning which may be corrected for future periods. The data in Table 15.9 are in fact insufficiently detailed for this purpose; a breakdown (e.g. price/quantity aspects) would be needed for a serious review.

Table 15.9 also illustrates the reconciliation of the internal accounting information with that for external reporting. The difference stems from Furniture's use of variable cost inventory valuation internally, with 'product cost' for external reporting. The adjustment represents the fixed overhead on any increase or decrease

491

in inventory. (All were increases. Control and planning: chairs $100 \times £1.30 = £130$. Actual: [chairs $100 \times £1.30 + $ desks $50 \times £3.90] = £325$.)

For the sake of completeness Furniture's summarized planned and actual balance sheets for the end of the period are shown in Table 15.10. Comparative figures for the beginning of the period indicate that this was Furniture's first period of operation – which simplifies association of the end period balance sheets with previous data.

Table 15.10 Planned and actual balance sheets – Furniture

Opening balance sheet			Planned £	Actual £
	Fixed assets:			
24 000	Cost	24 000		
	Less depreciation	1 000		
			23 000	23 000
	Current assets:			
3 500	Materials		3 000	2 800
—	Finished goods and work-in-progress		500	1 020
—	Debtors		15 000	15 900
5 000	Cash		3 752	3 417
£32 500			£45 252	£46 137
25 000	Capital		25 000	25 000
—	Retained profits		3 152	3 412
			28 152	28 412
7 500	Debt to holding company		10 000	9 600
—	Taxation provision		2 100	2 275
—	Creditors		5 000	5 850
£32 500			£45 252	£46 137

Bibliographical references

[1] Amerman, G., The mathematics of variance analysis, *Accounting Research,* July 1953, pp. 258–69, October 1953, pp. 329–50, and January 1954, pp. 56–79.
[2] Argyris, G., *The Impact of Budgets on People,* Controllership Foundation, 1952.
[3] Bromwich, M., Standard costing for planning and control, *The Accountant,* 19 April 1969, pp. 547–50, 26 April 1969, pp. 584–87, 3 May 1969, pp. 632–34.
[4] Bruns, W. J. and D. T. DeCoster, *Accounting and its Behavioral Implications,* McGraw-Hill, 1969. (Section 4.)
[5] Chumachenko, N. G., Once Again: The volume-mix-price/cost budget variance analysis, *Accounting Review,* October 1968, pp. 753–62.
[6] Dearden, J., *Cost and Budget Analysis,* Prentice-Hall, 1962.
[7] Duvall, R. M., Rules for investigating cost variances, *Management Science,* June 1967, pp. 631–41.
[8] Henrici, S. B., *Standard Costs for Manufacturing,* McGraw-Hill, 1960.
[9] Hirschmann, W. B., Profit from the learning curve, *Harvard Business Review,* January-February 1964, pp. 125–39.

[10] Hofstede, G. H., *The Game of Budget Control*, Van Gorcum, 1967.
[11] Horngren, C. T., A contribution margin approach to the analysis of capacity utilization, *Accounting Review*, April 1967, pp. 254–64.
[12] Institute of Chartered Accountants in England and Wales (publishers), *Standard Costing: An Introduction to the Accounting Processes*, 1956.
[13] Ozan, T. and T. R. Dyckman, A normative model for investigation decisions involving multi-origin cost variances, *Journal of Accounting Research*, Spring 1971, pp. 88–115.
[14] Perrin, J. R., Budgetary planning and control, *The Accountant*, 15 August 1959, pp. 54–57, and 22 August 1959, pp. 89–90.
[15] Solomons, D., *Studies in Cost Analysis*, Sweet and Maxwell, 1968. (Section on cost control.)
[16] Sord, B. H. and G. A. Welsch, *Business Budgeting: A Survey of Management Planning and Control Processes*, Controllership Foundation, 1958.
[17] Taylor, F. W., *Scientific Management*, Harper, 1947.
[18] Whyte, W. F., *Money and Motivation*, Harper and Row, 1955.

Problems

15.1 What is meant by 'management by exception'? What do you consider are its major strengths and weaknesses?

15.2 The following are some possibilities for what a standard may represent:

1. Average past performance.
2. Performance of the average worker.
3. Achievable by the average worker.
4. Achievable under normal working conditions.
5. Performance of the 'first-class man'.
6. A fair day's work.
7. Realistically attainable but not too loose.
8. Optimal performance.
9. Technically achievable under perfect conditions.
10. A goal.
11. A forecast.
12. A planned result.
13. An estimate.
14. An objective.
15. An expectation.
16. A target.

Examine the implications for standard setting and the interpretation of variances in each case (grouping synonymous terms where appropriate).

15.3 Discuss the following views:

'Variance reports in standard costing attach too much importance to figures and no importance to reasons. Written explanations for variances should accompany each report which goes to a superior of the responsible manager.

'Any manager worth his salt can find a good excuse for a variance.'

15.4 Trubright Ltd. manufactures floor polish, which is sold in one gallon containers. The budgeted manufacturing and profit and loss account for the month of January appears below.

		£
Sales (10 000 gallons)		40 000
Standard manufacturing cost of sales:		
Materials	15 000	
Direct labour (2 000 hours)	2 000	
Manufacturing overheads – fixed	7 000	
– variable	3 000	
		27 000
		13 000
Administration expenses	4 000	
Selling expenses	5 000	
		9 000
Net profit		£4 000

Variable manufacturing expenses are assumed to be linearly variable with direct labour hours, and the administration and selling expenses are treated as fixed budgets. There were no opening or closing inventories.

During the month of January 11 000 gallons were produced, and the cost ledger discloses the following information:

	£
Materials used – at actual prices	17 000
– at standard prices	16 000
Wages paid to direct labour (2 100 hours)	2 160
Manufacturing overheads	11 000
Administration expenses	3 900
Selling expenses	5 400
Sales at actual selling prices (11 000 gallons)	42 000

Required:

(a) Operating report for the month of January, showing appropriate variances.

(b) Comments on the variances.

15.5 Data given below relate to the budgeted and actual direct labour costs for a department of Misogynist Ltd. in a recent month.

Budget:		
Output	9 000 units	
	Men employees	Women employees
Standard hours	1 000 hr	2 000 hr
Pay at standard rates	£900	£1 200

Actual:		
Output	8 400 units	
	Men employees	Women employees
Actual hours:		
working time	960 hr	1 840 hr
idle time	80	60
overtime	60	—
total	1 100 hr	1 900 hr
Actual pay	£1 030	£1 120

Overtime is paid at a premium of 50 per cent above the pay rate for ordinary time.

Calculate direct labour variances and comment on your results.

15.6 A pet food manufacturer established the following mix of ingredients per 1 000 cans of output for the month of February:

	Inputs per 1 000 cans lb	Costs per lb £
Ingredient 1	200	0·05
Ingredient 2	120	0·15
Ingredient 3	180	0·25
	500	

Actual output for February was 40 000 cans. Purchases and usage were:

	Purchased Cost £	Purchased Quantity lb	Quantity used lb
Ingredient 1	390	7 900	8 100
Ingredient 2	865	5 400	5 100
Ingredient 3	1 665	6 600	6 600

Calculate, and comment on, the price, mix and yield variances.

15.7 A production centre's flexible overhead budget and corresponding actual expenditure for the month of June are given below.

	Budget for 'normal' activity of 1 000 machine hours £	Actual expenditure in June £
Variable costs:		
indirect materials	750	819
Semi-variable costs:		
indirect materials	250	270
power	1 100	1 165
repairs and maintenance	220	190
Fixed costs:		
supervision	180	180
rent	600	600
depreciation	800	800
equipment rental	—	180
	£3 900	£4 204

Over the relevant range of output the flexible budget for semi-variable expenditure is increased or decreased for each machine hour by £0·20 for indirect labour and by £0·15 for repairs and maintenance. The allowance for power costs is made up of a standing charge of £100 per month plus £1 per machine hour.

A fixed allowance of £200 for equipment rental is added to the budget when machine hours exceed 1 000.

The actual machine hours worked in June were 1 050; earned output was 1 080 machine hours.

Required:

(a) A calculation of the amount of over- or underabsorbed overheads (with burden rate determined at the normal activity level of 1 000 machine hours).

(b) A two-way overhead variance analysis (spending and volume).

(c) A three-way overhead variance analysis (amended spending, efficiency and volume variances).

(d) A report showing variances on individual items of expenditure, presented for management use.

(e) Comments.

15.8 Cutlers Ltd. sells three types of table cutlery in units of one place setting. Budgeted and actual sales data for a recent period are shown below:

	Accent £	*Products* *Baroque* £	*Classic* £
Budget:			
Selling price per unit	10	8	5
Variable cost of sales	4	4	3
Variable profit margin	6	4	2
£ sales	4 000	8 000	20 000
Standard market share 8 per cent			
Actual:			
Selling price per unit	10	9	5
£ sales	7 000	8 100	21 000
Actual market share 9 per cent			

Calculate, and comment on, the price, mix, market volume and market share variances.

16

Control through internal resource allocation

. . . the number of officials and the quantity of work are not related to each other at all. The rise in the total of those employed is governed by Parkinson's Law and would be much the same whether the volume of the work were to increase, diminish or even disappear.

C. NORTHCOTE PARKINSON

16.1 The significance of resource allocation

The major activities to be considered in this chapter are administration, marketing, research and development (R & D), all the subject of programmed budgets; and capital projects arising from capital budgeting decisions.

There are hazards in generalizing about such diverse activities, but they share substantial problems in the control of efficient use of resources: results are difficult to monitor. The commitment of resources assumes importance not only for what is to be done (the decision aspect) but also for how it is to be done (the control aspect). Resource allocation* to specific purposes can influence the way in which an activity is undertaken and determine the volume of the activity. In the use of standards the standard setting process imposed certain assumptions about the way in which operations were to be undertaken, and standard rates permitted adjustment in the control criteria for volume changes.

At the commitment stage alternative allocations must be rigorously examined; in familiar decision terms this merely means the investigation of opportunities; but opportunities do not happen, they have to be created. The control atmosphere can act as an informal screening device for proposals: control appraisal which ignores the risk aspects of innovation or which does not give recognition to successful changes, will ensure safety-first proposals. Ideas may be encouraged by rewards for successfully adopted proposals, but an open-minded management attitude is equally important. The converse of considering new proposals is that old ways of conducting activities must be subject to equal scrutiny. In the programmed budget area this is often termed cost reduction: sporadic cuts across the board are the time-honoured arbitrary means of attempting to control such costs. It is much more effective for continuing and selective control if programmed budget proposals specify the costs of undertaking individual activities and/or the effects of marginal allocation changes, e.g. what would be added/cut if the allocation were ± 5 per cent, ± 10 per cent.

* In the present context resource allocation refers solely to internal allocation of the firm's resources, and not to external controls on the firm considered in section 3 of Chapter 13.

Resource allocation should not be interpreted merely in money terms: time and skills are important scarce resources for some activities (e.g. R & D). Increments of such scarce resources can be bought, but often at rapidly increasing marginal cost: crash programmes are expensive.

It was seen that variances from standards served purposes of financial control, progress monitoring and appraisal of results, but that spending variances had only financial control implications for programmed budgets (to which can be added capital budgets for present purposes). Such spending variances provide essential information, but they cannot indicate effectiveness in the use of resources. *Effectiveness*, meaning 'success in the accomplishment of purpose', is a term which does not prejudge either the nature of objectives for an activity or the methods of appraisal (e.g. qualitative or quantitative); the closeness of 'effective' to 'efficient' in the profit maximizing sense will depend on the choice of objectives and appraisal methods.

Progress monitoring and appraisal must be developed for the assessment of effectiveness in ways which are appropriate to each activity. In some areas measures can be approximated in profit terms. A major alternative approach adopts non-financial 'tasks' or objectives which can be regarded as surrogates for long-term profit effectiveness. These objectives represent goals which managers seek to achieve with a given resource commitment; for example an advertising manager might be given an objective (among others) of obtaining 20 000 mail order enquiries from a given advertising allocation.* Such intermediate aims serve a useful function in defining the responsibilities of subordinate managers, but if these aims are not to become ends in themselves it is necessary to reconsider periodically whether the goals remain consistent with efficiency in profit terms.

The essential problems to be borne in mind through succeeding sections are the commitment of resources, financial control (satisfied by reporting on the lines of Chapter 15), monitoring of progress and appraisal of results. Although expressed sequentially these aspects are interrelated: the last three can assist in a learning process for later allocation of resources – in relation to activities *and* the abilities of responsible individuals to use resources. To provide appropriate information it is essential that accounting data are broken down to specific functions (e.g. projects with the R & D group, with further subdivisions for tasks within a project) rather than by traditional expense categories (e.g. R & D salaries). The use of cost codes can assist in such categorization; see Chapter 14.

One difficulty of the interrelated nature of the resource allocation process is that executives with functional responsibilities may sit in judgment at the final commitment stage. Potential dangers are defensive attitudes to criticism and the possibilities of 'log-rolling'. It is important that the last word rests with those who have overall responsibilities (e.g. managing and 'outside' directors). An additional

*[15]; see also [2].

approach is to have periodic review by a small independent team from within or outside the organization; such a team would investigate non-manufacturing costs (and/or manufacturing overheads) for a particular function.*

16.2 Administration

Administration is a loose term sometimes used in relation to all non-manufacturing functions. We are excluding marketing and R & D because they will receive separate treatment. Some examples of the remaining functions are Accounting and Financial Services, Personnel, Legal Services, Property Management and Maintenance, Public Relations, Purchasing.

Administration costs are notorious for their tendency to develop an independent momentum in large organizations. This is the area in which Parkinson's Law is particularly applicable. There are ways in which some constraints can be placed on these costs.

(a) Variable elements

It has been explained that elements of administration expense which are variable with activity in the functional area can be incorporated into a flexible budget for spending variance calculation. The nature of variability will depend on the administration function: for example invoicing and credit department costs will *tend* to be variable with sales. It will often be necessary to incorporate step assumptions, e.g. fixed salaries mean that salary expense can be adjusted only by hiring and firing, and if small numbers of employees are involved in the functional area the short-run smoothing of expense with activity may be difficult.

An assumption of variability does not determine the appropriate cost rate – which brings us back to problems of standards. Since most administration budgets incorporate substantial elements for which the level of costs and activity is discretionary, it may be convenient to treat all elements as part of a programmed budget (incorporating plans, not goals). Goal aspects can then be treated in the manner of the next section.

(b) Task setting

The analysis of work methods and work measurement can be applied to routine tasks irrespective of any fixed cost assumption in the budget allocation. Work times

*See [4], p. 24.

can be investigated by activity sampling for typing (e.g. per page), for cleaning (per square foot), etc. The major problems are the selection of a work unit which validly represents work output without involving excessively detailed measurement, the improvement of working methods and environment, the attitudes of employees and the estimation of allowances for idle time.* Once these substantial problems have been overcome it is possible to set performance goals and to provide incentive payments either by bonuses related to extent of achievement above some given level or by measured day work. Thus the monitoring and review of work performance for use at the supervisory level can be based on the relevant work units.

The task responsibility of the manager of the total function is more complex. He is allocated resources in the programmed budget based on planned work performance. His goal is to ensure the performance of certain tasks (say maintaining credit granting and collections by the firm) with the resources put at his disposal. His performance must be reviewed not only in terms of the quantity of resources used, but also in terms of the quality of the service which is provided. It may be commendable for the typists in the credit department to have a high letter output, but this is irrelevant if the letters are not achieving results. Objectives can be explicitly specified for the manager (e.g. maintain an average collection period of x weeks and y per cent of bad debts); success lies in the extent to which objectives are achieved and in any economy in the use of resources.

(c) Subjective review

In any administrative area it is possible to report what is done and its cost; the important and more difficult question is that of cost effectiveness. Some subjective judgment of benefits is unavoidable. For example, the Public Relations department can collect newspaper cuttings and statistics on enquiries, but the assessment of resulting benefits to the firm can only be qualitative. The firm has to perform some functions in order to stay in business, like publishing accounts, but even here discretionary cost/quality aspects can arise.

Marginal adjustments can sometimes be approached on a 'see what happens' basis: services provided can be temporarily discontinued, and subsequent effects investigated. Internal accounting reports provide a good example. One draconian approach to an enormous variety of reports is said to have been adopted by an incoming treasurer of Macy's: distribution was suspended for all but the obviously important reports, until loud complaints from users indicated which reports were used by whom.†

* See [7], [28].
† [4], p. 23.

16.3 Marketing

Marketing in its broadest sense involves the interrelationships of product design and selection, pricing, advertising and selling/distribution. Aspects relating to product decisions and pricing were considered in Chapters 7, 9 and 10; some facets of inventory control are considered in Chapter 19. The present concern is with control of the advertising and sales functions. (The term 'distribution' is often used as a joint term for these two functions.) As used here the sales function relates to sales personnel and sales outlets. Commonly advertising and sales are separate functional units, often responsible to a marketing head: examples of several structures are provided by Oxenfeldt and Swan [23].

The aim of resource allocation to marketing should be to direct efforts into products, sales outlets, classes of advertising, etc., up to the point at which further commitment would render no net benefit to the firm. The problems of identifying net revenues with marketing efforts commonly lead to the adoption of intermediate aims, which are not always consistent with profit maximization.

(a) The selling function

A prior requisite to the allocation of resources in the sales area is an analysis of the effectiveness of existing selling efforts. The first difficulty to be overcome may be lack of appropriate data. A firm may have sales information and costs categorized by geographical area, but not by size and relative profitability of orders, and associated selling effort. Such data can be provided partially through the accounting system (e.g. margins on products) and partially by special investigation (e.g. activity sampling of salesmen's use of time). The rewards from the redirection of selling efforts can be substantial. Baumol and Sevin (in [29]) give a dramatic example:

> In one company, marketing expenses were cut nearly in half, from 22·8 per cent to 11·5 per cent of sales, and a net loss of 2·9 per cent on the books was turned into a net profit of 15 per cent, after shifting some effort from the 68 per cent of accounts which had been unprofitable.

The allocation of selling effort to different products and customer categories can be approached by use of programming. Total variable profit (sales − variable costs) can be maximized in a linear programming model, subject to such constraints as salesmen's time, warehouse capacity, etc. The effects of fixing constraints at different levels can be examined. In a linear programming model the number of 'optimal' product or customer categories would however be limited to the number of constraints (because the model maximizes the objective function in relation to each constraint: e.g. if salesmen's time were the only assumed constraint the model would choose the single category which maximized use of salesmen's time). Obviously some consideration must be given to potential demand by product and customer categories. Although such demands are extremely difficult to estimate, they can be formulated as constraints and the model can be used to examine the sensitivity of results for different plausible constraints. A simple model is examined by Baumol and Sevin in [29], although demand constraints are not incorporated.

One possible approach to the provision of information on selling effort would be the routine collection of data in relation to customer categories. Customers could be categorized by volume of purchases, say category 1 above £10 000, 2 £5 000– 10 000, 3 below £5 000. Such categorization can be relatively easily accommodated by reference numbers. Identifiable costs of selling effort could be assigned to these categories from salesmen's time records, as illustrated in Table 16.1. These costs have been designated as direct selling costs (direct in the sense that they involve selling to customers *and* in the sense that they have been identified with customer categories, although identification with specific sales is not feasible). Direct selling costs will include salesmen's remuneration and certain promotional devices applying to different customer categories, like in-store promotions.

Variances between actual and planned results permit the calculation of a profitability index which indicates the *relative* impact of selling effort. In Table 16.1 the indices suggest that redirection of effort, particularly away from category 2 towards category 1, would be beneficial. In effect the variances are being used as indicators of *marginal* revenue and *marginal* cost, implying that an index of 1·0 would represent optimality. However, it would be dangerous to rely heavily on the magnitude of the indices: they imply a causal relationship between sales and selling effort which has only limited validity. The effects of total market changes, advertising, planning errors, etc., must be borne in mind, but if these aspects can be assumed to apply equally to all customer categories they do not detract from the implications of the indices for the direction of selling effort *between* categories.

The approach can be similarly employed to examine the effect of relative marketing effort between different sales areas.* The total marketing impact in an area can be summarized in a profitability index, as shown in the last column of Table 16.1, for comparison with other areas. Again the impact of non-marketing influences on sales must be borne in mind, particularly if the sales areas differ substantially in their economic environments.

For the monitoring of performance in the sales area it is common practice to adopt a goal approach. There is need to ensure that the goals are not related merely to sales volume, but incorporate some relationship to relative profitability of different products. This can be achieved by formulating goals in terms of variable margins; commonly the same effect is obtained by differential commissions or bonuses for different classes of products, permitting some flexibility to the indivi-

---

*See the A.A.A. Report of the committee on cost and profitability analyses for marketing [3]; the treatment in Table 16.1 is partly based on a pre-publication conference discussion of the A.A.A. committee's report.

Table 16.1

	Sales area X Customer categories				Total
	1	2	3		
		£000's			£000's
Gross sales	400	500	200		1 100
less standard variable cost of sales	180	270	90		540
Standard variable profit	220	230	110		560
less direct selling costs	29	32	8		69
Direct selling earnings	191	198	102		491
				less advertising	26
				price promotions	8
				Sales area earnings	457
A Incremental* standard variable profit	44	(12)	(11)		21
B Incremental* direct selling costs	4	1	(3)		
				C Incremental* marketing costs	3
Incremental selling effort profitability index (A ÷ B)	11·0	(12·0)	3·7	Incremental marketing effort profitability index (ΣA ÷ C)	7·0

*Incremental = (actual − planned)

dual salesman in setting his own goals. Goal setting in the sales area has been criticized in relation to the occasional practice of setting ludicrously high goals so that they become impossible to accept as attainable by the employee. It has already been seen (section 2 of Chapter 15) that beyond a certain point tightness of goals becomes counter-productive.

(b) The advertising function

It was seen in Chapter 9 that advertising seeks to influence the customer in the firm's favour by providing information or influencing the customer's desires. A wide variety of media are available: in addition to the traditional message carrying media (papers, television, etc.) there are increasing numbers of promotional devices like give-aways and self liquidating offers. The control of advertising involves an attempt at optimal direction of resources in these diverse areas.*

Most firms devolve a large part of the implementation of their advertising plans onto an advertising agency, which becomes responsible for advertisement design and acts as go-between for media planning and payment. Very rarely is the agency

*A survey of the development of techniques is provided in [11]; for a comparison of techniques in two firms see [20].

given a primary decision-making responsibility. Two outstandingly successful exceptions resulted in the Hathaway shirts 'eye-patch' advertisements ('the agency men could do whatever they wanted with the advertising'*) and the Avis Rent-a-Car message that No. 2 tries harder. The agency viewpoint in the Avis case reveals some of the problems of the agency/firm relationship:

> ... most clients put our ads through a succession of Assistant V.P.s and V.P.s of advertising, marketing and legal until we hardly recognise the remnants. If you promise to run them just as we write them, you'll have every art director and copywriter in my shop moonlighting on your account. †

Resounding advertising failures are usually less well publicized, but one comment by the chief executive of an American airline indicates that they are far from rare:

> It is easy for me to give you examples of instances in which we greatly increased advertising in some markets and got absolutely no business. If you want examples of advertising success, you will have to give me a little time to see if I can find one or two – there must be a couple.‡

Thus the problem of ensuring the effectiveness of advertising is of fundamental importance. Estimates of the profit impact of advertising can be made (although not without difficulty) in less clear-cut situations than those quoted above, and such estimates can be used in a continuing learning process for the re-direction of advertising allocations.

A classical method of testing advertising (and also new products) involves the use of a test segment of the market.§ This requires a market segment which, it is hoped, will be a microcosm of the market and yet will be effectively insulated from the remainder of the market. If the microcosm is a geographical area it is possible to monitor effects on sales, using the remainder of the market as a control group. A control group within a market segment can be obtained by split running of advertisements (in papers or on cable television); subsequent investigation can compare purchasing for exposed and non-exposed groups. The effect of direct mail advertising can be surveyed in a similar manner.** The results of mail order advertising are relatively easy to monitor when sales orders come in with an advertising coupon attached.

The limitations of testing can be substantial. The test microcosm may imperfectly represent the total market, particularly since competitors may act to influence the results of a test if they have an opportunity. The impact of advertising over time is complex and combines a borrowing effect (advertising can induce purchases now which would have been made later) and a retention effect (advertising now can influence later purchases, although this influence decays over time). Consequently rigorous testing can be lengthy and expensive. In these circumstances tests are

---

* [23], p. 14.
† [27], p. 2.
‡ [23], p. 13.
§ See [6].
** [4], p. 90.

often concentrated on communication goals (e.g. did the advertisement change the *attitudes* of customers to the product), which are not necessarily consistent with sales effects. Some estimate of profit impact however inadequate, is better than none at all.

For consideration of the global resource commitment to advertising see section 7 of Chapter 9 and also J. L. Simon in [29].

16.4 Research and development

Definitions of research and development abound, but briefly research is search for new knowledge and development is concerned with application of newly acquired knowledge. Research can be divided into *basic* and *applied*, denoting respectively the search for new knowledge *per se* and the search for knowledge relating to a specific problem. Development includes the development of new or improved products and processes, their associated engineering development and their testing and evaluation. R & D activity within firms consists predominantly of applied research and development.*

The relative importance of R & D to a firm depends on the technological nature of its industry, although no firm is insulated from innovation. The firm's control problem concerns a very hazardous activity; risk and uncertainty are inherent. Some published success rates (not on a consistent basis) are 50 per cent in applied research projects [8], 30 per cent for new products launched [9], and 1 in 60 of new product ideas [12]. The last statistic is derived from the Booz, Allen and Hamilton data for 51 companies illustrated in Figure 16.1. This provides a useful representation of the atrophy process; at each successive stage a discarded idea has been the subject of greater outlay by the firm.

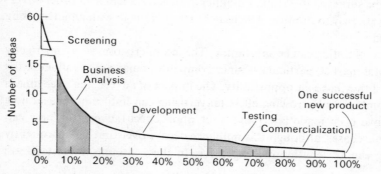

Figure 16.1 Mortality of new product ideas. Source: *Management of New Products,* Booz, Allen and Hamilton, Inc., 1960. Reproduced, with permission, from Dean [12].

*The proportions of total expenditure on R & D activities within British industrial firms in 1967/68 were: basic research 3 per cent, applied research 19 per cent, development 78 per cent [13].

(a) Major determinants of success and failure

The major problems of R & D can be appreciated by examining the success and failure of new products and processes. It would be idle to pretend that the determinants of successful innovation are unanimously agreed in the literature of this area. However some tentative generalizations can be made, subject to the qualifications that the relative importance of different elements in failure are not the same for all industries and that success depends on getting *all* the major elements right.

The bases for our brief generalizations are two studies in Britain (SAPPHO) and the United States (Conference Board) which adopted different methods,* but produced broadly consistent results. The consideration of user needs and marketing emerged as overwhelmingly important: awareness and analysis of the requirements of the market took pride of place, with advertising/publicity, selling and distribution as subsidiary elements. (*But* for the chemicals industry considered in isolation, the SAPPHO study ranked R & D strength as most important.) The more successful firms in the SAPPHO study were more receptive to (or better organized to obtain) outside advice, not only in relation to customers needs but also on specialized scientific and technical problems.

The elimination of product defects prior to launch was of substantial importance in both studies: loss of time in launching was preferable to a premature launch. Timing was given some importance: the SAPPHO study indicated that rapid completion of the *research* stage alone was associated with success in the chemicals industry, but in the scientific instruments industry there was support for the commonly held view that there are advantages in being second into the market with a new product.

Other important factors contributing to failure in the Conference Board study were underestimation of costs and actions of competitors; these aspects are not directly comparable with the SAPPHO consideration of competitive *environment* and forecasting/planning *methods*. On forecasting and planning the SAPPHO study revealed that most firms undertook systematic approaches, although the setting of time limits was by no means universal; little relationship was discovered between techniques adopted in these areas and successful innovation, but in this respect the report adds:

> It is important not to over-interpret our findings. They do *not* mean that there is no need to plan, to estimate, to control and to provide incentives for innovation, but only that there is no evidence from our observations that the use of such techniques in itself distinguishes successful from unsuccessful attempts to innovate.†

---

* The British SAPPHO study [24] examined pairs of successful and failed innovations in the chemicals and scientific instrument industries, a bare majority (54 per cent) in British organizations. The American Conference Board study [9] surveyed firms on causes of failure of new products over a wide range of American industry. SAPPHO's failures either did not obtain a worthwhile market share or made a loss; Conference Board's failures did not meet expectations in some important respect.

† [24], pp. 26–27.

Two further important aspects emerged from the SAPPHO study. In the chemicals industry there was a strong association between success and the power/seniority of individuals responsible for the overall progress of the project, but this relationship did not hold for the generally smaller firms in the scientific instruments industry. In both industries a larger team engaged on the specific project at the peak of development activity was associated with successful innovation.

(b) The control framework

Resource allocation to R & D projects must be related to an examination of the factors discussed above. However it is impossible to examine *all* aspects of *all* ideas before *any* commitment. Selection must often take the form of a sequential process* in which uncertainty is successively reduced by the expenditure of resources: at each stage a proposal can be re-appraised, and if necessary replanned in the light of knowledge acquired. The importance of the sequential approach depends on initial knowledge; this is clearly more appropriate to research in a new area than to development of a kind successfully completed in the past.†

The formal framework for control of R & D varies considerably between firms;‡ the principal elements are considered below.

1. Initial screening of ideas – commonly on an informal basis within the R & D function, in co-operation with other interested segments of the firm. Creativity within the R & D function and attitudes to innovation within the firm are major determinants at this stage.
2. Analysis as a basis for a formal proposal, incorporating consideration of the major factors relevant to success.
3. Commitment – allocation of resources on the proposal, with later commitments and/or revisions as work progresses.
4. Progress monitoring – periodic reporting (e.g. monthly) of financial expenditure and of progress towards achievement of objectives stated in the original commitment. For some projects a qualitative interim assessment of progress may have to be adopted, but for many projects it is possible to quantify progress towards objectives by using networks, to be considered in the next section.
5. Review and re-appraisal – when progress is lagging, or when substantial new information is made available by completion of a stage in the project, but in any case routinely at intervals (e.g. quarterly or annually). An overall review of the R & D function at annual intervals (in terms of profit contributions by

---

*Previously discussed in section 5(a) of Chapter 6.

†See [19], Chapter 2 and [1], Chapter 8 for further consideration of uncertainty reduction and R & D.

‡See [12].

successful projects and assessment of ongoing projects) is often the major instrument of central management control.

The R & D function may be split between a research segment and a development segment; such a separation in the Bell Telephone Laboratories is described by Fisk in [10]. This permits a different control approach to areas which can have substantially different problems; a less structured sequential approach (with longer time span for review) can be adopted in the research area.

The determination of the total R & D commitment should ideally proceed by comparison of marginal projects with competing demands for resources by other segments of the firm, although substantial qualifications are necessary regarding the nature of this comparison. Obviously the risk/uncertainty and long term nature of projects must be considered. Capital budgeting approaches can be adapted for these considerations (see Chapters 11 and 12): often an index is used which ranks projects according to the total of scores given to important factors in the decision; such an approach can be helpful in 'quantifying' the largely qualitative judgments which prevail at the early research stages of a project.*

The continuing nature of the R & D commitment is less amenable to quantification. Skilled teams cannot be expanded overnight for specific projects; part of the purpose of research as a search activity is to find the unexpected; certain activities within the R & D area are concerned with collecting and disseminating information which is not identifiable with specific projects (e.g. library and testing facilities). Consequently comparison of the global R & D commitment with competing demands must be made on partially quantified evidence in the context of a long term view of several years.

Resource commitment is commonly expressed as a total funding of facilities (salaries, laboratories, etc.) with little earmarking to specific projects; large companies may have several independent groups, each with its own funding. The advantage of such funding to a group lies particularly in the *research* area, where decentralization of decisions on specific lines of exploration can have benefits in encouraging the creativity which is crucial to this activity (see Allison [1]).

This type of decentralization is obtained at the expense of administratively imposed capital rationing, discussed earlier in section 1 of Chapter 12. The quasi-independent group must select its own projects within the financial constraints (which are not necessarily entirely rigid if particularly attractive marginal projects can be used to justify a changed commitment). One approach to such selection of projects within the American Cyanamid Company is described by Bobis, Cooke and Paden in [8].

---

*See [22] for an analysis of such scoring models.

16.5 Capital projects

The principles of investment decisions relating to capital projects were considered extensively in Chapters 11 and 12; the present concern is with controlling the efficient use of resources on committed projects. Two aspects will be examined. The first concerns the planning and control of complex projects, where network techniques can be used not only for 'in-house' capital projects but for any project involving the co-ordination of interrelated activities. The second concerns the review of completed capital projects, which may provide limited lessons for similar projects in the future.

(a) Network control of projects

Networks provide an analytical framework for planning and control of interrelated activities. The basic technique* is commonly termed Critical Path Analysis (CPA), and dates from about the mid 1950s. Previously Gantt charts† were used in the control of project times, but these are inadequate for analysing interlinked times although they still have uses in some areas.

Networks can be used to deal with a variety of problems at many levels of sophistication. Construction projects, new product development and the organization of clerical procedures provide just three examples which indicate the breadth of applications. Networks involving more than a few hundred activity times cannot be handled economically by manual methods, and developments have centred around computer applications, for which a variety of packages are available.‡ Two major methods were developed about 1958: CPM (Critical Path Method) developed by du Pont and PERT (Program Evaluation Research Task, now usually called Program Evaluation and Review Technique) by the US Navy. The former employed single time and cost estimates whereas the latter accommodated three estimates.

Initially the basic elements of CPA will be introduced using single estimates for time and cost, before reviewing some extensions of the technique.

(i) *CPA introduced*

The stages of a project can be analysed in terms of *activities* leading to *events*. These terms are defined :§

---

* For introductory treatments of CPA see Lockyer [17]; Staffurth [25], pp. 13–24; Williams, pp. 7–16 in [26]; Levy, Thompson and Wiest, pp. 352–68 in [5].
†See [17], Chapter 7.
‡ Problems of flows through highly complex networks can be treated by (deterministic) linear programming models of the transportation type (see Appendix C); the methods will not be considered here – see [14], Chapter 10, [26], pp. 123–35.
§These definitions follow [25].

Activity: an operation or process consuming time and possibly other resources;
Event: a state in the progress of a project after the completion of all preceding
activities but before the start of any succeeding activity.

A project sequence can be represented by an arrow diagram which constitutes a
network;* at the arrow heads are the events (or nodes), commonly shown as circles.
An exceedingly simple project for the acquisition of a new machine is illustrated in
Figure 16.2.

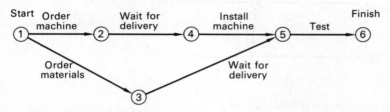

Figure 16.2 Network for a new machine

The assignment of a number to each event permits the definition of both events
and activities; for example, activity 3–5 means the activity commencing at event 3
and ending at event 5.

Certain rules and conventions apply to networks:

1. All activities entering an event must be completed before any activity leaving
   that event can be commenced, and all activities must have a beginning (or *tail*)
   event and an ending (or *head*) event.
2. Time elapses from left to right, although the network is not drawn to scale.
3. No two events can have the same number, and the tail event of an activity has
   a lower number than its head event (e.g. 5–3 is not permissible). The use of
   consecutive numbers is unnecessary; it may be convenient to leave gaps in the
   sequence for later rescheduling.
4. Dummy activities, which do not involve the lapse of time, may be inserted.
   This can be done to distinguish two parallel activities between common
   events or to represent the dependence of an activity on some prior event. For
   example, in Figure 16.3(a) the representation of two activities between events 1
   and 2 is ambiguous, nor does the network reveal that the commencement of
   activity 5–7 depends on the completion of activity 2–4. These aspects are
   clarified by the use of dummy activities in Figure 16.3(b).

With the assignment of estimated (e.g. 'most likely') time for the completion of
each activity a network can be used to determine the *critical path* – by determina-

*A network was defined earlier in Chapter 12 as a connected graph with no closed loops, where the
network was there termed as a tree diagram or decision tree.

511

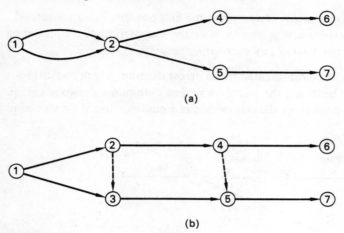

(a)

(b)

Figure 16.3 (a) Invalid sequence. (b) Valid sequence

tion of the *longest* activity route from start to finish of the project. All activities along the critical path are critical in the sense that a delay in any one of them will delay completion of the entire project (if all other estimated times are met). The estimated completion time for the project is given by the sum of the activity times along the critical path. It is, of course, the importance of the critical path which gives CPA its name.

Figure 16.4 illustrates a network with estimated time (in working weeks) and cost shown for each activity; the critical path is shown by the darkened arrows. Other additions are statements of the earliest time by which an event can be reached, and the latest time by which the event must be reached if the entire project is not to be delayed; these times are shown in consecutive boxes in Figure 16.4. The *earliest* time (T_E) is calculated as the sum of activity times via the *longest* route to the event. The latest time (T_L) is computed by working backwards from the terminating event; for example, event 9 must be reached by (17 minus 2) weeks.*

The difference between the earliest and latest times at which it is estimated an event can occur $(T_L - T_E)$ is termed *slack*. This represents the maximum time by which an event could be delayed without delaying the entire project; the events with zero slack are shown on the critical path in Figure 16.4. A scheduled target

---

*Considering event j, denoting tail events by i and head events by k, duration of the activity $d(i, j)$ or $d(j, k)$, and for clarity dropping the symbol T and using only the subscripts E (earliest event time) and L (latest event time), times for event j will be $E_j = max\ E_i + d(i, j)$ and $L_j = min\ L_k - d(j, k)$. This is illustrated below for event 4 from the network in Figure 16.4:

j	E_j	L_j
4	max of $1 + 5$ (2–4 path)	min of $10 - 4$ (4–8 path)
	$3 + 1$ (3–4 path) $= 6$	$10 - 1$ (4–6 path) $= 6$

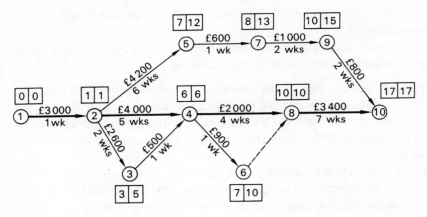

Figure 16.4 Network with single-time estimates for activities

time T_S may be imposed for the terminating event or for intermediate events in the network; in this case $T_L = T_S$ for the target event, and preceding values can be computed by working backwards through the network. If $T_S < T_E$, *negative* slack results; an event with negative slack is termed *hypercritical*. Negative slack is common in the initial programming of a network – improvement, via rescheduling and diversion of resources, is a fundamental purpose of the analysis.

The boundaries within which an activity can be scheduled without necessarily affecting completion time of the project are given by its *Earliest Start Time* ($= T_E$ for its tail event) and its *Latest Finish Time* ($= T_L$ for its head event). The total available time flexibility in relation to an activity within these boundaries is termed *total float*, and is given by:

[Latest finish time – Earliest start time] – duration of activity.

An activity which has a zero total float is critical – for example, the critical activity 4–8 in Figure 16.4 may be compared with the non-critical activity 3–4 which has a total float of 2 weeks.

Total float is widely used in the scheduling of activities (e.g. to match use of facilities against availability). Clearly rescheduling which reduces the total float of one activity may affect the total float of succeeding activities – if activity 2–3 loses one week of its total float so does activity 3–4. Thus with the use of total float it is necessary to check on the effect for the whole network, since a new critical path could emerge from the treatment of each activity independently. More rigorous analysis of float can be undertaken by decomposing total float into subsidiary float elements, according to the relationship of the head and tail slacks.*

If an attempt is made to reduce activity times in order to reduce overall project time, the activities must of course be on the critical path for the reduction to be

*See [17], Chapter 5; [26], pp. 13–14.

effective; otherwise float on non-critical activities is being reduced to no purpose and usually at some cost.

Now that the basic technique has been introduced this is an appropriate stage at which to summarize the steps in critical path analysis.

1. Understanding of the logic of the system under consideration. This can only be done in relation to the specific practical application.
2. Construction of the network. This can elucidate the logic of the system; in some cases analysis of the system may be the sole objective and the study can stop at this point.
3. Provision of estimates for activity durations.
4. Satisfaction of objectives. The major objective can take several alternative forms: completion by a target date or minimization of time (with or without cost constraints), the minimization of cost, smoothing of the use of resources (e.g. for crucial plant requiring continuous production flow). Some of these cost and resource aspects will be considered later; it should be noted that the results for different criteria will not be consistent with each other. Criteria may in fact be forced upon the firm, e.g. by customer requirements.
5. Investigation of alternative approaches. For example, can the assumed operating methods be changed, should additional resources be bought or hired from outside?
6. Implementation and control of the network. Checking and updating are essential.

(ii) *Uncertainty of activity durations*

The use of single-time estimates for each activity evades the problem of uncertain activity durations inherent in almost any project.

PERT/Time* goes a short way towards the consideration of uncertainty by adopting three estimates which are then used to calculate the (*single*) expected time for each activity – thus an average supplants the single-time estimate considered previously. The three PERT estimates for duration of each activity are: *optimistic* (if all goes well), *most likely*, and *pessimistic* (excluding 'acts of God'). It is evident that such estimates can yield skewed probability distributions with the most likely time (the mode of the distribution) not equal to the expected time (the distribution's mean). On the basis of their research the original PERT team adopted certain types of beta distribution as most closely representing the characteristics of the three-time estimates.

The approximate expected time of each activity, t_e (the mean of the distribution), and its standard deviation σ_{t_e} for the assumption of a beta distribution can be derived from the three-time estimates by:

*See [21] for a wider treatment.

514

$$t_e = \frac{a+4m+b}{6}$$

and
$$\sigma_{t_e} = \frac{b-a}{6};$$

where a = optimistic time, b = pessimistic time, m = most likely time.

The calculated expected times are used in the same way as the single-time estimates: the earliest time by which an event can be reached (T_E) and the latest time by which the event must be reached (T_L), slacks, floats, and the critical path are all derived in the manner considered earlier. In Figure 16.5 three-time estimates and the corresponding expected time t_e for each activity have been substituted for the single-time estimates previously shown in Figure 16.4. Costs have been omitted on this occasion.

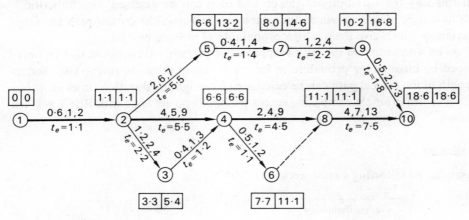

Figure 16.5 PERT/Time network

With PERT/Time the probability of meeting a target date T_S can be calculated by assuming that, with a large number of activities preceding the event having random distributions, the probability distribution of T_E for the target event will be approximately normal. The slack for the target event can be expressed as a multiple of standard deviation, σ;

$$\frac{T_S - T_E}{\sigma}$$

where
$$\sigma = \sqrt{\sum_{i=1}^{n} \sigma_{t_e i}^2}.$$

The value of the result, when compared against a table for the normal distribution, gives the probability of meeting the target date.

The major weakness* of the PERT method is that the computation of the critical path is still *deterministic*: it does not cater for the variability of activity durations. In fact, with variability of activity durations, *every* path through the network has some probability of being the longest. Moreover, one path can have the highest probability of being critical at one stage of the project and another path can be critical at a different stage; in other words there is no fixed critical path and some activities will be critical at some times and not at others.

Some idea of the variability of the duration time for a PERT path can be gained by calculating its variance, adopting the assumption that all activity times along the path are independent so that the variance is given by the sum of the variances for all activities on the path, $\sum_{i=1}^{n} \sigma_{t_e i}^2$ (where σ_{t_e} is calculated from the formula given earlier).

In this way the variability of the critical path can be assessed, and 'subcritical' paths can be identified which have durations less than the critical path but large variances which give them a high probability of proving critical.

As an alternative to the PERT approach a probabilistic network can be developed by introducing probabilities for multi-valued duration times. The average length of the critical path can be calculated by weighting duration times for probabilities. An example comparing such a probabilistic network with PERT is given below.

Example

Assume the following simple network:

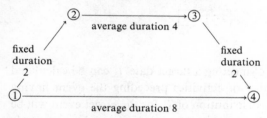

The following data are given concerning the variability of duration times for activities 2–3 and 1–4:

	Time (weeks)	Probability
2–3	3	0·5
	5	0·5
1–4	7	0·8
	12	0·2

---

*Another important limitation is that the assumption of a beta distribution imports certain errors which could be reduced by employing a triangular distribution. See [18].

The PERT (deterministic) model would use the average times for activities 2–3 and 1–4, which gives two critical paths:

$$\left.\begin{array}{l} 1-2-3-4 \\ 1-4 \end{array}\right\} \text{both with an overall duration time of 8.}$$

The probabilistic model would take the durations of 2–3 and 1–4 for each probability, and weight the resulting critical path lengths for probability:

Probability	2–3	1–4	Critical path: Length	Weighted
0·4	3	7	7	2·8
0·4	5	7	9	3·6
0·1	3	12	12	1·2
0·1	5	12	12	1·2
				8·8

Thus the weighted average of the critical path lengths is 8·8 weeks, in contrast with the 8 weeks calculated for PERT.

If the PERT critical path is the overall critical path with probability p and the PERT computed average duration of this path is D_p, the duration of the overall critical path is:

$$pD_p + (1-p)(D_p + e) = D_p + (1-p)e > D_p;$$

where e is an error term (> 0) attributable to the PERT adoption of average times. This error is additional to bias which can arise from a tendency for forecasters to underestimate modal time for PERT.

PERT's deterministic calculation for the critical path gives a downward (optimistic) bias for duration time of the project compared with a probabilistic weighted average which incorporates the variability of activity durations. This can be particularly serious if there are many parallel paths through the network.* However, practical investigations suggest that the approach of taking the sum of the variances as an indicator of path duration variability is commonly validated by the effect of compensating errors.

(iii) Costs and resource allocation

The networks above focused on meeting target date or minimizing time. Costs and resource allocation were mentioned earlier, and some approaches to the incorporation of these criteria will be outlined.

*See [18].

PERT/Cost* extends PERT/Time by the addition of cost estimates for activities. Either a single-cost estimate or three-cost estimates may be employed. In the latter case expected cost can be derived by adopting a beta distribution assumption as in PERT/Time. These approaches give estimates for control purposes but they do not provide a vehicle for analysing the interrelationships of cost and time.

The time-cost problem can be seen as one of trade-off between time and costs. Cost as a function of time for each activity can be assumed to take the form of a U-shaped curve: rapid completion of an activity can entail acquiring resources at premiums, the use of wasteful methods, etc., whereas a lengthy duration involves the accretion of period costs over time.† With a cost minimization objective the minimum cost point of the curve for each activity would be selected, and cost would therefore determine time. However, when there are target times to be met an optimal time-cost combination would minimize cost *subject to the time constraints.* The Resource Allocation Procedure Supplement‡ to PERT/Cost adopted this sort of trade-off procedure for significant activities of a project.

An alternative procedure adopts two time-cost estimates: 'normal' and 'crash'. The first is the *minimum cost* of an activity, with its corresponding time; the second is the *minimum time* to perform an activity, with its corresponding cost. Effectively these two points can be regarded as representing the left-hand side of the U-shaped time-cost curve (with crash cost above normal cost) although linearity is assumed between the two points. The 'crashing' approach can be used to select the minimum cost combination which will meet the time requirements for the project; alternatively time for the project can be minimized subject to a total cost constraint. The cost of crashing can be calculated by comparing cost for the crashed project with the computation of minimum cost.

A further approach is offered by the PERT Time–Cost Option Procedure.§ Three time estimates are made: for the *most efficient plan,* which is the network plan which would be chosen in the absence of constraints; for the *directed date plan* which is developed to meet the specified completion date, and for the *shortest time plan* which would meet the project requirements in the shortest time. The most efficient plan is modified to produce the directed date plan, which in turn is adapted to give the shortest time plan. Revised cost estimates are required only for activities affected by the modifications in the second and third plans, otherwise the original cost estimates for the efficient plan remain. Thus three cost estimates are provided for the significant elements of the network, which permits review of the cost impact of the time objectives.

* See DeCoster in [5], pp. 369–80 for a good introduction, and [21] for more extensive treatment.
† The appropriate costs for consideration in this context are those which are avoidable in the absence of the activity. In practice network costing adopts conventional direct and indirect costs, the latter implying the usual arbitrary features of overhead cost allocation.
‡ NASA/DOD Resource Allocation Procedure Supplement; see DeCoster in [5] and Ross in [16].
§ See DeCoster in [5].

Finally the resource allocation approach* can be used when there are resource constraints (e.g. limited skilled manpower for working on the project at any one time, plant with limited capacity, etc.); in this case time–resource criteria apply in place of the time–cost criteria discussed above. Activities are ranked in some order of time priority; total float commonly provides a partial basis for such ranking. The allocation may be undertaken by assigning resources to the entire network in priority order of activities or by allocating for one period at a time through the network. Resource shortages will involve planning adjustments to times or the acquisition of additional resources.

(iv) *Review of progress*

Cost and time progress on a project can be reviewed by analysis of achievement and expected future cost/time requirements at a specific date, commonly termed a *freeze* date. Project activities can be reviewed individually or summarized into tasks associated with areas of the project (the latter, of course, requires prior analysis of activities). A simple review schedule for task costs is illustrated in Table 16.2; estimated costs to completion have been added to actual incurred expenditure to give latest estimated expenditure. Comparison with budget (updated for previous revisions if appropriate) gives the cost variances for the review period. A similar analysis can be made for time. The cost variances can be split between spending and performance elements (to be considered for the total project below) and serve to trigger investigation in the usual cost control manner.

Table 16.2 Review schedule for task costs

Task	Actual incurred expenditure (1)	Estimated expenditure to completion (2)	Latest estimated expenditure (3) = (1)+(2)	Budget (revised) (4)	Cost variances for review period (4)−(3)
	£	£	£	£	£
1	60	15	75	80	5 F
2	40	80	120	100	20 U
3	20	140	160	130	30 U

An overall view of a project's progress in terms of costs and time is illustrated† in Figure 16.6. The *original expenditure curve* can be derived by summation of budgeted expenditure for each activity, as developed in the network. Subsequent budget revisions for cost and time are incorporated into the *revised expenditure curve*. Data on costs incurred and *budget 'value' of work done* can be estimated up to the freeze date. Budget 'value' of work done is similar in concept to standard cost of inputs for standard costing, but estimation for incomplete activities is dependent

---

* See [26], pp. 43–56.
† From Staffurth, ed., [25].

on technical judgment: 'value' will be the completed work proportion of estimated cost for an activity. From these data two control variances can be obtained:

SPENDING VARIANCE:

[actual incurred cost] – [budget 'value' of work done]

PERFORMANCE VARIANCE:

[budget 'value' of work done] – [revised budget cost]

These two variances explain the current budget variance shown in Figure 16.6. In this case the spending variance indicates greater expenditure than the revised budget for the work done; the performance variance shows that work is running

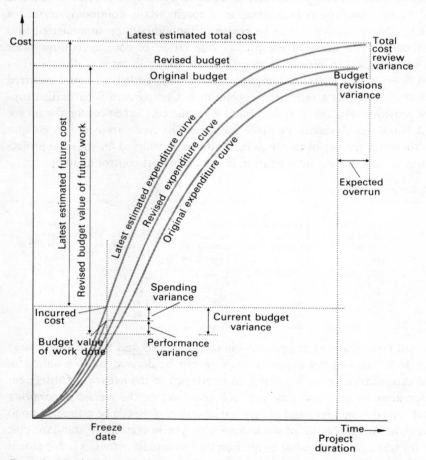

Figure 16.6 Project progress chart. Source: Staffurth, ed., [25]; reproduced (and modified) with permission.

ahead of the schedule assumed in the revised expenditure curve at the last review. The latter variance is therefore inherently favourable; it explains that portion of the expenditure which has occurred prematurely through rapid progress on the project since the last review.

The projection of the *latest estimated expenditure curve* can be derived by re-estimating costs for incomplete activities; the finishing time for this curve compared with the original finishing time gives the latest *expected overrun* on the project. (Comparison with revised time would give overrun since revision.) The latest estimated expenditure curve becomes the revised expenditure curve for the purpose of the next review.

As always in cost calculations it is usual practice to include allocated overheads in the determination of costs. This can only be justified as a very crude indicator of opportunity cost (when fixed resources being used for this project could be diverted to other purposes), but the time element acts as a similar indicator in this type of analysis.

Responsibility for variances and for the overall progress of the project would rest with a project manager, or sometimes less distinctly with a committee for a project overlapping different functional areas of the firm.

(b) Review of capital expenditure

The review of capital expenditure after it has taken place can have two major objectives:

1. The disclosure of shortcomings in the assets or their use which can provide lessons for the acquisition of similar assets in the future.
2. The disclosure of forecasting bias or the provision of sanctions against wild forecasting.* A manager who wishes to acquire a new facility may be naturally over-optimistic when the interests of his department are at stake. Bias should be eliminated at the capital budgeting stage, but it may be difficult to accomplish when prior analysis depends heavily on the expertize of interested parties.

A 'post-audit' approach to review would involve the estimation of net revenue or cost savings produced by an asset, after a period of say one year. The approach is workable for independent assets, but where a new asset is interdependent with old assets there is a choice between assuming unrealistically that all incremental net revenue relates to the addition and investigating the complex causes of variations in net revenue. Detailed investigation may be worthwhile only for major assets with objective 1. in mind.

* See also the discussion of control of estimating and forecasting in section 3(a) of Chapter 18.

A second approach, more appropriate for ongoing control purposes, provides that estimated net revenue or cost savings from capital expenditure are automatically translated into control budget revisions. Thus the responsible manager has a defined interest in the validity of the capital budgeting projection; subsequent amendments can be justified in the usual context of control budget determination. This does not imply any assumption of certainty in the benefits of capital expenditure: the results of risk-taking emerge as specific amendments. Amendments over a series of capital additions might be expected to be normally distributed around the expected values for net revenues or cost savings; any marked bias would suggest a need for investigation. If amendments are never necessary this suggests safety-first proposals or the existence of slack in the budget.

Bibliographical references

[1] Allison, D., ed., *The R & D Game*, M.I.T. Press, 1969.
[2] American Accounting Association, Report of the committee on non-financial measures of effectiveness, *Accounting Review*, Supplement 1971, pp. 165–211.
[3] American Accounting Association, Report of the committee on cost and profitability analyses for marketing, *Accounting Review*, Supplement 1972, pp. 575–615.
[4] American Management Association (publishers), *Control of Non-manufacturing Costs*, Special Report No. 26, 1957.
[5] Anton, H. R. and P. A. Firmin, *Contemporary Issues in Cost Accounting*, Houghton Mifflin, 1966.
[6] Becknell, J. C. and R. W. McIsaac, Test marketing cookware coated with 'Teflon', *Journal of Advertising Research*, September 1963, pp. 2–8.
[7] Birn, S. A., R. M. Crossan and R. W. Eastwood, *Measurement and Control of Office Costs*, McGraw-Hill, 1966.
[8] Bobis, A. H., T. P. Cooke and J. H. Paden, A funds allocation method to improve odds for research success, *Research Management*, March 1971, pp. 34–49.
[9] Cochran, B. and G. C. Thompson, Why new products fail, *Conference Board Record I*, 1964, pp. 11–18.
[10] Cockcroft, Sir J., ed., *The Organization of Research Establishments*, Cambridge University Press, 1965.
[11] Cohen, S. I., The rise of management science in advertising, *Management Science*, October 1966, pp. 11–28.
[12] Dean, B. V., *Evaluating, Selecting and Controlling R & D Projects*, A.M.A. Research Study 89, American Management Association, 1968.
[13] Department of Education and Science and Ministry of Technology, *Statistics of Science and Technology*, HMSO, 1970.
[14] Hadley, G., *Linear Programming*, Addison-Wesley, 1962.
[15] Humble, J. W., ed., *Management by Objectives in Action*, McGraw-Hill, 1970.
[16] Livingstone, J. L., ed., *Management Planning and Control*, McGraw-Hill, 1970.
[17] Lockyer, K. G., *An Introduction to Critical Path Analysis*, 2nd edn., Pitman, 1967.
[18] MacCrimmon, K. R. and C. A. Ryavec, An analytical study of the PERT assumptions, *Operations Research*, January/February 1964, pp. 16–37: reprinted in *Managerial Economics*, ed. G. P. E. Clarkson, Penguin, 1968.
[19] Marschak, T., T. K. Glennan Jr. and R. Summers, *Strategy for R & D*, Rand Corporation, 1967.
[20] Marschner, D. C., Theory versus practice in allocating advertising money, *Journal of Business*, July 1967, pp. 286–302.
[21] Miller, R. W., *Schedule, Cost and Profit Control with PERT*, McGraw-Hill, 1963.
[22] Moore, J. R. and N. R. Baker, Computational analysis of scoring models for R & D project selection, *Management Science*, December 1969, pp. 212–32.
[23] Oxenfeldt, A. R. and C. Swan, *Management of the Advertising Function*, Wadsworth, 1964.

[24] Science Policy Research Unit, University of Sussex, *Success and Failure in Industrial Innovation,* Centre for the Study of Industrial Innovation, 1972.
[25] Staffurth, C., ed., *Project Cost Control Using Networks*, Operational Research Society and Institute of Cost and Works Accountants, 1969.
[26] Thornley, G., ed., *Critical Path Analysis in Practice,* Tavistock, 1968.
[27] Townsend, R., *Up the Organisation,* Fawcett, 1970.
[28] Whitmore, D. A., *Measurement and Control of Indirect Work,* Heinemann, 1971.
[29] Williams, T. H. and C. H. Griffin, *Management Information,* Irwin, 1967; Part III, Analysis of the distribution function.

Problems

16.1 You are an executive employed by a company which produces a wide range of durable consumer goods. Last year the company made a substantial loss. You have been asked to organize an investigation, and provide preliminary evaluations, of the effectiveness of the company's expenditure in the following areas:

(a) Administration.
(b) Marketing.
(c) Research and development.
(d) A new £300 000 plant which went into production last year.

What sort of information would you seek and what sort of difficulties would you expect to encounter?

16.2 You have been asked to suggest performance objectives and work units for the following activity areas:

(a) Costing department.
(b) Wages office.
(c) Personnel department.
(d) Legal department.
What suggestions can you make?

16.3 The marketing organization of a firm is divided into three geographical areas: North, Midlands and South. Budgeted and actual sales and marketing cost data for a recent period are shown below.

	North	Midlands £000's	South
Budget:			
Sales	140	210	280
Standard variable costs	70	105	140
Segmental marketing costs	10	15	20
Actual:			
Sales	155	220	320
Standard variable costs	75	110	150
Segmental marketing costs	12	14	24

Calculate and comment on the variances for incremental marketing effort.

16.4 Flash Ltd. manufactures electrical goods. The company has centralized R & D and advertising departments.

Spending on R & D projects is determined by central management, after consultation with appropriate managers in the operating segments. R & D costs for products which go into production are charged to the operating segments, and are written off over four years. The R & D costs of abortive projects are borne centrally.

Advertising budgets for each production segment are determined as a fixed percentage of budgeted sales for the year; the segments are charged with expenditure as it is incurred. The managers of the operating segments select advertising methods in consultation with the advertising department.

What do you consider are the strengths and weaknesses of Flash's approach to expenditures on R & D and advertising?

16.5 The research department of a motor manufacturer has a proposal for a safety innovation which a preliminary test suggests might reduce serious injuries in accidents by as much as 75 per cent. The innovation involves structural changes to models which would affect their external appearance. Discuss the general problems of investigating and evaluating the proposal.

16.6 Track Ltd. is undertaking a project. From the data below draw a network for the project. Determine the critical path and expected completion time. What would be the most pessimistic estimate for completion time if *all* activities went badly?

Activity	Estimated times (weeks)			
	a	*m*	*b*	t_e
1–2	3	4	8	4·5
1–3	5	6	13	7
1–4	1	2	3	2
2–5	3	6	9	6
3–4	5	11	14	10·5
3–6	9	11	19	12
4–6	1	2	6	2·5
4–7	4	9	11	8·5
5–6	5	10	12	9·5
6–7	3	4	11	5

Progress is being reviewed ten weeks after commencement. Activities 1–2, 1–3, 1–4 and 2–5 are completed. Work is in progress on activities 3–4 and 3–6, and the updated three-time estimates for these activities are:

	a	*m*	*b*
3–4	4	5	6
3–6	5	7	12

No other activities have been commenced, nor have any other amendments been made to the estimated times.

What is the expected time to completion from the review date? How much slack is there for completion by the originally expected time?

16.7 A project is being undertaken by the Wheeling division of Dealing Ltd. Shown below are the original estimates for time and costs, together with data for the first review date 4 weeks after commencement of the project.

	Time		
		At review date	
Activity	Original estimate	Time spent	Estimated time to completion
	weeks	weeks	weeks
1–2	2	3	0
1–3	3	3	0
2–4	6	1	6
2–6	8	0	8
3–4	1	1	0
3–5	7	1	5
4–5	1	0	1
5–6	5	0	5

	Costs				
	Original budget		At review date		
Activity	To completion of activity £	To review date £	Budget value of work done £	Actual expenditure £	Estimated expenditure to completion £
1–2	1 200	1 200	1 200	1 400	0
1–3	700	700	700	750	0
2–4	1 800	300	100	500	2 000
2–6	3 000	0	0	0	3 000
3–4	400	400	400	350	0
3–5	4 100	600	700	660	3 330
4–5	200	0	0	0	300
5–6	1 900	0	0	0	1 900
	£13 300	£3 200	£3 100	£3 660	£10 530

Prepare an appropriate report for management showing the time progress of the project and the spending and performance variances for costs at the review date.

16.8 Formulate the problem of determining the longest path in a network as a linear programming problem.

17
Control through profitability measures

The inherent weakness in the centralized, functionally departmentalized operating company and in the loosely held, decentralized holding company became critical ... when the operations of the enterprise became too complex and the problems of coordination, appraisal, and policy formulation too intricate for a small number of top officers to handle both long-run, entrepreneurial and short-run operational administrative activities. To meet these new needs, the innovators built the multidivisional structure with a general office whose executives would concentrate on entrepreneurial activities and with autonomous, fairly self-contained operating divisions whose managers would handle operational ones.
A. D. CHANDLER JR. [7]

17.1 Profitability measures and responsibility

The use of profitability measures in control is associated particularly with the divisionalization of large business organizations. It was explained in Chapter 13 that the multidivisional organization is an administrative device for offsetting the forces limiting firm size; this device permits structured decentralization of responsibility. Strategic or entrepreneurial problems remain the responsibility of central management (alternative terms are: top management, general office, peak coordinators, executive committee) and tactical or operational responsibility is delegated to managers of quasi-autonomous operating divisions. Inherent in this approach is the provision of staff assistance to central management in its decision and control activities and appropriate staff support for responsibilities at division level.

The division manager heads a segment which often approximates in organization to that of a unitary firm. He is responsible for both revenue and expense elements in his division, and it is appropriate that an important measure (although not necessarily the sole measure) of his effectiveness should be based on profit. There are variations in the functions and degree of responsibility delegated to such segments: for the present purpose it will be convenient to define a division as any segment of the firm for which a profitability measure is used for control purposes.

The control purposes of profitability measurement for divisions can be stated as:

1. *Ex ante* specification of an objective to guide the (tactical) decision making of divisional managers.
2. *Ex post* appraisal of divisional performance by central management (and implicitly self-appraisal by divisional management).

This view of divisional responsibilities and the purposes of measurement will determine the choice of profitability measure. A major alternative view is exemplified by Solomons [19] who includes substantial strategic elements in divisional responsibilities and adds a third purpose of measurement: 'to guide top management in making decisions,'* subject to qualifications. This last purpose has been excluded above on the grounds that an *ex post* measure can permit reward/penalty judgments concerning the responsible manager and can trigger investigation (both appraisal functions) but central management should make decisions about the future of a division on expectations more detailed than the extrapolation of a single measure.

The fundamental areas of concern are the need for measurements to be consistent with the responsibilities of divisional management and the need to ensure that delegation does not sacrifice the interests of the firm to the sectional interests of the divisions. These are implicit in the N.A.C.A.'s succinct summary of the requirements for effective delegation of profit responsibility:†

1. Delegation of authority to make decisions with respect to important factors affecting profits.
2. Pricing interunit transfers on a basis which objectively measures income attributable to each profitability unit.
3. Staff assistance and managerial tools needed to exercise general management functions at the divisional level.
4. Avoidance of joint responsibility for costs and revenues.
5. Centrally established and administered policies to coordinate divisional operations in the interests of the company as a whole.

(a) Defining divisional responsibilities

The establishment of quasi-autonomous divisions requires the definition of separable activities on bases such as product class, geographical market or operating function (say manufacturing and retailing). Overlap between the interests of divisions can rarely be avoided entirely, but to the extent that overlap occurs the benefits of delegation are correspondingly diminished by the necessity for central management mediation in essentially tactical areas. Some firms have set up large numbers of multifunction segments with conflicting or ill-defined market interests, but there is some evidence by Chandler‡ that problems of coordination and control tend to lead to subsequent reconstruction into a smaller number of more clearly differentiated segments.

The degree of autonomy granted to divisions varies between firms but the freedom of divisions is usually substantially circumscribed: thus the term 'quasi-autonomous'. Central management neglect of its controlling powers is not a recipe for success.§

*[19], p. 83.
†[13], p. 8.
‡[7], pp. 348, 360 and 369.
§For examples of the effects of neglect see [7], pp. 122–25 and p. 188.

The legal form of a division is largely irrelevant to autonomy; a wholly-owned subsidiary can be administered in an entirely centralized manner. A parent company with only a controlling majority of a subsidiary's equity does have a legal and moral responsibility to refrain from deliberately sacrificing the interests of the minority shareholders to the interests of the parent, although such oppression must amount virtually to expropriation before the law intervenes.

In any organization there are many decisions which emerge as the outcome of interaction between several interested individuals. For assignment of responsibility it is necessary to identify the *principal* decision maker, in relation to whom the other interested individuals have only persuasive power. It is a function of staff advisers and line subordinates to make proposals (preferably with an analysis of alternatives); the individual who chooses between proposals is the responsible decision maker.

Decision responsibilities which are almost invariably reserved to central management are investment* (in excess of some low limit) and senior appointments; delegation of these powers would be equivalent to abdication of strategic control. Pricing policy is usually a central responsibility, although it tends to be regarded as a tactical divisional responsibility when the product range is very wide, as in retailing organizations.† The control of cash balances and the purchasing function are normally centralized to permit cash pooling and purchasing economies (increasingly with associated debtor collection and creditor payment to permit data processing economies), as are company-wide services like public relations. Responsibilities for R & D and advertising are often delegated, subject to spending constraints. The fundamental areas of divisional responsibility are ongoing control of operations and the selling function.

A profitability measure summarizes the performance of divisional responsibilities and must be defined as consistently as possible with them. Although the importance attached to the measure may be very considerable in some firms it is evident that any measure which attempts to summarize the complex implications of responsibility and control in a single figure must have imperfections. The choice of measure will lie with the least imperfect; even so a profitability measure must be seen in the context of a variety of controls used by most firms. These are of two major kinds: *constraints* within which the division must operate, such as central management policies, resource allocation, determination of objectives; and *transmission of information* to the centre, not only financial data, but also data on such matters as industrial disputes, R & D progress, etc.

---

* For support of this view see [7] p. 11, [19] p. 14, [22] p. 441. However, a reported example of what appears to be fully delegated investment responsibility is given in [20] p. 67 ('I am responsible for determining my capital expenditures, research and development program, and new product program'), and an assumption that divisionalization entails investment autonomy is made in [8], p. 205.

† For example the importance of the Annual Price Study in General Motors contrasts with the delegation of pricing by Sears in [7], pp. 151 and 272.

Definition of divisional responsibility would seem to require that the manager be given a specific objective expressed either as a single figure or as a range of acceptable performance. Such a figure would be set in the context of the perceived opportunities for the division, which requires interaction and a certain amount of mutual trust between divisional and central management. The objective could be based on planned performance or a goal. A goal which exceeds the planned result need not imply any lack of candour between divisional and central management: one British division of a major international company regularly adopts a profitability performance goal in excess of that required by central management.

(b) Interdivisional transfers

Delegation of profit responsibility requires the setting of prices for interdivisional transfers to ensure that tactical decisions are made in the interests of the firm.

The rules for optimal transfer pricing were considered in Chapter 9. When the intermediate market can be regarded for practical purposes as perfectly competitive the transfer price can be equated with market price; certain savings like delivery costs can be deducted from this price. Where there is no intermediate market or an imperfectly competitive market, it was seen in Chapter 9 that transfer prices must be determined by joint consideration of both supplying and using activities: the optimal transfer price is the marginal cost for the division supplying the intermediate product, at that level of output which will equate marginal cost and marginal revenue *for the firm*. This requires either central intervention or the exchange of data between divisions; the latter could be ineffective without substantial mutual trust between the divisions, given the data imperfections particularly for marginal revenue.

The marginal costs are those which are expected to vary with output during the transfer pricing period, for the given capacity. Some care may be needed for step costs, but as a first approximation it would be possible to assume constant variable costs per unit of output (not, of course, merely direct costs) in order to guesstimate the relevant range of output. More detailed investigation of cost variability could be confined to this range. Marginal revenue is much more difficult, and can only be approached in an iterative manner by examining the effects of price changes (if the final market is not for practical purposes perfectly competitive).

Transfer pricing can include services as well as goods. The same principles should apply, although the quantification of the output of some services entails difficulties.

Transfer pricing must inevitably entail an iterative approach to optimality, using administrative or programming methods:* amendments must be made to in-

---

*See e.g. [2], pp. 228–33, and [22].

529

corporate changes in the economic environment. For control purposes it is necessary to predetermine transfer prices; revisions may become unavoidable during a period if fresh informational content is needed to influence the decisions of segment managers towards optimality. *

The marginal cost approach to transfer pricing is concerned with the short-run. Since the supplying division is forced to supply at marginal cost and all benefits from imperfect markets go to the transferee division, there is no inducement for the supplying division to increase capacity – which is entirely compatible with centralized investment decisions. Admittedly it would be possible for a transferor and transferee division to reach a capacity decision jointly, and to arrange a fixed subsidy payment which would not detract from the tactical advantages of marginal cost pricing. *But* the magnitude of this payment would be arbitrary at best (say 50/50 sharing of benefits) and at worst would reflect bargaining strengths. The bargaining element defeats much of the purpose of profitability measurement as an indication of efficient operations, *unless* the subsidy payments lead to an amendment of the profit objectives assigned to each division – which renders the subsidy redundant anyway.

The subsidy approach is basically a window dressing device which permits the transferor division to show an accounting profit where it would otherwise show losses or a smaller profit. Subsidies are superfluous if performance is appraised in relation to specific profit objectives – it is the variance which matters. Nevertheless the subsidy approach is an improvement over the transfer pricing of many firms which adopt standard product costs, including both fixed and variable elements; the irrelevance of allocated fixed costs to short-run decisions should not need further repetition.

(c) Measurement categories

Various profitability measures are available for assessing divisional performance. The major split between the measures depends on the view taken of the responsibility of the divisional manager, thus:

Profit centre: a segment of the firm for which a manager is made responsible for profit, but not for the level of segment investment;

Investment centre: a segment of the firm for which a manager is made responsible for profit in relation to the level of segment investment.

Some indication of the adoption of such centres, with a breakdown of the mea-

* When there are many transfer prices reflecting interdependencies between divisions (and departments) the administrative problem of revising transfer prices sufficiently frequently to avoid misallocation of resources may become insurmountable. See the discussion of this type of problem in section 5 of Chapter 18.

sures used for investment centres, is given by a 1966 survey of large American companies (by Mauriel and Anthony [11]):

	Per cent (rounded)
Companies having:	
No profit or investment centres	18
Profit centres but not investment centres	21
Investment centres, with performance measured by:	
return on investment	31
both return on investment and residual income	25
residual income only	4
	— 60

This survey did not indicate the profit concepts employed for profit centres.

The meanings of these terms will be considered in the following sections. It will be convenient to consider 'residual income' with the other absolute profit measures, leaving 'return on investment' (a ratio measure) for separate treatment.

17.2 Profit measures

Table 17.1 shows the ways in which 'profit' could be calculated for divisions; it can be seen that the definition of a measure depends on where the line is drawn for deductions. The split after controllable profit indicates two alternative routes: the left-hand side follows conventional procedures for calculating net profit, while the right-hand side introduces interest deductions for assessing the performance of divisions as investment centres. The major measures for consideration are asterisked in Table 17.1; they are controllable profit, traceable profit (usually termed contribution margin in the American literature), net profit, controllable residual income and net residual income.

(a) Controllable profit

The rationale of controllable profit is that the measure of divisional performance should encompass only those costs and revenues for which the divisional manager has principal responsibility. A great deal must depend on the definition of 'controllable', but the earlier arguments that divisions have (or should have) tactical responsibility will provide a guideline.

It is fundamental to the controllable profit concept that divisional performance is not assessed simply on the global amount of controllable profit, but on the difference between a predetermined objective and achieved profit – on the variance

531

Table 17.1 Potential profit measures for divisions
(This table has been adapted from Amey [2] p. 128 and Solomons [19] pp. 72 and 82).

REVENUE – from external sales
– from internal transfers
less variable costs

VARIABLE PROFIT
less controllable divisional overheads

*CONTROLLABLE PROFIT
less depreciation and expenses (e.g.
leasing) on divisional fixed assets

less noncontrollable divisional overheads	*less:* interest on controllable investment;
	non-operating losses (*add* gains);
	fixed 'subsidy' charges by (*add* charges to) other divisions for internal transfers.
*TRACEABLE PROFIT *less* allocated nondivisional expenses	*CONTROLLABLE RESIDUAL INCOME *less:* interest on noncontrollable divisional investment;
	noncontrollable divisional overheads;
	incremental central expenses chargeable to division.
*NET PROFIT *less* taxation on divisional income	*NET RESIDUAL INCOME *less* taxation on divisional income
NET PROFIT AFTER TAX	NET RESIDUAL INCOME AFTER TAX

* Major measures for consideration.

principle of budgetary control. The divisional manager's objective is to produce a particular profit with the resources put at his disposal for the period. This objective can be set either by programming methods incorporating consideration of the opportunities and resources of the firm or by the conventional iterative process of budget determination.* The controllable profit does not stand alone: it is merely part of a complex control process.

The component items of controllable profit will be discussed in turn, and then the reasons for *not* deducting certain items will be considered. In the course of this discussion it will become evident that controllable profit is our preferred measure.

(i) *Variable elements*
Costs and revenues which are variable with the tactical decisions of divisional

* See [2] Chapter 9, [10], [17].

management in a particular period are appropriately included in controllable profit. Clearly sales revenue and variable production costs are relevant, although it may be noted that if any elements are affected by central management *diktat* during the period (say firm-wide pay rates) it may be necessary to revise the period's objective.

Also appropriate for inclusion are any other costs which vary with the division's tactical decisions. In this connection avoidable interest costs which are incurred by reason of divisional decisions affecting working capital are relevant. It was explained earlier that cash balances, debtor collection, creditor payment and purchasing are commonly centrally administered (the first almost invariably so): working capital levels arising from central administrative decisions (e.g. speculative central stockpiling) would not be a divisional responsibility. Items which are variable with the division's tactical selling and production decisions (e.g. debtors, divisional inventories) involve a current period interest cost for the firm, either causing borrowing or preventing lending, and an interest charge variable with the levels of these controllable items is appropriate. This short-run interest charge is of a different character from a long-run cost of capital charge on *all* resources (fixed or variable) entrusted to the division for the period: such a charge will be considered in connection with residual income.

It may be noted that for all internal control purposes it is desirable to value inventories at variable cost; it was seen in Chapter 14 (appendix) that a fixed overhead or period cost element in inventory valuation can distort the profit measure.

(ii) *Controllable divisional overheads*
It is appropriate to deduct controllable overheads for which the divisional management has spending responsibility, because although these may be substantially fixed they are variable at the margin by reason of tactical decisions: for example, the costs of accounting and selling carried on within the division. When control of advertising is delegated to the division it is relevant to deduct advertising costs, although the overlap of advertising with long-run profitability makes centralized review of advertising policy both desirable and usual.

R & D is unquestionably a strategic activity, and it is not a relevant charge against short-run controllable profit. However, there are often substantial advantages in a close interrelationship between R & D and a division on such matters as marketing implications, and it has been seen that divisions *may* have their own R & D groups. Control and performance appraisal for R & D can be appropriately handled quite separately from controllable profit. A separate budget allocation can be established, and if division management has general responsibility for ongoing control this can be exercised through short-run reports of the sort considered in Chapter 16. Overall appraisal (e.g. annual) can serve as central management's primary vehicle of control in this area. As new products emerge they will in any case require (centralized) investment decisions and the revision of controllable profit objectives.

(iii) *Exclusion of depreciation and fixed asset costs*

The fundamental reason for the exclusion of depreciation is that investment is a strategic decision area; divisions typically do not (and should not) have principal responsibility for significant investment or disinvestment of fixed assets. The proposals of divisions may be guided by some form of cut-off rate for capital budgeting decisions or by a global capital spending constraint. These are inadequate devices because they reconcile opportunities for different divisions imperfectly or not at all; overall consideration is necessary for any approach to optimality in the firm's investment decisions. However these devices are rarely used in isolation: they commonly have a crude screening function, and expected cash flows are subject to centralized overview. It follows from centralized strategic responsibility that depreciation of fixed assets and similar costs of long-run leasing commitments are excluded from controllable profit.

There are other reasons for excluding such costs. Routine profit reporting for control purposes is concerned essentially with the short-run (e.g. monthly) to provide an early warning of areas out of control; in the short-run fixed assets are fixed, and irrelevant for tactical decisions. Depreciation relates to past investment decisions, often made before the present manager was appointed; its inclusion gives an indication of the joint effect of the wisdom of those *past* investment decisions and *current* performance in the use of assets, but it does not disentangle the two aspects. Finally, depreciation calculations used by firms rarely reflect the current cost environment, but are based on the same historic cost calculations as external reports; Mauriel and Anthony [11] reveal that only $2\frac{1}{2}$ per cent of 981 respondent companies adopted a different depreciation basis for internal reporting.

It is important that the division manager does not regard fixed assets as free goods. This danger is avoided by centralized vetting and decision-making on fixed asset proposals above a certain limit and by the amendment of the controllable profit objective for the projected cash flows of *all* investments. (Subsequent explicit amendment of objectives was discussed in section 5 of Chapter 16.) It is equally important that the manager should be given an incentive to initiate disposal of uneconomic or excess resources; his controllable profit objective is reduced, and his economy of resources could be explicitly recognized as a favourable 'resource variance'.

Repair and maintenance costs pose a problem. Divisional managers can determine spending on these items, which are therefore appropriately charged to controllable profit, but the level of repairs and maintenance may affect both current operating efficiency and asset life. The problem does not concern the many assets for which obsolescence is likely to determine asset life, but only those for which technical life is the determinant. The division manager will be reluctant to incur expenditures which prolong technical life when he is not principally responsible for investment. A partial solution is to treat significant repairs as capital expenditure (since they produce benefits in future periods) and to have centralized monitoring of the *levels* of repair and maintenance expenditure – a variance outside certain limits would trigger investigation.

(iv) *Exclusion of noncontrollable and allocated general overheads*

By definition these items are not the responsibility of the division: they include central administration costs and fixed costs of facilities used jointly with other divisions. When such costs are variable with the tactical decisions of the division it is appropriate to estimate transfer prices and charge to controllable profit on the basis previously discussed.

(b) Traceable profit

Traceable profit* is used here to denote the profit, arising from the activities of the division, which can be identified without arbitrary cost allocations. It includes a charge for depreciation, etc., and noncontrollable divisional overheads in addition to the components of controllable profit. Both these aspects have been discussed. It may be noted that the term noncontrollable divisional overheads as used here includes only fixed costs which are unambiguously identifiable with the division – say the division manager's salary. Costs which are variable with the division's tactical decisions have been charged with variable costs.

(c) Net profit

The deduction of allocated nondivisional expenses provides no additional information for controlling the division's activities, and in view of the arbitrary nature of most allocation methods the deductions may even induce managers to act contrary to the interests of the firm. Consider the allocation of administration overheads as a percentage of sales: from the division manager's viewpoint this is a variable cost which he should consider in relation to marginal sales, which conflicts with the firm's interests if the overheads do not in fact increase proportionally with sales.

The use of net profit in connection with divisional performance measurement is undoubtedly common.†

---

* This term has been adopted instead of the widely used 'contribution margin' in order to avoid possible confusion with contribution in the sense of revenue minus variable costs – i.e. variable profit.
† For example, see [14] with regard to profit calculations used for return on investment.

(d) Controllable residual income

Residual income is the excess of net earnings over the cost of capital on divisional investment.*

The rationale of controllable residual income is, like controllable profit, that the measure of divisional performance should encompass those costs which the divisional manager controls, but the level of divisional investment is assumed to be a principal responsibility of divisional management. The divisions are charged with interest on investment at the firm's cost of capital in order to make divisional interests coincide with those of the firm as a whole.

Since residual income is a widely used investment centre measure which embodies a substantially different viewpoint from that advanced for controllable profit it will be convenient to examine the major differences between the measures in turn.

(i) *Depreciation*

Residual income is calculated after a charge for depreciation (and long-run leasing) on fixed assets controlled by the division; assets not identifiable specifically with the division and redundant assets retained on the directions of central management would not qualify.

The reasons for excluding depreciation from controllable profit were that investment is fundamental to centralized strategic responsibility, that reporting for ongoing control is essentially concerned with short-run elements, that depreciation relates to an amalgam of past decisions, and the evidence that most companies adopt historic cost depreciation. Residual income is based on an assumption of divisional investment responsibilities which rejects the first three points, and adopts an essentially long-run view of divisional performance measurement.

The amendment of the depreciation charge from historic cost may appear to be a relatively simple matter, but it raises issues of some difficulty which relate to the basic assumption of residual income.

Assume that a division purchased a fixed asset, some mining rights, for £100 000 at the beginning of the year; at that time the expected value assigned by the division was £130 000 NPV. By the end of the year the original rights would have cost £150 000, or would have sold for £140 000, either because the mineral market had changed or because the mineral deposits proved richer than was originally expected. (For the moment a constant value of the monetary unit is assumed.) With the benefit of hindsight the division now considers the original NPV should have been £170 000. Which figure should be used as the base for charging mineral ore consumed in the period?

It can be argued that either historic cost or original NPV provide the relevant

*[19], p. 63.

base for calculating depreciation to permit *ex post* appraisal of the division's investment decision* – but the depreciation charge ceases to reflect the economic environment in which the division is operating. Residual income becomes an inadequate indicator of current operating performance, because the benefits from the holding gain will trickle into residual income as the asset is consumed; in the absence of further major changes the division manager can rest on his laurels. If on the other hand the depreciation charge is amended to reflect some appraised value at the end of the period, much of the benefits of the 'wisdom' of the decision must be excluded from residual income – which defeats the long-run measurement objective. A solution might be achieved by an adjunct to the residual income statement, specifically recognizing holding gains and losses as they occur on the lines considered for the accounts of firms in Chapter 3. This is not a method which has so far been advocated for residual income.

A related problem concerns changes in the 'value' of the monetary unit, for which *general* price level changes provide an indicator. The above example assumed a stable monetary unit, but if the general price level had risen by 10 per cent in the period another depreciation viewpoint becomes available. Depreciation can be based on historic cost updated for changes in the monetary unit (e.g. depreciation on average of the year £105 000 or end year £110 000). This approach seems consistent with the investment centre viewpoint: it is preferred by Solomons [19] for residual income and by the N.A.A. [14] and the B.I.M. [6] for return on investment calculations. Such updating is, of course, merely putting original outlay into current money terms: the amended depreciation charge does not reflect any economic changes specifically relating to the asset since purchase. Residual income continues to incorporate, without distinction, the effect of both past investment outlays and current operating decisions.

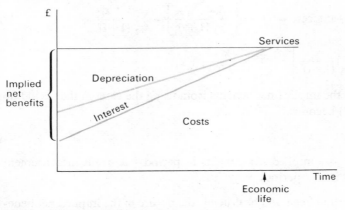

Figure 17.1 Implied net benefits of an asset

*E.g., see [8].

537

The interest charge against·residual income has implications for depreciation. The joint effect of deducting depreciation and interest on the opening balance of fixed assets is to charge the income calculation with the implied net benefits from use of the asset in a period. In Chapter 3 it was seen that depreciation plus interest on the opening asset balance gave an implied value for the net benefits of owning the asset in a period. This is illustrated in Figure 17.1: the linear graphs are merely illustrative, and are not intended to prejudge the pattern of implied benefits.

The equivalence of depreciation plus interest charge to the implied net benefit of the asset in a period is intuitively obvious, but can be demonstrated algebraically. We first define the following quantities:

x_t the implied net benefit from using the asset in the period up to time t. (The nature of this benefit is left undefined.)

n the asset's estimated remaining economic life from time 0 (the beginning of the current period)

i interest rate

$\sum_{t=1}^{n} \dfrac{x_t}{(1+i)^t}$ book value of the asset at time 0, which must be equal to the present value of (undefined) net benefits over remaining life

$\sum_{t=2}^{n} \dfrac{x_t}{(1+i)^{t-1}}$ book value of the asset at time 1 (the end of the current period).

Depreciation for period 1 is the difference between book values at time 0 and time 1, and interest is calculated on book value at time 0. Thus:

$$\text{Depreciation} + \text{interest} = \sum_{t=1}^{n} \frac{x_t}{(1+i)^t} - \sum_{t=2}^{n} \frac{x_t}{(1+i)^{t-1}} + i\left[\sum_{t=1}^{n} \frac{x_t}{(1+i)^t}\right] \quad (1)$$

This gives:

$$\text{Depreciation} + \text{interest} = (1+i)\left[\sum_{t=1}^{n} \frac{x_t}{(1+i)^t}\right] - \sum_{t=2}^{n} \frac{x_t}{(1+i)^{t-1}} \quad (2)$$

But:
$$(1+i)\left[\sum_{t=1}^{n} \frac{x_t}{(1+i)^t}\right] = \sum_{t=2}^{n} \frac{x_t}{(1+i)^{t-1}} + x_1.$$

Since x_1 represents the implied net benefits from using the asset in the period up to time 1, equation (2) becomes:

Depreciation + interest = x_1

= implied net benefits in period 1 (current measurement period).

Clearly the depreciation basis will be crucial: the nature of the implied net benefits will vary with the choice of the depreciation base. Some of the major possibilities are shown below.

Depreciation base		*Nature of implied net benefits*
Past data base	Historic cost	Expected replaceable benefits when purchased, in money terms at acquisition
	Historic cost updated for changes in the monetary unit	Expected replaceable benefits when purchased, in current money terms
	Original NPV	Expected cash flows when purchased, in money terms at acquisition. (Updating to current money terms would be feasible)
Current data base	Current realizable value	Minimum net benefits required to justify retention of the assets
	Current replacement cost	Current replaceable benefits

If residual income were concerned with measuring divisional management's use of resources in a single period there would seem to be a case for adopting some current data base for the assets in the period. For a similar firm-wide purpose replacement cost was preferred in Chapter 3, with qualifications. But such an approach is alien to the purpose of residual income as an indicator of investment success. Thus in respect of the objective given to the divisional manager, residual income is caught on the horns of a dilemma which is examined below.

1. The divisional manager's objective can be stated simply as 'maximize residual income'. Presumably any positive residual income must be regarded as satisfactory, but a positive residual income provides no indication of current performance because past and current decisions are inextricably mixed.
2. The divisional manager can be given an explicit residual income objective for the current period, expressed as a single figure or as a range of acceptable performance. How is this objective to be set? Presumably in relation to currently perceived opportunities – but depreciation and interest charges on past data become simply superfluous. Performance is assessed on *closeness to the objective*, and the objective has pre-empted the effects of past investment decisions. The objective could, with much less effort, be stated gross:

$$\left[\frac{\text{Residual income objective}}{\text{Depreciation and interest}}\right] \quad \left[\begin{array}{l}\text{Objective} \\ \text{ex depreciation and interest}\end{array}\right]$$

Since depreciation and interest on fixed assets are fixed for the period their exclusion or inclusion would not make any difference to the manager's short-run decisions. (Although there might be some differences if general price level adjustments are made *and* the general price level proves different from the original assumptions of the objective.)

What if assets are added or disinvested in the period? The residual income objective must presumably be updated; for the remainder of the period the position is as before.

Consequently it would seem that divisional objectives for residual income must either be set in terms which do not distinguish the effects of current and past performance or they must pre-empt the effects of past decisions and defeat the purpose of residual income for the evaluation of the results of past investment.

(ii) *Interest on controllable investment*

The rate of interest usually proposed for the interest charge on all controllable investment is the firm's cost of capital, defined for this purpose by Solomons* as the expected earnings yield on the current market price of an all equity company, or the weighted cost of capital in a company financed by debt and equity. This is intended as a measure of the opportunity cost† of the capital employed in the division.

Consider first the interest charge in relation to a division's capital investment‡ in fixed assets. Such a charge does not in fact measure opportunity cost (= highest-valued alternative foregone). The firm's cost of capital is an indicator of the *firm's current* opportunity cost of money, which is incompatible with money embodied in the *division's* fixed assets by reason of *past* investment decisions; an interest charge relating the two does not reflect consideration of opportunities for employing the division's assets in the period being appraised. Opportunity cost (correctly specified) is relevant to making decisions about the assets' future, not to reviewing past employment of resources.

From the divisional viewpoint the interest charge on depreciated fixed asset outlays imputes a cost to the division for *using* the assets. If the return which can be obtained from an asset in the current period is insufficient to satisfy the long-run expected earnings yield of equity shareholders (among other suppliers of long-term funds) the manager may be encouraged to dispose of the asset. This can lead to sub-optimal decisions on assets which do not meet the imputed cost, but for which employment in the division is the best available opportunity for the firm.

On the grounds considered above, the interest charge for divisional capital investment is conceptually invalid.

*[19], pp. 157–58.
†[19], p. 156.
‡See [3] and [9] for further consideration of this aspect.

On the question of interest costs to the firm which are variable with tactical decisions affecting working capital, an interest charge to the division is relevant – as was seen for controllable profit. But such interest is a variable cost of the current period, not an imputed long-run cost of capital.

(iii) *Non-operating gains and losses*

If a division is held responsible for investment in fixed assets it is consistent to hold it responsible for gains and losses on disposal of those assets. Even so, it is not inevitable that the divisional manager's interests will coincide with those of the firm: his horizon is likely to be shorter, particularly if he is in difficulties with current performance or if he expects to move from the division. He may also be more risk-averse. Thus the manager may choose a gain which boosts current residual income in preference to uncertain benefits in the future, contrary to the interests of the firm.

It may appear that valuation of the division's assets at realizable value would overcome this problem. It has been seen that the adoption of such a current value is not consistent with the purpose of residual income; moreover the use of realizable value alone would not ensure diversion of assets to more profitable use within the firm.

(iv) *Fixed 'subsidy' charges or receipts relating to internal transfers*

The effect of such subsidies in relation to transfer pricing has been discussed. In themselves they are innocuous for control purposes, because their fixed nature does not affect short-run decision making. However, the arbitrary manner of their determination means that an income figure after such an adjustment must not be taken as an indication of profitability of a division in isolation.

(e) Net residual income

This measure, whether before or after tax, is intended to help central management to 'judge the results of the investment in the division as distinct from the results achieved by its managers'.* As Table 17.1 showed, the items charged after controllable residual income are noncontrollable divisional overheads, incremental central expenses and interest on noncontrollable investment.

The noncontrollable divisional overheads are those costs clearly identifiable with the division, but not determined by decisions in the division. The incremental central expenses are estimates of costs incurred centrally because of the existence of the division: the view has already been advanced that any central costs which are variable with divisional decisions should be charged to controllable profit. To the extent that divisible fixed costs are unambiguously identifiable with the con-

*[19], p. 127.

tinuance of the division their deduction at this stage provides an estimate of certain avoidable central costs associated with the division: these are essentially traceable costs. Any assignment of indivisible fixed costs enters into the area of arbitrary allocation and is unlikely to provide relevant indications of avoidable cost.

Assuming that net residual income has not been charged with arbitrary cost allocations, and that the pre-tax measure is adopted, the major differences between net residual income and traceable profit are the subsidies on internal transfers and the interest charges. These two measures of division results can be compared.

Either measure could be used as a trigger mechanism to indicate to central management the need for investigation when the reward from investment in the division is 'unsatisfactory'. But 'unsatisfactory' can only be interpreted as not meeting plans, which should trigger an investigation of the plans and their implementation. For such a purpose the previously discussed limitations of the transfer subsidy and the interest charge would apply equally to net residual income. In any case it is clear that neither measure alone could provide the basis for any decision about the division's future: they both include depreciation charges which are unlikely to reflect alternative use of resources, they inadequately reflect interdependencies with other divisions and most important of all they relate to past results not future expectations.

Traceable profit does have an advantage in that it may be used to fulfil external reporting requirements, to be considered in section 4.

Tax is a relevant consideration in considering investment in divisions, since different activities, countries, and even locations within a single country are not taxed equally; but clearly it is future tax, not past tax, which is relevant.

17.3 Return on investment

Return on investment (ROI) is an investment centre measure. It is intended to indicate performance in the use of resources entrusted to divisions.* It is the most commonly used profitability measure for the appraisal of divisional performance, despite a substantial volume of criticism of its validity.†

(a) The ROI measure

The measure is determined by current period profit expressed as a percentage of the investment in divisional assets. Profit and investment can be defined in a variety of ways. Such definitions are relatively unimportant compared with the central fact

---

*Adoption in practice is not necessarily associated with any particular degree of investment autonomy, but Solomons [19], p. 151, proposes that the use of the rate of return should be confined to situations in which the division has little or no control over the level of its investment.

† For examples see [2], [10], [11], [16], [19], [21].

that ROI is a ratio measure. It was seen in section 4 of Chapter 11 that any ratio method is unreliable for ranking investments; therefore appraisal of divisional performance on ROI provides the manager with an objective which can be inconsistent with the interests of the firm.

ROI is an *average* return on the division's investment. The manager of a division with a stable ROI of 20 per cent can improve performance either by accepting (or proposing) only incremental projects which promise an ROI in excess of 20 per cent or by disinvesting projects currently yielding less than 20 per cent. If the relevant cost of capital to the firm is, say, 10 per cent, the manager is probably not supporting projects which would be acceptable to the firm, quite apart from questions of risk and comparisons with projects of other divisions.

ROI objectives are more commonly set equal to the firm's cost of capital, the average corporate rate of return, or the corporate rate of return plus x per cent,* than to some specific rate for the investment centre. Whatever the ROI objective the divisional manager has a positive incentive to improve his performance by a safety-first approach of supporting only projects which offer a substantial margin over his objective.

An objective of maximizing ROI is consistent with profit maximization when investment is a fixed constant; it is obvious that for any given denominator in the ROI calculation the maximization of the ratio will entail maximization of the profit numerator. If investment were centrally determined and fixed in a short control period an ROI objective would coincide with the interests of the firm – but in this case the ratio is redundant. In fact the working capital element in divisional investment makes it improbable that investment will be fixed.

(i) *Defining profit*
Views on the appropriate definition of profit for ROI run virtually the whole gamut of profit measures which have already been considered.† Adopted concepts usually, although not invariably, employ a consistent asset base.

(ii) *Defining the investment base*
A substantial amount of discussion of ROI has been concerned with the determination of the asset base; to a large extent the problems are analogous to those discussed for profit measures. The working capital element need not be further considered, except to reiterate its variable nature.

Some firms (notably du Pont [1]) adopt undepreciated historic cost of fixed assets for the investment base, on the grounds that the deduction of depreciation

---

* Adopted by 14, 32 and 15 per cent respectively of the companies in the Mauriel and Anthony survey [11].
† See [6] p. 2 and [14] pp. 19–23.

from the denominator of the ratio produces rising ROI over the life of assets which yield constant cash flows. Apart from the irrelevance of past cost to current asset use and the questionable presumption that assets typically produce constant cash flows, a rising return from assets over life is certainly implausible.

The internal rate of return method of depreciation* is an attempt to overcome the limitations of ROI calculated on a conventionally depreciated asset base by reconciliation of the ROI and IRR concepts. A depreciated value is assigned to an asset equal to the present value of the (originally) expected cash flows over the remaining life of the asset, discounted at the IRR. *If* the expected cash flows were achieved the ROI would be equal to a constant IRR in every period, as demonstrated below.

$$\text{ROI} = \frac{\text{Profit}}{\text{Investment}}$$

$$= \frac{\text{Cash flow} - \lceil \text{asset book value time } 0 - \text{asset book value time } 1 \rceil}{\text{Asset book value time } 0}$$

The IRR method of depreciation gives:

$$\text{ROI} = \frac{x_1 - \left[\sum_{t=1}^{n} \frac{x_t}{(1+\rho)^t} - \sum_{t=2}^{n} \frac{x_t}{(1+\rho)^{t-1}} \right]}{\sum_{t=1}^{n} \frac{x_t}{(1+\rho)^t}}$$

where the terms are as defined in section 2(d) *except* that x_t is originally expected cash flow from using asset in the period up to time t and ρ is IRR calculated on originally expected cash flow.

The IRR depreciation method reduces† to:

$$\text{ROI} = \frac{\left[\sum_{t=1}^{n} \frac{x_t}{(1+\rho)^t} \right] \rho}{\left[\sum_{t=1}^{n} \frac{x_t}{(1+\rho)^t} \right]} = \rho$$

---

*For advocacy of this method see [5] pp. 260–71 and [8].

†In the numerator x_1 and the *second* part of the expression in square brackets give:

$$x_1 + \frac{x_2}{(1+\rho)} + \ldots + \frac{x_n}{(1+\rho)^{n-1}}$$

from which is deducted the *first* part of the expression in square brackets:

$$\frac{x_1}{(1+\rho)} + \frac{x_2}{(1+\rho)^2} + \ldots + \frac{x_n}{(1+\rho)^n}$$

Since $x_1 - \frac{x_1}{1+\rho}$ equals $\frac{x_1\rho}{1+\rho}$, etc., the difference between the two expressions gives

$$\left[\sum_{t=1}^{n} \frac{x_t}{(1+\rho)^t} \right] \rho$$

Thus the IRR depreciation measure makes ROI reconcilable with IRR. However, quite apart from the limitations of IRR, this is an *ex ante* reconciliation; when achieved cash flows differ from expected cash flows (as they must in the absence of perfect foresight) the ROI calculation no longer equals IRR, and the rationale usually advanced for this method disappears. Even if depreciation were recalculated to incorporate actual past cash flows it would still (presumably) be applied to the historic cost of the asset. This emphasis on past outlays is similar to that considered for residual income; the ROI measure using IRR depreciation is equally irrelevant to appraisal of current period performance.

(b) Disaggregated ratios

The use of ROI is often associated with a breakdown of the components of the measure. The initial breakdown is:

$$ROI = \frac{Profit}{Investment} = \frac{Sales}{Investment} \times \frac{Profit}{Sales}$$

Such disaggregated ratios suffer from similar limitations to ROI: they are averages which can mask wide variations between different areas of the division's activities, and an increase in a ratio does not necessarily mean that the division has acted in the interests of the firm because increases can be achieved by avoiding activities which offer modest, although adequate, returns.

The ratio approach to divisional control was pioneered, and is still used, by E. I. du Pont de Nemours & Co. It is noteworthy that for du Pont these simple ratios represent a summarization of divisional data which are reported in their component details (costs, working capital assets, etc.). Even before 1918 du Pont's central management were provided with such information as annual forecasts updated monthly and detailed investment analyses.* Thus the ratios must be seen in perspective as a part of a much more sophisticated system of control.

17.4 Postscript on external reporting for segments

External reporting by the firm on the activities of its segments is analogous to performance measurement for divisions, but the analogy must not be overstrained. Management has an active control role, access to a wealth of data concerning divisions and the firm, and the power to determine divisional structure. The external user of segmental reports is, it will be assumed, the investor who has a relatively passive interpretative role, must be satisfied with 'objective' measures of perfor-

* [7], pp. 60–61 and 66–67.

mance, and might well prefer different segmental information from that following the lines of the divisional structure. The same measurement concepts need not necessarily be appropriate for both types of user.

From the investor viewpoint a major need for a breakdown of information on the activities of firms has been expressed succintly by Mautz*

> ... a conglomerate company is defined as one which is so managerially decentralized, so lacks operational integration, or has such diversified markets that it may experience rates of profitability, degrees of risk, and opportunities for growth which vary within the company to such an extent that an investor requires information about these variations in order to make informed decisions.

This definition is wide. Without entering into semantics it is evident that the important point at issue is that investors would ideally like a breakdown of data for any company within which there are substantial variations in 'rates of profitability, degrees of risk, and opportunities for growth', whether or not such a company would be conventionally regarded as a conglomerate. The major areas of investor interest are likely to be products (or product classes) and geographical distribution of activities; these areas may not necessarily coincide with the divisional structure. In Britain† companies are required to publish data in these two major areas.

The Companies Act 1967 (Section 17) requires annual publication of data for a company‡ carrying on business of two or more classes that, in the *opinion of the directors*, differ substantially from each other. The data requirements are:

1. The proportions of sales divided between the classes.
2. The approximate extent to which, *in the opinion of the directors*, the business of each class 'contributed to, or restricted, the profit or loss of the company for that year before taxation'.

As a condition for Stock Exchange quotation companies are required to comply with the General Undertaking of the Federation of Stock Exchanges. This requires, among other things, annual publication of a statement showing a geographical analysis (figures or percentages) of trading operations, where the company trades outside the United Kingdom. Usually this analysis seems to be interpreted as referring to sales, although some companies give profit figures; the geographical areas are usually broad continental classifications.

Neither the Companies Act nor the Stock Exchange regulations require details of net assets. Since the classification of business is dependent on the opinion of the directors, and both sets of data can be included in the directors' report without audit, the requirements are not formally onerous.

* [12], p. 26.
† Disclosure requirements also apply in the USA; see [18] for a chronicle and extensive bibliography of the debate preceding adoption in 1969.
‡ A company which is neither a holding company nor a subsidiary is exempted if sales do not exceed £250 000 (1972).

The regulations provide no indication of the appropriate profit concept to employ for classes of business. True to tradition in such matters the majority of companies allocate all overheads to class results.

The concept of controllable profit, which was advanced for performance appraisal of responsible division managers, may not be appropriate for the investor whose concern is with investment appraisal and not control. The investor is forced, unlike management, to extrapolate from past divisional or segment results – because they represent a major data source in relation to segments of the firm. Traceable profit, unencumbered by arbitrary allocations, would appear to provide the investor with the most 'objective' basis on which to undertake his analysis. A similar view is taken by Backer and McFarland [4].

Problems of transfers between divisions cause difficulties for external reporting (see e.g. Solomons in [15]). It could be argued that the marginal cost concept could still be applied for external reporting, but since firms typically include overhead allocations it must be recognized that these allocations are likely to remain in the external reports. However, there is a strong case for indicating the basis of transfers and for showing their amount separately: some firms do provide the latter information.

Bibliographical references

[1] American Management Association (publishers), *How the du Pont Organisation Appraises its Performance*, Financial Management Series No. 94, 1950.

[2] Amey, L. R., *The Efficiency of Business Enterprises*, Allen and Unwin, 1969.

[3] Amey, L. R., Divisional performance measurement and interest on capital, *Journal of Business Finance*, Spring 1969, pp. 2–7.

[4] Backer, M. and W. B. McFarland, *External Reporting for Segments of a Business*, National Association of Accountants, 1968.

[5] Bierman, H. and A. R. Drebin, *Managerial Accounting*, Macmillan, New York, 1968.

[6] British Institute of Management and the Centre for Interfirm Comparison (publishers), *Efficiency Comparisons within Large Organisations*, 1962.

[7] Chandler, A. D., *Strategy and Structure: Chapters in the History of the American Enterprise*, M.I.T. Press, 1962.

[8] Flower, J. F., Measurement of divisional performance, *Accounting and Business Research*, Summer 1971, pp. 205–14.

[9] Gabor, A. and I. F. Pearce, A new approach to the theory of the firm, *Oxford Economic Papers*, October 1952, pp. 252–65.

[10] Henderson, B. D. and J. Dearden, New system for divisional control, *Harvard Business Review*, September/October 1966, pp. 144–60.

[11] Mauriel, J. J. and R. N. Anthony, Misevaluation of investment center performance, *Harvard Business Review*, March/April 1966, pp. 98–105.

[12] Mautz, R. K., Identification of the conglomerate company, *Financial Executive*, July 1967, pp. 18–26.

[13] National Association of [Cost] Accountants (publishers), *Accounting for Intra-Company Transfers*, Research Series No. 30, 1956.

[14] National Association of Accountants (publishers), *Return on Capital as a Guide to Managerial Decisions*, Research Report No. 35, 1959.

[15] Rappaport, A., P. A. Firmin, and S. A. Zeff, *Public Reporting by Conglomerates*, Prentice-Hall, 1968.

[16] Shillinglaw, G., Toward a theory of divisional income measurement, *Accounting Review*, April 1962, pp. 208–16.

[17] Shillinglaw, G., Divisional performance review: An extension of budgetary control, in *Management Controls: New Directions in Basic Research*, eds. C. P. Bonini, R. K. Jaedicke and H. M. Wagner, McGraw-Hill, 1964.

[18] Skousen, K. F., Chronicle of events surrounding the segment reporting issue, *Journal of Accounting Research*, Autumn 1970, pp. 293–99.

[19] Solomons, D., *Divisional Performance: Measurement and Control*, Irwin 1965.

[20] Sord, B. H. and G. A. Welsch, *Business Budgeting*, Controllership Foundation, 1958.

[21] Vatter, W. J., Does rate of return measure business efficiency?, *N.A.A. Bulletin*, January 1959, pp. 33–48.

[22] Whinston, A., Price guides in decentralised organisations, in *New Perspectives in Organisation Research*, eds. W. W. Cooper, H. J. Leavitt and M. W. Shelly II, Wiley 1962.

Problems

17.1 'The company's central management remains ultimately responsible for the efficient operation of the division and normally fulfils this duty by measuring the division's performance – generally by means of a divisional profit and loss account. If the division's performance is shown to be satisfactory, the central management considers that it has fulfilled its duty at least until the next occasion for checking on performance. If the divisional profit and loss account reveals unsatisfactory performance, this is a signal for some form of action by central management – perhaps to supervise more closely the division's affairs or to replace the manager.

'... the way in which the division's performance is measured will have a profound effect upon the way in which the divisional manager will make decisions. The most important decisions with which he is concerned are those concerned with capital investment.' [8], p. 205.

Compare the above statement with other views of the delegation of responsibility to divisions and examine the implications for performance measurement.

17.2 'Transfer pricing is necessary to permit delegation of profit responsibility, but optimal transfer pricing requires centralized decision-making.'

Discuss this paradoxical statement.

17.3 'Management of an industrial enterprise ... must ... rely to some extent on returns in the form of figures. However, returns in the form of absolute figures (even the most important ones) may be positively misleading unless they are related to something else – preferably a constant.

'To take a very simple example, it may not be sufficient to know that profits are being maintained if the amount of capital employed to achieve these profits is constantly rising. Those same profits ... may show a constantly diminishing return on capital employed. And it may be that, had that fact been known and appreciated from an early date, some managerial action might have been possible to arrest the decline.

'The use of ratios, however, presupposes some sort of yardstick to measure the effectiveness or adequacy of the ratio that has been achieved. It is not sufficient to know that the return on capital employed is 15 per cent per annum unless one knows what ... [it] ... should or could be.

'There is always the yardstick of past performance which may indeed be a useful indicator of progression or regression, but inevitably the use of ratios will point to the need for comparison with the performance of other firms in similar – and sometimes dissimilar – businesses.'

Consider the above quotation in relation to the uses and limitations of ROI (here equivalent to return on capital employed) for internal appraisal of performance of *segments* of a firm.

17.4 The performance of the Fables division of a firm is appraised by the residual income method, and the division manager has power to dispose of redundant assets. The division has, among other assets, equipment with written down book value of £30 000. For residual income calculation purposes the equipment is depreciated at £3 000 per year (10-year life, nil scrap value). Residual income is charged with interest at 10 per cent per year on written down value.

The manager of the Fables division considers that the equipment's expected cash flows, net of out-of-pocket costs, will be £4 000 per year for 5 years and £1 000 per year for a further 5 years, giving an *expected* PV* of £17 517. However, he estimates a 0·1 probability of PV below £8 000 and a 0·1 probability of PV above £22 000. An opportunity to sell the equipment has occurred; after the current year the disposal value of the equipment will be negligible. Residual income will be charged with any book loss on the disposal of the equipment.

If the equipment can be sold for £16 000, do you consider sale or retention to be in the (apparent) interests of:

(1) The firm.
(2) An ambitious division manager who considers that his imminent promotion depends on high profit performance in the current period.
(3) A newly appointed division manager.
(4) A newly appointed division manager who has a period of grace during which losses and gains on disposal of redundant assets are not brought into residual income.

17.5 'ROI, measured as net profit divided by book value of an asset, will equal IRR if the book value of the asset is stated as the PV of future cash flows discounted at the project's IRR. Thus IRR depreciation overcomes the usual asset valuation difficulties associated with the appraisal of performance on the basis of ROI.'

The above view was adopted by Janus Ltd. The IRR depreciation method was first applied to a single asset, with cost £18 426, expected life 9 years, nil scrap value, expected cash flows £4 000 per year.

Required:

(a) Calculate ROI for years 1, 2 and 9 if the expected cash flows are achieved.
(b) Calculate ROI for years 1, 2 and 9 if the actual cash flows are £3 000 in each of those years, and the original IRR depreciation is adopted.

* Or EMV – see section 3(c) of Chapter 12.

    (c) Calculate ROI for years 1, 2 and 9 if the actual cash flows are £5 500, £5 400 and £4 700 respectively in those years, and the original IRR depreciation is adopted.

    (d) Comment.

17.6 A company recently established two new plants for the manufacture of adhesives (plant *A*) and components (plant *C*).

    Both plants cost £200 000. The decision to invest was made on identical expectations for each plant. The expectations were: £240 000 PV of future cash flows discounted at cost of capital 8 per cent per year, economic life 20 years, nil scrap value. Expected cash flows were £20 000 in year 1 and £25 000 in year 2; both plants achieved expectations in year 1.

    In year 2 *plant A* earned a cash flow of £30 000. Of this £10 000 was derived from the sale of a waste product which had been assumed valueless for the original investment decision.

    In year 2 *plant C* earned a cash flow of £15 000. Towards the end of the first year a staple component had been rendered obsolete. The major customer for this component had been forced by a competitor's innovation to redesign its own products. Plant *C* was reorganizing and partially retooling to manufacture new components in year 3. The plant manager believed that cash flow of £20 000 had been lost on the redundant component.

    Assuming that cash flows approximate to controllable profit, calculate the residual income in year 2 for each plant (adopting straight line depreciation). Discuss the appraisal of performance and the assumptions of the original expectations. To what extent would appraisal of performance be assisted by adopting different measures for the asset valuation (e.g. replacement cost, realizable value, adjustment for general price level changes)?

18

A critique of accounting controls

The baby figure of the giant mass, Of things to come at large.
— TROILUS AND CRESSIDA

In this chapter the ideas discussed in Chapters 5–6 and 13–17 will be critically examined. In those chapters we traced through the processes of plan formation, decision-making to implement plans, the recording of data on observed outcomes and the various means by which internal control was exercised over these observed results. Depending on the form of the control, certain measures of performance were calculated showing the degree of conformance of actual to planned behaviour. In Chapter 13 some first indications were given that all was not well with accounting control systems. Having described the main kinds of accounting controls in use we now carry this probe a little further.

18.1 The scope of control

Every firm, it has been said, is a control system. It has enterprise goals, detailed in an overall plan such as a comprehensive system of budgets, and an estimate of its current position, so that its decision-making may be seen as its response to the gap between its current position and its planned position.* According to this view, business behaviour is an iterative process. In a somewhat similar way business plans, once made, become an integral part of the internal control system – directly or indirectly, as will be explained later. As mentioned in Chapter 5, the very existence of the budgeting process may constrain the firm's planning. We begin to discern various levels of control, ranging from control in the large to controls in the small. At the top of this hierarchy of controls lies the economic control of the enterprise, which is governed by both external and internal controls, as shown in Chapter 13. It is no part of our present purpose to catalogue the whole array of detailed controls in the small. Prominent among them, however, will be a set of financial controls which will include the usual accounting controls, in particular:

> Control of revenue flows⎱
> „   „ expense flows⎰ and of the relation between them
>
> Control of cash flows;

---

*This is the 'industrial dynamics' of J. W. Forrester and others at M.I.T.

Control of asset structure ⎫
    ,,   ,, claims structure ⎬ and of the relation between them

Control of the firm's rate of growth.

The non-financial controls might include control of time,* product quality and data-information flow, to name only a few. The 'principle of exceptions' incorporated in most accounting control systems, the standardized operating rules referred to earlier, and the careful design of the information system (including the accounting control subsystem) are examples of the attempt to control the data flow within the organization, and information costs. Long-term contracts of various kinds (relating to purchases or hirings and sales), indeed any action taken by the firm to *stabilize* its activities (the example of production smoothing comes to mind) result not only in a reduction in the amount of information required to control the activities in question but also provide *controlled information* [24]: a number of future events can be identified, predicted and controlled by a single piece of information. Against this economy in information costs, of course, must be set the costs of stabilization (e.g. the costs of developing and computing a production smoothing model, and any resulting increase in inventory-related costs). As always, it is unwise to consider one part of the system in isolation; whether we are concerned with planning, decision-making or control we should be concerned with the effects on the costs, revenues and net worth of the firm as a whole.

Until comparatively recently, the typical accounting control techniques of standard costing and budgetary control, first introduced in the 1910s in the United States, have undergone virtually no development; flexible budgeting represents one of the very few advances. Nor were these systems subjected to a really critical examination. Accountants tinkered with the mechanics of the systems, rarely stopping to enquire whether they were properly designed, and whether they succeeded in doing what they were supposed to do, viz. control. To a considerable extent progress on this front had to await developments in other fields: in cybernetics (the science of control), organization theory, operations research, computation facilities, and the shift in emphasis away from an aggregative, outward-looking, normative theory of the firm to positive, inward-looking theories of decision-making within business organizations.

To help illustrate the points to be made in the remainder of the chapter, Figure 18.1 is offered as an attempt to represent the essential elements in an accounting control system.†

---

*Control of time needs to include control over the lead time between feasibility study and decision as well as control of decision implementation. This lead time depends on the 'quality' of top management, particularly its attitude to risk-taking. Research and development affords an example: the points of transition between research, development and commercial exploitation may often be critical. Military experience draws attention to the excessive lead times found in these crucial 'awaiting decision' stages. When to enter the market with a new product is another example.

† Some of these elements were briefly referred to in section 4 of Chapter 13. The diagram is an elaboration of the one used by Ashby [5] and reproduced in [37].

The diagram consists of three time frames, t_0, t_1 and t_2; the current period is t_1. E_1 represents the firm's environment in period 1, containing all the variables exogenous to the internal control system and to certain other related systems shown in the diagram; in cybernetics E is characterized as a variety generator, the source of all disturbances to the system which it is sought to control. R denotes the reactions of agents of the firm* to changes in the environment and to the performance targets set (at S). At the beginning of the period the firm draws up plans, budgets (P_1). These are the result of forecasts made towards the end of the previous period (F_1 in time frame t_0) and are influenced by the goals of the business (G). Contrary to the exposition of Ashby, Beer and Williamson, however, we have separate budgets as plans (P_1) and budgets as controls or performance programs (S). The reason for introducing P as a separate element will be given in section 2.

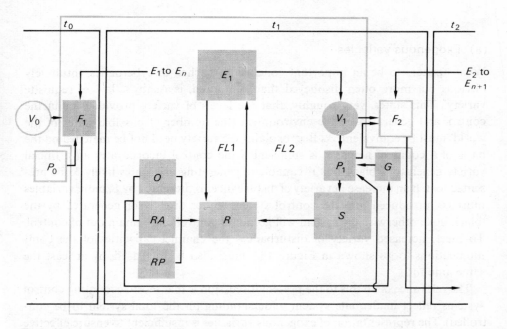

Figure 18.1 An accounting control system

The disturbances originating in E are broadly of two types: those that result in an adaptive response which is a change in degree, without any change in S (i.e. without revision of the budget), and those for which the appropriate response is a change in kind, calling for budget revision (replanning). The former minor changes form a feedback loop between E and R, labelled $FL1$; the latter are signalled by a change in certain essential variables (V_1), which triggers a change in plans and

---

* Using this term to mean all personnel other than top management.

related performance targets via the step mechanism S. This, then, is the second feedback loop ($FL2$). Unlike the first, it operates first on top management. The grey line indicates the boundaries of the control system in period t_1.

The diagram also shows three other influences which are thought to affect the responses of the firm's agents: the form and structure of the organization (O), the assignment of functions (role assignments) within the organization (RA), and the firm's reward-penalty system (RP). The first two are also shown as possibly influencing goal formation. In making its forecasts for period t_2 (and its longer range forecasts), the firm is shown as drawing upon information relating to the current period (earlier periods could also be included) from the revised budgets (P_1) and the most up-to-date values of the essential variables (V_1), as well as forming anticipations and making estimates concerning the relevant parts of its entire future.

(a) Exogenous variables

What appears to be an important conclusion reached in cybernetics, intuitively obvious but more often disobeyed than honoured, is Ashby's 'law of requisite variety'. This states, very roughly, that the levels of variety provided for in the control and generated by the environment (the number of possible states of the world) must be equivalent. As Beer explains it,* variety need not be matched on the basis of a count of items; it is sufficient if the control incorporates an artificial variety generator ('black box')† capable of generating any states likely to be presented to it. If an increase in variety of disturbances is presented by E, more variables must be introduced into the control system, either directly or generated by the 'black box', otherwise the system will go out of control and remain out of control. To meet increased variety of disturbances the channel capacities of the communications loops shown in Figure 18.1 must also be increased, by at least the same amount.‡

The relevance of all this to the present discussion is that most accounting control systems reflect inadequate system understanding (of the total system to be controlled). The representation of exogenous variables is insufficient to ensure effective control; many variables external to the system are unrepresented in it, the system does not include a cybernetic device for generating variety, and apart from transmission of the original budget performance program the second loop ($FL2$) is relatively unused. The variety of disturbances issuing from E is not matched by the requisite variety at R.

As stressed in Chapter 13, the firm is subject to external as well as internal

*[9], p. 280.
† *Ibid.*, p. 293.
‡ To allow for increased 'noise' as well as increased transmissions.

controls. To be effective, the internal control system must recognize the existence of these external variables and adequately incorporate them.

(b) The boundaries of the system

Where does the process we have just been discussing end, or to put it another way, where do we draw the boundaries between what is 'controllable' and what is 'non-controllable'? It has been the habit in accounting to assume that the boundaries of the accounting control system are coextensive with the boundaries of the firm; activities undertaken within the firm are regarded as controllable, those outside the firm as noncontrollable. Such an assumption is extremely simplistic and almost always invalid. The reason was stated in section 4 of Chapter 13. The 'relevant' external variables to be included are not only those elements of the environment which are thought to be subject to some degree of control by the firm, but also elements normally regarded as noncontrollable if they interact with internal variables. It is necessary to incorporate them in the control model in order to monitor the interactions. An example might be the current and expected prices and levels of advertising expenditure of competing firms.

This is further illustrated in an interesting case quoted by E. B. Roberts [27] which is worth reporting at length. Essentially it shows that what were thought to be externally-induced (and noncontrollable) disturbances in fact originated within the firm, but were controllable only by extending the boundaries of the control system beyond the organizational limits of the firm. The firm in question did not have any formal production smoothing control system to regulate production, finished goods inventory and employment. It responded to fluctuations in sales orders without foresight. When sales orders increased, inventories were at first run down until it was clear that the increase was not just a temporary fluctuation. If the fluctuation outlasted this response, production and employment had then to be increased more than proportionately to rebuild inventories as well as to meet the higher order rate. Similarly when sales orders fell, production and employment fell more than proportionately in order to reduce the excessive inventories which had been built up. Consequently even relatively small variations in sales order rate generated wide swings in production (via order backlog), inventories, employment, and hence profitability.

For the solution to this problem it is necessary, first, to obtain better data on expected sales, and to smooth these data (e.g. by averaging) to eliminate possibilities of chance variations being passed on to the works. Together with frequent checks on inventory and the order backlog, and adjustment of the work force to meet the desired production rate (a function of the current volume of sales and the order backlog), this should be enough to remove the wide swings in production,

555

inventories and employment.* The establishment of such a control system will in general reduce the magnitude and periodicity of demand-induced fluctuations but will not eliminate the underlying causes unless the boundaries of the control system enclose all parts of the firm's environment relevant to this set of activities.

The case cited by Roberts was of a company manufacturing electrical components. Competition depended heavily on product reliability and delivery time rather than on price. The firm's customers were other firms who used the components in the manufacture of the products they sold, a fact which was not considered in the firm's budgetary control system. What in fact happened was that when customers received orders for their products they despatched orders for components, the time at which these orders were placed depending partly on the lead time of the component manufacturer. The latter changes affected the rate at which customers released new orders, which in turn affected the company's lead time, forming a feedback loop not considered in the company's control system:

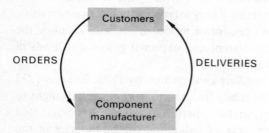

Figure 18.2 Firm-customer feedback loop

Suppose demand for the customers' products temporarily increases, then falls back to its previous level. This will be passed on to the component manufacturer in increased orders. But since the latter experiences sizeable fluctuations in order rate even under normal conditions, due to lack of control, some time will elapse before this change in order rate is noticed. In the meantime inventories will be run down and the order backlog increased, thereby lengthening the delivery period. As a result, customers will tend to order further ahead and to maintain the higher order rate originally caused by the temporary increase in demand for their products, which by now has returned to its original level. When the component manufacturer finally notices the higher sales he will increase his work force to a level higher than is justified by the current order rate, in order to deal with the order backlog and reduced inventory. Lead times to customers drop, and their ordering falls below its initial rate before the increase in demand. It is clear from this that order rate fluctuations can be generated independently of the basic pattern of demand for the customers' products.

*Such a procedure is formalized in the dynamic production smoothing model of Holt *et al.* [21], which has been referred to earlier.

The inadequacy of the component firm's control system, designed to damp down the effects of exogenous disturbances, in fact amplified them. To eliminate these unnecessary fluctuations what was needed was not control of inventory, order backlog or employment, but stabilization of factory lead time, using inventory to absorb random order rate fluctuations. The lesson to be learnt from this case is that it is a common mistake to draw the boundaries of a business control system to conform with the organizational boundaries of the firm, whereas the key to effective control may lie outside the organization. In other words the distinction between controllable and noncontrollable variances in performance is, in general, not as simple as accountants usually take it to be. The swings in customers' orders were apparently beyond the control of the component manufacturer. Certainly the ordering decisions of customers were no part of the company's formal organization. What was needed was stabilization of the input to customers' ordering decisions, viz. the delivery delay, which lay within the company's control. But to elicit this fact the interactions between delivery period and customer ordering rate had to be brought within the component manufacturer's control system, and monitored. That is, the control system had to extend beyond the firm. More generally, the control system must mirror the underlying realities, not be modelled on some convenient, but arbitrary and artificial, accounting or organizational classification. Design of the control system calls for a broad outlook. It is not the routine operation it is usually made out to be. Control systems often suffer through being designed at too low a level in the firm, by people who do not possess the necessary expertise, and whose outlook is not sufficiently broad, to identify the relevant variables and to comprehend the relationships and interrelationships between the underlying economic forces which they represent.

(c) The subdivisions of the system

A further aspect of the division between controllable and noncontrollable variations concerns the subdivisions of the control system. The subgoals set for parts of the organization are sometimes referred to as 'second-order control'. In the earlier discussion of decision-making the importance of allowing for interdependencies was repeatedly stressed. Likewise in control systems, what is needed is a way of partitioning the organization so that goal-striving behaviour in each subdivision is consistent with achievement of the goals of the organization. It must not be possible to optimize any subdivision without at the same time optimizing the whole. This means that the control system, as it applies to subdivisions, must incorporate all interactions with other subdivisions and satisfy all constraints on the organization as a whole.

As Churchman has pointed out,* one of the most serious defects of accounting

*[14], Chapter 13.

control systems as commonly designed is their concept of the closed system. Control subdivisions usually coincide in practice with organizational subdivisions. Because there is often a basic conflict between the administrative lines of authority and responsibility reflected in a firm's organizational structure and the economic relationships between its activities, this equation of organizational subdivisions with control subdivisions and the erroneous treatment of the latter as closed systems, unaffected by the operations of other subdivisions with respect to the goals of the organization, is bound to result in under-achievement (suboptimal performance if the firm pursues an optimizing goal).

(d) Intertemporal interdependencies

What has just been said regarding organizational subdivisions is also true of temporal subdivisions. Performance in one period is not unrelated to performance in subsequent periods. Adapting the argument of the previous section, we require some way of subdividing the organization's dynamic activities so that each time period can validly be considered a closed system within which the objective is to achieve some goal or goals (performance targets) in a way that is consistent with achievement of the firm's goals over time. In other words, budgets from period to period must be economically consistent. Just as it does not make sense for one organizational subdivision to achieve its objective at the expense of other subdivisions and of the firm as a whole, so it would be myopic to fulfil targets in one period at the expense of a more than offsetting reduction in performance in future periods.

It can confidently be said that in practice one or more of the three forms of interdependence referred to in subsections (b)–(d) go unrecognized in accounting control systems. Together with the paucity of exogenous variables included in the control data, this goes a long way towards explaining why economic control and financial control (typically exercised through various accounting devices such as budgetary control and standard costs*) are generally very different things.

(e) The control model

To the earlier remarks concerning the possible irrelevance for control purposes of organizational boundaries and structure and the artificial nature of time subdivisions in the continuum of events must now be added a word on accounting classifications. It should be evident that the model which underlies the budgetary control and standard costing systems should be an accurate representation of the activities to be controlled. If these activities are subject to a separate partial control

---

* For purposes of this chapter these can be regarded as one and the same thing: both prescribe desired levels of attainment.

(i.e. decision model), then the model underlying the accounting control system should be structurally consistent with this model: the latter should be an isomorphic mapping of the former. Otherwise a system is being 'controlled' which does not in reality exist, and management is being misinformed.* Beer contends† that in this situation there is no need for the accounting control, that it is an unnecessary duplication.‡ This view ignores the importance of budgets (planning, and by extension, control budgets) as embodiments of business plans and policies, the need to coordinate the firm's various activities, to ensure that resources and funds are available when needed and are efficiently utilized over time.

18.2 The nature of accounting controls

A brief reference was made in section 6(e) of Chapter 13 to the fact that budgets may serve duel functions, as plans and as controls. Cyert and March§ in fact distinguish four different roles of business plans in general: as goals, schedules of resource requirements, theories and precedents. Our interest here concerns budgets as plans and as controls.

Consider, first, the budget as an overall *plan* of business operations. Plans are concerned with internal resource allocation. The important points to be taken into account in drawing up plans, as we have seen in Chapter 5, include specifying the goals of the enterprise explicitly, the resources it expects to be able to command during the period, including any constraints on resource availabilities, generating all the feasible alternative courses of action open to the enterprise, predicting the outcomes of these alternatives, and selecting that set of alternatives which will achieve the prescribed goals (whether these be of an optimizing or satisficing nature) subject to the constraints and to various kinds of interdependencies, including intertemporal ones. All this is premised on the assumption that there is no communications or control problem: plans are perfectly executed. Finally, we stipulated that data for the planning budgets (operating and long-term) must be founded on economic principles.

The effectiveness of a *control* budget, by contrast, is measured solely by the results it produces, and not by any relation the data it contains may have to economic reality. If, for example, it is desired to minimize a certain cost, a control budget of £700 which produces a cost of £1 000 is to be preferred to a budget of £1 000 which produces a cost of £1 200, despite the greater predictive accuracy of the latter.

It follows, in the words of an oft-quoted remark attributed to Charnes and

* [9], p. 340 *et seq.*
† [9], p. 341.
‡ See also [17], [33] and [1].
§ [16], pp. 111–12.

Cooper, that 'a good plan ... does not necessarily yield a good control', and that 'good planning data and good control data are not necessarily the same'. Intuitively, one would be surprised if budget planning data which were the result of an optimization, for example, yielded the most effective control, i.e. brought about the greatest degree of conformance to these optimal targets. To believe that controls based on optimal plans would be effective would be to assume a very high threshold of discouragement, which is not in general characteristic of human behaviour.

In practice business budgets commonly serve as both plans and controls. The norms of which they are comprised are generally what is described in the accounting literature as 'currently attainable' rather than 'ideal' or optimal. As Stedry has remarked,* if the budgets and standards represent this kind of norm 'an "approach to standard" implies little more than an approach to a level of performance which was *a priori* assumed to be approachable, or perhaps more important, capable of betterment'.

Our purpose in raising this issue is to point out that there is a fundamental difference between the task of resource allocation undertaken in the pursuit of certain objectives (regarding planning budgets as providing a broad framework within which subsequent resource allocation and other decisions are expected to be taken) and the task of coordinating the activities of men and machines in an effort to ensure a predetermined degree of efficiency and the nearest approach to fulfilment of the planned objectives. This is why we separated P and S in Figure 18.1. It should be added that this separation at this stage rests on no more than general reasoning. The principles governing the exact relation, for any particular firm, between the control budget and the planning budget have yet to be worked out. Like the relations between planning budgets, plan revisions and subsequent decisions, we can only advance this as a topic worthy of continued research.

18.3 The internal control process

(a) Control of forecasting and estimating

Whether or not plans and controls coincide, plans become an integral part of the internal control mechanism, because as already stated a plan implies some sort of control to enforce it. And, as we saw in Chapter 5, plans involve *forecasts* ('relevant anticipations') of exogenous variables as well as *estimates* of the future course of variables within the firm's control. In other words the performance which the controls seek to regulate is measured in relation to an *ex ante* standard; expectations, together with control and the reward–penalty system, determine observed behaviour.† For both planning and control purposes considerable importance

---

*[34], p. 11.

† For a contrary view, involving measurement of performance in relation to an '*ex post* optimum', see [33] and [17]. The view expressed above is elaborated, and the contrary view critically examined, in [1].

attaches to the accuracy of these forecasts and estimates. Typical accounting controls to a very large extent concentrate on the implementation process, the putting into effect of plans, to the exclusion of the role of forecasting and estimating. It is our contention that, since in conditions of uncertainty the control norms must be expectational measures (or more strictly derivatives of the latter), control should encompass the forecasting and estimating activities which precede the setting up of the controls as well as the customary feedback comparisons which accompany their implementation.

This is an area calling for further investigation. In both aspects of control there is a need for much stronger links to be forged between the accounting control system and the firm's reward-penalty system. Usually only the plan implementation aspect is recognized as calling for the application of incentives.* In attempting to exercise some measure of control over forecasting and estimating connected with the planning and control budgets the possibility arises of building into the reward–penalty system an inducement to forecasters and estimators to achieve greater accuracy, by developing scoring rules based on histories of their subjective probability assessments in relation to observed results, appropriately adjusted.†

(b) Control of program implementation

We have already alluded to certain desirable characteristics of the control process, e.g. that it should be consistent with *economic* control of the enterprise, that accounting controls should be as rich in their representation of relevant exogenous variables as of endogenous ones, and that the boundaries and subdivisions of control should be correctly drawn and any other significant interdependencies taken into account. It may also be added that timeliness is of the very essence of control; a scheme which only discovers the causes of a variation after it has ceased is useless, as of course is a scheme which costs more to operate than the benefits it yields. The example of the electrical components manufacturer illustrated the importance of both the coverage and timeliness of the control. In short, controls are only useful if they are effective and economically justified.

(i) *Effectiveness of controls*
The question arises as to how effective most existing accounting control systems are. How many of them succeed in controlling? To be effective a system must reduce both the amplitude and periodicity of fluctuations in the variables it purports to control. One piece of evidence is based on a study, by means of simulation, of control systems (accounting and other) in over 1 000 organizations over a period of several years.‡ This study concluded that many systems, thought to be efficient

---

* Consider, for instance, the literature on socialist economics.
† For an analysis along these lines, though not related to accounting controls, see [38].
‡ Part of the industrial dynamics project conducted at M.I.T.

by the organizations operating them, did not control effectively, even exerted a disequilibrating effect, and sometimes created new problems. It is hoped that some of the reasons for this malfunctioning are given in this chapter.

(ii) *Self-regulation*

Beer states* it as a principle of general control theory, supported by 'the logical theorems of network theory, the mathematical theorems of information theory, the strategic analysis of the theory of games, and by other scientific sources', that viable control systems cannot be entirely regulated from outside; they must rely on some degree of self-regulation. It would appear likely that as the degree of complexity and the uncertainties of the system to be controlled multiply, the greater will be the need for the system to incorporate self-adaptive elements. That is to say, the act of going out of control must *automatically* trigger the necessary responses to bring the system back under control.†

A somewhat similar point is made by Shillinglaw‡ in the course of some discerning remarks on control. The need for delegating responsibility in an organization of any size leads to the presumption that a good control system should rely heavily on self-correction. This in turn involves certain implicit assumptions: that budgetary targets are sufficiently demanding to call forth strong efforts by those whom they are supposed to control, and that the latter are adequately motivated to meet or exceed the targets, the motivation being supplied by the entire reward structure of the firm.

We shall return to the question of the reward–penalty system in a moment. For the present it may be added that efforts to increase a control system's capacity for self-adaptation are likely to be more successful the more highly automated is the control system and the more closely the 'law of requisite variety' is observed in designing it. One way of obviating the need of the organization to adapt to every change in its environment and to reduce disturbances to manageable proportions is to build threshold responses into the control system. If the disturbance is less than some predetermined amount it is, in effect, channeled into *FL1*; only if it exceeds this amount is it allowed to generate step-function adaptation via *V* in *FL2*.§**

(iii) *Measurement problems*

To be effective, controls must measure whatever they are designed to control appropriately; more specifically, they must present the relationship measured in structurally true form [18]. The meaning of this is made clear by the following

---

* [9], p. 261 *et seq.*
† Sometimes referred to as the principle of error-controlled negative feedback.
‡ [29], in [10].
§ Ashby [6], p. 66.
** [34], p. 171.

example. Statistics on industrial disputes are commonly reported as 'number of disputes' or 'man-days lost per thousand employees' per year. This measure gives the impression that the disputes are spread over the whole work force in a random manner. Is such a measure structurally valid? While many natural events are found to be normally distributed, the distribution of social and economic events is non-normal, often exponential in form. In a particular firm the great majority of departments, employing (say) 95 per cent of the work force, might not register a single serious employee grievance during a given period. But one department, employing only a handful of men, may have bad employee–management relations and a heavy incidence of grievances – say one per man per year compared with five per thousand men per year for the works as a whole.

Drucker, who cited this example, went on to suggest that if the department with the heavy incidence of disputes happened to be the final assembly department through which all the firm's production must pass, and if workers in this department went out on strike when their grievances were neglected by a management which had been misled by its own control (the statistical average), the impact could be very serious. In fact this was reported to be an actual case, and to have bankrupted the firm in question.

It is easy to think of further illustrations; for example, 90 per cent of a company's turnover frequently comes from no more than 5 per cent of the number of products it produces, while 90 per cent of the total number of orders it receives account for only 5 per cent of total sales volume but for 90 per cent of distribution costs. How many managements, we may ask, receive control information which is in what we have called structurally true form? Probably only a small proportion. Traditional information systems, the accounting subsystem certainly not excepted, often conceal rather than highlight structural importance. Yet this is an essential prerequisite of an effective control system. If he does not have information in this form, the manager not only lacks knowledge; his efforts are automatically directed where they can have least effect. Many existing control systems may, in varying degree, misrepresent and misinform in this way.

(iv) *Assigning causes*
Although a control budget carries with it the concept of a desired level of attainment, it does not of itself guarantee the attainment of its objective. It merely shows, by throwing out 'variances', to what extent the control has been effective. Control as such consists in the action taken in response to the feedback of information comparing observed results with desired results. This response may call for an investigation of the 'variances', i.e. an attempt to find assignable causes for as much of the variation as possible.

While the relative size of the 'variances' may give some idea of which areas need to be investigated first, and of the intensity of search required, what is needed is a rather more precise procedure, a systematic search technique for finding and correcting (or modifying) the root causes of controllable 'variances' ('controllable' having been correctly defined) which will also determine priorities in the order of search. That is, efforts should be directed where they can produce the greatest results, thus economizing on scarce information and management resources. Most attention should be given to the (generally) small number of 'variances' which account for the bulk of the disturbance. In this way management can be given a great deal more control. This needs to be qualified, however, by saying that great care needs to be taken to trace small evidences of instability which, if constantly repeated, may become very serious. These signs that a destabilizing policy is being pursued which has explosive tendencies may easily go undetected.

Strictly, any such investigation should be preceded by tests to establish the amount of variation that could be expected due purely to chance, using probability theory, only the statistically significant 'variances' being investigated. It would be foolish to incur considerable expense in trying to track down a 'variance' which could have been due to chance. At the same time it is doubtful whether tests of significance would be justified on a cost–benefit basis, and they would involve certain statistical problems.

As much attention should, of course, be directed towards favourable as towards unfavourable 'variances' (in practice the treatment is often not symmetrical), and to ensuring that the system does not discourage offsetting 'variances' in different departments which are on balance favourable. Too often in practice a cost centre is penalized for exceeding its target even though this results in a greater increase in revenue elsewhere in the firm.* The control is not consistent with achievement of the firm's goals.

As a final comment, it is possible that control systems based on the 'principle of exceptions' may give too much attention to the dispersion and not enough to the mean, the control target. It is the latter which is of primary importance, since it determines the meaning to be attached to the former. As Arrow observes:†

> Dispersion is not bad in itself; it is only bad because it may and usually does indicate a policy which will also lead to intolerably low average characteristics. But we must not overlook the more fundamental importance of the average characteristic.

There is, however, some disagreement on this point by accountants. Evidently it depends on the view which is taken of the budgets. By separating the planning and control budgets we have viewed the latter as control targets, designed to bring about (but not necessarily identical to) planned objectives. Other writers‡ regard budgets merely as providing benchmarks for performance evaluation:

* If causality is not in doubt the latter 'variance' should be assigned to the cost centre.
† [4], in [10], p. 324.
‡ E.g. Shillinglaw [29].

The budget is a standard, not a target, and for some items [one is tempted to ask 'which?'] it is the average *deviation* that is to be minimised rather than the average cost.

Shillinglaw quotes Wagner,* who examined the question as to whether aggregate control systems of the type we have been talking about were compatible with 'Operations Research – oriented segments' of the business (i.e. with activities, the decision-making models for which employed various optimization techniques). Wagner's conclusion, based solely on inventory control models, seems to be that almost always they are not.

While we cannot enter fully into this question here, it would seem to us that aggregate accounting controls, however devised and however frequently revised, should never be thought of as providing more than a *framework* within which subsequent decisions are taken. The feedback comparison can only be inconsistent with the objective of the decision model and with the firm's overall objectives (taking for granted that these are mutually consistent) by virtue of being based on earlier data if, as should be the case and as was stated in section 1(e), the control conforms to the structure of the underlying processes represented in the decision model. What appears also to be implied by Wagner, that the inconsistency springs from the complexity of the decision model ('an Operations Research model') as well as from the degree of aggregation of the control system, is not borne out by Beer (*ibid.*), though it may well be that in order to meet Wagner's objection at least some elements of the cybernetic control model on which Beer's argument is premised would have to be built into the accounting control.†

(c) Uncertainty

Arrow believes‡ that the existence of uncertainty is 'one of the key factors – perhaps *the* key factor – in understanding controls'. Uncertainty arises, first, because one part of the organization is not perfectly acquainted with the activities of other parts, a problem involving information economics. Secondly, there is uncertainty about the external environment. Greater control over the environment, by fuller representation of relevant variables in the control system and by drawing its boundaries correctly, and the need for the system to be capable of adaptive response to changes in kind as well as degree, have been referred to. We also saw in Chapter 13 that the

* [36] in [10].

† Beer's cybernetic system, as we understand it, would provide for more or less continuous updating of the control targets. The more frequently control targets are revised, the more the difference between objectives of minimizing cost deviations and minimizing target cost becomes a semantic one. The 'ultrastable' control systems which Beer and Ashby speak about, after all, are capable of adapting after disturbances *of an unexpected kind*, i.e. of a kind not foreseen by the designer of the system. In these circumstances a 'meta-control' mechanism can be designed to provide implicit control: closure of the system is obtained by imposing a higher-order control. Such systems have been developed and applied in real-life situations – see [9], Chapters 12 and 13.

‡ [4], in [10].

presence of uncertainty was one of the principal reasons for establishing firms. As Arrow observes, it is very difficult to differentiate between control losses which result because the external environment is uncertain, and those due to poor performance by a manager or operative. *

18.4 Behavioural considerations

(a)   Motivation and incentives

The setting of a performance target, we have seen, is not sufficient to ensure or even invite compliance. In addition to the problems involved in designing the control system on the assumption that whatever system is devised will operate with maximum efficiency we have the further problem of how to achieve maximal efficiency of the control.† Some incentive must be offered to those affected to encourage their compliance. This problem does not arise in the standard theory of the firm, for it is there assumed that entrepreneurs make decisions and that these decisions are perfectly executed; the agents of the firm are will-less. This is of course a gross oversimplification, and does not help at all in dealing with real problems of budgetary control. When employees have some freedom as to how they operate it is necessary to specify standards against which their performance may be judged so that they have a guide to what is expected of them.

But let us stay with economic theory a little longer, and begin by considering market-determined performance targets. This is in line with our distinction between external and internal controls operating on the firm in Chapter 13. We shall, in fact, broaden the discussion to consider the entire economy, i.e. we shall look at the question from a social, economic efficiency point of view. Readers are cautioned not to confuse this with our main discussion.

In a perfectly competitive situation a guide to the level of performance expected is provided by the market, for if entrepreneurs and employees are not wholly efficient and yet are able to earn 'normal' profits this means that the efficient firms in the industry can earn above-normal profits. There will therefore be 'entry' into the industry, price-cutting, and inefficient producers will be forced out. Thus the market enforces a series of promotions and dismissals (for accomplishment and failure), making clear to all managements and employees what performance is expected of them. In a hypothetical world of universal perfect competition the choice of a target for budgetary control purposes would therefore be a trivial problem. It would merely be necessary to choose a cost target at the technological

---

* This point is also made in the concluding remarks in [1].
† In this section we have drawn on part of an unpublished paper by our former student, K. P. Gee; it is for the most part a précis of Stedry's approach [31].

minimum for an operation and let employees work to it – if the fact that employees are not machines with given technological capacities could be ignored.

But as already noted the best target for control purposes is an optimal one only if each employee has an automatic incentive to work with maximum effort, which is true only of universal perfect competition. In any other market situation (i.e. if there are market imperfections *anywhere* in the economy), if 'optimal' (second best) goals were set with penalties for non-attainment, since the goal is effectively un-attainable no matter how great the reward for achieving it is made, the expected value of that reward would be zero. And since the net expected value of rewards and penalties would therefore be negative, such a system would cause discontent, and workers would not agree to it, being freed now to some extent from market sanctions. Even if no penalties were attached to non-attainment of the goals the latter would still not lead to effort maximization, because employees would regard them as unreasonable. They would therefore feel under no compulsion to try to attain these goals, and their performance would be likely to drift further and further away from them.

Here we break off the discussion of market-determined goals in terms of eco-nomic efficiency in resource allocation *vs.* second best. For the remainder of the discussion we shall be concerned with the more important, and certainly more realistic, question of the relation between the firm's goals and those of individual workers and managers.

In the real world individuals not only have differing potentials but (at least in industrialized nations) few people have to work at full capacity merely to hold down their jobs. Man works for more than the satisfaction of his physiological needs (food, clothing, shelter). One rationalization of man's perennial wanting for more than he already has is provided by Maslow's hierarchy of needs,[*] which suggests that as soon as one want is satisfied another is ready to take its place: after physio-logical needs come the need for safety, for affiliation, for esteem and for 'self-actualization'. The firm provides a vehicle through which the employee can satisfy his wants by obtaining pecuniary and other rewards: these rewards will be asso-ciated with employee performance which is consistent with the goals of the firm.

The question at issue is how performance targets can be determined to give employees the maximum incentive to work towards the firm's goals. The answer, says Stedry, will depend on the *aspiration levels* of individual employees. 'Aspira-tion level' is defined by psychologists as the level of future performance in a familiar task which an individual, knowing the level of his past performance in that task, explicitly *undertakes* to reach. Thus employees' aspiration levels are reflected in the cost and output targets they set themselves when the question is put to them in this form, and in the targets to which they agree after negotiation with higher manage-ment. Since management will in general try to commit employees to higher per-

[*] Summarized in [20], p. 51.

formance levels than they originally set themselves, the aspiration level for any employee depends upon, but is not necessarily equal to, the budgeted level which management desires.

In general it may be safely concluded that the aspired level of cost will be lowered in response to a lowering of the budgeted level of cost which management attempts to impose. If, as is customary, there are rewards for attaining budgeted targets and penalties for failure (interpreting rewards and penalties in a broad sense), each employee will implicitly determine a point at which the rewards are satisfactory to him. He will then examine the relationship between this 'satisfactory' point and the budgeted cost level desired by management, find out how much it changes for a given change in the latter, and change his aspiration level accordingly in response to any change in the budget.

Stedry carried out an experiment to examine the relationship between aspiration levels, individual performance and an externally-imposed budget. He assumed that

$$\text{Actual achievement} = f(\text{Budget level, Aspiration level})$$

The experimental design was as follows:

Budget \ Aspiration level	α Not asked for	β Stated before seeing budget	γ Stated after seeing budget	Average
A: Implicit				
B: Explicit – Low				
C: Explicit – Medium				
D: Explicit – High				
Average				

Stedry exposed the volunteers in his test to various levels of budget targets, and found that where attainment of a goal was rewarded and non-attainment penalized,[*] performance was significantly affected by the type of budget used and by the way in which aspiration levels were determined. He discovered that an *implicit budget* (where the subject is not told what goal he should attain) gave the best performance, closely followed by a 'medium' and a 'high' budget, the latter terms referring to moderately difficult and very difficult targets, respectively. A 'low' budget was found to yield significantly poorer results. Stedry equated this low budget

---

[*] Rewards/penalties were not a variable in the experiment.

with the widely adopted conventional criterion that standards should be 'attainable but not too loose', which implies a standard attainable by the average employee. Whether Stedry's medium budget more appropriately reflected this criterion is perhaps debatable. Assuming, however, that it did not Stedry's experiment certainly gave no reason to assume that an 'attainable but not too loose' budget is always, or even generally, the best.

The success of the implicit budget might suggest that explicit goals are redundant; there are areas of activity in most firms where performance is assessed on 'qualitative' or unspecified criteria. But this interpretation would neglect the important finding of a strong *interaction* between budget target and personal aspiration levels.* The subjects of the experiment who received relatively difficult budget targets *before* they announced their aspiration levels (i.e. stated what they undertook to achieve) performed better than any other group (including the implicit budget group), while those who received relatively difficult targets *after* announcing their aspiration levels produced the lowest performance of all. The reason for this might be that the high-performance group formed their aspirations with the high budget level in mind, while the low-performance group rejected the high budget after forming aspiration levels based on their previous performance. If this is true it has implications for many so-called participatory budgeting schemes, in which the employee plans his own budget, then takes it to his supervisor, who gives him a higher target without first successfully gaining the employee's genuine acceptance at a psychological level.

The psychological rejection of a target which is very tight in relation to the individual's aspiration level was a key finding of Stedry's experiment. The main results are summarized in the orderings:

$$A > C > D > B;$$

$$\gamma > \beta > \alpha.$$

The implications for the relationships between aspirations, budgets and actual expense levels are demonstrated in Figure 18.3†:

Interrelated with the problem of setting the target performance levels is the problem of what the rewards for achieving, and penalties for failure to achieve, the target level should be. It seems reasonable to hypothesize that management can increase the propensity of employees to aim at the budget target by increasing the positive reward for its attainment and the negative reward for its non-attainment – in the form of immediate bonuses or longer-range incentives such as promotion for continued good performance, or the absence of these. (Whatever form the incentive takes, pecuniary or otherwise, we need to distinguish between offering an incentive and the incentive effect. In the case of pecuniary incentives the supply of effort may

---

*Significant at 1 per cent level in Stedry's study.
†Reproduced, with slight modification, from Hofstede [20], with permission.

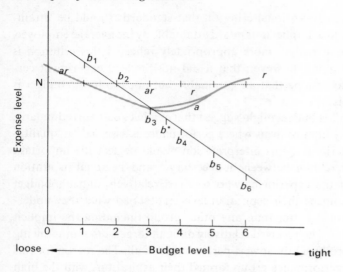

Figure 18.3 $b_1 b_6$ is alternative explicit budget levels set by management, ranging from very loose (b_1) to very tight (b_6); r is actual expense incurred; a is subject's aspiration level; N is expense level without a budget (= Stedry's implicit budget); b^* is optimal budget level, given the alternatives and constraints considered, the forecasts and estimates.

be highly inelastic (greater desire for increased leisure than for higher income which requires an increase in intensity of work). The desire for money income is known to vary greatly from one person to another.)

Taking the limiting case, if the above hypothesis were always true, the effort-maximizing reward–penalty system would appear to require dismissal for non-compliance with the budget. But in order to avoid too many dismissals budget levels would have to be set well above expected cost, to allow for random fluctuations in performance. Further, there would be little incentive for an employee to drive the cost under his control far below the budgeted level (although this level would now be well above expected cost), because with such a reward–penalty system a fear of the budget target being made progressively harder to attain if he performed too well would be likely to dominate over the desire to impress management with superior performance.

Stedry concludes that there is no single reward–penalty system which will induce maximum effort from all employees in all circumstances. Ideally, he believes, both reward–penalty systems and budget targets should vary from employee to employee, depending on their motivation. The more easily an employee is discouraged, the lower his personal target should be; the more ambitious he is, the more he will respond to a system with large rewards for success and large penalties for failure. Clearly the amount of psychological information needed about each employee in order to operate such a system to obtain maximum individual efficiency would be forbiddingly large.

Some doubt has been cast on Stedry's conclusions because of the way he measured the psychological variable 'aspiration level'. It has been found from other studies that the difference between actual and aspired results is greater when test subjects are asked what they *hope* to achieve (as Stedry asked) than when they are asked what they *expect* to achieve. Becker and Green* contend that Stedry measured his major independent variable inaccurately but add: 'his work is valuable heuristically because it highlights a possible relation between budgets, budgeting, and motivational performance.'

Later work† has supported the interrelationship between standards and aspiration levels, and would seem to indicate the importance of considering the aspiration levels of different individuals in formulating budget goals. Much more controversial is the question of the method of goal determination, for which the two extreme points of the potential scale can be termed 'imposed' (by higher management) and 'autonomous' (determined solely by the subordinate) – with 'participation' somewhere between the two. Stedry's budgets were imposed but in this respect his results cannot be translated with any confidence to the firm situation because his subjects were students in a 'laboratory experiment' who were not informed of their performance as the experiment progressed. An individual within a firm will have some knowledge of past performance which will influence his aspiration level.‡ Moreover, Stedry's study adopts the traditional budgeting assumption that each individual reacts to the budget *as an individual*, whereas there is evidence that group reactions are important,§ particularly at the shop-floor level. (Stedry's concern was with budgets of lower management, but these must have repercussions at operative level.)

Stedry adopted the view that the very low performance by his experimental group which received difficult budgets *after* formulating aspiration levels indicated a justification for imposed budgets. A participatory situation in which upper management decides on a high performance budget after the employee submits a low performance budget based on his aspiration level would elicit the lowest performance from the employee. There are three limitations to this view. As already indicated, the subordinate's aspiration level is likely to be influenced by his knowledge of operations (even if he were not supplied with formal information on results); there would seem to be no grounds for believing that his acceptance would necessarily be greater with an imposed budget unrelated to his prior aspiration level than with a subsequent upward amendment to his own proposal. A genuine

* Becker and Green [7]; see also Stedry's reply [35], their rejoinder [8], and Charnes and Stedry [12] and [13]. The first three are reprinted in [11].
† See [20], Chapter 8.
‡ See Benston in [11], pp. 161–72 for discussion and evidence on this point.
§ See references given in section 2 Chapter 15.

participatory system would place most emphasis on influencing the subordinate's aspirations *before* the submission of a budget (which would appear to be a justifiable approach in the light of Stedry's findings); participation is not an annual budgeting formality. Finally, if the subordinate did submit an inadequate budget the superior's reactions (except in a pseudo-participatory system) would not be an unexplained amendment: an effort to convince and gain genuine acceptance is implicit in a participatory process.

Knowledge in this area is still incomplete, but there is little reason to suppose that either extreme of imposed or autonomously developed goals would provide a single best target for performance in all business situations. There is, however, some evidence that a mixture between the influences of superior authority, participation (i.e. quasi-autonomous elements) and external reference points can yield better performance than the extremes of the scale. This mixture was referred to earlier in Chapter 15 and provided the basis for Hofstede's plausible 'improved model' of the effect of participation in standard setting, which was reproduced in Figure 15.2.

Stedry's concern that budgets should represent goals in the control context need not be identified with the use of imposed budgets and the 'manipulative' viewpoint (although it commonly is). The use of goals intended to motivate for improved performance is not incompatible with the open use of (different) plans. The distinction might well be welcomed by lower management, as is indicated by Hofstede's quote from a subordinate manager:

> Sometimes reality is lost in the standards, they're just too loose.... Top plant management ... ought to set two standards, one for financial purposes and one as an objective.*

(b) The reward–penalty system

In the foregoing we have referred a number of times to the firm's reward–penalty system, meaning by this the whole range of benefits offered to, or withheld from, employees, including wage and salary payments, cash bonuses, share options, paid holidays, promotion, and so on. This system has an important role to play in making a control effective, i.e. in inducing behaviour which is consistent with achievement of the firm's goals as embodied in the planning budget, so long as the latter contains the best information available at the point when action is taken to implement the plan. Equally, the reward–penalty system should encourage managers to override the plan where this has ceased to be the case, providing it is done in a way consistent with the firm's objective. That is, the accounting control system and the reward–penalty system should be mutually consistent in economic terms, and both encourage goal-striving behaviour. The relationship was displayed in Figure 18.1. In Shubik's words [30]:

*[20], p. 166.

A goal of good management should be to design a reward system for those who take risks in making decisions in such a manner that the rewards to the individual correlate positively with the worth of the decision to the organisation (taking into account the attitude of top management to variances as well as to expected gain).

The reward-penalty system, together with the level at which performance targets are set and (subjects' aspiration levels), provide the motivation to reach and possibly exceed these targets.

In practice, however, the two are often in conflict. Stedry illustrates with a hypothetical example.* A department is operating at full capacity but the departmental manager, on his own initiative, finds some more labour, for which he has to pay premium rates, and takes on an additional order which increases the profit of his department. Under normal standard costing practice the manager might be held responsible for an unfavourable cost 'variance'. He might get no credit for increasing his department's profit (which we assume increases the firm's profit). The 'principle of exception' reporting may have the effect of preventing such profitable work being taken on, i.e. it may act against the firm's objective. In the same way the system should be, but seldom is, designed to prevent the postponement of necessary expenditure in one period (e.g. expenditure on maintenance or advertising) in order to improve that period's measure of performance if such a postponement will be at the expense of future performance. It is surely possible to ensure more consistency between these systems without attempting to meet the requirement to which Stedry's investigations led him, referred to in the previous section.

The problem of providing incentives to individual managers to achieve the goals of the enterprise, as Arrow points out (*ibid.*), bears a formal similarity to the problem of how to motivate workers in a collectivist economy (and to marginal cost pricing by public enterprises). Briefly stated, the argument is as follows. The economic theory of distribution states that in a market economy a firm should employ a factor in such quantity that its marginal value product equals its marginal cost. That is, in the case of labour (of which management is a specialized kind), a person should be paid his marginal profitability: the whole of any cost saving or increase in profits attributable to his efforts alone should be paid over to him. (This leads to an optimal allocation of management labour and is a condition of profit maximization by the firm, irrespective of the structure of factor and product markets.) Suppose the specialized kind of labour called management is in fixed supply in the short run. Its marginal cost then becomes infinitely high, and under the above rule the manager's remuneration would become astronomical. If it can be assumed that the relation between increased effort and increased reward ceases at a level which is low relative to the reward in question, and beyond this point the factor makes the same total effort regardless of reward, the factor need only be paid a proportion (possibly quite small) of its full marginal profits, provided that it receives the same

*[31], p. 138.

proportion in every use.* This assumption would seem to be justified in many cases by the experience of firms which operate 'suggestion' schemes.

In a completely collectivist society the analogy is that all factors of production with the possible exception of labour are collectively owned – and regulation of labour and of what shall be produced by the State has much the same effect as State ownership of labour. There are no factor markets. The allocation of factors among different uses is effected by administrative rules; accounting prices, no longer represented by payments of money, are fixed and adjusted to market forces. The rules used in fixing these prices would ensure that (1) the marginal value product of a factor was the same in all uses, subject to the total supply of the factor being employed; (2) that the quantity of a factor used by any enterprise was such that the marginal value product of the factor was proportional to its price, with a further rule (scale rule) for determining when the output of the State-owned enterprise should be expanded and contracted. In addition to the problem of fixing these accounting prices for factors of production (there is a market for consumers' goods, though the supplies coming on to it are arbitrarily fixed by the State), there is a problem of providing incentives: labour is no longer motivated by self-interest; actual payments to factors are replaced by book entries. As Phelps Brown aptly put it,† 'It is hard to get soldiers to bother about taking cover when they are under fire from blank cartridges'. The calculus of accounting prices is useless unless people obey the rules and are motivated as strongly by an abstract ideal (economic socialism) as by competition and self-interest.

The parallel with marginal cost pricing as a method of resource allocation some-times advocated for use by enterprises administered 'in the public interest' of course refers to the problem of how to ensure at the same time that total receipts cover total costs. The two rules (price $= MC$ and $TR > TC$) conflict whenever there is any fixity in factor intakes, resulting from fixed supply, indivisibility, or from the factor being durable and specific.

Arrow concludes that the answer to the problem of providing incentives for managers in a privately-owned firm is some form of profit-sharing, that even a very small proportion of his marginal profitability may be quite large to the manager, and sufficient to provide adequate incentive. At the same time there may be trade-offs between pecuniary incentives and other aspects of the labour bargain.

(c) Other behavioural aspects

From a growing literature we can only cull a few further contributions which seem to us significant. Argyris [2], in his field researches, found that budgets were thought of as pressure devices used by management on supervisors. Because of the un-

* Cf. the earlier quotation from Shubik.

† [26], p. 222; parts of Chapters 7 and 8 are relevant to the present discussion.

favourable reactions they produced they tended to be self-defeating in the long run. Argyris made two recommendations: first, unlike Stedry, he believed that acceptance of budgets by genuine participation was crucial. Secondly, accounting staffs needed to be trained in human relations.

Hofstede [20] conducted a study of budgeting, planning and management information systems in five Dutch companies. Due to the wide coverage of the inquiry no attempt will be made to summarize his findings here. The reader who consults his book will receive the bonus of a useful survey of other work in this field. One novel idea of Hofstede's, referred to in the title of his book, is to regard a system of budgetary control as a competitive game, capable of generating positive motivation (team spirit) in the players (workers and subordinate managers) to beat the 'opponent' (the budget), in contrast to the negative motivation usually encountered (workers, and even subordinate managers, regarding the system as the opponent).

McGregor [25] and Likert [23] are concerned with wider human aspects of organizations but their work has considerable relevance for accounting controls. McGregor distinguishes two fundamental management attitudes. Briefly, 'theory X' assumes that people do not like work and must be coerced into working for corporate objectives; 'theory Y', like the Calvinist ethic, assumes that work is as natural as rest or play, and that people will work most effectively under self-direction when they commit themselves to personal objectives consistent with those of the firm. The management attitudes will be reflected in (among other things) the way in which the accounting control system is used.

Among other questions studied by McGregor have been the inappropriateness of formal leadership and hierarchical authority for exercising control in business organizations; identification of the basic needs of the person subjected to a control; peer group formation by managers, the development of group norms and group reaction to the budget (as in the case of workers); and subjective appraisal of performance.

Likert adopts a four system classification of management, of which the fourth 'participative group' approximates to 'theory Y'. His research (and that of others in this area) indicates that a shift to a participative system may take as long as two or three years to effect. Initially performance may decline, but there is substantial evidence of long-run gains in productivity and profits (for example, in one plant productivity declined for eight months from an index of some 120 per cent to 110 per cent, but rose over the succeeding nineteen months to almost 150 per cent). Conventional accounting control systems which are concerned with the short-run are inadequate indicators of the long-run impact of organizational changes: in particular imposed cost reduction schemes can produce short-run accounting improvements at the expense of long-run debilitation of the firm's organization and profits. Likert is concerned that the firm's very important assets of human organization and customer goodwill should not be entirely neglected in accounting reports, but that 'human asset accounting' should be developed for reporting.*

Simon's contributions are too numerous to catalogue.† In addition to initiating the important ideas mentioned in Chapter 6, studies undertaken by him and his collaborators have ranged over such topics as the role of the accounting staff in systems of budgetary control; unanticipated consequences of budget systems; ways of avoiding negative motivation by staff (as distinct from line workers); the relation between the amount of felt participation and the degree of control achieved; the relation between organizational slack and intergroup conflict; staff-line communication problems; and the consequences for control of choice between organizational subdivision into profit centres and expense centres.

18.5 Nonprofit controls

The performance of a business enterprise must ultimately be measured in economic terms, primarily in the form of some measure of profitability. However, as we have seen, it is likely that most accounting control systems have design defects and operate very imperfectly. The effectiveness of economic control with respect to the goals of the enterprise is probably not of a very high order. In these circumstances, at least until such time as improved systems can be developed and made operational, it would seem unwise to put all one's trust in the mechanical measures generated under 'management by exception' reporting. Supplementary measures, both quantitative and qualitative, may be desirable. (An example of the latter would be the quality of the human resources employed by the firm, the effectiveness of its personnel selection and promotion procedures and reward–penalty system.)

The typical modern business operates a host of controls. Controls proliferate with growth in size of the firm (whether measured by the volume of transactions or the size of its administrative staff) and in its complexity (the number of distinct processes it operates, the number of separate operating units, its degree of vertical integration or diversification), and with the extent to which control is decentralized. Behind the aggregate financial controls we have been talking about there will be a variety of partial controls, e.g. transfer prices, various forms of statistical control, control of time spent on various tasks (critical path analysis), control of data-information flows, and so on.

What is true of aggregate controls is also true of most of these partial controls, i.e. they are less than fully effective. Consider economic transfer pricing. While such schemes are likely to score well, relative to alternative devices, on grounds of informational efficiency (they help to solve the first problem of uncertainty referred to in section 3(c) above), economic transfer prices can never provide an entirely

* See also [22].

† A number of references in addition to [31] are cited in the bibliography to [20].

satisfactory solution to the problem of internal resource allocation between departments or divisions, and its control. Arrow has pointed out* that they run into the same sort of difficulties as marginal cost pricing by public enterprises in external markets; and because they cannot be estimated with certainty, frequent changes will be needed if resource allocation is not to be distorted. This means, moreover, that probability information is needed to implement the scheme, which qualifies the above remark about the informational efficiency of this method. With the possibility of a large number of interdependencies between the departments concerned, leading to externalities, this might very well mean that the scheme becomes impractical because of the sheer number of prices involved, a circumstance which may not be much alleviated by using thresholds to eliminate small-scale externalities.

Our principal preoccupation in this chapter has been with quantitative controls of the 'management by exception' type. Not all controls rest on this principle; and readers will recall our reference to 'management by objective' in Chapter 16 as an example of a control of another kind.

*[4], in [10], p. 319. See also [19].

Bibliographical references

[1] Amey, L. R., Hindsight *vs.* Expectations in Performance Measurement, in *Readings in Management Decision*, ed. L. R. Amey, Longman, 1973.

[2] Argyris, C., *The Impact of Budgets on People*, Controllership Foundation, New York, 1952.

[3] Argyris, C., Human problems with budgets, *Harvard Business Review*, January–February 1953, pp. 97–110; reprinted in [32].

[4] Arrow, K. J., Research in Management Controls: A Critical Synthesis, Chapter 17 in [10].

[5] Ashby, W. R., *Design for a Brain*, 2nd edn., John Wiley, 1960.

[6] Ashby, W. R., *An Introduction to Cybernetics*, John Wiley, 1956.

[7] Becker, S. W. and D. Green Jr., Budgeting and employee behavior, *Journal of Business*, October 1962, pp. 392–402; reprinted in [11] and in [32].

[8] Becker, S. W. and D. Green Jr., Budgeting and employee behavior: a rejoinder to a 'reply', *Journal of Business*, April 1964, pp. 203–05; reprinted in [11] and in [28].

[9] Beer, S., *Decision and Control*, John Wiley, 1966.

[10] Bonini, C. P., R. K. Jaedicke and H. M. Wagner, eds., *Management Controls: New Directions in Basic Research*, McGraw-Hill, 1964.

[11] Bruns, W. J. and D. T. DeCoster, eds., *Accounting and its Behavioral Implications*, McGraw-Hill, 1969.

[12] Charnes, A. and A. C. Stedry, Investigations in the theory of multiple budgeted goals, Chapter 10 in [10].

[13] Charnes, A. and A. C. Stedry, Exploratory models in the theory of budget control, in [15].

[14] Churchman, C. W., *Prediction and Optimal Decision*, Prentice-Hall, 1961.

[15] Cooper, W. W., H. J. Leavitt and M. W. Shelly, eds., *New Perspectives in Organization Research*, Wiley, 1964.

[16] Cyert, R. M. and J. G. March, *A Behavioral Theory of the Firm*, Prentice-Hall, 1963.

[17] Demski, J. S., An accounting system structured on a linear programming model, *Accounting Review*, October 1967, pp. 701–12.

[18] Drucker, P. F., Controls, control and management, in [10].

577

[19] Gordon, M. J., A method of pricing for a socialist economy, *Accounting Review*, July 1970, pp. 427–43.

[20] Hofstede, G. H., *The Game of Budget Control*, Tavistock, 1968.

[21] Holt, C. C., F. Modigliani, J. F. Muth and H. A. Simon, *Planning Production, Inventories and Work Force*, Prentice-Hall, 1960.

[22] Likert, R., *New Patterns of Management*, McGraw-Hill, 1961.

[23] Likert, R., *The Human Organization: Its Management and Value*, McGraw-Hill, 1967.

[24] Malmgren, H. B., Information, expectations and the theory of the firm, *Quarterly Journal of Economics*, August 1961, pp. 399–421, reprinted in *Readings in Management Decision*, ed. L. R. Amey, Longman, 1973.

[25] McGregor, D., *The Human Side of Enterprise*, McGraw-Hill, 1960.

[26] Phelps Brown, E. H., *A Course in Applied Economics*, Pitman, 1951.

[27] Roberts, E. B., Industrial dynamics and the design of management control systems, Chapter 6 in [10].

[28] Rosen, L. S., ed., *Topics in Managerial Accounting*, McGraw-Hill, 1970.

[29] Shillinglaw, G., Divisional performance review: An extension of budgetary control, Chapter 8 in [10].

[30] Shubik, M., Incentives, decentralized control, the assignment of joint costs and internal pricing, *Management Science*, April 1962, pp. 325–43; a slightly revised version appears in [10].

[31] Simon, H. A., H. Guetzkow, G. Kozmetsky and G. Tyndall, *Centralization vs. Decentralization in organizing the Controller's Department*, Controllership Foundation, 1954.

[32] Solomons, D., *Studies in Cost Analysis*, Sweet and Maxwell, 1968.

[33] Solomons, D., Performance measurement – a broader view, paper read to annual conference of American Accounting Association, Lexington, Kentucky, 1971 (unpublished).

[34] Stedry, A. C., *Budget Control and Cost Behavior*, Prentice-Hall, 1960.

[35] Stedry, A. C., Budgeting and employee behavior: a reply, *Journal of Business*, April 1964, pp. 195–202; reprinted in [11] and in [28].

[36] Wagner, H. M., Budgetary control in inventory systems, in [10].

[37] Williamson, O. E., *Corporate Control and Business Behavior*, Prentice-Hall, 1970.

[38] Winkler, R. L., Scoring rules and the evaluation of probability assessors, *Journal of American Statistical Association*, September 1969, pp. 1073–78.

Problems

18.1 In the literature, business budgets are variously regarded as:

(1) a standard, providing a benchmark for evaluating performance;
(2) a target, acting as a motivational device;
(3) a pressure device used by management.

Discuss these views and their implications for the design of the budgeting and any related systems.

18.2 'The seemingly plausible notion of "responsibility accounting", as it has been interpreted, has held control accounting back for more than half a century. It is now obvious that "responsibility" must be fundamentally redefined.'
Examine this view.

18.3 Suppose for a moment that business control budgets are optimal budgets. Carefully examine the argument that performance should be measured, not in relation to such an *ex ante* optimum, but rather in relation to an *ex post* optimum (i.e. an optimum with hindsight), because 'no measure of per-mance which mixes up capacity to perform and capacity to predict can be free from serious criticism'.

18.4 '... the management scientist is ... skeptical about managerial accounting, in any of its forms. The managerial accountant wants to generate "scores" of departmental performance, or "cost centers" which can be examined for their utilization of resources. But insufficient thinking goes into the identification of these scores and centers. ...'

C. W. Churchman.

Do you accept this criticism?

18.5 What do you understand by the term 'self-adaptive' as applied to accounting control systems, and what is its importance? How self-adaptive do you think the majority of such systems are in practice at the present time?

18.6 Describe and examine some of the problems that are brought to light when a systems approach to the problem of control is adopted.

18.7 What do you think of the argument, quoted in section 4(b), that the way to make accounting controls effective is to introduce some form of profit-sharing for managers and supervisors?

Part 4
Accounting and financial management

19

Working capital management

. . . 'liquidity' and 'carrying costs' are both a matter of degree . . .
J. M. KEYNES [10]

19.1 The working capital ambit

Working capital was defined in Chapter 2 as consisting of current assets less financing provided by current liabilities. Thus working capital management is concerned with the volatile short term elements of the firm's resources and financing: inventories, debtors, short term holdings of securities, cash, short term borrowing and trade creditors.

The function of working capital is to *work*: the *holding* of current assets is costly in terms of out-of-pocket costs and/or opportunity costs. The costs associated with working capital holdings provide an inducement to swift turnover of assets, low current asset balances and high current liabilities. In opposition to these cost considerations is the fact that the lower are current asset balances (and the higher are current liabilities) the greater the risks for the firm – of being out of stock, of being unable to pay trade creditors, etc. The essence of working capital management is a trade-off between costs and risks. However, cost minimization under assumptions of certainty can provide preliminary solutions in some problem areas.

A major function of working capital management is to control the many actions affecting working capital which are taken at operating levels of the firm, where cost/risk attitudes can conflict with the firm's interests. The risk of occasionally being unable to meet demand may appear overwhelmingly important to a storekeeper who is not fully aware of the cost consequences of high inventory. Conversely a salesman could be concerned with completing a sale almost to the exclusion of considering the risk that the customer may default. Guidelines must be established to yield the appropriate cost/risk balance from the firm's viewpoint.

The firm's decisions must be made in the context of constraints which can apply to working capital as a whole or to certain component items. Trade credit is rarely unlimited, short term borrowing facilities have ceilings, warehouse capacity is commonly fixed in the short-run. In addition the firm may employ certain policy guides to the overall working capital structure, constituting self-imposed constraints. Commonly these relate to accounting ratios :* a firm might adopt a quick asset ratio of x and/or a current ratio of y as a rule of thumb for minimum acceptable levels.

Most working capital decisions are essentially short-run, made in the context of a

---

* Discussed in Chapter 4.

582

given long term capital structure and given operating capacity. However, it must be remembered that working capital has implications for long-run decisions. When an investment decision is being made the associated working capital balances (inventory and debtors minus creditors) required to sustain certain assumed levels of operation clearly represent investment outlays relevant to the decision. They will be recouped as working capital is liquidated with reductions in operating levels or at the end of the investment's life.

19.2 Inventory control

Stockholding decisions involve consideration of interrelationships between demand and the replenishment of goods, with associated costs and financial constraints. Problem solving in this area is termed inventory control (or stock control), which includes both inventory planning and the implementation of plans. There is a substantial literature devoted to inventory control, encompassing models for a wide variety of problems encountered by firms. The present discussion will merely indicate certain principal aspects relating to inventory, particularly concerning the determination of relevant costs, and provide a glimpse of inventory models.*

Inventory consists of both purchased goods (either finished goods or raw materials) and goods manufactured internally by the firm. Attention will be largely directed to the former group; the inventory problem has similar characteristics in both cases, but production scheduling adds a further complex dimension for internally manufactured goods.

A noteworthy characteristic of inventory is that a small proportion of items or products commonly account for a high proportion of demand; for example 80 per cent of a firm's sales activity may relate to 10 per cent of the product range. Consequently substantial cost savings can be obtained from analysis which improves inventory holding for a small group of items.

The motives for stockholding by firms are basically the same as those originally advanced by Keynes for the holding of cash:† transactions, precautionary and speculative motives.

The holding of goods for *transactions* purposes alone can be distinguished where demand for the goods is assumed to be known with certainty and they can be replenished either immediately or with a certain waiting period. It is worthwhile to hold some inventory in these circumstances, because although there are costs of

---

*The interested reader is referred to the following range of texts: Beranek [5] for simple models and relationships to other aspects of working capital; Buchan and Koenigsberg [7] for a succinct introductory chapter on fundamentals and studies of applications of a range of models; Morrell (ed.) [11] for a compact treatment of the more typical problems arising in manufacturing industry; Starr and Miller [14] for a good 'intermediate' text; Hadley and Whitin [9] for a wide spectrum of models.

†[10], Chapter 15; similarities and differences for holdings of cash and goods are examined by Keynes, pp. 226–27.

carrying goods there are also costs of re-ordering and it is evident that some balancing of costs must take place: any household carries stocks of easily replenishable goods on a similar principle, rather than buying 'hand-to-mouth'.

The *precautionary* motive arises because demand for goods and/or the waiting period for replenishment are not known with certainty; it is necessary to hold safety stocks, for which the balance between carrying costs and the costs of being out of stock is relevant.

Finally the *speculative* motive is related to expected price changes: a firm may increase inventory in expectation of a price rise or decrease it below the 'usual' operating level in expectation of a price fall. The anticipated gains from a price rise must be balanced against carrying costs, or the anticipated savings from buying after a price fall must be balanced against the net cost of being out of stock in the interim period. The crucial element in speculative holding is the (commonly intuitive) expectation of a price change: with given expectations appropriate calculations can be made. Speculative holding of goods will not be examined further.

In section 2(b) the basic economic order quantity model will provide a solution for pure transactions, followed by an extension in the context of financial constraints. The precautionary motive is applicable to safety stocks in section 2(d).

(a) Relevant costs for inventory control

The relevant costs for an inventory decision, as for any decision, are those which are variable with the actions under consideration. These costs need not, and in very many cases will not, coincide with the costs designated as variable in the routine accounting records. Three possible approaches can be used for the less amenable costs: adjustment of available accounting data for the purpose in hand, separate investigation/estimation of cost elements, or the use of an inventory model to 'backtrack' from an assumed decision to discover if the implied costs seem plausible.

The major categories of costs associated with inventory are procurement costs, carrying costs and stockout costs.

(i) *Procurement costs*

These are incurred in acquiring a batch of goods. Two distinct elements can be distinguished. The first is the cost of the goods themselves, either the price paid or the cost of manufacture. It is convenient to treat these acquisition costs as constant per unit, although quantity discounts would make this assumption invalid and necessitate separate investigation.* Acquisition cost per unit would not in itself be relevant to the inventory decision, because it would be incurred even if no inventory

*For treatments of quantity discounts see [7], [9], [11], [14].

were held, *but* it will be seen that acquisition cost is relevant as a measure of funds tied up in inventory for the calculation of carrying costs.

The second category concerns costs caused by the act of acquiring a batch of units. Goods purchased by the firm incur an *order cost*, the costs of clerical time spent in ordering, processing the invoice and payment, arranging for delivery, etc. Goods manufactured by the firm may incur a similar '*set-up cost*': the cost of setting up equipment for a production run, administrative arrangements for production scheduling, etc. The major elements of both order and set-up costs are independent of the *quantity* of units in a batch and can be deemed fixed in relation to quantity; where procurement elements are variable with quantity (e.g. costs of unloading) it is usually convenient to include them in the cost of goods.

A major difficulty in estimating order cost, and to a lesser extent set-up cost, is that they are likely to include significant cost elements common to different functions, particularly in the administrative area. An estimate of the relevant opportunity cost is required for the basic EOQ model which will be considered shortly; employee time is commonly a substantial element, and a costing at the appropriate wage rate can be adopted as an indicator.

(ii) *Carrying cost*

Carrying cost of inventory includes several component elements:

1. *Interest* on the 'value' of goods carried in inventory. This is an opportunity cost: if stockholding were lower the funds released could be employed elsewhere or borrowing could be reduced. The appropriate interest charge would depend on the relevant opportunities for the released funds.

The 'value' of funds employed in inventory will be the acquisition costs which would be avoided if inventory were reduced, or the acquisition costs which would be incurred if inventory were increased. Inventory decisions relate to goods which the firm intends to replace; consequently the appropriate measure of value should be replacement cost for the decision period. This value will be termed cost of inventory.

2. *Storage costs* include such out-of-pocket costs as the running expenses of warehousing (light, heat, wages, rent), *provided* these expenses are variable with the inventory decision under consideration. When warehousing is owned by the firm the depreciation cost as such is irrelevant; the usual considerations of opportunity cost and capacity constraints apply. If there is spare capacity (owned or committed for renting in the period) the opportunity cost is zero: if there are alternative uses the value of the best alternative is the opportunity cost of storage. In capacity constrained situations the inventory decision should be made in the context of the constraints,* although approximate opportunity costs may be employed in the

* E.g. see [9], pp. 54–61, pp. 304–07.

simpler models. Clearly outlay costs are relevant for warehouse acquisition decisions which incorporate inventory considerations.

3. *Deterioration costs* include such elements as breakages, evaporation and pilferage; *insurance* against losses is also relevant. These costs have an approximately linear relationship to the time held in stock.

Obsolescence is a further cost associated with carrying inventory. A charge for obsolescence may be included on a similar basis to deterioration costs, but this implies that obsolescence is continuous over time, whereas its uncertain incidence really makes it inappropriate for incorporation in this simple (deterministic) manner.*

The different elements of carrying cost do not have identical behaviour in relation to inventory, but for inventory models it is necessary to make simplifying assumptions. It is therefore common practice to assume that carrying cost per period for a unit of inventory is a constant proportion of its value. This assumption is defensible in relation to the major elements of interest and deterioration, but not for all carrying costs (e.g. labour costs involved in storage).

(iii) *Stockout cost*

Represents the opportunity loss which occurs when the firm is unable to meet a demand for a good; it may include loss of profit margins on sales or the additional costs of filling backorders, and also the cost of lost goodwill affecting future sales. By nature the stockout cost is particularly difficult to estimate.

Only the above three groups of costs will be recognized in the following subsections, but the list is not exhaustive. We have ignored costs of the inventory information system, and also cost interrelationships in dynamic systems† which need to be considered jointly with regard to potential cost savings (e.g amalgamation of orders to a single supplier).

(b) Deterministic inventory models

(i) *The basic EOQ model*

The simple economic order quantity (EOQ) model has provided the basis for many applications and extensions since its development around the 1920s. The model to be considered here is concerned with purchased goods; it is intrinsically identical to the economic lot size model applicable to batches of goods manufactured within the firm, the only difference being that EOQ incorporates an order cost while ELS incorporates a set-up cost.‡

---

* For consideration of obsolescence see [9], pp. 309–10, 349–50.
† Starr and Miller [14] term these 'systemic costs'.
‡ The ELS model was the forerunner of the EOQ model, and is attributed to F. W. Harris, 1915.

The EOQ model adopts a fixed order quantity: this quantity is re-ordered at a regular replacement interval. The objective is the selection of the order quantity which minimizes costs of inventory policy; implicitly examination of the overall profitability of the inventory item takes place outside the model. The assumptions of the model are stated below.

1. Demand is certain, constant and continuous over time (e.g. sales are not made at discrete intervals).
2. *Lead time* (the time between placing an order and receiving it) is certain and constant.
3. All prices and costs are certain and constant.
4. Demand cannot be postponed, which means that backordering is not permitted. With this assumption the system will never be out of stock, provided it is worthwhile to carry inventory at all.
5. There is an infinite time horizon, unless the optimal replacement interval coincidentally divides into the (finite) time horizon an integral number of times. This is because average costs being minimized include an order cost occurring at replacement *intervals*.

The first two assumptions exclude the precautionary motive for holding inventory; the third excludes the speculative motive.

Under these assumptions it will be evident that it is feasible to re-order when inventory is just sufficient to satisfy demand during lead time. Thus the pattern of inventory levels will take the form shown in Figure 19.1.

The time between orders (= time between deliveries with constant lead time) is termed the *order cycle*. Since inventory declines uniformly over the order cycle the average inventory must be half the order quantity.

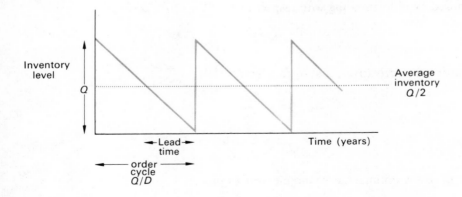

Figure 19.1 Inventory for basic EOQ model

The following notation will be adopted, assuming a demand period of one year:

Q = order quantity in units
D = annual demand in units
C = unit cost of good
I = carrying cost of inventory as percentage of unit cost C per year
A = cost of placing an order (or set-up cost per batch in ELS model).

From Figure 19.1 it can be seen that the average number of units in inventory is given by $Q/2$. Each unit involves a money cost C for funds tied up in inventory, and the percentage carrying cost of inventory value is I, so that IC = carrying cost *per unit* per year. (IC can be expressed as an absolute money amount without necessarily employing I as a percentage of unit cost – thus components of carrying cost which are not variable with the money value C, such as handling costs during storage, can be incorporated directly into IC.)

The carrying costs of average inventory is therefore given by:

$$\text{annual carrying costs} = \frac{ICQ}{2}. \tag{1}$$

The number of orders in a year is given by D/Q. Since each order incurs a cost A:

$$\text{annual order costs} = \frac{AD}{Q}. \tag{2}$$

Thus, where V = annual variable costs of inventory policy:

$$V = \frac{ICQ}{2} + \frac{AD}{Q}. \tag{3}$$

Treating Q as a continuous variable, the annual costs of inventory policy can be minimized by differentiating with respect to Q:

$$\frac{dV}{dQ} = \frac{IC}{2} - \frac{AD}{Q^2},$$

and setting the derivative equal to zero, giving:

$$Q^2 = \frac{2AD}{IC}$$

and

$$Q^* = \sqrt{\frac{2AD}{IC}} \tag{4}$$

where Q^* is the optimal (i.e. economic) order quantity.*

---

*This gives an absolute minimum because $\dfrac{dV}{dQ} = 0$ and $\dfrac{d^2V}{dQ^2} > 0$.

The expression in (4) is the core of the EOQ model; orders of Q^* units minimize the sum of order costs and carrying costs.

The minimum cost of inventory policy, V_{min}, can be derived by substituting for Q in (3):

$$V_{min} = \frac{IC}{2}\sqrt{\frac{2AD}{IC}} + AD\sqrt{\frac{IC}{2AD}}$$

$$= \sqrt{2ADIC} \tag{5}$$

Numerical examples using the basic EOQ formula from (4) will be given in section 2(c).

The EOQ formula in (4) shows that for transactions purposes optimal order quantity (and average inventory $Q^*/2$) will vary with the square root of demand: thus there are important economies of scale for items with a high level of demand or high unit cost. This square root relationship contrasts with the linear assumptions which are implicit in the orthodox analysis of accounting data, for example the sales/inventory and current ratios considered in Chapter 4.

The square root formula also means that EOQ is not highly sensitive to errors in the input data. This is fortunate in view of the nature of some of the'estimations which must be employed.

(ii) *EOQ with backordering*

In some situations demand not met from available inventory can be postponed as backorders to be met from the next delivery of goods to the firm (or from the next batch manufactured). This requires that customers (or production needs within the firm) will wait. Backorders are unlikely to be costless; they may involve additional administrative costs, a higher rate of returned goods by customers, loss of goodwill and sometimes specific penalty costs. All costs of backorders will not necessarily be proportional to units and the length of time of shortage, but as with carrying costs in the basic EOQ formula it will be convenient to assume proportionality.*

Retaining deterministic assumptions as before, it can be worthwhile for the firm to incur some backorder costs on postponed demand. Effectively backorder costs are balanced against the costs which would otherwise be incurred for carrying inventory to meet demand towards the end of the order cycle.

In addition to the notation used previously (Q = order quantity, D = demand, C = unit cost, I = carrying cost, A = order cost) the following will be adopted:

B = backorder cost per unit per time period (here per year)
M = maximum inventory, assumed $\leqslant Q$

---

*This treatment follows [7] pp. 338–42, and [8] pp. 205–07 and pp. 224–25. For consideration of a fixed element in backorder costs see [9], pp. 42–47.

T_1 = time during order cycle for which inventory is held
T_2 = shortage time during order cycle
T = order cycle (= Q/D as fraction of a year).

Figure 19.2 shows the inventory and shortage when backordering occurs. The maximum shortage, just prior to a delivery, is given by order quantity minus maximum inventory, $Q - M$.

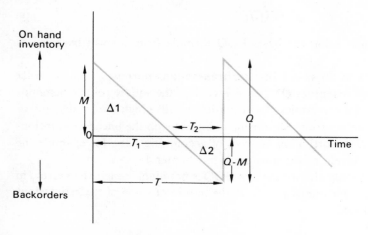

Figure 19.2 Inventory and backorders

It can be seen from Figure 19.2 that $\Delta 1$ and $\Delta 2$ are similar triangles, and since $T = T_1 + T_2$:

$$\frac{T_1}{M} = \frac{T_2}{Q - M} = \frac{T}{Q};$$

thus $\qquad T_1 = \frac{M}{Q}T \quad \text{and} \quad T_2 = \frac{(Q - M)}{Q}T \qquad (6)$

Average inventory over time T_1 is $M/2$ and the average shortage over time T_2 is $(Q - M)/2$. Unit carrying and backorder costs applied to the average inventory and shortage during the order cycle give total carrying and backorder costs. Thus total variable costs of inventory policy for *one order cycle*, V_c, composed of order cost, carrying costs, and backorder costs, is given by:

$$V_c = A + IC\frac{M}{2}T_1 + B\frac{(Q - M)}{2}T_2 \qquad (7)$$

Substituting for T_1 and T_2 from (6) gives:

$$V_c = A + \frac{ICM^2}{2Q}T + \frac{B(Q - M)^2}{2Q}T$$

The *annual* costs of inventory policy, V, are obtained by multiplying total costs for the order cycle by the number of orders D/Q:

$$V = \frac{AD}{Q} + \frac{ICM^2}{2Q}T \cdot \frac{D}{Q} + \frac{B(Q-M)^2}{2Q}T \cdot \frac{D}{Q} \tag{8}$$

But since $T = Q/D$, (8) becomes:

$$V = \frac{AD}{Q} + \frac{ICM^2}{2Q} + \frac{B(Q-M)^2}{2Q} \tag{9}$$

Differentiating (9) with respect to M and Q and setting equal to zero gives:*

$$\frac{\partial V}{\partial M} = \frac{ICM}{Q} - \frac{B(Q-M)}{Q} = 0$$

and

$$\frac{\partial V}{\partial Q} = -\frac{AD}{Q^2} - \frac{ICM^2}{2Q^2} + \frac{B}{2} - \frac{BM^2}{2Q^2} = 0$$

Simplification yields:

$$M = \frac{BQ}{IC+B} \tag{10}$$

and

$$Q^2 = \frac{2AD}{B} + \left(\frac{IC}{B}+1\right)M^2 \tag{11}$$

Substituting in (11) for M from (10) gives:

$$Q^{**} = \sqrt{\frac{2AD}{IC}} \cdot \sqrt{\frac{B+IC}{B}} \tag{12}$$

where Q^{**} is the economic order quantity with backordering.

The optimal maximum inventory holding, M^*, can be similarly derived from (11) as:

$$M^* = \sqrt{\frac{2AD}{IC}} \cdot \sqrt{\frac{B}{B+IC}} \tag{13}$$

The basic EOQ formula appears as the first square root term for both Q^{**} and M^*. Thus in the backorder case (with $B > 0$) it can be seen from (12) that the economic order quantity is greater than under the basic formula (because $[B+IC]/B > 1$): on the other hand maximum inventory is less (because $B/[B+IC] < 1$).

The maximum shortage, $Q^{**} - M^*$, depends on an optimal balance between carrying, order and backorder costs. It can be seen from (12) and (13) that as B

---

*The solution which follows applies only where the optimal values of Q and M do not lie on the boundaries, i.e. $0 < Q^{**} < \infty$ and $0 < M^* < \infty$.

approaches zero the optimal shortage becomes very large, and that with increasing B both Q^{**} and M^* approach the values given by the basic EOQ formula.

If sales cannot be backordered, but are lost when a stockout occurs, then in a deterministic system the basic EOQ formula would require no amendment. This can be seen intuitively: if the potential loss from foregoing (known) additional sales is greater than their carrying costs then carrying the required inventory is worthwhile; if the cost of lost sales (in lost profit, goodwill and administrative costs) is less than the carrying costs there is no point in carrying the inventory. The argument will be demonstrated more precisely,* adopting the following additional notation:

π = cost of a lost sale (lost profit on the sale, loss of goodwill, administrative costs)

T_1 = time during order cycle for which inventory is held (in this case = Q/D)

T_2 = shortage time during order cycle (in this case all potential sales during T_2 are lost).

On average there will be $D/[Q+DT_2]$ order cycles per year. Cost of inventory policy for one order cycle is given by:

$$V_c = A + \frac{ICQ}{2}\cdot\frac{Q}{D} + \pi DT_2 \tag{14}$$

The annual costs of inventory policy are given by multiplying by the number of orders, $D/[Q+DT_2]$;

$$V = \frac{AD}{Q+DT_2} + \frac{ICQ^2}{2(Q+DT_2)} + \frac{\pi D^2 T_2}{Q+DT_2} \tag{15}$$

Differentiating with respect to T_2 and Q and setting equal to zero gives:†

$$\frac{\partial V}{\partial T_2} = -\left[AD^2 + \frac{ICDQ^2}{2} + \pi D^3 T\right](Q+DT_2)^{-2} + \frac{\pi D^2}{Q+DT_2} = 0 \tag{16}$$

$$\frac{\partial V}{\partial Q} = -\left[AD + \frac{ICQ^2}{2} + \pi D^2 T\right](Q+DT_2)^{-2} + \frac{ICQ}{Q+DT_2} = 0 \tag{17}$$

Simplifying (16) and (17) gives:

$$\frac{AD}{Q} + \frac{ICQ}{2} - \pi D = 0 \tag{18}$$

and

$$-AD + \frac{ICQ^2}{2} - \pi D^2 T_2 + ICQDT_2 = 0 \tag{19}$$

*This proof follows Hadley and Whitin [9], pp. 47–50.

†In a similar manner to the backorders case, this solution requires $0 < T_2^* < \infty$ and $0 < Q^* < \infty$.

Solving for Q^* in (18) gives:

$$Q^* = \frac{\pi D}{IC} \pm \sqrt{\left(\frac{\pi D}{IC}\right)^2 - \frac{2AD}{IC}}. \tag{20}$$

Three possible relationships between the costs of lost sales and the costs of inventory policy can be considered.

1. $(\pi D)^2 < 2ADIC$; i.e. the annual costs of lost sales are less than the annual costs of an inventory policy in which no lost sales are incurred (equation (5) gave the costs for such a policy). In this case there is no real solution to (20) because the expression under the square root sign is negative. Incurring the costs of lost sales all the time would be cheaper than operating an inventory system.
2. $(\pi D)^2 > 2ADIC$, the reverse of the previous case. With this relationship:

$$\frac{\pi D}{IC} > \pm \sqrt{\left(\frac{\pi D}{IC}\right)^2 - \frac{2AD}{IC}} \tag{21}$$

so that there would be two positive values of Q^*.

By substituting in (19) for Q^* from (20) the following equation can be produced:

$$DT_2 = -\frac{\pi D}{IC} \pm \sqrt{\left(\frac{\pi D}{IC}\right)^2 - \frac{2AD}{IC}}. \tag{22}$$

But the relationship stated in (21) means that $T_2 < 0$, from (22). Thus it is not worthwhile to lose sales, and inventory policy using the EOQ model would minimize costs.

3. $(\pi D)^2 \doteq 2ADIC$. If this were the case, $Q^* = \pi D/IC$. Substitution into (18) produces:

$$(\pi D)^2 = 2ADIC \tag{23}$$

Thus *any* value of T_2 would be optimal; the basic EOQ formula (with $T_2 = 0$) would produce as good a policy as any other.

(c) Financial constraints

The EOQ solution, in the forms shown above, implies unlimited access to funds for financing inventory. This implication may not be valid: a firm may have limited credit with its suppliers and may be unable to borrow beyond a certain level, at least in the short-run. The firm will usually have some flexibility in obtaining funds, but management may wish to reserve this flexibility or may consider that available sources of funds would be prohibitively expensive.

When the firm's inventory decisions are subject to a funds constraint the use of Lagrangean multipliers provides a method of determining policy. Such a constraint applies to the value of inventories as a whole and it is therefore necessary to examine the problem of minimizing total costs of inventory policy with regard to total inventories rather than item by item.

Adapting equation (3) in the previous subsection to the requirements for total inventories:

$$V = A \sum_{j=1}^{n} \frac{D_j}{Q_j} + I \sum_{j=1}^{n} \frac{C_j Q_j}{2} \qquad (24)$$

where V is total cost of inventory policy, A is order cost (irrespective of item) and C_j, D_j, Q_j are the unit cost, demand and order quantity respectively for the jth item, $j = 1, 2, \ldots, n$.

Equation (24) is to be minimized subject to the constraint:

$$\sum_{j=1}^{n} \frac{C_j Q_j}{2} = M,$$

where M is the money amount available for investment in (average) inventory.

The Lagrangean expression can be formed:

$$L = A \sum_{j=1}^{n} \frac{D_j}{Q_j} + I \sum_{j=1}^{n} \frac{C_j Q_j}{2} + \lambda \left[\sum_{j=1}^{n} \frac{C_j Q_j}{2} - M \right].$$

Minimizing L over Q_j and λ by taking their derivatives and setting equal to zero gives:

$$\frac{\partial L}{\partial Q_j} = -\frac{A D_j}{Q_j^2} + \frac{I C_j}{2} + \frac{\lambda C_j}{2} = 0 \qquad (25)$$

$$\frac{\partial L}{\partial \lambda} = \sum_{j=1}^{n} \frac{C_j Q_j}{2} - M = 0. \qquad (26)$$

These equations can be solved simultaneously to obtain values of λ and Q_j.

An example

Pinch Ltd. has just three inventory items, for which cost per unit, annual demand and the resulting cost of goods are:

Item	Cost per unit, C_j £	Annual demand, D_j	Annual cost of goods, C_j, D_j £
1	45	360	16 200
2	20	1 000	20 000
3	3	3 750	11 250

Order cost $A = £10$ and carrying cost $I = 10$ per cent per year.

In the absence of a (binding) constraint the EOQ's given by equation (4) would be calculated:

$$Q^* = \sqrt{\frac{2 \times 10 \times 360}{0 \cdot 10 \times 45}} = 40, \text{ etc.,}$$

giving:

Item	Initial EOQ
1	40
2	100
3	500

Thus average inventory would be:

$$\tfrac{1}{2}[(40 \times £45) + (100 \times £20) + (500 \times £3)] = £2\,650.$$

But assume that Pinch Ltd. in fact has a constraint of £2 000 on average inventory held for transactions purposes. Inserting data into expressions (25) and (26) gives:

$$-\frac{10D_j}{Q_j^2} + \frac{0 \cdot 10C_j}{2} + \frac{\lambda C_j}{2} = 0 \tag{27}$$

$$\sum_{j=1}^{n} \frac{C_j Q_j}{2} - 2\,000 = 0. \tag{28}$$

From (27):
$$Q_j = \sqrt{\frac{20D_j}{C_j(0 \cdot 10 + \lambda)}} \tag{29}$$

Substituting for Q_j in (28) gives:

$$\sum_{j=1}^{n} \sqrt{C_j D_j} \cdot \sqrt{\frac{20}{0 \cdot 10 + \lambda}} = 4\,000, \tag{30}$$

$$\lambda = 20 \left[\frac{\sum_{j=1}^{n} \sqrt{C_j D_j}}{4\,000} \right]^2 - 0 \cdot 10.$$

From the original data we can calculate:

$$\sum_{j=1}^{n} \sqrt{C_j D_j} = 127 \cdot 27 + 141 \cdot 42 + 106 \cdot 06 = 374 \cdot 75$$

Thus
$$\lambda = 20 \left(\frac{374 \cdot 75}{4\,000} \right)^2 - 0 \cdot 10 = 0 \cdot 076$$

595

λ indicates the reduction in inventory policy costs which could be achieved by an increment of £1 per year beyond the funds constraint; this shadow price applies only at the margin. Negative λ would indicate that the funds constraint was not binding.

The new EOQ formulated in the context of the funds constraint can be derived from (29), or the money amounts can be derived rather more easily from (30):

Item	Q^*_j	$C_j Q^*_j$, £
1	30	1 359
2	75	1 509
3	377	1 132
		4 000

The above figures have been rounded: the values for Q^*_j are in fact a constant proportion ($\simeq$ 75 per cent) of the original values: this is the ratio of the funds constraint to the original average total value (£2 000/£2 650).

The new order quantities will be more costly than those originally calculated, because the constraint has reduced inventory below the 'economic' level. In this case total costs will be £15 more, which is the cost of reducing average inventory by £650.

In this approach total costs are not considered in relation to the constraint: although average inventory is reduced by £650 the firm must find the extra inventory policy costs £15 from somewhere. This difference is minor, particularly in view of the estimated nature of the cost data.

(d) Safety stocks

When demand and/or lead time cannot be treated as effectively certain, the precautionary motive for stockholding is relevant. In addition to the holdings for transactions purposes it is necessary to employ safety stocks to absorb variations in the calls on inventories.

The effect of a safety stock is illustrated in Figure 19.3 where demand is no longer certain but lead times remain constant.

Order quantity calculated on (mean) expected demand can be calculated in the deterministic manner already considered. The safety stock constitutes a separate component of inventory which *on average* will be carried all year round.* On the right-hand side of Figure 19.3 there is an upended probability density function for

---

*In fact the independent calculation of order quantity and safety stock implied here is not strictly valid, but sufficiently close for the present purposes. See [14], pp. 120–25 and also [9], Chapter 4.

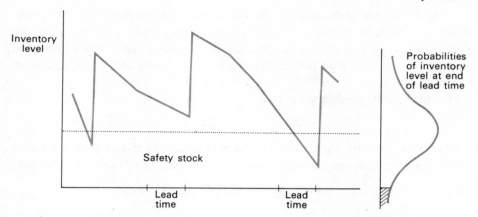

Figure 19.3 Variable sales with constant lead times

stocks remaining on hand at the end of lead time, illustrated here quite arbitrarily as a normal distribution. EOQ based on mean expected demand would leave sufficient inventory to meet demand during lead time on 50 per cent of occasions – because demand during lead time would be less than the mean for half the time. The remaining 50 per cent of variations in demand would either be met by safety stocks or would result in stockouts.

If the inventory policy is optimally determined the safety allowance will be that for which the probability of stockouts balances the expected costs of depletion against carrying charges for the marginal unit stocked. The technique will not be examined here. The alternative approach is to select a specific risk of stockout by arbitrary policy decision. In either case an assumption about the probability distribution of demand is required. Past data on demand can be examined to justify the adoption of a particular distribution; often it is convenient to assume that whole classes of inventory items share some characteristic distribution.

For an illustration of an arbitrarily determined probability of stockouts, consider a firm which requires that there shall be only one chance in 100 of being understocked on a particular inventory item. Sales occur in a random manner and the Poisson distribution is assumed to be appropriate. A convenient characteristic of the Poisson distribution is that standard deviation is given by the square root of the mean; thus only average demand during lead time need be known in order to determine the distribution. The direct normal distribution may then be used as an approximation to the Poisson distribution for small probabilities.

If I_0 = number of units on hand at the beginning of the period which will reduce the probability of running out of stock during the next period to 1/100, and

d = average demand during lead time,

then $I_0 = d + 2 \cdot 326\sigma = d + 2 \cdot 326\sqrt{d}$

2.326σ either side of the mean of the normal distribution (the 2 per cent probability level) includes all but 1 per cent of cases on either side of the mean. We are concerned with only one tail of the distribution; inventory needs to be sufficient to meet all but the 1 per cent probability of stockouts shown as the shaded area in Figure 19.3.

The firm's safety stock is given by:

$$I_0 - d \ = \ 2.326\sqrt{d}$$

If lead time is one week and average weekly demand is 24 units, a safety allowance which would on average give a stockout only one week in 100 can be calculated:

$$I_0 = 24 + 2.326\sqrt{24} = 35.4, \quad \text{say 36 units,}$$

and safety allowance $= 12$ units.

When the probability of stockouts is selected by policy decision it is still possible to calculate an implied cost of stockout to permit managerial assessment of the plausibility of stockout costs.*

The above discussion considered briefly only that type of amendment to the deterministic approach which accommodates demand variations. Variations in lead time could be treated in a similar manner, but to deal with variations in both demand *and* lead time would require a different approach. Simulation can be used to tackle this type of problem.† Moreover the discussion has been concerned exclusively with static models; significantly different treatment is required to accommodate dynamic changes in the determinants (demand, lead times, prices) of inventory policy.‡

19.3. Trade credit

The granting of trade credit to debtors and the taking of credit from creditors are important aspects of working capital management, but they have been subjected to much less analysis than the inventory control problem.

(a) Trade debtors

The major quantitative controllable variables relevant to credit granting are succinctly stated by Beranek [4] as:

> ... (1) amount of cash discount, (2) length of credit period, (3) level of collection expenditures, (4) the customers to whom we would offer terms, and (5) the magnitude of the line of credit.

* See e.g. [11], pp. 27–34.
† See [7].
‡ See e.g. [9], Chapter 7.

These categories will provide a convenient basis for our short discussion.

(i) *Cash discount*
Cash discount is granted for prompt payment; credit terms might be expressed as 2 per cent cash discount for payment within 7 days, otherwise payment in full within 30 days. An unconditional discount would be simply a price reduction.

The cash discount is usually set much higher than prevailing interest rates; in the above example 2 per cent for 23 days would be usurious. Thus there is an element of price reduction to encourage customers to take the discount.

For the firm the discount is a cost which can bring a number of possible benefits: increased sales (via the price reduction element), reduced interest on average funds tied up in debtors, reduction in bad debts (if weak payers are encouraged to take the discount) and reduction in collection expenses (payment reminders, etc.). Thus the potential effect on the firm's net profit arising from a decision to *increase* cash discount offered to customers could be expressed:

$$\Delta\pi = \Delta M + i\Delta D + \Delta B + \Delta E - \Delta C;$$

where Δ denotes increments arising from the cash discount decision, π = net profit, M = variable profit margin on sales (revenue − variable costs of sales), D = average level of debtors in period, i = interest rate (opportunity cost) on funds, B = bad debts, E = collection expenses, C = cash discount expense. (Reverse signs on right-hand side of equation for decrease in cash discount.)

A firm will have difficulty in forecasting the incremental effects of discount changes. Moreover the danger of antagonizing customers by frequent discount policy changes may prevent an iterative approach – although the diversified firm has opportunities for experimenting in different segments. However, probability estimates can provide a framework for examining the discount decision. Given a range of probability estimates of the proportion of customers whose payments will be influenced by the discount change it is possible to calculate an expected profit by quantifying the anticipated consequent changes in average debtors and expenses of collection. ΔM and ΔB are likely to be very difficult to estimate, but their values may not be material for the small range of discount normally considered by firms.

(ii) *Length of credit period*
An increase in the credit period can augment sales, possibly via new customers, in a similar manner to cash discount. It can also attract weak payers to the firm. The associated costs are interest on the increased funds tied up in trade debtors, perhaps increased bad debts and increased collection expenses.

Using the same notation as before, the effect of an *increased* credit period can be summarized.

$$\Delta\pi = \Delta M - i\Delta D - \Delta B - \Delta E.$$

Working capital management

(iii) *Expenses of collection*

A change in the level (or nature) of collection activity can affect bad debt experience and the average funds tied up by debtors; it may also affect sales in a manner analogous to changes in the length of the collection period. The effects of collection activity on debtor levels and bad debt experience can be estimated by experimenting with collection intensity for different segments of the debtor population, to give an estimate of the profit effect of *increased* collection expenditure:

$$\Delta\pi = i\Delta D + \Delta B - \Delta E.$$

(iv) *Selection of creditworthy customers*

A profit criterion for the selection of creditworthy customers requires that expected profit from sales to a customer should be greater than (or at least equal to) expected bad debt loss.

Assuming the percentage variable profit margin (m) to be an appropriate estimate of incremental profit from each £1 sale, and given probability estimates of whether the customer's debt will prove good ($P(G)$) or bad ($P(B)$), expected profit rate per £ sales $E(\pi_r)$ can be derived:

$$E(\pi_r) = mP(G) - (1-m)P(B)$$

For example, if $m = 0.29$, $P(G) = 0.8$ and $P(B) = 0.2$, then:

$$E(\pi_r) = 0.29(0.8) - (0.71)(0.2) = 0.09.$$

The variable profit margin should be calculated after deducting estimated costs associated with the sale (e.g. interest costs for funds tied up by the debtor). It should also be noted that $E(\pi_r)$ should be compared with any relevant competing sales opportunities.

It would be unduly burdensome to make such calculations for each specific sale (unless very large sums were involved) and in practice credit granting decisions rarely balance expected profit explicitly against expected bad debt loss. Usually a dichotomous distinction is made between creditworthy and not creditworthy. The major bases for the distinction are ratings from credit agencies, trade and bank references, etc., 'intuition', and the use of accounting ratios from final accounts where the customer is a business firm. One technique adopted for the assessment of credit granting to individuals is a numerical credit rating: weights are assigned for items from the personal history of individuals and a cut-off point is determined to distinguish between good and bad risks.*

Beranek [4] and others have proposed that a cut-off point for credit granting to business firms could be based on accounting ratios incorporating an explicit trade-off between expected profit margin and the expected loss from non-payment. The

* E.g. see [12].

600

probabilities of non-payment associated with values of an accounting ratio can be established from past data for customer firms; it may be recalled from Chapter 4 that there is evidence to support an association between 'poor' ratios and company failure.

Assuming that debt/total assets were adopted* as the ratio for determining creditworthiness, an investigation of past data for a particular class of customers could produce probabilities for customers proving 'good' or 'bad' during a period; such a hypothetical relationship is shown in Figure 19.4 where D/T = debt/total assets.

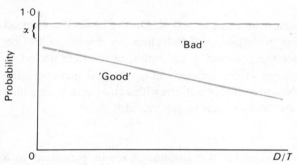

Figure 19.4 Probabilities for creditworthiness

If a linear probability relationship is valid over the observed range of D/T, probability of not receiving payment for a sale, $P(B)$, as a function of D/T is:

$$P(B) = \alpha + \frac{\beta D}{T}$$

where $\alpha \leqslant 1$ and $\beta > 0$. Similarly

$$P(G) = 1 - \left(\alpha + \frac{\beta D}{T}\right).$$

It was seen earlier that the expected profit rate per £ sales was given by:

$$E(\pi_r) = mP(G) - (1 - m)P(B)$$

Substituting for $P(G)$ and $P(B)$ gives:

$$E(\pi_r) = m\left(1 - \alpha - \frac{\beta D}{T}\right) - (1 - m)\left(\alpha + \frac{\beta D}{T}\right).$$

The firm will wish to avoid transactions which offer $E(\pi_r) < 0$; thus the cut-off point can be calculated by setting $E(\pi_r) = 0$ in the above equation. The result is:

$$\frac{D}{T} = \frac{m - \alpha}{\beta}.$$

* Our example is similar to Beranek's.

For example, where $m = 0.29$ as before, and from analysis of past data $\alpha = 0.05$ and $\beta = 1.0$ the cut-off point would be a ratio of 0.24 for D/T:

$$\frac{D}{T} = \frac{0.29 - 0.05}{1.0} = 0.24.$$

The firm will grant credit to customers with ratios below the cut-off point, which has been calculated to maximize expected profit from business with credit granting customers. This approach does assume that the probabilities of collection associated with particular values of the accounting ratios will not change with changes in the economic environment.

The above analysis was confined to a single period. On the basis of collection experience the firm's estimates of probabilities of collection can change: collection in one time period can enhance the prospect of collection in the next period. A decision tree analysis* for the current credit decision can be adopted, incorporating anticipated probabilities for a sequence of transactions with a customer, from which an expected value for the current decision can be calculated.†

(v) Credit limits

A specific limit is usually established for the amount of credit permitted to a customer at any one time. The limits are determined on similar information to that used for the credit granting decision: one test of the validity of a proposed limit is the standard enquiry to a customer's bank – 'Is X good for $£y$?' Such limits act as a constraint on loss through dealing with a particular customer.

(b) Trade creditors

The major elements to be considered in the use of trade credit facilities are cash discounts and the firm's credit image. Cash discounts should clearly be taken if the discount exceeds the short-run value of funds (after considering constraints) over the potential credit period.

The firm's image with trade creditors is a qualitative matter. Credit can be 'stretched' by deferring payment beyond the due date, but repeated stretching has obvious dangers. Trade creditors are most likely to countenance flagrant stretching by customers who are powerful in either purchasing or financial terms: in the latter case stretching is paradoxically easiest for those who need it least.

19.4 Cash and near-cash

We saw in section 2 that the reasons for holding cash or stocks of goods depended

---

*See Chapter 12.

†See Beranek [4] and Bierman [6]; the latter develops a dynamic programming model which is more versatile in accommodating the characteristics of the problem.

on transactions, precautionary and speculative motives. The last motive is bound up with expectations regarding interest rates and inflation/deflation, and need not detain us in our consideration of cash needs for operations of the firm. Following subsections will deal with two deterministic approaches essentially concerned with transactions, and will conclude with some observations on other aspects of the cash problem.

In order to meet its commitments a firm will maintain cash balances in bank current-accounts, notes and coin: these assets provide liquidity without return. Consequently most firms maintain secondary sources of liquidity which are less expensive in terms of opportunity costs. These can take the form of near-cash assets: readily marketable securities or short term deposits with financial institutions, which have a safety stock function or provide a resting place for temporarily surplus funds. But other secondary sources of liquidity are available: a firm can borrow short term, it may have an established overdraft limit or line of credit with a bank, it can temporarily stretch payments to creditors, it can factor debtors (effectively sell a proportion of the claims against debtors). Consequently most firms have flexibility in short run cash management, which makes the problem complex to manipulate in optimizing terms.

(a) The cash budget

The cash budget has probably been used in some form ever since money was invented.* It merely involves projecting cash balances on the basis of forecast

Table 19.1 A cash budget

	January £	February £	March £
Receipts:			
From debtors	9 000	12 000	9 000
Cash sales	4 000	3 000	5 000
	13 000	15 000	14 000
Payments:			
Creditors, wages, etc.	12 000	14 000	11 500
Equipment		5 000	
	12 000	19 000	11 500
Net cash flow	1 000	(4 000)	2 500
Balance, end month December £3 500	4 500	500	3 000

*E.g. 'For which of you, intending to build a tower, sitteth not down first, and counteth the cost, whether he have sufficient to finish it?' *St. Luke's Gospel*, Chapter 14, v. 28.

receipts and payments. Deficits indicate the need to borrow, to rephase receipts or payments, or to cut expenditure. Commonly a desired minimum balance is adopted (the precautionary motive) to accommodate forecasting errors. Cash in excess of the minimum balance will be diverted temporarily or permanently to other uses.

A very simple cash budget for three months is illustrated in Table 19.1. The cash budget has an important place in the budgeting of the firm, as was seen in Chapter 15, but it does not in itself consider the opportunity cost of holding cash or purport to produce an optimal cash balance.

(b) The transactions balance

The transactions demand for cash can be analysed in a similar manner to that used for inventory. Baumol [3] has adapted the inventory EOQ model to the cash situation; his notation will be used here.

Assume that demand for cash during a period (say one year) is known with certainty and takes the form of a steady stream, so that operating receipts minus payments are constant over time. This total demand in the year is denoted by T. The cash balance in hand has a carrying cost (per £) equal to an interest rate i, either on borrowed funds or on funds diverted from short term investments. The act of obtaining cash to replenish the cash balance involves a cost: borrowing must be arranged or fees must be incurred in selling securities. This cost can be termed a 'broker's fee' denoted by b; it corresponds to the order cost in the inventory model. Each replenishment amount is assumed to be a constant, C, paid into the cash balance at equal intervals throughout the year.

Following the method of the inventory model, the total costs for cash balances throughout the year is given by:

$$\frac{bT}{C} + \frac{iC}{2}.$$

Differentiating with regard to C and setting the derivative equal to zero gives:

$$-\frac{bT}{C^2} + \frac{i}{2} = 0:$$

thus

$$C^* = \sqrt{\frac{2bT}{i}}.$$

The result for optimal replenishment amount C^* resembles the EOQ formula. Although no firm's transactions would fully meet the assumptions of the model, it provides some guidance on the nature of the balance required for transactions purposes. As with inventory the square root relationship for cash indicates 'economies of scale'; the average cash balance for transaction purposes ($C^*/2$) does not increase linearly with transactions.

(c) Some other aspects

A safety stock of cash can be determined from the investigation of variability of past cash demands. Non-operating expenditures and receipts, such as capital outlays and interest payments, would have to be excluded; their incidence can in any case be forecast with substantial accuracy. It might seem that a firm could not countenance a cashout, but the flexibility afforded by near-cash assets and borrowing must be remembered: cash can be replenished swiftly from these sources, although at a cost. An 'outage' on all liquid resources (cash, near-cash and borrowing facilities) would be another matter.

The cost of a cashout is difficult to determine, and may depend on the nature of the cash demand being made; for example, payments for wages cannot be stretched in the same way as payments to trade creditors. However, it is still possible to select a safety balance based on a management determined risk of cashout, on the lines considered earlier for inventory. Archer [1] investigated the net cash flows of a firm over four years and produced a frequency distribution which permitted the calculation of the average cash balance for operating transaction purposes (at the mean of the distribution) and the precautionary balances required for given risks of cashouts. The firm in fact carried an average balance implying a 0·05 probability of cashout. A more complex investigation by Buchan and Koenigsberg* examined cash holdings by a chain of supermarkets and the influences on demands for cash. From the analysis of past data a formula for cash requirements was developed which permitted simulation of the cashout position for any average amount of cash carried. Comparison with past performance showed that the model permitted maintenance of the existing average cash with a 30 per cent reduction in cashouts or alternatively the existing cashout position could be maintained with an accompanying reduction of 39 per cent in average cash holding.

It was said earlier that the firm's short term financing decisions are made in the context of constraints like limited borrowing facilities and limited ability to stretch payments. An optimal cash decision would incorporate specific consideration of the constraints. A potentially fruitful approach by Robichek, Teichroew and Jones [13] involves the analysis of short-run financing in a (deterministic) linear programming model: as usual with linear programming some consideration of uncertainty can be accommodated by testing the effects of different values for inputs to the model.

Bibliographical references

[1] Archer, S. H., A model for the determination of firm cash balances, *Journal of Finance and Quantitative Analysis,* March 1966, pp. 1–11; reprinted in [2].
[2] Archer, S. H. and C. A. D'Ambrosio, *The Theory of Business Finance,* Macmillan, New York, 1967.

*[7], Chapter 5.

[3] Baumol, W. J., The transactions demand for cash, *Quarterly Journal of Economics*, November 1952, pp. 545–56; reprinted in [2].
[4] Beranek, W., *Analysis for Financial Decisions*, Irwin, 1963.
[5] Beranek, W., *Working Capital Management*, Wadsworth, 1966.
[6] Bierman, H., *Financial Policy Decisions*, Macmillan, New York, 1970.
[7] Buchan, J. and E. Koenigsberg, *Scientific Inventory Measurement*, Prentice-Hall, 1963.
[8] Churchman, C. W., R. L. Ackoff and E. L. Arnoff, *Introduction to Operations Research*, Wiley, 1957.
[9] Hadley, G. and T. M. Whitin, *Analysis of Inventory Systems*, Prentice-Hall, 1963.
[10] Keynes, J. M., *The General Theory of Employment Interest and Money*, Macmillan, London, 1949.
[11] Morrell, A. J. H., ed., *Problems of Stocks and Storage*, I.C.I. Monograph No. 4, Oliver and Boyd, 1967.
[12] Myers, J. H. and E. W. Forgy, The development of numerical credit evaluation systems, *Journal of the American Statistical Association*, September 1963, pp. 799–806; reprinted in K. J. Cohen and F. S. Hammer, *Analytical Methods in Banking*, Irwin, 1966.
[13] Robichek, A. A., D. Teichroew and J. M. Jones, Optimal short term financing decision, *Management Science*, September 1965, pp. 1–36.
[14] Starr, M. K. and D. W. Miller, *Inventory Control*, Prentice-Hall, 1962.

Problems

19.1 X is starting a business. He has contracts to supply 6 000 units of a product at a constant rate over the next year. Information relating to the product is shown below.

Purchase price per unit	£5
Sale price per unit	£6
Cost of placing one order	£7·50
Carrying cost (storage, insurance, etc.) of one unit of inventory for one year *excluding* interest	£0·40

All sales and purchases will be made on 'cash on delivery' terms. Order costs and carrying costs (including interest) will be met at the end of each inventory cycle.

X's bank will allow him an overdraft on the security of his inventory. The overdraft will be equal to 50 per cent of the inventory (purchase) value held at any time by X; the interest charge will be 8 per cent per year. The remaining 50 per cent of funds to finance inventory will be provided by X, who considers his opportunity cost to be 16 per cent per year.

X will maintain the overdraft at the maximum permitted level by withdrawing profits and employing any temporarily surplus funds for other purposes. Ignore uncertainty.

How much cash should X introduce into the business initially to finance optimal order quantities?

19.2 Vapour Ltd. will sell 20 000 units of an inventory item in the coming year.

Order cost is £8; carrying cost is £0·50 per unit per year. The assumptions of the basic EOQ model are applicable.

Required:

(a) What is the optimal order quantity?

(b) How many orders should be placed during the year?

(c) What is the cost of inventory policy?

(d) Assume that Vapour Ltd. estimates order cost could be somewhere in the range £6 to £10 and that carrying cost could be somewhere in the range £0·30 to £1. Recalculate the extreme values for (a), (b) and (c) above.

19.3 Use the original data for Vapour Ltd. in problem 19.2 (i.e. demand 20 000 units, order cost £8, carrying cost £0·50). Vapour Ltd. is able to supply customers through backorders; the backorder cost per unit is £2·50 per year. What is the optimal order quantity and the maximum inventory holding?

19.4 Data for annual demand, purchase costs and selling prices of Lambda's inventory items are given below.

Item	Annual demand Units	Cost per unit £	Selling price per unit £
Gadgets	7 200	4	6
Ratchets	1 000	5	9
Widgets	900	50	70

The firm has an order cost of £12 and a carrying cost of 12 per cent per year on unit cost for all inventory items.

Lambda's customers all take one month's credit; the company obtains, on average, credit of £5 000 from its suppliers. Lambda has determined that only £7 000 will be available to finance average working capital (inventory + debtors − creditors).

Determine the appropriate inventory policy in the context of the funds constraint. If Lambda is currently borrowing at 8 per cent per year (which has been incorporated in the carrying cost) at what interest rate would it be worthwhile to borrow in order to provide a marginal increment to working capital?

Ignore uncertainty.

19.5 A company's store for raw material X was recently destroyed by fire. A new store is to be erected; its capacity has to be decided.

The company forecasts that 100 000 tons of X will be consumed at a constant rate each year for the life of the store. X costs £200 per ton; when it is held in store it deteriorates in value at the rate of 3 per cent per year. The order cost for each delivery is £15.

The new store will be erected from prefabricated units. Each unit has a capacity of 300 tons and costs £2 000, including erection costs. Any number of units can be erected, but it would be prohibitively expensive to erect a 'made-to-measure' store with a capacity which is not a multiple of 300 tons. The store will have a life of 20 years and will be valueless at the end of that time. (Land value can be ignored; the store will occupy a worthless corner of the factory site.)

The company's cost of capital is 7 per cent per year. Assume that all data are certain.

Required:

(a) Calculations for the capacity of the store the company should erect, on the basis of the above information.

(b) Mention three ways in which your answer might be affected if the simplifying assumptions of the question did not apply, stating in each case the conditions under which the optimal capacity for the store would be increased or decreased.

19.6 SP Oils Ltd. sells fuel oil for heating, supplying domestic, industrial and commercial customers.

You have been asked to review the company's practices regarding credit given to customers. Discuss the information you would seek and examine the problems of determining credit policy.

19.7 Sam Tate is establishing a firm which is to be incorporated as Static Ltd. An estimated profit statement for the first year's trading, together with information on transactions, is shown below.

		£		Settlement of transactions
Materials:				
initial purchase		500		
purchases during year		10 000		Credit period 4 weeks
Wages		11 000		Paid weekly
Expenses		9 000		Average credit period 2 weeks
Depreciation		2 000		
		32 500		
Less ending inventories:				
materials	500			
finished goods	2 000			
		2 500		
		30 000		
Directors' remuneration		3 000		Paid at end of year's trading
Sales		£33 000		Credit period 6 weeks

Assume a working year of 50 weeks and that all payments and receipts occur at the first instant of the relevant week (e.g. wages for the preceding week are paid on Monday morning).

Static will purchase and pay for £20 000 equipment and £500 materials immediately the year's trading commences. Materials will be maintained at £500 by weekly replenishment. Production will be maintained at a constant rate throughout the year and costs will be incurred at a constant rate. Sales will be £500 per week for the first 10 weeks and £700 per week thereafter.

Static can borrow from its bank on overdraft, but the bank requires that the company's balance sheet at the end of the year must show a current ratio of 2 (otherwise future borrowing will be jeopardized). Static will issue share capital before commencing operations to ensure that this requirement will be met, on the basis of the estimated figures.

Exactly how much capital will Static issue? What will be the maximum overdraft during the year, if all the assumptions are met?

Discuss the problems which the assumptions of the question have avoided.

20

Long-term financing

So far as uncertainty is concerned, it is supposed that – unless otherwise stated – people think whatever they think about the future.
J. E. WALTER, 'Dividend policy: its influence on the value of the enterprise (in [1]).

20.1 The capital structure

The firm's asset holdings are financed from a variety of sources represented on the claims side of the balance sheet. The problems of capital structure are concerned with the mix of these claims.*

Decisions on the composition of claims involve consideration of the two major elements of cost and risk to the firm – which of course have related implications of returns and risk for the providers of finance. A relatively heavy reliance on long-term finance provides the firm with stability in its financing position – both the firm and the providers of finance are committed for better or worse. However, in imperfect and incomplete markets† not all firms have unlimited access to long-term finance: quoted firms which are financially weak in the opinion of the market may have considerable difficulty in raising long-term (or any) finance; unquoted companies tend to rely heavily on internally generated funds and to obtain their borrowed funds from relatively short-term bank loans.

The relative costs of short-term and long-term finance will depend upon current interest rates and the firm's expectations of future changes: short-term rates tend to be more volatile than long-term rates.‡ A firm can to some extent reduce both costs (of unnecessary funds) and risks (of fund shortages) by matching the maturities of claims against the expected maturities of assets: this matching occurs to a limited degree for any firm which has a spectrum of assets and claims, although to a much greater degree for financial institutions where the maturities of many assets are determinate.

Thus the division of long-term from short-term financing is arbitary; it is, however, both conventional and convenient. We shall in this chapter concentrate on equity financing and long-term debt such as debentures and loans, although most of the discussion would apply equally to short-term borrowing on a 'roll-over' basis, and we shall refer simply to debt. Preference capital will be ignored; the fact that it commits the firm to specific future payments makes it very similar to debt (except in the eyes of the tax authorities). We shall also ignore hybrid debt/equity claims

---

* See [28] for a theoretical analysis of optimal capital structure.
† On the implications of incomplete markets see [14].
‡ See [16], pp. 168–77 for an explanation of this phenomenon.

like convertible debentures and a host of important real world problems like stock options and debt refunding decisions.* Even so we shall provide only a sparse outline of certain fundamental aspects concerning long-term capital. In recent years substantial analysis has provided valuable insights into the company financing area; however it will be seen that this is a living area in which some central issues remain unsettled.

We shall be making use of the terms profit and earnings, interchangeably. The difficulties of defining profit/earnings/income, let alone measuring them, are already familiar. For the models in the following sections the terms profit and earnings can be assumed to mean the increment in value† of the underlying assets of a firm in a particular period – *before* meeting interest payments when debt is under consideration. For the simpler models which adopt the discounting of a constant perpetual stream these earnings will equal net cash flows under static assumptions (because, with stable prices and age distribution of assets, depreciation = replacement outlays). The actual measurement of earnings, as used by investors for analysis and projection of expectations or as used for the empirical testing of hypotheses on capital structure, must of course rely on accounting data which are less than perfect. In fact the accounting data, *with* other available information concerning the firm, provide only a base for an investor's projection of an anticipated cash flow stream to which a discount rate can be applied.‡

The other major strand in the discussion will concern risk. Two basic assumptions of the behaviour of investors are that they prefer higher expected wealth to lower wealth (*ceteris paribus*) and that they are risk averse, which can be taken to mean that they would choose an investment offering a lower standard deviation of probable returns in preference to an investment with the same expected value but higher standard deviation. It has been shown by Sharpe [29] that investor selection of an efficient combination of investments which maximizes individual investor utility (expected returns per unit of outlay *vs.* risk) will in market equilibrium produce a linear capital market line of the kind illustrated in Figure 20.1. This coincides with the conventional assumption of capital market behaviour, that the market presents the investor with two prices – the price of time (the prime or default-free interest rate) and the price of risk (which is the additional expected return per unit of risk borne). Sharpe's analysis also suggests that, if investors can diversify their portfolios to escape all but the risks resulting from swings in economic activity, only the responsiveness of the securities' rate of return to the level of economic activity is relevant in assessing risk. This supports (part of) the conventional view that the investor will require a lower/higher expected return on securities as their vulnerability to changes in the general economy is smaller/greater.

---

* For a good coverage of a variety of models for decisions in this area see Bierman [5].
† Value = market value, which in perfect markets is unambiguous (entry price = exit price).
‡ As in the capital budgeting context – see Chapter 11.

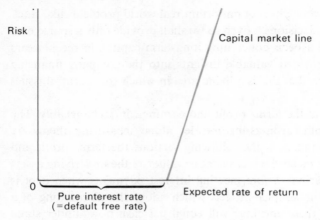

Figure 20.1 Rates of return in capital markets. (*Source:* Sharpe [29]; reproduced with permission.)

20.2 Dividends, retentions and valuation

Retained earnings provide a substantial source of equity financing; clearly the retention decision is the obverse of the dividend decision. Dividends which reduce the available internally generated funds below the planned investment outlays would (in the absence of surplus funds) require either the curtailment of the firm's investment programme or the raising of external finance. The latter is a relatively simple solution *if* the firm has access to a near perfect capital market.

The second possible implication of dividends, which will occupy our attention, is controversial: dividend policy may affect the price of the firm's shares and consequently the valuation of the firm and the cost of obtaining finance.

At this stage it will be convenient to assume an all-equity firm.

(a) Dividends stream valuation

According to the 'traditional' view dividend policy affects the valuation of the firm. A justification for this view is that uncertainty increases with time and investors will prefer a 'bird-in-the-hand' – a dividend distribution close at hand over a distant return of the same expected value (but with greater dispersion).*

The dividends stream approach to share valuation assumes that investors determine the price of a share as the discounted present value of expected future dividends. It will be seen later that under appropriate assumptions this is identical with an earnings stream valuation: the crucial issue concerns the nature of the discounting process under uncertainty.

*See [13], p. 56 and pp. 62–63.

612

A now classic dividend stream model is that originally advanced by Gordon and Shapiro [12] and later developed by Gordon [13] in connection with an empirical study. The basic model assumes that the value of a share (= current market price) will be equal to the present value of the share's expected dividends over the potentially infinite life of the firm; that is the same as saying that the stockmarket valuation of the firm's total equity is equal to the present value of the total dividend stream, a formulation which will be adopted here.

Stockmarket valuation of an all-equity firm was defined earlier in section 4(d) of Chapter 11 as the number of issued shares multiplied by current market price per share. It is in this sense that value of the firm's equity is being used in this chapter. In fact the marginal investor's estimate of present value will determine market price: the summation of current market price of shares will not determine the price at which *all* existing shareholders would be prepared to sell, nor the price which might be paid for the total equity by a takeover bidder. Unless otherwise stated we shall avoid these difficulties by assuming that common expectations are held by shareholders and that no single transactor can significantly influence market price.

For the development of the Gordon/Shapiro model it is convenient to assume that total dividend, D_t, for time t is paid in a continuous stream over time and is discounted continuously* at k, the return 'required' by investors (i.e. the rate at which investors discount expected receipts). The current value of the equity, V_0, is the value of the infinite dividend stream, given by:

$$V_0 = \int_0^\infty D_t e^{-kt} dt \qquad (1)$$

Assume that a company is expected to retain a constant fraction b of its profit,† π_t, at time t; the company is expected to earn a rate of return r on its retentions and to finance (net) investment entirely by retained earnings. Since dividends are the obverse of retentions:

$$D_t = (1-b)\pi_t. \qquad (2)$$

The earnings at time 1 (π_1) will therefore be equal to profit at time 0 plus earnings on the retentions made at time 0:

$$\pi_1 = \pi_0 + rb\pi_0 = \pi_0(1+rb).$$

Thus if earnings grow continuously at rate rb, earnings at time t are given by:

$$\pi_t = \pi_0 e^{rbt} \qquad (3)$$

---

* See Appendix A for continuous discounting. In the present context k and br (to be introduced shortly) are continuous rates of interest (= δ in Appendix A).

† For the present we are ignoring taxation.

From equation (2): $D_t = (1-b)\pi_0 e^{rbt}$

Substituting for D_t in (1) gives:

$$V_0 = \int_0^\infty (1-b)\pi_0 e^{rbt} e^{-kt}\,dt \tag{4}$$

Provided k is greater* than rb, integrating and simplifying (4) gives:

$$V_0 = \frac{(1-b)\pi_0}{k-br}. \tag{5}$$

The return required by equity shareholders is therefore given by:

$$k = \frac{(1-b)\pi_0}{V_0} + br. \tag{6}$$

Thus k is made up of the (observable) current dividend yield *plus* investor expectations of future growth in dividends, which are dependent on the expectations of the return which will be earned on retentions. *If* it could be assumed that investors adopt the current retention rate for b and the average return on capital employed as a measure of r, this would provide a measure of the current cost of equity capital to the firm. The leap from the observed (past) measures to investor expectations is a big one.

The basic model suggests a valuable analytical framework, but it must be viewed in the light of qualifications which can be only touched upon here.† First, the possibility of raising funds on the market is ignored: growth is assumed dependent on the retention decision. There is evidence that companies have a predilection for a consistent pay-out ratio,‡ so the assumption that b has a long-run stability has some support: this does not mean that such behaviour is optimal for a company, although it does suggest that investors may incorporate this tendency to stability in their expectations. The values of r and k are more difficult. The *average* return on *book value* will almost certainly not be the same as r which is the rate of return on *incremental investment*: management could, however, be guided by their own estimate of r (which, if valid, would determine earnings in the long-run). Moreover, the model suggests that for an optimal dividend decision the firm should choose between *either* $b = 0$ (where $k \geqslant r$) or $b = 1$ (where $k < r$); in the latter case the value of the firm given by equation (5) would be equal to zero. Nil retentions when $k \geqslant r$ would be to the advantage of the shareholders; however, a zero value for shares which do not currently pay a dividend is inconsistent with market observation – clearly investors may have an expectation of future returns in the absence of a current dividend.

* It will be seen from (5) that $k \leqslant rb$ gives negative or infinite V_0; neither is plausible.
† See Gordon's own treatment in [13], and also [23], [27], pp. 50–66.
‡ See e.g. [17] and [34], pp. 25–33.

Values of b between 0 and 1 can be explained if r and/or k are not constant over time. The term r may be a reducing function of b: this would be consistent with an apparently commonsense hypothesis that firms do not have unlimited opportunities to invest at constant rates of return, but that increments to investment offer declining marginal returns. The alternative, chosen by Gordon in [13] is that k is an increasing function of b: retentions are regarded by shareholders as riskier* because their benefits are more distant. This is a central assumption of a 'dividend policy effect' – the dividend decision *would* affect the value of the firm. Before turning to a different viewpoint we can observe that the alternative assumptions about r and k are not mutually exclusive, and therefore exceedingly difficult to test empirically.

(b) Earnings stream valuation

The basic dividends stream model is formally consistent with an assumption that investors value an *earnings* stream. The valuation equation in (5) can be re-expressed as:

$$k - br = \frac{\pi_0}{V_0} - \frac{b\pi_0}{V_0},$$

which gives:

$$k = \frac{\pi_0}{V_0} + b\left[r - \frac{\pi_0}{V_0}\right]. \tag{7}$$

Thus the rate of return required by investors is composed of the *current earnings yield* plus the firm's return on retentions in excess of the earnings yield. This 'premium' effect can be seen in terms of the firm's equity valuation by a different re-expression of (5):

$$kV_0 = \pi_0 - b\pi_0 + brV_0,$$

which gives:

$$V_0 = \frac{\pi_0}{k} + \frac{brV_0}{k} - \frac{b\pi_0}{k}. \tag{8}$$

It can be seen from (8) that valuation depends on:

1. The capitalization of the currently expected earnings stream, π_0/k.
2. *Plus* the expected increments to the earnings stream through investment, brV_0/k. Since brV_0 is the increase in firm earnings it could be expressed as $\Delta\pi_0$.
3. *Minus* the present value of funds required to provide investment, $b\pi_0/k$.

---

*In fact a *constant* discounting rate k (for risky returns) would in itself imply increasing risk through time – see Robichek and Myers [27], pp. 79–83, and also Chapter 12.

Provided the firm can raise funds on the market at the prevailing rate k (without transactions costs) the value of the firm to existing shareholders depends not upon retentions but upon the capitalization of the stream of earnings from existing assets and the stream of earnings from new investment: the shareholders would not suffer from any shortfall of retentions below investment.

Considering a current period decision to issue additional equity capital ΔE_0 which would yield a perpetual stream of future earnings $\Delta \pi_0$, the net value of the firm to the existing equity shareholders would be given by:

$$V_0 = \frac{\pi_0}{k} + \frac{\Delta \pi_0}{k} - \Delta E_0.$$

Thus the crucial point of either retention or fund raising is whether the (expected) value added to the firm by investment exceeds the value of the required funds. The assumption of a constant k in the above analysis is subject to a substantial qualification: there is no *a priori* reason to assume that the rate k for the existing stream of income should apply to the incremental stream – the latter may have different risk characteristics.

Modigliani and Miller [21] – henceforth MM – have cast fundamental doubts on the validity of the traditional theory that dividend policy affects valuation. Their view is that a change in dividend policy, given investment policy, implies only a change in the distribution of the total return in any period between dividends and capital. The earnings stream valuation developed above is, of course, consistent with such a viewpoint.

MM prove their point conclusively under assumptions of perfect markets, rational behaviour and perfect certainty. However, uncertainty is at the core of the dividend policy argument, and traditional theorists have remained unconvinced by their proof under uncertainty. Essentially, by assuming that even under uncertainty investors 'are indifferent as to whether a given increment to their wealth takes the form of a cash payment or an increase in the market value of their holdings of shares' MM assume away much of the ground on which the traditional argument depends.

(c) Some conclusions

There is considerable statistical evidence of positive relationships between share prices and dividends,* but the 'dividend' and 'earnings' theorists are divided in their interpretation of the evidence. The reasons for this continuing difference of opinion can be seen in the context of some major possible reasons why market prices may be affected by dividend policy in the real world:

---

* For some empirical studies see [9], [11], [13], [25].

1. Differentials in taxation between dividends and capital gains may affect relative values of dividends and gains to investors.
2. Many investors may depend on their shares for current income, and may have strong preferences for a high pay-out ratio.
3. Investors give a greater weight to a dividend expectation than to a corresponding retention because the latter will have a greater dispersion of returns which makes it riskier.
4. Investors adopt dividends as a surrogate for management expectations of future earnings, so that a change in dividend leads to a change in share price via changed investor expectations of earnings.

Neither of the first two possibilities offer conclusive reasons for a systematic effect of dividend policy on prices of widely traded shares, although they may well be influential for the unquoted and closely controlled company. Investors are subject to a wide spectrum of personal tax rates (upwards from zero on charities and pension funds), which would produce a wide range of tax induced preferences. Similarly there is likely to be a spectrum of preferences for current and future income. In both cases the reasoning by MM is relevant:

> Each corporation would tend to attract to itself a 'clientele' consisting of those preferring its particular payout ratio . . . if there were a 'shortage' of some particular payout ratio, investors would still normally have the option of achieving their particular savings objectives without paying a premium for the stocks in short supply simply by buying appropriately weighted combinations of the more plentiful payout ratios . . . this process would fail to eliminate permanent premiums and discounts only if the distribution of investor preferences were heavily concentrated at either of the extreme ends of the payout scale.*

The major differences between the dividends and earnings theories centre around possibilities 3. and 4. If the former is valid dividend policy can have a continuing effect on the valuation of the firm. If the latter is true the effects of dividend policy on share price can be only temporary: a change in dividend which is not vindicated by a subsequent change in the earnings of the firm will cease to influence share price. MM accept hypothesis 4., which they refer to as the 'informational content' of dividends.†

Thus the *tactical* importance of dividend policy is generally agreed, which means that dividend changes cannot be lightly made by management. However, on the case for a long-run dividend effect, which would mean that management could lower the long-run cost of capital by dividend policy, the verdict must be 'not proven'.

* [23], p. 431. The MM comments are made in the context of a 'classical' corporation tax system (to be considered again very briefly in section 3(c)), in which tax effects would favour retentions, if anything – because the company bears the full corporation tax on earnings *and* the investor pays personal tax on dividends. Under an imputation system the withholding tax on dividends is effectively retained by the firm so that, in principle, dividends to shareholders bear the same total tax burden as retentions. But differences still exist between personal tax rates on dividends and capital gains.

† See [25] for an attempt to isolate the informational content of dividends in an empirical study.

20.3 Debt/equity policy

Debt involves a commitment to pay specific money amounts in interest and eventual redemption (irredeemable debt securities are rare, but not unknown, for
companies). The right of equity shares to participate in the residual earnings of the
firm carries no such determinate commitment, so that shares can be expected to
yield a greater rate of return on outlay. Thus, in accordance with the 'capital market
line' of section 1 long term lenders to a firm can be assumed to require a lower rate
of return than the firm's equity shareholders. Whether this can make debt a cheap
method of financing is the crux of the debt/equity controversy to be considered in
section 3(b) below.

The reader may observe that published yields on fixed interest company debt
are commonly substantially higher than the earnings yields on equity shares,
which is the opposite of the above assumption. This phenomenon can occur for
three reasons:

1. The expected growth element in earnings yield, discussed earlier, is not part
   of the observed equity yield.
2. The contractual interest rate on debt (the *observed* rate currently required by
   the market) may be higher than the expected rate of interest because the
   probability of receiving the full amount of payments is not unity.
3. Whereas equity earnings incorporate something approaching a built-in
   inflation escalator (i.e. earnings tend to rise with inflation) so that current
   earnings may be projected in approximately real terms, no such escalator
   attaches to interest on debt. Thus lenders are likely to increase the contractual
   interest rate to compensate for any expected inflation.

Our discussions of market behaviour will be in terms of *expected real* interest
rates: thus the estimated interest rate elements attached in 2. and 3. have been
deducted and similarly the equity rate of return is in expected real terms (as was
implied in the preceding section). The *risk* premiums attaching to the rates of return
to compensate for uncertainty remain.

In practical terms disentangling the expected real rate would be no easy task; for
example, in a period of considerable uncertainty over future inflation the required
interest rates might conceivably be higher than equity rates not only in money
terms but also in real terms – if inflation effects gave anticipated interest (in real
terms) a greater dispersion than equity returns. This awkward possibility will be
conveniently ignored.

(a) Operating and financial leverage

A firm can obtain the use of many assets in two alternative ways: by hiring or by
purchasing. Hiring entails an obligation to pay certain amounts for the use of

assets, and can involve varying degrees of commitment on the part of the firm and the asset's owner. Since our focus is on the long-term we shall assume hiring under leasing contracts.

Purchase can be financed either by borrowing or by equity capital (retentions or new shares). Borrowing entails an obligation to pay certain amounts for the use of funds, and can involve varying degrees of commitment on the part of the firm and the lenders. Thus there are substantial similarities between leasing and borrowing, and the firm has a three-way choice between leasing, borrowing and equity financing.

In the business situation in which profits are uncertain the effect of obtaining assets by commitment to pay a fixed amount instead of through a (variable) obligation to equity shareholders is to increase the dispersion of rates of return to existing shareholders. This effect is usually termed gearing in Britain and leverage in North America; we shall adopt the latter term since it has wider currency.

The increase of variability of shareholder returns through a hiring commitment is termed operating leverage and via borrowing is termed financial leverage. The terms gearing or leverage in isolation normally refer to financial leverage: in this context the usual measure of leverage is the debt/equity ratio.

The effects of operating and financial leverage are illustrated by use of a simple profit–volume graph in the following example.

An example

Three new companies, X, Y, and Z were formed with initially identical ordinary share capital. They are about to commence manufacturing operations, which are identical in all respects except for the method to be used to acquire a particular asset.

Common data for each of the three firms are:

Full capacity sales	£30 000 per year
Fixed operating costs	£8 000 per year
Variable profit ratio	50 per cent.

The above data are certain; the demand is uncertain, but with expected sales value of £24 000 (i.e. expected profit is £4 000).

Each firm must acquire an identical asset with the conveniently static characteristics of being non-depreciable (or appreciable), non-realizable and not subject to repair or maintenance. No tax considerations are involved in the means of acquiring the assets.*

---

*The implausibility of these assumptions indicate that lease/buy and debt/equity decisions are much more complex than this example might imply: only the latter over-simplification will be mitigated later.

X   rents its asset for £1 000 per year on an indefinite lease

Y   purchases its asset for £20 000 by issuing 5 per cent irredeemable debentures

Z   purchases its asset for £20 000, obtaining that sum by the issue of further equity shares equal in number to those held by the original shareholders.

The profit available for distribution to the shareholders of both X and Y will be given by [0·5 (£ sales) −£8 000 −£1 000] and the slice of profit available for original shareholders in Z is $\frac{1}{2}$ [0·5 (£ sales) −£8 000]. The potential range of profit for shareholders in the three companies is shown in Figure 20.2.

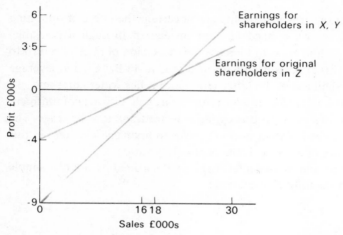

Figure 20.2 Profit–volume graph for leverage

Thus the position of X and Y is essentially similar: X has opted for an additional fixed element in its operating costs while Y has opted for a fixed element in its financial costs. This illustrates the danger of assuming that firms facing the same business environment are necessarily equally 'risky' (in the same risk class) *before financial leverage* is added.

The shareholders of Z have sacrificed a variable slice of their earnings: their expected returns will be lower than the return to shareholders in X and Y (£2 000 as against £3000) but their earnings are relatively more secure. Although at, say, £28 000 sales they would have an earnings slice of only £3 000 compared with £5 000 for the levered companies, they would obtain £500 at sales of £18 000 while the levered shareholders earned nothing.

(b) The debt/equity controversy

The determination of the debt/equity mix poses a similar problem to that of dividend policy: is there an optimal debt/equity mix which will maximize the value of the firms and consequently minimize cost of capital? In the traditional view there is; this suggests that for moderate degrees of leverage debt is 'cheap' relative to equity financing, perhaps because very many investors (e.g. financial institutions) have to buy low-risk investments and therefore pay a superpremium for safety which is not eliminated in imperfect markets.* The result is a U-shaped average cost of capital curve which offers a minimum cost of financing. This view is illustrated in Figure 20.3, where k is the (expected) rate of return required by shareholders, i is the (expected) interest rate required by lenders to the company, ρ is the average cost of capital and B/E is the debt/equity ratio which measures leverage (given by borrowing B divided by equity E). For the present discussion debt and equity are, of course, being considered as market values not book values. At the higher levels of B/E in Figure 20.3 (and Figure 20.4 considered below) the curves for k and i are broken to indicate that we shall defer the problem of highly levered companies. Note that $k > \rho > i$ in conformity with the usual assumptions about the behaviour of required market rates of return under uncertainty.

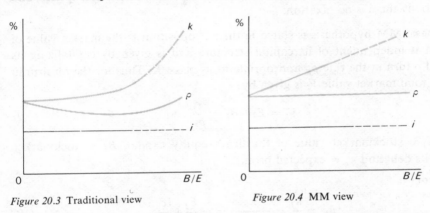

Figure 20.3 Traditional view   *Figure 20.4* MM view

The opposing view, again strongly represented by MM,† is that (in the absence of taxation) cost of capital is a constant, equal to the rate of return required by investors in a corresponding unlevered firm: the firm cannot alter this cost merely by splitting the firm's earnings between different classes of investor. Thus the rate of return required by shareholders from their uncertain slice of residual profits will change with increasing leverage to precisely offset the effect of greater debt. The corresponding curves for k, ρ and i are shown in Figure 20.4.

(i) *The* MM *hypothesis*
The MM assumptions which support development of their basic hypothesis‡ are summarized below:

*The superpremium argument is advanced by Durand [8].
† [20]; see also [21], [22], [24], [25], [26].
‡ In [20].

1. Assets used by firms yield an uncertain stream of profits extending indefinitely into the future. It is assumed that the average profit (before interest) per time period, π_R, is a finite random variable subject to a (subjective) probability distribution. Although investors may have different views as to the shape of the probability distributions it is assumed that they are all in agreement as to *expected* profits, which can be expressed as a constant (annual) amount $\pi = E(\pi_R)$. The expected rate of return of a share is π divided by the market value of the issued shares.

2. Firms are divided into 'equivalent return' classes which are homogeneous so that the shares of the different firms in each class are perfect substitutes for each other. This means that each firm within a class would have the same $\rho = k$ in the absence of leverage.

3. Shares and debt are traded in perfect markets, all debts of firms or individuals carry the same certain rate of interest i (which implies no bankruptcies) and initially there is no taxation.

The basic MM hypothesis is stated in their Proposition I: the market value of any firm is independent of its capital structure and is given by capitalizing its expected return at the rate ρ_K appropriate to its class, K. Thus for the jth firm in class K, total market value V_j is given by:

$$V_j = E_j + B_j = \frac{\pi_j}{\rho_K} \qquad (9)$$

where E_j = stockmarket value of the firm's equity capital, B_j = stockmarket value of its debt and π_j = expected profits.

Thus from (9),

$$\rho_K = \frac{\pi_j}{V_j} = \frac{\pi_j}{E_j + B_j} = \frac{k_j E_j}{V_j} + \frac{i B_j}{V_j}, \qquad (10)$$

where k_j is the expected yield on equity shares in the firm.

From the above follows Proposition II, hypothesizing that the required rate of return on equity will be equal to the capitalization rate for a *pure* equity stream *plus* a risk premium which will precisely compensate for the financial risk introduced by leverage, in contrast to the traditional view of under-compensation for moderate leverage.

By definition:

$$k_j = \frac{\pi_j - i B_j}{E_j}, \qquad (11)$$

and from (9);

$$\pi_j = \rho_K (E_j + B_j). \qquad (12)$$

Substituting for π in (11) gives Proposition II:

$$k_j = \rho_K + (\rho_K - i)\frac{B_j}{E_j}. \tag{13}$$

MM prove that if Proposition I (and therefore II) does not hold under the assumed conditions 'arbitrage'* will take place to restore the stated equalities. Their proof is given in algebraic terms in Table 20.1 with a corresponding numerical illustration for companies Y and Z considered earlier. The initial figures are based on an assumption that the total equity slice of expected profits for levered Y (£3 000) and unlevered Z (£4 000) are both capitalized at the same rate $k = 0.10$, which would be consistent with an extreme traditional hypothesis that moderate leverage does not affect k.

Table 20.1 The MM 'arbitrage' proof

Two companies in the same equivalent return class		Y	Z
		£	£
Total expected return identical for both companies	π	4 000	4 000
Y has some debt	B	20 000	
Z wholly equity financed	E	30 000	40 000
Market value of levered firm greater than unlevered	V	50 000	40 000
Firms and individuals borrow at same interest rate	i	0·05	0·05

A shareholder in Y can increase his return (without change of risk) by switching to Z and adopting home-made leverage:

Shareholder holds a fraction of the total shares of Y...............	α	0·01	
*earning a return	$R_Y = \alpha(\pi - iB_Y)$	30	
He sells his shares for..	αE_Y	300	
and borrows..	αB_Y	200	
using both sums to purchase shares in Z, obtaining a fraction	$\dfrac{\alpha(E_Y + B_Y)}{E_Z}$		$\dfrac{500}{40\,000}$
of the shares and earnings of company Z			
After allowing for interest payments on personal borrowing his return on the new portfolio is...	$R_Z = \dfrac{\alpha(E_Y + B_Y)}{E_Z}\pi - i\alpha B_Y$		
*	$= \dfrac{\alpha V_Y}{E_Z}\pi - i\alpha B_Y$		40

Comparing the returns (asterisked) before and after the arbitrage it can be seen that the original $V_Y > V_Z$ must give $R_Z > R_Y$: thus it pays owners of Y's shares to sell, depressing E_Y and V_Y, and to buy shares in Z which raises $E_Z(= V_Z)$.

---

*MM's use of the term has been criticized for contravening normal usage: switching would be more accurate. See [10].

The assumptions of the MM proof have been subject to considerable questioning.* Some of the more important limitations are that the proof depends on the existence of 'equivalent return classes', may imply objective rather than subjective probability distributions for possible outcomes and adopts partial rather than general equilibrium analysis. Further, it is not evident that the proof can apply in the real world of imperfect markets where there are disparities between the borrowing powers and interest rates for firms and individuals, and both firms and individuals can go bankrupt. Stiglitz [33] has shown that the MM hypothesis can hold in a general equilibrium context without the assumptions of equivalent return classes (or risk classes), perfect capital markets or the agreement between individuals of the probability distribution of outcomes. More intractable are the assumptions that individuals can borrow as easily and cheaply as firms and that there are no bankruptcies, but even here Stiglitz showed the MM propositions could hold hold with the aid of some assumptions about short selling and margin trading.

(ii) Taxation

The tax effects of debt in a company's financial structure are less controversial.† Interest is deductible in the calculation of profit for corporation tax purposes, but in most countries dividends are not. In a 'classical' corporation tax system‡ profits before dividends and retentions bear corporation tax in full whereas interest is deductible *before* calculating the corporation tax burden. Thus with a 50 per cent corporation tax rate, gross company earnings of £200 could provide £100 for equity shareholders or £200 for debt holders; debt is cheaper by reason of the tax effect. The same basis for calculating corporation tax applies in an 'imputation' system but the personal taxation on dividends which a company withholds as agent for the tax authorities is offset against the corporation tax liability: thus on dividends, as compared with interest payments, the firm bears the residual between the corporation tax rate and the withholding tax rate. Consequently debt is cheapened by the excess of the corporation tax rate over the withholding tax (if equity value is given by an infinite dividend stream).

The effect of tax on debt financing is considered by MM [24] in a correction to their original leverage paper, of which certain rudiments will be used here. The same meaning will be attached to π, i and B as before; note that π represents expected *pre-tax* earnings, and i is still assumed constant irrespective of leverage.

---

*See e.g. [10], [32], pp. 102–04, [35].

† But see [6], [22].

‡ The 'classical' system applies in the USA and several European countries, the imputation system in Britain (from 1973) and France. Canada has a modified imputation system: the individual shareholder obtains a dividend credit against personal taxation (from 1 January 1972 the shareholder gets $33\frac{1}{3}$ per cent dividend credit, but calculates his tax on four-thirds of the dividend); income earned from investment by a private (not a public) company is taxed at the full rate and there is a refund of 25 percentage points to the extent that this income is distributed.

The following notation will be added:

τ_c corporation tax rate

τ_r residual corporation tax rate (for classical system $= \tau_c$; for imputation system $= \tau_c -$ withholding tax rate)

π^τ expected earnings after tax burden on company

ρ^τ the rate at which investors in an unlevered company capitalize expected after tax earnings (for the 'equivalent return class' under consideration)

V_L market value of a levered company under corporation tax

For the levered firm:

$$\pi^\tau = \pi(1 - \tau_c) - iB(1 - \tau_r) + iB.$$

Since the net of tax income $\pi(1 - \tau_c)$ for an unlevered firm will be capitalized at ρ^τ and it can be assumed that the interest elements will be capitalized at i, the market value of the levered firm is given by:

$$V_L = \frac{\pi(1 - \tau_c)}{\rho^\tau} + B\tau_r.$$

Thus debt financing increases the value of the firm by an amount equal to the debt issued times the (residual) corporation tax rate. It might appear that if taxation were the only element making for an optimal leverage policy, value would be maximized by an all debt capital structure!

(iii) *Interest rates*

What happens to k and ρ if the interest rate on debt is not a constant over all levels of leverage, but lenders demand higher interest rates from highly levered firms? To quote MM 'economic theory and market experience both suggest that the yields demanded by lenders tend to increase with the debt-equity ratio of the borrowing firm'.* Remember that *expected* yields are at issue, which will be lower than observable rates when there is some probability of default. However, rising interest rates would be consistent with the usual assumptions of risk aversion by investors.

Since the MM hypothesis makes ρ a constant, increasing interest rates must have an offsetting effect on k, which may go so far as to cause k to decline in the manner envisaged by MM in Figure 20.5. This shape of the k curve is unconvincing;† it suggests that at some stage in the leverage spectrum investors are willing to *give*

* [20], p. 273.
† See [6], [27], [31]. Robichek and Myers [27] (pp. 48–49) show that when debt is being substituted for equity a declining k is conditional on the marginal rate of interest $i' > k$. Solomon [31] shows that under the different assumption of adding debt to a given amount of equity the condition for k to decline is $i' > \rho$. Thus incremental debt *with prior claims to earnings* would yield more than subordinated equity (substitution) or a pure equity stream (addition).

premiums for risk whereas previously the market *demanded* premiums for risk, and conflicts with the capital market line analysis mentioned in section 1. In fact MM appear to suggest that leverage is unlikely to go so far as to produce a falling k, since they refer to the point as 'of no practical consequence'.*

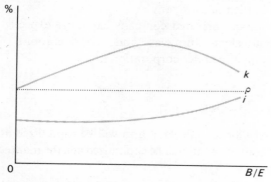

Figure 20.5 MM hypothesis with increasing interest rate

A suggestion by Robichek and Myers [27] provides an alternative explanation of the upper end of the leverage scale. As leverage increases investors may reduce their estimates of π, because an increasing debt burden can lead to interruptions to the firm's planned investment. In perfect markets mandatory interest payments would not cause the firm to reject profitable investment – fresh capital could be raised; but in imperfect markets highly levered companies with poor operating results have difficulty in capital raising. The average cost of capital would increase at high leverage levels, but in a way which is consistent with the basic MM thesis – *through reduction of the expected earnings stream*, not by the mere division of the stream between different claimants.

(iv) *Some conclusions*

The Robichek and Myers suggestion for the behaviour of cost of capital with high leverage would rescue the MM thesis from the paradoxical optimality of the all debt firm under taxation. The tax advantages of debt would induce a firm to increase leverage to the point at which the anticipated 'interruption' effect of further leverage on the cost of capital (via expected earnings) offsets the incremental tax benefits. Thus the cost of capital would have a U-shaped curve, in conformity with the traditional view. However, the reasons for optimality would be substantially different from those of the traditional theory and the analysis does provide an explicit framework within which to approach the debt/equity decision.

The basic difference between the MM theory and the traditional view of the inherent cheapness of debt remains. The problems of empirical proof are enormous.

*[22], p. 524.

A fundamental difficulty is that the whole question of the cost of capital is concerned with expectations of returns required by investors and of the earnings of firms – which do not lend themselves readily to analysis from observed data. Despite a number of studies* the empirical issue is unresolved, although the weight of theoretical analysis rests with the MM thesis and its developments.

20.4 Cost of capital implications

Much discussion of optimal financing decisions is concerned with an associated aim of determining the cost of capital for investment decision making. At its strongest this viewpoint is expressed by MM:

> ... the cut-off point for investment in the firm will in all cases be ρ_k [the cost of capital for the firm's 'equivalent return' class].†

Some limitations of such an approach were considered earlier (in section 4(d) of Chapter 11). Even with perfect capital markets a new investment could change the riskiness of the future earnings stream and put the firm into a different risk class *after* the investment is undertaken – so that current ρ would be irrelevant for the decision. Although a cut-off rate can be roughly adjusted for the risks of different investment decisions, the explicit consideration of subjective probability distributions (considered in section 3) provides a superior approach, certainly for significant investment projects.

This does not mean that the financing decision is devalued in importance, or that financing is divorced from investment.‡ It means that an estimate of the current, risk adjusted, average cost of capital provides no simple solution for the consideration of the risk (and with imperfect markets, the utility) aspects of investment decision-making.

The choice of financing is, of course, undertaken in terms of conventional rates, although it has been seen that the disentangling of expected rates from observed rates is in itself no easy task. An alternative expression of market value relationships can be reconciled with the use of default-free rates in investment decision-making. This method is considered by Bierman and Smidt;§ they term it a risk-premium approach, as against the conventional 'risk-discount' approach.

---

*For a review of empirical work see [19], pp. 441–52. Studies bearing on debt/equity (and in many cases dividend policy) are contained in [2], [7], [20], [25], [35]. A study of share prices which goes direct to expectations (of investment advisers) appears in [18].

†[20], p. 288; but see a verbal comment by Miller in the discussion in [3], p. 51: 'No one has suggested that you use our concept of cost of capital to discount nonstandard items or additions to assets that will change the nature of your asset mix.'

‡For an examination of the problems of the interrelationships of market valuation and capital budgeting see [15].

§[4], pp. 170–76.

Assume that the observed market values for company Y considered in section 3 were in fact £30 000 for equity and £20 000 for debt, and that estimates have been made for $k = 0{\cdot}10$ and $i = 0{\cdot}05$. The risk-discount approach calculates an average cost of capital by weighting each rate according to the proportions of equity and debt in total capital thus:

	Market value £	Weight w	Rates on equity and debt	Weighted average
Equity	30 000	0·6	$k = 0{\cdot}10$	$kw_E = 0{\cdot}06$
Debt	20 000	0·4	$i = 0{\cdot}05$	$iw_B = 0{\cdot}02$
	£50 000			0·08

Here the cost of capital is 0·08. This is commonly termed the *weighted average cost of capital*; the concept is not different from that adopted in this chapter so far. But some warnings are necessary. The weighted average is sometimes calculated on book values of equity and debt: given the lack of any relationship between market yields and book values such an exercise would be futile. The weighted average, on market values, can be used to examine the effects of financing by, say, an increase in debt: the effect of associated changes in earnings expectations must be considered *and* assumptions about changes in k with risk must be imported. Even if the MM hypothesis is not accepted, the traditional view would contemplate *some* increase in k with increasing debt, certainly at moderate debt levels.

The risk-premium approach again uses observed market values for debt and equity, but discounts expected cash flows at the default-free rate of interest. The expected cash flows are management's expectations in this case: management does not need to rely on the projection of a single earnings figure. Assume the previously adopted expected total earnings stream of £4 000 per year in perpetuity for Y. Of this the interest commitment to lenders was £1 000: the residual goes to shareholders. The streams (in perpetuity), discounted at an assumed default-free discount rate of 0·04, produce the present values of £75 000 and £25 000 shown below. The difference from market value represents a management estimation of the risk-premiums.

	Market value £	Present value of expected cash flows (here = earnings in perpetuity) £	Risk premium £
Equity	30 000	75 000	45 000
Debt	20 000	25 000	5 000
	£50 000	£100 000	£50 000

Financing could be considered in such a framework: for example, the effect of a proposal to issue incremental debt could be examined in terms of the anticipated risk premium rather than in terms of rates of return. Of course it must be remembered that management would be working outwards towards an estimate of market values. Assumptions about the reactions of the market must be inherent in both approaches.

Bibliographical references

[1] Archer, S. H. and C. A. D'Ambrosio, eds., *The Theory of Business Finance*, Macmillan, New York, 1967.

[2] Barges, A., *The Effect of Capital Structure on the Cost of Capital*, Prentice-Hall, 1963.

[3] Bierman, H., Capital structure and financial decisions, in *Financial Research and Management Decisions*, ed. A. A. Robichek, Wiley, 1967.

[4] Bierman, H. and S. Smidt, *The Capital Budgeting Decision*, Macmillan, New York, 1971.

[5] Bierman, H., *Financial Policy Decisions*, Macmillan, New York, 1970.

[6] Brewer, D. E. and J. B. Michaelson, The cost of capital, corporation finance and the theory of investment: Comment, *American Economic Review*, June 1965, pp. 516–24; reprinted in [1].

[7] Brigham, E. F. and M. J. Gordon, Leverage, dividend policy and the cost of capital, *Journal of Finance*, March 1968, pp. 85–104.

[8] Durand, D., Costs of debt and equity funds for business: Trends and problems of measurement, *Conference on Research in Business Finance*, pp. 215–54, National Bureau of Economic Research, 1952; reprinted in [1] and [30].

[9] Durand, D., *Bank Stock prices and the Bank Capital Problem*, Occasional Paper No. 54, National Bureau of Economic Research, 1957.

[10] Durand, D., The cost of capital, corporation finance, and the theory of investment: Comment, *American Economic Review*, September 1959, pp. 639–55; reprinted in [1].

[11] Friend, I. and M. Puckett, Dividends and stock prices, *American Economic Review*, September 1964, pp. 656–82.

[12] Gordon, M. J. and E. Shapiro, Capital equipment analysis: The required rate of profit, *Management Science*, October 1956, pp. 102–10; reprinted in [30].

[13] Gordon, M. J., *The Investment, Financing and Valuation of the Corporation*, Irwin, 1962.

[14] Hirshleifer, J., *Investment, Interest and Capital*, Prentice-Hall, 1970.

[15] Lerner, E. M. and W. T. Carleton, The integration of capital budgeting and stock valuation, *American Economic Review*, September 1964, pp. 683–702; reprinted in [1].

[16] Lerner, E. M. and W. T. Carleton, *A Theory of Financial Analysis*, Harcourt, Brace and World, 1966.

[17] Lintner, J., Distribution of incomes of corporations among dividends, retained earnings and taxes, *American Economic Review*, May 1956, pp. 97–113.

[18] Malkiel, B. G. and J. G. Cragg, Expectations and the structure of share prices, *American Economic Review*, September 1970, pp. 601–17.

[19] Mao, J. C. T., *Quantitative Analysis for Financial Decisions*, Macmillan, New York, 1969.

[20] Modigliani, F. and M. H. Miller, The cost of capital, corporation finance and the theory of investment, *American Economic Review*, June 1958, pp. 261–97; reprinted in [1].

[21] Modigliani, F. and M. H. Miller, The cost of capital, corporation finance and the theory of investment: Reply, *American Economic Review*, September 1959, pp. 655–69; reprinted in [1].

[22] Modigliani, F. and M. H. Miller, The cost of capital, corporation finance and the theory of investment: Reply, *American Economic Review*, June 1965, pp. 524–27; reprinted in [1].

[23] Modigliani, F. and M. H. Miller, Dividend policy, growth, and the valuation of shares, *Journal of Business*, October 1961, pp. 411–33, reprinted in [1].

[24] Modigliani, F. and M. H. Miller, Corporation income taxes and the cost of capital: A correction, *American Economic Review*, June 1963, pp. 433–43; reprinted in [1].

[25] Modigliani, F. and M. H. Miller, Some estimates of the cost of capital to the electric utility industry, 1954–57, *American Economic Review*, June 1966, pp. 333–91.

[26] Modigliani, F. and M. H. Miller, Reply to Heins and Sprenkle, *American Economic Review*, September 1969, pp. 592–95.

[27] Robichek, A. A. and S. C. Myers, *Optimal Financing Decisions*, Prentice-Hall, 1965.

[28] Schwartz, E., Theory of the capital structure of the firm, *Journal of Finance*, March 1959, pp. 18–39; reprinted in [1].

[29] Sharpe, W. F., Capital asset prices: A theory of market equilibrium under conditions of risk, *Journal of Finance*, September 1964, pp. 425–42; reprinted in [1].

[30] Solomon, E., ed., *The Management of Corporate Capital*, Free Press of Glencoe, 1959.

[31] Solomon, E., Leverage and the cost of capital, *Journal of Finance*, May 1963, pp. 273–79; reprinted in [1].

[32] Solomon, E., *The Theory of Financial Management*, Columbia University Press, 1963.

[33] Stiglitz, J. E., A re-examination of the Modigliani–Miller theorem, *American Economic Review*, December 1969, pp. 784–93.

[34] Walter, J. E., *Dividend policy and enterprise valuation*, Wadsworth, 1967.

[35] Weston, J. F., A test of cost of capital propositions, *The Southern Economic Journal*, October 1963, pp. 105–12; reprinted in [1].

Problems

20.1 Obtain published financial data and current share prices for three companies in a single industry. Use the basic Gordon–Shapiro model for share price to analyse the component elements which determine share price. What problems do you encounter?

20.2 Discuss the following quotation:

> 'If the steel industry is nationalized we do not know the terms under which this might be brought about, but it might not be out of place to give some figures of the value of the company's shares based on differing methods of valuation. These have been as follows:
>
> | | |
> |---|---|
> | Stock market valuation | £2·35 |
> | Dividend yield basis | £2·85 |
> | Balance sheet value | £2·25 |
> | Current replacement cost | £3·70 |
> | Capitalization of earnings | £3·45 |
>
> 'From the above it would seem that any figure of less than, say, £3 could only be described as unfair expropriation.'
>
> Chairman's annual statement, The United Steel Companies Ltd., 1964.
> [Prices have been amended to decimal currency.]

20.3 Growth Ltd. has an issued share capital of 10m. shares, nominal value 50 pence each. The market price of the shares has been steady at £2·70 per share for some time.

The company plans the following transactions:

1. An expansion programme to exploit a particularly favourable investment opportunity. £6m. will be required, which Growth intends to raise by a rights issue to shareholders at £1 per share. Growth estimates that the programme will augment the firm's market value by £8m. (before deducting the £6m. outlay).

2. The takeover of Plum Ltd. for £4·5m., to be satisfied by the issue of shares in Growth Ltd. The directors of Plum will recommend their shareholders to accept the offer. Growth's directors estimate that the acquisition will augment the market value of Growth by £5·5m. (before deducting the £4·5m. outlay).

No hint of either proposal has yet affected the market. It is intended to announce the impending rights issue a few days before the takeover bid, although the rights issue will be made *after* the takeover has been completed.

The appropriate valuation of Growth's shares in the offer to the shareholders of Plum is under consideration, and the following suggestions have been made:

1. The rights price of £1.
2. The current market price of £2·70.
3. The current market price of £2·70 less a discount of 10 per cent, as the increased issue of shares will reduce the market price.

Comment on the above suggestions, and develop your own estimate of the valuation (and therefore the number) of Growth's shares to be offered in the takeover bid. What principles are involved? Do you consider that Growth should defer the announcement of the impending rights issue until after the takeover has been completed?

20.4 The directors of PPP Ltd. are meeting in July 19–6 to consider the declaration of an interim dividend for the current half-year. They have been presented with accounting data which show:

| | Year to 31 December 19–6 | |
	First half (actual) £ m	Second half (expected) £ m
Net profit before tax	8·8	8·3
Corporation tax	2·9	2·8
Net profit after tax	5·9	5·5

PPP undertakes papermaking, printing and publishing. The profit reduction in 19–6 has been occasioned partly by a general economic downturn and partly by the reorganization of the company's papermaking plants. By early 19–7 the company will have completed the reorganization of its plants; trading conditions are expected to improve towards the end of that year.

The proposal before the directors is that an interim dividend of $3\frac{1}{2}$ per cent should be paid on the ordinary shares, with the intention of paying a final dividend of 5 per cent. The corresponding dividends in 19–5 were 4 per cent and 6 per cent. Some directors are worried about the effect of the dividend on the company's share price.

Give your views on the proposed dividend cut. The data below may be relevant.

	19–1	19–2	19–3	19–4	19–5
Average price of £1 ordinary share in PPP	£1·88	£1·20	£3·00	£2·70	£2·10
			Percentages		
Ordinary dividends as % of distributable profit (after tax and preference dividends)	35·4	42·7	51·0	38·8	52·4
Ordinary dividends as % of ordinary share capital	7·5	6·0	7·25	9·4	10·0
Average dividend yield on PPP's shares	4·0	5·0	2·4	3·5	4·8
Average dividend yield on quoted industrial shares	6·0	6·0	4·5	5·0	5·5
			£ m		
Net profit before tax	15·3	13·2	13·4	21·3	22·6
Net profit after tax	10·2	7·5	7·6	14·2	15·1
Ordinary dividends	3·6	3·2	3·9	5·5	7·9
Equity (ordinary share capital plus reserves)	115·4	122·7	126·3	143·3	150·0

Balance sheet of PPP Ltd. at 31 December 19–5

	£ m		£ m
Preference shares	17·5	Fixed assets	105·7
Ordinary shares	79·0	Current assets:	
Reserves	71·0	inventories	44·4
		debtors	28·3
	167·5	cash and near-cash	23·0
Corporation tax	7·5		95·7
Current liabilities (including final dividend)	26·4		
	201·4		201·4

(PPP was established many years before 19–1. There have not been any significant changes in market prices or financial structure since 19–5.)

20.5 Sharp is an enterprising student at the University of Erewhon. He has secured from the university authorities a sole franchise to instal a coffee machine in a university building.

The conditions of the franchise are that Sharp must provide the coffee machine for 50 months, pay the university £2 per month (for the use of electricity, water and floorspace) and charge a constant price of £0·03 per cup for the entire period.

Sharp has made two other contracts:

1. With Instafresh Ltd., who will supply plastic cups and ingredients at a constant price of £0·01 throughout the 50 months.
2. With Blunt, a slot machine servicer, who will service, maintain and replenish the machine at a constant wage of £8 per month throughout the 50 months. Blunt will make all necessary payments, paying to or from a separate business bank account at the end of each month, so that Sharp will have no responsibilities regarding the operation of the machines.

So far Sharp's outlay in organizing the venture has been negligible.

Sharp has two possible ways of acquiring the coffee machine (same model, and Blunt's duties unchanged in either case):

I. By renting the machine from Instafresh Ltd., at a constant rental of £7 per month throughout the 50 months. Payments would commence at the end of the first month.
II. By purchasing the machine from Instafresh Ltd. for £235. The machine can be assumed to have a physical life of exactly 50 months (with no repair costs apart from those covered by the agreement with Blunt) and a nil scrap value.

Sharp does not have funds currently available for purchase, but Rich (a fellow student) is prepared to do either of the following:

(i) Lend £235 to Sharp, at interest of 1 per cent per month. Sharp would pay Rich a constant amount at the end of each month, sufficient to redeem the debt and interest precisely within the 50 months.

(ii) Provide £235 capital for a partnership with Sharp. Rich is indifferent to risk, in the sense that he is prepared to accept an expected return of 1 per cent per month regardless of the dispersion of the return.

Sharp and Rich are agreed in their expectation that the sales from the machine may range from 400 to 1 400 cups per month, with equal probability for all sales within that range (i.e. the probability distribution is rectangular).

There is no taxation in Erewhon, no price changes occur, and performance of the contracts mentioned above is certain. Sharp could satisfy any losses he may incur but he would prefer to arrange matters so as to minimize his liability for such losses.

Assume that *no depreciation* is deducted in the calculation of profit and that all profit is withdrawn by the owner/s of the business each month.

Required:

(a) A break-even graph for the venture and Sharp's income-volume graph, illustrating the effects of the three possible methods of financing (in monthly terms).

(b) Calculation of the appropriate profit sharing ratio for the partnership mooted under II(ii).

(c) Conventional opening balance sheets under options II(i) and II(ii). Assume that capital will be owned in profit sharing ratios, along the lines of a limited company.

(d) Discuss the implications of your analysis.

Calculate to nearest £.

1 per cent interest table:

n	$(1+i)^n$	v^n	$a_{\overline{n}\rvert}$	$s_{\overline{n}\rvert}$
50	1·64	0·61	39·2	64·46

20.6 Data for Gear Ltd. are shown below:

	£
Market value of:	
equity	8 000
debt	8 000
	£16 000
Expected earnings before interest	£1 600
Interest payable on debt	£640

Gear intends to make an investment of £2 000, raising the required finance by a debt issue. Assume that the risk class of the company remains unchanged, the new lenders require the same return as the average rate on the existing debt and investors share the company's expectations that gross earnings will be raised by £200 per year. Ignore taxation and adopt the Modigliani–Miller assumptions.

Required:

(a) Calculate the rate of return required by the ordinary shareholders before and after the debt issue.

(b) Assume that the new investment puts Gear into a new risk class. Lenders for the new debt will require 8·5 per cent interest (original lenders unchanged) and shareholders will require a rate of return of 13·5 per cent. What is the new weighted average cost of capital if Gear raises £2 000 debt? What must the incremental expected gross earnings of the company be if the value of the firm is to remain the same as in part (a)?

(c) The original earnings and interest were given before tax. Assume that Gear bears a corporation tax of 25 per cent on earnings net of interest, under a classical corporation tax system. If the £2 000 debt issue raises expected gross earnings by £200 per year, risk class and interest rates remaining as in the original data, what happens to the value of the firm and the value of the equity?

Appendices

Appendix A

Interest

1. Many accounting texts discuss present value and nothing more. While this may be all that is required for many investment decision calculations, in other decision calculations it is not. The treatment of the mathematics of interest provided here should be adequate for most problems likely to be encountered. The reader with no previous exposure to the subject is recommended to work out the problems provided in order to make sure he understands the main ideas.

The following standard actuarial symbols will be used: i, $i^{(m)}$, v, δ, d, $d^{(m)}$, δ'; $s_{\overline{n}|}$, $a_{\overline{n}|}$, a_∞, $s_{\overline{n}|}^{-1}$, $a_{\overline{n}|}^{-1}$. They will be defined as we proceed. Throughout, interest is referred to as a rate per period (discrete case) or as a rate (continuous case), not as a rate per cent. Thus a rate of interest of 5 per cent will be written as 0·05.

(a) Discrete interest calculations

In most cases in practice interest is calculated at discrete intervals of time, e.g. yearly, half-yearly or quarterly. For generality we therefore use the word 'period' rather than 'year'.

(i) *Single payments*

If we are concerned with a single sum of money we may wish to know how much it will accumulate to at interest over a number of periods, or alternatively how much a future sum is worth now. We use the term '*amount*' to denote the result of the first calculation and '*present value*' to signify the second.

Amount We define i as the *effective rate of interest per period*, the rate which is actually operating on the sum.

$£1$ at interest for one period will amount to $(1+i)$

" " " " two periods " " " $(1+i)+i(1+i) = (1+i)^2$

" " " " n periods " " " $(1+i)^n$;

and the amount of $£P$ at i per period for n periods is $P(1+i)^n$. There are tables of $(1+i)^n$ for a range of values of i and n.

Present value It follows that if $£1$ amounts to $(1+i)$ in one period, the present value of $(1+i)$ due in one period's time is 1. By simple proportion the present value of $£1$ due in one period's time is $1/(1+i)$. This is denoted by the symbol v. Similarly the present value of $£P$ due n periods hence is $P/(1+i)^n = Pv^n$. Tables of v^n are available. (Anticipating what follows, tables of d are not usually provided; d is most easily calculated as $1 - v$.)

Effective and nominal rates Interest is frequently quoted as an annual rate, compounded more than once a year, e.g. 4% per annum compounded quarterly. The 4% is here a rate in name only; it is known as a *nominal rate*. This is recognized by using the symbol $i^{(m)}$, where m is the number of compoundings per year; m is *not* an index. In the case mentioned the nominal rate is $0.04^{(4)}$.

To show that this is not an effective rate we note that if interest had been compounded once a year the amount at the end of the year would have been $(1 + i) = 1.04$. But if interest is compounded quarterly we have

$$(1 + i) = \left(1 + \frac{i^{(m)}}{m}\right)^m = (1.01)^4,$$

which works out at slightly more than 4% a year:

$$(1.01)^4 - 1 = 0.0406.$$

Interest *calculations* are always made in terms of effective rates. The effective rate corresponding to 4% p.a. compounded quarterly is:

either (i) $\qquad (1.01)^4 - 1 = 0.0406 \; per \; annum \left[\left(1 + \frac{i^{(m)}}{m}\right)^m - 1\right]$

or (ii) $\qquad \left(1 + \frac{i^{(m)}}{m}\right) = (1 + i)^{1/m};$

$$(1 + i)^{1/4} = 1.01$$

i.e. the effective rate *per quarter* is 0.01 [i.e. $i^{(m)}/m$].

Simple interest The interest to which we have been referring is compound interest; and whenever 'interest' appears without qualification it means compound interest.

Simple interest is used as an approximation to true (compound) interest only for periods shorter than the period of compounding ($n < 1$). For such periods simple interest always exceeds compound interest; the two are equal when $n = 1$.

We are concerned, therefore, with an approximation to the value of

$(1 + i)^{1/n} - 1$

$$= \frac{i}{n} - \frac{(n-1)}{2!}\left(\frac{i}{n}\right)^2 + \frac{(n-1)(2n-1)}{3!}\left(\frac{i}{n}\right)^3 - \frac{(n-1)(2n-1)(3n-1)}{4!}\left(\frac{i}{n}\right)^4 + \ldots,$$

a rapidly converging series for all ordinary values of i.

At simple interest, 1 amounts in $1/n$ year at interest i per annum to

$$\begin{aligned} S &= \text{principal} + \text{interest} \\ &= \quad 1 \quad + \quad I, \end{aligned}$$

where
$$I = \text{principal} \times \text{rate} \times \text{time} = \frac{i}{n}.$$

That is, simple interest includes only the first term of the expression (binomial expansion) for compound interest.

Discount Interest and discount are separate but related, merely different ways of looking at the same thing. Interest is based on the principal (P above), while discount is based on the amount, which we will in this section denote by S. That is, the (average) rate of discount is $(S - P)/S$ and the rate of interest is $(S - P)/P$.

Corresponding to the treatment of interest, d is the effective rate of discount per period, and $d^{(m)}$ the nominal rate of discount payable m times a year. On a loan of £1, payment of i at the end of a period corresponds to payment of d at the beginning of the period. Hence

$$d(1 + i) = i, \quad \text{or} \quad i - d = id.$$

From this relation, putting $S = 1$ and $P = v$,

$$d = 1 - v = \frac{i}{(1 + i)} = iv = i(1 - d).$$

The present value of £1 due n periods hence is $(1 + i)^{-n}$ at an effective rate of interest i, or $(1 - d)^n$ at an effective rate of discount d. It will readily be seen that

$$(1 - d)^n = (1 + i)^{-n}.$$

Despite the above statement that interest is based on P and discount on S it should be noted that in most of the cases in which *discounting* is employed, and in particular in investment decision calculations, the 'discount rate' is in fact an interest rate; i.e. to discount for one period we multiply by $(1 + i)^{-1}$, not by $(1 - d)$. (If $i = 0.05$, $d = 0.0476$ approximately.) The reason for this is that the interest rate, i (and not d) has a definite economic meaning in the decision calculation. In fact discount rates as such are very seldom used outside of certain financial transactions such as discounting a bill of exchange.

The relations between i, v and d are displayed in the table below.

Value of	In terms of		
	i	d	v
i		$\dfrac{d}{1-d}$	$\dfrac{1-v}{v}$
d	$\dfrac{i}{1+i}$		$1-v$
v	$\dfrac{1}{1+i}$	$1-d$	

(ii) *Series of payments: annuities*

The term 'annuity' is used to describe a series of payments. The frequency of the payments need not be annual. We shall confine ourselves to *fixed annuities*, i.e. a uniform series of payments per period for a number of periods. Varying annuities are subject to the same general principles, but are more difficult to evaluate.

Annuities may be classified:

1. According to when they are payable:
   An *immediate* annuity is one which is payable at the end of each period;
   An *annuity-due* is payable at the start of each period, while
   A *deferred* annuity becomes an immediate annuity in k periods ($k = 1, 2, \ldots$).
2. According to their duration:
   An *annuity-certain* is a series of payments for a fixed number of periods. It may be of any of the types referred to in 1.
   A *contingent* annuity is one where the term depends on some uncertain event (an example is a whole life annuity).

As with single payments, so with an annuity we may wish to know its amount or present value.

Present value $= a_{\overline{n}|}$

Amount of an annuity Consider a series of payments of £1 per period for n periods at interest i. At the end of the nth period:

the payment just made is worth (in £s)	1
,, ,, made one period ago is worth	$(1+i)$
,, first payment, made $(n-1)$ periods ago, is worth	$(1+i)^{n-1}$.

The sum of this geometric series gives the amount of the annuity, $s_{\overline{n}|}$:

$$s_n = 1+(1+i)+(1+i)^2 + \ldots +(1+i)^{n-1}$$

$$= \frac{(1+i)^n - 1}{i}.$$

Tables of $s_{\overline{n}|}$ are available; alternatively, they may be constructed from the table of $(1+i)^n$ by continuous addition.

If the uniform periodical payments are of £x, the amount of the annuity at interest i is $xs_{\overline{n}|_i}$.

Present value of an annuity Considering the same series,

the present value of the first payment is v

" " " " " second " " v^2

" " " " " last " " v^n.

The sum of this geometric series gives the present value of the annuity, $a_{\overline{n}|}$:

$$a_n = v + v^2 + \ldots + v^n = \frac{1 - v^n}{i}.$$

Tables of $a_{\overline{n}|}$ are available; they can be constructed from the v^n table by continuous addition.

The present value of a series of payments of x per period for n periods at interest i is $xa_{\overline{n}|_i}$.

Special case: present value of a perpetuity A special case of more than passing interest concerns the present value of an infinite annuity, called a perpetuity, and denoted by a_∞. This is the limiting value of $a_{\overline{n}|}$ as $n \to \infty$:

$$\lim_{n \to \infty} a_{\overline{n}|} = \lim_{n \to \infty} \frac{1 - v^n}{i}$$

which, since $v < 1 = 1/i$.

Reciprocal functions of $s_{\overline{n}|}$ and $a_{\overline{n}|}$: individual annuity payments Alternatively, we may know the values of i, n and either $s_{\overline{n}|}$ or $a_{\overline{n}|}$ and wish to find the size of the individual payments. These are given by two reciprocal functions, $s_{\overline{n}|}^{-1}$ and $a_{\overline{n}|}^{-1}$, as shown below:

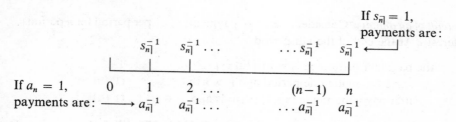

That is, if the amount of the annuity for n periods at interest i is £1, the uniform periodical payments are $s_{\overline{n}|}^{-1}$; and if the present value of the same annuity is £1, the uniform payments are $a_{\overline{n}|}^{-1}$. For an annuity whose amount (present value) is £x the individual payments are $xs_{\overline{n}|}^{-1}$ and $xa_{\overline{n}|}^{-1}$, respectively.

$s_{\overline{n}|}^{-1}$ is sometimes referred to as the sinking fund payment required to produce 1 in n periods. Tables are usually provided only for $a_{\overline{n}|}^{-1}$; $s_{\overline{n}|}^{-1}$ may be obtained from the relation $s_{\overline{n}|}^{-1} = a_{\overline{n}|}^{-1} - i$, which the reader may verify for himself from the formulae for $s_{\overline{n}|}$ and $a_{\overline{n}|}$. Neither of the reciprocal functions has been included in Appendix B.

Repayment of a loan Accountants may on occasion be concerned with loan repayments, and it may be useful to note that there is no essential difference between the purchase of an annuity and the making of a loan repayable by equal instalments of principal and interest. If A, a lender, makes a loan of X, repayable by equal instalments, R, of principal and interest over n years at interest i per annum, this is equivalent to A purchasing an n-year annuity of R per annum for a sum of X, the value of the annuity being calculated at the rate of interest charged on the loan.

We may thus calculate the equal instalments of principal and interest, the apportionment between principal and interest in each instalment, and the principal outstanding after payment of any instalment.

1. *The fixed instalment, R*

$$X = Ra_{\overline{n}|} \text{ at } i \text{ per period}$$

$$R = Xa_{\overline{n}|i}^{-1}$$

[$a_{\overline{n}|}^{-1}$, the annual instalment of principal and interest for n periods to repay a loan of £1, consists of the interest, i, on 1 plus the sinking fund payment, $s_{\overline{n}|}^{-1}$, required to repay 1 at the end of n periods.]

2. *Capital outstanding*
   To find how much of the principal is outstanding after the rth instalment has been paid:

$$(n-r) \text{ payments of } R \text{ remain to be paid;}$$

therefore the principal outstanding must be the present value of these payments, or $Ra_{\overline{n-r}|}$. Substituting for R from 1., this may be written

$$\frac{Xa_{\overline{n-r}|}}{a_{\overline{n}|}}.$$

3. *Apportionment of instalments*
   Again consider the rth instalment:

The interest due at the end of the rth period will be one period's interest on the capital outstanding at the beginning of the rth period, i.e. immediately after payment of the $(r-1)$th instalment.

The principal outstanding at the beginning of the rth period is the present value of $(n-r+1)$ instalments of R, or $Ra_{\overline{n-r+1}|}$. Therefore the interest in the rth instalment is $iRa_{\overline{n-r+1}|}$; and the principal in the rth instalment is

$$R - iRa_{\overline{n-r+1}|} = Rv^{n-r+1}.$$

Only one of these formulae is of course required.

643

(b) Notes on the use of interest tables

As already indicated, interest tables are available for use in discrete interest calculations for the functions $(1+i)^n$, v^n, $s_{\overline{n}|}$, $a_{\overline{n}|}$ and $a_{\overline{n}|}^{-1}$. Extracts of the first four are provided in Appendix B. It is important that the reader should understand what is and is not permissible in the use of these tables. This note is provided for that purpose.

1. Interest must be expressed in terms of an effective rate before the tables can be used.

2. The tables are constructed on the assumption that payment dates coincide with the dates at which interest is calculated, i.e. at the *end* of each period. If this is not so modification of the tabulated values becomes necessary. In the case of annuities this assumption means that the first payment is made at the end of one period. If this is not the case either the rate of interest must be changed to an equivalent rate compounded/discounted in agreement with the periodicity of the payments, or the payments must be changed to equivalent payments on the compounding dates (or we could write down the value of the typical payment and sum these values by ordinary algebra).

   The following are the corresponding relationships when payments are made at the beginning of each period:

End of period	*Beginning of period equivalent*
Payments of x per period	$x/(1+i) = xv$ per period
Amount of n payments of 1 per period $(s_{\overline{n}|})$	$s_{\overline{n}|}v$ or $(s_{\overline{n+1}|}-1)$
Present value of n payments of 1 per period $(a_{\overline{n}|})$	$a_{\overline{n}|}v$ or $(a_{\overline{n-1}|}+1)$
Uniform periodical payments for n periods whose amount is 1 $(s_{\overline{n}|}^{-1})$	$s_{\overline{n}|}^{-1}v$ or $(s_{\overline{n+1}|}-1)^{-1}$
Uniform periodical payments for n periods whose present value is 1 $(a_{\overline{n}|}^{-1})$	$a_{\overline{n}|}^{-1}v$ or $(1+a_{\overline{n-1}|})^{-1}$

3. *Values of i or n not given in tables*

   For *rates* not given in the tables, $(1+i)^n$ or v^n may be obtained by using logarithms, or the binomial theorem for a positive or negative integral index, respectively. Thus if 1 % tables were not available, the amount of 1 after three years at 4 % p.a. compounded quarterly could be found from:

$$(1+0\cdot01)^{12} = 1+12(0\cdot01)+\frac{12\times11}{2!}(0\cdot01)^2+\frac{12\times11\times10}{3!}(0\cdot01)^3+ \ldots$$

$$= 1+0\cdot12+0\cdot0066+0\cdot00022+0\cdot000005+ \ldots$$

$$= 1\cdot12683 \text{ approximately.}$$

The present value of 1 due in 10 periods' time at 0·8 per cent would be:

$$(1+0·008)^{-10} = 1 - 10(0·008) + \frac{10 \times 11}{2!}(0·008)^2 - \frac{10 \times 11 \times 12}{3!}(0·008)^3 + \ldots$$

$$= 0·92340 \text{ approximately.}$$

For *periods*, to obtain the value of $(1+i)^n$ or v^n when n (integral) lies beyond the range of the tables:

$$\left.\begin{array}{l} (1+i)^n = (1+i)^j(1+i)^k \\ v^n = v^j v^k \end{array}\right\} \quad \text{where } j+k = n.$$

j and k would be chosen for values which *are* tabulated.

[Simple interest is always used for broken periods (i.e. periods shorter than the period of compounding); e.g., the amount of 1 at 4% per annum for $10\frac{3}{4}$ years would be $(1·04)^{10}\{1+\frac{3}{4}(0·04)\}$.]

4. The interest tables may be entered backwards, as with tables of logarithms, to obtain i, v or n. Straight line interpolation is employed in practice as an approximation. This assumes that the functional relationship between i and amount/present value is linear, which it is not, but the approximation is satisfactory for normal sums, rates and periods.

5. It should be carefully noted that, due to the assumption on which interest tables are constructed, the present value of a *single sum*, x, due in n periods' time, is xv^n; but the present value of a *series* of 20 payments of x, the first to be made in n periods' time, is $xa_{\overline{20}|}v^{n-1}$.

6. To obtain $s_{\overline{n}|}$ and $a_{\overline{n}|}$ when n is outside the range of the tables:

$$s_{\overline{n+m}|} = s_{\overline{n}|} + (1+i)^n s_{\overline{m}|};$$

$$a_{\overline{n+m}|} = a_{\overline{n}|} + v^n a_{\overline{m}|}.$$

(c) Continuous compounding and discounting

So far it has been assumed that interest is calculated at discrete intervals of time. In stating that 1 amounted to $(1+i)$ in one period, the effective rate of interest, i, measured the *average* rate of growth. In fact, of course, the process is one of continuous growth, and for some purposes it is more convenient to work in terms of the continuous rate of interest (also called the instantaneous rate and the 'force of interest').

The continuous rate of interest, denoted by the symbol δ, is the limit approached as the interval of measurement (the period of compounding or discounting) is made smaller and smaller. The relationship between the continuous, effective and nominal rates of interest is explained below.

Appendices

(i) *Compounding*

A rate of interest compounded m times a year, a nominal rate, was denoted by $i^{(m)}$.

The continuous rate is *defined* as

$$\delta = \lim_{m \to \infty} i^{(m)}.$$

Also, as explained above,

$$i = \left(1 + \frac{i^{(m)}}{m}\right)^m - 1.$$

The binomial expansion of the RHS gives

$$i = \left[1 + i^{(m)} + \frac{m(m-1)}{2!}\left(\frac{i^{(m)}}{m}\right)^2 + \ldots\right] - 1$$

for positive integral m.

(1)

We also know that the pure number e, whose approximate value is 2·71828, is defined as

$$e = \lim_{m \to \infty} \left(1 + \frac{1}{m}\right)^m,$$

which by Taylor's series

$$= 1 + \frac{1}{1!} + \frac{1}{2!} + \ldots;$$

and that

$$e^x = \lim_{m \to \infty} \left(1 + \frac{x}{m}\right)^m$$

$$= 1 + \frac{x}{1!} + \frac{x^2}{2!} + \ldots \quad (x \neq 0)$$

(2)

As $m \to \infty$ (i.e. as we make the interval of compounding shorter and shorter), $i^{(m)}$ by definition $\to \delta$, and (1) becomes

$$i = \left[1 + \delta + \frac{\delta^2}{2!} + \ldots\right] - 1 \quad (\delta \neq 0)$$

(3)

(Readers who may have had difficulty following this last point are asked to consider the third term on the RHS of (1) as $m \to \infty$:

$$\frac{m(m-1)}{2!}\left(\frac{i^{(m)}}{m}\right)^2 \to \frac{\infty(\infty)}{2!} \cdot \frac{\delta^2}{\infty(\infty)}, \quad \text{or} \quad \frac{\delta^2}{2!}\Bigg)$$

646

From (2) and (3), $i = e^{\delta} - 1$, and

$$e^{\delta} = (1+i) = \left(1 + \frac{i^{(m)}}{m}\right)^m.$$

Generalizing this result from $t = 1$ to $t = n$,

$$e^{n\delta} = (1+i)^n = \left(1 + \frac{i^{(m)}}{m}\right)^{mn}$$

(ii) *Discounting*

In the case of continuous discounting we begin with the relation

$$v = (1+i)^{-1} = \left(1 + \frac{i^{(m)}}{m}\right)^{-m}.$$

On the assumption that the numerical value of $i^{(m)}/m$ is less than unity, the binomial expansion of the expression on the RHS above forms the converging series

$$1 + \frac{(-m)}{1!}\frac{i^{(m)}}{m} + \frac{(-m)(-m-1)}{2!}\left(\frac{i^{(m)}}{m}\right)^2 + \frac{(-m)(-m-1)(-m-2)}{3!}\left(\frac{i^{(m)}}{m}\right)^3 + \cdots$$

$$= 1 - i^{(m)} + \frac{m(m+1)}{2!}\left(\frac{i^{(m)}}{m}\right)^2 - \frac{m(m+1)(m+2)}{3!}\left(\frac{i^{(m)}}{m}\right)^3 + \cdots \quad (4)$$

This time we make use of the relations

$$e^{-x} = \lim_{m \to \infty}\left(1 + \frac{x}{m}\right)^{-m} = 1 - x + \frac{x^2}{2!} - \frac{x^3}{3!} + \cdots \quad (x \neq 0).$$

As $m \to \infty$, $i^{(m)} \to \delta$, and (4) becomes

$$v = 1 - \delta + \frac{\delta^2}{2!} - \frac{\delta^3}{3!} + \cdots \quad (\delta \neq 0) \qquad (5)$$

$$= e^{-\delta}.$$

That is,

$$e^{-\delta} = (1+i)^{-1} = \left(1 + \frac{i^{(m)}}{m}\right)^{-m} \quad ; \text{ and for } t = n$$

$$e^{-n\delta} = (1+i)^{-n} = \left(1 + \frac{i^{(m)}}{m}\right)^{-mn}$$

(iii) *Annuities with continuous interest*

1. *Amount of annuity* Consider an annuity of £A a year for five years, first payment in one year's time, with interest at i per annum.

In discrete terms the amount of the annuity is

$$As_{\overline{5}|_i} = \sum_{t=1}^{5} A_t(1+i)^{5-t}$$

If compounding is continuous, since $(1+i)^t = e^{t\delta}$, the amount is

$$\int_1^5 Ae^{\delta t}\,dt = A\left\{\left[-\frac{1}{\delta}e^{\delta(5-t)}\right]_{t=5} - \left[-\frac{1}{\delta}e^{\delta(5-t)}\right]_{t=1}\right\}$$

$$= A\left\{\left(-\frac{1}{\delta}\right) - \left(-\frac{1}{\delta}e^{4\delta}\right)\right\} = \frac{A}{\delta}(e^{4\delta}-1).$$

2. *Present value of annuity* Given the same data, the present value of the annuity is: with discrete discounting

$$Aa_{\overline{5}|_i} = \sum_{t=0}^{5} A_t v^t;$$

with continuous discounting

$$\int_0^5 Ae^{-\delta t}\,dt = A\left[-\frac{1}{\delta}e^{-\delta t}\right]_0^5 = A\left[\left(-\frac{1}{\delta}e^{-5\delta}\right) - \left(-\frac{1}{\delta}\right)\right]$$

$$= \frac{A}{\delta}(1-e^{-5\delta}).$$

Bibliography

Readers wishing to go beyond the material covered in this appendix are referred to:

Todhunter, R., *Text-Book on Compound Interest and Annuities-Certain*, Institute of Actuaries, London, 3rd edn., 1937 (if available), or its modern counterpart:
Donald, D. W. A., *Compound Interest and Annuities-Certain*, Cambridge University Press, 1963.

Problems

A.1 What sum will £1 amount to at the end of n years at (a) 5% p.a. effective, (b) 5% p.a. compounded quarterly, and (c) 5% continuous?

A.2 What is the present value of (a) £250 due in three years' time at 5% p.a. compounded half-yearly, (b) £1 000 000, due 40 years hence at 12% compounded quarterly?

A.3 In how many years will £1 amount to £1·75 at 3% compounded half-yearly?

A.4 At what rate per cent per annum compounded half-yearly will £1 amount to £4·8 in 20 years?

A.5 (a) Write down the formula for determining the annual depreciation charge in respect of an asset being depreciated by the sinking fund method, where C = acquisition cost, n years = expected working life and S = scrap value, if interest is i per annum.

(b) Given the information in (a), write down the formula for the depreciation rate using the diminishing balance method.

A.6 Evaluate the following:

(a) The amount of 10 annual payments of £100 each, the last of which was made five years ago, at 5% p.a.

(b) The present value of 10 annual payments of £100 each at the end of the year, the first payment to be made five years hence, at 5% p.a.

A.7 Z is buying a house. He pays £5 000 down and agrees to pay £200 every quarter for the next 10 years. The seller charges interest at 10% compounded quarterly. Answer the following questions, treating the last three independently of one another, by writing down the appropriate expressions; calculations are not required:

(a) What was the price of the house?

(b) If he missed the first 12 payments how much must he pay at the time of the 13th to bring himself up to date?

(c) After making eight payments he wishes to discharge the remaining indebtedness with a single payment at the time of the ninth regular payment. How much must he pay in addition to the regular payment then due?

(d) If he has missed the first 10 payments, how much must he pay when the eleventh is due to discharge his entire indebtedness?

A.8 Express in terms of δ, the continuous rate of interest, the equivalent nominal rate of interest payable quarterly.

A.9 (a) The value of a series of fixed annual payments at the end of each year for 25 years, interest at 5% p.a., amounts to £5 000. What is the annual payment?

(b) If the present value of the series of payments in (a) is £5 000, what is the annual payment?

A.10 Derive by calculus expressions in terms of the corresponding discrete symbols for the amount, $\bar{s}_{\overline{n}|}$, and present value, $\bar{a}_{\overline{n}|}$, of an annuity of 1 per period, payments at the end of each period, when interest is compounded continuously at a constant rate δ. [The bars on s and a denote continuous interest.]

A.11 Prove that the continuous rate of interest and the continuous rate of discount are equal, i.e. that $\delta = \delta'$.

Appendix B

Interest tables

Future amount of £1 n periods hence, interest rate i per period. $(1 + i)^n$

n	$2\frac{1}{2}\%$	3%	4%	5%	6%	7%	8%	9%	10%	12%	14%	16%	18%	20%
1	1·02500	1·03000	1·04000	1·05000	1·06000	1·07000	1·08000	1·09000	1·10000	1·12000	1·14000	1·16000	1·18000	1·20000
2	1·05063	1·06090	1·08160	1·10250	1·12360	1·14490	1·16640	1·18810	1·21000	1·25440	1·29960	1·34560	1·39240	1·44000
3	1·07689	1·09273	1·12486	1·15763	1·19102	1·22504	1·25971	1·29503	1·33100	1·40493	1·48154	1·56090	1·64303	1·72800
4	1·10381	1·12551	1·16986	1·21551	1·26248	1·31080	1·36049	1·41158	1·46410	1·57352	1·68896	1·81064	1·93878	2·07360
5	1·13141	1·15927	1·21665	1·27628	1·33823	1·40255	1·46933	1·53862	1·61051	1·76234	1·92541	2·10034	2·28776	2·48832
6	1·15969	1·19405	1·26532	1·34010	1·41852	1·50073	1·58687	1·67710	1·77156	1·97382	2·19497	2·43640	2·69955	2·98598
7	1·18869	1·22987	1·31593	1·40710	1·50363	1·60578	1·71382	1·82804	1·94872	2·21068	2·50227	2·82622	3·18547	3·58318
8	1·21840	1·26677	1·36857	1·47746	1·59385	1·71819	1·85093	1·99256	2·14359	2·47596	2·85259	3·27841	3·75886	4·29982
9	1·24886	1·30477	1·42331	1·55133	1·68948	1·83846	1·99900	2·17189	2·35795	2·77308	3·25195	3·80296	4·43545	5·15978
10	1·28008	1·34392	1·48024	1·62889	1·79085	1·96715	2·15893	2·36736	2·59374	3·10585	3·70722	4·41144	5·23384	6·19174
11	1·31209	1·38423	1·53945	1·71034	1·89830	2·10485	2·33164	2·58043	2·85312	3·47855	4·22623	5·11726	6·17593	7·43008
12	1·34489	1·42576	1·60103	1·79586	2·01220	2·25219	2·51817	2·81267	3·13843	3·89598	4·81790	5·93603	7·28759	8·91610
13	1·37851	1·46853	1·66507	1·88565	2·13293	2·40984	2·71962	3·06581	3·45227	4·36349	5·49241	6·88579	8·59936	10·6993
14	1·41297	1·51259	1·73168	1·97993	2·26090	2·57853	2·93719	3·34173	3·79750	4·88711	6·26135	7·98752	10·1472	12·8392
15	1·44830	1·55797	1·80094	2·07893	2·39656	2·75903	3·17217	3·64248	4·17725	5·47357	7·13794	9·26552	11·9737	15·4070
16	1·48451	1·60471	1·87298	2·18287	2·54035	2·95216	3·42594	3·97031	4·59497	6·13039	8·13725	10·7480	14·1290	18·4884
17	1·52162	1·65285	1·94790	2·29202	2·69277	3·15882	3·70002	4·32763	5·05447	6·86604	9·27646	12·4677	16·6722	22·1861
18	1·55966	1·70243	2·02582	2·40662	2·85434	3·37993	3·99602	4·71712	5·55992	7·68997	10·5752	14·4625	19·6733	26·6233
19	1·59865	1·75351	2·10685	2·52695	3·02560	3·61653	4·31570	5·14166	6·11591	8·61276	12·0557	16·7765	23·2144	31·9480
20	1·63862	1·80611	2·19112	2·65330	3·20714	3·86968	4·66096	5·60441	6·72750	9·64629	13·7435	19·4608	27·3930	38·3376
21	1·67958	1·86029	2·27877	2·78596	3·39956	4·14056	5·03383	6·10881	7·40025	10·8038	15·6676	22·5745	32·3238	46·0051
22	1·72157	1·91610	2·36992	2·92526	3·60354	4·43040	5·43654	6·65860	8·14027	12·1003	17·8610	26·1864	38·1421	55·2061
23	1·76461	1·97359	2·46472	3·07152	3·81975	4·74053	5·87146	7·25787	8·95430	13·5523	20·3616	30·3762	45·0076	66·2474
24	1·80873	2·03279	2·56330	3·22510	4·04893	5·07237	6·34118	7·91108	9·84973	15·1786	23·2122	35·2364	53·1090	79·4968
25	1·85394	2·09378	2·66584	3·38635	4·29187	5·42743	6·84848	8·62308	10·8347	17·0001	26·4619	40·8742	62·6686	95·3962
30	2·09757	2·42726	3·24340	4·32194	5·74349	7·61226	10·0627	13·2677	17·4494	29·9599	50·9502	85·8499	143·371	237·376
35	2·37321	2·81386	3·94609	5·51602	7·68609	10·6766	14·7853	20·4140	28·1024	52·7996	98·1002	180·314	327·997	590·668
40	2·68506	3·26204	4·80102	7·03999	10·2857	14·9745	21·7245	31·4094	45·2593	93·0510	188·884	378·721	750·378	1469·77
45	3·03790	3·78160	5·84118	8·98501	13·7646	21·0025	31·9204	48·3273	72·8905	163·988	363·679	795·444	1716·68	3657·26
50	3·43711	4·38391	7·10668	11·4674	18·4202	29·4570	46·9016	74·3575	117·391	289·002	700·233	1670·70	3927·36	9100·44

Present value of £1 to be received n periods hence, interest rate i per period. $v^n = (1+i)^{-n}$

n \ i	2½%	3%	4%	5%	6%	7%	8%	9%	10%	12%	14%	16%	18%	20%
1	0·97561	0·97087	0·96154	0·95238	0·94340	0·93458	0·92593	0·91743	0·90909	0·89286	0·87719	0·86207	0·84746	0·83333
2	0·95181	0·94260	0·92456	0·90703	0·89000	0·87344	0·85734	0·84168	0·82645	0·79719	0·76947	0·74316	0·71818	0·69444
3	0·92860	0·91514	0·88900	0·86384	0·83962	0·81630	0·79383	0·77218	0·75131	0·71178	0·67497	0·64066	0·60863	0·57870
4	0·90595	0·88849	0·85480	0·82270	0·79209	0·76290	0·73503	0·70843	0·68301	0·63552	0·59208	0·55229	0·51579	0·48225
5	0·88385	0·86261	0·82193	0·78353	0·74726	0·71299	0·68058	0·64993	0·62092	0·56743	0·51937	0·47611	0·43711	0·40188
6	0·86230	0·83748	0·79031	0·74622	0·70496	0·66634	0·63017	0·59627	0·56447	0·50663	0·45559	0·41044	0·37043	0·33490
7	0·84127	0·81309	0·75992	0·71068	0·66506	0·62275	0·58349	0·54703	0·51316	0·45235	0·39964	0·35383	0·31393	0·27908
8	0·82075	0·78941	0·73069	0·67684	0·62741	0·58201	0·54027	0·50187	0·46651	0·40388	0·35056	0·30503	0·26604	0·23257
9	0·80073	0·76642	0·70259	0·64461	0·59190	0·54393	0·50025	0·46043	0·42410	0·36061	0·30751	0·26295	0·22546	0·19381
10	0·78120	0·74409	0·67556	0·61391	0·55839	0·50835	0·46319	0·42241	0·38554	0·32197	0·26974	0·22668	0·19106	0·16151
11	0·76214	0·72242	0·64958	0·58468	0·52679	0·47509	0·42888	0·38753	0·35049	0·28748	0·23662	0·19542	0·16192	0·13459
12	0·74356	0·70138	0·62460	0·55684	0·49697	0·44401	0·39711	0·35553	0·31863	0·25668	0·20756	0·16846	0·13722	0·11216
13	0·72542	0·68095	0·60057	0·53032	0·46884	0·41496	0·36770	0·32618	0·28966	0·22917	0·18207	0·14523	0·11629	0·09346
14	0·70773	0·66112	0·57748	0·50507	0·44230	0·38782	0·34046	0·29925	0·26333	0·20462	0·15971	0·12520	0·09855	0·07789
15	0·69047	0·64186	0·55526	0·48102	0·41727	0·36245	0·31524	0·27454	0·23939	0·18270	0·14010	0·10793	0·08352	0·06491
16	0·67362	0·62317	0·53391	0·45811	0·39365	0·33873	0·29189	0·25187	0·21763	0·16312	0·12289	0·09304	0·07078	0·05409
17	0·65720	0·60502	0·51337	0·43630	0·37136	0·31657	0·27027	0·23107	0·19784	0·14564	0·10780	0·08021	0·05998	0·04507
18	0·64117	0·58739	0·49363	0·41552	0·35034	0·29586	0·25025	0·21199	0·17986	0·13004	0·09456	0·06914	0·05083	0·03756
19	0·62553	0·57029	0·47464	0·39573	0·33051	0·27651	0·23171	0·19449	0·16351	0·11611	0·08295	0·05961	0·04308	0·03130
20	0·61027	0·55368	0·45639	0·37689	0·31180	0·25842	0·21455	0·17843	0·14864	0·10367	0·07276	0·05139	0·03651	0·02608
21	0·59539	0·53755	0·43883	0·35894	0·29416	0·24151	0·19866	0·16370	0·13513	0·09256	0·06383	0·04430	0·03094	0·02174
22	0·58086	0·52189	0·42196	0·34185	0·27751	0·22571	0·18394	0·15018	0·12285	0·08264	0·05599	0·03819	0·02622	0·01811
23	0·56670	0·50669	0·40573	0·32557	0·26180	0·21095	0·17032	0·13778	0·11168	0·07379	0·04911	0·03292	0·02222	0·01509
24	0·55288	0·49193	0·39012	0·31007	0·24698	0·19715	0·15770	0·12640	0·10153	0·06588	0·04308	0·02838	0·01883	0·01258
25	0·53939	0·47761	0·37512	0·29530	0·23300	0·18425	0·14602	0·11597	0·09230	0·05882	0·03779	0·02447	0·01596	0·01048
30	0·47674	0·41199	0·30832	0·23138	0·17411	0·13137	0·09938	0·07537	0·05731	0·03338	0·01963	0·01165	0·00697	0·00421
35	0·42137	0·35538	0·25342	0·18129	0·13011	0·09366	0·06763	0·04899	0·03558	0·01894	0·01019	0·00555	0·00305	0·00169
40	0·37243	0·30656	0·20829	0·14205	0·09722	0·06678	0·04603	0·03184	0·02209	0·01075	0·00529	0·00264	0·00133	0·00068
45	0·32917	0·26444	0·17120	0·11130	0·07265	0·04761	0·03133	0·02069	0·01372	0·00610	0·00275	0·00126	0·00058	0·00027
50	0·29094	0·22811	0·14071	0·08720	0·05429	0·03395	0·02132	0·01345	0·00852	0·00346	0·00143	0·00060	0·00025	0·00011

Future amount of an annuity of £1 for n periods, interest rate i per period. $s_{\overline{n}|} = \dfrac{(1+i)^n - 1}{i}$

n \ i	$2\frac{1}{2}\%$	3%	4%	5%	6%	7%	8%	9%	10%	12%	14%	16%	18%	20%
1	1·0000	1·0000	1·0000	1·0000	1·0000	1·0000	1·0000	1·0000	1·0000	1·0000	1·0000	1·0000	1·0000	1·0000
2	2·0250	2·0300	2·0400	2·0500	2·0600	2·0700	2·0800	2·0900	2·1000	2·1200	2·1400	2·1600	2·1800	2·2000
3	3·0756	3·0909	3·1216	3·1525	3·1836	3·2149	3·2464	3·2781	3·3100	3·3744	3·4396	3·5056	3·5724	3·6400
4	4·1525	4·1836	4·2465	4·3101	4·3746	4·4399	4·5061	4·5731	4·6410	4·7793	4·9211	5·0665	5·2154	5·3680
5	5·2563	5·3091	5·4163	5·5256	5·6371	5·7507	5·8666	5·9847	6·1051	6·3528	6·6101	6·8771	7·1542	7·4416
6	6·3877	6·4684	6·6330	6·8019	6·9753	7·1533	7·3359	7·5233	7·7156	8·1152	8·5355	8·9775	9·4420	9·9299
7	7·5474	7·6625	7·8983	8·1420	8·3938	8·6540	8·9228	9·2004	9·4872	10·089	10·730	11·414	12·142	12·916
8	8·7361	8·8923	9·2142	9·5491	9·8975	10·260	10·637	11·028	11·436	12·300	13·233	14·240	15·327	16·499
9	9·9545	10·159	10·583	11·027	11·491	11·978	12·488	13·021	13·579	14·776	16·085	17·519	19·086	20·799
10	11·203	11·464	12·006	12·578	13·181	13·816	14·487	15·193	15·937	17·549	19·337	21·321	23·521	25·959
11	12·483	12·808	13·486	14·207	14·972	15·784	16·645	17·560	18·531	20·655	23·045	25·733	28·755	32·150
12	13·796	14·192	15·026	15·917	16·870	17·888	18·977	20·141	21·384	24·133	27·271	30·850	34·931	39·580
13	15·140	15·618	16·627	17·713	18·882	20·141	21·495	22·953	24·523	28·029	32·089	36·786	42·219	48·497
14	16·519	17·086	18·292	19·599	21·015	22·550	24·215	26·019	27·975	32·393	37·581	43·672	50·818	59·196
15	17·932	18·599	20·024	21·579	23·276	25·129	27·152	29·361	31·772	37·280	43·842	51·659	60·965	72·035
16	19·380	20·157	21·825	23·657	25·673	27·888	30·324	33·003	35·950	42·753	50·980	60·925	72·939	87·442
17	20·865	21·762	23·698	25·840	28·213	30·840	33·750	36·974	40·545	48·884	59·118	71·673	87·068	105·93
18	22·386	23·414	25·645	28·132	30·906	33·999	37·450	41·301	45·599	55·750	68·394	84·141	103·74	128·12
19	23·946	25·117	27·671	30·539	33·760	37·379	41·446	46·018	51·159	63·440	78·969	98·603	123·41	154·74
20	25·545	26·870	29·778	33·066	36·786	40·995	45·762	51·160	57·275	72·052	91·025	115·38	146·63	186·69
21	27·183	28·676	31·969	35·719	39·993	44·865	50·423	56·765	64·002	81·699	104·77	134·83	174·02	225·03
22	28·863	30·537	34·248	38·505	43·392	49·006	55·457	62·873	71·403	92·503	120·44	157·41	206·34	271·03
23	30·584	32·453	36·618	41·430	46·996	53·436	60·893	69·532	79·543	104·60	138·30	183·60	244·49	326·24
24	32·349	34·426	39·083	44·502	50·816	58·177	66·765	76·790	88·497	118·16	158·66	213·98	289·49	392·48
25	34·158	36·459	41·646	47·727	54·865	63·249	73·106	84·701	98·347	133·33	181·87	249·21	342·60	471·98
30	43·903	47·575	56·085	66·439	79·058	94·461	113·28	136·31	164·49	241·33	356·79	530·31	790·95	1181·9
35	54·928	60·462	73·652	90·320	111·43	138·24	172·32	215·71	271·02	431·66	693·57	1120·7	1816·7	2948·3
40	67·403	75·401	95·026	120·80	154·76	199·64	259·06	337·88	442·59	767·09	1342·0	2360·8	4163·2	7343·9
45	81·516	92·720	121·03	159·70	212·74	285·75	386·51	525·86	718·90	1358·2	2590·6	4965·3	9531·6	18281
50	97·484	112·80	152·67	209·35	290·34	406·53	573·77	815·08	1163·9	2400·0	4994·5	10436	21813	45497

Present value of an annuity of £1 for n periods, interest rate i per period. $a_{\overline{n}|} = \dfrac{1-v^n}{i}$

n	2½%	3%	4%	5%	6%	7%	8%	9%	10%	12%	14%	16%	18%	20%
1	0·9756	0·9709	0·9615	0·9524	0·9434	0·9346	0·9259	0·9174	0·9091	0·8929	0·8772	0·8621	0·8475	0·8333
2	1·9274	1·9135	1·8861	1·8594	1·8334	1·8080	1·7833	1·7591	1·7355	1·6901	1·6467	1·6052	1·5656	1·5278
3	2·8560	2·8286	2·7751	2·7232	2·6730	2·6243	2·5771	2·5313	2·4869	3·0373	2·3216	2·2459	2·1743	2·1065
4	3·7620	3·7171	3·6299	3·5460	3·4651	3·3872	3·3121	3·2397	3·1699	3·0373	2·9137	2·7982	2·6901	2·5887
5	4·6458	4·5797	4·4518	4·3295	4·2124	4·1002	3·9927	3·8897	3·7908	3·6048	3·4331	3·2743	3·1272	2·9906
6	5·5081	5·4172	5·2421	5·0757	4·9173	4·7665	4·6229	4·4859	4·3553	4·1114	3·8887	3·6847	3·4976	3·3255
7	6·3494	6·2303	6·0021	5·7864	5·5824	5·3893	5·2064	5·0330	4·8684	4·5638	4·2883	4·0386	3·8115	3·6046
8	7·1701	7·0197	6·7327	6·4632	6·2098	5·9713	5·7466	5·5348	5·3349	4·9676	4·6389	4·3436	4·0776	3·8372
9	7·9709	7·7861	7·4353	7·1078	6·8017	6·5152	6·2469	5·9952	5·7590	5·3282	4·9464	4·6065	4·3030	4·0310
10	8·7521	8·5302	8·1109	7·7217	7·3601	7·0236	6·7101	6·4177	6·1446	5·6502	5·2161	4·8332	4·4941	4·1925
11	9·5142	9·2526	8·7605	8·3064	7·8869	7·4987	7·1390	6·8052	6·4951	5·9377	5·4527	5·0286	4·6560	4·3271
12	10·258	9·9540	9·3851	8·8633	8·3838	7·9427	7·5361	7·1607	6·8137	6·1944	5·6603	5·1971	4·7932	4·4392
13	10·983	10·635	9·9856	9·3936	8·8527	8·3577	7·9038	7·4869	7·1034	6·4235	5·8424	5·3423	4·9095	4·5327
14	11·691	11·296	10·563	9·8986	9·2950	8·7455	8·2442	7·7862	7·3667	6·6282	6·0021	5·4675	5·0081	4·6106
15	12·381	11·938	11·118	10·380	9·7122	9·1079	8·5595	8·0607	7·6061	6·8109	6·1422	5·5755	5·0916	4·6755
16	13·055	12·561	11·652	10·838	10·106	9·4466	8·8514	8·3126	7·8237	6·9740	6·2651	5·6685	5·1624	4·7296
17	13·712	13·166	12·166	11·274	10·477	9·7632	9·1216	8·5436	8·0216	7·1196	6·3729	5·7487	5·2223	4·7746
18	14·353	13·754	12·659	11·690	10·828	10·059	9·3719	8·7556	8·2014	7·2497	6·4674	5·8178	5·2732	4·8122
19	14·979	14·324	13·134	12·085	11·158	10·336	9·6036	8·9501	8·3649	7·3658	6·5504	5·8775	5·3162	4·8435
20	15·589	14·877	13·590	12·462	11·470	10·594	9·8181	9·1285	8·5136	7·4694	6·6231	5·9288	5·3527	4·8696
21	16·185	15·415	14·029	12·821	11·764	10·836	10·017	9·2922	8·6487	7·5620	6·6870	5·9731	5·3837	4·8913
22	16·765	15·937	14·451	13·163	12·042	11·061	10·201	9·4424	8·7715	7·6446	6·7429	6·0113	5·4099	4·9094
23	17·332	16·444	14·857	13·489	12·303	11·272	10·371	9·5802	8·8832	7·7184	6·7921	6·0442	5·4321	4·9245
24	17·885	16·936	15·247	13·799	12·550	11·469	10·529	9·7066	8·9847	7·7843	6·8351	6·0726	5·4509	4·9371
25	18·424	17·413	15·622	14·094	12·783	11·654	10·675	9·8226	9·0770	7·8431	6·8729	6·0971	5·4669	4·9476
30	20·930	19·600	17·292	15·372	13·765	12·409	11·258	10·274	9·4269	8·0552	7·0027	6·1772	5·5168	4·9789
35	23·145	21·487	18·665	16·374	14·498	12·948	11·655	10·567	9·6442	8·1755	7·0700	6·2153	5·5386	4·9915
40	25·103	23·115	19·793	17·159	15·046	13·332	11·925	10·757	9·7791	8·2438	7·1050	6·2335	5·5482	4·9966
45	26·833	24·519	20·720	17·774	15·456	13·606	12·108	10·881	9·8628	8·2825	7·1232	6·2421	5·5523	4·9986
50	28·362	25·730	21·482	18·256	15·762	13·801	12·233	10·962	9·9148	8·3045	7·1327	6·2463	5·5541	4·9995

Appendix C

Notes on linear programming

This appendix is not intended to teach the reader linear programming, on which a number of excellent books are available,* but rather to acquaint him with some of the main features of this technique, which we apply at various points in the text and consider to be essential equipment for anyone working in the management accounting area, as in so many other business areas. What is provided here is little more than a glossary, and the reader would be very unwise to treat it as a substitute for a thorough understanding.

1. Definition

Hadley [5] defines the technique in the following way. 'Optimization problems' refers to the general class of problems which seek to maximize or minimize a numerical function of a number of variables (or functions), where the variables (or functions) are subject to certain constraints. Mathematical programming problems constitute the subset of the latter where classical optimization techniques such as the differential calculus (variables) and calculus of variations (functions) cannot be applied. *Linear* programming (which dates from about 1947) is one form of mathematical programming, in which all relations among the variables of the problem are linear (i.e. straight line relationships); in particular they must be linear in the objective function to be optimized *and* in the constraints.

2. General form

The linear programming (henceforth LP) problem presents itself in a number of different forms. The *general* problem, which happens to be the form most used in this book, is: A linear objective function in r variables is to be maximized or minimized subject to a set of s linear constraints in these variables which may be equations or inequalities. The problem is to find non-negative values of the variables which satisfy the constraints and optimize the objective function. In symbols:

$$\text{Maximize or minimize } z = c_1 x_1 + \ldots + c_r x_r$$

$$\left. = \sum_{j=1}^{r} c_j x_j \quad \right\} \quad \text{objective function}$$

*A short list would include [5], [4], [3]; an excellent short introduction appears as Chapters 5 and 6 in [2].

subject to: (1) $a_{i1}x_1 + a_{i2}x_2 + \ldots + a_{ir}x_r \geqslant, =$ or $\leqslant b_i$

$$(i = 1, \ldots, s)$$

i.e. $\displaystyle\sum_{j=1}^{r} a_{ij}x_j \gtreqless b_i \quad (i = 1, \ldots, s)$ } constraints

where $s >, <$ or $= r$, and where for any one of these s constraints only one of the signs $\leqslant, =$ or $\geqslant$ holds.

(2) $x_j \geqslant 0 \qquad (j = 1, \ldots, r)$} non-negativity restriction

The a_{ij}, c_j and b_i are known constants.

3. Linearity assumption

This implies, in the objective function, that if the profit from (cost of) n units is π, for example, for $2n$ units it will be 2π, and so on. In the constraints linearity implies that *processes* are subject to constant returns to scale. Constant unit prices for inputs and outputs over the range of the problem are implicit in this.

4. Other forms of the problem

Some of the other forms of the problem, each with application to a large class of problems but which will not be refered to further, are:

1. *The transportation problem*: the problem of minimizing the cost of transporting people or goods from m sources to n destinations. It is the special form of the general problem when $a_{ij} = 1$ for all i and j.
2. *The assignment problem*: a variation of the transportation problem (e.g. the allocation of m different facilities, such as machines or personnel, to n different tasks). The general problem reduces to the assignment problem when $a_{ij} = 1$ and $b_i = 1$ for all i and j. (The assignment problem can also be regarded as a special form of integer (or discrete) programming problem, see later.)

5. Some essential terms

1. *Feasible solution*: a set of values $(x_1, x_2, \ldots, x_r)$ which satisfies the constraints.
2. *Feasible region*: the set of all feasible solutions.
3. *Basic feasible solution*: a feasible solution containing no more than i positive x_j values, i.e. an extreme point (corner point) of the feasible region.
4. *Optimal feasible solution*: the feasible solution which optimizes the value of the objective function. It is represented by an extreme point, or an edge, of the feasible region (an infinity of optimal solutions in the latter case).
5. *Isoprofit (isocost) line*: families of parallel lines showing different values of the objective function.

Geometric illustrations of a maximization and a minimization problem follow:

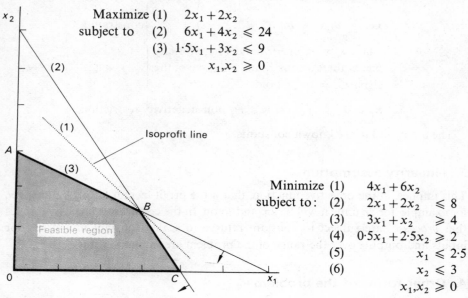

Maximize (1) $2x_1 + 2x_2$
subject to   (2) $6x_1 + 4x_2 \leqslant 24$
            (3) $1 \cdot 5x_1 + 3x_2 \leqslant 9$
                $x_1, x_2 \geqslant 0$

Minimize (1) $4x_1 + 6x_2$
subject to: (2) $2x_1 + 2x_2 \leqslant 8$
            (3) $3x_1 + x_2 \geqslant 4$
            (4) $0 \cdot 5x_1 + 2 \cdot 5x_2 \geqslant 2$
            (5) $x_1 \leqslant 2 \cdot 5$
            (6) $x_2 \leqslant 3$
                $x_1, x_2 \geqslant 0$

Figure C.1

Basic feasible solutions: points O, A, B and C
Optimal feasible solution: point B

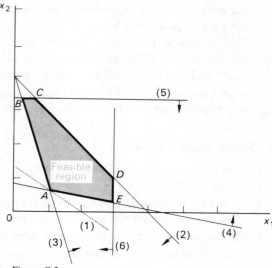

Figure C.2

Basic feasible solutions: points A, B, C, D, E
Optimal feasible solution: point A

6. Solution methods

In cases involving only two variables the problem may be solved geometrically, as above. Generally, however, algebraic solution is necessary. This involves introducing *slack variables* to convert the inequality constraints into equations. The slack variables represent the additional amount of the input required to make the constraint binding. For example, in the minimization problem $2x_1 + 2x_2 \leqslant 8$ would become $2x_1 + 2x_2 + x_3 = 8$, and $3x_1 + x_2 \geqslant 4$ would become $3x_1 + x_2 + x_4 = 4$. The slack variables are subject to the non-negativity restriction and are assumed to make no contribution to the value of the objective function.

Solution of the problem consists of an iterative procedure, a systematic search among the extreme (corner) points of the feasible region until no further improvement in the value of the objective function is possible. From the geometrical illustrations it will be apparent that if the isoprofit (or isocost) line happens to be parallel to a constraint line then all points on this particular constraint line will be optimal solutions to the problem, i.e. the solution will include some non-basic feasible solutions.

If two constraint lines happen to pass through an extreme point the basic feasible solution is said to be *degenerate*. (This is why a basic feasible solution was defined as a feasible solution containing no more than i positive x_j values in 5 above.) Degeneracy leads to 'cycling', i.e. the iterative solution procedure keeps returning to the same extreme point and the value of the objective function is not improved from one iteration to the next. This can be resolved by shifting one of the constraint lines very slightly and proceeding to solve the modified problem. (The latter procedures are known as 'perturbation techniques'.)

The *simplex method*, and variations of it, is one algebraic method for solving LP problems which appears to be the most efficient method in many cases. The procedure will not be described here; readers can refer to one of the books mentioned earlier. The method guarantees* that, in non-degenerate problems, the optimal solution will be reached in a finite number of steps (iterations), and that each iteration will approximate more closely to the optimal solution than the last. A common rule-of-thumb is that the number of iterations involved in a particular problem will be approximately $1 \cdot 5s$ to $2 \cdot 0s$, where s is the number of constraints. Large problems require the computer.

More efficient computational procedures (than the simplex method or one of the revised simplex techniques) have been devised to deal with special forms of the LP problem and with problems of large dimensions. Most of the remaining computational problems arise in connection with the *general* form of the problem.

---

*That is, the procedure is an algorithm (see Chapter 6).

7. Duality

An important theorem in LP states that for every maximization problem (the *primal* problem) there is a corresponding minimization problem (the *dual* problem), and vice versa, such that, if feasible solutions exist,

$$f_{max} = g_{min}$$

where f and g denote the objective functions in the primal and dual problems, respectively. The relationships between primal and dual problems are set out below for three different types of constraints in the primal problem [1]:

(a)   *Primal*   *Dual*

$$(1)\ \max f = \sum_{j=1}^{r} c_j x_j \qquad\qquad (3)\ \min g = \sum_{i=1}^{s} b_i u_i$$

$$\text{subject to } (2) \sum_{j=1}^{r} a_{ij} x_j \leqslant b_i \qquad\qquad \text{subject to } (4) \sum_{i=1}^{s} a_{ij} u_i \geqslant c_j$$

$$x_j \geqslant 0 \qquad\qquad u_i \geqslant 0$$

(b) Objective functions as before

$$\text{subject to } \sum^{r} a_{ij} x_j = b_i \qquad\qquad \text{subject to } \sum_{i=1}^{s} a_{ij} u_i \geqslant c_j$$

$$x_j \geqslant 0 \qquad\qquad \text{No non-negativity restrictions on}$$
the u_i.

(c) Objective functions as before

$$\text{subject to } \sum_{j=1}^{r} a_{ij} x_j \leqslant b_i \qquad\qquad \text{subject to } \sum_{i=1}^{s} a_{ij} u_i \geqslant c_j$$

$$(i = 1, \ldots, m) \qquad\qquad (j = 1, \ldots, p)$$

$$\sum_{j=1}^{r} a_{ij} x_j = b_i \qquad\qquad \sum_{i=1}^{s} a_{ij} u_i = c_j$$

$$(i = m+1, \ldots, k) \qquad\qquad (j = p+1, \ldots, r)$$

$$x_j \geqslant 0 \qquad\qquad u_i \geqslant 0$$

$$(j = 1, \ldots, p) \qquad\qquad (i = 1, \ldots, m)$$

remaining x_j unrestricted   remaining u_i unrestricted

Since $\min g = -\max(-g)$, every minimization problem can be converted into an equivalent maximization problem, and vice versa.

Apart from the relationships between the inequality or equality signs, notice the following relationships between primal and dual problems, described here by reference to the numbers in parentheses in case (a):

1. The coefficients c_j in (1) are the same as the constants on the right-hand side of (4).
2. The coefficients b_i in (3) are the same as the constants on the right-hand side of (2).
3. The coefficients a_{ij} in (2) are arranged horizontally, in (4) vertically:

(2) $a_{11}x_1 + a_{12}x_2 + \ldots + a_{1s}x_s \leqslant b_1$ (4) $a_{11}u_1 + a_{21}u_2 + \ldots + a_{s1}u_s \geqslant c_1$

$\qquad a_{21}x_1 + a_{22}x_2 + \ldots + a_{2s}x_s \leqslant b_2$ $a_{12}u_1 + a_{22}u_2 + \ldots + a_{s2}u_s \geqslant c_2$

$$\ldots \qquad\qquad\qquad \leqslant b_r \qquad\qquad \ldots \qquad \ldots \qquad \geqslant c_r$$

4. the number of variables in (2) equals the number of constraints in (4), $= r$.

The variables u_i in the dual problem may be interpreted as the imputed costs (or shadow prices) of the s constraints b_i in the primal problem. The optimal solution of the dual problem gives the values of these costs corresponding to the optimal solution of the primal problem. (In practice the two problems are solved simultaneously.) If $x_j > 0$ in the optimal solution of the primal problem the jth dual constraint,

$$\sum_i a_{ij}u_i,$$

is binding, the value of u_i^* indicating how much the primal objective function could be improved (by eliminating lost profits or higher costs) if this constraint could be eased by one unit. If $x_j = 0$ in the optimal solution of the primal problem the jth dual constraint is not binding (i.e. not used up to the limit c_j). Similarly in the optimal solution of the dual problem, $u_i > 0$ if the ith primal constraint is binding, and is zero if it is not. This property of the dual variables has considerable economic significance.

8. Integer solutions

In ordinary LP the x_j are assumed to be continuously variable. In some problems, however, it does not make sense for the x_j values to be other than whole numbers, and serious errors may result from using an ordinary LP formulation and rounding simplex solution values to the nearest whole number. The rounded solution may be either infeasible or nonoptimal. In Figure C.3, for instance, the nearest integer solution is infeasible and the nearest feasible integer solution is nonoptimal:

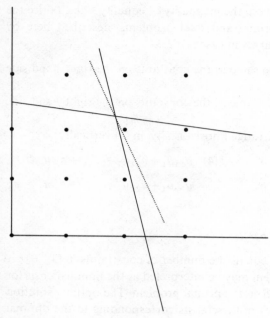

Figure C.3

A modified form of LP called *integer* (*or discrete*) *programming* is capable of obtaining optimal, integer solutions to such problems. The interpretation of the dual variables described in the previous section does not apply if the problem is an integer programming problem or 'mixed integer' LP problem (in which *some* of the variables may take on only integer values).

9. Uncertainty

We have been assuming so far that in all of the LP problems formulated the values of the coefficients (in the primal problem the c_j, a_{ij} and b_i) were given and accurate. In practice a major task in developing realistic LP models is the ascertainment of reliable numerical values for these coefficients. Consequently it is often desirable to study the behaviour of solutions when the coefficients are varied, either singly or a number at a time. This type of investigation which results from uncertainty about the numerical values of the coefficients is called *parametric programming* (or sensitivity analysis).

When some or all of the coefficients are random variables the method of analysis is called *stochastic linear programming*. One special case of this type of programming is called *chance-constrained programming*, where the chance constraint is formally expressed, e.g. as under:

Form of constraint under certainty:

$$\Sigma a_{ij}x_j \leqslant b_i$$

corresponding chance constraint, where the probability (P) is $0{\cdot}75$:

$$P[\Sigma a_{ij}x_j \leqslant b_i] \geqslant 0{\cdot}75.$$

10. Nonlinearities

Extensions of the technique of LP to problems in which the objective function and/or constraints are nonlinear in form are known as *nonlinear programming*. If a nonlinear objective function is convex,* it may be approximated by a series of line segments and treated as a LP problem. Algorithms have been developed for some but by no means all of the remaining cases.

Bibliographical references

[1] Arnoff, E. L. and S. S. Sengupta, Mathematical programming, in *Progress in Operations Research, Volume I,* ed. R. L. Ackoff, John Wiley, 1961, pp. 103–210.
[2] Baumol, W. J., *Economic Theory and Operations Analysis*, Prentice-Hall, 2nd edn., 1965.
[3] Boulding, K. E. and W. A. Spivey, *Linear Programming and the Theory of the Firm*, Macmillan, New York, 1960.
[4] Dorfman, R., P. A. Samuelson and R. M. Solow, *Linear Programming and Economic Analysis*, McGraw-Hill, 1958.
[5] Hadley, G., *Linear Programming*, Addison-Wesley, 1962.

---

*The connecting arc joining any two points on the curve representing the objective function never lies above the line connecting the two points; see [2], Chapter 7.

Author Index

Accountants' International Study
  Group, 109
Ackoff, R. L., 141, 180, 589
Allen, R. G. D., 162
Allison, D., 508, 509
American Accounting Association,
  22, 27, 31, 50, 51, 418, 499, 503
American Institute of Certified Public
  Accountants, 114, 406, 433
American Management Association,
  500, 501, 505, 543
Amerman, G., 458, 474
Amey, L. R., 172, 174, 180, 192, 244,
  247, 258, 259, 297, 310, 334, 529,
  532, 540, 542, 559, 560, 566
Andrews, P. W. S., 228
Ansoff, H. I., 141, 149
Anthony, R. N., 198, 531, 534, 542,
  543
Anton, H. R., 61
Archer, S. H., 605
Argyris, C., 449, 574
Arnoff, E. L., 589, 658
Arrow, K. J., 148, 163, 254, 258, 564,
  565, 573, 577

Ashby, W. R., 387, 388, 552, 562
Backer, M., 547
Bailey, M. J., 311
Bain, J. S., 385
Baker, N. R., 509
Barges, A., 627
Baumol, W. J., 146, 162, 165, 166, 176,
  214, 220, 222, 223, 239, 249, 307,
  331, 333, 348, 381, 389, 502, 503,
  604, 654
Baxter, W. T., 87, 93, 249
Beaver, W. H., 132, 133, 134, 135
Becker, S. W., 451, 571
Beckmann, M. J., 148
Becknell, J. C., 451
Bedford, N. M., 22, 27
Beer, S., 388, 554, 562, 565
Bell, P. W., 79, 88, 92, 103
Benston, G., 131, 287, 571
Beranek, W., 583, 598, 600, 602
Berle, A. A., 381
Bernhard, R. H., 304, 315
Bierman, H. Jr., 27, 278, 302, 309, 544,
  602, 611, 627
Bird, P., 124

Birn, S. A., 501
Blaine, E., 135
Board of Trade (Working Party
    Reports), 191
Bobis, A. H., 506, 509
Bonbright, J. C., 76
Bonini, C. P., 562, 564, 565, 577
Booz, Allen and Hamilton, 506
Bostwick, C. L., 22
Boulding, K. E., 14, 16, 164, 180, 227,
    383
Brewer, D. E., 624, 625
Brigham E. F., 627
British Institute of Management and
    the Centre for Interfirm
    Comparison, 537, 543
Bromwich, M., 474
Bruns, W. J., 571
Buchan, J., 583, 584, 589, 598, 605
Budd, A. P., 241
Burnham, J. H., 381
Byrne, R., 362
Carleton, W. T., 330, 337, 610, 627
Carlson, S., 143
Chamberlin, E. H., 383
Chambers, R. J., 75, 88
Chandler, A. D. Jr., 141, 380, 387,
    392, 527, 528, 545
Charnes, A., 281, 282, 362, 571
Chou, Y., 286, 287
Chumachenko, N. G., 484
Churchill, N. C., 32
Churchman, C. W., 14, 31, 157, 171,
    180, 388, 557, 579, 589
Clarkson, G. P. E., 234, 241
Coase, R. H., 16, 140, 170, 172, 256
Cochran, B., 506, 507
Cohen, K. J., 141, 144, 148, 153, 162,
    215, 234, 238, 239, 240, 241, 242,
    244, 262, 264, 351, 368, 387
Cohen, M. R., 30

Cohen, S. I., 504
Cooke T. P., 506, 509
Cooper, W. W., 281, 282, 362, 577
Copeland, R. M., 135
Cottle, S., 124
Cournot, A., 143, 233
Cragg, J. G., 627
Crossan, R. M., 501
Cushing, B. E., 135
Cyert, R. M., 17, 18, 21, 141, 144,
    151, 153, 155, 161, 162, 182, 215,
    234, 238, 239, 240, 241, 242, 244,
    257, 262, 350, 351, 368, 380, 386,
    387, 398, 559
Dascher, P. E., 135
Dean, B. V., 338, 348, 506, 508
Dean, J., 194, 195, 211, 212, 236, 255
Dearden, J., 446, 532, 542
De Coster, D. T., 518, 571
Demski, J. S., 27, 559, 560
Department of Education and Science
    and Ministry of Technology, 506
Dill, W. R., 161
Dodd, D. L., 124
Donald, D. W. A., 648
Dorfman, R., 14, 211, 212, 222, 232,
    244, 250, 654
Drebin, A. R., 544
Drucker, P. F., 389, 563
Duguid, A. M., 303
Durand, D., 616, 621, 623, 624
Duvall, R. M., 489
Dyckman, T. R., 175, 489
Eastwood, R. W., 501
Edgeworth, F. Y., 233, 366
Edwards, E. O., 79, 88, 92, 93, 103
Edwards, R. S., 88, 244
Edwards, W., 21, 32, 371
Egginton, D. A., 70
Emery, J. C., 385
Farrell, M. J., 208

Feigenbaum, E. A., 234
Feltham, G. A., 27
Fisher, I., 292, 305
Fisk, J., 509
Flower, J. F., 247, 528, 537, 544
Forgy, E. W., 600
Forrester, J. W., 551
Fouraker, L. E., 27
Friend, I., 616
Gabor, A., 240, 540
Gardiner, J., 385
Girshick, M. A., 219
Glennan, T. K. Jr., 508
Gonedes, N. J., 134
Gordon, M. J., 265, 577, 612, 613,
    614, 615, 616, 627
Goudeket, A., 88, 104
Gould, J. R., 172
Graham, B., 124
Grayson, C. J., 371
Green, D. Jr., 451, 571
Griffin, J. M., 215
Guetzkow, G., 573, 576
Haavelmo, T., 219
Hadley, G., 510, 583, 584, 585, 586,
    589, 592, 596, 598, 654
Hague, D. C., 162, 214, 215, 235
Hanssmann, F., 167
Harcourt, G. C., 75, 86, 104, 107
Henderson, B. D., 532, 542
Henderson, J. M., 147, 162, 216, 233
Hendriksen, E. S., 75
Henrici, S. B., 459, 469
Hepworth, S. R., 134
Hertz, D. B., 362
Hicks, J. R., 142, 144, 237, 264
Hillier, F. S., 353, 360, 361, 362
Hirshleifer, J., 258, 293, 299, 305, 310,
    311, 320, 321, 331, 610
Hirschmann, W. B., 450
Hitch, C. J., 180

Hoel, P. G., 175
Hofstede, G. H., 448, 449, 450, 451,
    489, 567, 569, 571, 572, 575, 576
Hohn, F. E., 179
Holmes, M. E., 338, 347, 348, 349
Holt, C. C., 145, 176, 177, 267, 300,
    556
Horngren, C. T., 406, 474
Houthakker, H. S., 219
Howell, J. E., 181
Humble, J. W., 499
Humphreys, E. N., 245
Hurwicz, L., 234
Ijiri, Y., 26, 31, 38, 88, 281, 282, 283,
    435, 437
Imperial Chemical Industries Ltd., 288
Institute of Chartered Accountants in
    England and Wales, 44, 45, 108,
    109, 114, 406, 484
Institute of Cost and Works
    Accountants, 191, 200, 405, 420
International Business Machines
    Corporation, 429
Jaedicke, R. K., 27, 31, 53, 127, 128,
    132, 278, 281, 435, 437, 562, 564,
    565, 577
Johnston, J., 175, 214, 215, 219, 227,
    287
Jones, J. M., 605
Jureen, L., 219, 287
Kaldor, N., 383
Karlin, S., 148
Keynes, J. M., 303, 583
Khinchin, A. I., 22
Knight, F. H., 169, 400
Koenigsberg, E., 583, 584, 589, 598,
    605
Kohler, E. L., 405
Kortanek, K., 362
Kozmetsky, G., 573, 576
Lancaster, K., 150, 188, 227, 293

Lanzillotti, R. F., 244
Laski, J. G., 303
Lawrence, F. C., 245
Leavitt, H. J., 577
Leibenstein, H., 212
Lerner, E. M., 337, 610, 627
Lesourne, J., 227, 323
Lev, B., 22, 26, 133
Levy, F. K., 510
Lewis, J. P., 162
Lewis, W. A., 93, 172
Lieberman, G. J., 361, 362
Likert, R., 575, 576
Lintner, J., 337, 614
Little, I. M. D., 134
Livingstone, J. L., 435, 437
Lockyer, K. G., 393, 510, 513
Luce, R. D., 163, 364
Lundberg, E., 147, 302
Lusztig, P., 334
Lutz, F. and V., 143, 323
Lyle, P., 286, 287
MacCrimmon, K. R., 516, 517
McAdams, A. K., 175
McFarland, W. B., 547
McGregor, D., 575
McIsaac, R. W., 505
Malcolm, R. E., 135
Malkiel, B. G., 627
Malmgren, H. B., 16, 17, 246, 552
Manes, R. P., 283, 417
Manne, A., 215
Mao, J. C. T., 283, 627
March, J. G., 17, 18, 21, 141, 151, 155,
    182, 234, 242, 257, 350, 380, 386,
    387, 398, 559
Markowitz, H. M., 366
Marschak, J., 19, 27, 176
Marschak, T., 508
Marschner, D. C., 504
Marshall, A., 11, 75, 77, 382

Martin, A. D., 367
Mason, P., 65
Massé, P., 143, 147, 148, 296, 298,
    338, 340, 347
Mathews, R. L., 200
Mattesich, R., 38
Mauriel J. J., 531, 534, 542, 543
Mautz, R. K., 546
Means, G. C., 381
Meij, J. L., 94
Merrett, A. J., 116
Merwin, C. L., 133
Michaelson, J. B., 624, 625
Miller, D. W., 583, 584, 586, 596
Miller, M. H., 309, 614, 616, 617,
    621-8
Miller, R. W., 514, 518
Modigliani, F., 18, 144, 145, 148, 176,
    177, 179, 264, 267, 300, 309, 556,
    614, 616, 617, 621-8
Montgomery, D. B., 246
Moonitz, M., 38
Moore, C. L., 283
Moore, J. R., 509
Morgenstern, O., 32, 365
Morrell, A. J. H., 583, 584, 598
Muth, J. F., 18, 145, 176, 177, 267,
    300, 556
Myers, J. H., 600
Myers, S. C., 614, 615, 625, 626
Nagel, E., 30
Näslund, B., 362
National Association of Accountants,
    258, 276, 535, 537, 543
National Association of [Cost]
    Accountants, 527
National Computing Centre, 29
Naylor, T. H., 233, 234, 239, 242, 260
Nerlove, M., 148, 254
Neumann, J. von, 32, 365
Nielsen, O., 31

Novick, D., 156
Onsi, M., 22, 27
Oxenfeldt, A. R., 245, 249, 502, 505
Ozan, T., 489
Paden, J. H., 506, 509
Palda, K. S., 254
Papandreou, A. G., 238
Pareto, V., 366
Parker, R. H., 65, 75, 86, 104, 107
Paton, W. A., 132
Patrick, A. W., 277
Pearce, I. F., 240, 244, 540
Penrose, E. T., 380, 383, 385, 386
Perrin, J. R., 447, 490
Phelps Brown, E. H., 574
Porterfield, J. T. S., 304
Prais, S. J., 219
Preinreich, G. A. D., 341, 345
Prince, T. R., 14
Puckett, M., 616
Pye, G., 311
Quandt, R. E., 147, 162, 165, 166, 176,
    216, 233, 307, 331
Raiffa, H., 27, 163, 364
Rayner, A. C., 134
Risk, J. M. S., 429
Roberts, E. B., 389, 555
Robichek, A. A., 278, 605, 614, 615,
    625, 626
Robinson, E. A. G., 244, 383
Rosen, L. S., 578
Ross, N. S., 383
Ross, W. R., 518
Ryavec, C. A., 516, 517
Saaty, T. L., 165
Samuels, J. M., 192
Samuelson, P. A., 212, 214, 303, 654
Savage, L. J., 353
Scarf, H., 148
Schiff, M., 128
Schlaifer, R., 27, 175, 355, 364

Schneider, E., 146, 227
Schultz, H., 227
Schwab, B., 334
Schwartz, E., 610
Science Policy Research Unit,
    University of Sussex, 507, 508
Scitovsky, T., 146
Sengupta, S. S., 658
Sevin, C. H., 502, 503
Shannon, C. E., 22
Shapiro, E., 309, 613
Sharpe, W. F., 366, 611, 612
Shelly, M. W. III, 577
Shepard, R. N., 32
Shillinglaw, G., 388, 532, 542, 562, 564
Shubik, M., 6, 164, 234, 257, 572, 574
Simon, H. A., 18, 145, 164, 165, 166,
    168, 176, 177, 181, 234, 241, 267,
    282, 300, 380, 387, 395, 556, 573,
    576
Simon, J. L., 506
Singh, A., 134
Skousen, K. F., 546
Smidt, S., 175, 302, 309, 627
Smith, A., 76
Smith, V. L., 143, 148, 295, 296, 312
    338, 340, 341, 343, 345, 347, 348,
    417
Solomon, E., 320, 624, 625
Solomons, D., 86, 192, 527, 528, 532,
    536, 537, 540, 541, 542, 547, 559,
    560
Solow, R. M., 212, 654
Sord, B. H., 447, 448, 451, 489, 528
Sorter, G. H., 131, 406
Spivey, W. A., 16, 227, 654
Sprouse, R. T., 53, 127, 128, 132
Stackelberg, H. von, 234
Staffurth, C., 510, 519, 520
Stamp, E., 66
Starr, M. K., 583, 584, 586, 596

Staubus, G. J., 88

Stedry, A. C., 32, 560, 562, 566, 571

Steiner, P. O., 250

Steuer, M. D., 241

Stigler, G. J., 11, 162, 190, 227, 250

Stiglitz, J. E., 624

Summers, R., 508

Swan, C., 502, 505

Sweezy, P. M., 234

Sykes, A., 116

Taylor, F. W., 447, 448

Teichroew, D., 181, 605

Terborgh, G., 338

Theil, H., 22, 26

Thompson, G. C., 506, 507

Thompson, G. L., 510

Thornley, G., 510, 513, 519

Todhunter, R., 648

Townsend, R., 505

Tversky, A., 21, 32, 371

Tyndall, G., 573, 576

U.N. Dept. of Economics and Social Affairs, 156

Urban, G. L., 246

U.S. Congress sub-committee of Joint Economic Committee, 156

U.S. Dept. of Defense and NASA, 393

U.S. Senate Hearings, 201

Van Horne, J. C., 367

Vatter, W. J., 542

Vernon, J. M., 233, 234, 239, 242, 260

Vickers, D., 143, 180, 214, 296, 299

Vickrey, W., 30, 31,

Wagner, H. M., 348, 562, 564, 565, 577

Walter, J. E., 614

Weingartner, H. M., 306, 312, 331, 333, 336, 353

Welsch, G. A., 447, 448, 451, 489, 528

Weston, J. F., 624, 627

Whinston, A., 258, 528, 529

White, G. E., 135

Whitin, T. M., 583, 584, 585, 586, 589, 592, 596, 598

Whitmore, D. A., 501

Whitmore, G. A., 334

Whyte, W. F., 448, 449

Wiest, J. D., 510

Wiles, P. J. D., 228

Williams, D., 510

Williamson, O.E., 238, 380, 383, 384, 385, 386, 387, 388, 389, 390, 392, 552

Winkler, R. L., 561

Wold, H., 219, 287

Wright, F. K., 93

Yamey, B. S., 46

Subject Index

Accounting
  aims, *see* Accounting 'principles'
  allocation in, 404–27, 518n, 521,
    535, 542, 547: *see also* Costing,
    absorption; Proration
  and economics, 11–13
  and Statistics, 13
  conventions, 43, 45, 50, 68n, 69n,
    70, 85, 93, 97–100, 108–9, 126,
    402, 406, 430, 433
  entity reports, 7, 38–46, 53–70,
    84–92, 101–14, 123–35
  identities, 46–53
  management, 8, 161, 171
  period, 9, 42, 396
  'principles', 10: *see also* Accounting
    conventions, unit of
    measurement
    conservatism, 45
    consistency, 44, 162
    continuity, 44, 88
    disclosure, 45
    objectivity, 44, 82, 85–6, 88, 91,
      108, 162
  prospective, 7, 171
  provisions, 57–8
  recording systems, 46–58, 91–2,
    401–39, 452, 454–6
  retrospective, 7, 171
  scope of, 6–9
  stewardship function, 7, 10
  unit, *see* Entity
  unit of measurement, 41–2, 44–5,
    90–1, 109–13, 124, 537
Accounting data/information
  and employees, 42, 134
  control of the economy, 13
  external and internal uses, 9–11,
    42–4, 101, 123–4, 406, 427–8
  external interpretation measures,
    124–34
  nature, 11–13
Accounting variances
  labour
    idle time and overtime, 461–3
    mix, 459–61
    pay-rate, 457–8
    quantity, 457–8
  manufacturing overheads, 470
    'efficiency', 475–6

spending, 472–3, 475–6
   volume, 472–6
margin
   market share and volume, 479–82,
      485–6
   mix, 482–5
   volume, 478–83, 485–6
materials
   mix, 465–8
   price, 463–5, 467–8
   quantity, 463–5, 467–8
   scrap and spoilage, 468–9
performance, 520–1
revision, 490
sales
   area earnings, 503–4
   price, 478–80
   volume, 478–9
spending, 476–7, 499, 520–1
Activity index, 407–8, 413, 421–2,
      424–8, 470–6
Administration, 446, 500–1
Advertising, 188, 225, 234, 239, 249–56
   deferred expense, 128, 135
   dynamic aspects, 253–5
   function, control of, 446, 528
   imperfect competition and
      monopoly, 249, 251–3
   marginal value product of, 252–3,
      275
   measurement problems, 255–6
   nature of, 249–50
   oligopoly, 249, 253, 255
Assets
   current, defined, 56
   fixed, defined, 56
   forms, 79
   intangible and tangible, 58
   wasting, *see* Depreciation

B.O.T. Working Party reports, 191

Booz, Allen and Hamilton, 506
Break-even graphs, 271–6, 283–4
Budget(s)
   as controls, 446–53, 487–92, 551–76
   as plans, 150–5, 451–2, 490–2,
      553–4, 558–60
   as pressure devices, 448–9, 574
   cash, 62, 452, 603–4
   comprehensive, 152
   consistency, 151–3, 451–2, 490–2,
      558
   explicit/implicit, 568–72
   flexible, 153, 155, 470–6, 552
   operating, 446, 451–3
   period, 150–1, 397, 452
   programmed, 446, 452–3, 476–7,
      498–9
   responsibility centres, 150, 447,
      451–2
   revision, 151–3, 276, 521, 553–4
   targets, nature of, *see* Control(s),
      targets/standards
Budgeting
   continuous, 398, 489–90
   interim revision, 398, 490
   participatory, 449–50, 569, 571–2,
      574–6
   periodic, 398, 489–90
Burden rates, *see* Costing, absorption

Calculus, 162, 182
Capital budgeting, 146–50, 201, 254
   adding new products, 195–7
   borrowing/lending by owners, 292,
      299, 308, 310–11, 320n, 322, 332,
      334
   capital market imperfection, 296–7,
      299, 301, 305–6, 309–12, 332–4,
      341
   capital rationing, 296–7, 300, 305–6,
      309–12, 330–7, 509

cost of capital, 129, 195–6, 201,
    304–9, 334, 536, 540, 627–8
criteria, 294, 297, 301, 303–12
    incorporating owners' utility,
        306–8, 310–12, 319–22, 333–7
    ratio methods, 305, 544–5
    utility-free rules, 303–6, 309–10,
        313–19, 330–3
decision responsibilities, 528,
    534
discount rates, 283, 302–3, 306–9,
    311, 332–7, 339, 343, 346
dividend policy, 310, 312, 320,
    335–7
    optimal, 336
dynamic models, 148–9
economic life, 93–4, 197, 293, 295,
    299, 301, 338
expansion of capacity, 293
financial investment by firm, 333n
financing of investment, 307, 309,
    321n, 322, 330: *see also* Capital
    structure
interest rates, 81, 213, 294, 308,
    333
irreversibility, 148, 295–6
nature of investment, 147–8, 292–6,
    309
obsolescence, 338, 345n, 347–8
optimal investment, 296, 301, 308,
    310, 322
'post-audit', 521
reinvestment assumptions, 304–5
replacement, 293, 301
    'adverse minimum', 347n
    assets that deteriorate, 337–48,
        368–9
    assets that fail, 348–50
    'inferiority gradient', 346, 347n,
        348
    'next-year test', 344

optimal, 298, 337–50
optimal length of service, 338–40
partial, 340
pure, 342, 345–7
timing, 341, 343–6
resource constraints, 297, 300, 330
retirement, 338–40
'scale obsolescence', 295n, 313, 338
scope, 146, 300
static models, 147–8, 292–322
time preferences, 293–4, 299–300,
    306–10, 321–2, 333, 334n, 336
timing of investment, 147, 298
Capital structure: *see also* Dividend
    policy
    and cost of capital, 308, 620–9
    financial leverage, 127, 132–3, 620–7
    operating leverage, 43–4, 618–20
    optimal, 43, 321n, 610–11
'Cash flow', 65, 132
Cash flows, 196–7, 200, 297, 301–2,
    332
    and funds statements, 62
    correlated over time, 359–61
    discounted, 80–2, 302–6, 312, 332
Code of accounts, *see* Information
    systems, coding
Companies (legal aspects)
    Acts, 39, 43, 53, 59, 66, 546
    dividends, 52–3, 104
    shares, 39, 47, 52–3, 66–7
    undistributable reserves, 47, 59, 69
Competition
    after-sales service, 188, 237
    'entry' of new firms, 212, 232, 236,
        244n, 245, 249
    government regulation, 212, 383
    non-price, 188, 235–7, 249
    product improvement, 188, 234, 237
Compound interest and annuities, 162,
    222–3, 338

amount, 638, 641, 648
and simple interest, 347, 639–40
continuous compounding/
    discounting, 645–8
discrete compounding/
    discounting, 638–45
effective and nominal rates, 639
present value, 638–9, 642, 648
Computational methods, 163
algorithmic, 181, 352
'direct search', 181
heuristic, 181
iterative, 334
Computers, electronic, 181
capacity, 163, 181
Conference Board, 507
Consolidated reports, 66–70
Contribution, *see* Profit, variable
Control(s): *see also* Feedback
accounting control process, 276,
    394–8, 420–3, 445–7, 487–90,
    561–6
amplitude and periodicity of
    fluctuations, 555, 561
and efficiency, 43, 380–1, 388–9,
    391, 445, 448, 566–7
and goal congruence, 394, 398, 423,
    534, 541–2, 572
and growth of the firm, 381–7
and networks, 510–21
assigning causes, 488–9, 563–5
behavioural aspects, 566–76
    group reaction, 448–9, 571, 575
    individual aspiration levels,
        448–50, 567–73
    motivation, 398, 449, 505, 562,
        566–76
boundaries and subdivisions of the
    system, 391, 395, 555–8
controllability, 389, 395, 420, 423,
    555, 557

costs of management (coordination),
    383–5
degree of, 391–3
delegation of responsibility
    (decentralisation), 384–5, 392,
    394–5, 447, 526–9, 576
divorce of ownership and, 381–2
enterprise (=external+internal
    controls), 380, 383, 388, 551,
    561
external, 386–90, 392, 553–5, 558,
    561, 565
    market, 382–3, 389–91
    'system', 386, 388–91
    willful control agents, 386,
        389–91, 395n
for entity reporting, 66
goals, *see* Control targets/standards
internal, 551–2, 561–2
    anticipatory action, 390
    incentives, 385, 390, 448–9, 560–1,
        566–74
    interfirm comparisons, 390
    intertemporal comparisons, 390
    investment centre measures, 392,
        530–2, 536–45
    manipulation, 390–1, 572
    organizational innovation, 387–8,
        390, 575
    performance checks, 388–91,
        520–1
    performance standards, *see*
        Performance standard
    planning, 385, 390, 551, 554,
        560–1
    profitability measures, 392,
        526–45
    response to feedback
        comparisons, 381, 392, 394,
        487–90, 563
    scheduling, 390

spending allowances, 392, 446, 476–7, 528, 533

technical standards, 392, 448

limits, 488–9

loss of, 381

'management by objectives', 499, 501, 577

meta-, 565n

model, accounting, 552–4, 557–9

non-profit, 499–501, 505–6, 576–7

of trade credit, 598–602

of data-information flow, 552, 576

of forecasting and estimating, 521–2, 560–1

of time, time-cost, 393, 499, 517–21, 552, 576

period, 150–1, 397, 452

plans and, 391, 393, 398, 451, 490–2, 554, 559, 560, 564

qualitative, 389n, 499, 501, 505–6, 508, 569, 575

self-adaptive, 166, 389, 392, 562, 565n

statistical, 392–3, 489, 576

targets/standards, nature of, 151, 393, 396–8, 445–50, 529, 552–4, 559, 560, 562, 564–9, 573, 576

techniques, 'principle of exceptions', 385, 393–4, 396–8, 552, 564, 573

budgetary control, 385, 393–4, 446, 551–76

standard costing, 385, 393–4, 445–92, 551–76

theory of the firm, 226, 242, 381–3, 566

timeliness of, 392, 397, 561–2

uncertainty, 382–4, 560–1, 565–6, 576–7

Cosmetic reporting, 134–5

Cost(s)

allocated, *see* Accounting, allocation in

and expense, 56, 174

apportionment, 405n

average, 16, 272–4, 403–18, 421–8, 430–8

avoidable, 172–4, 189, 199, 248n, 270, 533, 542

centre, 403–5, 451–2

common, 190–1, 404: *see also* Costs, fixed; Costs, indirect

comparability, 201–2

controllable, 420, 423, 428, 532–4

direct, 404, 406–19, 422, 425, 428, 452–69, 487, 518n

distribution, 225, 477

economic, *see* Cost, opportunity

equation, 172, 190

equivalent replacement, *see under* Depreciation

ex ante and *ex post*, 172

expansion/contraction, 196, 312–13

fixed, 172–3, 197, 240n, 261, 270–3, 275–80, 282, 284–6, 419–20, 423–4, 426–8, 435–9, 453–4, 470–6, 541–2

full, 243n

function, 172, 215, 260, 285–6, 347–8

historic, 41, 45–6, 79, 82, 85, 88n, 91, 97, 101–6, 108–9, 114–15, 126–7, 134–5, 433–4, 534, 536–8, 543–5

implicit opportunity, 174, 198, 344, 423, 521, 541–2

indirect, 404–28, 455–6, 469–77, 487, 518n

interest on capital, 147n, 532–3, 543–5

joint, 173, 191, 218

'learning effect', 198n, 226, 449–50

long run, 196, 214, 219, 220, 240, 248, 262, 385, 394

marginal, 16, 18, 172, 196, 218–19, 224, 231, 239, 242, 252, 258–9, 272–5, 383, 418, 503, 529, 573
minimum average, 188, 208, 210–11, 214–15, 216–18, 232
non-controllable, 420, 428, 532–3, 535, 541
opportunity, 154, 172–4, 188, 196, 198–200, 226, 247–8, 256, 306–9, 332–5, 339
overhead, *see* Costs, fixed; Costs, indirect
product, 405, 407–18, 423–7, 452, 454
replacement, 79–80, 82, 86–8, 91–2, 101–7, 111–13, 114, 116–18, 431–4, 539, 585
reproduction, 88
retainer, 96, 116, 419
selling, 188–9, 210, 249, 252–3: *see also* Advertising
semi-variable, 419
separable fixed, 173n, 198
shape of SRAC curve, 215, 274
shut-down, 173n
step, 275, 419–20, 470, 500, 529
standard, 432–8, 445–7, 452–77
start-up, 173n
'sunk', 154
traced segment, 404–5, 407, 410–11, 418
transport, 224
'uncontrollable', 420n
user, 96, 116, 339n, 419
variable, 172, 187, 223, 236, 270–3, 276–80, 284–6, 419–20, 422, 426–8, 435–9, 453–4, 456, 470–7, 500, 532–3, 535, 541
Cost-benefit analysis, 18, 300

Costing
absorption, 405–9, 411–18, 424–7, 434–9, 470–6
'direct', 424
job and batch, 412–13
joint product, 413–18
'marginal', 245, 424
period, 397
process, 408–12
variable, 245, 419–20, 424, 434–9, 541
Critical path analysis, 393, 510–19, 576; *see also* PERT
Cyanamid Company, 509

Data specification
and information, 6, 14–15, 180, 427–9
data limitations, 176
estimation problems, 162, 175
for decision, 161, 170–6
in economic and accounting 'plans', 154
in linear programming, 226
measurement problems, 171, 447
whose domain?, 161–2, 170–1
Debt
and equity, *see* Capital structure, financial leverage
and lenders, 45, 113, 123–4, 132, 134
in entity reports, 46, 64, 111–13, 124
interest rates, 103n, 610, 618, 625–6
Decentralization, 180, 257–8: *see also* Control, delegation of responsibility; Organization, multidivisional
optimal, 257n
Decision(s)
alternatives, 154, 163, 168
and information, 237, 241–2, 246n, 248

computational methods, 163, 181
constraints, 163–5, 168–9
  binding, 169, 192, 333
  regarded as goals, 165
criterion, *see* Decision rules
elements, 163–70
group, 163
horizon, 172, 177, 200, 350
information costs, 28
intertemporal, 147, 293
objective(s), 163–6
  mutual consistency, 164
problem identification, 170
proximate decision problem, 177
qualitative, 161, 241
relevant costs, 171–4: *see also* Data
  specification, and information
reversibility, 177, 202
routinizing, 15
sequential, 148, 176–7, 240, 245,
  508
single, 176–7
tree, 356, 358, 511n, 602
unstructured, 170
Decision rules, 166
approximative, 347–8
illogical, 191–2
optimal, 164
optimally imperfect, 176
standard, 15, 19, 241, 243, 254–5,
  297, 350
Decision theory
general, 163
statistical, 18, 26–7, 175n, 242
Demand
changes in, 295–6, 300, 312–13, 338
consumers' tastes, 249–50
forecasting, 287–8
level of, 237, 244
price elasticity, 250, 252–3, 255n,
  261

Depreciation
accounting, 9, 51, 57–8, 93–108, 419
and divisional performance, 534–40,
  543–5
and obsolescence, 93, 96, 534
and residual benefits, 95–100,
  114–17
economic, 93–4, 214
equivalent replacement cost, 95–6,
  114–17
eventual replacement, 106–7
non-fund, 64
Discounts, 57, 271, 598–9, 602
Disinvestment decisions, 197–8, 295,
  312–13
Distribution methods, 225–6, 236, 246
Disturbance, random, 178n
Diversification, *see under* Production
Dividend policy, 84, 90, 104, 129,
  612–17: *see also* Capital
  budgeting, dividend policy
du Pont de Nemours & Co., 510, 543,
  545
Dynamic programming, 148n

Economic efficiency, 380–1
Economics
concepts, principles, reasoning, 13n,
  76–8, 154, 162, 170
Economies/diseconomies of scale,
  188n, 189, 203, 214, 225, 236, 385
Economist Intelligence Unit, 102
Entity
economic, 8, 39–41
legal, 8–9, 38–9, 66
operating, 41
reports, *see under* Accounting
Excess capacity, 203, 210, 223
Expectations, 8, 17–19, 21, 141, 155,
  167, 182, 241, 388, 560–1
anticipations, 141, 188, 560

estimating planning/decision
    variables, 141–2, 198, 554,
    560–1
forecasting exogenous variables,
    141, 176–7, 188, 553–4, 560–1
'relevant anticipations', 145, 264,
    554, 560–1
External
    economies/diseconomies, 223
    reports, *see* Accounting, entity
        reports

Fallacy of composition, 308n
Feedback, 350, 553, 556, 562n
    automatic response to, *see*
        Control(s), self-adaptive
    double, 388
    step-function response, 388, 394,
        554, 562
    threshold response, 387n, 562
Firm(s)
    behavioural theories, 40, 234, 240–2,
        257, 380n
    dynamic theory, 12, 262–4
    failure, 133–4
    multinational, 224, 393
    multiproduct, 181–91, 243
    nature of, 150n
    neoclassical theory, 12, 17, 40, 143,
        187, 213–20, 232–5, 260–2
    reasons for forming, 16–17, 140
    size of, 385, 386n, 392, 576
First-in-first-out, *see* Inventories, cost
    flow assumptions
Funds flow statements, 53, 61–6

Gains
    borrowing, 110, 111–13, 115
    fictional, 110–12
    holding, defined, 92
    operating, defined, 92

real, 110–13
General Motors, 528n

Harris, F. W., 586n
Heuristic problem solving, 149
Human capital, 149, 576

Income: *see also* Profit
    and substitution effects
        of advertising, 256
        of price changes, 256
    residual, 531–2, 536–42
    smoothing, *see* Cosmetic reporting
    statements, 59–61, 103–5, 111–13
Index numbers
    output, 219
    price, 101–7, 109–14
Indifference curves
    constant revenue and outlay, 190n,
        208, 221, 250
    risk-return, 366–8
    time preferences, 311
Indivisibilities
    input availability, 189, 193, 214,
        219–20, 295, 312, 574
    input utilisation, 193, 210, 211, 295
    product demand, 193
Industrial dynamics, 551n, 555–7,
    561n
Information
    advantage, 188
    and imperfect competition, 188
    and theory of the firm, 21
    complete (exact) and incomplete
        (inexact), 17–18, 164, 241
    'controlled', 16, 29, 552
    data and, 6
    data-information flow, *see*
        Information systems,
        communication
    defined, 6

economics
  cost of information, 16, 19, 27, 145
  firm's existing stock of
    information, 18
  marginal cost of information, 18
  value of exact information, 32–3
  value of inexact information,
    33–5, 565
  knowledge and, 6
  loss, 26, 28, 34, 384
  market and internal, 16–18
  operationalizing, 384–6
  optimally inexact, 176n
  production function, 21
  timeliness, 15, 17, 422, 455–6
Information system(s)
  accounting, 14–22
    design of, 27–8, 401–3, 427–9
  coding, 18, 28–9, 429
  communication, 8, 17, 19–22, 29,
    385, 395, 554, 559, 576
    biasing, 21, 241, 388
    'decoupling', 384, 387
    filtering rules, 21
    'noise', 19, 21, 26n, 28, 384, 388,
      447, 554n
    routing rules, 21
    simple/compound control loss, 387
    the price system as a
      communication system, 16–17
  computer-based, 15, 28–9, 429
  concept of, 14–16, 20
  external and internal, 7
  integrated, 15, 29
  management, 6, 15, 402–3, 528
  'open-ended', 8, 45
  optimal, 14, 21
  processing, 15, 19–22, 385
  'real-time', 15
  search and collection, 17–19, 168,
    171, 241, 368

storage and retrieval, 19, 29
  uncertainty avoidance, 28
Information theory
  aggregation, 26
  amount of information in a
    message, 22–6
    optimal amount, 28
  concept of 'information', 22
  efficiency, 15, 26, 576–7
  purpose, 17
  redundancy, 26
Input(s)
  availability, 212
  capital goods, services of, 214, 292,
    295, 312
  defined, 214
  fixed, 213, 221
  marginal value product, 573–4
  'price efficiency', 209
  prices, 208, 211, 217n
  productivity, 208–9, 575
  role of time, 214
  variable, 213–14
Integration, 200–1, 576
Interdependence, 168–9, 179–80, 209
  advertising and price, 250
  amount of investment and discount
    rates, imperfect capital markets,
    332
  consumption and investment, 292–3,
    299–300
  cost (technological), 189–90, 217,
    218n, 219, 297, 557–8, 577
  demand, 189–90, 218n, 219, 297,
    557–8, 577
  demand determinants, 255
  expected returns of investment
    projects, 360, 367
  external and internal variables, 380,
    388–9, 555, 557
  external effects, 179

intertemporal (dynamic), 148, 154,
  178n, 298, 305, 558
investment, 297–301
markets, 187n
oligopolistic, 233–4
physical, 297–8, 305
production, 154
production and investment, 143,
  147, 296, 299
production, investment, financing,
  143, 299
replacement of items that fail, 349
serial, 298–9, 340
statistical, 299, 350
transfer pricing, 259
Inventories
  carrying costs, 437, 465, 585–6
  control, 583–98
  cost flow assumptions, 109, 430–4
  cost identification assumptions, 430,
    434–9
  turnover, 129–30
  valuation, 9, 50, 57, 77–8, 91–2, 101,
    104n, 109, 135, 276–7, 405–6,
    425, 429–39, 491, 585
  work-in-progress, 407, 412, 454
Investment centre – defined, 530
Investment decisions, see Capital
  budgeting

Lagrangean multiplier, 216, 239, 260,
  263, 367n, 594–6
Last-in-first-out, see Inventories, cost
  flow assumptions
Limiting factor, see Decision rules,
  illogical
Linear programming, 162, 193
  'activities' (processes), 220–1, 655
  applications, 220–5, 311, 332–6, 465,
    502–3, 510, 529, 532, 654–5
  assignment problem, 655

chance-constrained, 361–2, 660
constraints, 221, 654–5, 657–9
contrasted with break-even analysis,
  279–81
contrasted with burden rate data,
  426–7
degeneracy, 657
dual variables, 332–3, 335, 658–9
goal programming, 281–3
general LP problem, 654–5
integer restrictions, 659–60
method of partitions, 165n
nonlinearities, 215n, 661
parametric programming, 352–3,
  660
satisficing in relation to, 165
simplex method, 657
slack variables, 282, 657
stochastic programming, 361–2, 660
transportation problem, 655
Liquidity, 59, 130–2, 582, 602–5

Managerial discretion, see Market,
  blurring of
Market
  blurring of the, 190, 381, 383
  incomplete, 321n, 610
  narrowing/widening, 189, 194, 256:
    see also Income and
    substitution effects
  segments, 271
  share, 189, 234, 244, 479–82, 485–6
  size of, 383
Market structure
  duopoly, 242
  imperfect competition, 188, 231, 273
  monopoly, 212, 231, 245
  oligopoly, 188, 231, 248
  perfect competition, 187, 231
Marketing
  advertising, see Advertising

function, control of, 485, 502–6

Matching concept, 51, 401, 430: *see also* Accounting 'principles', continuity

Measurement
  error, 13, 30
  fundamental and derived, 30–1
  fundamental measure scales, 31
  in accounting, 6, 8, 30, 171, 562–3
    desirable properties, 31
  multi-dimensional, 31–2
  theory, 30–2
    formal properties of a measure, 30, 171

Models
  assumptions, 169
  decision, 163, 169
  deterministic, 142, 144–5, 148, 179, 352–3
  dynamic, 12, 142, 144–5, 148–9, 177–9, 200, 253–5, 262–4
  incorporating learning, 166, 241
  indeterminacy, 310–12, 322, 332–4, 336
  initial conditions, dynamic models, 177
  multiperiod, 147n, 178
  planning, 140–58
  probabilistic, 142, 145–6, 148n, 179, 353–68, 516–17
  short-run price-output, 270–83
  static, 12, 142, 144–5, 147–8, 177–9, 251–3, 301

Money capital, 10, 214
Monte Carlo methods, 362

Nonlinear programming, 334, 367
Numerical solution methods, *see* Computational methods

Objective(s), corporate, 163–6, 297

conflict of, 40, 388
earnings per share, 127
formation and revision of, 241, 387, 554
maximizing present value of firm, 40, 262–4, 338
maximizing stockmarket value of firm, 308–9, 336–7
multiple, 237, 240, 242
non-maximizing, 240, 257, 386
personal vs., 398, 575
profit maximization, 40, 164, 187, 231, 237, 275, 282
rate of return maximization, 240
revenue maximization, 239–40
'satisficing', 84, 164–6, 237, 240, 243, 276, 283
utility maximization, 84, 238–9

Operating cycle, 57
Opportunity loss, 33
Optimality
  and computation costs, 176
  and heuristics, 181
  and quality of firm's information, 18, 176
  learning included as a goal, 166
  length of planning horizon, 178–9
  maximal and optimal decisions, 176
  omitted variables, 182–3
  range of decision variable(s), 164–5

Optimization, 164
  constrained, 164–5, 216
  general, 180n
  joint, 337
  partial, 143, 180n

Organization(al)
  business, forms of, 11, 381–2, 395
  coalition, 17, 19n, 40, 238, 256–7
  centralized, 387
  hierarchical levels, 384, 387–8, 395–6

multidivisional, 387–9, 526–47
role assignments, 554
slack, 18, 238, 257, 387, 576
structure, 182, 226, 237, 241, 380,
    384, 386, 391, 396, 554
  innovation in, 384, 387, 392, 526
theory, 15, 241n, 380, 386–9, 552

Performance
  budgeted, 393, 446–7, 487–90, 520–1
  economic vs. financial, 140
  measures, 8, 89, 392, 447, 499–500,
      526–9, 530–2
  standard, 392, 394, 445–52, 488–90,
      499–501, 503–4, 508–9, 519–21
  subjective appraisal, 575
PERT, 514–18
Plans/planning
  and control, 154
  and decisions, 141, 161
  anticipations, *see* Expectations
  assumptions, 149
  budgeting process as constraint on,
      155, 241
  budgets as, 150–3
  communication, 155
  computation, 154–5
  corporate financial, 336–7
  degree of disaggregation, 154
  economic and accounting
      treatment, 153–5
  goal formation, 155, 182
  horizon, 140, 144, 166–8, 178–9,
      187, 301, 340
    fixed, 167–8
    optimal, 166
    shifting, 167
  influence of information system,
      154–5
  investment, in economics, 146–9:
      see also Capital budgeting

long-range economic, 149–50
organization structure, 155
planning variables, *see* Expectations
production, in economics, 142–6
representation of prices, 154
state of firm's information, 142
strategic, 141, 168, 387
tactical
  administrative, 141
  operating, 141
view of time, 141–2, 144–5
Plant
  flexible/specific, 210, 223, 351
  location, 223–5
  maintenance, 211, 338
  utilisation, 212, 345n, 347n
Price system
  as communication system, 16
  as computing device, 163, 187
Price control, 235
Price(s)
  entry, *see* Cost, replacement
  exit, *see* Value, (net) realizable
  level changes, general, *see*
      Accounting, unit of
      measurement
  level changes, specific, *see* Cost,
      replacement; Value, (net)
      realizable
Pricing
  at standard cost, 394
  collusion, 234
  competitive bidding, 246–7
  'cost-plus', 198n, 243–5
  discontinuous producers, 246n
  formula, 242–5
  government contracts, 247–8
  independent price policy, 188, 231,
      235–6
  in neoclassical theory of firm
      discriminating monopoly, 258, 261

imperfect competition, 232–3, 260
  monopoly, 232–3, 236
  multiplant monopoly, 262
  oligopoly, 233–6
  perfect competition, 232, 235
joint products, 261
marginal cost, 271, 573, 577
maximization of management's
    utility, 238–9
multiple products, 191, 260
negotiation, 246
number of buyers, 231, 234, 236n
price discrimination, 236, 261–2, 271
price leadership, 234–5, 274–5
'price points', 194
price stability, 188, 236
revenue maximization, 239–40
size of competitors, 236
tactical aspects, 244n, 271
target market share, 234, 240, 244
target rate of return, 243
Principle of exceptions, 19: *see also
    under* Control(s)
Probability, 13, 162n
  Bayes' theorem, 175
  conditional, 351, 357, 370
  joint, 351, 357, 370
  subjective, 175, 247, 353–5, 362, 368,
    561
Process analysis, 220–1
Product(s)
  branding, 188, 194, 250
  complementary, 189–90, 246
  defined, 214
  elasticity of substitution, 235n
  estimated life cycle, 189, 196, 236
  homogeneity/differentiation, 188–9,
    231, 236, 252
  intermediate, 199–203, 256–9
  joint, 191, 212, 217–19, 413–18: *see
    also* Costing, joint product

marginal rate of substitution, 235n
  marginal, ratio of, 217
  multiple, 191, 215–16, 223, 278–81
  quality, 198
  storability, 236
  substitute, 189–90, 213, 232, 235,
    236n
Product decisions, 187–203
  adding products, 194–8, 506–8
  dropping products, 194–5, 197–8
  make/buy, 200–3
  mix, 189–98, 212, 223, 276
  product line, 189, 194–8, 246
  sell/process further, 199–200
Production
  capital intensity, 188, 243n, 292
  centre, defined, 403
  diversified, 189, 194, 392, 576
  function, 17, 21, 172, 209, 211,
    213–20, 249, 260
  period of, 146n
  plans, 142–6, 262–4
  rate of, 187–9, 209–10, 214
  runs, 189
  scale, 211–12, 243n, 293, 339–40
  smoothing, 145n, 188, 194, 240, 552,
    555, 556n
Profit
  centre, defined, 530
  concepts, 75–6, 89–90
  controllable, 531–5, 541, 547
  expected, defined, 278
  measurement, 50–2, 56, 75–6, 90–2,
    101–14, 134–5, 276–7, 415–17,
    435–9, 530–42, 545–7
  realized, 50n, 104
  retained, 52–3, 59, 67–9
  traceable, 532, 535, 542, 547
  unrealized, 69–70
  variable, 191, 272–3, 276–81, 427–8,
    477–86, 503–4, 532

-volume graphs, 277–81
Program budgeting (PPBS), 156–8
Proration
  of capital among products, 198
  of costs, 404–5, 410–11, 420–4, 473
  of revenue and expense between
    periods, 9, 240

Quantitative methods, 13, 162

Rationality
  economic, 164, 237
  bounded, principle of, 164, 387
Research and development, 211, 351
  control of, 446, 506–9, 528, 533,
    552n
  deferred expense, 88, 135
Resource allocation
  internal, and control, 499–522
  'timeless' and intertemporal, 294
  with critical path analysis, 519
Return on investment (capital
    employed), 126–7, 133, 542–5,
    614–15
Returns to scale
  constant, 221
  nonconstant, 188n
Revenue
  average, 273–4
  cross marginal, 190
  function, 260, 264, 272–5, 287–8
  marginal, 190, 218, 231, 239, 242,
    252, 258–9, 272–4, 383, 503,
    529
Reward-penalty system, 258n: *see also*
    Control(s), internal, incentives
Risk, *see also* Uncertainty
  business, *see* Uncertainty
  financial, 11, 618–27
  first-and higher-order, 351
  spreading, 194

SAPPHO, 507–8
Sears, 528n
Segmental reports, 545–7
Service centre – defined, 403
Simulation, 178, 181, 241–2, 362–3,
    561
Social costs and benefits, 179
Socialism, economic, 257, 561n
  accounting prices, 257, 573–4
Solution
  analytical, 181
  heuristic, 181, 237
  necessary and sufficient conditions,
    181–2, 200–1, 216–17, 239,
    260–3
Statistical methods, 13, 215, 219,
    285–8: *see also* Probability;
    Decision theory
Stockmarket measures
  dividend yield, 10, 129, 308–9,
    612–17
  earnings per share, 126–8
  price-earnings ratio and earnings
    yield, 10, 128–9, 308, 615–17
  share price, 10, 82–3, 124, 133–4,
    308n, 309, 612–17, 621–9
Stocks and flows, 12, 53
System(s)
  analysis, 6, 15–16, 156, 554
  approach, 14, 554
  defining the system, 14–15, 554
  management by, 15, 156–8
  objectives, 14
  theory, general, 14

Taxation, 59, 60–1, 83–4, 90, 108, 126,
    213, 238–9, 256, 302, 433,
    541–2, 617, 624–6
Technique of production, 187, 208–27
  information, 210–11, 226
  long-run, 214–15, 222–3, 293

short-run, 213–15, 221–2, 293
Technological change, 194, 216, 227,
    338, 343, 345–7, 392
Theories
  degree of aggregation, 241–2
  normative, 154, 166, 237, 552
  positive, 154, 237, 257, 552
Theory of capital, 292, 294
Theory of games, 234, 365
Theory of investment of the firm,
    292–4
Theory of teams, 19n
Transactions
  composition, 48–50
  conversion, 50–2
  proprietorship, 52–3
Transfer prices, 170, 203, 256–9, 576–7
  and external market structures, 257
  and non-marginal adjustments, 170,
    259
  and theory of the firm, 256–7
  at standard cost, 259
  control aspects of, 259, 423, 527,
    529–30, 541
  incentives, 258
  information costs, 258
  interdependencies, 259
  optimal, 256–9, 576–7

Uncertainty, 142, 169–70, 201, 243
  and investment decisions, 293, 299,
    300, 303, 308n, 347, 350–68
  certainty equivalents, 81, 354
  chance-constrained programming,
    361–2
  expected monetary value, 354–9
  expected utility, 363–5
  payback period, 303, 352
  portfolio selection theory, 366–8
  probability distribution of
    monetary value, 359–61

risk-adjusted discount rate, 81,
    308n, 352, 615
  sensitivity analysis, 276, 283,
    352–3
  simulation, 362–3
  and risk, 28
  and short-run price-output
    decisions, 276–8
  and statistical sampling, 13
  as reason for forming firms, 16n
  avoidance, 28, 350–1
  due to market imperfections, 16, 252
  reduction, 508
  risk estimation, 169, 351
  risk preference, 169–70, 351, 355,
    363–8, 388, 552n, 611–12
Utility function
  general, 76–7, 238
  group, 336
  linear in money, 335n
  management's, 84, 238–9
  two-valued, 164

Valuation
  inventories, *see* Inventories,
    valuation
  present value, 80–7, 91, 98–100, 140,
    196
  wasting assets, *see* Depreciation
Value
  and goodwill, 87, 118
  and profit, 75–6
  current, 42, 79–80: *see also* Cost(s),
    replacement, Value, (net)
    realizable
  deprival, 87n
  expected, *see* Uncertainty and
    investment decisions, expected
    monetary value
  future, 42, 78–9, 80–2, 107
  in accounting, 12, 75

in economics, 12, 75–8
(net) realizable, 79–80, 82, 86–8,
     109, 430
nominal or par, 47, 67, 69
past, 42, 79: *see also* Cost(s),
     historic
present, *see* Compound interest and
     annuities, present value;
     Valuation, present value
to firm, 83–8
to shareholders, 82–3, 89–90
Variables
     endogenous, 141n, 178n
     essential, 553
     ex ante, see Expectations
     exogenous, 141n, 178n, 388, 554–5
     external, 154

internal, 154
omitted, 182–3
Variances, *see* Accounting variances

Welfare economics, 180, 300, 302n
     second best, 180n
Working capital
     and entity reports, 56–7, 62–5
     and solvency, 130–4, 582–3
     associated with investment in fixed
          assets, 147, 300, 302, 583
     divisional, 528, 533, 541, 543
     management, 582–605
     return on, 146, 300
     risk/uncertainty, 582–3, 596–8,
          600–2, 605
     window dressing, 131–2